COGNITIVE PROCESSES IN THE PERCEPTION OF ART

ADVANCES IN PSYCHOLOGY 19

Editors

G. E. STELMACH

P. A. VROON

NORTH-HOLLAND
AMSTERDAM · NEW YORK · OXFORD

COGNITIVE PROCESSES IN THE PERCEPTION OF ART

Edited by

W. Ray CROZIER
School of Psychology
Preston Polytechnic

and

Antony J. CHAPMAN
Department of Psychology
University of Leeds

1984

NORTH-HOLLAND
AMSTERDAM · NEW YORK · OXFORD

© Elsevier Science Publishers B.V., 1984

All rights reserved. No part of this publication may be reproduced, stored in a retrieval system, or transmitted, in any form or by any means, electronic, mechanical, photocopying, recording or otherwise, without the prior permission of the copyright owner.

ISBN: 0 444 87501 8

Publishers:
ELSEVIER SCIENCE PUBLISHERS B.V.
P.O. Box 1991
1000 BZ Amsterdam
The Netherlands

Sole distributors for the U.S.A. and Canada:
ELSEVIER SCIENCE PUBLISHING COMPANY, INC.
52 Vanderbilt Avenue
New York, N.Y. 10017
U.S.A.

PRINTED IN THE NETHERLANDS

PREFACE

This book is based on a small group of the 150 or so papers presented at the International Conference on Psychology and the Arts -- a 5-day conference held in September 1983 under the auspices of The British Psychological Society. Symposia and individual papers were designed to advance psychological approaches to the creation, performance, consumption, and appreciation of works of art. A range of art-forms was in evidence, including architecture, dance, literature, music, painting and drawing, photography, and sculpture; and continuing debates within experimental aesthetics were pursued -- the effects of familiarity upon liking, the determinants of preference for simple forms, and relationships between levels of arousal and judgments of pleasingness. The full assembly of papers can be seen in abstract form in the Bulletin of The British Psychological Society (1983, Volume 36, pp. A113-A140), and some of the papers are available in full in special issues of Leonardo (1983, Volume 16, pp. 161-256), Visual Arts Research (1984, in press), and Music Perception (in preparation).

The clear message from the Conference was that, while the vitality of established approaches (such as psychoanalysis and experimental aesthetics) is still maintained by the advocates of those approaches, there has in recent years been a marked shift in emphasis towards the investigation of cognitive processes. Just as cognitive psychology has achieved some dominance within experimental psychology, so its concepts and methods are now being applied with growing success to the study of the arts. And just as every shift in emphasis within a scientific discipline brings fresh problems to the fore and allows one to regard old problems in new ways, so too this approach has focused psychologists' attention in new ways: for example, attention is now focused upon developmental aspects of the production of and sensitivity to the arts, upon the perception of representational pictures, and upon music perception and memory. This volume is intended to reflect and advance these trends within the psychology of art.

Selected conference speakers were asked to rewrite their contributions. In particular they were invited to explore the theoretical rationale for their cognitive approach and to relate their own research to its context. Taken together, the chapters circumscribe an important new area of application of cognitive psychology, and they make a significant advance in our understanding of the processes underlying the perception of works of art. They have been grouped in six sections for ease of reference, but not too much should be made of these divisions: one of the characteristics of the cognitive approach has been a move away from sharp distinctions between theoretical and empirical advances and between different art forms or media. Hence, for example, Kose draws upon empirical studies of the development of children's symbol use to illuminate his analysis of Cassirer's and Goodman's philosophical approaches, while Bartlett applies the 'event perception' hypothesis to the study of photographical material and melodies.

At the start of Section I, our introduction argues that twentieth-century trends within the arts strongly suggest that the simplification strategy adopted generally by psychologists has failed to do justice to the complexity of artistic phenomena. We propose that cognitive psychology is in a good position to remedy that failure: (1) by reflecting and offering a study of the important part that cognition plays in aesthetic appreciation; and (2) by providing a firm foundation for experimental aesthetics through identifying the processes involved in the perception of works of art.

In Section II four chapters discuss symbols and meanings in the arts. Traditionally the psychological approach to symbolism and to meaning in the arts has been most clearly identified with psychoanalysis and its emphasis upon unconscious processes and latent meanings. The chapters in this volume take a broader view: Kose and Smythe review a range of philosophical and psychological perspectives on symbols; Hudson is critical of the psychologists' neglect of the meanings of art-works and recommends the adoption of a hermeneutic approach; and Konečni provides an empirical investigation of the 'success' of art-works in communicating their creators' intentions.

In Section III four chapters take a developmental perspective on the arts. Both Pratt and Willats examine children's drawing abilities and they consider relationships between looking and drawing: the differences in their models of the drawing process demonstrate the complexity of this much studied yet still mysterious set of skills. The chapter by Blank, Massey, Gardner, and Winner provides an empirical study of children's sensitivity to expression in paintings. Dowling's longitudinal investigation traces the development of the spontaneous singing of two preschool children, and he reports experiments on the recall and recognition of songs.

Sections IV and V consider the application of models and concepts from cognitive psychology to the study of the perception of visual arts and music respectively. In Section IV Hock investigates the perception of information about relative location in photographs; Purcell examines his aesthetic preference model through an experiment using photographs of houses, and he analyses relationships among judgments of preference, attractiveness, interest, and goodness-of-example; while Walk describes an experimental investigation of dance and the perception of emotion.

In Section V, Bartlett outlines an event-perception hypothesis of memory and applies it to the recognition of visual scenes and the recognition of melody. Deutsch takes two approaches to the notion of 'musical space': a review of attempts to arrive at musical analogues of visual perception phenomena, and a discussion of the illusions which occur when several streams of music are organized. McAdams, too, is concerned with musical organization. His chapter introduces the concept of 'auditory image' as a metaphor for research on auditory organization, and a thorough review of such research is provided. The chapters by Vīķis-Freibergs and by Pressing offer complementary approaches to an important but neglected phenomenon within the arts, viz improvisation. Vīķis-Freibergs draws upon computer technology to give an account of relationships between spontaneity and tradition in Latvian folk-song; while Pressing attempts to isolate common properties of improvisation in different art-forms and, in outline, he presents a psychological model of the cognitive processes underlying them.

Section VI deals with issues in experimental aesthetics and reflects the growing realization within this field of the importance of cognitive processes. Boselie and Leeuwenberg draw upon the concept of 'cognitive representation' as part of a model designed to improve upon the formulae proposed by Birkhoff and by Eysenck for relationships between beauty and stimulus properties of order and complexity. Temme argues that cognitive set and task expectations play significant roles in mediating the effects of familiarity upon preference. Apter is critical of the notion of 'optimal level of arousal' which is central to contemporary theories in experimental aesthetics. He points to its failure to show why people should seek out arousal-increasing experiences and proposes an alternative account in terms of pairs of meta-motivational modes rather than one underlying motivational dimension. He uses these to relate a variety of artistic phenomena to theoretical concepts of cognitive synergy and paratelic and negativistic modes. Finally, Marks provides a review of synesthesia in the arts and discusses relevant aspects of his extensive research into cross-modal associations in children.

The chapters in this volume indicate the variety of topics in the arts which can be illuminated by the systematic examination of cognitive processes. The perception of musical and pictorial material can be investigated in depth without the problem of making assumptions about artistic value which have dogged past research in the arts. In these pages there are studies focusing on children's singing, copying, looking at photographs and abstract paintings; the appreciation of music (including jazz and rock music as well as classical); folk-song and dance; poems and literary passages; houses; and photographs. The range of methods adopted is also broad: there are intensive studies of individuals, experimental manipulations of variables, multivariate analyses of large sets of judgments, analyses of the writings of artists, composers, performers, and critics, and the recording of a culture's traditions. These chapters suggest something of the renewed vigour which has recently characterized the psychology of art, and they should stimulate further advances in the understanding of underlying cognitive processes.

In organizing the Conference Programme we were assisted by an Advisory Group: B.Beit-Hallahmi (Israel), D.Deutsch (USA), W.J. Dowling (USA), G.Eckblad (Norway), H.J.Eysenck (UK), R.Frances (France), H.Gardner (USA), M.A. Hagen (USA), L.Halasz (Hungary), L.Hudson (UK), J.M.Kennedy (Canada), V.Konečni (USA), M.S.Lindauer (USA), P.Machotka (USA), R.Nicki (Canada), D.O'Hare (New Zealand), W. Sluckin (UK) and J.F.Wohlwill (USA). As well as gratefully acknowledging the assistance of members of that Group, we thank friends and colleagues who helped in diverse ways. In particular, we should like to identify Sandra Crozier, Paul Greenhalgh, Hugh Harrison, Julia Hawkins, H. Gwynne Jones, Dave Müller, and Dave Oborne; and our Conference Stewards Dave Morrison, Julia Hawkins, Greg Bolton, Jim Brooks, Richard Dzadiek, Jacqui Eastlake, Nina Edge, Lincoln Grove, Luke Shepherd, and Wendy Sherrat. The major contribution made by Wendy Sheehy is available for all to see: she typed the camera-ready copy for this book; and Siriol David, Bill Sollitt and Mavis Walton were also invaluable at various stages in the production of the book. We offer our thanks to all these people.

W. Ray Crozier
Preston Polytechnic

January 1984

Antony J. Chapman
University of Leeds

CONTRIBUTORS

APTER, M.J., Department of Psychology, University College Cardiff, Wales, UK.

BARTLETT, J.C., Program in Psychology and Human Development, University of Texas at Dallas, Richardson, Texas, USA.

BLANK, P., Boston College, and Harvard Project Zero, Harvard University, Cambridge, Massachusetts, USA.

BOSELIE, F., Psychological Laboratory, University of Nijmegen, The Netherlands.

CHAPMAN, A.J., Department of Psychology, University of Leeds, England, UK.

CROZIER, W.R., School of Psychology, Preston Polytechnic, England, UK.

DEUTSCH, D., Department of Psychology, University of California, San Diego, La Jolla, California, USA.

DOWLING, W.J., Program in Human Development and Communication Sciences, University of Texas at Dallas, Richardson, Texas, USA.

GARDNER, H., Harvard Project Zero, and Boston Veterans Administration Medical Center, Boston, Massachusetts, USA.

HOCK, H.S., Department of Psychology, Florida Atlantic University, Boca Raton, Florida, USA.

HUDSON, L., Department of Psychology, Brunel University, Uxbridge, England, UK.

KONECNI, V.J., Department of Psychology, University of California, San Diego, La Jolla, California, USA.

KOSE, G., Institute for Cognitive Studies, Rutgers University, Newark, New Jersey, USA.

LEEUWENBERG, E., Psychological Laboratory, University of Nijmegen, The Netherlands.

MARKS, L.E., John B. Pierce Laboratory, Yale University, New Haven, Connecticut, USA.

MASSEY, C., Boston College and Harvard Project Zero, Harvard University, Cambridge, Massachusetts, USA.

MCADAMS, S.,Institut de Recherche et Coordination Acoustique/Musique, Centre Georges-Pompidou, Paris, France.

PRATT, F., Department of Psychology, University of Stirling, Scotland, UK.

PRESSING, J., Department of Music, La Trobe University, Bundoora, Australia.

PURCELL, A.T., Department of Architecture, Sydney University, New South Wales, Australia.

SMYTHE, W.E., Department of Psychology, University of Toronto, Canada.

TEMME, J.E., Institute of Social Psychology, University of Utrecht, The Netherlands.

VIKIS-FREIBERGS, V., Department of Psychology, University of Montreal, Canada.

WALK, R.D., Department of Psychology, George Washington University, Washington, DC, USA.

WILLATS, J., Faculty of Art and Design, North East London Polytechnic, London, England.

WINNER, E., Boston College, and Harvard Project Zero, Harvard University, Cambridge, Massachusetts, USA.

CONTENTS

Section 1

INTRODUCTION

Cognitive Processes in the Perception of Art
W.R. Crozier and A.J. Chapman (editors)
© Elsevier Science Publishers B.V. (North-Holland), 1984

THE PERCEPTION OF ART: THE COGNITIVE APPROACH AND ITS CONTEXT

W. Ray Crozier and Antony J. Chapman
Preston Polytechnic   University of Leeds

> 'Aesthetic phenomena are certainly among the most complex of all those with which the behavioral sciences have to deal.' (Berlyne 1971)

THE COMPLEXITY OF AESTHETIC PHENOMENA

Aesthetic experience was one of the earliest topics to be incorporated in the discipline of experimental psychology as it began to emerge in the fourth quarter of the nineteenth century. A substantial literature on aesthetics has developed in the intervening years; and a variety of psychological approaches has been brought to bear on questions concerning the production and appreciation of works of art. Two generalizations may be made with some confidence about the corpus of research which has accumulated. The first is that there is considerable pessimism about the heuristic value of the work. Munro (1963), for example, doubted that the scientific methods of psychology were appropriate for the study of many of the processes that are important in the perception of art; and Child (1969) suggested more assertively that the 'coarse categorizations' and the 'vigorous and broad sweep of the scientific approach' are not adequate for the study of art. Not only has psychology seemed to contribute rather little to the understanding of the processes which underlie artistic creation and reactions to art-works, but within psychology the study of art has seldom been regarded as a distinctive area. Partly because of the uncertain status of artistic phenomena within the discipline, textbooks and courses in psychology have paid scant regard to such phenomena. Psychology's neglect of aesthetics generally is unfortunate for various reasons: for example, because of the persistence and ubiquity of art through time and across cultures, its significance in the lives of individuals, the esteem with which the arts are held in society, and so on.

The second point to be made is that since 1876, when Fechner initiated the empirical approach to art through his book 'Vorschule der Aesthetik' psychology has been characterized by different 'schools'; there has been continual dispute about the proper subject-matter of the discipline and about the theories and methods which should be applied to it. In many cases, the various approaches -- such as Behaviourism, Gestalt Theory, Psychoanalysis, Humanistic Psychology, Information Theory, and Cognitive Psychology -- have made distinctive contributions to the arts. One consequence has been that particular artistic phenomena have been selectively examined and then assimilated to preferred theories and methods of working, and hence these phenomena have escaped broad and systematic investigation as distinctive phenomena in their own right. Approaches to the arts have often been superficial and fragmentary and, as Kose points out in his chapter, traditional approaches to the study of art often reveal more about the workings of psychological investigations than they do about art.

Fechner's research programme advocated the strategy of studying aesthetics 'from below'. The proposed focus of study was to be the impact upon the perceiver of the elements of aesthetic stimuli (such as lines, shapes and colours). When confronted with complex phenomena, it was seen as a useful scientific strategy to begin with some simplification. It was assumed that synthesis might subsequently be possible and that the study of reactions to simple stimuli could help us comprehend responses to actual works of art. The results emanating from this approach have been disappointing, and this we now illustrate by considering that approach within the context of artistic 'behaviour' since the time of Fechner's seminal publication.

We begin by taking painting as an example of developments in the arts. Fechner's investigation of lawful relationships between the 'formal' elements of artworks and the spectator's response to those elements was undertaken in late-nineteenth century Germany. In that society at that time the visual arts were characterized by academicism, with art schools and academies comprising the centres of artistic activity; and painting was held to serve educational purposes and the 'elevation' of society. Some idea of the role of tradition may be gleaned by considering the example of a notable and (for the period) original artist, Hans von Marees (1837-1887). He was then painting landscapes which were based on his study of Italian Renaissance art and on his memories of the Roman countryside. However, at the same time, developments were taking place in France which were to usher in the 'modern movement', a century of continual change in the arts. While there is debate as to the origins of these changes -- for example, many would consider the key work to have been Courbet's painting, 'The Painter's Studio', which was exhibited in Paris in 1855 -- we may note here that Monet's painting 'Impression: Sunrise' (1872), which gave rise to the name of the Impressionist movement, is almost contemporaneous with Fechner's publication. The Impressionist paintings of artists such as Monet and Manet must be some of the most popular paintings in the world (and possibly the last school with which people in general feel comfortable); and they are now regarded as national treasures and centre-pieces of the galleries which exhibit them. Yet, as is well known, the reaction at the time was strikingly different: the loose handling of paint so admired today resulted in the pictures being described as incomplete, and paintings were greeted with indignation. Rosetti is quoted as having said in 1864, 'the new French school is simply putrescence and decomposition'.

The group of artists who in 1916 founded the Cabaret Voltaire in Switzerland questioned the value of art through a series of Dadaist or anti-art works which were intended to outrage and which instigated a theme in artistic practice which is still current. The twentieth century has been a period of unprecedented change in the arts which has been rapid and often bewildering. The bewilderment may be detected, for example, in the titles of some of the books which have chronicled or commentated upon such change -- 'the shock of the new', 'art at the edge' and 'the anxious object'. This has been a century of 'modern art' although by now many of the products which typify that term and which are thought 'modern' and difficult are some sixty to eighty years old. In the visual arts, movements followed one another in quick succession -- surrealism, analytic cubism, synthetic cubism, futurism .... abstract expressionism, hard-edge .... conceptual art, happenings, performance art, earth art, op, pop, photorealism, and so on. So frequent have been the developments that the psychologist observing artistic behaviour might be forgiven for facetiously describing the task facing the psychology-of-art as being less one of accounting for lawful relationships between aesthetic experience and the elements of line, form and colour, and more one of explaining preferences for novelty or the unexpected. A corresponding state of affairs is to be found when, instead of painting, one considers sculpture, music, architecture, dance, drama or poetry.

Many such trends in the arts provide a serious challenge to the researcher who seeks to provide an explanation for artistic behaviour. One such trend is the dominant position within the 'artworld' of the 'avant-garde' and the promotion of avant-garde art as 'official art' (as Brighton, 1977, terms it). (Official art is supported by an elite group of art historians, dealers, critics, artists, and museum staff, who confer status upon it while withholding status from other artistic products). 'Originality' and 'artistic creativity' are now synonymous in ways that may seem natural or obvious to us, but which have not been seen as such in previous periods and in other cultures. Thus, in this volume Vīķis-Freibergs, in a chapter which offers a detailed discussion of the nature of tradition within Latvian oral literature, writes as follows:

> 'The folk poet differs from the modern poet in several ways. First, she or he had a functional role to play in everyday occurrences and did not cater to a selected elite of the population. In this role, they were expected to exhibit a high degree of skill in performance, but there were no demands from society that they be original or necessarily different from other singers'.

A second trend is the artist's mistrust of the 'pleasing' or the 'beautiful' or the 'tasteful', and an embracing of materials and techniques which strenuously avoid such labels. Hence some of the hallmarks of contemporary art are strident colour relationships, dissonant and unmelodic structures in music and poetry, and the preference for accident and the primitive over the crafted and the sophisticated. Cubist painters like Braque and Picasso incorporated various materials in their pictures, such as pieces of newspaper and wallpaper, matchboxes, cardboard and sand, and now it is not out of the ordinary to find a wide range of materials and textures incorporated into painting and sculpture, and 'non-musical' sounds like coughs, sneezes or even silence included in pieces of music.

There has, too, been a blurring of distinctions between art forms: performance art and happenings draw upon music, drama, dance and the visual arts; poetry can become 'concrete'; and painters embrace the three-dimensional. To take a particular example, the Dadaist artist, Schwitters, produced sound-poems, where poetry became an increasingly formal arrangement of pure, meaningless sounds suggested by musical forms (Rubin, 1969). There is also an intense consciousness of the status of the work of art, a consciousness perhaps most strikingly exemplified by the artist Duchamp signing a urinal and displaying it in an exhibition, but also widespread in such practices as land art or conceptual art, or the delight in objects trouvés, impermanent works of art, art outside museums, and so on. More often than not these works are incomprehensible or greeted with anger or ridicule by members of the public.

All these trends point to the difficulties facing any psychologist who attempts to frame explanations for artistic phenomena; and it seems, as Arnheim (1966) has argued, that psychologists have tended to cling to conventional notions about art instead of tackling these difficulties. Machotka (1983) has made the point that much of psychological research into pictorial perception has in fact addressed questions which have been of only marginal interest to picture-makers since the seventeenth century. There are yet further problems. The study of the perception of art is already the subject matter of disciplines, such as art history or art criticism, which utilize psychological concepts and terminology in their accounts; and, to the extent that their practitioners are often trained in art or are members of the 'artworld', these disciplines are closer to art than is psychology. Psychology has to establish its relationship with these disciplines and if it is not to be restricted to empirical investigations of a mundane kind, it will need to develop theory and methodology adequate for the complexity of artistic phenomena.

Neither psychology nor the arts exist in a social or cultural vacuum; and the one can influence the other. The impact of psychoanalysis upon art movements, individual artists, and art criticism has been considerable (see, for example, the review provided by Spector, 1974); and many of the trends identified above had their origins in Freudian work -- in artists' discoveries of 'sexuality' and the 'unconscious'. Gestalt psychology has influenced theory and practice in painting and architecture (cf. Lang, 1984). Vitz (1979) has detected a large number of what he terms 'parallels' between twentieth-century developments in the study of perception and in visual art: there are sometimes similarities between scientific diagrams and images in painting; and techniques for incorporating randomness into visual displays are common to artistic and scientific investigations. Vitz explains these parallel developments in terms of a shared attitude of analytical reductionism which has, it is asserted, characterized thinking in the modern period. Potter et al (in press) discuss both literature and social psychology as constructions of language-users in society, and they argue that neither has a privileged perspective on the other. From these lines of argument, it is clear that psychology must not adopt a stance which purports to view the arts 'from outside' as static or predictable relationships between a stimulus (however complex) and responses. The psychological study of the arts can influence and provide a fresh stimulus for the arts; and both the arts and their psychological study are responsive to broader trends within society.

Psychology should not be seduced by 'artworld' claims about the appeal of artifacts and of artistic perception. One point is clear: the audience for the arts (i.e., for painting, sculpture, classical music, opera, ballet and theatre) is a minority of the population. A second point is that in broad terms the composition of this audience is to a marked extent predictable, particularly in terms of social stratification: Dimaggio and Useem (1978), for example, reviewed over 200 American studies and were able to conclude that the 'rate of consumption of the high arts in the United States varies significantly by social class'. Studies have consistently demonstrated that the ranks of those who attend museums and theatres, opera, symphony concerts and ballet performances are dominated by the well-educated and wealthy: most attenders are professional people. Blue-collar workers and those with little education are virtually absent. By contrast the 'popular' arts such as jazz, rock music and the cinema are consumed at more comparable rates by members of all social classes.

But if exposure to the high arts is both limited and socially stratified, the audience for pictures (still and moving), for music, for drama and for literature has surely never been larger. To illustrate this point, let us examine some statistics on television viewing in Britain (with its population of some 55 million inhabitants). On an average evening, 38 million people will view television, while 5 million will view video-cassettes. Only 0.5% to 2% of the adult population watch visual arts programmes on television; but, while such programmes are therefore placed towards the bottom of the viewing lists, their audiences are larger by a factor of 10 than the record-breaking 6-week attendances at London's Tate Gallery (Read, 1983).

Under the pressures of commercial competition advertisers invest in graphic design which, as Caudle (1983) has shown, uses devices common to art such as visual incongruity and metaphorical symbolism; and of course, additionally, well-known works of art are sometimes incorporated into advertisements. Contemporary Western society is immersed in visual images and Konečni (1982) has made much the same point with regard to music. Music is no longer restricted to elite groups or to special occasions: it has penetrated into every corner of people's lives -- their homes, cars, factories, supermarkets, and public places -- and it accompanies many activities and social encounters. As Konečni (p. 499) points out, this has implications for the study of the perception of the arts: 'what seems needed is a broader perspective on music appreciation, one that transcends the narrow, elitist, and arbitrary definitions of what constitutes good and serious music and also takes into account the reality of music appreciation in our time'. In similar vein, Crozier and Chapman (1981) argued that, in selecting stimuli for experimental studies, an exclusive reliance upon 'artworld' definitions and standards gives rise to a small and unrepresentative sample of stimuli; in their everyday lives the subjects in studies would generally draw upon a far broader range of stimuli for their aesthetic experiences.

We conclude this section by reiterating the view that the arts are complex, multi-levelled phenomena which will continue to defy simple generalizations. It is improbable that any one psychological explanation will ever suffice. Psychological theory will need to treat the arts in their complexity. In our view it will not be found sufficient to adopt conventional notions about the nature of artistic perception, and nor will it prove possible to assimilate the arts to a simple form of psychological model.

PSYCHOLOGICAL THEORIES OF THE ARTS

The psychological schools that have made the most substantial contributions to the understanding of the perception of art have been psychoanalysis, Gestalt theory and experimental psychology (including behaviourism). Each is associated with a large body of research, and each has attempted to explain the perception of art in terms of more general psychological processes (cf. Arnheim, 1956; Berlyne, 1971; Hogg, 1963; Kreitler and Kreitler, 1972; Spector, 1974). In fact each provides only a partial account of the psychological processes underlying the perception of works of art, and in particular cognitive processes have been neglected until recently. The strengths and weaknesses of each approach are briefly outlined in the following sub-sections.

Psychoanalysis

Psychoanalysis is the psychological theory which has had the most impact on artistic practice and criticism. Its influence has been evident since the early experiments of the Surrealists into automatic writing and the recording of dream images; and it remains evident today, for example, in literary theory (Eagleton, 1983). Its impact may be thought surprising to the extent that Freud himself never wrote extensively or developed systematic theory on the arts; he had little interest in the art of his contemporaries and was disparaging about artists' attempts to investigate the unconscious (Spector, 1974). Also, his major retrospective account of the psychology of the artist Leonardo seems seriously flawed: apart from a mistranslation which undermines the plausibility of the interpretation of Leonardo's childhood memory (Farrell, 1963), it is highly selective in specifying which aspects of the artist's work might be considered of psychological significance. For example, the portrayal of St Anne is held to be of particular significance because the depiction of the Saint as a young woman is deemed to be unusual, yet this disregards the fact that by Leonardo's time there had been a longstanding cult of St Anne, and it was one which tended to depict saints as youthful. Additionally, Freud ignores many of the details of composition which are peculiar to the artist. His account of the perception of art stressed that the sources of the pleasure which the spectator obtains are in the unconscious; art provides for the spectator an 'incentive bonus' in the sense that it allows enjoyment of material which would otherwise threaten the ego, and he or she is unaware of the sources of the pleasure obtained from contemplating a work of art.

Freud's theory of art has been severely criticized, not the least because it was concerned only with the content or latent content of the work, and paid no attention to questions of form: the objective aspects of the work were neglected, such that there was no discussion about aesthetic matters of line, colour or form in painting. Little attention was paid to the medium involved; so that, for example, there was no mention of the specific qualities of painting or sculpture. The enjoyment of a work of art was not seen as rewarding in itself, but only as a means to another end. No doubt these weaknesses can be attributed to the fact that Freud never studied artistic phenomena or the perception of works of art in their own right. Works of art were selected for discussion because they were interesting from a psychoanalytic point of view, and from that perspective a minor work like Jensen's 'Gradiva' was as rich in meaning as a masterpiece by Dostoyevsky. The distinctions which Freud failed to make are precisely those which are central to artistic criticism and to the psychology of the perception of art.

Nevertheless, Freud did focus attention on unconscious processes in the perception of art, and he provided fresh constructs for discussing symbolism in the arts. His approach instigated a considerable literature on psychoanalysis and the arts, and vigorous debates continue: hence, for example, a number of papers at the International Conference on Psychology and the Arts (Cardiff, 1983) presented research within the psychoanalytical framework. Also Freud has provided concepts which have been of value for more empirical approaches to the arts; for example, Martindale has made use of the concept of 'primary process' in his theory of historical change in the arts, including painting, poetry, and music (Martindale, 1975; Martindale and Uemura, 1983).

Gestalt Theory

Gestalt psychology, too, has influenced artistic practice and discussion: for example, Gestalt principles were taught at the Bauhaus school of art and design in Germany under Gropius, and that school has had a key role in the development of modern art and architecture. One of the most notable contributors to the psychological analysis of the perception of art, Rudolf Arnheim, has drawn heavily upon Gestalt theory (e.g., Arnheim, 1956, 1966). Then again, one of the points originally made by von Ehrenfels in favour of 'whole' perception (as opposed to associationism) referred to the example of the melody, and this is a gestalt because it is more than the sum of its elements and it can be transposed. From Gestalt psychology have emerged two principal notions in discussions of art: the 'good gestalt' and the theory of expression. The first refers to the organizational principle of the tendency towards a good form -- that is, the simplest form possible -- and its reflection in the compositional balance of works of art. Arnheim (1956) and Kreitler and Kreitler (1972) have applied the concept of 'good gestalt' to the perception of formal qualities in works of art, such as balance and rhythm, line colour and shape. The presence of organizational factors like similarity, proximity and good continuation in the structure of individual works may be discussed in these terms; or generalizations can be made about the predominance of simple forms in primitive stages of artistic development.

The Gestalt theory of expression asserts that the perception of expressiveness in a work of art is direct and unmediated; to perceive a colour at all, for example, demands perception of its expressiveness -- the warmth or liveliness of the colour. The Gestalt approach disputes the view that this is due to learnt associations: perception is not derived from experience and is not culturally variable. Instead expression is explained in terms of the principle of isomorphism: 'processes which take place in different media may be nevertheless similar in their structural organization'(Arnheim,1966). The principal weakness of this view is that the theory of the organization of the brain, upon which the principles of good gestalt and isomorphism rest, has not received empirical support; and within the psychology of perception, Gestalt theory is better known for its demonstration of organizational factors than for its explanation of those factors. Also, from eye movement studies we know that visual perception results from a series of discrete samples of the stimulus, and this casts doubt on the principles of isomorphism as an explanation of expressiveness.

Nevertheless Gestalt psychology has proved fruitful for the discussion of the perception of art. Arnehim has drawn attention to formal aspects of works of art which have been neglected in other approaches and he has attempted to relate the perception of art to more general principles of perception. The question of the expressiveness of art-works has not been sufficiently studied within psychology, but some recent research has suggested that it does not depend on past experience (Lindauer,1984): physiognomic properties appear to be 'in' the stimulus, even if the stimulus is a 'nonsense' figure -- they do not seem to be imposed by the perceiver from memory. In summary the Gestalt account is a partial one and, in concentrating on questions of form, it ignores issues to do with the content of works of art (such as meaning and symbolism).

Experimental Psychology

Fechner's original studies have given rise to a considerable literature upon aesthetic preferences, and several of the questions which Fechner addressed remain topics for inquiry today. For example, a substantial body of research has addressed the psychological status of the 'golden section' -- the belief that rectangular figures are more pleasing if the ratio of the longer side to the shorter side approaches 1:0.62 (cf. McManus, 1980). One recurring ambition has been to discover lawful relationships between aesthetic preferences and properties of simple geometric forms, a project instigated largely by Birkhoff's (1932) formulation of the relationship between beauty (M), order (O) and complexity (C). Birkhoff claimed that the amount of pleasure obtained from a figure was best represented by the equation $M = O/C$. Eysenck (1942) provided data to support the view that the equation $M = O \times C$ provides a better fit and, in the present volume, Boselie and Leeuwenberg now present a formula which they argue provides a still better fit to aesthetic judgments. More significantly, Boselie and Leeuwenberg move away from considering order and complexity as properties of the stimulus: rather, they emphasize what they describe as the subject's 'cognitive representation of two qualities which, according to the knowledge embedded in the representation system, are incompatible'. They conclude that preference data will require an explanation in terms of cognitive processes rather than any stimulus-response regularities.

Experimental aesthetics has placed relatively little emphasis on theory constructions: instead the emphasis has been upon data collection and the search for regularities within preferences. The research orientation has incorporated a number of assumptions: for instance, that the origins of aesthetic preferences are biological, and that artistic behaviour serves adaptive functions. Eysenck (1961) proposed that there is 'some property of the central nervous system which determines aesthetic judgments, a property which is biologically derived, and which covers the whole field of visual art'; and Humphrey argued as follows:

> 'considered as a biological phenomenon, aesthetic preferences stem from a predisposition among animals and men to seek out experiences through which they may *learn* to *classify* the objects in the world about them. Beautiful 'structures' in nature or in art are those which facilitate the task of classification by presenting evidence of the "taxonomic" relations between things in a way which is informative and easy to grasp'. (1973, p. 432)

The most sustained attempt to place art within a biological perspective has been the 'new experimental aesthetics' of Berlyne (1971, 1974), which linked aesthetic behaviour to exploration. The pervasiveness of artistic activity and its presence in varied cultures throughout the world led Berlyne to propose that artistic activity grows out of some fundamental characteristic of the human nervous system. His account emphasized the psychophysiological concept of 'arousal'. The level of arousal in the nervous system could be increased by external stimulus patterns, including the collative variables of novelty, complexity, surprisingness, and puzzlingness ('collative' in the sense that information from two or more sources is being compared). Berlyne proposed that the characteristics on which the pleasingness (or hedonic value) of a stimulus depended were also the ones which determine the level of arousal, and he formulated relationships among hedonic value and arousal potential:

> 'a work of art is regarded as a stimulus pattern whose collative properties, and possibly other properties as well, give it a positive hedonic value'. (Berlyne, 1974, p. 8)

Berlyne's theory stimulated a considerable amount of research (see, for example, Day, 1981) which has in recent years given a fresh impetus to the psychological investigation of art. From studies of specially prepared simple stimuli there has been substantial support for the theory's predictions; and, to their credit, researchers in the Berlyne tradition have gone beyond subjective statements of preference and ratings of pleasingness to introduce a range of response measures into experimental aesthetics. However, Francès (1976) has questioned the generalizability and universality of the equations between collative variables and judgments of pleasingness and interest. By obtaining different patterns of results for students and manual workers of the same age in France and in Hungary, he has shown that the form of relationships is not independent of socio-cultural factors; and he has recently suggested that the mediating variable is differential exposure to the norms and values of the 'artworld' (Francès, 1983).

Research with works of art has been less convincing and has not received as much attention as that with specially constructed stimuli. In part this balance of attention may be due to Berlyne's conviction that the scientific approach should begin with the simplest phenomena and only gradually work its way up to the more complex. Another reason is the problems posed to the Berlyne approach by art-works. Works of art are over-determined: even the simplest is replete with meanings, and it is a moot point whether they can be considered as the sum of their elements or described or constructed along Berlyne's dimensions. The research that has been carried out with works of art (typically reproductions), such as multivariate analyses of judgments to detect factors (e.g., complexity) underlying judgments (e.g., Berlyne, 1974) is generally considered 'suggestive', but it does not show that art-works directly affect the nervous system in the kinds of ways proposed by the theory. Indeed discussion of the arousal-increasing or moderating qualities of art-works -- for example, abstract paintings -- is often highly speculative (cf. Berlyne, 1971). Also, insufficient attention is paid to individual differences in reactions to works of art and a great deal of necessary research has yet to be conducted. Some of Berlyne's observations have yet to be tested: for example, he suggested that through increased exposure one can 'learn the redundancies and transitional probabilities that characterize particular art forms, styles, and cultural traditions' (Berlyne, 1971).

One recent debate within this paradigm has concerned the effects of the familiarity of a stimulus upon its pleasingness. Berlyne proposed an inverted-U function relating familiarity and affect, and explained this function in terms of the relationship between hedonic value and arousal potential which, as we have already noted, is held to be dependent on collative variables such as novelty and familiarity. This account has been disputed by Zajonc (e.g., Zajonc et al, 1974) whose 'mere exposure' hypothesis holds that pleasingness is enhanced by increasing familiarity rather than being diminished by exposure as predicted by Berlyne. In this volume Temme presents data from several experiments to test these rival predictions. His results suggest the relevance for the effects of exposure of a distinction between two cognitive sets adopted by subjects: an 'aesthetic' set (where subjects approach the task as one involving aesthetic appreciation); and a 'meaning' set (where they see the task as involving guessing meanings). The chapter by Temme indicates the importance of cognitive set and task expectations in mediating the effects of mere exposure, and it suggests that some of the findings in this area may be due to experimental artefacts.

A theory advanced by Kreitler and Kreitler (1972) again focuses on the pleasure afforded by works of art. Pleasure is interpreted within a homeostatic model of motivation: it is associated with a rise in tension followed by a reduction in tension. The authors discuss why people should seek out and persist in enjoying tension increasing (and hence presumably displeasing) encounters with art-works, and hence they face up to the problem posed by a tension-reduction model through incorporating a number of modifications. Their first modification is as follows:

> 'a major motivation for art is tensions which exist in the spectator of art prior to his exposure to the work of art. The work of art mediates the relief of the preexisting tensions by generating new tensions which are specific'. (1972, p. 16)

That is, a spectator seeks out art-works which increase tension (which effects are mitigated, however, by the anticipation of tension reduction) and which serve as a cue for the reduction of the more diffuse, cue-less arousal which exists prior to the spectator's encounter with the work. The adoption of this view (which is akin to the Hebbian notion of a stimulus acting as both an elicitor of arousal and as a cue for action to reduce arousal upon which it draws) is intended to resolve the apparent contradictions of deriving pleasure from an arousal-increasing stimulus.

Kreitler and Kreitler emphasize that pleasure is not the whole of art experience, and they note that much discussion of the arts has concerned what they term the 'more' in art. That is to say, works of art do more than evoke emotional experiences: they have varied functions in promoting ethical, political, religious, spiritual and other goals of society; works of art have 'meaning'. To account for these pervasive aspects of art they propose the concept of 'cognitive orientation':

> 'the theory of cognitive orientation shows that a stimulus turns into a cue only after it is subjected to a series of processes designed to determine its meaning and the relations of this meaning to the meanings of other concomitant stimuli, external and internal'. (1972, p. 23)

They assert that cognition is as important as arousal for determining aesthetic experience; spectators are clearly concerned with establishing the meanings of art-works, while an important motive for seeking out such works is the opportunity to extend one's cognitive orientation and to test its dimensions. In this regard Kreitler and Kreitler may seem to resemble Berlyne, but the Kreitlers argue against an interpretation of exploration in terms of some optimal level of arousal or complexity: they maintain that this is subservient to the motive of extending cognitive orientation. Their 1972 book is an important work in which they demonstrate a profound grasp of the arts as basic psychological principles are applied to a range of phenomena (from the elements of colour, line, form, harmony, melody, and rhythm) to a range of art forms (including music, dance, painting, sculpture and literature). However the many significant points which they make do not disguise an uneasiness invoked by a tension-reduction model (however modified); and an appeal to some pre-existing diffuse tension within the individual seems hardly to account for the enormous amount of 'work' that is invested by the individual as a spectator of art.

One of the most persistent critics of theories which emphasize optimal levels of arousal has been Apter (e.g., 1982). In his contribution to this volume he outlines his reveral theory of motivation and applies it to the arts. He substitutes the notion of a single dimension of arousal with that of pairs of metamotivational modes. Also, he distinguishes the telic and paratelic modes: in the telic mode the goal of behaviour is primary; and in the paratelic mode the focus is upon the activity itself rather than the goal. In the telic mode high arousal tends to lead to anxiety, and arousal reduction gives pleasure or relaxation; whereas in the paratelic mode high arousal is actively sought by the individual, and low arousal leads to boredom. With this distinction Apter is able to meet the problem faced by Kreitler and Kreitler, viz that people, in the apparent pursuit of pleasure, seek out increases in arousal; and in the present book Apter interprets many artistic phenomena in terms of the paratelic mode. He argues that the arts utilize a number of devices (such as providing special locations) to ensure that the paratelic rather than the telic mode is induced: failure would render increases in arousal threatening and aversive (rather than desirable). Apter applies his theory to explain how it might be that the arts produce enjoyable experiences.

COGNITIVE PROCESSES IN THE PERCEPTION OF ART

As indicated already, the approach which is broadly described as 'experimental aesthetics' has shifted its emphasis from stimulus properties to cognitive issues -- such as cognitive representations, cognitive set, and cognitive orientation. These developments parallel trends within psychology more generally where cognitive psychology has achieved a dominant position. It is not appropriate to consider 'cognitive psychology' as a new school within psychology which is opposed to previous experimental approaches. Rather it is indicative of changes in emphases -- new concepts have been introduced and there is increased methodological sophistication. At first sight, this might not seem a productive paradigm for the study of artistic phenomena: two of its principal roots might be considered unsympathetic to the kinds of creativity that distinguish the production and appreciation of works of art. First, cognitive psychology is a rather sophisticated variant of a mechanistic view of man: it is sophisticated in the sense that developments in the computer and in information technology have permitted a relatively elaborate mechanistic metaphor; also, the bias within cognitive psychology has been towards the use of verbal material and linguistic performance and away from pictorial and non-language sound stimuli. Second, cognitive psychology has in part developed out of a European structuralist tradition. In particular Piaget focused attention on cognitive development and he advanced concepts which have been central in contemporary thinking about cognition. But, as Gardner and others have pointed out, the French intellectual tradition within which structuralism has developed has been associated with 'the denigration of humanistic philosophy and the arts, accompanied by the exaltation of logical-mathematical thought and geometrical reasoning' (Gardner, 1981, p.17). Heuristic models of man as machine or man as scientist might seem to offer little to the psychology of art. However, on the evidence of the papers presented at the International Conference on Psychology and the Arts and the chapters in this volume this is clearly a pessimistic if not totally unwarranted viewpoint. Partly because of the new inputs from cognitive psychology the arts are now being analysed with unprecedented vigour by psychologists. Various reasons are to be found in the biases of cognitive psychology: for example, there is a concern with people's representations of the world; there is a related concern with the role of symbols in thought; perceptual processes are seen as extended in time; and there is an emphasis on human skills, viewed as complex sequences of behaviour. We now examine each of these examples, briefly in turn, and we refer to chapters in this volume to illustrate their value for understanding the perception of art.

Cognitive psychology is largely the analysis of how people construct and manipulate mental representations of the external world. This perspective has given rise to core concepts like the 'schema' or the 'mental image' which have been fruitful for the psychological investigation of art. Schemata are pre-existing conceptual frameworks; organized predispositions through which individuals respond to the external world in characteristic ways. They are 'frames' for the individual to attribute meaning to events, objects and people. They are not fixed or static: through processes of 'accommodation' and 'assimilation', as Piaget terms them (cf. Flavell, 1963), the schemata are modified and become elaborated during the person's transactions with the environment. In the process of assimilation the individual interprets and behaves towards the environment in terms of his or her existent cognitive system; in accommodation the schema is modified to adapt to the environment. Schemata originate in action, and the construct has proved useful to cognitive psychologists in relating perception to action. For example, Neisser describes schemata as 'cognitive structures that prepare the perceiver to accept certain kinds of information rather than others and thus control the activity of looking' (1976, p. 20); 'the schema accepts information as it becomes available at sensory surfaces and is changed by that information: it directs movements and exploratory activities that make more information available, by which it is further modified' (1976, p. 54).

Several of our authors rely on the concept of schema as outlined above. For example, Pratt studies the copying of line drawings, and he monitors looking (recording eye movements) and drawing (hand movements). His data have led him to abandon any thoughts of a simple dichotomy between knowing and seeing, of the kind that has featured in analyses of drawing. Instead he postulates a concept of knowledge-guided-looking, similar to Neisser's concept of schemata and perceptual cycles. Pratt writes,

> 'We came to see knowledge-guided-looking as providing a means of control; both over visual input from the model (to be copied) and over what aspect of that input is utilized in acts of drawing: we came to see this process of control in terms of a perceptual cycle ... which not only involves the possibility of modifying what aspects of the model are attended to, but also the possibility of modifying the knowledge base of drawing acts'.

Willats provides an alternative account of the relationship between looking and drawing. It is one that emphasizes a distinction between those drawing systems which are based on projective geometry and those based on a broader class of denotation systems which say what the marks in a picture stand for. Willats argues that the developmental process, at least in its early stages, involves an interaction between the production of drawings (which make sense according to some denotation system) and the child's dissatisfaction with these products. There is dissatisfaction because they do not meet additional criteria: they can not be derived from the object by projective geometry, or they do not depict the object from a sufficiently general direction of view.

A similar kind of knowledge base to that proposed by Pratt is postulated by Dowling in his longitudinal study of the spontaneous singing of two children. He holds that the most parsimonious account of the course of development is provided by the development and elaboration of schemata, defined as 'systematic patterns in the abstract knowledge listeners have about musical structure' and 'the knowledge the child has at a given stage of development concerning how a song should be constructed'. Dowling speculates about whether the same or similar schemata function in both music production and music perception.

Purcell, too, draws upon the concept of schema in discussing aesthetic reactions to environmental stimuli. He has developed a model of aesthetic reactions which is couched in terms of the arousal or tension consequent upon a conflict between the current stimulus and what has been expected. This model is similar to accounts by Berlyne and by Lasher et al (1983), but Purcell stresses the prominent part played by mental organizations, or schemata. He argues that a current stimulus is not compared with some fixed list of attributes, in order to test for some discrepancy; but rather the stimulus is compared with schemata, characterized by a hierarchical structure and by prototypes rather than lists of attributes. In his chapter Purcell tests predictions of his model by analysing ratings of attractiveness, interest and preference when stimuli depart in varying ways from some prototype.

The application of the concept of schemata in perception and memory is not without its critics. A notable critic is Gibson (1979). He denies that in perception there is any part played by mental events such as memories, or unconscious inferences, or schemata. In Gibson's theory information is available in the environment which is both necessary and sufficient for perception; in particular there are available those characteristics of the stimulus array which remain invariant across change and which are 'picked-up' directly by the perceiver without the need for any further 'information' processing. In the present volume Bartlett outlines a theory of memory expressed in Gibsonian terms. It is a theory which is antithetical to accounts of memory in terms of schemata, and Bartlett applies it to questions concerning recognition memory for photographic sequences and for melodies. The theory has three major postulates: (1) the event perception hypothesis, that sequences of stimuli extended in time can function as units in memory; (2) the basis of memory is the pick-up of invariants over time, and these invariants also specify alternative stimuli to those presented; and (3) memory is essentially veridical -- that is to say, then, that the notion of assimilation is rejected. Bartlett shows how these postulates might be applied to memory for music. For example, atonal melodies are more difficult to remember than tonal melodies, and this might be explained in terms of schemata and assimilation: memory for atonal melodies is distorted in the direction of tonality. However, Bartlett presents evidence for an alternative explanation: melodies are perceived as events, and this allows for the extraction of invariants which contribute to their coherence as events and which specify other melodies which were not presented. Atonal melodies will have a greater range of optional others, and hence will be more difficult to remember. Walk, in his chapter, also considers event perception, and he describes an experiment which uses points of light to depict emotion and dance.

A further focus on the study of mental representations has been upon mental imagery and this, too, is reflected in the present volume. Deutsch provides an extensive review of visuo-spatial analogues for musical processing, drawing upon historical sources, the writings of composers, and much current research in music cognition. She poses such questions as: can transformations be performed in 'musical space' which are analogous to those in vision? The composer Schoenberg (1951) answered this question in the affirmative:

> 'Just as our mind always recognizes, for instance, a knife, a bottle or a watch, regardless of its position and can reproduce it in the imagination in every possible position, even so a musical creator's mind can operate subconsciously with a row of tones, regardless of their direction, regardless of the way in which a mirror might show the mutual relations, which remain a given quantity'.

Deutsch places in historical context the goal of abstract geometrical representation of musical structure, and she discusses research into representations of pitch structures, relationships between keys, and timbre.

Analogies between visual and musical percepts are addressed also by Marks in a chapter which reviews research on synesthesia. There he notes the ambitions of composers who have been influenced by Newton's analogy between the colours of the spectrum and the notes of the diatonic scale, and he discusses artists who showed evidence of strong synesthesia. McAdams, in his chapter on auditory organization, addresses questions such as how far, when listening to a recording of an orchestra, one can separate out the sounds of instruments, and so 'parse' the single source into multiple 'virtual source images'; or how one can similarly separate out melodies and chords, and group textures. He argues that research into auditory organization is aided by utilizing the metaphor of the 'auditory image', defined as a 'psychological representation of a sound entity exhibiting a coherence in its acoustic behaviour'. He shows that the adoption of this metaphor allows for a multi-levelled approach to auditory orgnization and that it can illuminate studies of sequential and simultaneous organization and interactions between them. Adopting the metaphor also has benefits for communication between musicians and psychologists in that it offers a common language for discussions of a range of musical phenomena.

As Lasher et al (1983) have pointed out, cognitive psychology is likely to offer insights into aesthetic behaviour because of the central role which it ascribes to the representation of the external world through abstract symbols and because of the traditional conception of art as a symbolic representation of the world. Within the psychology of art, current research into symbols has been considerably influenced by the philosopher Nelson Goodman (cf. Perkins and Leondar, 1977). While the term 'symbol' has frequently featured in art criticism and has figured prominently in psychoanalytic accounts of the arts, Goodman's seminal work, 'Languages of Art' (1968), has clarified the meaning of the term. That work has also stimulated a large number of empirical enquiries, particularly into the development of symbol use in the arts. Goodman showed that symbolism is not restricted to representational art-works: abstract or formal painting or sculpture, performance works, and musical compositions can also be said to be symbolic, in that they exemplify some of their properties, and that to exemplify could properly be said to symbolize; also an art-work which is non-representational may have expressive properties and hence can again be said to symbolize an emotion or idea.

In 1966 Goodman founded a research group, Harvard Project Zero, which has carried out a sustained programme of research into the development of artistic production and sensitivity. It has emphasized the development of abilities to use and understand symbols in art, and one of its explicit goals has been 'to analyze and classify the types of symbol systems and symbolic reference characteristics of different art forms (and) to identify and study experimentally the skills and abilities required for the understanding and manipulation of art symbols' (Howard, 1971, p. 64). The work of this group is represented here in a chapter by Blank, Massey, Gardner and Winner, which considers the ability of five- to ten-year-olds to perceive expression in paintings. The children were asked to point to the painting which was best described by a given mood term, or to match paintings according to mood; and through careful experimentation, the Project Zero researchers were able to show that even children of pre-school age are sensitive to expressive properties in works of art.

Three further chapters consider conceptual issues in the study of symbols. Smythe critically reviews three kinds of symbol systems current in psychology -- conventional, mythopoetic, and physical. In the first system the relationship between the symbol and what it stands for is determined by convention; the second system, mythopoetic, is most closely associated with psychoanalytic theory and characterizes symbols as having deep or hidden significance; and the physical system refers to 'a machine that produces through time an evolving collection of symbol structures' (Newell and Simon, 1976, p. 116) -- a small and well-defined set of operators, as in a computer program, is sufficient to compose any arbitrary calculation. Smythe suggests that it is a 'central dogma' of contemporary cognitive psychology that physical symbol systems can be used to explain people's use of both conventional and mythopoetic systems. He goes on to argue that this central dogma is severely flawed; and he concludes that human symbolic activity is not to be reduced to one system, but that a number of such systems need to be identified and studied.

Hudson, too, in his chapter is critical of the current dominant approaches within psychology. He argues that hermeneutics is a more productive approach to the arts, and it is one which he believes will avoid the trivializing of complex phenomena: he sees other approaches as trivializing in that way. Hermeneutics is the interpretation of meanings: it involves the sifting and evaluation of various 'readings' of 'texts' -- the term 'text' being extended to incorporate paintings, photographs, and other artefacts. Such 'readings' require detailed attention to the art-object, a knowledge of its history, and appreciation of the context within which the reading takes place. Clearly hermeneutics is in direct opposition to more traditional approaches in experimental aesthetics (with their reliance upon simple response measures and brief presentations of large numbers of stimuli). Hudson's own work (e.g., Hudson, 1982) provides one of the few applications of this approach in the psychological literature.

Kose contrasts Nelson Goodman's and Ernst Cassirer's approaches to the study of symbols in art. They share an aversion to reductive explanations of art, and they both focus on the concept of symbol. Nevertheless they differ in how they see the relationship between a work of art and its meaning. Kose summarizes the differences in this way:

> 'artistic meaning, for Goodman, is determined by convention and by the characteristics of a particular symbol system. While for Cassirer, meaning in art, or its "symbolic pregnance" is mutually determined by the interweaving of a ".. perceptive phenomenon, given here and now, to a characteristic total meaning ..." .... the significance of art is in the particular way in which the intention to do art is carried out'.

That is to say, for Cassirer symbols do not have an independent conventional meaning that can be easily transmitted; rather, symbolic meaning is mutually determined by the relationship between the total intention behind the work and the specific embodiment of that intention in forms and materials. Kose also considers the implications of these two theories for empirical enquiries into symbol use in the arts. He briefly reviews some of the findings of the Harvard Project Zero group; and he suggests that some of the results about individual differences in the acquisition of symbol systems, and the many factors which influence such acquisition, call into question the validity of Goodman's analysis of the organization of symbolic meaning. Kose also outlines his own research into children's understanding of the meanings of drawings and photographs, and he suggests how these illustrate the complexity of pictures and the problem of generalizing about competence in pictorial symbol systems across different kinds of pictures.

Konečni adopts an empirical approach to the 'meaning' of art-works, in that his studies investigate the success of claims made by artists about the messages communicated to the spectator by their art-works. His approach is to take artists' statements or 'manifestoes' and to examine whether the meanings which are claimed therein are detected by groups of subjects. Typically the subjects are college students with no specialized knowledge of the arts. Five separate experiments provide little evidence of successful communication. Konečni has written a provocative chapter: many artists and commentators on the arts would dispute that works should be expected to 'communicate' in the sense that he has in mind, and many artists are known to be averse to any discussion about their work, other than perhaps elusive or indirect discussion. Nevertheless there is an important point here: art-works do have meanings and these require some shared symbol system of the kinds discussed by Smythe and Kose. But, as we have argued above, works of art are produced and appreciated within a context, and their interpretation requires shared values and expectations. There are many illustrations of this. Let us consider one (well-publicized) example: to display a neat array of household bricks in a prestigious gallery is to many people 'meaningless', and any interest or pleasure that they might potentially derive from this array is overwhelmed by this sense of meaninglessness; that kind of reaction may sometimes be the goal of an artist, but, more generally, it may be a straightforward reflection of a gulf between the norms and values of an 'artworld' and those of public. Whether the gulf is relatively wider at some times or in some cultures is a matter for discussion. What Konečni has shown is that, contrary to the claims that many artists might make for the universal significance of their work, spectators must bring something to the work of art in order to appreciate it. Psychologists have yet to tackle in any depth the question of what that 'something' is (Crozier and Chapman, 1981).

Another aspect of cognitive psychology, mentioned earlier, has been its emphasis on considering the process of perceiving as extended in time. Cognitive psychologists postulate that a number of information processing stages intervene between the presentation of a stimulus and an overt response. Our subjective impression when looking at a picture, for example, might be that we take it in 'at a glance' or that our eyes sweep across it in a 'glance curve' (Gordon, 1981), but it is clear now that such impressions are not correct. Eye-movement analysis shows that our perceptions are actually constructed from integrating many discrete samples of the picture, and the fact that visual attention is biased towards certain 'informative' parts of the pictures is indicative of processes of inference and of guidance of fixations. In models of information processing these processes have been specified through the postulation of a sequence of stages between 'input' and 'output' and these models have recently been applied to the perception of works of art. Marschalek (1983), for example, has discussed developmental changes in aesthetic responses in terms of stages of attention, perceptual memory, short-term memory, and processing capacity.

Hock's chapter discusses the factors which influence the precision with which people can remember the spatial location of objects in a picture. He considers a number of factors including short-term memory for location information and the effects of perceptual grouping on the spatial resolution of the visual system. Research is cited which shows that following a fixation there is a rapid decrease in the precision of information about location that is necessary to make sense of a complex scene. Also, the perceptual grouping which is required for a spectator to establish thematic relationships in the picture tends to decrease the accuracy with which the spectator retrieves information about location. Usually a viewer's main concern when inspecting a picture is to determine its content rather than make judgments about the precise location of objects in it. Hock proposes a model for retrieving information about location in terms of the viewer constructing 'imaginary perspectives' -- imagining what the scene would look like from different perspectives, and using these to encode location information. His chapter represents much of what is distinctive about the cognitive approach to the perception of pictures: it emphasizes stages of processing, processing-capacity limitations, and the evolution of 'strategies' or 'heuristics' to simplify the spectator's task and bring it within capacity.

Improvisation has been a favoured artistic technique for centuries across different art forms, and when it is performed in 'real-time' (as for example in jazz music) it can involve remarkable performance skills. In the chapter by Pressing the point is made that

> 'fluent musical improvisers can produce unbroken complex and coherent melodic strings of notes of nearly arbitrary length at speeds up to circa 10 notes/second. This is close to the limited reported values of kinesthetic reaction time ... ' .

Pressing provides an overview of improvisation in many art forms. He compares performers' accounts and critics' accounts in an effort to extract elements which seem common to the different media. Then he considers these common elements in terms of research into cognitive processes, particularly research into the distribution of attention across tasks, information processing capacity limits, memory processes, and skills. Skilled performance itself involves a chain of mechanisms leading from input to output: for example, the coding of incoming data, the evaluation of possible responses, the choice of response, and its execution and timing. Questions are raised about the role of automaticity in skill, the concurrent running of processing stages, and the role of feedback and feedforward loops in the maintenance of skilled performance. Improvisation is a set of skills fundamental to many psychological tasks but, as Pressing reminds us, research on high levels of skilled performance has not been much studied by psychologists; and much of the information on improvised performance has been embedded within a specialized literature on the arts. Pressing is able to bring the expertize and sensitivity of a cognitive psychologist and a musician to illuminate the complexity of improvisation. Cognitive psychology offers sophisticated analysis of skilled performance; but, as research is only beginning to examine perceptual processes in the performance of art, so we await the instigation of the corresponding investigation into the perception and enjoyment of improvisation.

CONCLUSIONS

Returning here to our opening quotation, it is impossible not to concur with Berlyne that the arts are highly complex phenomena with many dimensions. We would expect that a variety of approaches will be required to elucidate the psychological processes underlying the perception of art. Within experimental psychology the dominant tradition has been experimental aesthetics. This has generated a large number of empirical studies into relationships between aesthetic responses and stimulus properties, and it has encouraged some theory development, most notably Berlyne's contributions. However, the strategy of 'aesthetics from below' has resulted in insufficient attention being paid to works of art, and conclusions derived from the study of specially contrived stimuli have not been applied successfully to the perception of art works. Often, indeed, as Hardiman and Zernich (1977) have concluded, the direct study of responses to works of art has tended to result in a series of isolated investigations which has not been sufficient to develop theory or even to build up a coherent knowledge base.

The examination of cognitive processes seems to us to be potentially fruitful for a number of reasons: (1) As researchers have attempted to forge theories within experimental aesthetics they have necessarily attributed importance to cognitive processes. (2) Such processes have been largely neglected by the major theories of aesthetic reactions -- like psychoanalysis, or approaches which rely upon the concept of arousal -- as these have focused on an interpretation of the pleasure afforded by art in terms of drive-reduction, whether sublimated or not. Yet one could hardly deny that cognition is important in the appreciation of art -- the enjoyment is often derived from exploring works of art, from detecting patterns and rhythms, from comparing works by the same or different artists, from solving puzzles etc. -- and here the concept of 'cognitive orientation' is illuminating (cf. Kreitler and Kreitler, 1972). (3) A full understanding of aesthetic responses will require an analysis of how artworks are perceived, and a sound foundation for experimental aesthetics can emerge from cognitive psychologists applying their models and methodologies to the investigation of the perception of pictures and the perception of music. At the very least, they can provide some direct evidence on the parts allegedly played in the perception of art by processes such as isomorphism or glance curves. (4) Cognitive psychology introduces a broader set of dependent variables into experimental aesthetics: it breaks away from an over-reliance on measures of preference and liking, and judgments of pleasingness and interest. It is not obvious from an examination of art criticism or from artists' discussions that these traditional measures reflect the most salient constructs with which spectators confront art-works. (5) In the past an erroneous assumption has been salient, to the effect that in order to pursue the psychological study of art rigorously one is obliged to forego the analysis of responses to actual art-works and to adopt a research strategy like 'aesthetics from below'. The chapters in this volume demonstrate that pictures, drawings, songs, and pieces of music can be studied directly with methodological rigour and sophistication.

Finally, we would say that the study of cognitive processes should help to break down a compartmentalization in the investigation of art. Previously, emotional responses have been studied separately from cognitive aspects, and social psychological perspectives have been virtually disregarded. Now recent research within mainstream psychology -- research into cognition and affect, and into social cognition -- promises possibilities for more integrated theories of the perception of art. That is the hope for the future. Meanwhile this volume demonstrates progress thus far in the new field of the cognitive psychology of art.

REFERENCES

Apter, M.J. (1982). The Experience of Motivation: The Theory of Psychological Reversals. London: Academic Press.

Arnheim, R. (1956). Art and Visual Perception: A Psychology of the Creative Eye. London: Faber and Faber.

Arnheim, R. (1966). Towards a Psychology of Art: Collected Essays. London: Faber and Faber.

Berlyne, D.E. (1971). Aesthetics and Psychobiology. New York: Appleton-Century-Crofts.

Berlyne, D.E. (1974). Studies in the New Experimental Aesthetics. New York: Wiley.

Birkhoff, G.D. (1932). Aesthetic Measure. Cambridge, Massachusetts: Harvard University Press.

Brighton, A. (1977). Official art and the Tate Gallery. Studio International, 193, 41-44.

Caudle, F.M. (1983). Psychological aspects of art in American magazine advertising. Paper presented at the British Psychological Society, Welsh Branch, International Conference on Psychology and the Arts, Cardiff.

Child, I.L. (1969). Aesthetics. In: G. Lindzey and E. Aronson (Eds.) Handbook of Social Psychology. Volume 3. London: Addison-Wesley.

Crozier, W.R. and Chapman, A.J. (1981). Aesthetic preferences, prestige and social class. In: D. O'Hare (Ed.) Psychology and the Arts. Brighton, Sussex: Harvester.

Day, H.I. (1981). Advances in Intrinsic Motivation and Aesthetics. New York: Plenum.

Dimaggio, P. and Useem, M. (1978). Social class and arts consumption: the origins and consequences of class differences in exposure to the arts in America. Theory and Society, 5, 141-161.

Eagleton, T. (1983). Literary Theory. Oxford: Basil Blackwell.

Eysenck, H.J. (1942). The experimental study of the 'Good Gestalt': a new approach. Psychological Review, 49, 344-364.

Eysenck, H.J. (1961). Sense and Nonsense in Psychology. Harmondsworth: Penguin.

Farrell, B. (1963). Introduction to S. Freud, Leonardo. Harmondsworth: Penguin.

Fechner, G.T. (1876). Vorschule der Aesthetik. Leipzig: Breitkopf and Haertel.

Flavell, J.H. (1963). The Developmental Psychology of Jean Piaget. New York: Van Nostrand Reinhold.

Francès, R. (1976). Comparative effects of six collative variables on interest and preference in adults of different educational levels. Journal of Personality and Social Psychology, 33, 62-79.

Francès, R. (1983). Perceptual interest and aesthetic preference, or switching of hedonic power based on educational background. Paper presented at the

British Psychological Society, Welsh Branch, International Conference on Psychology and the Arts, Cardiff.

Gardner, H. (1981). The Quest for Mind. Chicago, Illinois: Chicago University Press.

Gibson, J.J. (1979). The Ecological Approach to Visual Perception. Boston, Massachusetts: Houghton-Mifflin.

Goodman, N. (1968). Languages of Art. London: Oxford University Press.

Gordon, I. (1981). Left and Right in Art. In: D. O'Hare (Ed.) Psychology and the Arts. Brighton, Sussex: Harvester.

Hardiman, G.W. and Zernich, T. (1977). Preferences for the visual arts: A review of recent studies. Perceptual and Motor Skills, 44, 455-463.

Hogg, J. (1969). Psychology and the Visual Arts. Harmondsworth, Middlesex: Penguin.

Howard, V.A. (1971). Harvard Project Zero: A fresh look at art education. Journal of Aesthetic Education, 5, 61-73.

Hudson, L. (1982). Bodies of Knowledge. London: Weidenfeld.

Humphrey, N.K. (1973). The illusion of beauty. Perception, 2, 429-439.

Konečni, V.J. (1982). Social interaction and musical preference. In: D. Deutsch (Ed.) The Psychology of Music. New York: Academic Press.

Kreitler, H. and Kreitler, S. (1972). Psychology and the Arts. Durham, North Carolina: Duke University Press.

Lang, J. (1984). Formal aesthetics and visual perception, and questions architects ask. Visual Arts Research, in press.

Lasher, M.D., Carroll, J.M., and Bever, T.G. (1983). The cognitive basis of aesthetic experience. Leonardo, 16, 196-199.

Lindauer, M.S. (1984). Physiognomy and art: approaches from above, below and sideways. Visual Arts Research, in press.

Machotka, P. (1983). Perception, psychology and the study of art. Paper presented at the British Psychological Society, Welsh Branch, International Conference on Psychology and the Arts, Cardiff.

Marschalek, D. (1983). A review of basic cognitive processes and their relevance to understanding responses to works of art. Visual Arts Research, 9, 23-33.

Martindale, C. (1975). Romantic Progression: The Psychology of Literary History. Washington, DC: Hemisphere.

Martindale, C. and Uemura, A. (1983). Stylistic evolution in European music. Leonardo, 16, 225-228.

McManus, I.C. (1980). The aesthetics of simple figures. British Journal of Psychology, 71, 505-524.

Munro, T. (1963). The psychology of art: past, present, future. Journal of Aesthetics and Art Criticism, 21, 264-282.

Neisser, U. (1976). Cognition and Reality. San Francisco, California: Freeman.

Newell, A. and Simon, H.A. (1976). Computer science as empirical inquiry: symbols and search. Communications of the ACM, 19, 113-126.

Perkins, D. and Leondar, B. (1977). The Arts and Cognition. Baltimore, Maryland: Johns Hopkins University Press.

Potter, J., Stringer, P. and Wetherell, M. (in press). Social Texts and Context: Literature and Social Psychology. London: Routledge and Kegan Paul.

Read, J. (1983). 'I don't know why you bother'. Art and Artists, 203, August.

Rubin, W.S. (1969). Dada and Surrealist Art. London: Thames and Hudson.

Schoenberg, A. (1951). Style and Idea. London: Williams and Norgate.

Spector, J. (1974). The Aesthetics of Freud: A Study in Psychoanalysis and Art. Washington, DC: McGraw-Hill.

Vitz, P.C. (1979). Visual sciences and modernist art: historical parallels. In: C.F. Nodine and D.F. Fisher (Eds.) Perception and Pictorial Representation. New York: Praeger.

Zajonc, R.B., Crandall, R., Kail, R.V. and Swap, W. (1974). Effect of extreme exposure frequencies on different affective ratings of stimuli. Perceptual and Motor Skills, 38, 667-678.

Section 2

SYMBOLS AND MEANINGS IN THE ARTS

Cognitive Processes in the Perception of Art
W.R. Crozier and A.J. Chapman (editors)
© Elsevier Science Publishers B.V. (North-Holland), 1984

THE PSYCHOLOGICAL INVESTIGATION OF ART: THEORETICAL AND METHODOLOGICAL IMPLICATIONS[1]

Gary Kose
Rutgers University

The psychological study of art is not new. Psychological investigations have maintained a continual but nonetheless distant intrigue with so formidable a task as explaining art and the activities that surround it. Consideration of a psychology of art may be traced to philosophic investigations of aesthetics (see Munro, 1951 for review); and is clearly located in the early work of Fechner (1876), which served as a point of departure for European and American investigations (Ogden, 1938; Munro, 1948; Morgan, 1951). Art is among the most pervasive of human activities and the continual interest is certainly justified. However, it is also among the most complex of activities and has been approached with caution. It seems that art as a topic of study defies definition as a theoretical object and easily evades any one methodological attempt to study its workings. Traditional approaches to the study of art often reveal more about the workings of psychological investigations than they do about art.

Arnheim (1966), for example, takes as an agenda for the psychology of art '... the concept of equilibration ... drawn from such varied sources as the principle of entropy in physics, homeostasis in physiology, and the law of simplicity in Gestalt Psychology' (p. 21). Arnheim defines his interest in art in terms of the physical presence of its objects and the way they are perceived. His method of study involves examining the Gestalt principles concerning the perception of depth, figure-ground relationships, closure and sequencing principles as they apply to visual arts. Arnheim has argued the varied ways in which these principles work. His theoretical explication proposes the way in which perception organizes patterns within the work of art (Arnheim, 1969). Perceptual organization, in his theory, is directly related to the physical structure of a specific work. Arnheim's psychological account of art seems to be most directly concerned with art as physical objects, and the way in which they are perceived.

Experimental aesthetics, characterized by the work of Berlyne (1971, 1974), defines its interest in art in terms of psychological reactions. Berlyne used the term 'psychobiological aesthetics' to describe this interest. The methods of study are in the tradition of Fechner, stressing experimental rigour in measuring preferences and correlative physiological reactions to works of art. Theory within this approach is axiomatic, derived from information theory. Berlyne describes how complexity and conflict in a stimulus gives rise to 'hedonic' responses, such as preference, degree of pleasure, and curiosity. A psychological explanation of art derived from 'psychobiological aesthetics' would primarily concern the art of perceiving art.

Within the psychoanalytic tradition, there is a fundamental interest in the working out of a complex of physical needs and drives, which strive for symbolic expression. Such expressions are often manifest in works of art. From this approach the method of studying art involves a detailed analysis of a work or consideration of its relationship to biographic information from the creator's life or from the individual who is responding to it (e.g., Freud, 1964; Wolheim, 1974a). A common criticism is that both the defined interest and method of study are vague; however, this approach underscores the aspects of expression and subjectivity that are not easily discussed in the other approaches. From the psychoanalytic approach a psychological explanation of art would take into consideration the creation or projection of one's subjective relationship to art and its basis in affective complexes, whether as artist or audience.

While each approach has defined a focus of interest that touches on a fundamental aspect of art, it seems that no one approach addresses the complexity of art qua art. All three approaches are more purposely oriented towards the psychological perspective that motivates their interests rather than being oriented towards understanding the distinctive nature of art and artistic activity. Methodologies and the import of findings are relative to the particular perspective that directs each approach, and the investigation of art is in this sense a subsidiary interest that illuminates the range of psychological principles.

This difficulty in approaching the study of art reflects, to some degree, a certain positivistic assumption that has served historically as a model for psychological theories and methods.[2] Such an assumption is reductionistic in seeking an empirical or physical basis of explanation and manifests itself in two general tendencies. The first is revealed in the attempts to segregate or classify essential components, be they laws of perceptual organization, patterns of sensory pick-up or affective complexes; the second can be seen in attempts to identify systematic relationships between theoretical components and the phenomena of study, which often promises causal explanations.[3] This assumption and its manifestations seem restrictive when attempting to account for art. An alternative approach would have to maintain a purposeful orientation towards art and artistic meaning itself, while considering the variety of possible relationships between its objects, their production and perception. Such an alternative is a serious challenge to this fundamental assumption that must be met in order to establish a theoretical and methodological language for the psychological study of art.

This chapter examines an approach to the study of art that is represented by the philosophic works of Goodman and Cassirer, and considers the implications of this approach for psychological investigations. Both Goodman and Cassirer use the concept of symbol for discussing the nature of human activity. Symbol, in the broadest sense, is a relational term that allows for the consideration of the relationship between a symbol and its significance or meaning. An approach to the study of art in terms of symbols takes as its primary interest the relationsip between a work and its distinctive meaning. This approach, although vague, can serve as a check against any form of a positivistic assumption and reductive explanations.[4] Both Goodman and Cassirer share this orientation but differ in their accounts of the relationship between a symbol and its meaning. Consideration of their positions can serve in delimiting parameters in adopting this approach for psychological studies.

ART AS COMMUNICATION

Goodman's work is in the tradition of Analytic Philosophy, in which he distinguishes himself as a Nominalist. For Goodman, this distinction means adopting a method of describing the world rather than reducing it to essential properties or classes of relationships. This method is akin to that of structural linguistics. The basic terms used in such descriptions are referred to as 'individuals' (1972, p. 155). An 'individual' is purposely defined as an abstraction that can refer to whatever is irreducible in a given system. This abstraction allows a range of choices in what can be considered as an 'individual'. By definition an 'individual' cannot be concrete in any way and forbids consideration of ' ... allegedly occult entities as properties or classes' (Goodman, 1965, p.33). This type of nominalism provides a way of describing the world in terms of distinctive individual entities that come to form equally distinctive systems; and avoids reductionistic explanations. It is from this perspective that Goodman's discussion of art and symbols is best understood (see Black, 1971).

In *Languages of Art* (1968), Goodman states, 'The objective (of this work) is an approach to a general theory of symbols. Symbol is used here as a very general and colorless term. It covers letters, words, texts, pictures, diagrams, maps, models and more but carries no implication of the oblique or the occult' (p. xi). This work can be seen as Goodman's extension of structural linguistics to non verbal systems of meaning and provides an explanation of the varieties and functions of symbols. Goodman achieves this goal through his discussion of the way various artistic symbols establish semantic reference and operate in understanding. However, Goodman does not use art *en passant*. The problems that arise and help formulate his argument are closely linked to problems of art itself. Goodman's work is as much concerned with art as it is with a general theory of symbols.

Goodman develops an intricate argument that is difficult to summarize in its nuance and with the array of topics that it incorporates (e.g., see reviews by Savile, 1971; Wollheim, 1974b; Margolis, 1970). An appreciation of his theory can be garnered by considering his treatment of three issues: representation, expression and authenticity in art. Goodman begins by considering the way in which pictures can represent objects and events. His argument, in line with his general perspective, is directed against any position that would maintain that a picture represents because it shares certain properties or resembles some object or event. This argument is based on the difficulty of defining a criterion for establishing resemblance of any kind. Goodman quickly eliminates the theory that a picture is a copy or imitation of objects in the world. Such a theory does not, nor could not, precisely detail what information is needed in order to achieve a successful picture. Goodman also dismisses the use of the laws of perspective as a way of explaining how a picture represents.[5] Goodman notes the unlikeliness of actually seeing a picture in exact accord with the laws of perspective.

> Pictures are normally viewed against a background by a person free to walk about and to move his eyes. To paint a picture that will under these conditions deliver the same light rays as the object viewed under any condition, would be pointless even if it were possible. Rather the artist's task in representing an object before him is to decide what light rays, under gallery conditions, will succeed in rendering what he sees. This is not a matter of

> copying but of conveying. (1968, p. 13)

Goodman's position on the issue of pictorial representation is concise and directly opposed to such realist explanations.

> The plain fact is that a picture, to represent an object, must be a symbol for it, must stand for it, refer to it; and that no degree of resemblance is sufficient to establish the requisite relationships of reference. Nor is resemblance necessary for reference; almost anything can stand for anything else. A picture that represents -- like a passage that describes -- an object refers to and, more particularly denotes it. Denotation is the core of representation and is independent of resemblance. (1968, p. 5)

This argument proposes that pictorial representations, which ostensibly have an inherently natural relationship with what they represent, are ultimately symbols as are linguistic descriptions. The fundamental semantic relationship between a symbol and what it represents is one of denotation. Goodman accomplishes two objectives with this argument. First, he has brought together linguistic symbols with pictorial symbols, both being a function of a denotational relationship; and in so doing he justifies the utility of proposing a general theory of symbols. Secondly, in characterizing denotation in contrast to realist theories of representation, Goodman has stressed the conventionality of symbolic meaning. These two objectives serve as the distinguishing characteristics of Goodman's discussion of art and symbols.

Pictures, and more generally artistic symbols, do not just represent; they also can be expressive. A second issue that Goodman considers is an attempt to account for expression within his general theory of symbols. Goodman's treatment of expression begins by accepting the tentative distinction ' ... that representation is of objects or events while expression is of feelings or other properties' (1968, p. 46). He also notes that it appears that what is expressed is directly tied to the properties of the symbolic medium and can be directly perceived in contrast to representation that depends on convention. However, despite these apparent distinctions Goodman argues that expression depends on the same conventional semantic relationship as representation. He rejects the possibility that expressions can be directly perceived. A symbol cannot literally copy a feeling or emotion, and often an expression is remote from the symbol itself, for example, a painting expressing heat. Expression is not essentially different from representation, both are a matter of denotation, established by convention. In support of this argument Goodman notes the way in which expressions of feelings must be acquired and practiced for drama, as well as variations in the expression of feelings in different cultures. Goodman concludes,

> With representation and expression alike, certain relationships become firmly fixed for certain people by habit; but in neither case are these relationships absolute, universal or immutable .... representation and expression are both species of denotation. (1968, p. 50)

While Goodman demonstrates the usefulness of a general theory of symbols based on convention, his treatment of expression also indicates that symbols can function in different ways. Representation functions in being understood as a literal reference to objects and events, expression is understood as a possession of feelings and emotions. This difference is not an essential difference; the understanding of a symbol in either representational or expressive terms must be acquired in accord with conventional standards. Symbolic meaning, for Goodman, is then relative to a particular cultural context or symbolic system. This implication necessitates that symbolic meaning, in all its possible complexity, must be communicative.

Art, however, seems to run contrary to such a stipulation. In a classic sense, a work of art can be thought of as having essential qualities that are unique to that work and whose value is not exclusively defined in a relative sense, nor is it easily communicable. Artistic symbols can be distinguished in terms of their identity. Goodman considers the distinctiveness of artistic symbols in his discussion of authenticity and the identification of forgeries in painting. Goodman begins by questioning the purpose of distinguishing a perfect or near perfect forgery As in his discussions of representation and expression, he fails to find a criterion based on physical properties or distinctive features that justifies a search for or guarantees the authenticity of a painting. The distinction of authenticity is conventional. The historical context of a particular painting makes it a member of a particular group of authentic paintings, which ultimately defines its authenticity.

> My chance of learning to make this discrimination correctly -- of discovering projectible characteristics that differentiates Rembrandts from non-Rembrandts -- depends heavily upon the set of examples available as a basis. Thus the fact that the given pictures belong to one or the other is important for me to know in learning how to tell Rembrandt paintings from others (p. 110).

Goodman notes, however, that the discussion of authenticity is only pertinent for some art forms, such as painting but not for others, such as music. Again Goodman has maintained his argument for a general theory of symbols but is forced to make another functional distinction in the way symbols function in communicating their meaning. Similar to the distinction between representation and expression, Goodman distinguishes between autographic works of art, where there is no decisive test for identifying a work and its authenticity is defined by historical context, and allographic works of art, where there is no question of its identity or authenticity because of the notational characteristics of the symbols. Unlike the replete non-notational symbols in autographic art, notational symbol systems have clearly defined syntactic and semantic requirements. Notational systems are composed of distinct characters within the system. Semantically the characters must have specified referents, a minimum of redundancy and a means for signifying variations in meaning. The number system, the alphabet and music are typical examples. In general, notational systems are the pinnacle of articulation and unambiguous symbolization. The distinctive identity and meaning of notational symbols are in their structure or spelling. The distinction between notational and non-notational systems is an extremely practical aspect of Goodman's theory. This distinction provides a continuum for evaluating the communicative capacities and kinds of understandings that are possible in various symbol systems.

Goodman's theory of symbols has demonstrated a method of analysis that avoids any form of a positivistic assumption and explanation that reduces its topic of study to properties or relationships to things other than itself. Goodman's discussion of art in terms of a general theory of symbols is not reductive because the basic term of the theory does not carry any implications with it; it is defined in abstraction, devoid of any implications or content. And despite this formalization, it suggests a flexible and practical way of accurately describing various systems of meaning.[6] A vivid illustration of the workings of this theory can be seen in a rather simple example. Goodman reproduces a square, whose perimeter is marked off with harsh marks. Within the square are seven curved lines that are interwoven with one another. Each line is distinguished by certain properties, for example, one is composed of dots while another is a continuous line; the height of the curves; and a numeral associated with each line (p. 97). In all, a complex pattern emerges. However, Goodman renders every feature readable by revealing that the pattern is a spectographic analysis of various green pigments mixed with a chemical that cuases changes in the reflectant colour. When provided with the key the pattern is comprehensible in all its detail. The lines from right to left indicate wave length. From top to bottom the height of the curves indicate the percent reflectance. And each line, identified by its corresponding number, is given a label. Symbolic meaning is understood in terms of what the pattern denotes. The pattern represents a certain event and expresses certain aspects of that event; both what is represented and what is expressed are determined by denotation. These functions are carried out by both replete, non-notational symbols, for example, the numbers. Explaining this pattern and its complex meaning is not dependent on any one essential property or relationship. Understanding the pattern requires consideration of the inner workings of the components of the pattern itself.

The neat formalization and utility of Goodman's theory in describing the workings of symbolic meaning invites an important psychological question. Is Goodman's theory a unique product of his method of analysis or is it an accurate description of the ways symbols are actually produced, perceived and understood? Responding to such a question requires consideration of how the conventional standards that define symbolic meaning are communicated and acquired. The example given above does not allow consideration of these issues. The key to the pattern is merely given by Goodman. How symbols are established by convention is not addressed in his theory. It appears that this question is independent from and second to his philosophical analysis. While it may be that an answer can best be provided by psychological investigations, this question poses a more serious challenge to Goodman's assumption concerning the independent existence of coherent systems of symbolic meaning. Is it possible to understand the nature of symbols independent of the way in which they are produced and transmitted? In contrast, Cassirer begins his study of symbols by considering their direct relationship to human activity and understanding. Such an approach has consequences that are markedly different from Goodman's description of the structure and functions of symbols.

ART AS ACTION

In dealing with no less a problem than the 'crisis of man's knowledge of himself', that is the fragmentation of existence into various modes of thought and culture; Cassirer defines man as an 'animal symbolicum', suggesting that symbols provide an identity and a sense of unity to various kinds of experience (1944, p. 28). In contrast to Goodman's abstract and 'colorless' definition of symbol, Cassirer relates his notion of symbol directly to the nature of action and understanding. The most important aspect of symbols for Cassirer is that they are not ' ... passive images of something given ...' but are ' ... created by the intellect itself' (1955, p. 75). What the mind can know depends on the symbols it can create. Symbols do not enter into thinking and direct understanding, rather they are part of thought and constitute precisely what is known.

Cassirer's most striking example of what he means by symbol can be seen in his discussion of a simple plotted line, a Linenzug (Cassirer, 1957, pp. 200-202). First he considers the line as a perceptual event. The expressiveness of the line's properties are revealed, 'as we immerse ourselves in the design and construct it for ourselves, we become aware of a distinct physiognomic character in it. A peculiar mood is expressed in purely spatial determination ...' (p. 200). Next he considers the lines as a mathematical symbol, ' ... it becomes a graphic representation of a trignometric function'. Third, Cassirer discusses the line as a mythic symbol in which it embraces the sacred and profane. Here Cassirer makes an important note, 'Yet here it (the line) does not merely act as a sign, a mark by which the sacred is recognized, but proposes also a factually inherent, magical compelling and repelling power' (p. 201). Finally, he views the line as an ornament. In this sense what is appreciated is very distinct from either the mathematical or mythic discussions. The line can be discussed in an aesthetic sense, 'Here again the experience of spatial form is completed only through its relation to a total horizon which reveals to us through a certain atmosphere in which it not merely 'is', but in which, as it were, it lives and breathes' (p. 201).

Symbols, for Cassirer, do not have an independent and coherent conventional meaning that can be easily transmitted. Rather, symbols as symbolic forms are ways of conceptualizing the relationship between a certain direction of thought and the objects thought about. In his example, assuming a direction of thought such as the logic of mathematics, the mythical or the aesthetic will determine the properties of the line that will be brought to the fore and incorporated into symbolic meaning; these same properties are instrumental in influencing the further direction of a particular mode of thought. Symbolic meaning, in this sense, is mutually determined. Cassirer refers to this mutual determination as 'symbolic pregnance' and is defined as follows:

> ... the way in which a perception as a sensory experience contains at the same time a certain non-intuitive meaning which immediately and concretely represents ... we are not dealing with bare perceptive data ... Rather, it is the perception itself which by virtue of its own immanent organization, takes on a kind of spiritual articulation - which being ordered itself, also belongs to a determinate order of meaning ... It is this ideal interwovenness, this relatedness of the single perceptive phenomenon, given here and now, to a characteristic total meaning that the term 'pregnance' is meant to designate.(p. 202)

It is this notion of mutual determination, this 'symbolic pregnance', which is the foundation for understanding Cassirer's discussions of the various forms of symbolic meaning such as language, myth, science and art.

Cassirer never completed a major work on art; however, it is clear that it was an important topic for his understanding of symbols. His writings are replete with references to the arts. It is believed that he intended to complete a volume on art. While preparing a summary of his major philosophic work he stated in a letter, 'Already in the first sketch of the Philosophy of Symbolic Forms a particular volume on art was considered but the disfavor of the time postponed its working out again and again' (see Verene, 1977, p. 25). His actual writings on art are scant. Cassirer's relevance to understanding art has been maintained through the work of Langer (1953). Cassirer first makes reference to art in a paper entitled, *Mythic Aesthetics and Theoretical Space* (1969), and his most significant statement can be found in his summary work '*An Essay on Man*' (1944).

Cassirer begins his discussion of art by considering traditional arguments that view art as either an imitation of nature or an outpouring of emotions. Cassirer rejects both views since they imply that art passively reflects physical properties or an emotional inner life. In this way Cassirer, like Goodman, avoids any form of a positivistic assumption and reductive explanation. However, the fundamental difference between Goodman and Cassirer is in the way in which they describe what constitutes the symbols of art. Artistic meaning for Goodman is determined by convention and by the characteristics of a particular symbol system. While for Cassirer, meaning in art, or its 'symbolic pregnance', is mutually determined by the interweaving of a ' ... perceptive phenomenon, given here and now, to a characteristic total meaning ... ' This is not accomplished nor understood, in one instance of organization but rather in what Cassirer refers to as the 'formative process'.

> Art is indeed expressive, but it cannot be expressive without being formative. And this formative process is carried out in a certain sensuous medium ... for a great painter, a great musician, or a great poet, the colors, the lines, rhythms, and words are not merely part of his technical apparatus; they are necessary moments of the productive process itself ... All of this is not simply expression: it is also representation and interpretation. (pp. 141-142)

The significance of art is in the particular way in which the intention to do art is carried out. It is the interweaving of specific material and instances with this total intention that constitutes the 'symbolic pregnance' of a work of art. And it is an appreciation of this interweaving that is most important for both artist and audience alike in understanding art.

> Not even the spectator is left to merely a passive role. We cannot understand a work of art without, to a certain degree, repeating and reconstructing the creative process by which it has come into being. By the nature of this creative process the passions are turned into actions (p. 149).

As a result of his emphasis on the formative process in characterizing symbolic meaning in art, Cassirer cannot make the same functional distinctions that Goodman makes in his theory of symbols. Cassirer cannot specify and differentiate a symbol and what it represents from what it expresses. In the act of constructing an art symbol, the artistic intention influences what will be represented and expressed; while concomitantly the particular characteristics of the material at hand direct the intention in representing and expressing a certain meaning. The art symbol, its referent and what it expresses are constituted in the formative process of its creation. Consequently, identifying and distinguishing between art works is not a matter of considering just the historical context of the work, nor is it just a matter of reading the structural characteristics in the notations in the work. An art work is distinguished by the particular process of its construction. The formative process, for Cassirer, constitutes the products of art.

> The artist must not only feel the inward meaning of things and their moral life, he must externalize his feelings. The highest and most characteristic power of artistic imagination appears in this latter act. Externalization means the visible or tangible embodiment not merely in a particular material medium -- in clay, bronze or marble -- but in sensuous forms, in rhythm, color patterns, in lines and designs and in plastic shapes ... These formal elements are not merely external or technical means to reproduce a given intention; they are part and parcel of the artistic intention itself. (1944, pp. 154-155)

In Cassirer's discussion of art, symbolic meaning is not described as existing in an independently coherent system or language, as it is by Goodman. Rather, meaning in art is characterized as a particular form of 'symbolic pregnance', in which a particular intention or direction of thought is interwoven with the material at hand that achieves some type of externalization. It is this formative process that is at the core of meaning in art, and the particular course of this formative process is what distinguishes art from other symbolic forms.

> Art may be defined as a symbolic language. But this leaves us only with a common genus, not the specific difference ... There is, however, an unmistakable difference between the symbols of art and the linguistic terms of ordinary speech or writing. These two activites agree neither in character nor in purpose; they do not employ the same means, nor do they tend towards the same ends. Neither language nor art give us mere imitations of things or actions; both are representations. But a representation of sensuous forms differs widely from verbal or conceptual representations. (1944, p. 168)

As an example of how the distinctive formative process in art achieves symbolic form, Cassirer considers the difference between an artist and a scientist attempting to describe a landscape. If the artist is a painter then both his aim and his methods will differ from a geologist's description of a landscape. However, if the artist is a poet he will be using a linguistic medium, which is also of primary importance to any scientific description. Yet Cassirer maintains that the poet's direction and use of language will remain distinct from that of the geologist. The geologist's aim is empirical fact, achieved by using language in observation, comparison and induction. The poet, on the other hand will concern himself with the rhyme and rhythm of the language which constitutes the 'sensuous forms' of his art. Cassirer has provided an approach in which art is characterized, not as an independently coherent system of meaning, but rather, as a form of activity that is distinguished from other such activities by its direction and methods. This distinctiveness is fundamental to understanding the kind of meaning that art can reveal.

SYMBOL AND PSYCHOLOGY

In considering the psychological investigation of art, this chapter has suggested that art is a difficult topic to define, let alone study and understand. Traditional approaches, while discussing important aspects of art, seem restrictive with regard to the array of topics that could be discussed. It was suggested that this restrictiveness is not specific to any one theoretical enterprise but reflects a fundamental theoretical assumption and method characteristic of psychological studies. Psychological investigations tend to reduce art to empirical or physical properties, and fundamental relations. Consequently, art is then discussed in positivistic terms, neglecting the distinctiveness of the activities and objects of art. In noting this difficulty, the study of art cannot be seen as just another interesting topic, but rather is a topic that raises meta-theoretical questions about systems of psychological explanation.

The notion of symbol is often associated with discussions of art, and while it is vague and varies in the way it is used, it can be seen as a caution against positivism and reductionistic explanations. The juxtaposition of Goodman's and Cassirer's positions was intended to highlight aspects of this notion of symbol using it as a heuristic for asking questions about art. There are two important general issues that resonate in both positions. In discussing art, both Goodman and Cassirer struggle to describe the coherent organization of symbolic meaning, while simultaneously trying to account for the multiplicity of meanings that are possible of any symbol. The different way in which Goodman and Cassirer maintain consideration of these two seemingly contradictory issues marks the distinctiveness of their positions.

In Goodman's theory of symbols these two issues are clearly distant and kept separate. The coherent organization of meaning is the subject of Goodman's anatomization of symbol systems. In his explanation specific functions are differentiated (representation and expression), and distinctions in the structure of various systems are described (notational and non-notational) which allow for the evaluation of symbols in terms of their intelligibility. Goodman's discussion of the organization of symbolic meanings serves in providing clear distinctions as well as suggesting a criterion for evaluation in psychological studies of art. His focus on organization is not without a price. The origins of various symbol systems, how they change and vary in meaning are never addressed in any detail. These issues that concern the multiplicity of symbolic meaning, are described as being determined by conventional standards. This explanation serves in maintaining Goodman's Nominalist orientation, denying ' ... allegedly occult entities such as properties or classes'; however, it is silent with regard to how conventional standards are acquired and how they operate in the processes of producing and interpreting symbols. It is in this regard that psychological studies of art could complement Goodman's theory of symbols.

The work of Howard Gardner and Project Zero is already well known (See the chapter by Blank, Gardner and Winner, this volume). Taking their impetus from Goodman, this team of researchers have formulated and addressed a number of problems derived from Goodman's analysis of the organization of symbolic meaning. In a recent work Gardner (1982) has provided samples of these investigations. Following Goodman, symbol systems are defined by their unique structures. There are a variety of symbol systems, determined by convention, requiring conformity and a specific set of skills in order to produce or read meaning within a particular system. The visual arts, literature and music are typical examples. Gardner's most important contribution to Goodman's theory of symbols is in his stressing that the acquisition of symbol systems must be understood in relation to the overall pattern of human development. Acquiring proficiency in a symbol system is not simply a case of socialization or learning. Developments in cognitive capacities are an important determinant in gaining access to the conventional standards of a symbol system. Understanding the functions and structures of a symbol system is described as the result of an interaction between developing intellectual capacities and the rules and restrictions of the various systems within a culture.

An example can be seen in Gardner's description of the development of artistry in children (1982, pp. 86-91). Having investigated children's drawing ability and their use of literary language,[7] Gardner notes that despite differences between these two domains there is a common course of development. In both drawing and the use of metaphor, young children display a precocious disposition for novelty in their productions that is often aesthetically pleasing and is similar to more accomplished artistic productions. Around seven or eight years of age this disposition declines and children become obsessed with realism. Gardner refers to this period as the 'literal stage'. In an interesting series of studies Gardner suggests that children's precocious productions cannot be equated with more accomplished productions. These early productions are a result of the vast amount of experimenting that is characteristic of preschool children's intellectual capacity. They are not a result of mastery but are a reflection of the children's first encounters with the symbol systems of their culture. Gardner refers to this as a 'first draft of artistry'. The apparent decline is believed to be a result of children entering school and becoming aware of the conventional standards of symbol systems. The fact that younger children's productions are appreciated for having aesthetic value is itself a result of contemporary artistic conventions. Gardner's explanation stresses both the general disposition of the children and the way they come to terms with the conventionality of symbol systems. An individual child developing competency within a specific symbolic system should follow a similar course of development.

Gardner has already begun to closely examine the way individual children develop competency within various symbol systems (1982, pp. 110-126). In an ongoing longitudinal study, Gardner and his associates have been observing preschool children using a variety of symbolic media, such as story telling, drawing, block play and sculpture.[8] Preliminary findings reveal certain developmental trends that cut across media with regard to the children's planfulness, their ability to follow instructions and their seriousness of purpose. An outstanding finding is the predominance of consistent individual differences in the children's activities. Dichotomies have been proposed to characterize some of their individual styles, for example, verbalizers-visualizers, object-centred/person-centred, self-starters/completers. The children also express their individuality in the use of consistent themes in their various productions. An additional complication in assessing the children's symbolic competence was that their performance often varied depending on the particular task at hand, for example, directly copying a standard was most anxiety provoking and challenging, while freely producing or completing a project that was already started was most liberating and accessed more of the children's personal concerns. These task effects cut across various symbolic media.

While these findings are not conclusive, they are seen as providing a starting point for understanding productions within various symbolic media. Generally, children's work can be categorized according to their level of competence. The children's work can also be distinguished within an array of typical styles; such as visualizer, person-centred, etc. And, finally, early productions need to be characterized in terms of individual stylistic differences that stem from several factors, such as the child's general command of symbolization, the child's typical style, particular task demands within the media, recent events and consistent traits and motivations that characterize the child's life. Gardner and his colleagues suggest that understanding the productions and competencies within symbol systems necessitates thinking in terms of the interaction of multiple factors.

This work has profited from Goodman's discussion of the organization of symbolic meaning by the way in which it defines where to begin psychological investigation. On the other hand, this study appears to complement Goodman's theory of symbols by suggesting the way in which symbol systems are acquired and how meaning within the systems vary and change. However,in considering the myriad of factors that influence performance within symbol systems, this study brings into question the accuracy of Goodman's neat dissection of the organization of symbolic meaning. It seems from these preliminary findings that a clear distinction of symbol systems and the assessment of various levels of competency within a particular system cannot be made without being qualified by mentioning individual differences in style, specific task demands or life situations. And,moreover, any explanation in terms of the interrelatedness of these multiple factors would be merely descriptive and virtually meaningless, unless appropriate weights and vectors were assigned to these factors that specify their direction and importance within a symbol system. But even if such an explanation was provided, it would still run the risk of becoming what William James referred to as the 'psychologist fallacy', that is, to assume that such hypothetical constructs as level of competence, individual style, traits and motivation have fixed and distinguishable properties, possessing powers of their own. More importantly supporting such a fallacy violates the nominalist orientation that initiates and is a context for Goodman's theory of symbols. This orientation explicitly forbids consideration of such 'allegedly occult symbol systems and his way of accounting for changes and variations in symbolic meaning is so great that any psychological attempt to shorten the distance is antithetical to the very nature of the theory itself. Goodman has provided an explanation that details the external functions and structures of symbols but this explanation excludes a means for understanding the varying ways in which symbols take on psychological significance.

In Cassirer's discussion of art and symbols, his description of the organization of meaning and his account of variations and changes in meaning are indistinguishable. A symbolic form is mutually determined. Non-inituitive direction or intention provides the basis for continuity and organization, for example, as in the form of language, myth, science and art. The perceptive phenomena or materials at hand are the source of variation and change. 'Symbolic pregnance' is achieved by the interweaving of non-intuitive intention with the materials at hand. Neither his description of organization, nor the mechanism of change is clearly distinguished: they are circularly defined in terms of one another. The meaning of this close reciprocal relationship between permanent organization and change can only be understood in its 'formative process', that is, in the act of its construction. Symbolic meaning within this approach does not have an end point or level of completion; characterizing meaning in terms of the 'formative process' allows for an endless turning back to create new variations in meaning. Cassirer quotes Goethe who describes the experience of this kind of symbolic action:

> And thus began the bent of mind from which I could not deviate my whole life through; namely, that of turning into an image, into a poem, everything that delighted or troubled me, or otherwise occupied my attention, and of coming to some certain understanding within myself there upon, as well to rectify my conceptions of external things, as to set my mind at rest about them. The faculty of doing this was necessary to no one more than to me, for my natural disposition whirled me constantly from one extreme to the other. All the works therefore that have been published by me are only fragments of one great confession (Cassirer, 1979, pp. 209-210).

Cassirer brings back the mystery to symbols that Goodman's analysis tried to remove. However, while his description may capture the experience and significance in symbolization, it is difficult to adopt Cassirer's approach for psychological investigation.

Some recent studies of children's understanding of pictorial symbols indicate the importance of considering the formative process but also suggest the difficulty in adopting this position.[9] Despite the very early ability to perceive and recognize objects and events depicted in pictures, children's full understanding of the meaning of pictures is a more complex achievement. In one study (Kose et al, 1983) children between the ages of three- and six-years were asked to imitate various actions. The actions were presented by a live model and in one of three symbolic media: by way of a doll modelling the actions, in line drawings, and in black and white photographs depicting children performing the actions. All of the children could accurately imitate the live model. Also, all of the children could imitate the doll modelling the actions. However, the three-year-old children were often inaccurate when imitating the actions depicted in line drawings, and a significant number of three- and four-year-olds would not imitate the actions when they were depicted in the photographs. Instead, many of these children would describe what was depicted but would not use the photographs to direct their own action. One possible explanation for these findings is that playing with dolls and drawing are familiar representational activities, and the children understand the relationships that could exist between a doll or a drawing and the action it refers to. While photographs are more realistic and probably just as available as dolls and drawing, the children are not familiar with the process of producing photographs and do not fully understand the way in which they may represent actions.

In a second study (O'Connor et al, 1981) six-year-old children were presented with a problem and its solution using actual materials. The children were also shown a series of photographic slides depicting the same problem but ending in an illogical outcome. The order of presenting either the actual material or the slides was counterbalanced for equal numbers of children. After seeing both presentations the children were asked to compare the two endings and explain the discrepancy between them. It was found that if the children were shown the photographic slides before the actual problem they were most likely to argue that the illogical slides were correct. This same procedure was followed in another condition in which illogical drawings were used instead of photographic slides. In this condition no primacy effect was found. The children readily pointed out that there was a mistake in the drawings. It seems that the children assume a degree of fidelity in photographs while their understanding of drawings includes an awareness of the chirographic process and the possibility of mistakes.

In a third study (Seidman and Beilin, in press) four- and six-year-old children and adults were given the task of creating a series of drawings or photographs. The subjects were asked to talk about what they were doing and thinking as they produced their pictures. The findings showed a progression with age from viewing photography as a simple reflection of reality among the youngest children, to viewing photography as a medium which allows for control and alteration of reality. In the drawing task all three age groups displayed knowledge of the ability to control the medium.

In a final study (Kose, 1983) five-, eight- and eleven-year-old children were asked to produce either drawings or photographs of objects in various spatial relationships. The children were brought to an area in which two large containers were displayed. In one condition the children were presented with drawings of the containers in different spatial relationships: in the first, one container partially occluded the other; in the second, one container was enclosed by the other; and, in the third, the two containers were depicted in linear perspective. The children were then asked to reproduce the drawings. In a second condition the same procedure was followed except that the children were shown photographs of the three spatial relationships and were asked to reproduce them using a Polaroid camera. The findings showed that in the drawing condition the younger children could accurately reproduce the partially occluded and enclosed relationships but had difficulty representing perspective. In the photography condition the findings were reversed. The four-year-olds had difficulty reproducing all three relationships; and among the eight-year-olds reproducing the partially occluded and enclosed relationships were the most difficult, while reproducing the containers in perspective was easiest. The activities of drawing and photography are very different despite their both being pictorial symbols. The kind of control that is imminent in drawing makes representing certain spatial relationships easier than others. One important aspect may be that in drawing there is no requirement to establish a fixed station point. In photography gaining control over the medium is more difficult in certain ways, and establishing a fixed station point is essential to taking any photography. It appears that such differences in the process of constructing pictures are reflected in the kinds of pictures that are produced.

These studies demonstrate the complexity of pictures and the kinds of information they may involve. All of these studies bring into question the segregation of symbol systems in terms of the way in which they organize and present information. The findings of these studies are troublesome for any attempt at a generic classification in terms of pictorial symbols. In all of the studies the children's responses to drawing were markedly different from their responses to photography. Classifying both drawing and photography as two types of pictorial symbols could not account for these differences. On the other hand, there is no clear criterion for distinguishing drawing and photography as two different types of symbols. Both are two-dimensional representations. And while drawing and photography do differ in the kind of detail and realism they present, this is not a fundamental difference. Any drawing may be more or less detailed or realistic, and the same is true of any photograph. The only fundamental difference between these two pictorial forms is the formative process involved in their construction. The process of drawing is distinct from the process of taking a photograph, and this distinction is important, not only when producing such pictures but also when interpreting and understanding their meaning.

These studies also demonstrate the complexity of the ways children can relate to the information presented in pictures. These studies bring into question the evaluation of different levels of symbolic competence as a way of accounting for changes and variations in symbolic meaning. It is difficult to understand the variations in the children's responses to either the drawing or photography tasks in terms of differences in levels of symbolic competence. The children's competence with pictorial symbols varied not only between their use of drawings and photographs but also across the different tasks that were used in the various studies. Children's competence with photography, for example, depends on what task is being performed. While very young children can easily recognize and describe what is depicted in a photograph, three- and four-year-olds have difficulty imitating actions depicted in photographs. And while six-year-old children can accurately imitate actions depicted in photographs, they have difficulty evaluating the accuracy and truthfulness of information depicted in photographs. Specific task demands are closely linked to the kinds of symbolic competence that can be accessed. However, these studies have also demonstrated that task difficulty is partly determined by the symbolic media in which it is presented. The distinction between the children's symbolic competence and their ability to perform certain tasks is at best vague and hard to define making it virtually impossible to make a clear statement about an individual's level of symbolic competence. It appears that competence with symbols must be described in terms of the specific processes of interpretation and production within a particular context.

While these studies support an understanding of symbols in terms of Cassirer's notion of 'formative processes', such an approach is in essence negative, rejecting clearly defined organization of meaning and the discussion of competence with regard to symbols. It appears that Cassirer's notion is best defined by the remoteness of its interest and represents an esoteric topic of concern. However, the difficulty in adopting Cassirer's approach for the psychological study of symbols and art may be not in the remoteness of its interest but rather in its remoteness from current methods and theoretical languages. Methods and theories are often best suited to explain topics of interest that can be discussed in terms of clearly defined organizations, with segregated components and systematic relationships. The close relationship between organization and sources of variation and change implied in Cassirer's 'formative process' does not allow for explanations in such terms. The most important impact of Cassirer's approach to symbols and art is not in it suggesting a new set of topics and questions but in suggesting a different way of asking the same questions. His approach is not concerned with asking how segregated systems come together, the questions concern instead, how from the richness of experience and action, do systems of meaning become segregated and yet maintain a connection to the simplest action. Rather than anatomizing the symbol systems that constitute art, Cassirer's approach asks questions about what makes such systems emerge as distinct forms of experience in culture. This line of questioning is concerned more with attaining the intimate understanding of origins rather than the distant explanation of organization.[10]

Adopting this line of questioning suggests directions for studying symbols and art. Cassirer's account of the mutual determination of symbols raises questions about the way the intention to engage in a form of activity incorporates and interweaves specific materials in the course of creating or interpreting a distinct symbolic form. Few psychological investigations have examined the establishment of the intention to create or interpret art. Under what conditions do such intentions arise and how do they influence action and the use of materials at hand? Most importantly for Cassirer's position, this mutual determination must be studied within the 'formative process'. Symbolic meaning and the competence to relate to that meaning must be understood in the course of specific actions, as symbols are constructed and transformed over time towards a distinct externalized form. These suggestions require further evaluation. A starting point for beginning serious consideration of these suggestions is in recognizing that they carry with them a challenge to existing methodologies and theoretical languages. Meeting this challenge will depend on an openness to reflect on techniques and ways of thinking that have long been a sacred part of the history of psychology.

REFERENCE NOTES

1. The completion of this paper was supported by grant 2-02089 from the Research Council of Rutgers University. I thank Professors Melvin Feffer and Adrienne Harris, and Patricia Heindel and Leah Weich for their very helpful comments.

2. See J. Fodor, *The Language of Thought* (Crowell, New York, 1975, pp. 9-25), for a discussion of positivistic philosophies and psychological explanation. Positivism is used here to represent the general thesis that all of the events discussed by the various theories are considered to be physical events.

3. See J. Fodor, *ibid.*, for a discussion of the relationship between positivistic assumptions and reductionism. Also E. Gellner, in *Legitimation of Belief* (Cambridge University Press, London, 1974, pp. 32-70), provides a discussion of the roots of such strategies in Empiricist thought that have remained as essential characteristics of scientific thought (pp. 152-167). Finally, S. Toulmin, in *Human Understanding: The collective use and evolution of concepts* (Princeton University Press, New Jersey, 1972), describes how similar strategies have become a normative aspect of rational thought.

4. Although in a different context, this alternative is suggested by F. de Saussure in his *Course in General Linguistics* (McGraw-Hill, New York, 1966). This approach can also be seen in the work of C. Levi Strauss (e.g., see Structural Analysis in Linguistics and Anthropology, in: *Structural Anthropology*, Basic Books, New York, 1963, pp. 31-54) and J. Piaget (see *Structuralism*, Harper Tourchbooks, 1970).

5. This part of Goodman's argument is directed towards the positions of E. Gombrich (*Art and Illusion: A study in the psychology of pictorial representation*, Princeton University Press, New Jersey, 1961) and J.J. Gibson (see The information available in pictures, Leonardo, 4, 1971, 37-53).

6. Most recently this method has been elaborated in *Ways of World Making* (Hackett Publishing Co., 1978).

7. Gardner's studies of drawing are elaborated in *Artful Scribbles* (Basic Books, New York, 1980); and a review of work on children's figurative language can be found in the development of figurative language, with E. Winner, R. Bechofer and D. Wolf, in K. Nelson (Ed.) *Children's Language:*

Vol 1 (Gardner Press, New York, 1978).

8. The work that is presented is in collaboration with D. Wolf and A. Smith. An earlier presentation of this material can be found in, Styles of achievement in early symbol use, with J.M. Shotwell and D. Wolf, in M.L. Foster and S.H. Brandes (Eds.) *Symbol as Sense* (Academic Press, New York, 1980).

9. This work was conducted under the direction of Harry Beilin at the Graduate School and University Center of the City University of New York. A more extensive review can be found in H. Beilin, *Development of Photographic Comprehension, Art Education*. Special Issue: *Art and Mind*, 1983.

10. This argument was recently made by J. Glock in a discussion of Werner's Organismic Theory. See Piaget, Vygotsky and Werner, in S. Wapner, and B. Kaplan (Eds.) *Holistic Developmental Psychology* (Lawrence Erlbaum Assoc., New Jersey, in press).

REFERENCES

Arnheim, R. (1966). Towards a psychology of art. California: University of California Press.

Arnheim, R. (1969). Visual Thinking. California: University of California Press.

Berlyne, D.E. (1971). Aesthetics and Psychobiology. New York: Appleton-Century-Crofts.

Berlyne, D.E. (1974). Studies in the new experimental aesthetics: Steps towards an objective psychology of aesthetic appreciation. New York: Wiley.

Black, M. (1971). Review article: The structure of symbol systems. Linguistic Inquiry, 2, 515-538.

Cassirer, E. (1944). An Essay on Man. New Haven, Connecticut: Yale University Press.

Cassirer, E. (1955). The Philosophy of Symbolic Forms. Volume 1. New Haven, Connecticut: Yale University Press.

Cassirer, E. (1957). The Philosophy of Symbolic Forms. Volume 3. New Haven, Connecticut: Yale University Press.

Cassirer, E. (1969). Mythic aesthetics and theoretical space. Man and World, 2, 3-17.

Cassirer, E. (1979). The educational value of art. In: D.P. Verene (Ed.), Symbol, Myth and Culture: Essays and Lectures of Ernst Cassirer 1935-1945. New Haven, Connecticut: Yale University Press.

Fechner, G.T. (1876). Vorschule der Asthetik. Leipzig: Breitkopf and Hartel.

Freud, S. (1964). Leonardo da Vinci and a memory of his childhood. New York: Norton Publishing.

Gardner, H. (1982). Art, Mind and Brain: A Cognitive Approach to Creativity. New York: Basic Books.

Goodman, N. (1965). Fact, Fiction and Forecast. Indianapolis, Indiana: Bobbs-Merrill.

Goodman, N. (1968). Languages of Art. Indianapolis, Indiana: Bobbs-Merrill.

Goodman, N. (1972). A world of individuals. In: N. Goodman (Ed.) Problems and Projects. Indianapolis, Indiana: Bobbs-Merrill.

Kose, G. (1983). Children's conceptions of spatial relationships in drawings and photographs. Paper presented at the American Educational Research Association Annual Meetings, Montreal, Canada.

Kose, H., Beilin, H., and O'Connor, J. (1983). Children's comprehension of actions depicted in photographs. Developmental Psychology, 19, 636-643.

Langer, S. (1953). Feeling and Form. New York: Charles Scribner's Sons.

Margolis, J. (1970). Numerical identity and reference in the arts. British Journal of Aesthetics, 10, 138-146.

Morgan, D.N. (1951). Psychology and art today: A summary and critique. Journal of Aesthetics and Art Criticism, 9, 181-196.

Munro, T. (1948). Aesthetics as science: Its development in America. Journal of Aesthetics and Art Criticism, 6, 225-235.

Munro, T. (1951). Methods in the psychology of art. Journal of Aesthetics and Art Criticism, 9, 161-207.

O'Connor, J., Beilin, H. and Kose, G. (1981). Children's belief in photographic fidelity. Developmental Psychology, 17, 859-865.

Ogden, R.M. (1938). The Psychology of Art. New York: Charles Scribner's Sons.

Savile, A. (1971). Nelson Goodman's 'Languages of Art': A study. British Journal of Aesthetics, 2, 3-27.

Seidman, S. and Beilin, H. (in press). Effects of media on picturing by children and adults. Developmental Psychology.

Verene, D.P. (1979). Symbol, Myth and Culture: Essays and Lectures of Ernst Cassirer, 1935-1945. New Haven, Connecticut: Yale University Press.

Wollheim, R. (1974a). Freud and the understanding of art. In: R. Wollheim (Ed.) Art and Mind. Cambridge, Massachusetts: Harvard University Press.

Wollheim, R. (1974b). Nelson Goodman's Languages of Art. In: R. Wollheim (Ed.) Art and Mind. Cambridge, Massachusetts: Harvard University Press.

Cognitive Processes in the Perception of Art
W.R. Crozier and A.J. Chapman (editors)
© Elsevier Science Publishers B.V. (North-Holland), 1984

PSYCHOLOGY AND THE TRADITIONS OF SYMBOLIZATION

William E. Smythe

University of Toronto

The phenomenon of symbolization has been a matter of persistent concern for the student of aesthetics. A proper understanding of the nature and function of symbols would obviously be of great benefit for aesthetic inquiry in general and for psychological aesthetics in particular. However the notion of symbol has a much broader significance for psychology than this. Indeed there has long been a close relation between psychological theories and theories of symbols. Such diverse traditions as behaviourism, psychoanalysis, and modern computational or information processing psychology can each be seen to adopt or endorse a particular view of symbolization.

Early behaviourism, for example, readily accepted the idea of grounding all of symbolic behaviour on the notions of 'sign' and 'signalling' system, as developed in the then fledgling science of semiotics. A notable instance of this is Pavlov's (1927) description of language as a 'second signalling system'. Many early semioticians for their own part, in particular Morris (1938, 1946), had a distinct interest in the psychological theories of the behaviourists as a way of grounding their own enterprise. Psychoanalysis borrowed from a quite different tradition in the study of symbols. This tradition, emphasizing mythological and metaphoric aspects of symbolization, has enjoyed a long history in the study of artistic, literary, and religious symbolism. It well suited the psychoanalyst's task of attempting to capture the latent, psychodynamic forms of symbolization so characteristic of mental life. Finally, modern computational psychology has inheritied its notion of symbol from a much more recent source. This notion, which construes symbolization purely formally in terms of rules for the manipulation of meaningless tokens, has received great impetus from the profound developments in the study of formal logic and the theory of computation that have taken place mostly within the present century. In this way, modern computational models of mental processes owe a substantial debt to the work of mathematicians and logicians such as Church and Turing. Throughout all of this work, it has become evident that the concerns of psychological theory and of the theory of symbolization have never been far apart.

These three views of the psychology of symbols -- the behaviourist, the psychoanalytic, and the computational -- would be of little more than historical interest were it not the case that each one is still very much alive, if often in modified form, in contemporary psychology. Their mutual and harmonious coexistence is by no means a foregone conclusion however. In this chapter, the prospects for such a coexistence are examined in light of the statements of some prominent exemplars of each view in modern psychology. An inquiry of this kind should help to assess the existing prospects for a unified psychology of the symbol, a matter of no small importance for psychological aesthetics in particular, and for psychological theory in general.

THREE KINDS OF SYMBOL SYSTEM

Each of the views of symbolization here examined is associated with a particular notion of symbol system now current in the psychological literature. The three have been called 'conventional', 'physical', and 'mythopoetic' symbol systems. Before proceeding to examine each one in turn, it will be useful to identify the basic topic of this discussion in a very general way. The term 'symbol' may be taken very broadly to mean anything that refers, represents, or otherwise expresses or embodies meaning. Despite a considerable divergence of opinion on just what reference, representation, expression, and indeed meaning amount to, this definition may be taken to be generally accepted. Particular approaches to symbolization begin to diverge from one another only after some further qualification or constraint upon this definition is ventured.

For example, a contrast commonly drawn in earlier writings on the topic distinguishes symbols from signs as kinds of referring object (Cassirer, 1944; Langer, 1942) or, taking 'sign' as the more generic term, contrasted 'symbolic signs' with 'indexical signs' (Morris, 1938; Peirce, 1955). This contrast was seldom consistently drawn among different authors, although generally it was supposed that signs or indices were highly particular, being related to their referents either casually, materially, or automatically -- in a word, they were 'concretized', as opposed to symbols which were more arbitrary, deliberative, or conventional -- in a word, 'systematized'. A sign or index such as a deer track, for instance, obviously signifies the passing of a particular animal in a very different way than the linguistic symbol 'deer' refers to it. However the distinction breaks down once it is appreciated that neither systematization nor concretization can ever be wholly absent from any form of signification. For example, some system presumably underlies the experienced tracker's command of his craft; whereas, conversely, linguistic symbols can be derivative from more 'concretized' modes of signification, as etymological studies often show. More recent terminological practice is consistent with taking 'symbol' rather than 'sign' as the more generic term and, rather than classifying different kinds of signifying objects into disjoint categories, identifies instead the different (frequently overlapping) functions that symbols may subserve, such as indicating, naming, classifying, and so on.

An important initial observation is that no object is itself intrinsically a sign or symbol of anything. Rather, symbolization or signification is always relative to some principle of interpretation, the form of a fixed relation, as in the case of more 'indexical' symbols, or as an arbitrary rule in the case of more 'conventionalized' symbols, this third element is truly omnipresent in symbolic situations.

Conventional Symbol Systems

The study of symbolic phenomena from the point of view of conventional symbol systems, takes interpretants to be expressible as conventionally agreed upon rules. On this approach, symbol or sign is to be defined, as in the account of the modern semiotician Eco (1976), as *everything* that, on the grounds of a previously established social convention, can be taken as *something standing for something else*' (p.16). On this view, there are, then, no perfectly solitary, isolated acts of symbolization; in using symbols one always has some potential recipient of a message in mind with whom one is linked by means of some system of shared conventions, even if this recipient is only oneself on a later occasion, and the 'shared' conventions a mere mnemonic device. Thus an isolated Robinson Crusoe who finds the world in a grain of sand is not, on this view, behaving symbolically unless he has worked out some code by means of which to transmit his vision to another. Neither would symbolization, in this sense, be implicated in the recent case of another man who reportedly converses with a stone in hope of communing with eternity (Powell, 1982) for, as Eco insists, 'a single use of the stone is not culture' (p.24).

It is not necessary in this account that there be an actual recipient of a message, only that a means be provided, through the device of a code, for its possible receipt. Thus symbolic communication, or at least the receipt of codes, is held to be a methodological rather than empirical condition on the existence of symbolization or signification (Eco, 1976). The methodological strictures of this program, with all its emphasis on the consensually observable and conventionally codable, have much in common with those of radical behaviourism so it is not surprising to find historical connections between the two as earlier noted in the writings of Pavlov and Morris.

More recently psychologists have turned to the study of conventional symbolization for quite different reasons. The work of Bates, a developmental psychologist and cognitive theorist, is particularly exemplary of some recent trends. Bates (1979) and her colleagues have taken up the study of the development of conventional symbolization in children; and the notions of intention and convention figure prominently in her research programme, as in the work of semioticians. It will be recalled that Eco's definition of significance required not just that a symbol be governed by convention, but that it be 'taken' (i.e., intentionally) as such. Bates defines conventions as 'sounds or gestures whose form and function are agreed upon and recognized' (p.36) by some community and a symbol as an object 'that is related to its referent only through the conventions agreed upon by a community of users' (p.48). Intentional communication is then defined as 'signalling behavior in which the sender is aware a priori of the effect that a signal will have on his listener' (p.36).

Intentional signalling of this conventionalized sort constitutes what Bates calls the 'first moment' in the development of human symbolic capabilities. The second moment is described as 'the emergence of symbols and the discovery that things have names' (p.33). This is said to involve some means for 'objectification' of the symbol-referent relation, such that symbols can now be considered apart from their pragmatic role in communicating intentions and desires. The child at this stage might be said to have some grasp of what it means, abstractly and independently of any practical aim, for one thing to 'stand for' another; and this, for Bates, involves the child 'realizing that the vehicle (i.e., the symbol) can be substituted for its referent for certain purposes, at the same time realizing that the symbol is not the same thing as its referent' (p.38). A classic instance of the dawn of this second moment of symbolic awareness was noted by Helen Keller's teacher Mrs. Sullivan when she reported that 'Helen has taken the second great step in her education. She has learned that *everything has a name, and that the ... alphabet is the key to everything she wants to know'* (Keller, 1904, p. 315).

In describing and accounting for the process of objectification that mediates the traversal from the first to the second moments of symbolic competence Bates does not, however, fully subscribe to Eco's methodological condition on symbolization for, in her view:

> Symbolic activity includes symbolic communication. However, symbolic activity may also include some private and often idiosyncratic behaviors ... A complete situation of symbol use involves not two but four parts: the *objective, observable vehicle and its real world referent, and the subjective, psychological vehicle and its mental referent*.(pp. 43-46)

As an example, Bates cites the case of a child representing a spoon by means of his own stirring action. In this case, the objective symbolic value is taken as the conventionally recognized stirring motion that the child's own action -- the subjective vehicle -- aims to imitate; and the objective referent is an instance from the conventional category of objects called 'spoons', for which 'the entire complex of potential interactions with spoons in the child's repertoire, the "action package" that comprises the child's knowledge of spoons' (p.55) is the subjective referent. To acquire a symbol system, on this view, is to make the appropriate match of one's subjective symbolic vehicles and referents with their objective counterparts.

Bates' (1979) approach, like the research programs of Werner and Kaplan (1963) and Piaget (1962) which were its precursors, leads one to search for various patterns of family resemblance among processes such as vocalizing, gesturing, imitation, tool use, and manipulative play. Each of these may be said to involve in its own way a certain degree of communicative intention and convention. Indeed various specific relationships in the ontological development of each kind of the acquisition of the capacity for manipulating conventional symbols can be separated out from more general factors like overall intellectual development. Conventional symbolization in this way stands out as a distinct psychological phenomenon.

Physical Symbol Systems

A notion that at first seem to have much in common with the idea of conventional symbol systems, but is actually quite distinct from it, is the concept of 'physical symbol systems'. The term comes from the work of Newell and Simon (cf. Newell, 1980; Newell and Simon, 1976), who summarize the notion in the following way:

> A physical symbol system consists of a set of entities, called symbols, which are physical patterns that can occur as components of another type of entity called an expression (or symbol structure) ... A physical symbol system is a machine that produces through time an evolving collection of symbol structures.(Newell and Simon, 1976, p.116)

The paradigmatic instance of such a machine in contemporary culture is, of course, the digital computer. Digital computers are sometimes described as 'universal machines', in recognition of their capacity to simulate any well defined input/output function. One outcome of the profound modern developments in formal logic and the theory of computation as realized in the work of Church, Turing and others, is an exact mathematical account of what universality, in this sense, amounts to. In more pragmatic terms, it entails the theoretical sufficiency of a small and well defined set of basic operations to compose any arbitrary calculation. Typically included are those operations, familiar from computer programming, such as assigning a symbol to an expression; copying an expression; writing it onto or reading it from some storage medium; controlling the sequence of operations conditionally, as with expressions in the form 'IF ... THEN ...'; quoting an expression so that it may be treated as data, and so on.

Newell (1980) goes on to make the strong claim that *symbol systems are universal machines* (p.154). He explains what he means by this assertion in the following way:

> We do not have an independent notion of a symbol system that is precise enough to counterpoise to a universal machine, and thus subsequently prove their equivalence. Instead, we have *discovered* that universal machines always contain within them a particular notion of symbol and symbolic behavior, and that this notion provides us for the first time with an adequate abstract characterization of what a symbol system should be. Thus, tautologically, the notion of symbol system, which we have here called *physical symbol systems* is universal. (p. 155)

However, even lacking an independent characterization of symbol systems at the level of precision that Newell demands, a number of important differences between physical and conventional symbol systems are readily apparent.

As an example, consider how reference might be thought to be secured for the symbols of a physical symbol system. Newell (1980) accounts for it as a kind of composite of a more primitive relation called 'designation', that is defined as follows:

> Designation: An entity X designates an entity Y relative to a process P, if, when P takes X as input, its behavior depends on Y. (p.156)

It is further proposed that designation be transitive, such that 'if X designates Y and Y designates Z, then X designates Z' (p.157). Moreover, any symbol that aims to designate something in the environment external to the machine must do so by means of designating, in the right way, an 'interface' operation such as imputing a datum or commanding an action. Thus the designation of an external object -- 'external designation', as it might be called -- is typically a two-step process in which a symbol designates one or more of a limited set of interface operators which then directly designate the object in question. External designation may thus be said to presuppose and derive from 'internal designation' -- the designation of one symbol or expression by another; for as Newell would have it, 'the prototype symbolic relation is that of access from a symbol to an expression, not that of naming an external object' (p.169). It is important to note, however, that external designation is entirely constrained by the machine's intrinsic capabilities for receiving signals from and acting upon its environment. One is here reminded of Bates' (1979) 'potential spoon interactions', the subjective component of the child's reference to the class of spoons. For, just as the child's immediate knowledge of spoons is for Bates constituted by the total 'action package' of spoon-related behaviours in the child's repertoire, so does a physical symbol system have 'action packages' fixed by the behavioural possibilities of its set of interface operators. Moreover, this is as far as any physical symbol system can penetrate a field of reference; Bates' distinction between objective and subjective reference cannot even be formulated in the terminology of physical symbol systems. For all its emphasis on explicitness and physical realizability this notion of symbol systems turns out to be remarkably solopsistic.

Another definition that is central to the description of physical symbol systems concerns the notion of 'interpretation'.

> 'Interpretation': The act of accepting as input an expression that designates a process and then performing that process. (Newell, 1980, p. 158)

Again, a special role is reserved for symbols that designate 'operators' -- symbols that, in Newell's description, 'have an external semantics wired into them' (p. 159). These would include, in addition to the interface operators earlier mentioned, all of the directly physically realized operations internal to the system itself. It is proposed that the interpretation of any symbolic expression is then an iterative process that finally converges on a set of symbols designating such operators; in this way, it is suggested, we 'finally solve Tolman's problem of how his rats, lost in thought in their cognitive maps, could ever behave' (p. 159). So in the same way that the physical symbol system notion of designation eliminates this distinction between objective and subjective reference, this concept of interpretation obviates the need for notions like intention and convention. For 'interpretation', rather than being specified in the usual way in terms of the shared practices of some community of intentional agents, now becomes the description of a formally-defined process.

Bates' distinction between the objective and subjective components of symbolization, along with the accompanying notions of convention and intention, at least call attention to one sense in which symbolization may be said to be an achievement of mind. It is an achievement to the extent that it requires of an individual the acquisition, by some means or other, of a set of cultural objects conventionally taken as standing for something else. From the standpoint of physical symbol systems, symbolization is rather a 'given' of mind. It is not, that is to say, 'acquired' in any way, but is rather the prerequisite of a certain kind of system being able to exhibit any significant behaviour whatsoever. A physical symbol system, as a machine, has its symbols in virtue of its structure as a machine, and not because of any membership in a larger community of intentional agents. It rather comprises, from the outset, an 'unintentional community' unto itself.

Mythopoetic Symbol Systems

Yet a third conception of symbol system is familiar to psychologists from psychoanalytic (and particularly Jungian) theory; and has, apart from its influence in psychology, enjoyed a long tradition in the study of cultures, myths, and art forms. On this conception, as Howard (1980) characterizes it, symbolism is viewed as having to do exclusively with 'the metaphorical and allegorical, the esoteric, hidden, latent, deeper, more general, or recondite significance of things' (p. 503). A symbol, that is to say, is whatever bears some sort of 'mysterious' relation to its meaning, as if the basic relation between any referring object and its referent were not already mysterious enough. Whatever else may be concluded about the status of this notion of symbol system in contemporary psychology, it is the only one of the three here surveyed to have, in any significant way, captured the popular imagination. It is also the most difficult of them to define. Kaplan (1979), among the most recent of contemporary psychologists to have written from this perspective, makes the following attempt at a definition:

> I would like to urge that we take symbolization as referring principally to the attempts to use some medium to represent something -- some experiential content -- that is not tangible or visible to the subject. I am suggesting, then, that the prime form of symbolization occurs when *abstract intangible states of affairs are realized in a concrete medium.* (p. 220)

The symbolic attitude engendered by such attempts is dubbed, by Kaplan, the 'mythopoetic' attitude.

An example of what Kaplan here intends is the kind of symbolic play we engage in when pondering such 'nonsense' questions as: 'If Emerson were a kind of plant, what kind would he be?' The question is literally nonsense, although its literal reading may only be the surface manifestation of a deeper inquiry. This same sense of surface incongruity together with a deeper significance pervades talk of what is called mental and spiritual life. How else are we to take such literally puzzling expressions as 'grasping an idea', 'being struck by an impulse', the 'unity in trinity' of Christianity, or, from Zen Buddhism, 'the sound of one hand clapping'? These examples help to illustrate just how the mythopoetic conception of symbolization differs from the other two conceptions. It cannot be said, in respect of any of these expressions, that they are simply labels or descriptions for what is otherwise readily and independently available through other designatory means. They are in this way fundamentally distinct from Bates' conventional symbols, which are just labels for what is available through pre-formed action-packages like 'potential spoon interactions', and from Newell's physical symbols which refer by designating fixed interface operators. Rather one would say that what is 'meant' in mythopoetic contexts is part and parcel of its symbolic expression, and not an independently ascertainable, specifiable 'something else'. As Kaplan puts it, 'there is no clear indication of a 'something else' but rather an embodiment or incarnation of certain intangibilia in material form' (p.225).

On the mythopoetic conception, symbols may be characterized in one way as 'Janus-faced', as mediators 'between the domains of the spiritual or mental and the physical or corporeal' (Kaplan, 1979, p.226), or as another account would have it, 'between objective and subjective realities' (Chebat, 1974, p.37). The basic idea is that symbols constitute a medium of exchange between the tangible and sensible on one hand and the intangible or insensible on the other. Yet it is not lack of tangibility or sensibility per se that makes sensible qualities become as opaque to representation when considered apart from the entrenched vocabularies of symbols normally used to describe or depict them. Consider, for example, how one would undertake to describe the visual quality of 'redness' apart from the usual vocabulary of colour names or depict it in an uncoloured pictorial medium. Here is a situation ripe for the process of 'symbol formation' (Werner and Kaplan, 1963) -- the free or unconstrained invention of new ways of symbolizing or the novel usages of old ways. This is an aspect of symbolic behaviour that contemporary cognitive psychology has almost completely ignored. As Kolers and Smythe (in press) note, in surveying a number of recent cognitive proposals about mental representation, cognitive psychologists have pervasively confused the notion of representation with that of coding or categorizing. A cognitive 'theory' of representation typically begins by laying out some pre-formed domain of represented object or event-types and then considers various ways of coding or sorting them (cf. Anderson, 1976, 1978; Palmer, 1978). However, the question of how the objects or events are known in the first place, of how they are first symbolized, is never addressed.

Symbol formation, then, is at the heart of mythopoetic symbolization. The essence of the mythopoetic attitude would seem to lie just in this attempt to exceed the bounds of habitual or conventional symbolization. If mastery of a conventional symbol system involves careful compliance with a previously established set of constraints, mythopoetic mastery must be said to involve their selective violation. In this way mythopoetic symbol systems presuppose but are not determined by conventional symbol systems; indeed the propriety of even speaking of a 'system' in respect to mythopoetic symbolization is open to question.

Kaplan (1979) attempts to capture mythopoetic phenomena, not by appeal to any kind of system but, like Bates (1979), in terms of their principal 'moments' in psychological development. Kaplan refers to three such distinct moments as 'the embodiment of meanings in objects, the imaginative transformation of objects, (and) the externalization of thoughts and feelings at a remove from the pragmatic-utilitarian world of everyday occurrence' (p.224). The first of these moments -- 'the embodiment of meanings' -- would presumably coincide with the child's general apprehension of significance in objects and events around him, without his yet making a distinction between the 'pragmatic-utilitarian' significance of things and their 'mythological' significance; the second moment -- 'imaginative transformation' would be achieved once the child has access to such a distinction, and some ability to selectively shift his attention from one to the other side of it; the third moment -- 'externalization' -- implies some degree of freedom in making imaginative transformation, such that both the pragmatic and mythological significance of a thing are concurrently available to the child, even when only one aspect is being actively entertained. The dawning of the first of these moments is obviously quite early in development, if not largely present at birth. Achievement of the second but not the third moment would, for example, be implicated in the frequently noted cases of children who, after summoning up some phantom from their own imagination, then have difficulty making it disappear. The third moment would be characteristic of ordinary adult competence in the mythopoetic sphere.

The contrast between the mythopoetic and pragmatic-utilitarian stances, each taken phenomenologically as a form of 'being in the world', is then central to Kaplan's account. The principal aim of a theory of symbolization on this view, would be to account for the emergence of the former against the background of the latter. For Kaplan, this is to be understood, not in terms of rules and coded conventions, but as a form of 'dynamic schematizing activity' which is manifest in the body of the symbolizer, not in terms of an overt action observable to another, but as an 'internal gesture' experienced by the symbolizer himself.

TOWARD A UNIFIED APPROACH TO SYMBOLIZATION

In the notions of conventional, physical, and mythopoetic symbol system we have, then, three quite distinct proposals about the nature of symbolization. A unified theory of symbols of sufficient breadth of scope would do well to incorporate features of all three, showing how they all interrelate. How is this to be achieved?

The 'Central Dogma' of the Cognitive Sciences

There is an implicit dogma at work in much of the contemporary study of cognition that presumes at least a sketch of an answer. The dogma is in two parts. The first part supposes that physical symbol systems in some sense underlie or explain people's use of conventional symbol systems. Newell (1980) puts this supposition in the form of an explicit hypothesis when, in speaking of physical symbols, he asserts:

> It is a hypothesis that these symbols are in fact the same symbols that we humans have and use everyday of our lives. Stated another way, the hypothesis is that humans are instances of physical symbol systems, and, by virtue of this, mind enters into the physical universe (p. 136).

The analogy between this 'physical symbol system hypothesis', as it is called, and Crick's'central dogma of modern biology' is, for Newell, quite intentional. He goes on to say that:

> this hypothesis sets the terms on which we search for a scientific theory of mind ... the physical symbol system is to our enterprise what the theory of evolution is to all biology, the cell doctrine to cellular biology, the notion of germs to the scientific concept of disease, the notion of tectonic plates to structural geology (p. 136).

The physical symbol system hypothesis would appear to enjoy wide, if largely tacit, acceptance among modern cognitive psychologists. Bates (1979) gives her own endorsement of it in declaring, as her main task, the discovery of '*some sort of software package, a "program" than an individual child or adult "has", which permits generation of behaviors that are externally identifiable as "linguistic", "cognitive", or "social"*' (p. 6). For example, a child's subjective symbolic vehicles and reference with respect to spoons would be taken as the surface expression of an underlying 'spoon program' (p. 55).

If the first part of the central dogma thus constitutes a kind of working hypothesis for psychologists in the modern cognitive tradition, the second part may be seen to have much the same function in anthropological and linguistic studies in the semiotic tradition. This part of the dogma supposes that mythopoetic symbolization can be fully accounted for as the rule-governed meta-symbolic use of conventional symbols -- that is, in terms of rules that govern symbols that refer to other symbols. Suppose for example that, in response to the 'nonsense query' earlier posed about Emerson, I was to say that I find Emerson like an ivy plant. This might be taken to mean that I find Emerson rambling but enduring and majestic, or something of the sort. One way of describing this sample of symbolic behaviour is as making use of a linguistic symbol (S) denoting an object, in this case an ivy plant, that itself taken as a symbol (S), expresses certain qualities like, for instance, excursivity, durability and majesty. This, in any case, is the kind of account that Howard (1980), following the approach of Goodman (1968, 1978), would recommend. Howard makes his case with the aid of a number of other less idiosyncratic examples.

The central dogma takes this approach one step further in supposing that these meta-symbolic expressions can be fully encompassed by a closed system of rules. As Sperber (1975) characterizes this claim, it is 'to assert simply that to each (mythopoetic) symbol corresponds a fixed set of interpretations, that to each interpretation corresponds a fixed set of symbols or, in other terms, that a particular occurrence of a symbol selects certain pairs (symbol, interpretation) among a set defined in the very structure of symbolism' (p. 15). Thus, for example, one would be led to postulate a generative system of rules out of which my metaphor from within a given cultural or linguistic community, could be systematically derived. Note how well this second part of the dogma squares with the first part. Meta-symbolization is not only consistent with physical symbol systems but, given the designation of one symbol by another as the primary symbolic relation in such systems, must even be viewed as a basic function of them. A physical symbol system account of phenomena like metaphor would then be predicted on the simple observation that linguistic symbols, like any other kind representable in a physical symbol system, are amenable to the pervasive operation of quotation.

Problems with the Central Dogma

The central dogma of the cognitive sciences is, then, a compelling and influential one. It is increasingly apparent, however, that it may also be fundamentally mistaken. The dogma is as severely flawed in both its aspects.

We turn first to a consideration of the physical symbol system hypothesis, the view that the full range of human symbolic phenomena can be accommodated within and explained in terms of physical symbol systems. As an illustration of the principal weaknesses of this program, we return to an examination of the physical symbol system account of symbolic reference. As pointed out earlier, reference is thought to be secured for the symbols of a physical symbol system by means of external designation, where a token or symbol instance so designates an external object relative to some process if, given the token, the process then behaves in a way that depends on the object. It has also been noted that external designation, fixed as it is by the causal properties of a given machine, lacks all the public, consensual aspects that characterize the use of conventional symbol systems. More particularly, it can be shown that external designation is neither a necessary nor a sufficient condition of symbolic reference in the ordinary sense.

External designation is not a sufficient condition of reference, because there are many ways in which its defining conditions can be satisfied without implicating reference as normally understood. Someone turns the thermostat down in a room, for instance, and subsequently my teeth begin to chatter. One could presumably chart the physiological events underlying this process all the way from the immediate response of temperature sensitive cells in the skin to the final execution of the response of teeth chattering in the mouth. The activity of the temperature sensitive cells could then be viewed as a kind of 'token' activating behaviour, in the form of teeth chattering, that is clearly dependent upon the ambient temperature. Yet, for all this, the activity of these cells does not refer nor does it have demantic properties in anything like the way that my utterance 'It is cold in here!' does. I do not, in virtue of a reflex like chattering teeth in response to cold, refer to anything. External designation is also not strictly necessary for reference. I am confident, for example, that my use of the name 'Genghis Khan' refers to an actual historical individual though, thankfully, I am in no position to have my behaviour depend (in any direct way) upon him.

There are ways of amending the definition of external designation to forge a better correspondence with the requirements of reference. However none of these bodes well for the physical symbol system hypothesis. For instance it might seem that external designation could be made a sufficient condition of reference if construed not only relative to a process, but to an entire physical symbol system. In this way one might insist that not all but only certain causal contingencies among events, namely those constitutive of the functioning of the system in question, are constitutive also of designation; examples like the teeth chattering reflex might be thought to be excluded as symbolic behaviour therapy. The difficulty is in specifying just what these certain kinds of contingencies are. All of the formal apparatus of the theory of universal machines is of surprisingly little help in this regard; for the notion of a universal or Turing machine is so encompassing and non-specific as to include all sorts of perfectly ordinary (non-symbol using) systems under, of course, an appropriate description. For example, the physiological details underlying the teeth chattering reflex are probably complex enough, at some level of description, to have some sort of structural correspondence with a Turing machine, even if the chattering of teeth turns out to be a rather uninteresting computation in such a system. Indeed, any suitably complex system may have any number of alternative mappings onto formally distinct universal machines.

Proponents of computational theories characteristically require that cognitive behaviour be understood uniquely in terms of rules and representations (cf. Chomsky, 1980; Pylyshyn, 1980). This sort of account cannot be based merely on the possibility of establishing an arbitrary mapping relation between the nervous system and some universal machine, however. Rather, such an account already presupposes the propriety of one such mapping, moreover an interpreted one; for with any suitably complex system, it is entirely possible that mappings may be found onto distinct universal machines embodying mutually contradictory sets of rules. To speak of 'rules' and 'representations' in such a situation is to preferentially select one of the these mappings to the exclusion of the others. What is characteristically missing from computational theories of mental processes is the guiding principle for this selection; and if this can be supplied in terms of the intrinsic structure of the system being modelled, then it must be a matter of the extrinsic attribution of significance to it. This, at least, is the conclusion of two recent authors who have pondered the semantics of computational theories in some detail.

Heil (1981) makes his case by citing, as a general principle, the impossibility of any formal system containing within its intrinsic structure, no matter how detailed, its own rules of interpretation. At the outset of this chapter, it was pointed out that no object is intrinsically a symbol for something else. Indeed an essential feature of the notion of symbol on any view is that anything can be used to refer to anything else. If this feature is a truly general one, it would mean that any symbol instance, considered only with respect to its own intrinsic structure is, qua symbol, essentially ambiguous; and this is just what Heil's principle affirms. One can imagine various ways of augmenting the intrinsic structure of a symbol token with elements that encode rules of interpretation, but these latter must still themselves be interpreted, and so the essential ambiguity from structure to interpretation remains. Neither, as Heil goes on to show, can 'structural isomorphism' be appealed to as an independent representational principle. Rather, he concludes that interpretation 'is obtained only when the structure is used by some agent against a suitable linguistic background' (p. 333).

Smith (1982) takes this argument a step further in suggesting that such extrinsic semantic attribution is essential to the very notion of computation itself. Smith suggests that the description of a device as a computer is already in the domain of interpretation rather than of uninterpreted mechanical processes. If computational devices were to be described just as complex rule-governed artifacts, there would be no principle by means of which to distinguish them from things like steam engines and food processors. However a food processor, even one with a micro-programmed chip, is still just a device for transforming edible material; whereas a computer is not, in the same way, just a device for transforming electrical impulses. To speak of a device as a 'number cruncher', a 'word processor' or, more generally, as a 'formal symbol manipulator', is to impute to it operations defined on already interpreted entities, that is to say on 'numbers', 'words', and 'symbols'. This view of computation has led Smith to reconstruct, with notable success, aspects of modern computer programming practice with the aid of the same theoretical framework as used to analyze the semantics of natural languages. The suggestion is thus clear that, far from explaining the features of intention and convention in ordinary symbolic practice, a resort to computational theories actually presupposes them.

Other kinds of modification of the notion of external designation quickly lead to similar results. For example, one way of attempting to make external designation strictly necessary for reference would be to suppose that a person's physical symbols can inherit their designation from those of other people, and in this way, secure reference to that which (like long deceased historical individuals) cannot be directly causally efficacious for the symbolizer. This amounts to a simple extension of the transitivity property of designation outside the bounds of a particular physical symbol system. Thus, for example, though Genghis Khan can have no direct causal influence upon me, there is presumably some long and circuitous causal chain that connects my use of the name, through a series of passing of tokens of it from one individual to another, to the man himself. Again, however, any arbitrary chain of this kind cannot be said to secure reference; for example, there might also exist some long circuitous chain of grunts and groans, passed from one individual to another, that similarly connects me with Genghis Khan's chief manicurist, though I have never in virtue of this referred to any such person. Semantic theorists who have recently speculated about referential chains of this sort agree that the links of such chains are not just causal but intentional. Donnellan (1977b), for example, speaks of 'historical' rather than of merely 'causal' referential chains as a way of including motives, intentions, and the like as essential ingredients. Kripke (1980) goes on to propose that the intention of an individual to use a symbol with the same reference as the person(s) who passed it to him is a necessary though not sufficient condition for each link in such a chain. So, again, physical symbol system accounts of symbolic behaviour end up requiring, rather than explaining, intention and convention.

The second part of the central dogma -- that mythopoetic symbolization can be reduced to conventional symbolization -- is at least equally problematic. Since these deficiencies bear less directly on psychological issues, they are examined here only briefly. An extensive case against the semiotic account of ritual, myth and metaphor has, however, been put forward in a recent book by Sperber (1975). Sperber uses mostly anthropological evidence to make a number of points, one being that mythopoetic symbols cannot be in any way replaced or translated by their linguistic interpretations. If, for example, all that I mean by the metaphoric comparison of Emerson with an ivy plant was to attribute certain definite, nameable features such as 'excursivity','durability', and so on, one might wonder why I did not simply name them in the first place. Yet the linguistic reading remains, in itself, somehow less compelling and interesting than the actual metaphor (or the metaphor taken in conjunction with its linguistic reading). As Sperber notes, if the symbols underlying myth, metaphor and legend carry meaning only in this linguistically eliminable sense, then 'what they mean is almost always banal. The existence of spirits and the luxuriance of symbols are more fascinating than are their feeble messages about the weather' (p. 6).

Sperber argues against the reduction of mythopoetic symbolization to a semiotic system by pointing out that the interpretation of such symbols, rather than being fixed, must be seen as variable and context dependent. Moreover, the 'rules' that assign interpretations to the symbols must themselves be mythopoetically interpreted. For example, Freudian phallic symbolism is not a matter of the constant association of sexual significance with a particular kind of object, it is a way of taking objects that is malleable according to circumstance and (purportedly unconscious) motivation. Furthermore it would be very difficult to explain any rules governing this kind of symbolism, if they could even be formulated, to someone who had not already grasped its central idea. So in this way the symbolism is not 'explained' by rules, but is rather an essential condition on their application. Finally, mythopoetic symbol systems differ from conventional systems like languages in having neither a fixed alphabet of symbols or any fixed media for their instantiation (as in speech), nor any 'grammatical' connection with a particular language; mythopoetic signification is, it is argued, 'encyclopedic' rather than lexical or linguistic. For Jung, in particular, the study of this form of symbolization was one route to the discovery of the universals of mental life. All of these features together make a very definite case against a wholly semiotic or conventional treatment of mythopoetic symbolization.

Beyond the Central Dogma: Extensional and Personal Symbols

That the central dogma has problems, even severe ones, is no sure indication that it will be readily abandoned by students of cognition in the near future. The rejection of a dogma is always more palatable when something equally specific and systematic is available to take its place; and a precise alternative to this dogma is not yet clearly in view. However some recent developments in semantic theory and the theory of symbolization constitute significant departures from the central dogma and suggest new avenues for future inquiry. It will be appropriate to conclude this chapter with a brief overview of some of these developments.

The idea of conventional symbolization has figured prominently in what has been said to this point. The modern semiotic tradition is quite explicit in its commitment to conventional symbol systems; and, as argued above, the contemporary computational tradition in psychology quite thoroughly presupposes them. These two traditions have together had a profound influence on much of current thinking about cognition and symbolization.

The acme of conventional symbolization is the development of a 'notation' -- a symbol system that meets some rather exacting requirements on communicability. These requirements, as developed in Goodman's (1968) seminal work, bear on both the syntactic domain of the symbol instances themselves, and the correlated semantic domain of their reference. The syntactic requirements call for a collection of symbols so arranged that any symbol instance is considered to be an instance of just one symbol, and no symbol instance is indeterminate with respect to its belonging to one as opposed to another of the symbols. It is natural to describe the syntactic domain of a notation as formed of a collection of patterns or templates which specify objects in a non-overlapping way, and are each copiable or repeatable within some fixed and finite range of measurable variation. Similar requirements hold for the semantic domain of a notation. In particular, the referents of symbols must be categorized by them in a non-overlapping and determinable way. The semantic domain of a notation is most naturally conceived of as a set of classes each of which is specified by a finite list of necessary and sufficient conditions for determining any object to be in its membership. Though notationality is an ideal rarely realized exactly in practice, it is a useful yardstick for assessing the efficiency of a symbol system when precision of communication is at issue.

It may be convenient to think of a notation as a kind of well-specified 'game'. Games like chess, that involve the rule-governed manipulation of a specified set of elements are, for example, naturally described in notational terms. The 'syntax' of chess may be seen as comprised from the different kinds of pieces and the rules governing their movement on the board, both of which are patterns that may be endlessly repeated or copied; and the 'semantics' of the game might be described in terms of all necessary and sufficient conditions of winning. The reduction of all of human symbolic activity to a 'game' of this sort, involving the purely formal manipulation of a specified set of elements, is widely taken to be the principal goal of theory of cognition and symbolization. The underlying assumption must be that notationality is, at some level, coextensive with all of symbolization. However, recent theory in semantics and symbolization does not at all support this assumption.

Extensional symbols. One notable trend is in recent semantic theory, which under the seminal influence of authors like Kripke (1977, 1980), Putnam (1975) and Donellan (1977a,b) is beginning to consider semantic domains that are comprised on the basis of particulars rather than classes. Whereas classes are governed by specified membership conditions, particulars have properties or distinguishing features that are, for some reason, not all specifiable.

One case of special interest is what Goodman (1968) calls 'semantic density'. This feature is said to characterize any semantic domain so ordered that between any two referents, a third is possible. For example, height, conceived of as a physical continuum, would be characterized as a dense domain because no finite set of measurements could, in principle, determine an object to be 'exactly six feet tall'. The height of a person, conceived of in this way, for instance, is an utterly particular fact about that person. Another kind of particular has unspecifiable properties, not by virtue of a theoretical or mathematical indeterminacy, but because it is considered to be constituted by natural law rather than by prior stipulation. These are the 'natural kinds' spoken of by Putnam and Kripke, of which physical and chemical substances are the commonly preferred examples. While a term denoting a class, for example 'the set of all odd numerals' has its application fixed by a specified condition (e.g., non-integral divisibility by two), a term denoting a natural kind is said to refer to something whose essential properties are not yet articulated, and which may require an indefinite amount of empirical investigation to fully specify. Though any of the features of a particular substance, for example, may be open to question as essential, yet one and the same substance is intended as the referent of each use of the corresponding substance term, and does not change as the list of conventionally associated features or traits is modified. 'Gold' and 'Water', for instance may be considered to refer to the same substances now as before their chemical and atomic formulae were found, and to continue to do so even if these formulae should require modification in the future. In classical terminology one might say that, whereas for class terms intension (roughly the conventional definition of a term) determines extension (the reference of the term), in the case of natural kind terms it is more nearly the case that extension determines intension (Schwartz, 1977). A third kind of particular is considered to have no essential or defining properties whatever, known or unknown. These are what Ghiselin (1981) calls 'individuals'; where an individual is described as 'a single thing, definitely located in space and time' (p. 271). This includes not only individual objects, people, and so on, but functional aggregations like planetary systems, cultural groups and even, on one way of taking the term, biological species.

Despite their differences, symbols denoting particulars, whether they be semantically dense symbols, natural kind terms, or the 'names' of individuals, have in common that, rather than securing reference on the basis of a specified set of determining features they come to mean what they refer to. These are symbols that we take from the outset as 'designating a "something I am not sure what"' (Ghiselin, 1981, p. 271). For this reason, we may refer to them all as 'extensional symbols', as a way of contrasting them with conventional symbols which may be considered to refer, in principle, notationally.

Symbols may also be extensionally constituted in the syntactic domain. This is an aspect of symbolization that the work of Goodman has again shed considerable light on. Goodman (1968), for example, draws a distinction between allographic and autographic arts. Whereas the symbols of an allographic art are exactly copiable or repeatable, as novels or musical scores are, for example, the symbols of an autographic art, like painting or sculpture, are unique and not exactly copiable; they introduce the concept of forgery, for example. Autographic symbols, like other kinds of extensional symbols, are based on particulars, though the particular is now the symbol itself rather than its referent. Some such symbols are particular primarily in virtue of being dense; rough sketches in which any arbitrary spatial features may be signifying would be examples. Others, particularly aesthetic objects, are more naturally thought of as individuals, that is as objects with unique histories, the constitutive features of which are not fully specified. This kind of symbol cannot be accommodated in the terminology of type/token ratios as writers in the semiotic tradition are sometimes inclined to suggest (cf. Eco, 1976, pp. 183-184), for autographic symbols are, as particulars, objects for which no such distinction between type and token, or 'template' and 'copy' can even be drawn.

Extensional symbols, whether in the semantic or syntactic domain, are relative to a linguistic community of unspecifiable membership. This is another important respect in which they differ from conventional symbols. The community of users of a conventional symbol system may have arbitrary bounds on its membership, but these may in any case be specified to any required degree. For example, there may be some dispute about what extent of a person's command of the rules of the game qualifies him for membership in the community of 'chess-players', but the rules themselves remain fixed. In contrast, the qualifications that enable a person to make pronouncements on the use of scientific substance or species terms, on the exploits of historical individuals, or on the origin of autographic aesthetic objects, are not clearly specified in advance, for genuine discoveries on any of these matters may come from hitherto unexpected quarters. Whereas the membership criteria for a community of conventional symbol users are fixed, though arbitrary in application, those for a community of extensional symbol users are essentially indeterminate and open-ended.

The importance of extensional symbols for psychology is evident in the attention they have recently attracted in studies of categorization. Modern approaches to this phenomenon have come recently to reject the notion that categorization is wholly conventional and to give serious attention to categories as determined by the 'natural structure' of the perceived world (Rosch, 1978) or as clustered around instances (Brooks, 1978).

Personal symbols. One last kind of symbolic particular is beyond the scope of either conventional or extensional symbolic practices. These are the symbolic particulars directly realized as the experiences and performances of a person -- 'personal symbols', as they have been elsewhere designated (Kolers and Smythe, in press). This type of symbol subsumes a rather diverse collection of phenomena: on the experiental side are included all of the referential phenomenal events such as mental images, associations, perceptual experiences, thought episodes, and the like (as distinct from non-referring phenomenal events like pains, afterimages and sensory phantasms); on the performative side are all of the significant acts a person may perform like indicating, judging, carrying out a plan or intention, and so on. Despite this considerable diversity, all personal symbols have in common that they are particulars that are personally constituted. They are particulars in as much as they are never exactly repeatable; they are inevitably the experiences and performances of a person in a particular situation no two of which can exist, even for that person, in any common space where they can be matched or mapped one to another. An experience or performance is what it is at its own moment in time and does not properly exist at any other. Such symbols are, moreover, personally constituted in that they are always activated by an individual person and have no status apart from this activation. They are, for this reason, relative finally to a symbol-using community of one -- the individual whose activies are essential to their occurrence. They are personal, not in the way that the private mnemonic devices spoken of by semioticians are for, while any such device may be communicated to another on request, the experiences or performances of one person are uniquely his or her own and cannot, in the same way, become those of another. Devices like private mnemonics are, to use a term of (Kolers and Smythe, in press). merely 'adventitiously private'; whereas personal symbols must be considered, in virtue of their mode of constitution, as 'intrinsically private'.

The study of the phenomenon of symbolization must, for the psychologist, begin with a consideration of personal symbols, for in the domain of symbolic cognition, experience and performance provide the essential data. As brought out more fully elsewhere, the study of symbolic cognition, so grounded, would take on a very different character than it now has under the dominance of the central dogma of the cognitive sciences (Kolers, 1980; Kolers and Smythe, in press; Smythe, 1981, in press).

CONCLUSION

The scope of human symbolic activity is considerable by any reckoning. The symbol is a truly pervasive aspect of human experience. Whether in our intellectual lives, in scientific or aesthetic environments, or in the practical affairs of daily life, we are unavoidably surrounded and immersed in a world of symbols. The central dogma of the cognitive sciences would have us believe that all of this great diversity can be captured, finally, in terms of purely formal, notational symbol manipulation. The discussion in the latter part of this chapter has suggested an alternative. The picture that is beginning to emerge is that human symbolic activity, rather than deriving from a single type of symbol system, involves the manipulation of a number of fundamentally distinct kinds of symbol. The distinctions among 'conventional', 'extensional', and 'personal' symbols only begin to map out this territory. However, these distinctions are already an improvement on the conventional/physical/mythopoetic symbol system trichotomy, because they are based on a common principle. The principle is that different modes of symbolization are constituted by the functioning of symbol-using communities of varying scope. Further inquiry into the principles governing such communities and the activities of people within them may be the best way to advance the study of symbolic cognition.

REFERENCES

Anderson, J.R. (1976). Language, Memory and Thought. Hillsdale, New Jersey: Erlbaum.

Anderson, J.R. (1978). Arguments concerning representation for mental imagery. Psychological Review, 85, 249-277.

Bates, E. (1979). The Emergence of Symbols. New York: Academic Press.

Brooks, L. (1978). Nonanalytic concept formation and memory for instances. In: E. Rosch and B.B. Lloyd (Eds.) Cognition and Categorization. Hillsdale, New Jersey: Erlbaum.

Cassirer, E. (1944). An Essay on Man. New Haven, Connecticut: Yale University Press.

Chebat, J. (1974). Symbol: Towards a definition. International Journal of Symbology, 5, 31-39.

Chomsky, N. (1980). Rules and representations. Behavioral and Brain Sciences, 3, 1-61.

Donnellan, K.S. (1977a). Reference and definite descriptions. In: S.P. Schwartz (Ed.) Naming, Necessity and Natural Kinds. Ithaca, New York: Cornell University Press.

Donnellan, K.S. (1977b). Speaking of nothing. In: S.P. Schwartz (Ed.) Naming, Necessity and Natural Kinds. Ithaca, New York: Cornell University Press.

Eco, U. (1976). A Theory of Semiotics. Bloomington, Indiana: Indiana University Press.

Ghiselin, M.T. (1981). Categories, life and thinking. Behavioral and Brain Sciences, 4, 269-313.

Goodman, N. (1968). Languages of Art. Indianapolis, Indiana: Bobbs-Merrill.

Goodman, N. (1978). Ways of Worldmaking. Indianapolis, Indiana: Hackett.

Heil, J. (1981). Does cognitive psychology rest on a mistake? Mind, XC, 321-342.

Howard, V.A. (1980). Theory of representation: Three questions. In: P.A. Kolers, M.E. Wrolstad and H. Bouma (Eds.) Processing of Visible Language 2. New York: Plenum.

Kaplan, B. (1979). Symbolism: From the body to the soul. In: N.R. Smith, and M.B. Franklin (Eds.) Symbolic Functioning in Childhood. Hillsdale, New Jersey: Erlbaum.

Keller, H. (1904). The Story of My Life. New York: Grosset and Dunlap.

Kolers, P.A. (1980). Confusions of symbolization in mental representation. In: Philosophy of Science Association, Volume 2.

Kolers, P.A. and Smythe, W.E. (In press). Symbol manipulation: Alternatives to the computational view of mind. Journal of Verbal Learning and Verbal Behavior.

Kripke, S.A. (1977). Identity and necessity. In: S.P. Schwartz (Ed.) Naming, Necessity and Natural Kinds. Ithaca, New York: Cornell University Press.

Kripke, S.A. (1980). Naming and Necessity. Cambridge, Massachusetts: Harvard University Press.

Langer, S.K. (1942). Philosophy in a New Key. Cambridge, Massachusetts: Harvard University Press.

Morris, C.W. (1938). Foundations of the theory of signs. In: International Encyclopedia of Unified Science, Volume 1. Chicago, Illinois: University of Chicago Press.

Morris, C.W. (1946). Signs, Language and Behavior. New York: Prentice-Hall.

Newell, A. (1980). Physical symbol systems. Cognitive Science, 4, 135-183.

Newell, A. and Simon, H.A. (1978). Computer science as empirical inquiry: Symbols and search. Communications of the ACM, 19, 113-126.

Palmer, S.E. (1978). Fundamental aspects of cognitive representation. In: E. Rosch and B.B. Lloyd (Eds.) Cognition and Categorization. Hillsdale, New Jersey: Erlbaum.

Pavlov, I.P. (1927). Conditioned Reflexes: An Investigation of the Physiological Activity of the Cerebral Cortex. London: Oxford University Press.

Peirce, C.S. (1955). Logic as semiotic: The theory of signs. In: J. Buchler (Ed.) Philosophical Writings of Peirce. New York: Dover.

Piaget, J. (1962). Play, Dreams and Imitation in Childhood. G. Gattegno and F.M. Hodgson, translation. New York: Norton.

Powell, J.N. (1982). The Tao of Symbols. New York: Quill.

Putnam, H. (1975). The meaning of "meaning". In: K. Gunderson (Ed.) Minnesota Studies in the Philosophy of Science, Volume VII. Minneapolis, Minnesota: University of Minnesota Press.

Pylyshyn, Z.W. (1980). Cognitive representation and the process-architecture distinction. Behavioral and Brain Sciences, 3, 154-169.

Rosch, E. (1972). Principles of categorization. In: E. Rosch and B.B. Lloyd (Eds.) Cognition and Categorization. Hillsdale, New Jersey: Erlbaum.

Schwartz, S.P. (1977). Introduction. In: S.P. Schwartz (Ed.) Naming, Necessity and Natural Kinds. Ithaca, New York: Cornell University Press.

Smith, B.C. (1982). Semantic Attribution and the Formality Condition. Paper presented at the eighth annual meeting of the Society for Philosophy and Psychology, University of Western Ontario, May.

Smythe, W.E. (1981). Personal symbol systems. Paper presented at the seventh annual meeting of the Society for Philosophy and Psychology, University of Chicago, April.

Smythe, W.E. (In press). Mental imagery as a personal symbol system. In: A. Ahsen, A.T. Dolan and C.S. Jordan (Eds.) Handbook of Imagery Research and Practice. New York: Brandon House.

Sperber, D. (1975). Rethinking Symbolism. A.L. Mortan (Ed. and translator). London: Cambridge University Press.

Werner, H. and Kaplan, B. (1963). Symbol Formation. New York: Wiley.

Cognitive Processes in the Perception of Art
W.R. Crozier and A.J. Chapman (editors)
© Elsevier Science Publishers B.V. (North-Holland), 1984

TEXTS, SIGNS, ARTEFACTS

Liam Hudson
Brunel University

Psychology, it seems to me, is in an interesting state of transition, and I want to take stock. In particular, I want to look at those aspects of psychology that have come to be called 'soft'; to acknowledge certain disappointments and shortcomings, but at the same time to point to developments that hold the potential for excitement. I say something too about 'hard' psychology, the laboratory tradition, but this only in passing. It is the 'soft' and what might become of it that is my chief concern.

In the late 1960's, a great deal changed. A number of psychologists, myself among them, wrote books saying that the application of conventionally 'scientific' methods of research to the more complex or subtle aspects of human experience had proved barren: that the evidence of such research was trivial, trivializing, and the vehicle, often, for prejudices that were as unattractive as they were naive (Hudson, 1972). Such work was bad science, and a mockery of scholarly values. By the mid-1970's, people were saying 'All well and good, but where are the examples of something better?' What they sought were not sermons about the shortcomings of behaviourism but instances, exemplifications, of something that fell less short. I recall being shouted at for two hours to this effect by one of the great philosophers of science. My claim was that psychologists were well advised to think about their research before they did it. His counter-claim, thundering around the walls of my room in the Princeton Institute, was that I and my kind should get on with the doing.

The forms of 'soft' or 'alternative' psychology then taking shape were three. In retrospect, each has seemed to make a characteristic claim. The first, was that psychologists should abandon all thought of becoming scientists, and concern themselves with 'human relations'. The second was that, more or less by definition, human thought and action is 'socially constructed'. The third was that psychology should properly be conducted in the form of a 'critique'.

Of these, the 'human relations' option seemed at the time worryingly mushy. While stressing human potentiality, a noble theme, it did so in ways which threatened continually to remove it from the world of dispassionate knowledge to that of wise thoughts. Eastern religions, drug-induced states of heightened awareness, primal screams: these were not activities, it seemed, from which a patient accumulation of knowledge about the mind could easily be won. And so it has proved. There has been excitement, intuitive self-awareness in abundance; but, unless I am mistaken, the excitement has waned, the sense of heightened self-awareness has begun to fade.

The 'social construction' option has about it a grittier feel. Books have been written, academic careers built. Here, too, though, one has a sense of misgiving. The problem is simple: this is an approach that turns psychology into an outhouse of sociology. Instead of taking prior influences - whether biological, physical or social - as read, and attempting to make sense of the mind and its products as they now present themselves, the 'social construction' option leads to analyses indistinguishable from those pursued in the department of sociology.

An analogous objection faces the argument, often forcefully advanced, that psychology must take shape as a 'critique'. According to this view, human experience can only be studied if the inquiry is informed by theoretical beliefs that are themselves invested with some special political, moral or historical authority: Marxist, feminist, Freudian, or what you will. Such critiques can be illuminative and some are pursued in a spirit of considerable intellectual rigour; but, again, they turn psychology into something else - sometimes into politics, sometimes into philosophy or exegetics.

My point in criticizing these three strands in 'soft' psychology is not in the least to denigrate neighbouring activities, whether therapy, sociology, politics, philosophy or exigetics - or, on the other side, physiology, genetics or cybernetics. I want simply to claim back from these neighbours territory that is our own: to be able to say 'this is psychology' and 'this is how it is done'. If the 'human relations', 'social construction' and 'critical' options do not fit the bill, which will? My own answer leads back to a vein of thought referred to quite often in the recent past -- among others, again, by myself -- but not wholly grasped: to wit, *hermeneutics*.

Compared with the dignity of empiricism and its origins, unflaggingly but not entirely convincingly rehearsed, in the thought processes of Locke, Berkeley and Hume, the roots of the hermeneutic tradition are tenuous. They are also Teutonic. For it was on the Continent of Europe rather than in the British Isles that the conceptual problems of the historian and, then of the human as opposed to physical scientist, were first taken seriously. In search of precedents one is forced to gesture towards shadowy figures - William Dilthey, for example; and to do so uneasily because one has read their works only in translation and in scraps (see, for example, Dilthey 1972).

Behind Dilthey, one learns, stood Schleiermacher; and behind both stood generations of scholars committed to search for the best, the most defensible, reading of obscure or corrupted Biblical texts. The links between the supposedly 'soft' psychologist in the late twentieth century and the German Biblical scholar in the nineteenth century are these. Both are engaged in an activity that is essentially interpretative. Both are concerned to make sense. And both have, as their self-imposed discipline, the task of sifting alternative readings, weighing their respective merits in the light of what is given: the 'text'. In itself, the hermeneutic approach is little more than a slogan, certainly less than a recipe. It does have special attractions, though: and chief among them is precisely its concentration on a text; on what is tangibly, incontrovertibly *there*. The text is given in just the down-to-earth and reassuring sense that scientific apparatus or experimental data are. As with laboratory research, the hermeneutic formulation combines a respect for what is given with an urge towards the greatest degree of order that this respect for the given permits.

So far, so good. What it has taken longer to see is the implication of this formulation for what one actually does. In my own case, the lesson has taken the best part of a decade to sink in. Once grasped, however, the argument is almost embarrassingly simple. In my book *Bodies of Knowledge* I take the hermeneutic notion of psychology to heart (cf. Hudson, 1982). It is a book that adopts a point of view: the belief that in intimate matters and especially in our perception of the human body, we are characteristically ambivalent. It then explores this claim in terms of 'texts'; that is to say, paintings, sculptures, photographs of the body each memorable in its own right, and each of which can be shown to explore and exploit our ambivalences towards the body in a skilled and fastidious way. In practice, this meant taking specific images -- a particular Titian, Manet's *Olympia* certain Degas', a pin-up from the Pirelli Calendar -- and unpacking the meanings with which they are freighted. These analyses are not flights of fantasy any more than good archaeology or good detective work is. Rather, a painstaking effort to say how it is that these images achieve their effects. In the course of such an analysis, one must learn some art history, just as the study of the visual system forced one to learn some physiology and chemistry. You must know that the Titian you are discussing was dropped by Napoleon's army into a river and extensively patched up before it was returned. At times you even seem to trespass. But the analysis itself, the exploration of the carefully poised ambiguities of which such works of art consist, remains psychological: it deals with what we see, what we think, what we think we see.

Out of this first project has grown a second: a book, almost finished, built on Charles Darwin's claim (Rycroft, 1979) that dreams are a form of involuntary poetry. Our sleeping thought is involuntary, inventive and ambiguous; and certain of our waking thoughts -- notably those concerned with the construction and appreciation of works of art -- show these properties too. The analogies between sleeping and waking thought are explored by means of a scrutiny of certain poems, passages in novels, details in films, photographs. Again, there is the opportunity to work with texts, signs, to use what is unequivocally *there*.

What emerges is neither science nor entertainment. One deals neither with phenomena that are in principle clear and unequivocal, as the scientist hopes to, nor with the random. Instead, with arrangements that steer the mind in one direction or another, much as the plan of a landscape garden might. The analysis does not remove doubt or ambiguity; rather, it specifies as dispassionately as possible, how doubt and ambiguity arise. The raw materials are, to use Gass's phrase, 'containers of consciousness' and the surprises with which these are packed.

Having launched along this path and found it at least as straightforward as research with mental tests, say, or with the output from a sleep laboratory, what now interests me is the way in which certain simple prejudices have ruled both this and related inquiries out of account. The simplest prejudice of all, the basic currency of judgment in the academy at large, is the distinction with which I began: that between the 'hard' and the 'soft' (Hudson, 1967). Either this distinction says, we are trying to do science or we are engaged in something quite different: politics, therapy, journalism, self-expression. The arts in particular are seen as peripheral, or -- even worse -- as 'fun'; that is to say, as a simple emotional release that receives little professionally academic attention because it deserves none. Yet the briefest glance shows that poems, novels, paintings, photographs, plays, films or any quality are rarely fun, either for artist or for spectator; what is more, that they are at least as carefully poised, as subtly calculated in their effects, as any other genre of intellectual activity. Many take months, years, to put together, and at least as long to assimilate in any but a superficial way.

Just as the dichotomy between hard and soft has led to the exclusion of the arts from the arena, it has led us to ignore three further aspects of everyday life: to ignore the world of brands, logos and loyalties out of which much of our environment is fashioned; to ignore the activity of design, that sprawling empire in which, in a dozen ways, the material and the imaginative are married to one another; and, perhaps most significant of all, ignore the psychological implications of the machines on which we depend - the ones which serve our regal purposes, but, at the same time, invade and reshape our sense of what those purposes might be (Hudson, 1983). If art is 'fun' and therefore ignorable, advertising is 'immoral', design is 'cosmetic' and technology is a 'bore'. They can all be ignored together. Compared with the intellectual refinement, the heroic challenge, of the study of short-term memory, say, each of the facets of everyday life is made to seem evanescent.

It is no part of my intention to criticize the laboratory tradition in psychology. I take it as read, too, that none of us is in favour of slovenly argument or hand-waving. But I do want to emphasize the gravity and scope of these omissions; and to point out that they no longer seem natural if you adopt as a guiding principle, not the distinction between hard and soft, but the scrutiny of what is unequivocally *there* in the form of texts, signs and artefacts - what is there, moreover, not in simplified form, but in its full complexity.

Such texts, signs and artefacts pose three sorts of questions, only one of which is straight-forward. The straightforward question is the one of fact:

> *How, as a matter of fact, are the texts, signs and artefacts all around us used, construed?*

In addition, though, there are two further questions less obvious:

> *What must we grasp in order to explain their presence?*; and
> *Given their presence, what are their psychological implications?*

Let me explain, by means of examples. Among psychologists, the first issue causes no strain. There are a dozen techniques available to us with which to establish the ways in which texts, signs and artifacts are construed; systems of meaning in which they are enmeshed. If, in the course of such inquiries, we encounter surprises -- people treated as though they were artefacts, artefacts treated as though they were people -- they are at least surprises of a kind that is in principle familiar. The argument, however, is more far-reaching than such precedents imply: it reaches into our collective pasts and into our collective futures too.

Two thousand years ago, the Greeks created an object which, when excavated and closely examined, proved to be a system of differential gears, carefully tuned to the movements of the heavenly bodies: in a sense, a work of art, in a sense a piece of technology, an immensely elaborate toy. So the differential gear was invented earlier rather than later, one might say, but what follows? In the event, a great deal. I have watched Zeeman (1982) demonstrate that, looking back, deductively, one can establish what mathematics the Greeks must have possessed in order to bring this artefact into being. He reconstructed the calculations the Greeks would have had to perform in order to design it. The history of mathematics is thus written by peering back 'through' the artefact in question. Without his scholarly curiosity and vision, it would have been left as an ancient remnant, of prime interest only to the museum in which it happened to be lodged. We can peer 'through' too, using texts that are written, painted, photographed. We can examine Manet's *Olympia*, unpacking it in search of those aspects of its construction that, a hundred years ago, so successfully moved the Paris public to outrage. If Manet set many hundreds of thousands of teeth on edge, and did so with an image that now seems so innocuous, we must ask 'how'? Such analyses, almost always a matter of nuance and innuendo, are rewarding in their own right. Our capacity as a species to be moved by inanimate objects like paintings and books is, after all, one of our few redeeming features.

It would be a mistake, though, to be too restrictedly historical or aesthetic. As it happens the shock of Manet's *Olympia* had a great deal to do with the camera; and the camera, in its turn, is an eloquent instrument rather than a merely useful one. It invades and alters our imaginative lives. And in that there is an important clue. Our subject-matter in future may be concerned more with such invasions -- with the marriage, the miscegenation, of the imagination and the machine.

Traditionally, ergonomics has come to be seen as the most tedious of all psychology's branches, but only, I think, because we have addressed this extraordinary relationship of man to machine as though it must be mechanical on both sides. The assumption is absurd. As Marxists have reminded us, shifts in technology trigger irreversible shifts in consciousness, in sensibility. Critics like Berger (1972) have addressed such issues, but without quite grasping, it seems to me, what must be grasped; the comprehensiveness of psychological changes that technology triggers. For those interested, I would point as example to Mailer's (1979) remarkable book *The Executioner's Song*, about the death of Gary Gilmore, and the mounting sense of the bizarre with which this execution was surrounded. Without camera, tape-recorder, radio and television set these strange goings on could not have occurred. They embroil their participants,increasingly helpless, in their dream-like world of a 'media-event'. Actions of ordinary people take on significance, more and more, as raw material for the eventual screenplay. Around Gilmore, commonsense melts away and we are left, in the end, in a space more closely akin to that of the hallucination than the flat-footed empiricist in each of us cares to admit. A great deal of everyday experience, I would seek to suggest, now has this hallucinatory character to a more limited extent; an extent that may prove to grow as our dependence on the machines of communication itself grows.

All this, it might be said, is sweepingly innovatory, but spuriously so. In practice laboratory scientists clearly address themselves to a text and to its interpretation; in their care, a data-base - what people, animals or things can be seen to do. Far from disputing this connection, I would like to admit and capitalize upon it; to say that where the laboratory tradition in psychology has flourished, it has done so because those concerned have articulated for themselves an orderly sense of what their evidence means. They have created an interpretative core which gives their experimental studies point, rather than allowing one fact to breed from another. I would suggest that the shortcoming of the psychology that has been pursued outside the laboratory lies in our failure to transpose just this relation of text to interpretation to the more subtle problems of meaning that the complex aspects of human activity pose. One of the rewards of addressing ourselves to the arts in full seriousness, and to adjacent fields like that of design, is that their very nature fosters this transposition. When baffled or in disagreement, rather than drifting off into theory, we are drawn back, naturally, to a scrutiny of what such works say. If disposed to listen, we find that they answer us back with the same stubborn resolution that data bases offer to the scientifically inclined. It is on this tense and at times mysteriously indeterminate relation of text to interpretation that the vitality of psychology -- both supposedly 'soft' and reputedly 'hard' -- seems to be to depend.

REFERENCES

Berger, J. (1972). Ways of Seeing. BBC. Harmondsworth: Penguin.

Dilthey, W. (1972). The Rise of Hermeneutics. New Literary History, 3, 229.

Gass, W. (No date). On Being Blue. Godine.

Hudson, L. (1967). The stereotypical scientist. Nature, 213, 228.

Hudson, L. (1972). The Cult of the Fact. London: Cape.

Hudson, L. (1982). Bodies of Knowledge. New York: Weidenfeld.

Hudson, L. (1983). The Great Miscegenation - or the Joyous Union of the Imagination and the Machine. SIAD/Maurice Hille Lecture, the Society of Industrial Artists and Designers.

Mailer, N. (1979). The Executioner's Song. London: Hutchinson.

Rycroft, C. (1979). The Innocence of Dreams. London: Hogarth.

Zeeman, C. (1982). Differential Gears from the Ancient Greeks. Unpublished lecture, Brunel University.

Cognitive Processes in the Perception of Art
W.R. Crozier and A.J. Chapman (editors)
© Elsevier Science Publishers B.V. (North-Holland), 1984

ELUSIVE EFFECTS OF ARTISTS' 'MESSAGES'

Vladimir J. Konečni

University of California at San Diego

Analyses of work of art, broadly defined, imply a discussion of its components or characteristics, and its intended impact on the viewer, listener, or reader. Such analyses of artistic styles and individual works are clearly one of the most important functions of art history and criticism. Also, although some artists have been reluctant to discuss publicly their works and intentions, many have been eager to write about their art, for instance, in the so-called 'manifestoes' (writings by Klee, Kandinsky, Boccioni, Delaunay, Mondrian -- and countless others in the visual arts alone -- are examples of this; e.g., Hoffman, 1954; Long and Washton, 1980; Orbourne, 1979; Rosenberg, 1966, 1975).

Moreover, even in the absence of verbal analyses, artists implicitly give indications of their beliefs about the way in which the work of art affects or should affect the audience. The simplest decision, such as to hang a painting in a certain orientation, present the parts of a musical piece in a certain sequence, use short or long paragraphs, or place the actors in a scene in one, as opposed to another, place on the stage, reflect the painter's, composer's, writer's, and director's, respectively, belief about their work's optimal impact. Even in the extreme case, when a work of art consists of random events (some compositions by John Cage are examples of this), there are good reasons to conclude that the artist believes that either the very randomness of the work's components, or the particular method of producing the random events, or both, will have an impact on the audience. In short, there is a large body of writing by art historians, critics, and artists themselves about the specific components of works of art and their supposed perceptual, cognitive, and emotional impact; such writings are not to be confused with the philosophical, historical, or political speculations about the alleged real or desirable 'social functions' of art.

For many reasons, some of the verbal analyses of works of art are of only literary or historical value. However, many statements are more precise and explicit about the relative contribution of individual components to the work's overall alleged impact about the artist's intended 'message' (in the broadest possible sense), and about the ways in which the work was constructed in order to achieve the desired effect. Such statements can often be translated into propositions that are empirically verifiable. To the extent that the psychology of art and music is in part concerned with the perceptual, cognitive, and emotional effects of works of art on appreciators, and that it has the requisite methodological and experimental tools, it would seem that its practitioners could provide an important service to the artists by informing them of the extent to which the intended message is actually 'getting through' to the audience. In other words, is the audience perceptually, cognitively, and emotionally responding in the way that the artist (or critic) expects? Do certain parts of a work of art and its overall structure have the intended effects?

It can, of course, be argued that art is a completely spontaneous activity, that artists 'have to' create a work in a certain way, that artists neither consciously nor unconsciously show or should show any regard for the effect of the work on the audience and finally, that art is an entirely private activity. There is perhaps some truth to some such claims for some artists some of the time, but the very fact that artists do talk about the intended impact of their works and the components of these works, that at least some do hope for public, critical and social approval and acclaim (and that many apply for public funds or private support), and that art historians and critics do claim that they can discern the artists' intentions concerning the work's 'message' and the way that message is constructed, all suggest that much if not most art is meant to be presented, that it is more than an entirely private activity, and that it is therefore reasonable to submit artists' and critics' claims about the impact of works of art on the audience to psycho-aesthetic scrutiny.

In the remainder of this chapter, I present the results of 5 studies each of which attempted to evaluate empirically an explicit or implicit claim made by an artist, critic, or art historian about the intended perceptual, cognitive and emotional impact of an overall work of art or some of its components. In the different studies, paintings, literary works, dramatic performances, and musical pieces (classical and rock 'n' roll) were used as stimuli, and with a variety of audiences. All studies had the same format. First, an explicit or implicit claim by an artist, art historian or art critic about the impact, effect, or purpose of a work of art, that could be clearly translated into a testable form, was isolated. Next, original and modified (control) versions of the work were presented to subjects. Finally, the subjects rated the various versions' pleasingness, interestingness, emotional impact, and related characteristics or dimensions.

STUDY 1: ORIENTATION OF PAINTINGS

The decision to present a painting for viewing in a particular orientation is clearly one of the most basic statements an artist can make; it obviously reflects the artist's beliefs regarding the optimal impact of that painting on viewers. In representational art, of course, orientation is almost never at issue. In abstract art, however, a 'natural' orientation is often not obvious from the content of the painting; instead, the artist defines the proper orientation by hanging the painting in a certain way. This decision can be thought of as a fundamental part of the artist's 'message'.

Would that message be lost, or become weaker or distorted, if the unsuspecting viewers were to be presented with abstract paintings rotated 90° or 180° from the 'correct' orientation? Would such a rude intervention in the communication between the artist and the viewers -- an intervention which fundamentally alters the balance of a painting in terms of form and colour on the horizontal and vertical dimensions (Western paintings are very seldom symmetrical) reduce the pleasingness and interestingness of paintings?

A related issue, and one not limited to abstract art, is the lateral (left-right) organization of paintings. Gordon (1981) and others credit Wolfflin (1941) for suggesting that paintings are typically scanned from left to right (for whatever reason, such as hemispheric dominance or the reading sequence), and that the left-right scanning pattern is responsible both for the widespread lateral asymmetry in Western painting and the subjective impression of a pronounced change in the appearance of paintings following the right-left mirror reversal.

Subsequently Wofflin's ideas were refined considerably by Gaffron (1950, 1962) who proposed the existence of a 'glance-curve' -- a typical scan that begins at the bottom left and proceeds to the top right and into the three-dimensional space portrayed in the painting. The glance curve would explain, according to Gaffron, all the various changes that occur when a painting is mirror-reversed.

In an outstanding paper on the left-right organization of paintings, Gordon (1981) extracts no less than eighteen testable claims that have been made by Gaffron, Arnheim (1956), and others regarding the left-right differences in paintings, the most important of which is that 'pictures cannot be mirror reversed without losing much of their aesthetic quality ... when reversed, they appear less balanced, less well composed' (Gordon, 1981, p. 224).

However, after reviewing 8 relevant experiments, which have used a wide variety of subjects and paintings, Gordon (1981, p. 233) concluded: 'Overall, detection of original orientations is poor ... Even when above chance, the mean detection rate is typically only about 53 per cent ... Original orientations are not overwhelmingly preferred'.

The present study is a replication and extension of the work of Lindauer (1969), Swartz and Hewitt (1970), and Gordon and Gardner (1974). Within a single study, the effects of mirror reversal of representational works, and of mirror reversal and 90°-rotations and 180°-rotations of abstract works, were comprehensively examined. In addition, the study examined the effects of the knowledge of a painting's title (actual or fictitious) on various dimensions of preference.

Method

The subjects were 120 undergraduates (60 women, 60 men) from the University of California at San Diego and the University of California at Los Angeles. Demographic and art-related information was obtained from all subjects.

Thirty representational and 30 abstract works were used as stimuli (see Table 1), all painted in the twentieth century (to ensure aesthetic consistency and overlap of artists). In the correct orientation, all 60 paintings contained a left-right asymmetry in terms of form and colour. The terms 'representational' (R) and 'abstract' (A) are here used loosely. Paintings in the R group contained a variety of abstractions and distortions common in the movements represented (cubism, fauvism, metaphysicism, expressionism, 'die-Brücke', 'Blaue Reiter' and surrealism). All R-group paintings, however, were sufficiently representational that the correct position (in terms of top-bottom orientation) was in no doubt whatsoever. In contrast, A-group paintings were entirely ambiguous in this sense; there was nothing inthese paintings that revealed or dictated the correct top-bottom orientation (other than the artist's decision). Paintings in the A-group, in addition to those that are commonly classified as abstract in the narrow sense, included many surrealist, fauvist, cubist, futurist, 'Blaue Reiter' and Dadaist works.

TABLE 1

Representational works used in Study 1	
De Chirico	The disquieting Muses (1917)
Kandinsky	The blue horseman (1903)
Kandinsky	Beach cabins in Holland (1904)
Kandinsky	Russian beauty in a landscape (1905)
Kandinsky	A street in Murnau (1908)
Klee	In the mine (1913)
Klee	With the eagle (1918)
Klee	Landscape with yellow birds (1923)
Kokoschka	Old man Hirsch (1907)
Kokoschka	Marseilles (1925)
Léger	The mechanic (1920)
Léger	The dancer with keys (1930)
Léger	Four cyclists (1943-48)
Léger	The great parade (1954)
Magritte	Discovery (1927)
Magritte	Bather between light and darkness (1935)
Magritte	Personal valuables (1952)
Magritte	Euclidean walks (1955)
Matisse	Bathers by a river (1916-17)
Matisse	Interior at Nice (1921)
Matisse	Pink nude (1935)
Matisse	The big red interior (1948)
Munch	Village street in Elgersburg (1905)
Munch	Weeping woman (1906-7)
Munch	Death of Marat (1907)
Picasso	The old guitarist (1903)
Picasso	Mother and child (1921)
Picasso	Three musicians (1921)
Picasso	The rooster and the knife (1947)
Munch	Young people on the beach (1903-04)

Abstract works used in Study 1	
Boccioni	Elasticity (1912)
Duchamp	The transformation of a virgin into a bride (1912)
Ernst	Mother and children on planet Earth (1953)
Kandinsky	Improvisation 30 (1913)
Kandinsky	Improvisation 'Klamm' (1914)
Kandinsky	In the black circle (1923)
Kandinsky	Quiet (1924)
Kandinsky	Several circles (1926)
Klee	To the stars (1923)
Klee	Individual altimetry of layers (1930)
Klee	Drunkenness (1939)
Klee	The sailor (1940)
Kupka	Vertical planes, blue and red (1913)
Kupka	Philosophical architecture
Léger	Composition (1918)
Léger	Butterflies and flowers (1937)
Magritte	The false mirror (1928)
Malevich	Suprematist composition (1915-16)
Matisse	The king's sadness (1952)
Matisse	The snail (1953)
Miró	Catalon landscape, the hunter (1923-24)
Miró	Night bird (1939)
Miró	The white lady (1950)

Miró	The violet color of the moon (1951)
Mondrian	Oval composition (1914)
Mondrian	Composition red-yellow-blue in a square (1926)
Mondrian	Broadway boogie-woogie (1942-43)
Villon	Joy (1932)
Villon	Toward Chimaera (1947)
Villon	Icarus (1956)

Subjects, in groups averaging 10 people, saw all 60 slides for 60 seconds each. Each single subject saw a painting only once, in either the correct or mirror-reversed orientation for R-paintings, and either the correct, or 90°-rotated, 180°-rotated, or mirror-reversed orientation for A-paintings. When a new slide came on, the experimenter read either its correct title or a fictitious, unrelated, but not ridiculous title (e.g., 'Mother Nature' for Matisse's 'Pink nude'; 'Rocks III' for Klee's 'Individual altimetry of layers'), or no title at all. In other words, the R versus A (type of painting) factor was examined on a within-subjects basis; the orientation factor (2 levels for R-paintings, 4 levels for A-paintings) and the title information factor (3 levels) were between-subjects.

While viewing a slide, subjects rated the painting's pleasingness, interestingness, balance, emotional impact, appropriateness of title and willingness to buy a reproduction on 20 cm scales. These scales have been successfully used in prior work and their correlations are known (e.g., Konečni and Sargent-Pollock, 1977; Sargent-Pollack and Konečni, 1977). In addition, following the pleasingness, interestingness, emotional impact, and balance questions, the subjects indicated, in a multiple choice format, what made a painting pleasing, interesting, and so on (colour, composition, movement, subject, contrast and humour were among the options).

Results

When their effects were compared (in correct orientations), it was found that representational paintings were significantly (p .01, unless otherwise stated) more pleasing (M = 10.6), more desirable to own (M = 8.3), more balanced (M = 7.9, p .05), and had a greater emotional impact (M = 8.2) than did the abstract works (the respective means for A-paintings were 7.8, 6.8, 6.9 and 7.0). The two groups did not differ in terms of interestingness (Ms for R- and A-paintings were 11.2 and 11.0 respectively).

The absence of effects of orientation for both groups of paintings and all rating dimensions was quite striking. In terms of pleasingness, mirror reversal changed the means quite negligibly, for R-paintings to 10.4 (from 10.6 in the correct orientation) and for A-paintings to 7.9 (from 7.8). Mirror reversal had similarly weak effects on other dimensions of judgment for both groups of paintings.

The experimental analogue of hanging an abstract painting upside down (rotating it by 180°) similarily had no effect on any of the dimensions of judgment (M for pleasingness, for example, was 7.5). Only when an abstract painting was rotated 90° was there a decrease, albeit very small ($p<.15$), in pleasingness. (This result is analogous to that obtained by Lindauer, 1969).

These results would clearly lead one to regard Gordon's (1981, p. 233) conclusion that 'original orientations are not overwhelmingly preferred' as an understatement. Furthermore, no effect was found of art training or of the degree of exposure to art (Gordon came to a similar conclusion). Finally, no consistent pattern emerged regarding the reasons subjects gave for their pleasingness and other judgments (in terms of colour, composition, movement, etc.)

The original titles of the paintings fared rather worse than the original orientations. Fictitious titles were preferred significantly over the original ones for both R- and A-paintings (which did not differ from each other in terms of the judged appropriateness of the original titles). However, the judged appropriateness of titles was uncorrelated with the pleasingness, interestingness and other ratings. Also, there was no overall greater preference for paintings when titles (actual or fictitious) were given, as opposed to not given.

In summary, whatever the messages are that major twentieth century painters are sending by their paintings' orientations and titles seem to be altogether lost on many viewers.

STUDY 2: ROCK 'N' ROLL LYRICS

Rock 'n' roll (loosely defined) is a huge industry and its products have a gigantic world-wide audience. Listening to rock 'n' roll in cars, in clubs at work, and at home, while walking, roller-skating, and bicyling, is more than a casual past-time for many millions of people; it is the focus of many people's lives and relations, an integral part of the social fabric, and is at the core of several subcultures (cf. Konecni, 1982). To ignore this powerful musical medium on the grounds of inadequate artistic quality is to misunderstand seriously the reality of musical enjoyment in the daily lives of millions of men and women. Elitist standards cannot conceal the huge gulf that exists between rock 'n' roll, on one hand, and what may (perhaps correctly) be claimed to be the pinnacles of human musical achievement, on the other, in terms of influence, exposure, the frequency of listening, and the size of the audience -- all in favour of the former.

Predictably, the mushrooming of rock 'n' roll has been accompanied by a proliferation of specialized magazines (many with very large circulations), books, theorists, liner-note writers, and critics. Serious record reviews, interviews with musicians, and theoretical attempts, though they must vie for space with gossip columns and sensationalist hype, nevertheless abound. Much of the writing, perhaps in direct proportion to how well-informed it is (or how seriously it takes itself) is concerned with the lyrics of rock 'n' roll songs almost as much as with the music.

A number of rock 'n' roll artists, perhaps rightly so, have been hailed as genuine poets, others as influential social commentators that have spawned movements and subcultures and dramatically affected the course of a war. Rock 'n' roll lyrics have been seriously analyzed as indicators of changing social values on important topics such as sex, racial relations, war, patriotism, and economic conditions (e.g., Tosches, 1983).

There seems to be no question, then, that serious critics claim that they can discern a message in rock 'n' roll lyrics, a point amply corroborated by the artists themselves in statements they often make in interviews. The present study submitted these claims to experimental scrutiny.

Method

The subjects were 50 men and women from different walks of life, from the San Diego and Los Angeles areas, all under the age of 30. The study was conducted in a music studio at the University of California at San Diego.

A cassette tape (total listening time: 60 minutes and 56 seconds) was prepared. It contained 16 musical selections, 2 songs by each of 8 artists (see Table 2) presented in random order. The songs differed in familiarity, but were of similar duration. The artists represented a broad spectrum of musical styles (including hard rock, folk rock, punk, new wave, jazz, pop, and soul-pop), and were, with some exceptions, well established and widely popular. An important criterion for inclusion was the availability of a direct quote from the artist regarding the message, subject, or meaning of the song in question (see Table 2 for sources).

The subjects, in groups of 10, listened to all 16 selections. Unbeknownst to others, half of the subjects in each group received a list of the artists' names which matched the order in which their songs were played. While listening to a song, or in the interval between songs, the subjects answered a brief questionnaire about each selection. They were explicitly asked: 'What is the message/purpose of this song?' and given 4 options in a multiple-choice format. For each song, there was a correct choice (as defined by the artist in direct quotes in interviews or liner notes), an almost-correct choice (somewhat close in meaning, but with a key misinterpretation or omission), and two incorrect choices (plausible general statements, but entirely unrelated to the message of the song in question).

To assess familiarity, the subjects rated songs on a 10 cm very-familiar/completely-unfamiliar scale, and were also asked for the name of each song. Finally, they rated the pleasingness and interestingness of each selection on 10-cm scales.

Results

In response to the question about the message/purpose of the songs, the subjects chose the artist-defined correct alternative only 28% of the time (25% is chance; the percents were 29 and 27 for subjects who had and had not been, respectively, informed of the artists' identity). The almost-correct alternative was chosen 24% of the time (26% by the informed group, and 22% by the uninformed subjects). Thus, informed subjects chose one of these two alternatives -- to give them the maximum benefit of the doubt -- only 55% of the time, and the subjects who had not been told the artists' names actually performed slightly below chance, choosing the correct or semi-correct options a total of 49% of the time. For only 4 songs did over 50% of the subjects manage to divine the artist's message and choose the correct option (in the case of one of these songs, this was accomplished only by the informed subjects). For only 2 songs, one by James Taylor and one by the Waitresses, were the informed subjects significantly more accurate than the uninformed ones. Overall, two conclusions can be drawn: (a) For this sample of songs and subjects, the artists' messages were not 'getting through' above the chance level; and (b) being informed of the name of the author/singer of a song rarely made a difference in terms of the accuracy in deciphering the message.

The rated familiarity with the songs ranged from 2.8 (on a 10-cm scale) for one of the songs by the Waitresses, to 9.8 for Stevie Wonder's 'You are the sunshine of my life', with a mean of 6.7. Very few songs were rated as completely unfamiliar by more than a handful of subjects, and very few subjects rated more than one or two songs as completely unfamiliar. In other words, the selection of songs for use in the study was not too esoteric, and the subjects were generally quite familiar with the rock 'n' roll idiom (broadly defined). The rank-order correlation between the songs' familiarity and the frequency with which their messages were accurately understood was surprisingly low (.16). Furthermore, knowing a song's name was significantly associated (Chi-square) with correctly interpreting the artist-defined meaning in the case of only 4 songs.

TABLE 2 Musical selections used in Study 2

ARTIST	SONG NAME	ALBUM NAME	REFERENCE FOR THE INTENDED MESSAGE
Devo	Jocko-Homo Too Much Paranoia	Are We Not Men?	Rolling Stone, 25 January 1979
Herbie Hancock	Chameleon Sly	Headhunters	Rolling Stone, 6 October 1977
Keith Jarrett	Part I Part IIc	The Köln Concert	Rolling Stone, 25 January 1979
James Taylor	B.S.U.R Johnnie Comes Back	Flag	Rolling Stone, Interviews, 1967-1980, Rolling Stone Press, 1981
Pete Townsend	Empty Glass Just a Little is Enough	Empty Glass	"
The Waitresses	Wise up Pussy Strut	Wasn't Tomorrow Wonderful	Rolling Stone, 24 April 1982
Stevie Wonder	You are the sunshine of my life You've got it bad girl	Talking Book	Downbeat 13 September 1973
Frank Zappa	Wowie Zowie Trouble Every Day	Freak Out	Album Cover

On the average, the songs were rated as both quite enjoyable and interesting (the Ms were 7.9 and 7.4, on 10-cm scales; incidentally, the correlations between these 2 measures were .82 for the informed subjects and .75 for the uninformed, and significant). Thus, it seems reasonable to assume tentatively that the subjects did not reject the selections or fall asleep.

What then accounts for the low accuracy in the comprehension of the artists' messages? A number of possibilities suggest themselves. One is that the artists' ideas and intentions (as stated in interviews) are not captured by the songs' lyrics (but the interviewers are either unaware of this or reluctant to point it out). Another is that people actually do not regard the lyrics in rock 'n' roll as important and do not listen to them carefully, perhaps with the exception of truly seminal songs (though, in the present study, the subjects' attention would have certainly been drawn to the lyrics by having to answer lyrics-related questions after each song). A further possibility is that the artists' diction was so poor as to preclude the comprehension of the ideas expressed in the lyrics. Whereas poor enunciation may be an intentional (or unintentional) attribute of some singers and styles in rock 'n' roll, it is by no means ubiquitous, and the great majority of the songs used in the present study was characterized by perfectly audible and comprehensible lyrics.

Whatever the reason the fact is that often the artist-defined messages of the songs used in the present study were not 'getting through' to the listeners.

STUDY 3: STYLE IN LITERARY DISCOURSE

Close to the beginning of an influential essay on the renowned French essayist Roland Barthes (who died in 1980), Susan Sontag (1982) says of Barthes's writing style:

> Typically, his sentences are complex, comma-ridden and colon-prone, packed with densely worded entailments of ideas deployed as if these were the materials of a supple prose. It is a style of exposition, recognizably French, whose parent tradition is to be found in the terse, idiosyncratic essays published between the two world wars in the 'Nouvelle Revue Française' - a perfected version of the N.R.F.'s house style, which can deliver more ideas per page while retaining the brio, the acuteness of timbre' (p. 122).

And later, with apparent approval, on Barthe's views on the role of the literary critic: '... (T)he critic is called on to reconstitute not the 'message' of a work but only its 'system' - its form, its structure .. (p. 123)

Sontag thus focuses on (1) the critic as an interpreter of other writers' form (and formalisms) and (2) the stylistic conventions and formalisms - and especially the breach of these - used by the critic as a writer; hence the title of Sontag's essay. Throughout the essay, there are intimations (that can be traced to Shklovsky and others in the 1920's, as well as to numerous artists and critics in music, theatre and the visual arts) to the effect that sophisticated uses of formalisms, conventions, and departures from conventions themselves constitute a 'change in meaning' with psychological counterparts -- in the reader -- on both the intellectual and emotional planes. These claims should be empirically testable. Sontag contines:

> For the purposes of achieving an ideal digressiveness and an ideal intensity, two strategies have been widely adopted. One is to abolish some or all of the conventional demarcations or separations of discourse, such as chapters, paragraphing, even punctuation, whatever is regarded as impeding formally the continuous production of (the writer's) voice - the run-on method favored by writers of philosophical fictions, such as Hermann Broch, Joyce, Stein, Beckett.

> The other strategy is the opposite one: to multiply the ways in which discourse is segmented, to invent further ways of breaking it up. Joyce and Stein used this method too. (p. 127)

The present study attempted to examine the cognitive (comprehension of ideas, memory for detail, interest) and emotion-related (enjoyment) effects of tampering, in various ways, with fairly long excerpts from works written by Barthes, Beckett, Broch, and Stein. For good measure, an excerpt from Sontag's essay on Barthes was tampered with also (unlike the other 4 writers Sontage writes in a 'normal' style that she herself would probably call 'linear' as opposed to 'serial').

Method

The original excerpts and modifications used in this study are listed in Table 3. Six original excerpts, by 5 authors, were modified in various ways, depending on the form they were in. Continuous test or long paragraphs were broken into shorter paragraphs; very short paragraphs were fused together; long sentences were broken into shorter ones; and so on. Only one type of modification was applied to a particular original excerpt (except for 9, see Table 3). Every effort was made to preserve the original meaning, while interfering liberally with the formal aspects of the texts.

The 6 original excerpts and the 7 modifications (about 27 typewritten pages altogether) were read by 48 students in classroom settings. The students were from the University of California in San Diego. The 13 excerpts were arranged in 3 different quasi-random orders (16 subjects per order), but in no case did an original excerpt immediately precede or follow its modification. The 3 orders were about equal in terms of the number of times that original excerpts appeared in the sets before vs. after their modifications -- about 50% of the time in each order. The subjects read at their own pace (averaging about 4 minutes, 30 seconds per excerpt). After reading each excerpt, they first answered 3-4 questions designed to test memory for details and comprehension of general ideas in the excerpt (different questions were asked after the original and modified versions of an excerpt within a set). The subjects then indicated on 20 cm scales how much they enjoyed the excerpt, and what they thought of its content and style.

Results

The means for the original excerpts on the 20-cm enjoyment scale were all in the 6-8 range, with the exception of the excerpts by Stein (9.5) and Beckett (Ms = 9.4 and 9.1 for excerpts 5 and 3, respectively), which were enjoyed the most, and the excerpt 1 (Barthes), which was enjoyed the least (M = 5.7) (M = 7.4 for excerpt 10, Sontag). Similar results were obtained on the quality-of-content and style scales (the 3 correlation coefficients between these scales were all in .50 to .60 range and significant).

A more interesting finding was that none of the rather drastic and varied modifications led to any significant decreases in either the enjoyment of the excerpts or in the judged quality of their content and style (indeed, nonsignificant increases on some of these dimensions for some of the excerpts were obtained). Furthermore, there were no memory and comprehension deficits as a function of tampering with the texts; if anything, there was a trend ($p<.10$) for both memory and comprehension to improve in cases where continuous text (3 Beckett) or long, information-packed paragraphs (10 Sontag) had been broken into shorter paragraphs.

TABLE 3 Original excerpts and modifications in Study 3

	EXCERPT		EXCERPT
1.	R. Barthes. The pleasure of the text; *3.5 pp of text from pp. 11-15; this came to 3.5 pp in the typed version;	2.	Omission of wide gaps (with and without three asterisks) between paragraphs (original paragraphs preserved); 3 pp. of typed text;
3.	S. Beckett, Molloy * 1.5 pp. of text from pp. 27-28; 1.75 pp. of typed text;	4.	Continuous text broken into 8 paragraphs; 2.25 pp. of typed text.
5.	S. Beckett, Molloy * 1.5 pp. of text from pp. 151-153; 1.5 pp. of typed text.	6.	Fusion of 10 paragraphs into 2; 1.1 pp of typed text;
7.	H. Broch, The death of Virgil. * 1.75 pp. of text from pp. 80-82; 2.3 pp. of typed text;	8.	Shortened sentences; 7 sentences in the original, 18 in the modification; 2.3 pp. of typed text;
	Same as 7	9.	Shortened sentences (as in 8), and also continuous text broken into 6 paragraphs; 2.8 pp. of typed text;
10.	S. Sontag, Writing itself: On Roland Barthes.* One column from The New Yorker, p. 127; 1.2 pp. of typed text.	11.	Two paragraphs broken down into 11 (resulting mostly in one-sentence paragraphs); 1.7 pp. of typed text;
12.	G. Stein, Four in America*. 1.5 pp. of text from pp. 3-4 (the beginning of "Grant"); 2 pp. of typed text.	13.	Fusion of 15 paragraphs into 4; 1.6 pp. of typed text.

* See References for the exact edition used

These subjects clearly did not show an overall preference for either the dense run-on method, or the segmentation method (the two which Sontag discussed in her essay), or, for that matter, for the 'normal' method (Sontag's own). Also, there was clearly no increase in enjoyment as a function of attempts (the various modifications) to transform the extremes into more modal forms (in terms of sentence length, paragraphing, and so on). Rather, it seems to be the case, that for these excerpts, these stylistic modifications and judgment dimensions, and these subjects, the formalistic aspects simply did not matter -- although, as shown by the data, this unresponsiveness to form by no means implied a lack of either enjoyment or comprehension.

STUDY 4: ORDER OF MOVEMENTS IN BEETHOVEN'S QUARTETS AND SONATAS

> 'Why (is it that) the chronology of the themes of a masterpiece cannot be changed (?) Why does one thematic chronology sound good, another bad? If the movements of a great sonata or a symphony are switched around, the result will be musically inferior' (entry on 'criticism' in 'Britannica Book of Music', 1980, p. 229).

More musicologists and theorists of music composition, at least those concerned primarily with the 'classical style' and musical forms such as the sonata (as well as the symphony and the quartet, both of which can be thought of as derived from the sonata), would probably strongly agree with the above assessment (e.g., Barrett-Ayres, 1974; Newman, 1972; Rosen, 1971). They would probably also share some of the following sentiments regarding the structure, and the thematic development, relations and sequence both within and across the movements of a classical composition:

> 'Why does music unfold a particular structure? Why that kind of structure rather than another? The textbooks on form remain silent; yet this is a profound question. It is surely of paramount interest to know why music unrolls in one direction rather than another. Inspired music appears to carry within itself its own blueprint, according to which it propels itself across precise distances and in precise directions. If it is prematurely halted, diverted or too long continued ... it loses the sense of punctuality, the feeling of arriving on time, the knowledge of being in the right place at the right moment, which characterizes each stage of an emerging structure masterfully handled' (Britannica Book of Music, p. 230).

The first movement of a classical sonata often has the elements of exposition, development, and recapitulation (the 'sonata form') and is typically quite fast. The slow movement occupies the central portion of the piece and is meant to hold it together; it is often in an 'ABA' form or in a variations form. In a 4-movement sonata, there is typically a lighter movement, a minuet or a scherzo, which either precedes or follows the slow movement. The last movement is typically again fairly fast; Beethoven is often credited for being the first to switch the structural weight from the first to the last movement of a sonata and treating the whole as a dramatically developed plot (cf. Newman, 1972; Rosen, 1971).

Aspects of the sonata that appeal to purists of the classical style - the exposition-development-recapitulation sequence of the first movement, the ABA sequence of the slow movement, the fast-slow-light relief-fast structure of the whole piece - have also not escaped the attention of writers interested in the psychological - emotional and hedonic - effects of music (e.g., Berlyne, 1971; Meyer, 1956). Berlyne, in particular, was able to point to the sonata as an example of the serial use of arousal-raising and arousal-moderating devices (both within and across movements), with the intention of holding the listener's interest and keeping the arousal fluctuations going, but within a certain pleasurable range, avaoiding excess.

The crudest, but simplest and most direct, way to test some of these musical and psychological claims is to go back to the quote from the 'Britannica' at the beginning of this section and switch around the movements of a great sonata (perhaps this is the musical equivalent of hanging pictures upside down).

Method

The works used in this study were all by Beethoven. Precisely because of his frequent treatment of the sonata as a plot that is resolved in the last movement, and his being widely acknowledged as the supreme master of the thematic build-up and development, one would think that his pieces would be most likely to suffer (in terms of the listeners' enjoyment) if the sequence of the movements were to be changed.

Five works, 2 piano sonatas and 3 string quartets. spanning almost 30 years of Beethoven's life, were used (see Table 4). All are highly respected and well-known pieces of music (though none, to the best of my knowledge, has yet been made into a film score). All are in 4 movements, and all, with the possible exception of the D major sonata, have outstanding slow movements whose mood lingers on.

Two tampered versions of each piece were prepared. In Version A, the order of of the movements was: Last movement; first movement; 'light relief' movement (Scherzo in Sonatas, Op. 28 and Op. 106, and in Quartet, Op. 18; Menueto in Quartet, Op. 59; Vivace in Quartet, Op. 135; note that the 'light relief' movement is either the second or the third movement in these pieces); slow movement. This sequence of the movements breaks down the entire structure of the pieces. However, after reviewing the results obtained by using Version A, an ostensibly even less appealing -- musically and psychologically -- sequence of movements was created. Version B: Last movement; first movement; slow movement; 'light relief' movement. In contrast to Version A, Version B does not end with the beautiful, sensitive, affecting slow movements.

In the first part of the study, male and female students from the University of California at San Diego (none was a music major) came to the laboratory in groups of 10 and heard 1 of the 5 pieces, either the original or the altered version (Version A). Thus both the 5 pieces and the original-altered factors were between-subjects (for a total of 100 subjects). In addition, one piece, Sonata in B flat major, Op. 106 was heard in both the original and altered versions by a further 16 subjects (8 subjects heard the original first, 8 heard Version A first).

In the second part of the study, only the B flat major Sonata, Op. 106, and the C major Quartet, Op. 59, were used. Students in groups of 10 heard either the original or the altered version (Version B this time) of 1 of the 2 pieces (for a total of 40 subjects). Finally, an additional 18 subjects heard both the original and the altered Version B of the Sonata (9 in each of the 2 possible orders), and a further 16 heard both the original and the altered Version B of the Quartet (a half in each order).

In both parts of the study, after hearing the piece (or after hearing each of the 2 pieces, in the within-subject designs), subjects rated, on 10 cm scales, their enjoyment of the piece and their familiarity with it.

TABLE 4 Beethoven's works used in Study 4

1.* Piano Sonata No. 15 in D major, Op. 28 (Pastorale) (1801)
Allegro
Andante
Scherzo: Allegro vivace
Rondo: Alegro, ma non troppo

2.* Piano Sonata No. 29 in B flat major, Op. 106 (Hammerklavier) (1817/18)
Allegro
Scherzo: Assai Vivace - Presto
Adagio sostenuto
Largo - Allegro risoluto

3.** String Quartet in F major, Op. 18, No. 1 (1798-1800)
Allegro con brio
Adagio affetuoso e appasionato
Scherzo: Allegro molto
Allegro

4.** String Quartet in C major, Op.59, No. 3 (1808)
Introduzione: Andante con moto - Allegro vivaco
Andante con moto quasi Allegretto
Menueto: Grazioso
Allegro molto

5.** String Quartet in F major, Op. 135 (1826)
Allegretto
Vivace
Lento assai, cantante e tranquillo
Grave, ma non troppo tratto - Allegro

* Wilhelm Kempff, pianist
** Amadeus Quartet

All works recorded by Deutsche Gramophon

Results

The original versions of all 5 pieces were found quite enjoyable by the subjects in both parts of the study; the means were uniformly in the 6-7 range on a 10 cm scale (except for the F major Quartet, Op. 135, $M = 5.1$). The enjoyment ratings were virtually uncorrelated with the familiarity ratings, which stemmed, apparently (judging by the subjects' post-experimental comments), from their confusion about what the question meant: Knowing a piece's name? Opus number? Some themes? Familiarity with the whole work? and so on. (Such confusion often arises when a stimulus that is very 'large' -- in terms of content and duration -- is judged on a simple bipolar scale).

In the first part of the study, the astonishing finding was that there was literally no effect of changing the sequence of the movements (Version A) in terms of the rated enjoyment. On a between-subject basis, three of the original pieces and two of the Version A pieces were rated somewhat higher than their counterparts, but all these differences were negligible. In the case of the one piece (Sonata, Op. 106) which was heard in both the original and altered versions by an additional 18 subjects, there was a statistically nonsignificant primacy effect both for subjects who had heard the original version first and for those who had hear Version A first. (These findings prompted the construction of Version B pieces and the design of the second part of the study).

Despite the even more drastic re-ordering of the movements, in the second part of the study there was again no effect on enjoyment -- on a between-subject basis -- for either of the 2 pieces used (the means were again in the 6-7 range for both the original and altered versions). Even in the within-subjects design there was no significant difference for either piece when the altered version (Version B) was heard first. Finally, when the original versions were heard before the Version B pieces, significant difference ($p < .01$) were obtained in favour of the original versions ($M = 6.6$ for the Sonata, Op. 106, and $M = 5.2$, for its Version B; $M = 7.0$ for the Quartet, Op. 59, and $M = 5.4$ for its Version B).

In summary, only with an extreme modification of the order of the movements, and with the subjects forced to compare the original and the modified versions (in the within-subjects design), and only when the original version was heard first, did it emerge as the clearly preferred choice. This was so despite the fact that the pieces were great works in the classical tradition, with a clearly defined structure, by a grandmaster of thematic and structural development. Under these circumstances, it would seem reasonable to conclude that people, much as they may like a piece of music, sometimes ignore the implicit musical message -- whatever it may be -- that is contained in the order of the movements of a piece.

STUDY 5: FEATURES OF A THEATRICAL PERFORMANCE

It is a truism that the production of a play is a highly complex endeavour involving numerous elements and participants that are interposed between the play, as written, and its staging in front of an audience. In much of contemporary theatre, it is generally recognized that the director has a key function in this cooperative effort (e.g., Clurman, 1972; Dietrich, 1953; Samuels, 1972; Sievers, Stiver and Kahan, 1974). By working with actors in rehearsals, collaborating with set-, lighting-, and costume-designers, collaborating and planning the actors' movements on the stage (known as 'blocking'), the director is in a unique position to modulate the impact of the play on the audience. Numerous choices, from the use of the tiniest prop to the grandest gesture, have to be made, taking into account the size of the theatre, the shape of the stage, and perhaps less frequently, the type of the audience likely to attend.

Texts on theatre and individuals involved in it make certain assumptions about the intellectual and emotional impact that certain features of a dramatic performance have on the audience. Typically the stage can be said to be divided into parts (often nine) that are said to give an actor positioned in them different amounts of 'strength'. An actor facing the audience, or moving, or speaking, or being looked at by other actors, or standing isolated from a group, or more brightly lit, or having a more attractive costume, everything else equal, is thought of 'being in focus'.

Such factors, and their psychological effects on the audience, are believed to depend heavily on the shape of the stage and the distance from the audience. An intimate theatre with a thrust stage surrounded by the audience on 3 sides is believed to focus the attention of the audience members on the actors (and each other's reactions) and away from the set - quite unlike a larger theatre with a proscenium stage which de-emphasizes the actors and makes it possible for a more elaborate set to be effective.

Many of these assumptions appear intuitively reasonable and psychologically sound (in terms of the findings of modern social and cognitive psychology). Nevertheless, the details of the actors' movements on the stage in a specific scene are far removed from the textbook prescriptions about blocking; the actors' facial expressions, gestures and actions, as well as other features of the play, may in fact not have the effect that the director anticipates.

At least some of the assumptions discussed above can be tested by systematically questioning the members of the audience after a play. Ideally, one would want to study the effects of several different versions of a performance which would vary along specified dimensions. This being impractical, one of the next-best things is to study the effects of certain features of a performance carried out in the same way in very different theatrical settings. If the performance is specially designed to reach a particular type of audience, if it involves a new play and thus there is no overbearing history of past performances, and if the play is written or put together by the director personally, so much the better. The director can be asked to articulate the objectives and specify the theatrical devices by which they shall be attained. The actual impact of some of these devices can then be tested under different performance conditions. Such were the concerns of the present study. It capitalized on an opportunity to examine the effects of certain features of a theatrical performance on real-life audiences.

Method

The Old Globe Theatre in San Diego, a renowned company and the site of a major annual Shakespeare festival, carries out each year an 'educational tour' of schools, hospitals, convalescent homes, and correctional institutions. Typically, a new production, often an adaptation of an 'accessible' play, is created especially for the tour. Some past productions involved as many as 15-20 actors with full sets and costumes and one-hour versions of Shakespeare's plays.

In 1982, Kent Brisby wrote and directed 'A Shakespeare Mosaic' for the tour. The performance begins with a prologue which deals with Shakespeare's life and times; after this, there is a series of scenes adapted from various Shakespeare plays (see Table 5) connected by a narrative written by Brisby and a few Elizabethan songs. Four actors, a simple and functional set, and a number of props, including puppets (such as 8-foot tall witches in 'Macbeth') and rollerskates (Puck on rollerskates in 'A Midsummer-Night's Dream') are used. An electrical keyboard, a rhythm machine, and a base guitar are also used.

TABLE 5 Scenes from Shakespeare's plays used in the San Diego Old Globe Theatre's 'Mosaic' (Globe Educational Tour 11, Spring 1982).

1. Two Gentlemen of Verona, Act II, Scene 3;*

2. Macbeth, Act IV, Scene I;

3. A Midsummer Night's Dream, Act II, Scene 2; Act III, Scene I;

4. Much Ado About Nothing, Act III, Scene 3;

5. Romeo and Juliet, Act III, Scene I.

* The scenes were presented in the 'Mosaic' in the order given here.

The study examined the effects of 4 performances in 4 different schools in the San Diego area. A total of 412 children, 9-12 years of age, 200 boys and 212 girls, attended. The 4 schools are quite far apart geographically and rather different from each other in terms of the socio-economic status, race, and ethnic background of the students. The size of the audience varied from school to school: 52, 107, 130 and 123 children. Furthermore, in one school (52 children in the audience), the performance took place in the middle of the cafeteria, with the children seated on 3 sides, literally at the feet of the actors. Another school had a thrust stage, with the audience also on 3 sides, but a somewhat greater separation of the audience from the actors. The remaining 2 schools had conventional proscenium stages although the seating capacity differed considerably. Thus, the same performance was given in very different theatrical settings.

The study began by conducting an extensive interview with the director. The following points were extracted from this interview: (1) the primary purpose of the 'Mosaic' was to introduce children to the theatre in general and Shakespeare in particular in an unforbidding manner; (2) to attact and keep the children's attention -- attention being a necessary intial step for eventual enjoyment, according to Brisby -- certain theatrical devices were to be used: A lot of action; bright costumes; large or incongruous props; unexpected turns of action or speech; interesting juxtapositions; and audience participation (most of these would be easily classifiable as psychophysical, ecological, or collative variables that Berlyne (1971) thought were so important for aesthetic enjoyment); (3) the entire performance and its constituent elements, including blocking, were planned with an intimate, thrust-stage performing situation in mind - one that would emphasize the actors and the props, reduce the importance of the set, and facilitate audience participation; thus, according to the director, the play would not 'work' for children in a large theatre with a conventional proscenium stage.

After each of the 4 performances mentioned above, a questionnaire was administered to all the children in the audience. Two to 3 multiple choice questions with 3 options were asked about each of the 6 scenes listed in Table 5. These questions were quite hard and detailed, and were designed to test the children's memory (and thus attention during the performance) regarding specific theatrical devices which the director felt (in the interview) would attract the children's interest. Additional questions asked the children to rate their enjoyment of the entire performance, and their desire to see a play at the Old Globe, on a 10 point scale (the use of these was explained).

Results

Children's recall for the details of the 'Mosaic' was remarkably good. For 7 of the 13 questions, the correct option was chosen by over 90% of the 412 respondents; for 5 of the questions, by between 80% and 90% of the children; and for 1 question, by 74%. Accuracy increased somewhat with age, but was high for all age-groups, for boys and girls, and for all 4 schools.

'Mosaic' was furthermore uniformly enjoyed by all age-groups and in all the schools the mean on the enjoyment scale for the entire sample was 8.7 on a 10-point scale, and it did not fall below 8.0 for any age-group, at any of the schools (none of the age- and school-related differences was statistically significant). Ratings of the desire to see a play at the Old Globe were also high, but significantly lower than the enjoyment ratings.

The findings of this study are straightforward. The director's use of theatrical devices and blocking to attract the children's attention and make the experience enjoyable had precisely the effects that he had anticipated. In this case, one could say that the entire, quite detailed, artistic message got through to the audience for which it was intended. Paradoxically, however, this was the case even in theatrical settings in which, according to the director himself, the message should not have got through. For this audience and for this play, apparently, the shape of the stage, the distance from the actors, and the size of the theatre made very little difference.

DISCUSSION

The main findings of this series of studies can be succinctly summarized. (1) Mirror reversal did not decrease the pleasingness of representational and abstract twentieth century paintings; the latter were not affected by 180° and 90° rotations either. Fictitious titles were preferred to the original ones. (2) Subjects failed to guess, at a better than chance level the artist defined message/purpose of the lyrics of rock 'n' roll songs. (3) Drastic stylistic alterations of literary texts produced no decrement in enjoyment or comprehension; if anything, some alterations improved comprehension. (4) Extensive tampering with the sequence of movements of Beethoven's sonatas and quartets resulted in no decrease in enjoyment, except under highly circumscribed conditions. (5) Children did respond to a play in the manner anticipated by the director, but they did so even in settings that should have, according to the director, seriously interfered with the impact of the theatrical message.

In short, many explicit or implicit features of these diverse artistic messages were entirtely ignored by the audiences, contrary to the artists' and critics' expectations and claims, and despite the extraordinary calibre of many of the works. Indeed, the great majority of these diverse works were rated as very enjoyable by the subjects; it is just that they were unresponsive to some of the features that artists and critics thought important.

It is of interest to examine some of the possible criticisms of this series of studies. The most basic criticism is that a general conclusion is being drawn from a series of null effects. However, it is generally accepted in the philosophy of science that when a substantial number of studies - using different methods and domains of inquiry (different art media, in this case) but all asking the same basic question - all obtain a negative answer, this cumulative evidence begins to count. Besides, the point being made here is not that the artists' and critics' explicit or implicit claims are always inaccurate, but simply that they may be inaccurate more often than is commonly thought. There clearly are limits to how much can be accomplished by speculative and introspective reasoning alone about the human response to art, and this should be repeated again and again by the psychologists of art. Loath as artists, critics and scholars in the arts and humanities may be to embrace the experimental method, even when it is applied to the response to art (as opposed to its creation), they may realize (a) that it can serve a useful function, and (b) that their claims may well be submitted to experimental scrutiny. Both might make the speculative conclusions more cautious - a desirable outcome.

A related criticism is that 5 studies prove nothing and that additional studies concerning the effects of artistic messages would paint a different picture (perhaps an upside-down one?). This is quite possibly true, but it is worth pointing out that the five 'messages' examined in the present series of studies were not chosen on the basis of preconceived or informed notions that they were weak spots in the artists' and critics' armour and thus convenient targets if one wished to score an easy point (a possible exception is the mirror-reversal lack of effect in Study 1, given Gordon's, 1981, review). On the contrary, the research problems were chosen almost at random, reflecting mostly the professional and private interests of the author and his students and the availability of quotable claims by artists or critics regarding the work's impact. Indeed, the null effects came often as a considerable surprise.

A counter-rebuttal to the above would be that rather than dabble in all sorts of 'messages' and media, it would have been better to focus on one work of art, and examine its various messages in depth. I disagree. Depth seems premature in this relatively uncharted area and 5 null results regarding the impact of a single work of art most certainly could not lead to any generalizations. For the time being, the 'rake' research strategy (shallow but multipronged) seems better suited for planting the seed of doubt that the 'pick' strategy (deep, but perhaps zeroing on the wrong spot).

Actually, when one does dig deep in a spot in this general area, artists' and critics' claims often fare no better. For example, the experimental work by Deutsch (in press) and others shows that the perceptual configurations based on pitch proximity may completely override the effects of spatial separation; in other words, 'spatial separation (forcefully urged, for example, by Berlioz) by no means guarantees that music will be perceived in accordance with the positioning of the instruments' (Deutsch, in press). Also as part of his theory of 12 tone compositions, Schoenberg included octave separation as an example of an equivalence (together with transposition, inversion, and so on); yet, in her 'Yankee Doodle' experiments Deutsch demonstrated that interval class cannot be treated as a perceptual invariant.

Not all artistic domains yield themselves with equal ease to subtle experimental probing of their effects on an audience - theatre, dance and literature being notoriously difficult. Thus, experimentally asking simple, 'big' and direct questions in these areas (those who disagree may substitute these adjectives by 'rude', 'crude' and 'obnoxious') seems justifiable in order to challenge entrenched (but possibly false) ideas and set the stage for subtler (but more narrow) experimental work. Even in music and painting where more detailed experimental work is feasible, it is important to ask broad questions and re-examine statements that have been repeated without factual substantiation to the point of reification (or implicitly assumed as self-evident and therefore not aired).

At first thought, the most damaging of the present series of studies is that the subjects were not sophisticated enough, that they were not art connoisseurs. True enough, but this criticism can be seriously challenged on several different levels; a partial list follows: (1) An average student in California may not be an art connoisseur, but he or she is likely to be reasonably cultivated and well-educated, certainly on par with an average citizen almost anywhere (myths about everyone in Southern California being a surfer notwithstanding). The debater using the connoisseurship argument has thus already secluded him or herself in a rarefied corner. (2) Would this debater deny student surfers expertize even in rock 'n' roll (re. Study 2)? (3) Even if connoisseurs are, by definition, more discerning than the reasonably well-educated non-connoisseurs, this does not necessarily mean that they would respond differently to altered versions of artworks in all situations and in all art media. It would seem that one would be likely to find substantial memory-, prestige-of-communicator-, experimental-instructions-, duration-of-exposure, and experimental-situation-related effects, but these are empirical questions. Regarding the mirror-reversal of paintings, at the very least, according to Gordon's (1981) review of the literature and the present Study 1, no effects of art training and exposure to art have so far been obtained. (4) As Gordon (1981) has convincingly argued regarding the claims made by the glance-curve theory, many artists' and critics' statements are worded so as to imply applicability to all humans, not just a few connoisseurs. Fundamental - though complex - emotional, perceptual, memory, early-learning, and anatomical/physiological (e.g., hemispheric dominance) factors are said to be involved in scanning a painting, reading a text, or listening to the unfolding of a symphony. If so, why should connoisseurs be expected to respond differently from others in many art-related situations?

The above discussion naturally suggests even broader questions and dilemmas. Images arise of the artist in a desperate search for the essence of the human condition, portraying the heights and abysses found in all of us, yet finding nothing contradictory in claiming at the same time that the artist is painting or composing 'for himself and three other people he respects'. Also images of the artist who thinks of his total creative freedom as an inalienable right -- even if it is at the public expense. Perhaps, these are exaggerations, but the argument that many great artists were 'misunderstood' by their contemporaries and starved (and that we should correct this in our own time) is a poor one. It conveniently neglects the real possibility that for each starving misunderstood genius there must have been hundreds of starving misunderstood mediocrities who should have been misunderstood. Time and the marketplace sifted the wheat from the chaff; personally, I trust these long-term processes far more than the art-bureaucracy at the National Endowment for the Arts, and the contemporary critics and artists.

A cynical generalization from the findings of the present and similar studies is that with the exception of a few true geniuses and near-geniuses by and large, artists, art critics and art historians hypothesize the allegedly important dimensions of artworks without any reference to attributes actually responsible for the impact of artworks on the broader audience, and use these invented dimensions chiefly as vehicles through which to speak to each other and make points in their self-contained world. In this view, connoisseurs would be seen as participating rather passively in the artworld's doings, and treating the (mostly second-echelon) artists' and critics' opinions as prescriptions for taste formulation and art-purchasing behaviour. Others basically foot the bill (by paying taxes which pay for agency grants to artists, municipal commissions of artworks etc.)

A more gracious hypothesis concerning the reasons for the present findings is possible - although its implications for the social consequences of the artworld's behaviour are similar to those mentioned above. Various attributes of an artwork (content-related, style-related, etc.) may interact in complex ways, and only certain subsets of the higher-order interactions may produce the highly positive effects one finds (in terms of the rated enjoyment, pleasingness, interestingness, and so on). The critics, partly because of the inherent limitations of the purely speculative, nonexperimental reasoning and inference, and in part due to the prevalent linearity of human thought and language, may see the dimensions of artworks as related to each other in an additive, as opposed to an interactive, manner. Thus, their theories may be correct in providing accurate lists of important dimensions, while failing to capture the complicated ways in which these dimensions interact to produce the observed effects. In this view, experiments in the psychology of art of the kind described in this chapter could perhaps help sharpen the existing theories of the structure and effects of artworks.

REFERENCES

Arnheim, R. (1956). Art and Visual Perception. London: Faber and Faber.

Barrett-Ayres, R. (1974). Joseph Haydn and the String Quartet. New York: Schirmer Books.

Barthes, R. (1975). The Pleasure of the Text. New York: Hill and Wang. (Original in French, 1973).

Beckett, S. (1955). Molloy. In: Molloy; Malone Dies; The Unnamable. New York: Grove Press. (Original in French, 1951).

Berlyne, D.E. (1971). Aesthetics and Psychobiology. New York: Appleton-Century-Crofts.

Britannica Book of Music (1980). Garden City, New York: Doubleday/Britannica.

Broch, H. (1945). The Death of Virgil. New York: Pantheon Books.

Clurman, H. (1972). On Directing. New York: Macmillan.

Deutsch, D.A. (in press). Psychology and Music. In: M. Bornstein (Ed.) Psychology and the Allied Disciplines. Hillsdale, New Jersey: Erlbaum.

Dietrich, J.E. (1953). Play Direction. Englewood Cliffs, New Jersey: Prentice-Hall.

Gaffron, M. (1950). Right and left in pictures. Art Quarterly, 13, 312-331.

Gaffron, M. (1962). Perceptual experience: An analysis of its relation to the external world through internal proceedings. In: S. Koch (Ed.) Psychology: The Study of a Science, Volume 4. London: McGraw-Hill.

Gordon, I.(1981). Left and right in art. In: D. O'Hare (Ed.) Psychology and the Arts. Brighton, Sussex: Harvester.

Gordon, I. and Gardner, C. (1974). Response to altered pictures. British Journal of Psychology, 65, 243-254.

Hoffman, W. (1954). The Mind and Works of Paul Klee. New York: Praeger.

Konečni, V.J. (1982). Social interaction and musical preference. In: D. Deutsch (Ed.) The Psychology of Music. New York: Academic Press.

Konečni, V.J. and Sargent-Pollack, D. (1977). Arousal, positive and negative affect, and preference for Renaissance and 20th Century paintings. Motivation and Emotion, 1, 75-93.

Lindauer, M.S. (1969). The orientation of form in abstract art. Proceedings of the 77th Annual Convention of the American Psychological Association, 4, 475-476.

Long, R. and Washton, C. (1980). Kandinsky: The Development of an Abstract Style. Oxford: Clarendon Press.

Meyer, L.B. (1956). Emotion and Meaning in Music. Chicago, Illinois: University of Chicago Press.

Newman, W.S. (1972). The Sonata in the Classic Era. (Revised Edition). Chapel Hill, North Carolina: University of North Carolina Press.

Orbourne, H. (1979). Abstraction and Artifice in Twentieth Century Art. Oxford: Clarendon.

Rosen, C. (1971). The Classical Style. New York: Viking Press.

Rosenberg, H. (1966). The Anxious Object: Art and its Audience. New York: Horizon.

Rosenberg, H. (1975). Art on the Edge: Creators and Situations. New York: Macmillan.

Samuels, C.T. (1972). Encountering Directors. New York: Putnam.

Sargent-Pollack, D.N. and Konečni, V.J. (1977). Evaluative and skin-conductance responses to Renaissance and 20th Century paintings. Behavior Research Methods and Instrumentation, 9, 291-296.

Sievers, D., Silver, H. and Kahn, S. (1974). Directing for the Theatre. New York: W.M.C. Brown.

Sontag, S. (1982). Writing itself: On Roland Barthes. The New Yorker, 26th April, 122-141.

Stein, G. (1947). Four in America. New Haven, Connecticut: Yale University Press.

Swartz, O. and Hewitt, D. (1970). Lateral organization in pictures and aesthetic preference. Perceptual and Motor Skills, 30, 991-1007.

Tosches, N. (1983). Good Golly Miss Molly: Sex in popular music. Vanity Fair, April.

Wölfflin, N. (1941). Uber das rechts und links im bilde. In: Gedanken zur Kunstgeschichte. Basle, Switzerland: Schwabe.

Section 3

THE ARTS AND DEVELOPMENT

Cognitive Processes in the Perception of Art
W.R. Crozier and A.J. Chapman (editors)
© Elsevier Science Publishers B.V. (North-Holland), 1984

A THEORETICAL FRAMEWORK FOR THINKING ABOUT DEPICTION

Francis Pratt

University of Stirling

The ideas presented in this chapter come from four sources. They come from my experience as a professional artist: from my experience as a teacher of depiction; from the results of a series of experiments done at the University of Stirling (cf. Pratt, 1983, where may be found summaries of most of the experiments referred to in this chapter); and from the work of other psychologists. In essence, the chapter may be seen as an attempt to provide a chronological account of the steps by which I arrived at my present theoretical framework for thinking about depiction.

In all the experiments I have been studying people attempting to copy line drawings as accurately as possible. The people have been of various ages and levels of skill. They have included 7/9-year-old children, Psychology students and Art students. The line drawings they have copied have been of various kinds. They have included: drawings of objects; 'abstract' patterns (derived from the object drawings); and collections of separated straight lines of randomized length, angle and position on the paper. In many of the experiments, eye and hand movements were monitored. This made it possible to see whether the subject was looking at the model or at the copy and how looking behaviour related to line production.

In the first experiment (Phillips et al, 1978), we discovered that young children were better at making 'accurate' copies of an 'abstract' pattern than they were at making 'accurate' copies of a drawing of a cube. We explained this result in the language of the theory of 'intellectual realism'. We concluded that, when children copy 'familiar' objects, they are more influenced by 'what they know' than by 'what they see'. In contrast, when they copy 'unfamiliar' patterns, they are mainly influenced by 'what they see'. However, our experiments also showed that, even when making 'intellectually realistic' copies, children do a certain amount of scene-analysis. The interesting point about this scene-specific analysis was that it clearly involved very different patterns of looking than those used in the analysis of 'unfamiliar' models. This discrepancy led us to conclude that there must be a role for 'knowledge' guided looking strategies.

Later research gave ample support for this conclusion and reinforced our grounds for abandoning conceptualization in terms of a simple 'know'/'see' dichotomy. We came to see 'knowledge' as playing a central role, not only in generating drawing activity, but also, in generating looking activity; we came to see 'knowledge-guided-looking' as providing a means of control, both over visual input from the model and over what aspects of that input is utilized in acts of drawing; and we came to see this process of control in terms of a perceptual cycle (cf. Neisser, 1976) which not only involves the possibility of modifying what aspects of the model are attended to, but also the possibility of modifying the 'knowledge' base of drawing acts. Furthermore, we came to attach importance to the consequence of drawing acts and, in particular, to their capacity to provide new visual input. Thus, we came to appreciate the potential importance of the emerging copy as a means of affecting the 'knowledge' base of subsequent acts of looking at the model.

Our experimental results provided good evidence for the following assertions: (1) 'knowledge' is a necessary part of all acts of depiction done by people of all ages and of all levels of skill; (2) 'knowledge' is a main determinant of looking strategies; (3) the role of 'knowledge' in the organization of looking strategies is one of determining the 'level of description' to be used as the basis of analytic processes; and (4) 'good' copying performance (i.e., 'accurate' in terms of scene-specific and view-specific relations) can be equated with level of description accessed.

The last two of the above assertions need amplification. For this purpose it is necessary to say more about some of the models used in our experiments. As a preliminary to doing this, I want to make clear that in general in this chapter my use of specific examples is illustrative. I do not want to attach too much importance to the exact details. What I want to stress is the general characteristics.

Consider our cube model (this was derived from a 'real' cube by making a tracing on glass and is, therefore, 'in perspective'). It could be described in many different ways. Thus, it could be described: (1) as a cube (i.e., as a 3D object); (2) as three intersecting surfaces; (3) as a 'Y' in a hexagon (i.e., as two related 2D objects); (4) as three contiguous regions; (5) as a group of nine related straight lines; or (6) as a set of related end points of lines. These different modes of description can be categorized in terms of the number of relations between pairs implied by them. Thus, the 'object' description, since it related to a unified whole, implies no relations; the 'Y' in a hexagon, since it comprises two parts, implies one relation; the intersecting surfaces and the contiguous regions both imply three relations; the group of straight lines implies many relations; and the set of end points implies many more still. In short, the general characteristic that I illustrate is that the lower the level of description used, the greater the number of parts and of potential relations between parts implied.

It is worth noting here, for it has important implications in terms of what follows, that the description in terms of three intersecting surfaces refers to exactly the same aspects of the model as the description in terms of the three contiguous regions. The difference between them resides in the perspective from which the description emanates. Perception in terms of intersecting surfaces depends on prior perception of the model as a cube. Perception in terms of contiguous regions depends on prior perception of the model in terms of some kind of 'abstract' pattern.

Our abstract model, which can be described as an inverted 'Y' in a hexagon, can also be analysed in terms of different levels of description. In fact it shares all the modes of description applicable to the cube model except the first two (i.e., those that depend on or emanate from a perception of the model as a cube). In contrast, our separate straight line models can only be described in terms of relations between lines and points. They can only be analysed in terms of the lowest levels of description.

At each level of description visual analysis is accomplished by means of judgments involving fairly simple relations. Thus, shapes can be analysed in terms of such antitheses as 'above'/'below', 'to the right of'/'to the left of', 'touching'/'separate', or 'bigger'/'smaller'. Both linear and point relations can be analysed in similar antithetical terms. Even judgments relating to angles, lengths and position-of-end points of lines may be accomplished in the same way (cf. Pratt, 1983). It would seem that complex relations do not have to be analysed. This is possible because of the hierarchical nature of analysis. Complex relations are subsumed into the description of the parts being related. 'Knowledge' of these subsumed 'higher level' relations is implicit in all acts of analysis. Analysis of relations always depends on acts of looking that are controlled by some higher level description. The highest such levels would be the whole-object description.

A whole object description may be conceived in terms of sets of constraints on how an object might be structured. These constraints allow for a considerable degree of variance in respect of the details of how the parts might relate to one another. The same picture applies to part descriptions. These also imply constraints and allow for variance. However, the lower the level of description, the tighter the constraints and the less the variance.

When applied to the analysis of scenes, this conceptualization can be expressed in terms of degrees of scene-specificity. The lower the level of description, the more the analysis is subject to scene-specific and, indeed, view-specific constraints.

If analysis of relations always depends on looks that are controlled by higher-level descriptions, it follows that there is no way of analysing the highest level of description as such. By this I only mean that there is no way of analysing objects as such for the purposes of depiction. Of course object analysis is possible; it is a primary function of perception. However, it is accomplished by pre-conscious processes that remain obscure to psychologists. The very difficulty that psychologists have in pinning down the precise nature of these processes is support for the point I am making. The 'knowledge' base of analysis is not subject to analysis. Furthermore, the logic as it applies to the highest levels of description, also applies to the lower levels. Even the 'knowledge' base of analysis of straight lines is not subject to analysis (cf. Pratt, 1983, where the case for this assertion is presented). In short, analysis for depiction can only be analysis of relations between parts; it cannot be analysis of the parts themselves.

There are four aspects of the above that I want to emphasize: (1) Each descending level of description implies an increasing disintegration of the analytic task. Thus, there are only a few possible relations between shapes, more between lines and most between points. (2) Analysis for depiction is concerned with variance. It is concerned with relations that change according to viewing circumstances. In effect, they can be considered as 'novel' relations. There is much evidence that people's ability to maintain 'novel' relations in memory is severely limited (cf. Phillips, 1983). In particular, maintenance of 'accurate' information about line parameters is virtually impossible in parallel with concurrent drawing or looking activity. A consequence of this is that depiction can only be accomplished by means of a series of separate judgments of simple relations. (3) The model consisting of a group of straight lines is only capable of being analysed at the lowest levels of description. If, as I suggested, good copying performance can be equated with level of description accessed, this should mean that differences between people of different skill levels should be minimized when copying such models. This is what we found to be the case. We found no differences between art students and psychology students and surprisingly few between adults and children (cf. Pratt, 1983). (4) Access of the lowest levels of description from the perspective of the highest, involves a descent through levels. I am proposing that skill level can be related directly to an ability to make this descent. This point can be further elaborated by means of reference to the kind of copies of cubes made by people of different levels of skill and to the amount of looking between model and copy they indulge in.'

Here, for convenience sake, I propose four levels of skill. These can be defined by the copy type produced and not by the age group of the people. I have called the skill levels: (1) 'proto-realist'; (2) 'intellectual realist'; (3) 'unskilled looker'; and (4) 'skilled looker'. Definition by age group would be helpful. For example, the age range of the 'unskilled lookers' would include children of seven years (or even younger) as well as adults of all ages. These are the people who draw like my psychology students; who produce drawings of cubes that might loosely be said to 'look like' cubes (cf. our definition of 'correct' copy, in Phillips et al, 1978); and who look back and forth between model and copy between ten and fifteen times. However, these 'unskilled lookers' would be unlikely to represent 'perspective' in their copies of our cube models. The depiction of 'perspective' characterized the drawings of our 'skilled lookers'. All of these were art students and as a group they averaged more than twice as many looks between model and copy as compared with the 'unskilled lookers'. They averaged 32 looks. The 'intellectual realists' produced copies of the type that have been typically called 'intellectually realistic' and that will be familiar to students of children's drawings (cf. Phillips et al, 1978, for commmon types of such drawings). When making such drawings, the children seem to look about five times between model and copy. The last of my groups the 'proto-realists' include children who show signs of attempting to represent what they perceive, but can manage no more than a vague circular shape or an isolated square. I have no record of the looking behaviour of this group, but I would be surprised if they used more than one or two looks between model and copy.

I fully recognize that my categorization is crude and that drawings I have assigned to one group often show indications of 'progress' towards the next group. However, since these indications seem to be reflected in looking behaviour, this does not weaken the main point I am trying to make here. This is that there is a simple relation between copy-type and looking behaviour. Number of looks is a very good predictor of what category of copy-type will be produced.

Another way of categorizing the copies of the four skill groups would be in terms of the kinds of relations that are taken into consideration when making the copy. Thus, 'proto-realist' copies present a minimum of relations; 'intellectual realists' copies present relations between surfaces; 'unskilled lookers' copies present relations between surfaces and lines; and 'skilled lookers' copies present relations between surfaces, lines and points. In other words, increase in skill can be equated with increase in the number of levels of description presented in copies, and, as I suggested above, with increase in numbers of looks between model and copy.

These, then, were some of the ideas generated by thinking of our experimental results in terms of the theory of 'intellectual realism'. However, I was aware that the language of this theory, though providing much explanatory power, was somewhat vague. It generated as many questions as it suggested answers. Three questions in particular seemed worth following up: (1) If depiction always involves drawing 'what you know', can more be said about the mechanisms that enable this process?; (2) How do 'knowledge-driven' looking strategies affect the content of the 'knowledge' subsequently used to drive acts of depiction?; and (3) Does the structure of visual input affect the structure of the 'knowledge' used to drive acts of depiction? My search for answers to these questions led me to adopt the framework for thinking about depiction which is diagrammed in Figure 1. The diagram represents alternative cycles by means of which optical input is processed, responded to and, in turn, affected by those responses. Optical input is represented as going through a number of stages of visual processing before activating 'organized responses'. These stages correspond to progressive levels of abstraction, with each stage being predicted on the abstractions created by the previous stage of processing. The organized responses are influenced by plans, goals and expectations, as well as, on occasion, by non-visual inputs. The responses are made manifest in the form of various kinds of actions. 'Spinal' acts determine what aspects of the existing visual world are available to be perceived and make it possible physically to alter the contents of the visual world (e.g., by making a depiction) and by doing so, to affect the structure of optical light. 'Ocular' acts further refine the structure of optical input. In these ways, the organized responses affect subsequent visual processing.

One feature of the processes described by the diagram is the high degree of automaticity involved. Also worth emphasizing is the implication that control over what activates responses is to to a highly significant degree achieved by means of control over what goes into the visual processing system in the first place (cf. Gibson, 1979). The need for this mode of control may be taken as implying significant limits on the potential for control at higher levels of processing. As we see later, these limits can be seen in terms of: (1) effects of interference between visual and non-visual processing systems (due to the dominance over actions of the levels of processing concerned with organized responses); (2) effects of interference between different visual processing systems (which may be due to selective enhancement and suppression of the products of visual processing systems by non-visual higher level systems); and (3) limitations with respect to potential for change (e.g., with respect to enabling 'new' ways of perceiving the world).

My diagram can help in the elaboration of four points: (1) Organized responses are the product of inputs from a number of sources. Since visual input is by no means the only one of these sources, it is virtually impossible to make any assumptions about the relative contribution of visual and non-visual sources to any particular act of depiction. This is just another way of making the point that it is difficult to distinguish between the contributions of drawing 'what you know' and drawing 'what you see' to any particular copying act: (2) Since there is a number of independent visual processes, the same logic applies to the question of making assumptions about the relative contributions to any organized response of the products of any particular one of these systems. For example, in a 'familiar' place, for which reliable expectations have been developed, scant visual information could 'trigger' identification of some 'familiar' object. Thus, a vague colour impression might provide an 'adequate trigger' for some

FIGURE 1

A diagramatic representation of the framework for thinking about depiction

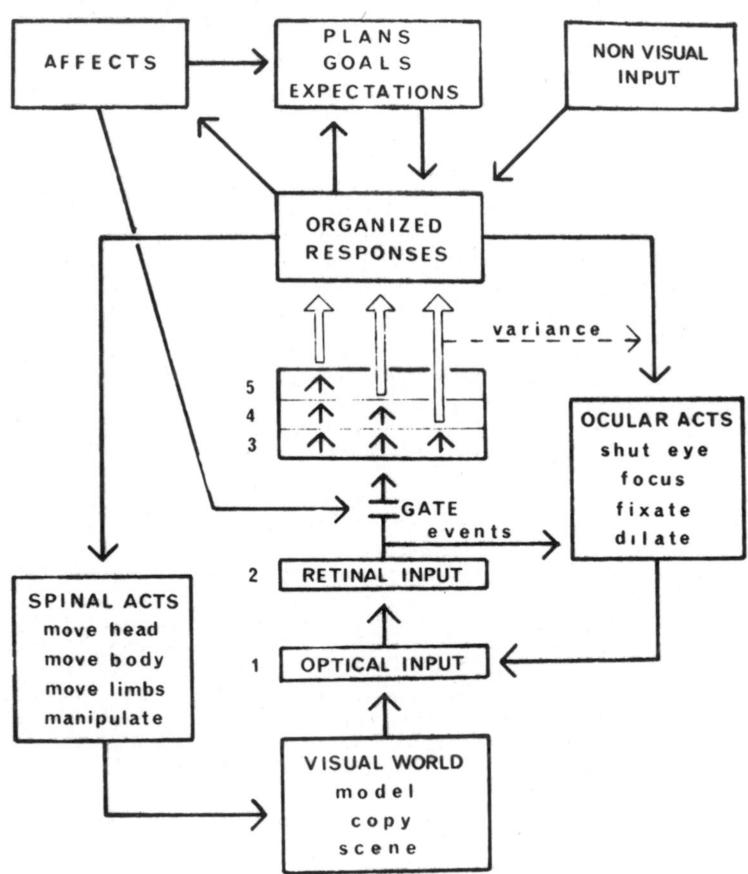

Note:
No claim is made that the connections shown are comprehensive. However, all of the connections shown can be justified in terms of known neurophysiological pathways (cf. Crowne, 1983; Hyvarinen, 1982). The numbers 1-5 refer to stages of visual processing. The divisions are schematic and should only be relied on in so far as they indicate a progression of levels of abstraction. The basis of the abstractions at each level are: (a) focus; (b) brightness, wave-length and events; (c) features (edges, nodes); (d) surface (colour, form); and (e) complex relations (surface layout, shape, depth). The diagram does not show either perceptual systems working in parallel or degrees of complexity of description.

organized response to an object. However, colour processes are by no means the only ones that could have provided the adequate trigger: (3) As I have already suggested, some degree of control over the way visual input is processed can be achieved by means of 'spinal' and 'ocular' acts. For example, standing still can prevent the use of motion parallax and shutting one eye must inevitably prevent the use of stereopsis: (4) Again, this is a point I have already introduced. It is that the nature of the visual information available from the visual world can impose constraints on which visual processes can be activated and, consequently, on which processes can trigger organized responses. Thus, for example, the same processes that can be inhibited by motionless, one-eyed looking, can equally well be inhibited by making the object of the organized response an image in a picture on a flat surface.

These four points depend on an interactive, cyclical notion of visual perception, in which interactions between visual and non-visual subsystems are important. One reason for this importance is that the interactions involved can affect what kind of information will dominate particular visual perceptions and the actions based on them; they can affect the nature of information picked up from the environment and/or the level of abstraction to which that information is raised. To illustrate these assertions, I turn to a description of the subsystems involved in colour perception. I am turning to colour perception at this point, partly to remind you that there are other aspects to depiction than shape; and partly because doing so enables the use of research findings that provide a convenient basis for the elaboration of my argument.

My description covers familiar ground. When light hits the retina it triggers a multitude of receptors. The individual receptors provide information about light intensity and wave-length. However, this information cannot be used unless it it is combined in various ways by means of inter-connecting neural pathways. Thus, processing wave-length combinations requires inputs from more than one receptor type. More complex interconnections are required to provide information about the 'brightness' ratios that underpin perceptions of contrast, edges and lines. These interconnections are organized in the form of centre/surround receptor fields. Perceptions of surface colour are provided by means of pooling information from many disparate receptor fields (cf. Zeki, 1980). The regions of the visual field contributing to such colour perceptions may be limited by 'figure'/'field' separation processes (cf. Gilchrist, 1980, and below). Finally, the most complex perceptions involving colour systems seem to depend on contributions of information from receptor fields distributed throughout the retina. These are perceptions of 'form', surface-layout, 'light' and 'space'. Thus, in summary, the various aspects of colour perception depend on a number of visual processes in which higher subsystems depend on input from lower ones. They depend on a hierarchical organization in which each level of processing bears a more complex relation to the visual input responsible for triggering it and, thus, may be said to produce information at a higher-level of abstraction.

In everyday perception the main role of colour is to help in the analysis of objects and scenes. It fulfills this role in combination with other perceptual systems. In many cases, the other perceptual systems provide alternative ways of arriving at similar results. For example, one role of colour is to help in 'figure'/'field' separation, but this can also be accomplished by systems depending on stereopsis, motion parallax and focus. Also, the same systems can help in the perception of surface and form. The question arises as to whether there is any kind of interaction between the different systems; whether some systems are given priority in terms of which triggers responses; or, whether there are other kinds of interference between them.

Take, for example, the case of 'figure'/'field' separation. This can be accomplished, not only by the above mentioned systems (i.e., those depending on motion parallax, stereopsis, focus and colour/brightness), but also by 'cognitive' systems (e.g., using 'overlap' information). The question might be asked, could the action of any of the non-colour systems interfere with the nature of the perceptual product of the colour/ brightness system? The answer would have to be, 'yes'.

The best experimental evidence for this assertion came from Gilchrist (1980). Other evidence comes from artistic practice. Both the move towards Abstraction in the latter part of the nineteenth century and the concurrent emphasis on respecting the 'integrity' of the picture surface, provide implicit support for Gilchrist's conclusion. They also supply ground for broadening their implications.

Gilchrist's experiments involved subjects making judgments about the colour appearance of parts of stimuli that were adjacent in terms of their retinal 'images' but which could be perceived as existing either in the same plane or on different planes. What he found was that, when they were perceived as being on the same plane, strong contrast affects occurred; whereas, when they were perceived as being on different planes, the brightness relation between 'figure' and 'field' had negligible effect on colour appearance. The changes in appearance due to changes in perception of planar relations were dramatic; white was changed to black and vice versa.

Gilchrist used two methods of changing perceptions of planar relations. In his first experiment he exploited the difference between monocular and binocular vision and, in the second, he used 'overlap' (i.e., 'cognitive') information. Thus, in the fist experiment, what the subjects actually saw depended on whether they looked at the stimulus array with one eye or with two. If they looked at it with one eye, they saw an arrangement of four colours on what appeared to be a flat surface. If they looked at it with both eyes, they saw two surfaces at right angles to one another. In effect, the one-eyed view of the stimulus extended the area within which colour interactions took place. Other ways of creating similar extensions of colour interactions are well known to artists and might well have been used by Gilchrist for further experimentation. For example, he might have presented his stimulus array at a greater distance; he might have presented it out-of-focus; or he might have presented it as a 2D array (i.e., as a depiction). All these methods could be expected to produce comparable results by preventing or reducing the interference with colour appearance produced by the activity of various form and depth perception systems. This is, presumably, why all of them, including the use of monocular vision, have been for so long part of the artist's stock in trade.

Also well known to artists are some of the implications of Gilchrist's finding relating to the power of cognitive processes to interfere with the perception of figure/field relations. They know that perceiving things as objects hinders analysis of relations which can be of central importance to their enterprise. It hinders analysis of figure/field and whole-field relations, whether they be of shape or of colour. Many traditional artistic aids and practices bear testimony to the struggle of artists against the dominance of object perceptions over other perceptual activity. A good example of such an aid is the perspective frame (sometimes called a 'reticule'; cf. Doerner, 1949). This, by means of subdividing scenes into a network of rectangles, facilitates analysis in terms of local relations and militates against the influence of whole-object perceptions over looking behaviour. It is significant that perspective frames were used by artists of all levels of skill, including the most skilled. This suggests that the presence of whole-object perceptions may hinder appropriate visual analysis for all people. Other examples can be found in any good 'how-to-depict' book (e.g., Edwards, 1979; Nicolaides, 1941).

Further evidence for artists' awareness of the negative influence of whole-object perceptions comes from the nature of formal developments in painting during the past hundred years. It has been responsible for the two most important of such developments. The first of these has been the flattening of pictorial space and the increasing emphasis on the physicality of the picture surface (cf. Greenberg, 1975, who shares the general opinion that the origin of these tendencies is to be found in the paintings of the Impressionists and of Cezanne). The flattening of pictorial space has been a primary characteristic of twentieth century colourist painters (cf. Matisse, Bonnard, Kelly, Kidner). One advantage it procures is the better appreciation of colour relations. The claim made here is that the reason for this advantage is that the flattening of pictorial space reduces the influence of object perceptions over the operation of perceptual systems involved in figure/field and whole-field colour perceptions.

The second main formal development has been the advent of non-figurative or 'abstract' paintings. The very word 'abstract' makes the point that needs to be made here. Artists were abandoning figuration so that they could paint pictures in which colour and shape relations could be experienced in isolation from object perceptions. The need to make such abstractions is evidence that the artists regarded object perceptions as interfering with the effects they were trying to produce in their paintings.

SUMMARY AND IMPLICATIONS

In the first part of this chapter, I argued that copying performance can be related to the level of description accessed. The lower the level, the more 'accurate' (i.e., the more view-specific) the results. I also suggested that there is a link between the level of description accessed and the number of looks. There is thus a three-way correlation between level of description accessed, level of performance and number of looks used. This correlation suggests that number of looks should be a good predictor of level of performance and, indeed, this suggestion was supported by our evidence.

Our experimental findings showed that differences between people of different levels of skill were at a minimum when copying models that could only be perceived in terms of the lowest levels of description (e.g., our separated straight-line models) and were at a maximum when copying models that were perceived in terms of the highest levels of description (e.g., our cube models). Our evidence suggested that, in practice, the level of description accessed in the first place was always the highest possible. Thus, access to the lowest levels (i.e., those required for view-specific depiction) always involved a descent through levels. The higher the level of the initial perception, the more stages there are to be descended through. Our evidence suggests that the ability to negotiate these stages may be the main characteristic of skilled performance. One indication of the diffiuclty of accomplishing successful descent is the widespread use by skilled artists of aids that enable them to inhibit whole-object perceptions and/or facilitate direct access to lower levels of description.

In the second part of the chapter, I introduced a diagram intended to help in an elaboration of ideas about processes involved in depiction. This diagram represents depiction in terms of perceptual cycles in which visual and non-visual inputs are capable of eliciting response in terms of 'spinal' or 'ocular' acts. Such acts can, in turn, influence the structure of subsequent visual input.

The relation between the products of visual processing and organized responses is not simple. If the function of visual processing is to provide 'adequate triggers' for organized responses, then there can be no certainty as to what aspect of visual input is providing that trigger. Nor is the triggering information necessarily used in the act it triggers. I gave the example of a vague colour impression triggering a response to a 'familiar' and 'expected' object. Suppose, for example, the response was to set about picking up the object. If it were, the act of picking up would most likely be done using information derived from motion parallax, stereopsis and/or focus. It would be less likely to rely on colour information.

However, the perceptual activity associated with the picking-up resonse would be task related. It would involve looking for situation-specific visual information. In the terms I was using earlier, it would involve looking for 'novel' relations. Furthermore, the information sought would be used to guide the act of picking-up. Thus, a perceptual cycle would have taken place during which task-irrelevant information would have facilitated access of task-relevant information.

Earlier, I proposed that task-relevant information in the context of our copying task could be described in terms of antitheses of the form 'above'/ 'below' or 'larger'/ 'smaller'. I also proposed that analysis for depiction can only be an analysis of relations between parts and cannot be an analysis of the parts themselves. A similar situation would seem to obtain with respect to colour analysis and description. This is a clear implication of Land's (1977) and Zeki's (1980) work on the mathematical and neurophysiological bases of colour perception. They show that colour perception depends on computations using information derived simultaneously from disparate parts of the visual field. However, when artists analyse colour relations in such disparate parts of the visual field, they have to do so by means of a sequence of comparative looks. Furthermore, they have to resort to analysis in terms of antitheses comparable to those used in shape analysis. For example, they would judge colours in terms of being 'greener'/'bluer' or 'brighter'/'darker'. It seems to me that a clear implication of this state of affairs is that direct use of the products of visual processing is impossible. These can only be used indirectly through the mediation of responses triggered by them. Such responses can be characterized in terms of verbal descriptions.

The difficulty of accessing lower-level descriptions relating to aspects of 'familiar' objects is evidence for the dominance of higher-levels of description over the organization of visual analysis. This can be described in terms of interference between alternative ways of processing the same visual input. Gilchrist's (1980) experiments show that there is also interference between different perceptual systems. Obviously, these kinds of interference could have significant effects on what information would be available to be used in acts of visual analysis. For example, Gilchrist's results imply that it would be more difficult to analyse figure/field relations when moving or when looking with two eyes, than when standing still and looking monocularly. This being so, it comes as no surprise that almost all the aids and practices traditionally used by artists to assist accurate depiction can be justified, at least in part, in terms of their capacity to inhibit the operation of unwanted perceptual systems and to undermine the domination of higher-level descriptions over acts of analysis. Amongst the artists' aids, a favourite has been the use of 2D images as models. Sometimes these have taken the form of sketches or studies prepared by the artist and sometimes they have taken the form of photographic images (cf. Sharf, 1968, who shows just how widespread has been the use of photographic images). A great advantage of such 2D images is that they inhibit the use of motion parallax, stereopsis and focus as aids to visual analysis. In this way, they promote the use of perceptual systems that are more suited to the analysis of the figure/field and whole-field relations upon which successful depiction depends. The same advantages apply to the use in the depicting process of feedback from the emerging depiction, since depictions are made on 2D surfaces.

The emerging depiction can provide other advantages as well. For example, it provides a rich source of low-level descriptions, particularly in the early stages of its production. These can be used as comparators. Thus, marks on the picture surface can be compared with corresponding parts of scenes. Comparisons help because they can provide a means of transforming the task; they enable the use of recognition memory, and by so doing, provide an opportunity for the utilization of same/different judgments.

The capacity for making same/different judgments may be of great significance. It may provide people with a tool for undermining the domination of object perceptions and for descending through levels of description, from complex to simple. Elsewhere (Pratt, in preparation) I have suggested that when similar things are compared attention may be attracted automatically to differences between them, in much the same way as unattended 'events' attract attention. The dashed arrow labelled 'variance' in my diagram (Figure 1) is intended to represent the possibility that the perceptual cycle involved may, in some circumstances, at least, by-pass cognitive levels of processing. The necessary comparisons may be provided, either by parallel processing of disparate parts of the visual field, or by sequential processing of the same part. In either case, the crucial point is that attention is drawn to differences between things that have much in common. It is also crucial to notice that these differences must invariably relate to component parts of what is being compared; that is to say, they must relate to elements that are capable of simpler description. In this way comparisons lead to a descent through levels of description. Furthermore, by so doing, they circumvent the domination of higher and more complex descriptions and promote an awareness of unique and formerly unnoticed aspects of scenes. In other words, by calling attention to variance, comparisons initiate a natural mechanism for seeing in new ways.

One of the puzzles that has confronted me, both as a teacher of depiction and as an experimental psychologist, is the degree to which people fail to take advantage of the opportunities afforded by comparative looking. Why do depictors not do more looking back and forth between scene and depiction, making comparisons between marks they have made and the elements in the scene to which those marks are intended to correspond? Two plausible answers to this question may be suggested. The first of these brings us back to a main theme of this chapter, namely the dominance of higher levels of description over perception; the second, related to the usability of 'novel' descriptions. (1) The higher the level of description the greater the number of different perceptions of the same thing must be accounted for in that description and, therefore, the more generalized it must be. This means that comparisons based on high-level descriptions are less likely to draw attention to differences than comparisons based on low-level descriptions. It follows that, in so far as high-level descriptions dominate perception, differences between things, particularly differences in details, will tend to be overlooked. Since, it would appear that domination of perception by high-level descriptions is the norm, it can be presumed that it will be very common for such overlooking to occur and for opportunities to make comparisons to be neglected: (2) Memory for 'novel' relations is extremely fragile (cf. Phillips, 1983). Specifically, it is disrupted by attempts to accumulate further information about other 'novel' relations and by various kinds of mental activity, including, it would seem, that employed in depicting activity (cf. Pratt, 1983, where experimental evidence for the disruptive effects of line production is presented and where some practical ways of circumventing the difficulties consequent upon the disruption are discussed). What this means is that depictors may be discouraged from making comparisons because there are intrinsic difficulties when it comes to using the information obtained as a basis for acts of depiction.

Finally, I would like to allude to the potential of non-verbal inputs in terms of affecting looking strategies and, consequently, depicting performance. There is abundant evidence that depictions (even young children's depictions) can be strikingly influenced by verbal instructions. It is generally easy to draw people's attention to aspects of scenes that they have previously overlooked. The fact that they failed to see these aspects without instruction can be taken as yet more evidence of the high degree of automaticity in the normal use of looking strategies. In general, this automaticity would seem to be a major obstacle to the acquisition of depicting skills.

Depictors through the ages have dealt with this obstacle in two ways. Either they have turned the automaticity to their own advantage, by using aids and strategies that discourage access to high level descriptions, encourage comparisons and enable appropriate storage of useful information; or, they have circumvented it by organizing their looking strategies on the basis of non-visual input. In effect, this means that they have depended on memories of what they have learnt from their own previous endeavours or what they have learnt from the accumulated wisdom of their predecessors.

ACKNOWLEDGMENTS

My experimental investigation of depicting skill was mostly done with the help of a Social Science Research Council grant. My thanks are also due to many members of the Psychology Department at the University of Stirling and, in particular, to Bill Phillips, Lindsay Wilson and Ranald Macdonald.

REFERENCES

Crowne, D.P. (1983). The frontal eye fields and attention. Psychological Bulletin, 93, 232-260.

Doerner, M. (1949). The Materials of the Artist. London: Harrup.

Edwards, B. (1979). Drawing on the Right Side of the Brain. Los Angeles, California: Tarcher.

Gibson, J.J. (1979). The Ecological Approach to Visual Perception. Boston, Massachusetts: Houghton Mifflin.

Gilchrist, A.L. (1980). When does perceived lightness depend on perceived spatial arrangement? Perception and Psychophysics, 28, 527-538.

Greenberg, C. (1975). Cezanne and the Unity of Modern Art. In: J. Wechsler (Ed.) Cezanne in Perspective. Englewood Cliffs, New Jersey: Prentice-Hall.

Hyvarinen, J. (1982). Posterior parietal lobe of the primate brain. Physiological Review, 62, 1060-1129.

Land, E.H. (1977). The retinex theory of color vision. Scientific American, 237, 108-128.

Neisser, U. (1976). Cognition and Reality: Principles and Implications of Cognitive Psychology. San Francisco, California: Freeman.

Nicolaides, K. (1941). The Natural Way to Draw. Boston, Massachusetts: Houghton Mifflin.

Phillips, W.A., Hobbs, S.B. and Pratt, F.R. (1978). Intellectual Realism in children's drawings of cubes. Cognition, 6, 15-33.

Pratt, F.R. (1983). Intellectual realism in adults' and children's copies of cubes and straight lines. In: D. Rogers and J.A. Sloboda (Eds.) The Acquisition of Symbolic Skills. New York: Plenum.

Pratt, F.R. (In preparation). A perspective on traditional artistic practices suggested by Gibson's critique of traditional experimental paradigms. In: M. Cox and N.H. Freeman (Eds.) Picture Production. Cambridge: Cambridge University Press.

Sharf, A. (1968). Art and Photography. London: Allen Lane.

Zeki, S. (1980). The representation of colour in the cerebral cortex. Nature, 284 (5755), 412-418.

Cognitive Processes in the Perception of Art
W.R. Crozier and A.J. Chapman (editors)
© Elsevier Science Publishers B.V. (North-Holland), 1984

GETTING THE DRAWING TO LOOK RIGHT AS WELL AS TO BE RIGHT: THE INTERACTION BETWEEN PRODUCTION AND PERCEPTION AS A MECHANISM OF DEVELOPMENT

John Willats

North East London Polytechnic

When children are learning to draw, what is it that they are trying to do? One answer might be that they are trying to make their drawings look like adult pictures: but if this is the case,then it has to be said that children are not very successful at it The commonest adult pictures in our culture must surely be photographs, but in order to make their drawings look like photographs children would have to use patches of tone or colour to stand for the intercepts of bundles of light rays as they are received by the eye or the camera. We have no evidence that children are trying to do this; in fact, the only adult artists who have tried to do this were the Pointillistes and, to a lesser extent, the Impressionists.

Another answer might be that children are trying to make their drawings look more like the real world. This may perhaps be true, but this is a proposition which is difficult to test, because the attempt to do so immediately raises all sorts of difficult questions about what the world looks like independently of any representational system.

A third, and I think more promising, approach is to say that what children are doing is trying to produce pictures which are better as *representations*.

What I mean by 'better as representations' is illustrated in the three drawings shown in Figure 1. Figure 1c is unambiguous, and shows a cube with a smaller cube removed from one corner. Figure 1b is ambiguous: it can be seen as a cube with a smaller cube removed from one corner, or as an internal corner with small cube stuck up into it, or as a cube with a smaller cube protruding at an unusual angle. Figure 1a is not only ambiguous, but can just as well be seen as a flat pattern. For a picture to be a good representation, it must be possible (1) to be able to recognize the object in the drawing, and (2) to be able to see the (three-dimensional) shape of the object in the drawing (cf. Wollheim, 1977). By these criteria, Figure 1c is a better representation than Figure 1b, and Figure 1b is a better representation than Figure 1a.

Figure 2 shows children's drawings of a similar object. One hundred and seventy children aged 4 to 13 years attending State Schools in East London were asked to draw this and several other objects (Willats, 1981b). They were encouraged to place the object in any position they wished. The drawings were assigned to classes based on (but not identical with) those described in Willats (1977a) and (1977b). Figure 2 shows representative drawings from each class, together with the mean ages of children in each class to the nearest half-year.

It is at once apparent that the drawings produced by the older children are better as representations than the drawings produced by the younger children; but the transition from class 1 to class 6 is not a smooth one. The drawings as a whole can be divided into two quite separate groups which cut right across the developmental sequence. In the first group, corresponding roughly but not completely to classes 2, 4 and 6, are drawings which can be assigned to one or other of the drawing systems; that is, drawings which can be derived from the stimulus object by projective geometry (Willats, 1977a, 1977b). In the second group, corresponding roughly, but again not completely to classes 1, 3 and 5, are drawings which cannot be derived from the stimulus object by projective geometry.

Figure 3 shows drawings in the first group; these accounted for about two thirds of all the drawings produced. The drawings in this group are all more or less acceptable as representations; in the right context they could be accepted as adult drawings. Drawings in class 2, for example, are in *orthographic projection* a system widely used by architects and engineers. Drawings in class 4, though of a type which is less familiar, are in *vertical oblique projection* a system sometimes used by painters and graphic designers and, though more rarely, by architects. Drawings in class 6, in isometric projection, oblique projection and perspective, are of a type familiar in ordinary adult pictures. Drawings in this first group, therefore, generally 'look right'.

FIGURE 1 Three drawings of a cube with a smaller cube removed from one corner. Drawings (b) and (c) are both in oblique projection, but (c) contains a T junction denoting the point at which a face partially occludes an edge, removing the ambiguity of drawing (b). Drawing (a) is in vertical oblique projection, and shows the object from a less general direction of view.

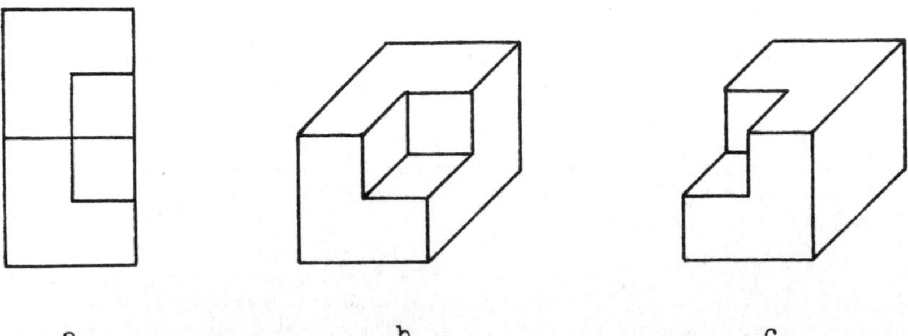

FIGURE 2 Children's drawings of a cube with a smaller cube removed from one corner, arranged into classes and showing the mean age for each class.

class	mean age
1	5.5
2	7.0
3	9.0
4	10.0
5	10.5
6	12.0

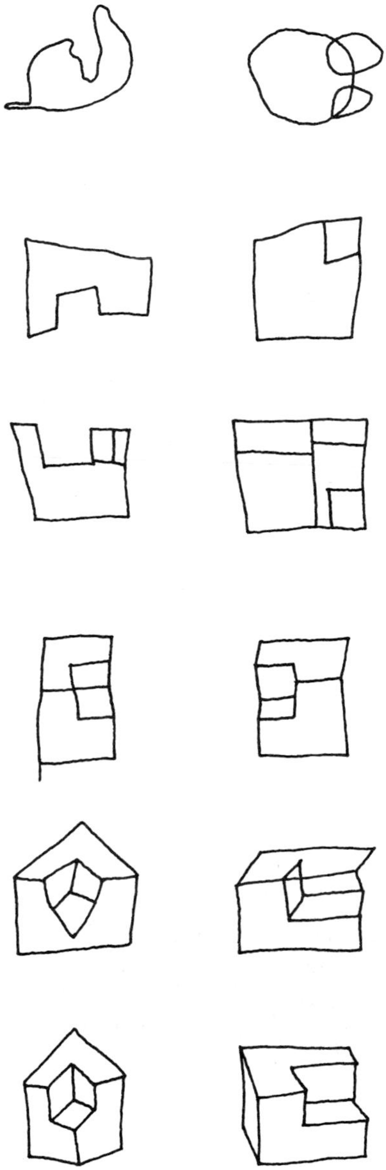

FIGURE 3 Drawings which can be derived from the stimulus object by projective geometry.

class	mean age	projection system
2	7.0	orthographic projection 
4	10.0	vertical oblique projection 
6	12.0	isometric and oblique projections 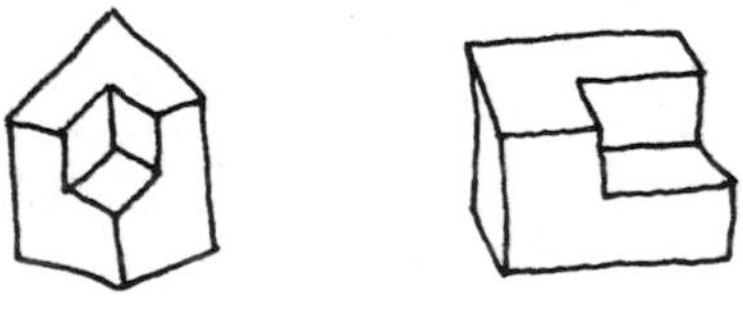

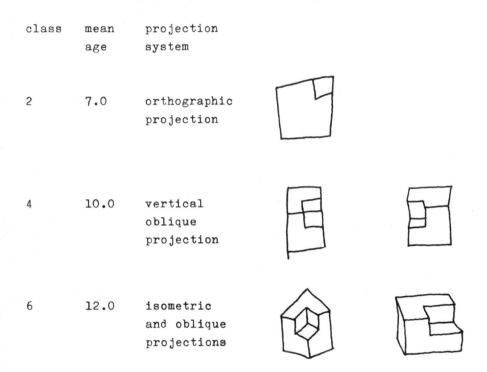

Not all of these drawings are, however, equally good as representations. Figure 4 shows the primary geometry of orthographic projection, and it can be seen that the projection rays are parallel, and intersect the picture plane at right angles in both the horizontal and vertical directions. As a result, drawings in orthographic projection show only the front, top or side faces of an object, so that the object is seen from a rather special direction of view. Of all types of drawing based on projective geometry, therefore, orthographic projections are the least good as representations.

Figure 5 shows the primary geometry of vertical oblique projection. Here, the projection rays intersect the picture plane at right angles in the horizontal direction, but at an oblique angle in the vertical direction. Drawings in vertical oblique projection show the front and top views of an object together, and are thus somewhat better as representations than drawings in orthographic projection.

FIGURE 4 The primary geometry of orthographic projection, the least general of all the projection systems. The projection rays intersect the picture plane at right angles in both the horizontal and vertical directions.

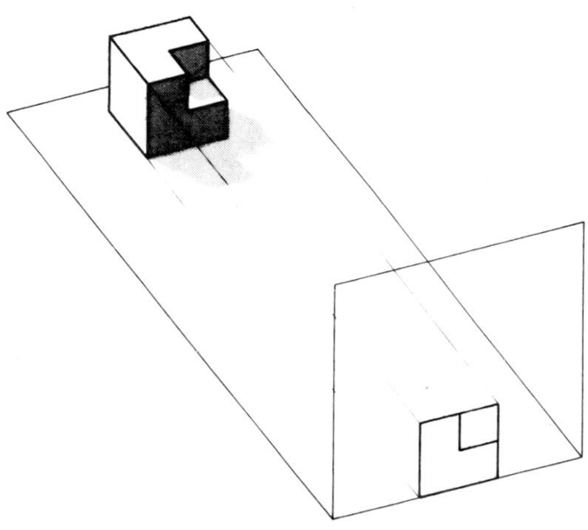

FIGURE 5 The primary geometry of vertical oblique projection. The projection rays intersect the picture plane at right angles in the horizontal direction, but at an oblique angle in the vertical direction.

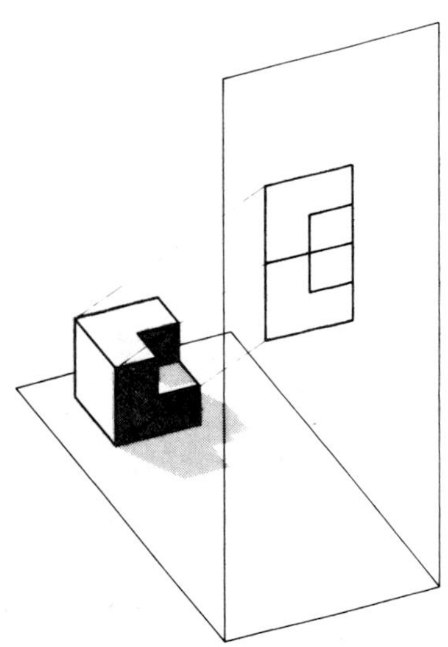

FIGURE 6 The primary geometry of oblique projection. The projection rays intersect the picture plane at an oblique angle in both the horizontal and vertical directions.

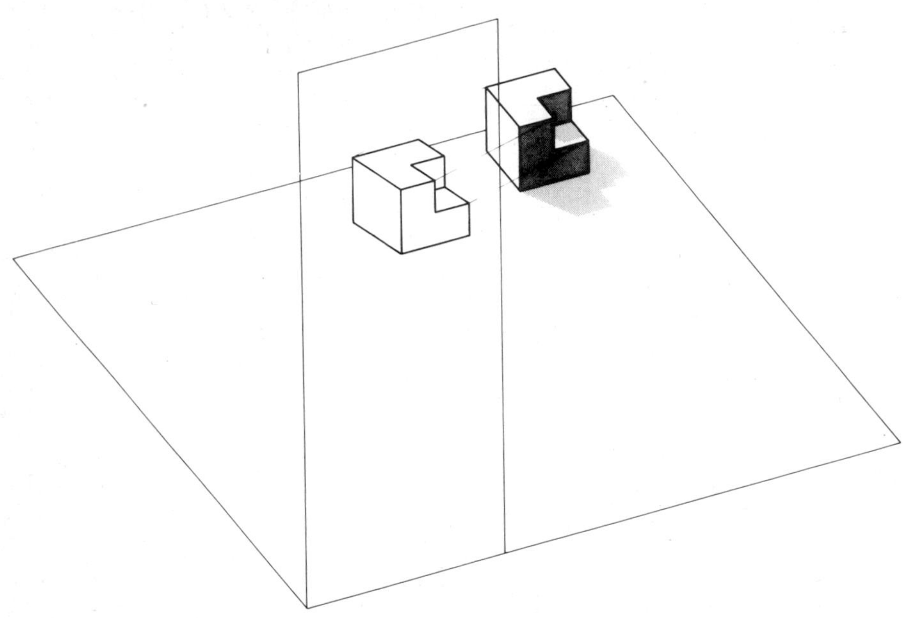

Finally, Figure 6 shows the primary geometry of oblique projection. The projection rays intersect the picture plane at an oblique angle in both directions, and drawings in oblique projection show the front, top and side views of an object together in the same drawing. Drawings in perspective are similar to drawings in oblique projection, but in perspective the projection rays are not parallel, but converge to the eye of the spectator. Drawings in perspective are not necessarily better as representations compared with drawings in oblique projection: in fact, Saenger (1981) found that children of all ages chose oblique projections as 'most realistic, clearest and best liked' even when they could produce drawings in perspective themselves. Perspective drawings do, however, show the apparent change in the size of objects with distance.

Since drawings in the first group could all be assigned to one or other of the drawing systems, they all correspond to possible views of the object, and therefore to possible images which could be received by the retina. Not all these drawings are equally good as representations, however. Drawings in oblique projection and perspective are better as representations than drawings in vertical oblique projection, and drawings in vertical oblique projection are in turn better than drawings in orthographic projection. Neglecting drawings in the second group, we can therefore say that as children get older they produce drawings which show objects from an increasingly general direction of view. As a result, drawings by older children are better as representations than drawings by younger children. This is very close to what Lewis said: the 'successive discovery of increasingly adequate methods of depicting three-dimensional relationships within the limits of a two-dimensional medium constitutes progress' (1963, p. 96)

But alas for this satisfyingly neat and tidy account of the acquisition of drawing ability, not all children's drawings can be described in terms of projective geometry. How can these other drawings be described, and what part, if any, do they play in the developmental process?

FIGURE 7 Drawings which cannot be derived from the stimulus object by projective geometry.

class	mean age	? system
1 & 2	-	?
3	9.0	?
5	10.5	?

Figure 7 shows drawings in the second group; with a few exceptions, these drawings were assigned to classes 1, 3 and 5 and accounted for the remaining one-third of the drawings obtained in the experiment. None of these drawings in the second group can be obtained from the stimulus object by projective geometry, and to adult eyes at least, and probably also to children (Kosslyn et al, 1977) they are all more or less unacceptable as representations: in other words, compared with the drawings in the first group, they all seem to have something wrong with them. They can all, however, be described in terms of the various *denotation systems*.

Denotation systems say what the marks in the picture stand for (Willats, 1981a). In any kind of picture, the marks in the picture, or *picture primitives*, stand for, refer to, or *denote* corresponding objects or entities in the real world, or *scene primitives*. In line drawings, for example, lines commonly stand for the edges of objects; while in photographs the marks in the picture, which may be Benday dots in a newspaper photograph, points on a television screen or grains on a photographic film, stand for the intercepts of small bundles of light rays. Scene and picture primitives may be classified according to the number of dimensions of space into which they can be extended. 0-dimensional primitives like points have no extension. 1-dimensional primitives like lines or edges can be extended in only one dimension. 2-dimensional primitives like faces or regions can be extended in two dimensions. And, finally, 3-dimensional or volumetric primitives like spheres, cubes, pillow-shaped objects (Marr and Nishihara, 1978), or flying saucers can be extended in three dimensions. In the following account of denotation systems the number of dimensions into which each primitive can be extended, or the dimensional index, is shown on the left-hand side of the analytical diagram, and the arrow stands for the 'denotes' relationship.

Taking drawings by the younger children first, we can say that in drawings of the type shown in Figure 8, the object is represented by a single region. Since in the case of this particular object the shape of the volume includes a local concavity, the shape of the corresponding region also includes a local concavity. This account is similar to suggestions by Arnheim (1954) and Piaget and Inhelder (1956) that young children represent the object as a whole.

Drawings like those shown in Figure 9 can be described by saying that they are based on a denotation system in which areas or regions stand for faces. Kennedy (1978) calls these 'fold out' drawings, and that seems a good name for them because it brings out the fact that in many of these drawings the regions represent the true shapes of faces, like the faces of a cardboard box. Similar drawings have been described by Lewis (1963), Minsky and Papert (1972), Kosslyn et al (1977), Hayes (1978) and Phillips et al (1978).

Finally in drawings like those shown in Figure 10, lines stand for edges: either all the edges of an object, or just those edges which can be seen from a particular point or direction of view.

This account of denotation systems, by concentrating only on drawings in the second group may have given the impression that drawings may be divided into those which can be described in terms of projection systems, and those which can be described in terms of denotation systems; but of course this would be incorrect. All drawings must be based on denotation systems of some kind, but not all drawings can be described in terms of projective geometry. To enable drawings to correspond to images which could be derived from the stimulus object by projective geometry, some extra constraint must be added to the denotation system.

FIGURE 8 The denotation system for some of the drawings in classes 1 and 2.

class

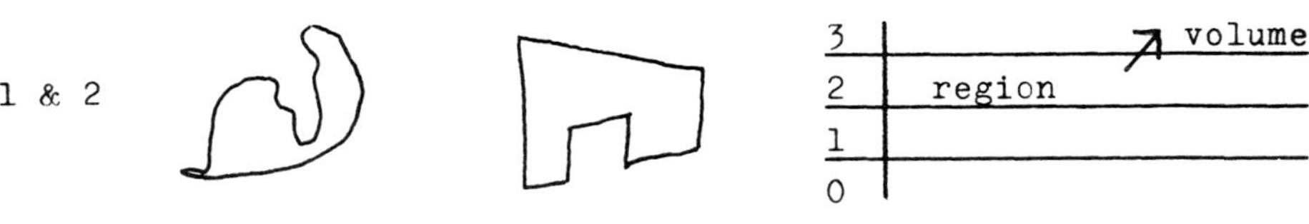

FIGURE 9 The denotation system for drawings in class 3.

class

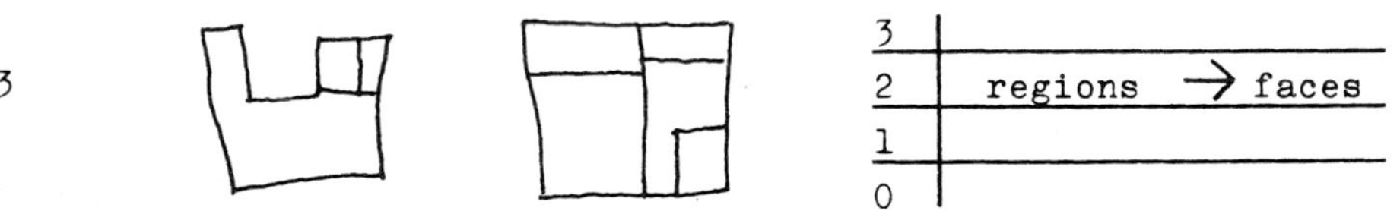

FIGURE 10 The denotation system for drawings in class 5.

class

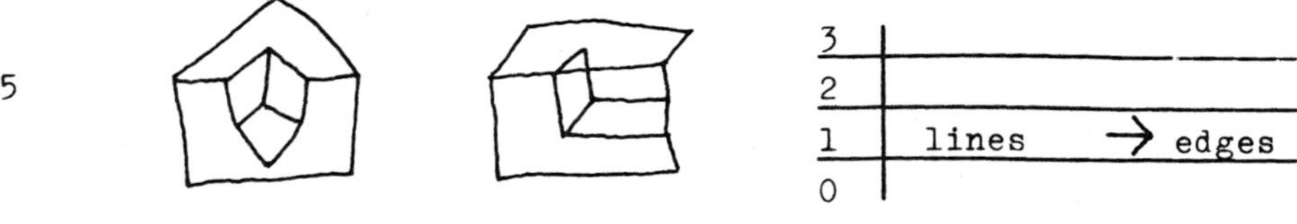

FIGURE 11 Representative drawings from the whole developmental sequence showing the associated projection and denotation systems.

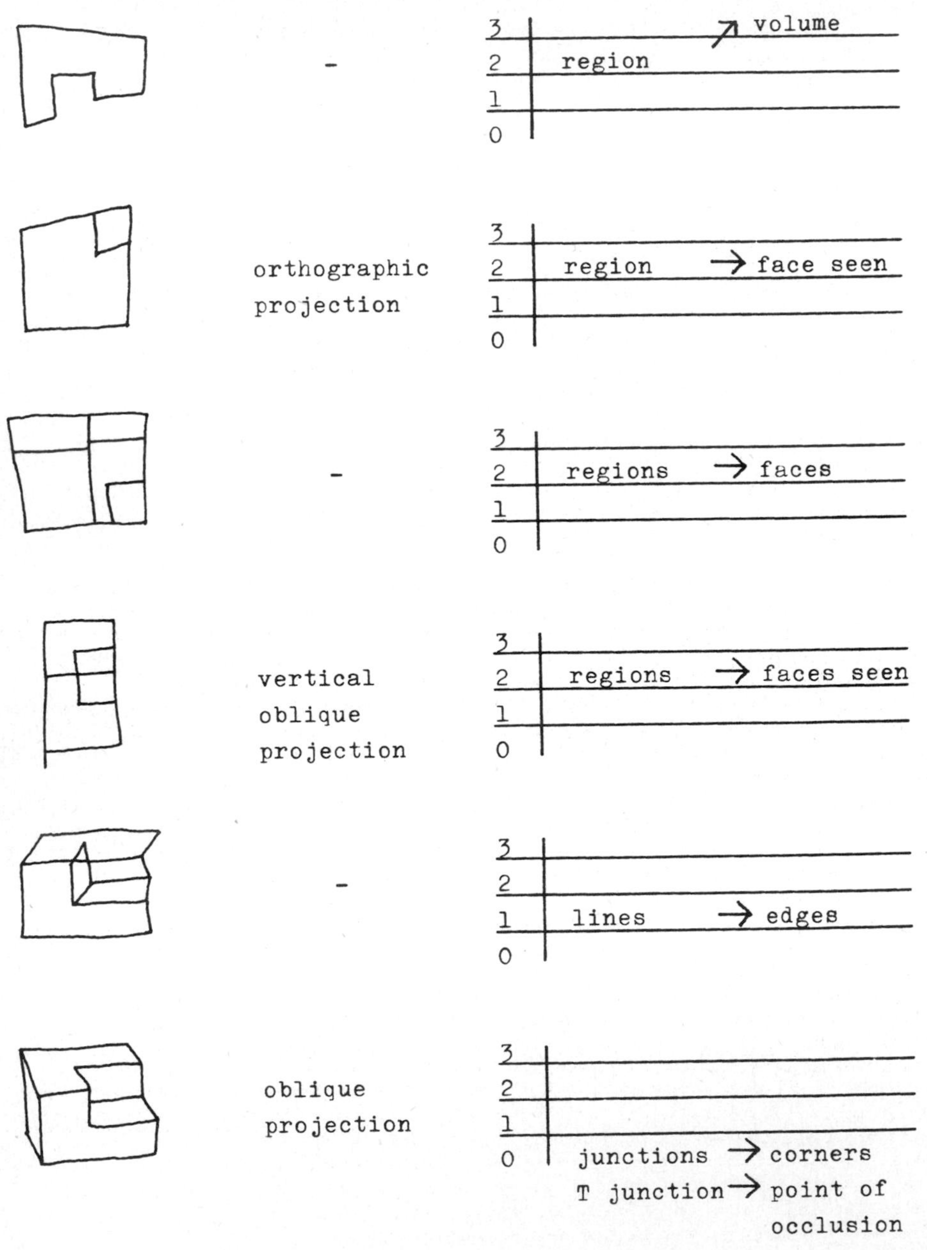

Figure 11 shows representative drawings from both the first and second groups, together with their denotation systems. At one extreme are drawings by the younger children, in which regions or areas are used to stand for the whole volume of the object. At the other extreme are drawings based on 0-dimensional primitives, in which line junctions are used to stand either for corners, or for the points in the visual field at which a face partially occludes an edge. The developmental sequence as a whole is thus marked by a progressive lowering of the values of the dimensional indices of the primitives on which the denotation systems are based. A sequence of this kind seems to have a natural basis, if Marr (1978) is correct in supposing that the analysis of the retinal image by the perceptual system follows the sequence: point primitives (retinal sensations); line primitives (the 'primal sketch'); two-dimensional primitives (the '2½ D sketch'); and finally three-dimensional (volumetric) primitives. We would expect pictures based on primitives having lower dimensional indices to be more effective as representations, since they can come closer to the unanalysed retinal images of objects seen from a general direction of view; and we would therefore expect children, as they get older, to use denotation systems based on progressively lower dimensional indices. The results of the experiment confirmed this prediction. Figure 11 shows the drawing systems which are associated with alternate stages in the developmental sequence. Drawings in any one of these stages may be derived from drawings in a previous stage by adding some additional constraint to the denotation system. For example, drawings in vertical oblique projection (stage 4) can be derived from the denotation system *regions denote faces* (belonging to the previous stage) by adding an additional constraint to form the system *regions denote faces which can be seen from a specific direction of view.*

This provides us with a clue to the nature of the developmental sequence as a whole: a series of longer stages during which children produce drawings which look right, divided by shorter transitional stages during which children produce drawings which look wrong. What seems to happen is that a drawing is first produced which makes sense in terms of some specific denotation system, but which (usually) looks wrong. The drawing is then modified in some way so as to get it to look right. In practice, this means modifying the drawing until it could have been derived from the object by projective geometry. This stage persists until the child becomes dissatisfied with the fact that the drawing system currently in use does not result in a sufficiently good representation: that is, it does not show the object from a sufficiently general direction of view. A new denotation system is then adopted, which again results in a drawing which looks wrong - and the whole process starts again. Two additional factors may be involved. In the earliest stages, drawings based on the denotative system in which a region is used to denote the whole volume of an object may, fortuitously, result in a drawing which looks right from the word go. For example, a square, drawn to denote the whole volume of a cube, already looks like a face. In this case, no modification of the drawing is needed, only the realization on the child's part that the drawing can be perceived or interpreted in terms of a more advanced system than the one by which it was produced. Finally, in the later stages of drawing development after oblique projection and perspective have been mastered, any further improvement can only be achieved by adopting a more sophisticated denotation system in which *false attachments* or what Guzman (1968) called 'nasty coincidences' are avoided, and T junctions denoting points in the visual field at which faces partially occlude edges are deliberately introduced. It is doubtful, however, whether many children reach this stage.

FIGURE 12 A simplified and idealized version of the whole developmental sequence, illustrated by children's drawings of a cube. The arrows show the transitions from one stage to the next.

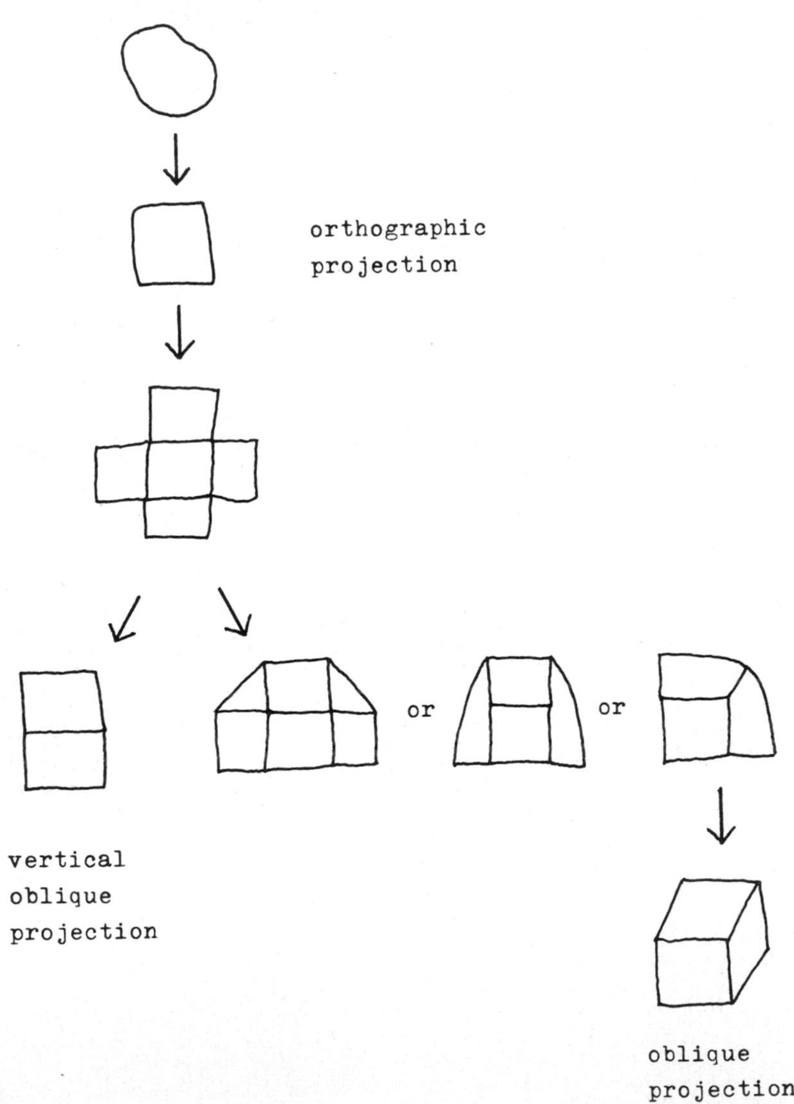

A rather simplified and idealized version of the whole developmental sequence, illustrated by children's drawings of a cube, is shown in Figure 12. The arrows show the transitions from one stage to the next. A child at the earliest stage of development will probably produce a closed curved form (Piaget's '*Jordan's curve*) as a drawing of a cube, and this is later modified to a square to show the flat faces. At this stage, the square denotes the whole volume of a cube; but sooner or later the child will realize that the square actually *looks* like a single face. This is the origin of orthographic projection, the earliest of the drawing systems to emerge. This stage persists for some time, until the child becomes dissatisfied with the fact that a drawing in orthographic projection shows only one face of the object, and begins to add more faces. This is logical enough, but inevitably results in a drawing which looks 'wrong' because the faces and corners will not join up properly. The child then tinkers around with the drawing in various ways, in an effort to get it to look 'right'. One solution is to stop drawing at the right moment: this results in a drawing in vertical oblique projection. An alternative is to add extra lines to the drawing in an attempt to force the corners to join up. Unfortunately this is not very helpful, and makes the drawing look worse rather than better. Another option is to look ahead a little, and distort the two faces on either side (usually the last two faces to be drawn). This is a more promising approach, because the oblique lines, originally added to make the corners join, begin to suggest edges in the third dimension. Finally, the child may look ahead still further, and draw an oblique line as the common edge between two faces. From this stage, it is only a small step to true oblique projection or perspective, in which lines stand for edges, and oblique lines stand for edges in the third dimension.

The process of development can thus be seen as the result of a series of interactions between production, and the child's perception of his or her own drawings. At each intermediate stage a drawing is produced which *is* right, in the sense of arising as the result of a sensible and logical solution to a problem, but which does not necessarily *look* right. This is Gombrich's (1960) theory of schema and correction; the only originality claimed for the present account lies in the details of the analysis.

In theory, this mechanism of interaction between production and perception would be sufficient to enable a child working in complete isolation to reach the stage of oblique projection. To reach the level of *naïve* perspective just one extra observation of the real world would be needed: the observation that objects appear to get smaller as they get farther away. To reach the stage of true perspective, one needs either a mirror, a sheet of glass, the price of admission to an old-fashioned Art School, or a book on perspective. In other words, either a bit of help or a lot of luck.

In practice, the transition from 'fold out' drawing to oblique projection is a complex one requiring several intermediate stages, and children are unlikely to make this transition unless they are brought up in a pictorially rich environment, or given some teaching, or both. Certainly Jahoda (1981) who tested schooled and unschooled adults in Ghana, concluded that 'the boundary between classes 3 and 4 (vertical oblique and oblique projection) represents a critical divide; in the absence of an environment rich in perspective drawings, it is not crossed.' (p. 142).

On the other hand, this argument cuts both ways. In countries like Britain and the USA, where there is a rich pictorial environment, nearly all the pictures available to children are in perspective or near perspective, so that adult pictures in the developmentally earlier systems such as orthographic projection and vertical oblique projection are rarely seen by children. This suggests either that children discover these systems for themselves, or that they see them used in pictures by older children. Probably very young children make their discoveries almost wholly on their own, and then when they are older and go to school they are influenced, at least in part, by seeing pictures by other children.

Thus, although the mechanism of development which has just been described, which depends on the interaction of children with their own pictures, could in theory account for the whole developmental sequence, in practice it is probably most important for the earlier stages of drawing. Perhaps this is why drawings by very young children sometimes seem fresher and more exciting than pictures by older children: they still have on them all the bloom of individual discovery.

ACKNOWLEDGMENTS

I thank the Faculty of Art and Design, North East London Polytechnic, for help in the preparation of the manuscript of this chapter; and the School of Graphic Arts, Royal College of Art, for supporting my attendance at The British Psychological Society, Welsh Branch, International Conference on Psychology and the Arts.

REFERENCES

Arnheim, R. (1954). Art and Visual Perception. Calfornia: University of California Press.

Gombrich, E.H. (1960). Art and Illusion. New York: Pantheon.

Guzman, A. (1968). Decomposition of a visual scene into three-dimensional bodies. Proceedings of the Joint Fall Computer Conference, 291-366. Washington, DC: Thomson Book Co.

Hayes, J. (1978). Children's visual descriptions. Cognitive Science, 2, 1-15.

Jahoda, G. (1981). Drawing styles of schooled and unschooled adults: a study in Ghana. Quarterly Journal of Experimental Psychology, 33A, 133-143.

Kennedy, J.M. (1978). Pictures and the blind. Paper presented at the American Psychological Association Meeting, Toronto, in the Symposium 'First Encounters of a Pictorial Kind'.

Kosslyn, S.M., Heldmeyer, K.H. and Locklear, E.P. (1977). Children's drawings as data about internal representations. Journal of Experimental Child Psychology, 23, 181-211.

Lewis, H.P. (1963). Spatial representation in drawings as a correlate of development and a basis for picture preference. Journal of Genetic Psychology, 102, 95-105.

Marr, D. (1978). Representing visual information: a computational approach. In: A.R. Hanson and E.M. Riseman (Eds.) Computer Vision. New York: Academic Press.

Marr, D. and Nishihara, H.K. (1978). Representation and recognition of the spatial organization of three-dimensional shapes. Proceedings of the Royal Society, London, B, 200, 269-294.

Minsky, M. and Papert, S. (1972). Artificial Intelligence Progress Report, Memo 252. Cambridge Massachusetts: M.I.T. Artifical Intelligence Laboratory.

Phillips, W.A., Hobbs, S.B. and Pratt, F.R. (1978). Intellectual realism in children's drawings of cubes. Cognition, 6, 15-33.

Piaget, J. and Inhelder, B. (1956). The Child's Conception of Space. London: Routledge and Kegan Paul.

Saenger, E.A. (1981). Drawing Systems: a Developmental Study of Representation. Unpublished doctoral dissertation. Department of Social Psychology, Harvard University.

Willats, J. (1977a). How children learn to draw realistic pictures. Quarterly Journal of Experimental Psychology, 29, 367-382.

Willats, J. (1977b). How children learn to represent three-dimensional space in drawings. In: G. Butterworth (Ed.) The Child's Representation of the World. London: Plenum Press.

Willats, J. (1981a). What do the marks in the picture stand for? The child's acquisition of systems of transformation and denotation. Review of Research in Art Education, 13, 18-33.

Willats, J. (1981b). Formal Structures in Drawing and Painting. Unpublished doctoral dissertation, North East London Polytechnic.

Wollheim, R. (1977). Representation: the philosophical contribution to psychology. In: G. Butterworth (Ed.) The Child's Representation of the World. London: Plenum Press.

Cognitive Processes in the Perception of Art
W.R. Crozier and A.J. Chapman (editors)
© Elsevier Science Publishers B.V. (North-Holland), 1984

PERCEIVING WHAT PAINTINGS EXPRESS

Paula Blank, Christine Massey, Howard Gardner and Ellen Winner

Boston College
Harvard Project Zero
Boston Veterans Administration Medical Center

What skills are needed to perceive 'aesthetic' properties of works of art, and what is the developmental history of these skills? To speak about aesthetic properties of art is not, as it might seem, tautologous. A work of art possesses countless properties, and only some of these, we argue, are relevant to its status as art.

Philosophers have long sought to specify those features which are unique to the arts - features which define works of art and which set them apart from non-works of art (e.g., Bell, 1913; Collingwood, 1938; Kant, 1952). The attempt to determine the necessary and sufficient features of art has, however, remained hopelessly vexed. Definitions have been criticized for their incompleteness, for example defining art as an 'artifact made with human skill' eliminates found art. Definitions have also been faulted for their over-inclusiveness (e.g., defining art as self-expression forces us to include a scream as a work of art).

In our view, the most successful approach to this problem is to be found in the writings of the philosopher Goodman (1976). While acknowledging that art cannot be defined in terms of necessary and sufficient features, Goodman proposes that when objects are treated as works of art, they tend to possess certain properties or 'symptoms'. One of the characteristic (but not necessary) symptoms of work of art is that they are 'replete'. This means that when we view an object as a work of art, more of its physical properties become important than when we are not treating this object as art. For instance, given a line drawing, we pay attention to the quality of the line (its thickness, texture, colour, etc.) as well as to what the line represents. If this same line were part of a diagram, map, or graph (i.e., not functioning as art), we would attend to fewer of the line's physical qualities; its texture and colour, for instance, would be irrelevant and thus usually ignored. In brief, when an object functions aesthetically, more of its properties are relevant than when this object functions outside the arts.

Another symptom of the aesthetic, according to Goodman, is 'metaphorical exemplification' (also called expression). Expressive properties are aspects which paintings convey, but which do not literally form part of the work. For instance, we may sense that a painting is loud, fiery or happy. Such nonvisual properties are not, of course, literally present in the work: a fiery painting is not hot to touch; a loud painting makes no noise; and a sad painting does not itself feel sad. Such terms apply only metaphorically to a painting. A painting literally possesses any number of properties -- its colour and shape, its style and composition. Moreover a representational painting literally denotes the objects presented. But to perceive what a painter expresses, it is necessary to go beyond the literal.

Whenever we go beyond the literal to perceive an object's expressive properties, this object begins to function aesthetically. Expression is not restricted to objects officially labelled as art, but may be found everywhere -- in rocks, trees, sunsets, even in rusted pieces of discarded machinery. Whether an object 'expresses' depends entirely on how we view it. A rock can express (e.g., strength, fierceness, stability) if it is viewed as an aesthetic object. Conversely, a painting can fail to express if the spectator sees only its literal properties (Goodman, 1976).

A third property central to objects when functioning as works of art is composition (cf. Arnheim, 1974). Art objects are structured so that the parts fit together in a balanced whole. Balance need not be (and is usually not) created by symmetry. Instead, balance is usually achieved by pitting the elements of a work against each other so that the parts seem anchored and stable. Of course all objects have some form of composition or structure. But it is primarily in art objects that composition becomes relevant to note.

If repleteness, expression, and composition are key properties of art objects, then viewers ought to perceive these properties when responding to works of art. We have sought to determine whether young children spontaneously perceive these properties, or whether such sensitivity must develop over time. We have undertaken a large scale programme of research to investigate how children respond to these three properties in three major art forms -- painting, literature and music. Through this study, we hope to determine whether sensitivity to aesthetic properties is a primitive (early-developing) or late skill. We also hope to determine whether there exists some form of 'pan-artistic' intelligence. For instance if a child is very sensitive to expression in the visual arts, is he or she also likely to be attuned to expression in other art forms? Or can sensitivity to one art form exist independently of skill in other art forms?

Through this research, we also hope to shed light on the relationship between child and adult art. Young children produce drawings and metaphors that adults perceive as aesthetically pleasing and also as similar in some respects to the works of twentieth century artists (e.g., Miró, Klee and e.e. cummings). Moreover, artists have often turned to children's art as a source of inspiration. The similarity between child and adult art is less often noted in works by older children (Gardner and Winner, 1981). Such works have lost the imagination of earlier works and have become conventionalized and rule-governed. Are young children who produce 'aesthetically pleasing' works sensitive to aesthetic properties? In other words, are their art works accidentally pleasing, or do children possess some control over the aesthetic properties of their works? If children who produce works reminiscent of Klee or Miro are insensitive to repleteness, expression, or composition, then the aesthetic aspects of their works may exist primarily in the eye of the beholder. On the other hand, if young children are sensitive to at least some aesthetic aspects of the arts, then the purported relationship between child and adult cannot be easily dismissed.

In this chapter, we focus on one art form - painting - and one aesthetic property - expression. By what means do works of art express properties that they do not literally possess? One possibility is that paintings express by means of what they literally represent: a painting of a weeping woman expresses sorrow: a painting of a sunny day expresses warmth; and a painting of a skyscraper expresses strength and power. While paintings often express through their content, what is expressed need not rest on what is represented. One can imagine a winter landscape painting that expresses warmth via the use of its colours; and a portrait of a serene-looking person may, through the texture of its paint, convey a sense of tension. But the claim that expression is independent of content is more convincing in the case of abstract works which, while they do not represent, seem always to express. Rothko believed that his paintings, which consist of fields of colour, were able to express the range of human emotions -- 'tragedy, ecstacy, doom' (Lark-Horowitz et al, 1973, p. 229). Even the simplest pattern of line or colour can be viewed in terms of its expressive properties (Arnheim, 1949; Cassirer, 1957); and adults display a high level of agreement about just what properties particular abstract patterns express (Gardner, 1974; Werner and Kaplan, 1963).

Thus, we can conclude that paintings express not only by their content but also - and perhaps more importantly - by their colour, shapes, composition, and texture. For instance, at least in our culture, acute angles are more 'tense' than right angles or curves; crowded compositions are more 'excited' than ones with a great deal of empty space; and bright colours are 'happier' than dark ones. It is quite remarkable that people seem to agree about what moods are expressed by particular configurations of colour, line or shape. How is it, one might rightly ask, that colours and abstract shapes by themselves are able to express moods? Perhaps shapes express because they remind us of postures associated with particular moods: for instance, droopy forms look like the sagging posture associated with sadness; jagged lines remind us of the stiff, forward posture associated with tension. But why should colours express moods? There seems to be no obvious similarity between brightness and joy, or darkness and sorrow. Nonetheless, the phenomenon is real, as everyone can attest. The phenomenon is the more surprising given that we do not have to experience the emotion expressed directly in order to perceive it. A sad picture may make us feel sad, but we need not feel sad to recognize the sadness conveyed by the picture. And certainly a fiery painting does not make our temperature rise.

A child confronted with a painting has no trouble reading what is literally there. Even a young infant sees its colours and forms and recognizes the similarity between two-dimensional pictures of objects and the objects themselves (DeLoache et al, 1979; Hochberg and Brooks, 1962). And, at least by three years of age, children can read depth in pictures (Olson, 1975). Thus, the ability to read pictorial representation is partially present at birth, and fully there a few years later. But what about the ability to perceive what is not literally there, to perceive what is only metaphorically there?

There have been a few studies of the child's ability to perceive expression in the visual arts. Children as young as three and four have been shown to be able to match nonvisual labels (e.g., happy/sad, or loud/quiet) to pairs of colours or lines, for instance, pre-school children tend to respond as do adults. Yellow is happy, violet is sad, thick lines are loud, thin ones are quiet. Thus, at least the rudiments of the ability to perceive expression are present by three years of age.

The ability to perceive expressed properties depends on the recognition of similarities between elements from different domains of experience. To perceive yellow as happy, for instance, one must be able to note connections between visual experiences and psychological ones; to perceive lines as loud, connections must be perceived between visual and auditory experiences.

Some such cross-modal connections may be perceived at a very early age, and this ability may perhaps even be innate. For instance, infants as young as one month can detect similarities between degrees of brightness and parallel levels of loudness (Lewkowicz and Turkewitz, 1980). And infants as young as nine months can detect links between broken lines and pulsing sounds, or between ascending arrows and ascending tones (Wagner et al, 1981). Thus, the raw ability to perceive auditory properties expressed in visual patterns may be innate. To date, no one has examined the onset of the ability to perceive psychological properties (e.g., moods) expressed in visual stimuli.

The ability to perceive expressive properties in simple abstract stimuli may be a far cry from the ability to detect those same properties in actual works of art. A few studies have explored children's ability to perceive expression using paintings and drawings as stimuli. While it is not until preadolescence that children spontaneously begin to describe expressive properties in paintings (Machotka, 1966), children have the capacity to perceive such properties at an earlier age (Carothers and Gardner, 1979). Ten-year-olds (but not seven-year-olds) are able to complete a picture of a representationally sad picture (a sad person) with an expressively sad tree and flowers (dead and wilting), and, conversely, a picture of a happy person with an expressively happy tree and flowers (alive and blooming).

Although seven-year-olds fail to complete a sad picture with expressively sad tree and flowers this does not allow us to conclude that they do not perceive the expressive properties of the tree and flowers. Perhaps they perceive the wilted flowers as sad but do not consider it important that a picture of a sad person contains elements that also express this emotion. A more direct test of the ability to perceive expression is one in which pictures expressing certain properties (e.g., happiness) must be matched to verbal labels (e.g., 'happy'). Taunton (1980) carried out such a study. Four-year-olds were shown sets of three pictures (reproductions of paintings) and were asked to select the one best described by one or two labels. For instance, given three paintings, children had to decide which one was 'hot'. If they failed to select the one considered appropriate by the designers of the task (graduate students in art education), they were given a second term (e.g., 'happy). The four-year-olds were able to select the appropriate picture at a level above chance, even with only the first verbal label. However, only a few children could justify their selections.

Some problems in the design of this study preclude the conclusion that pre-school children can perceive expression in paintings. The major problem was that not all of the terms used referred to expressive properties. The terms 'hot' and 'happy', to be matched to an abstract expressionist painting, certainly refer to expressive properties. However, other terms used in this study referred to literal rather than expressive properties. For instance, 'sneaky' and 'mean' were to be matched to a portrait painting (referring to the mood literally represented) and 'tired' and 'resting' were to be matched to a painting of a person reading (again suggesting properties that might be literally true of the depicted person). Thus children could have succeeded on many items simply by applying the terms literally. The reasons given by the children to explain their choices suggest that this is precisely the strategy adopted. For instance, 'tired' was matched to the painting of a person reading because 'she was reading a book and got tired'; 'fearful' was matched to a landscape painting including people because 'they are scared of that big rock'; and 'heavy' was matched to an abstract work with thick dark brush strokes because 'it's a suitcase with treasure'. Never, it appears, did children mention formal properties (e.g., 'heavy' because it is dark, or 'fearful' because of jagged lines). And when a few children volunteered to supply their own labels for pictures, they offered literal, content-oriented ones (e.g., 'beard') rather than expressive ones.

In our research, we sought to rectify this problem. We examined children's abilities to perceive moods expressed in abstract paintings. Abstract works were used so that children could not succeed by attending to content literally depicted. In a verbal task, children were asked to match a mood term to one of two abstract paintings presented as a pair. Since it is possible that children may perceive moods in paintings but perceive ones different from those noted by adults, we also devised a nonverbal task. A different set of children saw the same pairs of abstract paintings and were asked to match one of the members of each pair to a representational picture on the basis of similarity in mood. If children find it easier to group pictures by mood than to apply a mood label to a work, we can conclude that children perceive expression but do not use adult vocabulary to describe what they see.

We examined two mood dimensions: happiness (happy vs. sad) and excitement (excited vs. calm). These two contrasts were selected because they are among the most basic psychological dimensions differentiated by children and adults (Osgood et al, 1957). Moreover, we suspect that many paintings can be placed along one or both of these dimensions. To determine whether the ability to perceive expression was affected by the existence of a sharp mood contrast in the surrounding context, we developed two kinds of items. In half, we pitted pictures rated by adults as extremely happy (or excited) against ones rated as extremely sad (or calm). In the other half, the contrast was muted (e.g., somewhat happy vs. a tinge of sadness). We expected the context to prove important: only when a picture was pitted against its extreme opposite did we expect pre-schoolers to succeed.

To determine whether the ability to perceive expression was facilitated when all other salient factors were held constant, we constructed half of the items so that the members of a pair were painted by the same artist in the same style (e.g., a happy vs. a sad Rothko). In the other half, the members of a pair were painted by different artists in different styles (e.g., a Miró vs. a Soulages). We expected it to be easier to perceive the mood of a work when it was pitted against another work similar in all salient respects except mood. When paintings also differed in style, we expected children to be distracted from the task at hand. (Table 1 presents the study design schematically.)

Finally, in order to determine whether children could talk about expressive properties, we asked them to explain the choices that they made. The reasons given were classified into a number of different categories. If children could offer appropriate reasons for their selections, we could then rule out chance as a factor contributing to apparent success.

We administered the tasks to 30 children at each of ages 5, 6, 8 and 10 years (30 at each age, approximately equally divided between boys and girls). The children were selected at random from their classrooms, and no attempt was made to find children who were gifted in the visual arts.

TABLE 1

Design of Study

	HIGH CONTRAST	LOW CONTRAST
Same Style	4 items, 1 of each mood*	4 items, 1 of each mood*
Different Style	4 items, 1 of each mood*	4 items, 1 of each mood*

* Happy, sad, excited, calm.

To construct the items used in this study, we showed adults a series of abstract paintings and asked them to decide for each work whether it was predominantly happy, sad, excited or calm. After determining the mood most clearly conveyed by a work, these judges were then asked to rate, on an 8 point scale, the intensity of the mood expressed by each work. Only those items on which 9 out of 10 adults concurred were used.

Colour slides were made of 16 pairs of paintings. These pairs were constructed so that the 2 members of each pair contrasted in mood, either on the dimension of happiness (happy vs. sad) or on the dimension of excitement and tension (excited vs. calm). In addition, in half of the pairs the 2 members contrasted sharply in mood: one member was rated as extremely sad (or calm) while the other member was rated as extremely happy (or excited). The other half contrasted more subtly -- happy vs. a little sad, or mildly exciting vs. somewhat calm. Those which contrasted sharply were rated between 5 to 7 points apart on the 8 point scale; subtly contrasting items were rated only 1, 2, or 3 points apart.

Finally the pairs varied in style contrast. In half, the 2 members of a pair were by the same artist and were painted in the same style; in the other half of the items, the 2 members were by different artists and represented different styles. Thus, items differed according to 3 factors: mood dimension (happy-sad vs. excited-calm), degree of mood contrast (high vs. low), and similarity of style (same vs. different).

Fifteen children at each age were given a verbal labelling task: 18 were given a matching task. In the labelling task, children were shown the 16 pairs (in random order) and were asked to point to the one that was 'happier' or 'sadder' (for happy-sad items) or 'more excited' or 'calmer' (for excited calm items). The following instructions were used:
Are you in a good mood today? You know, sometimes people can have all kinds of moods and feelings. They can feel happy and full of fun, or sad and all alone; they can feel calm and relaxed, or excited and full of energy. Sometimes, pictures have a way of showing these moods and feelings too. I'm going to show you two pictures at a time, and ask you to pick the one that shows a certain mood.

It is possible that children may perceive a mood expressed by a painting, yet use different vocabulary to describe this mood than that used by adults. For instance, a child might see a painting that adults consider to express calm as expressing sadness or boredom instead. Thus, in the matching task children were shown each pair of slides along with a representational painting that had been previously rated by adults as either happy, sad, excited or calm (hereafter called the 'target). The task in this case was to select the member of the abstract pair that was most similar in mood to the target. For the 8 happy-sad pairs, 4 happy and 4 sad targets were used, for the 8 excited-calm pairs, 4 excited and 4 calm targets were used.

Every effort was made in the construction of items to insure that matches could not be made on some obvious basis besides mood. Because the targets were representational and the choices abstract, content matches were avoided. In addition, the possibility of matching by colour was eliminated: coloured targets were presented with black and white choices, and black and white targets were presented with coloured choices.

The targets were presented in the form of enlarged photographs. For each item, the target was placed on a table immediately in front of the child. The 2 slides were then projected onto a screen. Thus, children could easily look back from target to slides and vice versa. The following instructions were used to introduce the matching task:

> Are you in a good mood today? You know sometimes people can have all kinds of moods and feelings. They feel happy, or scared or angry or sad; they can feel bored, or nervous; they can feel sleepy or full of energy. Sometimes, pictures have a way of showing these moods and feelings too. I'm going to show you a picture, and ask you to think about what mood or feeling it shows. Then I'm going to show you two other pictures on the wall in front of you. I want you to pick which of the pictures on the wall has the same kind of mood as the first one I show you.

It is possible to select the correct picture by guessing. Indeed, a child who relied entirely on guessing would achieve a score of about 50% in either condition. This is a problem with any multiple-choice test, and must be taken into consideration in the interpretation of scores. To provide a measure on which one could not succeed by guessing, we also asked children to justify each choice made. After each item selection, children were asked: 'Why did you pick that one?' The types of reasons given were then categorized into kinds of appropriate or inappropriate responses.

While a task in which children are asked to give reasons for their choices avoids the problem of chance success, it introduces the opposite problem: children may fail to supply an appropriate reason even though they have correctly perceived the mood in a work. In this case, failure is not due to an insensitivity to expression in art but to an inability to talk about it -- either to name the mood, or to say why a certain mood is conveyed. Thus, while the choice scores may overrepresent children's sensitivity to expression, an analysis of the reasons given may underrepresent it. Because each of these measures by itself has a limitation, we thought it best to use both, and to weigh them against each other.

As indicated above, in this study there were 3 between-subject factors (Age, Condition, and Sex) and 3 within-subject factors (Mood - happy, sad, excited, calm; Contrast - high, low; Style - same, different). Because we could include no more than 16 items in either condition (due to time constraints in the administration of the task), it was not possible to examine the interaction of all 3 within-subject factors. Any such interaction would be based on only one item per cell. Thus, separate analyses were performed first with Mood, and then with Contrast and Style as the within-subject factors. Only those results significant at p .01 are reported below.

A 3-way (Age x Condition x Mood) analysis of variance was performed on the number of correct choices, with Mood as the repeated measures factor. All 3 main effects were significant: Age ($F = 17.15$; $df=3,104$; $p<.001$); Condition ($F = 17.49$; $df=1,104$; $p<.001$); Mood ($F = 6.64$; $df=3,312$; $p<.001$). The age effect was due to a steady increase with age in frequency of correct scores. Using the binomial probability test, we were able to determine that the scores of even the youngest children were significantly above chance ($p<.01$) in both tasks. The Condition effect occurred because the labelling task proved easier than the matching task. The Mood effect occurred because the lowest scores were elicited by items in which children had to select either the calm or the happy picture. However, a Condition x Mood interaction ($F = 7.81$; $df= 3,312$; $p<.01$) revealed that calm items were only difficult on the matching task: on the labelling task, calm items proved as easy as sad and excited ones. Moreover, although happy items were difficult in both tasks, they were considerably less difficult than were the calm items on the matching task (See Figure 1).

To examine the effect of Contrast and Style, the same analysis was repeated, this time with 2 within-subject factors (Contrast and Style). Only effects involving these factors are reported below, as all other effects duplicate those already reported.

There was a main effect of Contrast ($F = 43.10$; $df=1,104$; $p<.001$). As predicted, items with a high contrast between moods yielded higher scores than those characterized by low contrast. Contrast interacted with Condition ($F = 8.11$; $df=1,105$; $p=.005$). This interaction revealed that the greater ease of the high-contrast items occurred primarily in the Labelling task. In the Matching task, presumably because of its overall difficulty, high contrast items failed to elevate performance.

While there was no main effect of Style, this factor interacted with Condition ($F = 3.43$; $df=1,104$; $p=.067$). Contrary to prediction, in the Labelling Condition, items whose members were characterized by different styles were easier than some style items. However, in the Matching Condition, there was no difference between the two.

The kinds of reasons with which children justified their choices were classified into a number of different categories. Occasionally children gave more than one reason for a particular choice. In this case, all reasons were analysed. If the reasons fell into the same category, then only one reason score was given. However, if the reasons given represented more than one type of response, more than one reason score was given.

The reasons given following correct choices in the both Conditions were classified into 3 categories: Appropriate; Inappropriate - Related to Mood; and Inappropriate - Unrelated to Mood. In the Labelling task, the only type of response considered appropriate was one in which subjects identified those formal properties (e.g., colour, line, composition) that are the means by which moods are expressed -- for example justifying a work as happy because of its bright colours, or sad because of its dark lines. It is difficult to imagine how else one could respond appropriately when asked to explain why a picture is perceived as expressing a particular mood. Indeed, when the task was piloted with adults, this was the most frequent type of reason given.

FIGURE 1

Mean number of correct choices on each task for each mood.

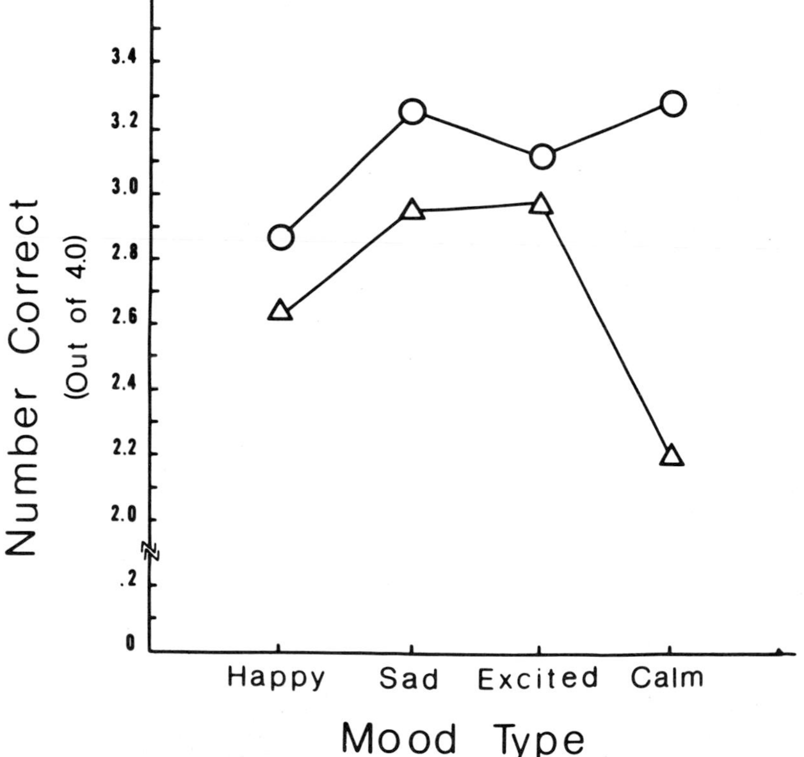

Five types of reasons given in the Labelling task were considered inappropriate yet related to mood. The mood term given by the experimenter might be repeated (a picture was chosen as happy 'because it is happy') or paraphrased (a picture was chosen as happy 'because its laughing'). Some mood-related content might be imagined in the abstract work (e.g., a picture is happy 'because it looks like a fun party'). Or the child might justify a work as expressing a particular mood by referring either to the artist's mood while painting (e.g., a picture is excited 'because the person who drew it was 'nervous') or to the mood that the work creates in the perceiver (e.g., a picture is happy 'because it makes me happy'). The latter 2 types of response are inappropriate because, like the other inappropriate but mood related reasons, these simply repeat or paraphrase the mood term supplied by the experimenter.

Two types of reasons given in the Labelling task were considered inappropriate and also unrelated to mood: content reasons, in which a child pointed to some imagined object in the work that is irrelevant to mood (e.g., noting a form that looks like a hat); and responses in which the child gave no reason at all or gave some unscorable or idiosyncratic reason. A description and frequency count of the 3 reason categories and sub-categories is given in Table 2.

As can be seen in Table 2, the most common reasons given at all ages in the Labelling task were appropriate ones. The frequency of appropriate reasons increased between 5 and 6 years, and between 8 and 10 years. However, even 5-year-olds offered formal reasons over one-third of the time. This finding buttresses the statistical fact, reported above, that the scores of the youngest children were significantly above chance.

It might be objected that formal reasons are not indicative of a sensitivity to expression. Perhaps the youngest children adopted a strategy of simply describing the physical characteristics of a picture when asked to give a reason for a particular selection. When this strategy follows a correct choice, one might argue, the response gives the false impression that children are sensitive to the means by which moods are expressed.

However, if children were simply describing the colours and lines in the picture without noticing their connection to the mood expressed, one would expect formal reasons to be as likely to support incorrect as correct choices. But this did not occur. Five-year-olds gave formal reasons almost twice as often following correct choices (70 times) as they did following incorrect choices (43 times). Thus, we can conclude that formal reasons are at least not entirely the result of the above-described strategy.

We can conclude that the reasons offered by children as young as 5 indicate considerable sensitivity to the means by which moods are expressed in paintings. Moreover, when one considers that a perceiver may sense the mood expressed in a work without being able to pinpoint and/or verbalize the formal properties responsible, the performance of the 5-year-olds begins to look even better.

TABLE 2

Reasons given following correct choice in labelling condition.

	REASON TYPE	DEFINITION	EXAMPLE	AGE GROUP 5	6	8	10	TOTAL
I.	Appropriate (Total=535)							
A	Formal	Formal properties of work relevant to mood are noted	H*:This has brighter colours' S: 'The lines are darker'	70	133	147	185	535
II.	Inappropriate - Related to Mood (TOTAL=419)							
A.	Repetition	Mood term supplied is repeated	H:'This one is happy' E:'It's excited'	29	36	85	48	198
B.	Paraphrase	Mood term is paraphrased	H:'It's laughing' E:'It's jumping around'	18	21	18	33	90
C.	Content	Person or event displaying relevant mood is described	H:'It looks like a fun party' C:'There's someone sleeping'	13	17	19	21	70
D.	Artist's Mood	Artist was in relevant mood when painting	E:'The person who drew it was nervous' H:'The person who drew it was in a good mood	0	4	22	22	48
E.	Perceiver's Mood	Work creates relevant mood in perceiver	H:'It makes me happy' E:'It makes me nervous'	3	2	4	4	13
			TOTAL	63	80	148	128	419

TABLE 2 (Continued).

III. Inappropriate - Unrelated to Mood (TOTAL=136)

	REASON TYPE	DEFINITION	EXAMPLE	5	6	8	10	TOTAL
A.	Content	Object unrelated to mood is located in abstract work	S:'There's a hat in it' C:'It's a person and a tree'	16	14	16	11	57
B.	Other	No response; unscorable		43	30	3	3	79
			TOTAL	59	44	19	14	136

* H,S,E,C refer to type of item for which reason was given (Happy, Sad, Excited, Calm).

The reasons given following correct choices in the Matching task were also classified into the 3 categories used in the Labelling task. These major categories were divided into subcategories somewhat different from those used in the Labelling task. Included as appropriate reasons were both formal reasons (as in the Labelling task) and ones in which the choice was described as expressing a mood (e.g., a picture was matched to a target representing a person smiling because 'it (the choice) is gay'). (The latter type of response could not be considered appropriate in the Labelling task since subjects were given the mood term and asked to find the work expressing this mood.) Children did not have to use the terms happy, sad, excited or calm to achieve a mood response -- any mood term, whether or not it was related to our classification of the item, was counted.

Inappropriate reasons related to mood include 3 of those used in the Labelling task: imagining some mood-related content, referring to the artist's mood, and referring to the perceiver's mood. (The other 2 types of reason in this category used in Labelling were not relevant to Matching). Inappropriate reasons unrelated to mood included those used in Labelling as well as 2 additional ones: target-matches, in which a work was selected because of some slight formal similarity between target and choice (e.g., 'both have squiggly lines') and target-associations, in which a work was selected because of some thematic associations between target and choice (e.g., this (target) is a boat and this (choice) is the map of the place he's going). The items were constructed so as to avoid any obvious physical similarities or thematic associations between the target and one of the choices. However, it is always possible to find some minor physical similarity between 2 works, or some association between the imagined content of 2 works. A description and frequency count of the 3 reason categories and sub-categories is given in Table 3.

TABLE 3

Reasons given following correct choice in matching condition.

	REASON TYPE	DEFINITION	EXAMPLE	AGE GROUP 5	6	8	10	TOTAL
I.	Appropriate (Total=586)							
A.	Formal	Formal properties of work relevant to mood are noted	H*:'This one is brighter'	52	44	61	119	276
B.	Mood	Mood of abstract work identified either directly (ex.1) or indirectly (ex.2)	H:'It's happy' S:'It's crying'	82	67	51	110	310
			TOTAL	134	111	112	229	586
II.	Inappropriate: Related to Mood (Total=105)							
A.	Content	Person or event (in abstract work) displaying relevant mood is described	S:'It looks like a funeral' E:'People are racing around'	10	6	15	20	51
B.	Artist's Mood	Artist was in relevant mood when painting	H:'He was happy when he made it' S:'The artist felt sad'	0	0	2	10	30
C.	Perceiver's Mood	Work creates relevant mood in perceiver	H:'It makes me happy' E:'It makes me nervous'	15	5	1	3	24
			TOTAL	25	11	18	33	105

TABLE 3 (Continued)

III. Inappropriate: Unrelated to Mood (Total=189)

	REASON TYPE	DEFINITION	EXAMPLE	5	6	8	10	TOTAL
A.	Content	Object unrelated to mood is located in abstract work	S:'There's a pile of rocks here' C:'These are blocks'	16	16	6	4	42
B.	Target-Match	Similarity between target and choice unrelated to mood is noted	H:'Both have spots' E:'There's a hat in both'	7	9	25	11	52
C.	Target-Association	Association between target and choice is made	E:'He (in target) is in a boat and these (in choice) are the places he's going' C:'This (in target) is a baby and babies like blocks and this one (choice) has more blocks	2	3	9	4	18
D.	Other	No response; Unscorable		22	34	18	3	77
			TOTAL	47	62	58	22	189

(*H,S,E,C refer to type of item for which reason was given (Happy, Sad, Excited, Calm).

As can be seen, at all ages appropriate reasons following correct choices far outnumbered inappropriate ones in the Matching task. Moreover 5-year-olds were as likely as 6-and 8-year-olds to offer appropriate reasons. (In fact, 5-year-olds gave slightly more appropriate reasons than did 6- and 8-year-olds!) Only the 10-year-olds gave more (and they gave considerably more) appropriate reasons than did the 5-year-olds. Once again, the fact that appropriate responses far outnumbered inappropriate ones buttresses the statistical claim that the scores of all age groups exceed what would be expected by guessing.

As mentioned above, any mood term justifying a match between a target and a choice qualified as a mood reason (one of the two appropriate types of reasons). It was thus possible to achieve such a score by describing a work very differently from our mood classification. For all but the calm items, children used mood terms similar to those by which the items were classified. Thus, works that we selected as happy were described as happy, joyful, funny, or silly; works selected by us as sad were described as sad, happy, lonely, depressed, upset, sorry, dismal, or dreary; and works selected by us as excited were described by the children as exciting, wild, restless, angry, mad, scary or crazy, rushing, or jumping. Calm items, however, presented a different profile. While children sometimes identified these items as did adults (as calm, quiet, dull, bored, peaceful, lazy, gentle, or sleeping) calm items were more often than not 'misidentified' by the youngest subjects as sad. A few children described calm items as happy, as 'not quite happy and not quite sad', or as having no mood at all. Recall that in the Matching task, children were least likely to make a correct choice given a calm target. Thus, it appears that children showed particular difficulty both in perceiving a shared mood between two 'calm' works, and in describing works as calm (or by some related term).

The results of this study demonstrate a high level of ability in children as young as five. Even pre-schoolers could perceive expressive properties in abstract paintings. Moreover, children described the moods expressed in happy, sad and excited works in terms similar to ones used by adult. It is only with paintings expressing a sense of calm that children appeared to perceive a different mood from that seen by adults. Where adults perceived a mood of calm, 5-year-olds perceived a mood of sadness, or they simply lacked the productive vocabulary to talk about calm works and resorted instead to terms such as 'sad'. It appears that, with respect to the visual arts, it is the child's production skills -- but not perceptual skills -- that set the child apart from the adult.

The role of context in highlighting the moods perceived was also demonstrated. When the 2 paintings pitted against each other contrasted sharply in mood, children were better able to perceive the mood of both works. A comparison to adults can be made here. While adults can perceive expressive properties even when the contrast with another work is subtle, the context of a work affects which mood(s) is perceived. Thus, Mondrian's 'Broadway Boogie Woogie' appears excited, almost frenzied, when contrasted to his more typical severe works; however, next to an abstract expressionist work, the Mondrian expresses orderliness, calm and repose (Gombrich, 1960).

Contrary to expectation, pitting works against each other that are similar in all salient respects except mood did not facilitate performance. The same-style pairs proved more difficult than the different-style pairs. It appears as if children were overwhelmed by the stylistic similarity between the 2 works in the former type. Blinded by the stylistic resemblance, they proved unable to detect the expressive difference. This same result has been demonstrated in the domain of music (Davidson et al, 1983).

How do these findings compare with other findings growing out of the research programme described earlier? Not all of the studies have been completed, so it is not yet possible to discuss patterns across the 3 properties and the 3 art forms. However, a few comparisons can now be made. To begin with, the perception of expression seems to be a very early emerging skill in music as well as in the visual arts (Davidson et al, 1983).

We do not yet know whether young children will be able to detect expressive properties in literature. However, we expect verbal expression to prove more difficult to detect because the denotational content of literature (its semantic meaning) is likely to interfere with the recognition of moods expressed by the rhythm or connotation of the words. We predict that only when the semantic content buttresses the expressive content will young children recognize literary mood. And if this is the only condition under which moods are noted, then we will be forced to conclude that children are responding to the semantic but not the expressive content of a verbal work.

Within the visual arts, expression appears to be perceived at a younger age than is repleteness (Blank et al, 1983). The same appears to be true with respect to music. Sensitivity to repleteness calls for attention to fine details in and of themselves; sensitivity to expression calls for a sensitivity to fine details only in so far as they convey moods. It appears as if children can respond to often minute stylistic differences more readily when these properties express differences in mood.

In our view, the most important conclusion to be drawn from this study is as follows. The fact that children can perceive expression in the visual arts at a young age means that the expressive properties that adults perceive in child art may be put there intentionally. This is a strong claim. A weaker claim, one more firmly supported by the present findings, is that young children are aware of the expressive properties in their works once they have produced them. Thus, the young child artist is similar in at least one respect to the adult artist.

ACKNOWLEDGMENTS

This research was supported by a grant to Ellen Winner from the Spencer Foundation. We are grateful to Nathan Knobler, of the Philadelphia College of Art, for help in the conceptualization of this study, and to Joseph Walters for assistance with data analysis. We thank Arnold Lanni, Assistant Superintendent of Schools, Arlington, Massachusetts; Mary Murphy Principal of the Dallin School, Arlington, Massachusetts; Joan Warren, Principal of the Bishop School, Arlington, Massachusetts; Frank Peros, Department of Art Education, Watertown Public Schools, Watertown, Massachusetts; and all of the teachers and students from the Arlington Public Schools who participated in this study.

REFERENCES

Arnheim, R. (1949). The Gestalt theory of expression. Psychological Review, 56, 156-171.

Arnheim, R. (1974). Art and Visual Expression. Berkeley, California: University of California Press.

Bell, C. (1913). Art. New York: F.A. Stokes.

Blank, P., Massey, C., Gardner, H. and Winner, E. (1983). Children's sensitivity to aesthetic properties of line drawings. Leonardo (in press).

Carothers, T. and Gardner, H. (1979). When children's drawings become art: the emergence of aesthetic production and perception. Developmental Psychology, 15, 570-580.

Cassirer, E. (1957). Philosophy of Symbolic Forms. New Haven, Connecticut: Yale University Press.

Collingwood, R. (1938). The Principles of Art. Oxford: Clarendon Press.

Davidson, L., Hall, J., Gardner, H. and Winner, E. (1983). Perceiving expression in music. Paper presented at the British Psychological Society, Welsh Branch, International Conference on Psychology and the Arts, Cardiff, Wales.

DeLoache, J., Strauss, M. and Maynard, J. (1979). Picture perception in infancy. Infant Behavior and Development, 2, 77-89.

Gardner, H. (1974). Metaphors and modalities: how children project polar adjectives onto diverse domains. Child Development, 45, 84-91.

Gardner, H. and Winner, E. (1981). First intimations of artistry. In: S. Strauss (Ed.) U-Shaped Behavioral Growth. New York: Academic Press.

Gombrich, E.H. (1960). Art and Illusion. Princeton, New Jersey: Princeton University Press.

Goodman, N. (1976). Languages of Art. Indianapolis, Indiana: Hackett.

Hochberg, J. and Brooks, V. (1962). Pictorial recognition as an unlearned ability: a study of one child's performance. American Journal of Psychology, 75, 624-628.

Kant, I. (1952). Critique of Judgment. Oxford: Clarendon Press.

Lark-Horowitz, B., Lewis, H. and Luca, M. (1973). Understanding Children's Art for Better Teaching. Second Edition. Columbus: Merrill.

Lewkowicz, D. and Turkewitz, G. (1980). Cross-modal equivalence in early infancy: auditory-visual intensity matching. Developmental Psychology, 16, 597-607.

Machotka, P. (1966). Aesthetic criteria in childhood: justifications of preference. Child Development, 37, 877-885.

Olson, R. (1975). Children's sensitivity to pictorial depth information. Perception and Psychophysics, 17, 59-64.

Osgood, C., Suci, G. and Tannenbaum, P. (1957). The Measurement of Meaning. Urbana: University of Illinois Press.

Taunton, M. (1980). An Initial Inquiry into Four-Year-Old Children's Understanding of Expressive Interpretations of Painting Reproductions. Paper presented at the National Symposium for Research in Art, University of Illinois, Urbana-Champaign.

Wagner, S., Winner, E., Cicchetti, D. and Gardner, H. (1981). 'Metaphorical' mapping in human infants. Child Development, 52, 728-731.

Werner, H. and Kaplan, B. (1963). Symbol Formation. New York: Wiley.

Cognitive Processes in the Perception of Art
W.R. Crozier and A.J. Chapman (editors)
© Elsevier Science Publishers B.V. (North-Holland), 1984

DEVELOPMENT OF MUSICAL SCHEMATA IN CHILDREN'S SPONTANEOUS SINGING

W. Jay Dowling

University of Texas at Dallas

During their second year children typically begin to sing spontaneously in a way clearly distinguishable from speech. I believe that regularities in the structure of these songs provide evidence for mental schemata controlling song production. In this chapter I describe the general pattern of development of children's singing, and then present an analysis of the spontaneous songs of two children illustrating schematic control over the melodic and rhythmic contours of the phrases used in the songs. Finally, I present a brief study of the children's memory for some of their own songs.

CHILDREN'S SINGING

Moog (1976) provides the most extensive description of the child's early music behaviour that we have. My observations are in general agreement with his. During the first year of life a baby produces babbling songs that are difficult to distinguish from the babbling of speech sounds. The infant uses this vocal play to explore the range of possibilities of the voice for pitch loudness and timbre. During the second year, as speech comes to be used increasingly for verbal communication, there is an increase in vocalizations that are clearly recognizable as songs. These early songs are different from speech in their use of discrete pitch intervals between more or less steady pitches of sustained vowel sounds, and in being rhythmically organized by a steady beat (at least within phrases). The pitch intervals the child uses are not those of the adult scale systems. The pitch wanders and sounds 'out of tune' to the adult ear. The wandering of the pitch involves both a high variability of interval sizes and a drift of what sounds to the adult like a 'tonal centre'. Identifiable variants of the 'same' song recur in the child's singing behaviour over periods of days or weeks, and then disappear to be replaced by new patterns. I have not observed any spontaneous song recurring over periods greater than 6 weeks, nor do such songs ever find their way into the basic repertoire of nursery tunes known to the average preschooler.

Table 1 lists the major points in this outline of the early development of the child's singing and of what typical songs are like around the age of 2 years. I have indicated with a 'Yes' in the column under each of 6 treatments ofearly childhood singing instances where their observations appear congruent with my general outline. Where there seemed to be no basis for deciding what the author thought, I have left a blank. I indicated disagreements with a 'No'. There are two areas of disagreement. Moorhead et al (1941-51) appear not to think the beat is as steady as I do. They contrast 'songs' with what they call 'chants' (of which more below), with the song characterized by 'its free and flexible rhythm (that of chant being rigidly confined in a beat structure)' (p.41). In my observations I found the beat nearly always to be steady within phrases, and often steady across phrases. The main exceptions to the latter were when the child paused for a breath or to think. The steadiness of beat was the most striking feature that distinguished songs from speech. In songs, speech rhythms appear adapted to the beat, rather than vice versa. In fact the adaptation of the speech rhythms of the words the child is singing to the beat structure of the song is the main source of rhythmic complexity in these songs.

TABLE 1

Observation of Various Features of Children's Singing. Reported in Previous Studies.

	STUDY					
	BENTLEY (1966)	DAVIDSON et al (1981)	MOOG (1976)	MOORHEAD et al. (1945-51)	OSTWALD (1973)	REVESZ (1954)
FEATURE:						
Babbling songs before 1 year		YES	YES		YES	
Increased singing between 1 and 2			YES			YES
Discrete pitches	YES	YES	YES	YES		YES
Pitch Wanders	YES	YES	YES	YES	YES	YES
Steady beat within phrase	YES		YES	NO		
Songs recur		NO				YES

The other dissension from the general picture I have been presenting is by Davidson et al (1981) concerning the memorability and recurrence of spontaneous songs during the second year. Davidson et al see external standard songs as the main source of ordered patterns in the child's singing behaviour during the second year. They characterize early spontaneous songs as 'unpredictable and unmemorable', and suggest that 'to the extent that (such a) tune exists at all as a recognizable entity, it does so on the basis of its lyrics, not its tonal or rhythmic structure'. In contrast, I have observed recurrences of distinctive spontaneous song patterns over periods of up to 3 weeks around age 1:6 in the 2 children studied. Even at that age the child knows how she puts a song together -- she remembers a song pattern, a schema. In fact, I found considerable evidence, here in agreement with the observations of Davidson et al, that when 2-year-olds produce standard songs they provide versions filtered through (or 'assimilated to') their own internal schemata.

MUSICAL DEVELOPMENT

These investigations were carried out in the context of existing theory and data indicating that the child develops the cognitive components of adult auditory information processing piece by piece over the first 8 years of life. Elsewhere (Dowling, 1982) I have reviewed evidence for a pattern of schema acquisition in which melodic contours (in the sense of ups and downs of pitch) are important even at the earliest ages, while the importance of stable tonal centres (the tonics of keys) appears later, around the age of 5 or 6. Still later, perhaps around 7 or 8, the child develops a sensitivity to the intervals of the musical scale and to violations of that pattern. This characterization of auditory cognitive development, in which the child is seen as acquiring components of adult cognitive skills that are retained and elaborated throughout life (rather than, say, discarded or radically restructured) is very similar to the general approach suggested by Keil (1981). And Krumhansl and Keil (1982) have provided a nice example of the child's continued growth in auditory sophistication through the elementary school years in the acquisition of more and more subtle differentiations in the hierarchical organization of the tonal scale system -- at each step adding on to the pattern that was there before.

Infants notice changes in melodic contours, and melodic and rhythmic contours dominate perception and performance during the preschool years. (There is even better evidence for the infant's ability to detect contour changes than when I wrote the earlier review. Trehub et al (in press) have shown that 9-month-olds can indicate contour changes with a conditioned head turning response. From this characterization of the child's acquisition of song patterns we would expect that the main thrust of the child's control over songs during the first 5 years of life would be in the direction of controlling melodic contours. That is, there is little control during these developmental periods over pitch consistency in the sense of a tonal centre or of scale intervals. The main focus of this chapter is on the analysis of contour control in spontaneous songs in age range from 1:0 to 3:6 years. I took repetition of phrase contours as evidence for schematic control of phrases, and in the following analysis I looked for evidence of organization of those phrases under the control of higher-level schemata. Essentially I was looking for clues to the syntax of the child's early language. But before turning to the analysis of the songs I wish to discuss briefly the notion of 'schema' and what I mean by it in this context.

SCHEMATA

I use the term 'schemata' to refer to systematic patterns in the 'abstract knowledge listeners have about musical structure', to borrow a phrase from Krumhansl and Castellano's (1983, p.325) useful discussion of the term. They suggest that 'schema' be used to refer to those aspects of abstract musical knowledge that are engaged in the perceptual process. In that sense a schema is like a description of regularities of stimulus structure that hold across numerous particular pieces of music. In this chapter I emphasize the function of schemata in controlling patterns on the output side, in governing song production. Production schemata are like 'plans' by which behaviour is generated. It may be that the same or similar schemata function in both aspects of music congition; that is, that there are truly 'sensori-motor' schemata underlying music perception and production. Such a possibility seems plausible, but further converging evidence is needed.

Another dimension involved in the characterization of schemata is that of the level of psychological reality they are thought to have. In terms reminiscent of Chomsky's (1965) outline of levels of reality for the syntax of a language, we might ask whether a schema is intended to function (1) simply as an efficient description of regularities of the external stimulus structure; or (2) as description of the knowledge the singer and listener has of the stimulus structure; or (3) as a description of the actual process by which that knowledge of the stimulus structure is applied. For verification description (1) would seem to refer to musiciological data, (2) to the sort of psychological data we have most readily available from scaling and memory tasks, and (3) to sorts of psychological data that we often wish we had more of but usually lack, that provide insights into underlying psychological processes. The types of schemata I discuss here mostly aim at level (2), being plans for the production of songs that display the knowledge the child has at a given stage of development concerning how a song should be constructed.

SONG SAMPLES

My two daughters, Calla and Erica, were born respectively on 10th June 1977 and 8th June 1979. Beginning in March 1978, I began to record samples of their vocalizations regularly, and I am continuing to do so. The observations reported below are based on recordings up to June 1982. The recordings were stereophonic and were made principally with a Superscope CS-200 portable casette recorder using its built-in condenser microphones, and with a TEAC CX-315 cassette tape deck using Sony ECM-200 condenser microphones. Occasionally I used a Superscope CD-302A cassette tape deck with the Sony microphones. I used Dolby noise-reduction with the latter two machines. The recordings were made on high-quality 90 minute cassette tape: early in the sequence for the most part on TDK D-C90 or Memorex MRX-1 (120 microsec bias); later in the sequence exclusively on Maxell UDXL-II-C90 or TDK SA-X-C90 (70 msec bias).

During the earlier years, before the children became used to the tape-recorder, the songs were sometimes hard to capture. Spontaneous songs are elusive in the sense that they occur at odd moments and the children are easily distracted from singing them. Moog (1976) cites the example of a mother who sang in answer to the song of a 2-year-old, who promptly stopped singing. I attempted to have a tape-recorder ready all the time to capture the songs as unobtrusively as possible. During the later years it was easier to record songs, since the children's singing was not interrupted when they noticed the tape-recorder. However, I was careful to record as many songs as possible in which the children were unaware of being recorded even at the later ages, as a check against the possibility that the children might sing differently under the 2 conditions.

The entire body of recordings consisted of 68.25 hours of tape. The first step in analysing the songs was to dub the songs from the original tape onto a tape consisting only of songs. This was done by a graduate student according to the following criteria. 'Singing' consisted of either florid vocal play or (more commonly) a period of vocalization consisting of relatively sustained vowels at mostly discrete pitch levels and having a relatively regular temporal organization or 'beat'. Singing was easily distinguishable from speech on the basis of those characteristics. A 'song' was defined as an instance of singing bounded by either salient intervals (30 seconds) or speech. Reliability checks with another student and myself disclosed little disagreement on what constituted 'singing', or when songs began and ended.

These criteria selected 579 songs comprising 4.87 hours of singing. The songs were distributed evenly across the 5 year period with at least one song recording per month for a mean of 2.23 songs per week. The songs had a mean length of 30.3 seconds, with a distribution having many brief songs and a few quite long ones. Figure 1 shows some examples of the songs. Songs typically had a beat that remained steady within each phrase, but they did not always carry across phrases, as Moorhead et al (1941-51) and Moog (1976) observed. Slight disruptions of the beat are marked in Figure 1 with commas between phrases; a severe disruption is marked with a *luftpauzer*. Note the contrast between preschoolers' ability to keep a steady beat in spontaneous singing and their general inability to match the tempo of an external beat (Shuter-Dyson and Gabriel, 1981). Contrary to earlier observations, songs with a single 'note' duration were rare. More complex rhythms typically arose from the adaptation of speech rhythms to the beat.

TABLE 2

Description of Spontaneous Song Samples from Two Children in Age Ranges 1:0 - 2:0 years and 3:0 - 3:6 years

AGE:	1:0 - 2:0		3:0 - 3:6	
CHILD	CALLA	ERICA	CALLA	ERICA
Number of Songs	27	14	40	40
Pot-Pourri	0	1	15	12
Original	27	13	25	28
'Chant'	1	2	9	0
Phrases/Song	8.56	5.43	6.13	8.65

Table 2 provides a description of the sample of 121 songs I analysed. The sample includes literally all the solo songs by either child in the age range 1:0 to 2:0, and the first 40 songs following the age of 3:0 -- for each child covering the age range of 3:0 to about 3:6. That there were fewer solo songs from Erica than from Calla between 1:0 and 2:0 reflects the social environment -- it was harder for her to do any activity alone than it had been for her older sister, and her parents were less free to leap into action to activate the tape-recorder than when there was only one child in the family.

Table 2 categorizes the sounds as either 'pot-pourri' songs (Moor, 1976) that were largely based on parts of external models (usually just one), and 'original' songs that were not. Figure 1(B) provides an example of a pot-pourri song based on an alphabet song using the tune of 'Twinkle, Twinkle'. The single pot-pourri song in the earlier sample from Erica is due to the influence of her older sister, who sang versions of 'Twinkle, Twinkle' quite often during that year. I think the term 'pot-pourri' is appropriate to describe all those children's versions of 'standard' songs that failed to copy the adult models exactly. Even when the children's songs were modelled on standard songs the songs were presented as filtered through the child's own song-production system, as Davidson et al (1981) noted in connection with children's versions of a song they were trying to learn. This is analogous to Brown's (1973) observations of children's modelling of adult speech, in which the child produces the adult sentence filtered through the child's own syntax. Clearly the songs of Figure 1(B) and (C) display such filtering.

Moorhead et al's (1941-51) distinction between songs into 'songs' and 'chants' was reflected in these data. The 'chant' is a distinctive performance style: musically simple, repetitive, and loud. Other songs were more complex and often private. Figure 1(B) and (C) present 'straight' and chant versions of an alphabet song. Chants were almost always social. Moorhead et al in their preschool setting found a preponderance of chants. I found relatively few. Both pot-pourri and original songs occurred in chant versions, and the numbers shown in Table 2 include both varieties. (That is, 'chant' is not a third way of categorizing the songs in Table 2, but rather 'chant' versus 'non-chant' is a cross-cutting pair of categories to 'pot-pourri' versus 'original'). In this sample they occurred mainly with the older sibling singing socially with the younger when the younger was too young to join in effectively: namely, in the 3-year-old sample from Calla. Chants certainly occurred when Erica was 3 and Calla 5, but not as solos; by then the children invariably sang them together.

The songs divided naturally into phrases, with average lengths of 5 to 9 phrases per song. Songs even at the age of one consisted of phrases having characteristic melodic (Dowling, 1978) and rhythmic (Monahan, 1983) contours with variants of the 'same' song appearing over periods of several weeks. The following analysis is based on that division into phrases, and the phrase contour served as the basic unit of analysis.

Division into phrases was easy and could be done with high inter-observer reliability. Formal description of the phrases in terms of melodic and rhythmic contour was more difficult and necessarily involved numerous acts of 'judgment'. The aim was to describe each phrase's melodic and rhythmic contour and decide which phrases differed from which others. To be different a phrase had only to differ in one contour element of either sort. Exceptions to that rigid rule arose when a phrase had different words that closely fitted the rhythm of a previous phrase, or when 'passing tones' were inserted into basically the same rhythmic outline. Examples of such variation are provided by the song 'Three Blind Mice' in which the third and fourth phrases ('See how they run') would be assigned the same phrase contour as the first and second ('Three blind mice'). The fifth through to the seventh phrases would have a different contour, while the eighth phrase ('As three blind mice') would be assigned the same contour as the first. The formal representation of 'Three Blind Mice' would thus be (AAAABBBA).

FIGURE 1

Examples of songs sung by the children at different ages: (A) by Erica at 1:3, (B) Calla at 3:2; (C) Calla at 3:2, 'chant' version; (D) Calla at 3:3; (E) Calla at 5:2 with cousin. Pitches are approximate, and the recurrence of a notated pitch does not necessarily indicate its exact repetition. "..." in the song text indicates repetition of the same words. Approximate tempos in quarter note values per minute were: (A) 68, (B) 132, (C) 160 and (D) 176.

I did all the formal descriptions of the songs before carrying out any further analysis, so the syntactic analysis did not influence the descriptions. (I was in fact surprised by the later results). I listened to each song several times on the tape of songs dubbed off the master tapes and made a rough diagram of the pitch and rhythmic contours of its phrases. This was difficult because the pitch wandered and was often indistinct. The rhythm was usually clear, but it was often hard to decide even with repeated listening whether a given rhythm was sung with the same or different pitch contour. Then I used the diagram and the heard song to write a formal characterization (like the one for 'Three Blind Mice') of the phrase contour pattern of each song. These patterns were used in the following analyses.

One example of the type of formal characterization I wrote for each song is the following description of Calla's 'Yeah, Yeah, Yeah, Yeah' song shown in Figure 2 of Dowling (1982, p. 417): (ABBCBBBBBCBB). There the judgment call involves the coding of the third phrase from the end. I chose to categorize it as a variant of 'C' (the fourth phrase), with an added passing tone. The songs in Figure 1 had the following descriptions: (A) (AAAAAB); (B) (ABBBBBBAC); (C) (ABBCBB); and (D) (AAAABCBCD).

STRUCTURAL PATTERNS

In my search for patterns in the higher-level organization of song structure I started by calculating phrase-contour type/token ratios (TTR) for the four samples. The TTR provides an overall measure of variety in the songs. The TTR has a value of 1.0 for songs with no repetition of phrase contours. Lower values reflect increased repetition - a TTR of .50 would mean that on the average each phrase contour would appear twice in a song. A song with the description (ABBCBBBBBCBB) for example would have a TTR of 3/12 or 0.25. The mean TTRs shown in Figure 2 reflect a trend toward greater variety in songs between the ages of 1 and 3. The shift in TTR from about .50 to about .59 was statistically significant ($F=4.10$; $df=1,117$; $p<.05$). No other effects in the Age x Child analysis of variance were significant.

The children's TTRs fell in the same range as those of 3 types of adult model. On the right side of the figure are TTRs from 24 nursery tunes common in the children's environment; 30 popular songs from the 1960's; and 30 Appalachian folksongs. The 24 nursery tunes were those that Calla could name as ones she knew at the age of 6. The popular songs were the first 30 in a book (Okun, 1971) that included songs of the Beatles, Simon and Garfunkel, Bob Dylan, etc. The folk songs were the first 30 in a standard collection (Sharp and Karpeles, 1968). For the adult songs I calculated the TTR on the first 8 phrases only, for more accurate comparison to the children's spontaneous songs which averaged about 8 phrases in length. For several of the folk songs this meant repeating a 4 phrase melody, for example. Thus the mean TTR for the folk songs is less than it would be in a typical performance where a 4 phrase melody would be repeated for numerous stanzas.

The overall shift of TTR in Figure 2 does not necessarily reflect a simple increase of sophistication with age. It is easy to imagine the TTR being pulled in opposite directions by various underlying tendencies in competition. The younger children often produce songs that simply repeat one element (low TTR), but also produce meandering songs with no repetition at all (high TTR) that display little evidence of higher-order structure. The older children include variety in their songs (increasing TTRs), but also display control over that variety through patterned repetition of contours (reducing TTRs).

The general pattern shown in Figure 2 masks more complex shifts in the details of pattern organization, to which I now turn.

FIGURE 2

Type/Token ratios for songs of the two children (Calla, solid line; Erica, dashed line) at ages 1:0-2:0 and 3:0-3:6 years, compared with TTRs from three types of adult model.

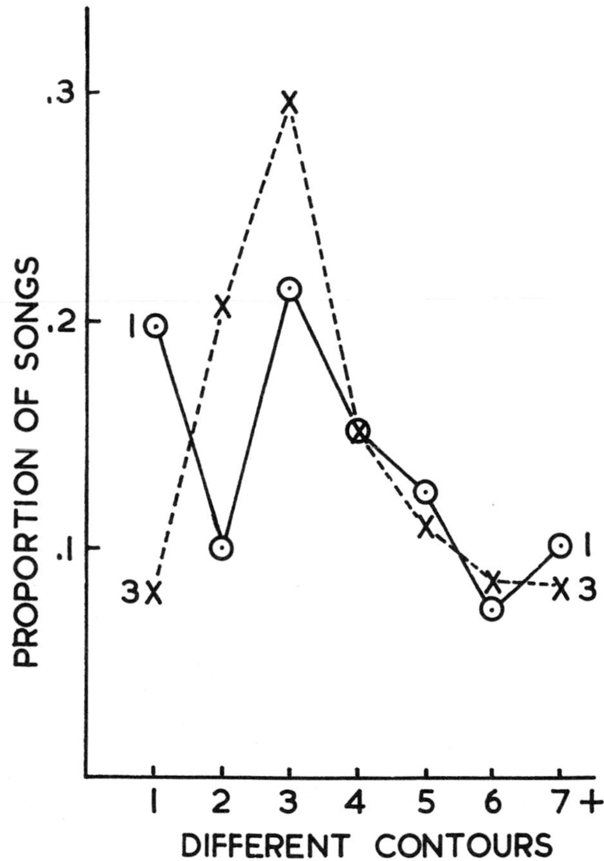

TABLE 3

Proportions of Songs of Different Syntactical Forms in Two Age Ranges for Two Children.

		AGE 1:0 - 2:0		AGE 3:0 - 3:6	
CHILD		CALLA	ERICA	CALLA	ERICA
TYPE OF STRUCTURE	EXAMPLE				
Simple Repetition (SR) (...XX...)	ABBCCD				
Delayed Repetition (DR) (...XY...X...)	ABAC	.44	.57	.40	.73
$\frac{DR}{DR + SR}$		.33	.34	.38	.45
Linear Sequencing (X Y Z etc.)	AABCCCDE	.56	.43	.60	.18
Two or Three Phrase Contours in Song with Repetition (X...Y...) or (X...Y...Z...) with at least one (...) non-empty	ABB ABAC	.30	.36	.60	.43
The above plus such songs having a single 'coda' element	ABBC ABCAD	.37	.43	.78	.68
The above rule plus (X..Y..Z)or(X..Y..Z..W) With at least one (...) non-empty					

NOTE Syntactic structures are in brackets ( ). X,Y,Z,W represent distinguishable phrase-contour elements. X^n represents n repetitions of X, n⩾1. '...' represents any string of phrase-contour elements and may usually be empty.

I describe a series of measures of syntactic organization, starting with ones that show mild effects of age difference and progressing to measures that show stronger effects. Table 3 presents an outline of these measures. Each entry in Table 3 names a structure and gives a formal definition of it. There follows an example, and proportions of songs displaying the particular structure for the 2 children at the 2 age levels. The notation represents distinguishable phrase contours with different majuscules. Thus (...XY... X...) means that some phrase contour X is repeated somewhere in the melody and that some different phrase contour Y intervenes between the repetitions of X. Dots indicate areas that may or may not contain other phrases (except where specified as non-empty, where they must contain some phrase.) Repeated iterations of a single phrase contour are indicated by superscripts Thus (X^3) means (XXX).

Repetition

Simple repetition is the repetition of a phrase contour without intervening material. Delayed repetition refers to repetition across intervening material. I supposed that increased use of delayed repetition would characterize the older children's songs, since that would demonstrate structural control over contour elements across a filled time delay. The proportion of songs containing delayed repetition increased for Erica across the age range, but decreased for Calla. The ratio of delayed repetitions to all repetitions (DR / DR+SR) increased somewhat for both children, and may indicate part of what happens between 1 and 3 years; namely, that the singers control contour repetitions over longer time spans.

Linear Sequencing

The next possibility I tested was whether the children at earlier ages were using a very simple grammar I call 'linear sequencing'. That is, they might have been constructing songs by first repeating a contour element, and then going on to another contour element and repeating it, and so on, without any returns to prior contour elements. This supposition was only partly true, with the proportion of such songs decreasing between 1 and 3 for Erica but not for Calla.

Variety of Phrase Contours

Next I looked at variety more directly by plotting the proportion of songs at the 2 ages containing different numbers of different phrase contours within the song, plotted in Figure 3. This showed a definite difference across age. The children at both ages had about the same number of songs using 4 or more different contours. However, between 1 and 2 the children had quite a few songs that simply repeated one contour. In contrast, the 3-year-olds were typically using the 2 and 3 phrase contours in a song and had very few one contour songs. This trend was also apparent in data from the individual children.

Table 3 shows the proportion of songs at each age that contain 2 or 3 contour elements and display some repetition; for example, (ABB) and (ABAC). Those proportions increase with age for both children. Figure 1(B) and the song in Figure 2 of Dowling (1982) provide examples of this form.

FIGURE 3

Mean proportions of songs of the two children at two different ages (1:0-2:0, solid line; 3:0-3:6, dashed line) as a function of the number of different phrase contours (types) in the songs.

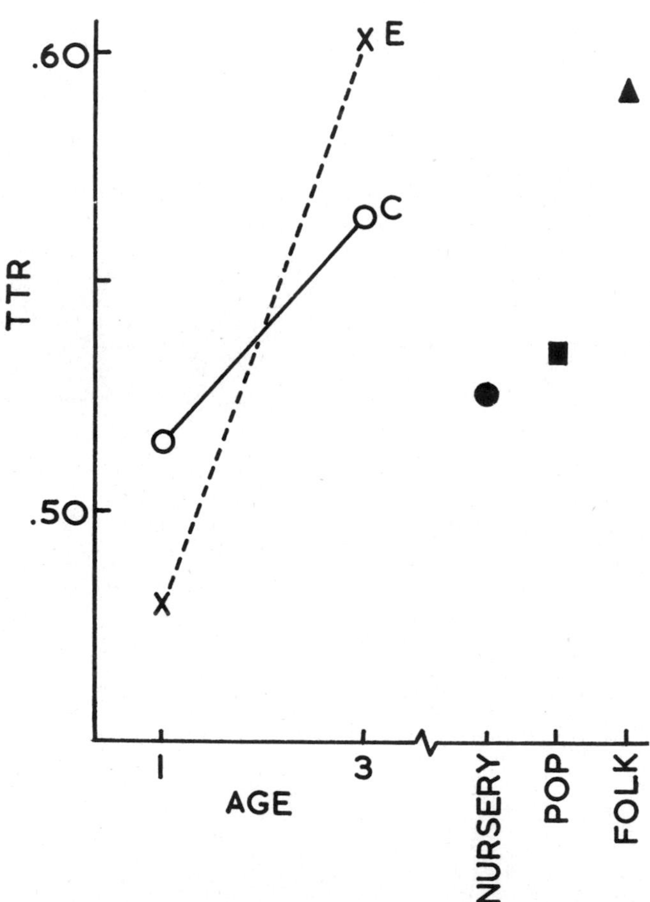

This relationship is strengthened if we add to the foregoing songs that have 2 or 3 elements involving repetition and having a 'coda' - a contour element that appears only once at the end of the song. Examples are (ABBC) and (ABCAD). The increases in the use of this form of song are dramatic across ages, going from about 40% to about 73%. This song structure appears to be very typical of 3-year-old singing, at least for these children. Examples of songs with codas are shown in Figure 1 (A) and (D).

It is interesting to compare this performance by 3-year-olds with the same data from the adult models. Of the 3 types of model I analysed, only the nursery songs approach the children's output for this type of song pattern. The folk and popular songs each showed a 17% incidence. Just as the children in Brown's (1973) study of language development tended to 'overproduce' the simple grammatical forms they were just acquiring, so these children go well beyond their models in exploiting this family of simple melodic forms. This is evidence of an inner-directed mechanism for song-form acquisition. The children achieve more and more effective schematic control over the songs they sing. They do this not by simply copying cultural models, but rather by developing more and more sophisticated mental representations in response to their musical environment.

MEMORY FOR SONGS

I turn now to tests of the two children's memory for songs they sang. A longitudinal study such as this provides an opportunity to test for recognition and recall of spontaneous songs they personally created. If the production of songs is under schematic memory control, and if the associated schemata change from time to time during development, then a song produced during one time period should be difficult to retrieve at a later time if the relevant schemata have changed. Schachtel (1947) proposed essentially this model as an explanation of 'childhood amnesia', the general inability of adults to recall events from their first three years of life (see, for example, Sheingold and Tenney, 1982). The same processes should result in failures of retrieval even later in childhood, while schematic organization is still undergoing change. Exceptions to this retrieval failure should occur in cases where the song was initially rehearsed over a long enough period to carry through periods of schematic change.

These tests were carried out when the children were between the ages of 3:6 and 4:6, and 5:6 and 6:6. To be suitable for testing a song needed to have been performed at least several times and then to have dropped out of use completely for at least 6 months. I found 5 spontaneous songs (3 for Calla and 2 for Erica) that met these criteria. The songs were tested 6 to 9 months following their last natural occurrence. An example of such a song, highly memorable to the adult listener, is shown in Figure 3. I also found a group of 8 standard songs that met the same criteria.

The memory tests I used are listed in Table 4. In order of administration they were: (1) recall cued by circumstances of initial generation (or words or title in the case of standard songs); (2) recognition of first phrase; (3) recall of a subsequent phrase cued by the first; and (4) recall of a subsequent phrase cued by partial words. Of course success on test (3) would obviate the need for test (4). In the case of the song in Figure 3, for example, I asked Calla if she remembered the song that she and her cousin Jennifer had sung on a hike we took in the Colorado mountains. I described the occasion, and Calla indicated familiarity with it. (She had viewed slides of their hiking and singing together several times during the intervening months). I asked if she could sing me some of the song they sang then. She could not remember it. Then I sang the first phrase and asked if it was the same song. She agreed that it was. I asked her if she could continue with the next phrase, but she could not. (With this song I added the information that the next phrase involved counting, but still with no success). Then I sang the tune of the second phrase 'Boop, boop, boop, boop, boop, boop, boop', but she still could not provide the words. These responses are indicated in Table 4 with N (for 'no') in all the columns but the second, where a Y (for 'yes') indicates agreement to recognizing the song.

Spontaneous Songs

The result in Table 4 suggest that the children's memory for their own spontaneous songs was at best weak. Though they always assented on the recognition test, they never recalled any parts of the song not presented in the test.

Lures

As a further check on the meaning of the children's positive recognition responses, I constructed 3 lures for each child to use in 'catch' trials. I tried to match the lures closely to the children's own styles from 6 months before the test. For the cued recall trials I attributed each song to a real time period, such as 'around the end of school', or 'just before your birthday'. There was a greater tendency to reject lures than to reject actual songs on the recognition test: 2 out of 3 lures were rejected. In one case where Calla was doubtful of the authenticity of the lure she nevertheless went on to invent a continuation of it -- definitely a reconstructive process in memory!

Comparison of hit and false-alarm rates in the recognition tests would seem to indicate better than chance accuracy in recognition of actual songs. However, one should keep in mind that the lures were only an adult's imitation of the children's styles. The lures could possibly have been distinguished from actual songs on the basis of style alone, apart from particular memories for the specific songs. That is, in terms of a knowledge-performance distinction the child may have known more about her own style at an earlier date than appeared in her song production at that time or than was apparent to the adult listener. Thus lures constructed by an adult could have unwittingly violated some unobserved principle of style. Further, the pairing of song and occasion could have been inappropriate from the child's point of view. One of Erica's 'No' responses, for example, when I introduced a lure with, 'I think you were singing this just before your birthday' was 'No, then we were just singing "Happy Birthday"'. Thus I think not very much should be made of the somewhat ambiguous degree of discrimination seen in the hit and false-alarm rates. I think it is a safe conclusion in view of these results and the complete absence of cued recall that the children's memory for their own spontaneous songs is weak, if not totally lacking.

TABLE 4

Responses to Tests of Memory for Spontaneous and Standard Songs and for Contrived Lures.

TEST:	EXTERNAL CUED RECALL	RECOGNITION, FIRST PHRASE	CUED RECALL, LATER PHRASE	WORDS OF LATER PHRASE GIVEN TUNE	NONE
Spontaneous Songs:					
Calla 1	N	Y	N	N	
2	N	Y	N	N	
3	N	Y	N	N	
Erica 1	N	Y	N	N	
2	N	Y	N	N	
Lures:					
Calla 1	N	N	N		
2	N	Maybe	Y		
3	N	N	N		
Erica 1	N	N	N		
2	N	Y	N		
3	N	N	N		
Standard Songs:					
Itsy-Bitsy Spider	CE	CE	CE		
Are You Sleeping	C	CE	CE		
Row, Row, Row	CE	CE	CE		
Hush, Little Baby		CE	C	E	
Good King Wenceslaus	C*	CE	E		
C: School Pageant (several songs)					C
E: Choir Songs					E
E: Preschool songs					E

* Calla sang the correct words to the tune of 'Yankee Doodle'

Standard Songs

The results with the standard songs tested after a 6-9 month delay were mixed. In Table 4 each child's initial (C or E) in a given column indicates success on that test. The songs divided into 3 groups: songs remembered quite well when tested with both recognition and recall ('Itsy-Bitsy Spider', 'Are You Sleeping' and 'Row, Row, Row Your Boat'); songs that were recognized and recalled with partial success ('Hush Little Baby' and 'Good King Wenceslaus'); and songs that were neither recalled nor recognized (Calla's school Christmas pageant songs and Erica's school music programme and church-choir songs). The third group of songs that were not remembered were distinguished by numerous practice trials during relatively short learning periods (less than 2 months). Though each song was learned to a criterion of 'memorization' suitable for group performance during that practice period, attempts at retrieval 6 to 9 months later failed completely.

The results of this study suggest that only songs that received numerous practice trials across a period of more than 2 months were well remembered 6 months later. This was true of both spontaneous and standard songs. This result is compatible with the schematic-control-of-song-production model developed here in that in such a view only songs that remained in the child's repertoire long enough to survive a change of schematic organization would be remembered after such a change.

An alternative characterization of these results is possible; namely, that distributed practice is more valuable than massed practice in song learning. Bahrick (1979) found that adults' retrieval of verbal materials when tested 6 months after learning was enhanced by spreading the learning trials over periods of months rather than massing them into a few days. But 'distributed practice' merely labels a phenomenon without providing an explanation. Bahrick presents evidence that suggests that his distributed-practice effect may have been due in some measure to the possibility of covert rehearsal of his materials. In the present case, covert rehearsal could occur only as long as production schemata remained relatively constant. The present results are compatible with both a 'distributed practice' and a 'schematic change' characterization. When a song fails to cross the boundary of a schematic change it drops out of the repertoire and becomes very difficult to retrieve at a later date.

Clearly some songs, usually standard nursery songs, remain in the child's repertoire from year to year. Four- and five-year-olds typically have about two dozen of these they can recall on demand (Dowling, 1982). The 24 nursery songs in the data comparisons above constitute Calla's list at the age of 6. The standard nursery songs that each child knows survive in the repertoire because of environmental support that keeps them in active use across relatively long time periods, perhaps spanning schematic changes. As Davidson et al (1981) note, these songs change with development in the direction of closer and closer approximations of the adult models. I encountered no instances of spontaneous songs making their way into the child's permanent repertoire.

ADDITIONAL OBSERVATIONS ON PITCH

During the next year I hope to be able to carry out a computer analysis of pitch patterns in the children's songs. Before then my observations on the use of pitches and intervals are necessarily less formal than I might wish.

However, I include some further observations because of their bearing on important issues.

A persistent observation that I believe to be based on very weak evidence, dating perhaps from studies by Werner (Révész, 1954), is that the interval of a descending minor third (-3 semitones) is basic to children's singing. An example is the occurrence of that interval in the taunting formula ('sol-mi-la-sol-mi') observed by Moorhead et al (1941-51). There was little evidence in the present corpus for a universal 'sol-mi-la-sol-mi' melody. That phrase pattern occurred exactly twice among the 121 songs in the sample analysed. When it occurred it was in game songs like 'Ring-around-a-rosie' but even there the final interval which in the model is a descending minor third was likely to be rendered as anything from a major second to a perfect fifth (-2 to -7 semitones). This variability also was characteristic on closer inspection of the descending minor thirds I previously reported from Calla at 1:8 years (Dowling, 1982, p. 416). These observations agree with those of Moog (1976) in finding no evidence for the universality of the interval of the descending minor third. (Moog even tried to teach an 18-month-old the 'sol-mi-la-sol-mi'pattern; without success). Moorhead et al (1941-51) found the descending minor third common only in social chants, and not in normal spontaneous songs. The cross-cultural evidence for the universality of a descending minor third outside of Europe is also weak. Blacking (1967), for example, found a definite preponderance of other intervals in children's songs of the African Venda.

There is reason to suppose that the perfect fifth might be a more universally occurring interval. One notion of the order in which children might acquire adult scale intervals is that they might acquire some more obvious large interval first and later fill in the smaller intervals within it. Whether that is the case or not, I did observe some instances of assimilation of various pitches of model standard songs to the perfect fifth. For example, the children at ages 4:5 and 6:5 sang together a variant of the taunting formula to the words, 'You'll never get more than us ...,' with the pitches 'mi-sol-sol-sol-sol-ti-sol-do', replacing the minor third 'sol-mi' with the perfect fifth 'sol-do'. Also, in singing together the chorus of the song 'Jimmy Crack Corn and I Don't Care' at ages 3:3 and 5:3 they sang the last occurrence of 'care' consistently on 'sol' instead of the 'la' of the model, substituting the fifth for the sixth degree of the scale. However, this assimilation of pitches to the fifth degree of the scale may simply be an example of regularizing less familiar intervals to better-known ones. Calla had learned the song 'Old Abe Lincoln Came Out of the Wilderness' at about the age of 5:6 years on the piano. In that version the melody contained chromatic alterations of pitches. Both children in singing it together at the ages of 4:2 and 6:2 substituted pitches of the major scale for the chromatic notes.

A concluding observation concerns the effects of early musical training. Both children started learning to play the piano at about 3:6 years, and due partly to a good teacher they both enjoyed the experience and learned much from it. I imagine their intonation during the pre-school years has benefited from the training, at least they often sing quite well in tune. They have good intonation on the standard songs they have learned, whether from learning to play them or from adult models (especially fanfares heard on television). However, contrary to what I would have expected from a theoretical model in which pitch is completely under the control of an internalized musical scale schema, their intonation in spontaneous songs often deviates from the scale. This is even true of Calla at the age of 6:6, and is particularly the case when she is not aware of being observed. (This is perhaps similar to the adult phenomenon of loosely controlled intonation while singing in the shower). The musical scale schema is a useful theoretical abstraction, but the actual reference standards people use in producing good intonation in singing are probably quite specific, and often tied to single instances of interval occurrence. (This is evident in the way in which a musician retrieves an arbitrary interval by finding an instance of it in a well-known tune (Dowling, 1978, p. 351). It seems plausible that generalization of precise intonation across the board to novel melodies requires considerable experience with a variety of well-learned instances -- more than a 6-year-old is likely to have had. It is nevertheless clear that pitch production at this age is not so much under the control of a pervasive scale schema, as it is guided by the occasional relevance of particular instances.

CONCLUSIONS

Two main conclusions I want to emphasize in closing concern the relationship between children's songs and adult songs. First, when the child imitates an adult song model the result is a version filtered through the child's own song syntax. As I noted above, this is analogous to what happens when the child imitates an adult sentence in speech. This filtering was evident in both the spontaneous pot-pourri songs of the present study and in children's versions of a standard song they were trying to copy in the study by Davidson et al (1981). Second, as Moorhead et al (1941-51) observed, in the child's syntax we can see the origins of the adult's more articulated and elaborate version. It does not seem far-fetched to suppose with Teplov (1966), that the child's singing lays the foundation for the adult musical ear. As Keil (1981) suggested, the adult's schemata are not so likely to be radical restructurings of the child's, but rather subtler elaborations of them. The same basic patterns of novelty and repetition are found in both. The simple codas of the children's songs grow into the complex codas of the adult's compositions.

When I was preparing this chapter I discussed it with my children and received their permission to present examples of their songs. I asked them if there was anything about the songs that I should be sure to mention. After thinking for a minute, they said, yes, I should be sure to say that singing is fun!

REFERENCES

Bahrick, H.P. (1979). Maintenance of knowledge: Questions about memory we forgot to ask. Journal of Experimental Psychology: General, 108, 296-308.

Bentley, A. (1966). Musical ability in children. London: Harrap.

Blacking, J. (1967). Venda Children's Songs. Johannesburg: Witwatersrand University Press.

Brown, R. (1973). A First Language. London: George Allen and Unwin.

Chomsky, N. (1965). Aspects of the Theory of Syntax. Cambridge, Massachusetts: MIT Press.

Davidson, L., McKernon, P. and Gardner, H. (1981). The Acquisition of Song: A Developmental Approach. In: Documentary Report of the Ann Arbor Symposium. Reston, Virginia: Music Educators National Conference.

Dowling, W.J. (1978). Scale and contour: Two components of a theory of memory for melodies. Psychological Review, 85, 341-354.

Dowling, W. (1982). Melodic information processing and its development. In: D. Deutsch (Ed.) The Psychology of Music. New York: Academic Press.

Keil, F.C. (1981). Constraints on knowledge and cognitive development. Psychological Review, 88, 197-227.

Krumhansl, C.L. and Castellano, M.A. (1983). Dynamic processes in musical perception. Memory and Cognition, 11, 325-334.

Krumhansl, C.L. and Keil, F.C. (1982). Acquistion of the hierarchy of tonal functions in music. Memory and Cognition, 10, 243-251.

Monahan, C.B. (1983). Melodic and rhythmic determinants of recognition of brief tonal patterns. Unpublished Doctoral Dissertation, UCLA.

Moog, H. (1976). The Musical Experience of the Preschool Child. (C. Clarke translation). London: Schott.

Moorhead, G.E. et al. (1941-51). Music of Young Children. Santa Barbara, California: Pillsbury Foundation.

Okun, M. (1971). The New York Times Great Songs of the Sixties. Chicago, Illinois: Quadrangle Books.

Ostwald, P.F. (1971). Musical behavior in early childhood. Developmental Medicine and Child Neurology, 15, 367-375.

Révész, G. (1954). Introduction to the Psychology of Music. Norman, Oklahoma: University of Oklahoma Press.

Schachtel, E.G. (1947). On memory and childhood amnesia. Psychiatry, 10, 1-26.

Sharp, C.J. and Karpeles, M. (1968). Eighty English Folk Songs from the Southern Appalachians. Cambridge, Massachusetts: MIT Press.

Sheingold, K. and Tenney, Y.J. (1982). Memory for a salient childhood event. In: U. Neisser (Ed.) Memory Observed. San Francisco, California: Freeman.

Shuter-Dyson, R. and Gabriel, C. (1981). The Psychology of Musical Ability. Second Edition. London: Methuen.

Teplov, B.M. (1966). Psychologie des aptitudes musicales. (J. Deprun translation). Paris: Presses Universitaires de France.

Trehub, S.E., Bull, D. and Thorpe, L.A. (In press). Infants' perception of melodies: The role of melodic contour. Child Development.

Section 4

PERCEPTION OF THE VISUAL ARTS

Cognitive Processes in the Perception of Art
W.R. Crozier and A.J. Chapman (editors)
© Elsevier Science Publishers B.V. (North-Holland), 1984

CHRISTINA'S WORLD: IMAGINARY PERSPECTIVES AND THE ENCODING OF SPATIAL ALIGNMENT RELATIONS[1]

Howard S. Hock

Florida Atlantic University

Under normal conditions, we pick up visual information by a continual series of saccadic eye movements. Our eyes fixate on points in the visual field for time intervals of approximately 200 milliseconds (msec), whereupon they rapidly move on to new fixation points. There is no attempt by our visual system to sample uniformly the information in a scene. Rather, our eyes tend to return continually to objects of thematic importance, so that much of the information in the scene does not receive detailed foveal vision (Yarbus 1967). Our experience of a coherent visual world is testimony to our ability to integrate this succession of overlapping samples of the visual field that only partially benefit from detailed foveal vision. This feat is all the more remarkable when it is realized that the location of objects in each visual sample is imprecisely coded. This was illustrated nicely in experiments by Wolford and Hollingsworth (1974) and Estes et al (1976).

Wolford and Hollingsworth (1974) presented strings of five consonants to the right of a fixation point. Since the consonant strings intercepted a visual angle of approximately one degree (1°), their presentation was essentially foveal (detailed foveal vision is limited to about 2° of visual angle). The consonants were presented for a brief duration that was adjusted for each subject to maintain overall performance at approximately 60% correct. Following the presentation of each stimulus, subjects were required to report the letters they had seen in the left-to-right order in which they were presented. Wolford and Hollingsworth (1974) found that approximately one-third of subjects' errors were position errors. These were letters that were correctly identified, but reported in the wrong position.

In a similar experiment, Estes et al (1976) extended their consonant strings outside the fovea (they subtended a visual angle of 5.3^{o} either to the left or right of fixation, and presented them for 150 msec in one condition and for 2400 msec, or until subjects' eyes left the fixation point, in the second condition. In the 150 msec condition approximately one-fourth of the subjects' errors were correctly identified items, but in the wrong position (a direct comparison with Wolford and Hollingsworth's results was precluded by many design differences, including greater inter-letter spacing in Estes et al's experiment than in Wolford and Hollingsworth's). Similar results were obtained by Estes et al in the 2400 msec condition; one third of the errors were now position errors. The results obtained in the 2400 msec condition were important because they showed that position errors were not due to limiations in subjects' ability to 'read out' information from a rapidly fading visual trace, as might be argued for the 150 msec condition.

The present chapter discusses a number of factors that influence the precision with which people remember the spatial location of objects in a scene, including the following: (1) the distinction between projective and relational spatial information; (2) short-term memory for location information; (3) the effects of perceptual grouping on the spatial resolution of the visual system; (4) the contribution of the perceiver's knowledge of rules governing the possible locations of objects in a scene to the encoding of spatial location information; (5) the importance of mutual constraints in the spatial relations among the objects in a scene; and (6) the distinction between automatic encoding and effortful memory strategies in the retention of spatial location information. Finally, I describe the results of two experiments which explore the effect of the perceiver constructing non-egocentric, imaginary perspectives on the encoding of spatial location information.

PROJECTIVE VS. RELATIONAL SPATIAL INFORMATION

By projective location information I mean the position of an object on a reference surface. The projective location of an object could be encoded in terms of its position on a table-top, on a wall, in a pre-defined matrix of possible locations, etc. Projective location can also be established on the basis of an object's position in the picture plane defined by the perceiver's line-of-sight. Whereas projective location information specifies the position of an object relative to a surface, relational location information specifies the position of an object relative to other objects. Relational location information can incorporate projective location information (e.g., A is to the left of B) and can also include nonprojective spatial information (e.g., A is supported by B), but it must always specify relations among objects. In general, relational information is invariant under changes in projective location. For example, the relation 'a cup on a saucer' remains the same whether the cup and saucer are on the left or right side of the table, and whether they are high or low with regard to the perceiver's line-of-sight.

The dissociation of projective and relational information pertains to orientation as well as location. It is well-known that certain paintings have the quality that some objects depicted in the painting (e.g., the road in *The Village of Becquigny*, by Theodore Rousseau) seem to be always oriented towards the perceiver, regardless of the latter's stationpoint. In an empirical assessment of this effect, Goldstein (1979) showed that various objects in *The Village of Becquigny*, differed in the extent to which they appeared to change their orientation, relative to the perceiver's line of sight, at different stationpoints. That is, some objects completely 'followed' the perceiver to new viewing locations while others did so only partially. As a result, two objects with similar projective orientations at one stationpoint might have much different projective orientations at another stationpoint. If projective orientations determined the relational orientations of the object depicted in *The Village of Becquigny*, the internal structure of the scene would change when the perceiver changes stationpoints. Goldstein, however, found that this was not the case. For example, objects oriented at right-angles to each other in the scene maintained that perceived relation at different stationpoints. In this way, Goldstein provided evidence for the dissociation of projective and relational orientation information.

Returning to my primary concern, the encoding of location information, the question at hand is why the level of projective position uncertainty is so high in experiments like those of Wolford and Hollingsworth (1974) and

Estes et al (1976), described above, (since their stimuli were simply rows of consonants, the location information that is relevant is projective). The conceptual difficulty is that for some purposes, extraordinarily precise projective location information is available to the perceiver. This was shown most impressively by Julesz's (1963) creation of random-dot stereograms. The stimuli Julesz generated were pairs of patterns involving 10,000 potential locations per pattern. Whether or not a dot was presented at a particular location was determined in a random fashion, with the exemption that a section of one pattern (in the early demonstrations the section was square) was repeated, with a slight horizontal shift, in the pattern with which it was paired. When viewed stereoscopically, the square section emerged from the random noise and a square composed of random dots was seen in front of a background, also composed of random dots.

The significance of Julesz' demonstration lies in that fact that when viewed individually, each of the dot patterns was completely formless. For the perceiver stereoscopically to combine the information in the two patterns the perceiver must encode the projective location of the individual dots with a very high degree of precision (in Julesz's demonstration to within $.008^{o}$). Unfortunately, this highly precise information is limited in its usefulness. This is indicated by experiments showing that precise projective location information is retrievable for only brief periods of time.

SHORT-TERM MEMORY FOR LOCATION INFORMATION

Ross and Hogben (1974) have created a version of Julesz's demonstration which they call a random-process stereogram. Ultimately, their patterns look like those generated by Julesz, but the differences lie in the way they are presented. Julesz presented all the information in his stereoscopic pairs of patterns simultaneously. In contrast, Ross and Hogben presented only one point at a time, for a very brief period of time (on the order of 0.1 msec), whereupon the next point was presented. What they relied on was the persistence of the points' visibility long after the brief stimulus was gone. They found that if they renewed the presentation of the points every 120-140 msec, all the points appeared as if they were continuously present. The experimental advantage of Ross and Hogben's procedure was that they could introduce a time delay between the presentation of corresponding points in the two patterns of the stereoscopic pair. This meant that subjects had to hold the location of each point in a pattern in memory until they could check for its binocular disparity with the corresponding point in its stereoscopic partner. Ross and Hogben found that delays of more than 50 msec destroyed the stereoscopic effect (i.e., the emergence of a form in depth).

This result does not mean that all location information is lost after 50 msec. Instead of testing for stereopsis, Hogben et al (1976) had subjects judge whether a pair of random-process patterns were symmetrical, again introducing a delay between the presentation of points for the two patterns. They found that judgments of symmetry perception can bridge longer time gaps than stereoscopic perception because less precise projective location information is required for the latter. It should also be recalled that the entire random dot pattern remains visible for even longer: 120-140 msec. Hogben and DiLollo (1974) have shown that information regarding spatial location remains available for that time interval. They did this by presenting dots one at a time until 24 of the 25 cells of a 5 x 5 matrix were filled. Subjects had no difficulty identifying the location of the missing dot, providing the 24 dots were all presented within an interval of 120 msec. It is interesting that Hogben and DiLollo's displays were relatively large, measuring more than 6° of visual angle vertically and horizontally. An experiment varying the disciminability of the dot locations, using Hogben and DiLollo's paradigm, could provide converging evidence that relatively precise location information is available for much less than 120 msec. Of further interest is the role of capacity. Although capacity does not seem to be a problem for stereoscopic perception, future research may show that the availability of spatial location information in Hogben and DiLollo's 'find the missing dot' task may be affected by the number of dots in the display.

It is important at this juncture to emphasize that although projective location information loses precision after 50 msec, it is not completely lost. In the section that follows I propose that this partial loss is due to the operation of mechanisms involved in perceptual grouping.

PERCEPTUAL GROUPING

The basis for my argument is that from the earliest stages of perception information is gathered in chunks or groups. It is because of this chunking that we tend to see texture, even in randomly generated patterns (Julesz, 1965). When there is cohesive structure to the visual field, the chunks of information that one gathered are influenced by the Gestalt laws of organization. Neisser (1967) refers to this early stage of processing as preattentive. I am proposing that the projective locations of primitive elements in the visual field are encoded with reference to the chunk or group into which they are incorporated. More specifically, I am suggesting that the projective location (X,Y) of the chunk is encoded on the basis of the centre-of-gravity of its elements, and the locations of the primitive elements are encoded as deviations with respect to the centre-of-gravity $(X+X_1, Y+Y_1)$, $(X+X_2, Y+Y_2)$, etc. In this way, the usefulness of location information regarding primitive elements depends on the retention of location information concerning the higher order units to which they belong.

It should be recalled from the discussion of short-term visual memory that after a very brief period of time (50 msec) it becomes difficult to retrieve large amounts of projective location information. Although this difficulty in retrieval could be equivalent for the centre-of-gravity and deviation components of the location code, the retrieval information is effectively in double jeopardy: (1) it may not be retrieved and (2) if it is retrieved it may be useless for many purposes (like stereoscopic vision) if the centre-of-gravity information is not retrieved with it. As a result, the retrieval of projective location information is biased toward the centre-of-gravity component of the location code. The results of a recent experiment by Coren and Girgus (1980) are consistent with this proposal. Their general finding was that the estimated distance between pairs of dots was affected by whether the dots belonged to the same perceptual group or different perceptual groups. For the purposes of this exposition, I focus on Experiment 2 of Coren and Girgus' five experiments. In this experiment subjects were presented with six vertical columns composed of small circles. The circles composing the two innermost columns were empty; the circles composing the four outside columns were filled. According to the Gestalt law of similarity, the two innermost columns, which were similar to each other by virtue of being composed of unfilled circles, should be perceptually segregated from the columns with unfilled circles. Coren and Girgus found that the estimated distance between circles belonging to different perceptual groups was greater than the estimated distance between circles belonging to the same perceptual group. Was this because being in the same perceptual groups decreased perceived distance; because being in different perceptual groups increased perceived distance; or a combination of both? The reason we have discussed this particular experiment in the Coren and Girgus study is that it is the only one which includes the control conditions necessary to make these distinctions. That is, subjects in this experiment also estimated distances between pairs of circles that were presented in isolation, and were therefore not subject to the organizational principles operating in the columnar arrays of circles described above.

When the results in the control conditions were taken into account, it could be concluded that the effect of perceptual grouping of circles on their perceived distance was due almost entirely to the presence of the circles in different perceptual groups increasing the perceived distance between the circles. Whether or not two circles were in the same perceptual group had little effect on estimates of the distance between them. This result was consistent with my hypothesis that the location code for individual elements is derived with reference to the perceptual group to which the element belongs. When the subjects moved their gaze from the array of dots to the bottom of the page, where they were to indicate their distance judgments, information regarding the projective location of the dots quickly became difficult to retrieve. As a result of the double jeapordy this placed on the deviation component of the centre-of-gravity plus deviation codes, subjects' estimates of the distance between circles tended to be biased toward the centres-of-gravity of the perceptual groups to which the circles belong. This bias toward the centre-of-gravity of perceptual groups is also consistent with the central shift in position errors obtained in both the Welford and Hollingsworth (1974) and the Estes et al (1976) experiments with consonant strings.

The idea of a centre-of-gravity plus deviation representation of projective location also helps explain the phenomenon of 'illusory conjunctions', which has been reported by Treisman and Gelade (1980). A typical instance of this phenomenon has been studied by Prinzmetal (1981). It involved the presentation of a short vertical line next to a short, horizontal line. When the pair of lines is presented for a brief period of time, subjects frequently report seeing a cross or 'plus' sign. Since the separation of the vertical and horizontal line segments in this experiment was approximately 3° of visual angle, the illusory conjunction must have occurred at a point in time when it was difficult to retrieve both the centre-of-gravity and the deviation components of the projective location codes for the line segments. The double jeopardy this places on the deviation codes would result in a tendency for both the vertical and the horizontal line to be perceived at the same location (i.e., at the centre-of-gravity). Direct support for this explanation comes from Prinzmetal's finding that the illusory conjunction of the vertical and horizontal line segments was more likely to occur when they were in the same perceptual group than when they were in different perceptual groups.

To summarize up to this point, I have been arguing that perceptual grouping, together with the quick onset of difficulty in retrieving both centre-of-gravity and deviation information, results in a reduction in the precision with which people remember projective locations. This loss in projective information may be the cost which our perceptual system must pay to make sense of the visual world. Perceptual grouping is of obvious necessity for form perception, and is also implicit in the encoding of relational location information in multi-object scenes. That is, when people form descriptive representations involving relations among a set of small units, they are in effect grouping those units into a larger unit. When the small units are objects and the larger units are scenes, rules governing the possible locations of objects in the scene influence the formation of descriptive representations involving relational location information.

RULE-GOVERNED OBJECT LOCATIONS

DeGroot (1965) has shown that chess masters can more accurately recall the positions of chess pieces on a chess board than novices. This was not due to chess masters having better visual memory than novices. The masters were superior to the novices when the to-be-recalled positions were from actual games, but not when chess pieces were placed in random positions on the chess board. It seemed from DeGroot's (1965) results that the chess masters' facility at forming descriptive representations involving rule-defined relations among the chess pieces was responsible for their superior recall.

Hock et al (1974) have studied the influence of rules governing the physically possible locations of objects in an experiment involving same-different judgments for pairs of simultaneously presented scenes. They used four types of hand-drawn scenes. For Type 1 scenes, the objects in each scene belonged together (i.e., are commonly found together), were in physically possible arrangements, and the arrangements were familiar. Type 2 scenes also comprised objects that belonged together and were in physically possible arrangements, but now their arrangement was unfamiliar. For Type 3 scenes the arrangement of objects was both unfamiliar and impossible. However, the objects in Type 3 scenes did belong together. Finally, there were no contextual relations among the objects in Type 4 scenes. The arrangements were unfamiliar, impossible, and involved objects that did not belong together.

On this basis, performance for the four types of scene could be contrasted to assess the effects of familiarity, physical possibility and belongingness on same-different comparison. Subjects were shown pairs of scenes; half of the pairs were the same and half were different. When the scene-pair differed, it was with respect to the identity of one of the objects; the scene-pair was otherwise unchanged (i.e., 'different' pairs always involved scenes of the same 'type'). Hock et al (1974) found that the only factor which significantly affected 'same' reaction time was whether or not the objects were in a physically possible arrangement. It should be noted, however, that this evidence for the effect of rules involving the physically possible locations of objects was obtained for arrays of objects that belonged together. Whether rules governing physical possibility would influence the processing of scenes in which the objects do not belong together could not be determined from Hock et al's (1974) results.

A more detailed analysis of the rules that govern the possible locations of objects in a scene has been provided by Biederman et al (1982). The stimuli Biederman et al (1982) used were outline drawings of real-world scenes. Either the scenes were normal (base scenes) or an object in an otherwise normal scene was subject to violations of rules involving support, interposition, size, position and probability. Support violations involve the inappropriate location of objects 'off the ground', interposition violations result in a tendency for two objects to be perceived at locations inappropriate to the size projected by the object onto the perceiver's retina (i.e., size violations are implicitly location violations), position violations involve objects being placed in locations in which they are not ordinarily found, and probability violations involve objects being placed in settings in which they are not ordinarily found. Biederman et al presented their scenes individually for a time interval (150 msec) sufficiently brief to prevent subjects from changing their point of eye fixation during the presentation. The name of the target object was provided prior to the presentation of the scene, and a location cue (a dot) embedded in a masking stimulus (a random array of lines) was presented immediately after the scene. Subjects were to respond 'Yes' or 'No' depending on whether the specified target appeared at the specified location. Beiderman et al (1982) found that each of the above mentioned violations, except for the interposition violation, reduced subjects' ability to detect accurately the target object.

Why is an object poorly detected when it is in a rule-violating relation with its context? Is it because the violation adversely affects the apprehension of the context, or is it because the violating object does not fit the context? This question was answered by testing detection performance for 'innocent bystanders'. These were objects that appeared in violated scenes, but were not themselves in violation. Biederman et al (1982) found that being in a violated scene did not affect the performance for the 'innocent bystanders' relative to being in a base scene. If the violation had reduced subjects' ability to identify the scene, the detectability of 'innocent bystanders' would also have been reduced. It was concluded, therefore, that violating objects were poorly detected because they did not fit the context in which they were presented, not because the context was improperly apprehended.

The research described above indicates that subjects' ability to process information in complex scenes is influenced by an internalized set of rules involving the physically possible locations of objects. When an object appears in a rule-violating relation to the rest of the scene, subjects seem to omit the violating object in developing a relational description for the scene. Since rule-violating objects are less likely to be grouped with other objects than nonviolating objects, the encoding of projective location information should be more precise for violating than for nonviolating objects, but the encoding of relational location information should be more likely for nonviolating than for violating objects. Evidence reported by Mandler and her colleagues is consistent with this hypothetical trade-off between the encoding of projective and relational location information.

Mandler and Johnson (1976), Mandler and Parker (1976) and Mandler and Ritchey (1977) have studied the retention of location information for organized and disorganized hand-drawn scenes. Their organized scenes comprised objects in familiar, three-dimensional layouts; their disorganized scenes comprised the same objects, but in an unfamiliar arrangement lacking three-dimensional spatial structure. For both the organized and disorganized scenes the objects were relatively dispersed and non-interactive. Subjects were instructed to study the pictures carefully so they could remember them. The instructions, it should be noted, did not specifically mention remembering location information. Following the presentation of the scenes subjects were presented pictures identical to those they had just seen (they were to respond 'same' for these stimuli) and transformed versions of the pictures they had just seen (they were to respond 'different' for these stimuli). One type of transformation involved moving one of the objects a relatively small distance to a new location. Another type of transformation involved interchanging the locations of two objects of approximately the same size and shape. Of particular interest were subjects' false alarms, which were incorrect 'same' responses to transformed versions of the previously presented stimuli.

In all of the studies cited above, Mandler and her colleagues found that the rate of false alarm errors for 'interchange' transformation was lower for organized than for disorganized scenes. This result was consistent with the conclusion that subjects more readily encoded relational location information for the organized than for the disorganized scenes. Another result that was consistently obtained in Mandler's experiments was that the rate of false alarm errors for the 'move' transformation was lower for disorganized scenes than for organized scenes. This result is, at first glance, counter-intuitive; organization usually facilitates retention. Let us, however, assume that the perceptual grouping of objects was more likely for organized than for disorganized scenes. This assumption is consistent with the evidence for the encoding of relational location information that was obtained with the 'interchange' transformations. Since I have argued previously that perceptual grouping tends to decrease the accuracy with which projective location information is retrieved, it would follow that Mandler's evidence that subjects could detect 'moves' less accurately for organized scenes could be attributed to greater perceptual grouping for the organized scenes compared with the disorganized scenes.

MUTUAL SPATIAL CONSTRAINT

In the above account of Mandler's research it was argued that subjects' ability to detect 'move' transformations depended on the encoding of projective location information. We felt comfortable with this interpretation because the objects in both Mandler's organized and disorganized scenes were spatially dispersed and noninteractive. Imagine, instead, a coherently organized scene in which two objects are touching. In this case, relational location information specifying the contact between the two objects would lead to greater sensitivity in the detection of small 'moves' than projective location information. The point is that the usefulness of relational location information is highly dependent on the structure of the scene. That is, the precision with which relational location information specifies the position of objects depends on the mutual constraints introduced by the relation. For example, minimal spatial constraint is 'exerted' when two objects are encoded as far apart along a dimension. That is, a wide range of different locations would be consistent with two objects being far apart. Greater spatial constraint is 'exerted' when one object supports another. The supported object must remain above and in contact with the supporting object.

I anticipate that future research will differentiate among two general classes of mutual constraint: position and alignment. Position constraints include the following spatial relations: far apart, close together, in contact (adjacent objects), horizontal support (one object leans against another), and vertical support (one object lies upon the other). Alignment constraints among objects are of particular interest in this chapter. They include the following relations: opposition (the fronts of two objects are facing each other), beyond (an object has a second, closer object between it and the perceiver), partial concealment (the closer object hinders sight of the other), complete concealment, and between (one object is between two others). Greater levels of mutual constraint, whether they involve position or alignment relations, should result in more precise encoding of the location of objects in a scene since less variability in location is allowed by more constraining spatial relations. This is particularly the case for alignment relations. Ludvigh (1953) has shown that the alignment of a dot between two other dots can be determined with extraordinary precision: to within less than .001° of visual angle when the outside dots are approximately 0.25^{o} apart, and to less than .003° of visual angle when the outside dots are slightly less than 1° apart.

AUTOMATIC VS. EFFORTFUL ENCODING

Although the presence of mutually constraining relations between objects is a necessary condition for relational location information to be useful, it is not a sufficient condition. It is necessary also for mechanisms involved in the encoding of mutually constraining relational information to be activated. This issue brings me to Hasher and Zacks' (1979) distinction between automatic and effortful processes in memory. They argue that automatic encoding proceeds without intention or effort, whereas effortful processes involve the intentional use of strategies to facilitate the encoding of information. Research concerned with the effect of intention on the encoding of spatial location information has often involved arbitrary collections of objects whose locations depend on projective location information. Park and Mason (1982) had subjects discriminate between pictures (or words) presented on either the left or right side of a slide, von Wright et al (1975) had subjects discriminate locations defined by positions within a 2 x 2 matrix, and Mandler et al (1977) had subjects discriminate locations defined by positions within a 6 x 6 matrix. In most cases, the intention to learn spatial location had little or no effect on performance in these experiments. When evidence was obtained indicating that intention improved performance, it tended to be when the objects were presented in realistic contexts (von Wright et al, 1975) or in an actual three-dimensional environment (Acredelo et al, 1975).

Implicit in Hasher and Zacks' (1979) concept of effortful processing are the following: (1) appropriate processing strategies are available to the perceiver to facilitate the effortful encoding of spatial location information; and (2) the subject matter allows for or affords the utilization of such strategies. That strategies appropriate for the effortful encoding of spatial location are not always available to subjects is indicated by improvement, with age, in children's ability to retain location information (Acredelo et al, 1975; von Wright et al, 1975). That the utilization of such effortful strategies depends on the suitability of the subject matter is indicated by evidence that intention, which has minimal effects on retention when location is defined by arbitrary positions on a projective surface (Mandler et al, 1977; Park and Mason, 1982; von Wright et al, 1975), becomes more of a factor when locations are defined by positions in realistic spatial contexts (Acredelo et al, 1975; von Wright et al, 1975).[2]

As indicated above, intention does not seem to be necessary for subjects to encode projective location information. In terms of Hasher and Zacks' (1979) model, the encoding of projective location information seems to proceed automatically. In contrast, intentions seem to be of greater importance when subjects are presented realistic scenes and have the opportunity to encode relational location information. This, however, should not be read as meaning that the encoding of relational information is invariably

FIGURE 1 Black and white photograph by Dorethea Lange reproduced from *To A Cabin*, by D. Lange and M. Mitchell, New York: Grossman, 1973. (Reproduced with permission of the Oakland Museum, Oakland, California).

effortful. Relations that give meaning to an event are probably encoded automatically. In Figure 1, for example, the encoding of the woman standing at the edge of the water and the boys playing in the sand probably proceeds without intention. These relations provide the perceiver with some ability to specify the location of these objects, but the relations are not especially constraining. More mutual constraint comes from noticing alignments among the objects. For example, the woman is directly beyond the older boy playing in the sand. Also, the young boy playing in the sand is directly between the girl walking in the water and the older boy closest to the camera. Discovering relations involving the alignment of objects develops highly precise location information. For the photograph in Figure 1 the encoding of alignment relations would probably be effortful. In other cases, however, I argue that the encoding of spatial relations involving alignments of objects occurs without effort. Whether automatic or effortful, the encoding of alignment relations among objects may depend on the ability of the perceiver to construct non-egocentric, imaginary perspectives in viewing the scene.

IMAGINARY PERSPECTIVES

In Figure 2, the boy at the top of the picture is looking at the book held by the boy on the right side of the picture. The first boy's view of the book is slightly obscured by the head of the boy holding the book. These spatial relationships can be apprehended when the perceiver of the scene adopts the perspective of the boy at the top of the picture. The potential benefit of so doing is that the alignment relations here are mutually constraining, increasing the likelihood that subjects will encode relatively precise relational location information for the objects in the scene. In terms of Hasher and Zack's (1979) model, the encoding of relational location information for the objects in this scene might proceed automatically if the construction of the perspective of the boy at the top of the picture were elicited by the information in the scene.

Imagined perspectives are of obvious importance in establishing where someone is looking or in visualizing an open view or path to a goal object. Also, establishing the relative spatial locations of objects in a scene can require imagining the relationship among objects from several different perspectives. For example, to determine whether an object is directly above another object it is necessary to determine whether the vertical alignment of the two objects is maintained over several different imagined perspectives. Finally, establishing functional relations between objects can require the coordination of more than one perspective. For example, imagining the viewing perspectives of the boys depicted in Figure 2 is necessary to establish that they are looking at the book. However, in order to determine whether their perspectives are appropriate for them to be observing the information presented in the book, it is also necessary to establish the range of viable viewing perspectives with reference to the book. This kind of visual thinking could differentiate between two different functional relations: (1) the boys are looking at the book; and (2) the boys are attending to its contents (i.e., they are reading).

Young children have limited ability to construct or imagine perspectives other than their own. In their famous three-mountain problem, Piaget and Inhelder (1948) found that children could not select photographs corresponding to nonegocentric views of the three-mountain scene until nine years of age.[3] Using a different procedure, but testing for similar abilities, Hardwick et al (1976) placed subjects behind a screen and had them

FIGURE 2 Black and white photograph by Margaretta Mitchell, from *To A Cabin* by D. Lange and M. Mitchell, New York: Grossman, 1973. (Reproduced with permission of the Oaklan Museum, Oakland, California).

aim a sighting tube at designated objects they had just seen in a room. They were asked to do this while imagining themselves at different locations in the room. Whereas 11-year-olds were moderately successful at this task, 6-year-olds could not do it. It is of interest, with regard to this developmental trend in children's ability to construct imaginary perspectives, that in von Wright et al's (1975) experiment with realistic contexts, evidence for effects of intention on the encoding of spatial location was obtained for 12-year-olds and adults, but not 5- or 7-year-olds. If the encoding of relational location information in von Wright et al's experiment was facilitated by the use of an effortful strategy involving imaginary perspectives, it would follow that the effects of intention would not emerge in the experiment until children reached an age when they could construct nonegocentric perspectives for the material presented in their scenes.

The integration of multiple perspectives of a real-world street scene has been studied, with adults, by Hock and Schmelzkopf (1980). Their study showed that subjects can integrate photographs taken in different directions from the same or different camera locations to form a schematic representation of the street scene. Once this representation was formed, subjects could discriminate camera locations for photographs taken in novel directions as well as photographs taken from novel locations. Also, experiments investigating the mental rotation of disoriented stimuli implicitly require that the perceiver imagine what the stimuli would look like from a perspective that would make them perceptually upright. For example, egocentrically disoriented letters must be imagined as upright in order to determine whether they are normal or mirror-image reversed (Cooper and Shepard, 1973). Finally, imaginary perspectives can be intentionally constructed in order to provide a gravitationally upright frame of reference for a newly-learned form. Hock and Sullivan (1981) showed this by having two groups of subjects view unfamiliar, random polygons with their heads tilted 45°. Subjects in the incidental condition were instructed to judge the goodness of form for the polygons; subjects in the intentional condition were instructed to remember the polygons. Hock and Sullivan (1981) found that subjects in the incidental condition encoded the information in the polygons on the basis of their orientation on the retina. It was only when subjects intentionally tried to remember them that they encoded the information in the polygons by imagining what they look like from an upright perspective.

The purpose of the research reported in this chapter is to provide evidence for the effects of nonegocentric, imaginary perspectives on the encoding of relational location information involving the alignment of objects in a scene. The stimulus selected for this purpose was Andrew Wyeth's painting *Christina's World*. As can be seen in Figure 3, a very strong imaginary perspective is provided in this painting by Christina's torso straining toward the house in the upper-right corner. In fact, Christina's body almost precisely fills a projective cone emanating from the door of the house. Of particular interest was how well someone looking at the painting would encode the location of the small barn on the horizon. In relation to the projective reference frame provided by the surface on which the scene is painted, the barn is in the top-centre of the painting. However, in terms of other objects in the scene, the barn is directly beyond Christina'shead and along the horizon to the left of the house toward which Christina is straining. We hypothesized that the imaginary perspective elicited by Christina's torso would result in subjects' encoding the location of the barn in terms of its alignment relations with the other objects in the

FIGURE 3 Andrew Wyeth, *Christina's World* (1948). Tempera on gesso panel (81.9 x 121.3 cm). Collection, The Museum of Modern Art, New York. Purchase. (Reproduced, with permission, from black and white photographs provided by the Museum of Modern Art).

scene (primarily Christina and the house) rather than its less projective location (i.e., the top centre of the painting). In Experiment 1, subjects' ability to determine the location of the barn was examined under two viewing conditions: (1) when the painting was upright and the imaginary perspective was strongly established; and (2) when the painting was rotated 180° and the imagined perspective was, at best, weakly established.

EXPERIMENT 1

Method

The first step in the experiment involved presenting a 15.6 x 23.4cm colour reproduction of Andrew Wyeth's Painting, *Christina's World* on a horizontal surface. The painting was presented in its normal upright orientation for 25 subjects, and rotated 180° for another 25 subjects. Each subject was instructed to try to remember the information in the picture, and was given approximately 10 sec to examine it. The colour reproduction was then removed and subjects were presented with 5 black and white photocopies of the painting. These comprised the test stimuli for the experiment. They were prepared by cutting off the top of the photocopies along the horizon line, removing the barn in the top-centre, but not the house in the upper-right corner. The barn was then reinserted into the photocopy at one of 5 locations along the horizon: at its original (0) location, displaced 0.7 cm to the left (-0.7), displaced 1.4 cm to the left (-1.4), displaced 0.7 cm to the right (+0.7), and displaced 1.4 cm to the right (+1.4)[4]. It should be noted that for all five options the barn remained at the top of the painting, and within the central-third of the painting in terms of horizontal location.

During the testing phase of the experiment, each subject was presented the five options placed in random arrangement. The test stimuli were presented in the same orientation as the initial presentation of the painting. Subjects were shown that the 5 alternatives differed with respect to the position of the barn along the horizon, and were instructed to select the photocopy that corresponded with the painting that they had previously examined. There was no limit to how long subjects could take to make their choice. If unsure, they were instructed to make their best guess.

Results

The percentage of subjects' responses for each of the five test stimuli are presented in Table 1. If subjects were merely guessing in choosing among the 5 alternatives, the expected value for each alternative test stimulus would have been 20%. The analysis of the data in the Upright condition indicated that the distribution of responses was significantly different from what would be expected if subjects were guessing. That is, as a result of the concentration of responses at the +0.7 alternative, the distribution of responses was significantly different from chance (χ^2 = 9.6, p<.05). In contrast, the distribution of responses for subjects in the Rotated condition was not significantly different from chance (χ^2 = 2.4, p>.05). The results therefore indicated that subjects had encoded the location of the barn when the painting was upright, and the imaginary perspective strongly established (although with bias toward the +0.7 alternative, which was more directly beyond Christina's head). When the painting was rotated 180° and the imagined perspective was, at best, weakly established, there was no indication that subjects had encoded the spatial location of the barn with sufficient precision to discriminate among the five test stimuli.

TABLE 1 Percentage of subjects' responses for each of the five locations of the barn during the testing phase of the experiment.

EXPERIMENT 1: Full View of Painting

	LOCATIONS OF BARN						
	-1.4	-0.7	0	+0.7	+1.4	χ^2	p
Upright	16.0	16.0	16.0	44.0	8.0	9.6	<.05
Rotated	8.0	20.0	24.0	24.0	24.0	2.4	>.05

EXPERIMENT 2: Partially Shielded View of Painting

	LOCATIONS OF BARN						
	-1.4	-0.7	0	+0.7	+1.4	χ^2	p
Intentional	12.0	36.0	24.0	28.0	0	10.0	<.05
Incidental	28.0	20.0	24.0	16.0	12.0	2.0	>.05

Discussion

The results of the experiment indicated that the encoding of relational location information does not proceed in a purely automatic manner. If it did, subjects would have been able to discriminate among the 5 alternative barn locations in the Rotated as well as the Upright condition. It should also be noted that subjects in this experiment were not specifically instructed to remember location information. This indicated that when the thematic content of a scene elicits the construction of a strong imaginary perspective, as in the Upright presentation of 'Christina's World', intentional strategies are not required to encode relational alignments among the objects in the scene. It followed, on this basis, that if a scene did not elicit the construction of imaginary perspectives, then subjects would have to be instructed to remember intentionally the location of objects in the scene. This hypothesis was tested in Experiment 2.

EXPERIMENT 2

The imaginary perspective elicited by *Christina's World* is the result of Christina's torso straining toward the house in the upper-right corner of the painting. Her head is turned away from the viewer of the painting, so no information is provided concerning her direction of gaze. In order to eliminate the imaginary perspective elicited by Christina, the bottom 45% of the painting was shielded with an opaque sheet of white paper so that Christina's entire torso was covered. Only her head and a small part of her neck could be seen, along with the remaining information in the upper 55% of the painting.

Method

The experiment followed the same general format as in Experiment 1. Subjects were shown the shielded version of *Christina's World* for approximately 10 sec and were then shown the same 5 test alternatives as in Experiment 1. The test stimuli were shielded in the same manner as in the initial presentation of the painting. During the initial presentation, one group of 25 subjects received the same instructions as Experiment 1; they were told to remember the information in the picture. Since they were not specifically told to remember location information, these subjects composed the Incidental condition in the experiment. The second group of 25 subjects were instructed during the initial presentation of *Christina's World* , to remember the locations of the main objects in the picture. Since they were specifically told to remember location information, these subjects composed the Intentional condition in the experiment. As in Experiment 1, all the subjects were tested individually (with regard both to the initial presentation of *Christina's World* and to the presentation of the five test alternatives).

Results

The percentage of subjects' responses for each of the 5 test stimuli are presented in Table 1. Subjects in the Intentional condition concentrated their responses in the middle 3 options (-0.7, 0, +0.7) resulting in a distribution that was significantly different from chance ($\chi^2 = 10.0$, $p < .05$). In contrast, the distribution of responses for subjects in the Incidental condition was not significantly different from chance ($\chi^2 = 2.0$, $p > .05$).

Discussion

The results of the experiment indicated that subjects encoded location information with sufficient precision to discriminate among the 5 different locations of the barn, but only when they intentionally tried to remember the location of the main objects in the painting. As in Experiment 1, the results provided evidence that the encoding of relational location information did not proceed in a purely automatic manner. Otherwise, subjects would have encoded the location of the barn in both the Intentional and Incidental conditions. The results therefore supported the hypothesis that in the absence of information that elicits the construction of imaginary perspectives, intention is necessary to activate mechanisms that encode relational location information for the objects in a scene.

CONCLUSIONS

The results of the two experiments reported in this study indicated that relational location information for objects in a scene is not encoded in a completely automatic fashion. If the subject matter depicted in the scene elicits the construction of imaginary perspectives, mechanisms involved in coding relational information are activated, apparently automatically. If, however, the subject matter depicted in the scene does not elicit imaginary perspectives, the strategic intention to encode relational location information is required. An examination of previously reported developmental data indicates that young children seem automatically to encode the location of objects in relation to projective reference frames. However the construction of nonegocentric perspectives is not something that young children do well, at least when they must do so strategically. Currently under investigation is whether young children who otherwise have difficulty constructing nonegocentric perspectives can do so with *Christina's World*, a stimulus which for adults seems to elicit such a construction without strategic intent.

Reviewing in my own mind the issues that have been discussed in this chapter, it seems to be that the key to all else is that the predominant concern of the perceiver is to determine the thematic content of a scene. This results in the activation (probably automatically) of mechanisms concerned with the organization of the visual field into a hierarchy of perceptual groups for the purposes of establishing the formal qualities of objects and encoding thematically important relations among objects. The effect of perceptual grouping, I have argued, is the formation of two-component projective location codes for the elements composing the group: a centre-of-gravity component based on all the elements incorporated into the group, and a deviation code specific to individual elements. I then went on to argue that 50 msec after moving one's fixation to a new point in a scene, it becomes difficult to retrieve both the centre-of-gravity and deviation components of the projective location codes for the previously sampled information. Hence, there is very quickly a sharp decrease in the precision of projective location information that the perceiver needs in order to make sense of a complex scene. This may be why our gaze must continually return to points of high thematic importance in sampling information from a scene (Yarbus, 1967). The cost of this biased sampling is that significant portions of the visual field may never be processed by high resolution mechanisms involving foveal vision, reducing the precision of projective location information in these regions. This cost may be further magnified by shrinkage in the effective functional field of view (i.e., tunnel vision) when the demands on foveal vision are complex (Ikeda and Takeuchi, 1975).

How then do we recover from these losses in projective location information? In most cases we probably do not. Thematic content is almost always more important to us than the specific location of objects. However, on occasions when we do concern ourselves with the location of objects in a scene, there are some remedies that can be taken. One is more uniformly to sample information in the scene (Yarbus provides some evidence to support this conjecture). A second remedy is intentionally to construct imaginary perspectives that allow for the encoding of highly constraining alignment relations among the objects in a scene (as suggested for Figure 1). If imaginary perspectives are elicited by the thematic content of the scene, as in *'Christina's World*, highly constraining spatial alignment relations may be encoded without intention or effort.

FOOTNOTES

1. The research reported in this chapter was supported by a grant from the Army Research Institute (#MDA903-82-V-0317). I thank Larry Malcus for his careful reading of the manuscript and the Department of Experimental Psychology, University of Cambridge, England where the work was completed.

2. Park and Mason (1982) found that the retention of location information (left vs. right side of a slide) was better when subjects were instructed to study the items and their location than when they were instructed to study only the items. They interpreted this as indicating that location memory was better under intentional instructions. This conclusion, however, was contradicted by their further evidence that the location of pictures was retained with essentially the same accuracy when subjects were instructed to study the items and their colour as when they were instructed to study the items and their position.

3. Masangkay et al (1974) have shown that children as young as three-years of age understand that other people have viewing perspectives that are different than their own. However, their ability to perform the visual transformations necessary to determine what the other person sees is age limited. Since the transformations required by Piaget and Inhelder's (1948) three-mountain task are relatively complex, children do not adequately display their nonegocentricity in this task until about nine years of age.

4. The displacement of 0.7 cm was equivalent to approximately one-third of the width of the barn.

REFERENCES

Acredelo, L.P., Pick. H.L. and Olsen, M.G. (1975). Environmental differentiation and familiarity as determinants of children's memory for spatial location. Developmental Psychology, 11, 495-501.

Biederman, I., Mezzanotte, R.L. and Rabinowitz, J.C. (1982). Scene perception: Detecting and judging objects undergoing relational violations. Cognitive Psychology, 14, 143-177.

Cooper, L.A. and Shepard, R.N. (1973). Chronometric studies of the rotation of mental images. In W.G. Chase (Ed.) Visual Information Processing. New York: Academic Press.

Coren, S. and Girgus, J.S. (1980). Principles of perceptual organization and spatial distortion: The Gestalt illusions. Journal of Experimental Psychology: Human Perception and Performance, 6, 404-412.

De Groot, A.D. (1965). Thought and Choice in Chess. The Hague: Mouton.

Estes, W.K., Allmeyer, D.H. and Reder, S.M. (1976). Serial position functions for letter identification at brief and extended exposure durations. Perception and Psychophysics, 19, 1-15.

Goldstein, E.B. (1979). Rotation of objects in pictures viewed at an angle: Evidence for different properties of two types of pictorial space. Journal of Experimental Psychology: Human Perception and Performance, 5, 78-87.

Hardwick, D.A., McIntyre, C.W. and Pick, H.L. Jr. (1976). Content and manipulation of cognitive maps in children and adults. Society for Research in Child Development Monographs, 41, Serial No. 166.

Hasher, L. and Zacks, R.T. (1979). Automatic and effortful processes in memory. Journal of Experimental Psychology: General, 108, 356-388.

Hock, H.S., Gordon, G.P. and Whitehurst, R. (1974). Contextual relations: The influence of familiarity, physical plausibility and belongingness. Perception and Psychophysics, 16, 4-8.

Hock, H.S. and Schmelzkopf, K.F. (1980). The abstraction of schematic representations from photographs of real-world scenes. Memory and Cognition, 8, 543-554.

Hock, H.S. and Sullivan M. (1981). Alternative spatial reference systems: Intentional vs. incidental learning. Perception and Psychophysics, 29, 467-474.

Hogben, J.H. and DiLollo, V. (1974). Perceptual integration and perceptual segregation of brief visual stimuli. Vision Research, 14, 1059-1069.

Hogben, J.H., Julesz, B. and Ross, J. (1976). Short-term memory in symmetry perception. Vision Research, 16, 861-866.

Ikeda, M. and Takeuchi, T.(1975). Influence of the foveal load on the functional field of view. Perception and Psychophysics, 18, 255-260.

Julesz, B. (1963). Stereopsis and binocular rivalry of contours. Journal of the Optical Society of America, 53, 994-999.

Julesz, B. (1965). Texture and visual perception. Scientific American, 212, 38-48.

Ludvigh, E. (1953). Direction sense of the eye. American Journal of Ophthalmology, 36, 139-142.

Mandler, J.M. and Johnson, N.S. (1976). Some of the thousand words a picture is worth. Journal of Experimental Psychology: Human Learning and Memory, 2, 529-540.

Mandler, J.M. and Parker, R.E. (1976). Memory for descriptive and spatial information in complex pictures. Journal of Experimental Psychology: Human Learning and Memory, 2, 38-48.

Mandler, J.M. and Ritchey, G.H. (1977). Long term memory for pictures. Journal of Experimental Psychology: Human Learning and Memory, 3, 386-396.

Mandler, J.M., Seegmiller, O. and Day, J. (1979). On the coding of spatial information. Memory and Cognition, 5, 10-16.

Masangkay, Z.S., McCluskey, K.A., McIntyre, C.W., Sims-Knight, J., Vaughn, B.E. and Flavell, J.H. (1974). The early development of inferences about the visual percepts of others. Child Development, 45, 357-366.

Neisser, U. (1967). Cognitive Psychology. New York: Appleton-Century-Crofts.

Park, D.C. and Mason, D.A. (1982). Is there evidence for automatic processing of spatial and color attributes present in pictures and words? Memory and Cognition, 10, 76-81.

Piaget, J. and Inhelder, B. (1948). The Child's Conception of Space. New York: Norton Company.

Prinzmetal, W. (1981). Principles of feature integration in visual perception. Perception and Psychophysics, 30, 330-340.

Ross, J. and Hogben J.H. (1974). Short-term memory in stereopsis. Vision Research, 14, 1195-1201.

Treisman, A. and Gelade, G. (1980). A feature integration theory of attention. Cognitive Psychology, 12, 97-136.

von Wright, J.M. Gebhard, P. and Karttunen, M. (1975). A developmental study of the recall of spatial location. Journal of Experimental Child Psychology, 20, 181-190.

Wolford, G. and Hollingsworth, S. (1974). Evidence that short-term memory is not the limiting factor in the tachistoscopic full-report procedure. Memory and Cognition, 2, 769-800.

Yarbus, A.L. (1967). Eye Movements and Vision. New York: Plenum Press.

Cognitive Processes in the Perception of Art
W.R. Crozier and A.J. Chapman (editors)
© Elsevier Science Publishers B.V. (North-Holland), 1984

The Aesthetic Experience and Mundane Reality

A.T. Purcell

Sydney University

Psychology and the arts have a long and chequered relationship. Certainly this relationship extends from the beginning of a scientific psychology. Fechner (1876) attempted to test experimentally the importance of the golden section by collecting preference data relating to rectangles of varying proportions and examining artworks for the presence of such relationships. This type of approach has reappeared intermittently since that time in a variety of contexts and using a variety of materials. Some variations to the basic paradigm have occurred: for example, Berlyne and his co-workers (e.g., Berlyne et al, 1974) have extended the response side of the paradigm to include sets of work regarded as representing different facets of the aesthetic response (calm/exciting, simple/complex) and factor analysed the correlation matrix obtained from the matrix of verbal responses by aesthetic stimulus material averaged across subjects. The resulting factors are regarded as identifying underlying dimensions of the aesthetic response and the aesthetic stimulus material (e.g., each painting) can then be given a score on each of the factors allowing an analysis of the aesthetic characteristics of the stimulus material as well as the aesthetic response.

Another perhaps less direct relationship between psychology and the arts arises from the continuing interest that has been shown in the psychology of creativity and the characteristics of creative people. This interest was often based in the area of ability testing (e.g., Guilford and Holley, 1949) or individual differences (e.g., Barron, 1958). Much of this early work was also related to popular conceptions of creativity and that creative traits were particularly associated with artists. Creativity was also considered to be something an individual either did or did not have and it was this particular ability which allowed creative individuals in the arts to produce material capable of eliciting aesthetic responses in other people. Thus many studies were conducted with people who were considered to have exhibited creativity in their output in an attempt to identify their particular abilities. The question of whether or not creativity is an ability possessed by all individuals but varying in degree or extent or an ability unique to particular individuals has in more recent years generated considerable debate. However, for a large part of its history in psychology and certainly as a continuing attitude held by the general public, both the individual who is creative, the work produced and, in the case of artists, the aesthetic response to that work, were regarded as different and distinct from other abilities and other types of human experience.

A basic assumption can therefore be identified in the two areas of psychology that have had most to do with the arts. It is an assumption about the separateness and difference between art objects and the responses to them and everyday human behaviour and experience. In all preference studies the stimulus material selected has only consisted of material identifiably the product of artistic endeavour, for example, sets of paintings. Similarly the response studied has been preference or some sort of verbal responses shown to be elicited by artistic material. Both aspects have great face validity. To study aesthetic responses one should obviously study the output of artists: people exhibit differential preference responses to what are considered to be good and bad example of artworks; preference is therefore an obvious measure of aesthetic response and so on.

The aim of this chapter, however, is first to argue that a full understanding of the aesthetic responses can only occur when it is placed in the context of a model which deals with the representation and processing of a particular class of information. This is not to say that the aesthetic response is the same as the experiences resulting from the representation and processing of information about mundane reality. Rather the aesthetic response is the result of a difference between the characteristics of a particular environment and the way this is organized and remembered and the existing cognitive structures concerned with ongoing everyday experience.

This general idea is not new. For example, Humphreys (1973) presented a convincing argument about the relevance of similarity and difference to the understanding of beauty and the idea of unity and diversity as the basis for the aesthetic response is widespread in aesthetic theory and throughout the history of the arts. Here I first review briefly some recent models of the organization of everyday experience developed in cognitive psychology and review recent work on the genesis of emotion. I then develop a model of the mechanism for the aesthetic response. The model is also sufficiently specific to permit experimental tests of its implications; and, in the second part of the chapter, I present the results of one such experiment.

THE ORGANIZATION OF EXPERIENCE

Most of us do not realize that every time we look at the same scene it will be different to the previous time we looked at it. Even two sequential glances at a scene will be different - the lighting can change, head or body movement and so on. The retinal image on which our visual experience of the scene depends is therefore varying to a greater or lesser extent through time, and yet we perceive the scene as constant. Similarily we are all aware of differences between instances of the same class of things seen on different occasions. For example, we are aware of the differences between the great variety of particular dogs we have seen, but recognize them all as dogs. The problem for the study of representation and processing of information about the environment therefore is how can our response be to the similarities between specific instances rather than to the differences. This is in fact a question about how we form categories which contain similar instances.

A very common approach until recently was to argue that we have a list of attributes stored in memory (the representation of the attributes being possibly different in short- and long-term memory) to which we compare the current instance. If the two match, they are treated as being similar. However, such an approach has a number of problems. We would all agree that a cow is an animal with four legs. Four legs would therefore appear to be one of the attributes on the criterial list. However, if we are exposed to a three-legged cow we still classify it as a cow. A fixed criterial list of attributes requiring the presence of all attributes before classification can occur has problems dealing with obvious aspects of our ability to respond to similar instances. Recently, however, a number of authors have elaborated models based on a proposal by Wittgenstein (1953) that family resemblance was the basis for category formation. This approach is particularly well illustrated by Rosch's work on natural categories (Rosch, 1977; Rosch and Mervis, 1975) and Smith et al's (1974) model of semantic memory. Rosch argues that categories are formed around particular instances that exhibit the largest number of attributes in common with all other members of the category. This example(s) is called the prototype. Other category members share greater or lesser numbers of attributes with the prototype. If an instance has many attributes in common with the prototype it will be considered a particularly good example of the category. Two non-prototypical examples can, however, share different attributes or partly overlapping sets of attributes with the prototype and still be considered as equally good members of the category. If this describes the category formation process the problem of the cow with three legs disappears - it would be recognized as a cow because it would have a large degree of overlap with the prototype cow. It would not, I expect, be regarded as the best example of a cow but probably an equally good example as a cow with no tail. This is what is meant by a family resemblance relationship and a similar idea occurs in Smith et al's (1974) concept of defining and characteristic attributes of a word's meaning. Rosch and her colleagues in an extensive series of experiments using a variety of converging methods have convincingly shown that such a process does occur in the formation of natural categories such as birds, vegetables, and furniture.

PROCESSING OF ENVIRONMENTAL INFORMATION

This does not, however, describe how the process occurs in ongoing everyday experience. It is a model of category formation, not of the use of such categories to solve the problem posed by variation in the input from the environment. A number of authors, however, have proposed that we build up, on the basis of our continuing experience of the environment mental structures called schemas, frames or scripts. These are mental organizations which process chunks of experience. These chunks deal with aspects of the environment such as whole scenes -- for example, kitchens, gardens, houses etc. -- and they contain different types of information about different aspects of the scene varying between very detailed perceptual information to more abstract, conceptual attributes and relationships. These schemas are also arranged in hierarchies which vary from the specific to the general -- robin, bird, mammal, animal, living thing. It is then argued that, at each of the levels of a hierarchy, is stored a set of attributes for objects and relationships, called the default values, which we match current experience against. If there is a sufficient match then we classify the particular object in immediate experience as a member of the category. These models make no explicit statement about the characteristics of default values: however, I propose that the default values found in these schemas are the attributes of the prototype.

A number of recent experiments have tested hypotheses derived from such models of our representation and processing of information about the environment. Particulary interesting from the point of view of this chapter, however, has been work where people's ability to recognize changes to scenes has been tested. For example, Friedman (1979) presented individuals with a number of everyday scenes and then tested their memory for various aspects of the scenes. A number of different types of changes had been made to the scenes prior to their presentation. Objects within the scenes had been classified as obligatory, non-obligatory and unexpected on the basis of prior ratings of the likelihood of finding these objects in a particular scene. Changes were made to each of these classes of objects, and it was found that only changes involving the introduction of unexpected objects into a scene were recognized and remembered. Friedman interprets this to mean that providing there is a sufficient fit to the default values at the relevant levels in the cognitive organization we respond as though the objects with those values had been present and therefore fail to detect and remember alterations to obligatory and non-obligatory objects. Ongoing experience therefore consists of matching current perceptual input to stored prototypes. Where a sufficient mismatch occurs, as when unexpected objects are present, we pay attention to and engage in extra processing of information about that aspect of the external situation.

EVERYDAY EXPERIENCE AND EMOTION

It is this aspect of the model of our representation and processing of information about the environment which provides the link to the experience of emotion. Most work in psychology on the emotions has been elemental in orientation: that is, it was argued that there were a number of independent types of emotion - happy, excited, drowsy and so on. However, Schachter and Singer (1962) demonstrated that emotion depended on autonomic nervous system arousal and the characteristics of the situation in which the arousal occurred. Thus different emotions such as happiness or anger could be induced in individuals with the same arousal level (resulting from injections of adrenalin) as a function of what happened to the aroused individual. When a confederate of the experimenter acted in a happy, joyful manner the subjects reported experiencing similar feelings; while if the confederate was angry and abusive the subject also experienced anger.

Findings such as this led Mandler (1975) to propose a model of the causation of emotional experience. Mandler argued that any interruption or blocking of ongoing behaviour results in autonomic nervous system arousal. He uses 'behaviour' in the general sense that in psychology includes mental activity as well as overt motor behaviour. The consequences of its intensity will depend on what happens subsequently -- whether the interruption can be overcome -- and the characteristics of the situation in which it occurred. Mandler's model therefore includes as another consequence of interruption or blocking, attention and further cognitive activity. The parallel with the work on the representation and processing of chunks of experience represented by Friedman's work is obvious - the presentation of unexpected objects within a scene leads to further cognitive activity and represents in Mandler's terms a blocking or interruption which will therefore result in emotional experience.

I would argue that the aesthetic response conforms to this model. That is, a work of art (and this applies to both more recent experimental art forms as well as the traditional) presents us with an environmental stimulus which contains unexpected (non-default) values; this constitutes a blocking of an ongoing response which results in attention and further activity and emotional experience. The extent of the response and the type will govern the characteristics of the emotion experienced. Thus the range of emotional aesthetic response can vary between pleasant, attractive feelings (at low levels of blocking and type of unexpectedness combined with successful processing of the discrepancy through excitement and extreme interest) to extremely negative emotions (resulting from extreme and unusual alterations to an expected pattern in association with failure to resolve the discrepancy by extra cognitive processing).

EXPERIMENTAL DESIGN

My experimental work has been based on the above model. Before discussing one experiment to illustrate the model I introduce a number of specific ideas about the way in which the experiments were done. Amongst the many methods Rosch has used to study whether or not prototypes are the basis of category formation is the rating of degree of goodness of example of a number of instances of the category. If instances of category vary in the number of attributes they share with the category prototype, it would be expected that ratings of widely distributed instances would vary all the way from low ratings, indicating very poor examples, to high ratings, indicating very good examples, and the highest rating being interpretable under the appropriate conditions as approximating the prototype.

If, as argued above, aesthetic responses vary in intensity and type depending on the extent and type of departure from the prototype, then careful selection of examples from the stimulus domain of interest should ensure varying degrees of extent and type of departure from the prototype.

Further the intensity and type of aesthetic response could be indexed by also having ratings of attractiveness, interest and preference. If the model is correct it would be expected that attractiveness would be more closely related to goodness of example than interest but not identical with goodness of example. The preference of response would indicate whether an overall aesthetic response was related to greater or lesser departure from the prototype. Similarily an examination of the relationships between poor examples, the least attractive, least interesting and least preferred should reveal whether or not the least attractive and least preferred closely related to poor examples or uninteresting examples.

The various ratings can be used to test this idea relatively directly. For each of the stimuli a mean value across respondents can be calculated for each of the scales. Measures of covariation or correlation coefficients can then be calculated which will indicate how similar the judgements on each pair of scales are. If attractiveness represents relatively small departures from the attributes of the prototype a high but not perfect positive correlation would be predicted. If interest represents greater departures from the prototype, lower correlations with goodness of example, ratings would be expected with higher correlations with attractiveness.

These relatively direct assessments of the model could however be misleading. Producing average scales for each type of rating imples that they are unidimensional: that is, the process by which the judgement was made took account of only one attribute of the stimulus. However, it is easy to imagine that the same degree of attractiveness, for example, could then be the result of different combinations of attributes: that is, the process may be multi-dimensional. Fortunately, it is possible to test this idea using the same set of rating-scale responses. Rather than simply averaging across individuals to give a mean score for each stimulus it is possible to calculate an index of similarity between each stimulus and all the other stimuli. This gives a set of measurements of the degree of similarity between all pairs of stimuli and this can be analysed to test how many underlying dimensions are required to account for the relationships between each stimulus and every other stimulus. Both types of analysis were used in the experiments to be reported. Thus correlation coefficients can be used to assess the relationships between the scales or subjective experiences, while measures of similarity are used to examine relationships between the stimuli for each scale separately.

Any type of stimulus material could be used to test this model; however, the results to be discussed come from a study using houses as the stimuli. This obviously reflects my interest in architecture. However, not only is architecture in general considered one of the arts, but the design of single houses has been an area of architecture where considerable efforts have been expended by architects attempting to realize the highest aesthetic aims. The study therefore involved a selection of 43 single, detached houses. The other advantage of using stimuli such as houses is that it is possible to identify examples ranging from the everyday suburban house where little conscious effort was expended on its aesthetic characteristics to houses where architects at the forefront of design are consciously and deliberately pursuing aesthetic aims. A sample of forty-two students drawn from all faculties and levels at the University of Sydney were paid to participate in the study. They were shown each of the slides four times and each time were asked to rate each slide in terms of goodness of example, interest and preference.

RESULTS

Correlations between Judgment Types

The first analysis consisted of calculating correlation coefficients between all pairs of ratings. These are presented in Table 1. A clearer idea of the relationship between each of the judgments can be gained from the graphic representation below Table 1 (see part A). This was obtained by carrying out a principal components analysis of the mean ratings for each house on the four judgment scales. Two principal components (the axes in the diagram) accounted for 98% of the variance. The location of each of the scales in this space is indicated. The horizontal factor (Factor 1) accounted for 68% of the variance and is obviously closely related to the goodness of example, attractiveness and preference ratings. Interest is more closely related to the vertical factor (Factor 2) and accounts for 30% of the variance, significantly less than the first factor. It is quite clear that this correlation reflects the relationships predicted by the model. Attractiveness is closely related to goodness of example, preference is very closely related to attractiveness but less closely related to goodness of example. Interest is slightly negatively correlated with goodness of example, slightly positively with attractiveness (neither significantly) and positively and significantly with preference although this correlation is quite small.

While not the main emphasis of the chapter, this diagram can be used to illustrate how another theme of continuing interest in aesthetics can be accommodated by the present model. The question of individual differences in aesthetic response, particularly as a function of variables such as social class or education, has recently been reviewed by Eysenck (1981). As well as collecting this data set from a widely distributed group of university students the experiment has also been conducted with a group of seventeen third-year architecture students. The results of a principal components analysis of their data are presented in Table 1 (B).

TABLE 1 Correlation coefficients between the rating scales and graphic illustration based on a principal components analysis of general sample (A) and architectural students (B).

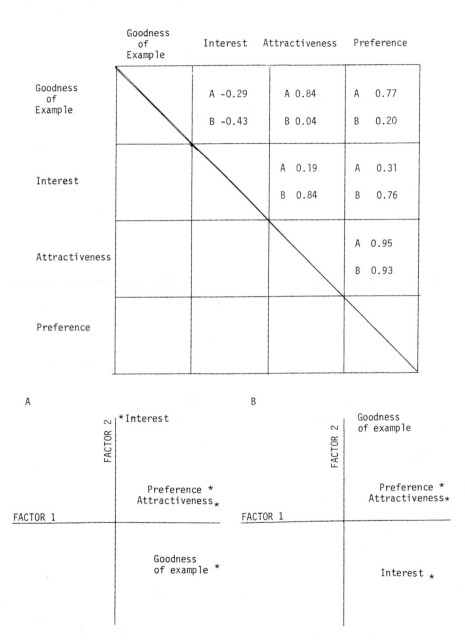

	Goodness of Example	Interest	Attractiveness	Preference
Goodness of Example		A -0.29 B -0.43	A 0.84 B 0.04	A 0.77 B 0.20
Interest			A 0.19 B 0.84	A 0.31 B 0.76
Attractiveness				A 0.95 B 0.93
Preference				

A

B

FIGURE 1 Multi-dimensional scaling of the goodness of example ratings of the architecture student group.

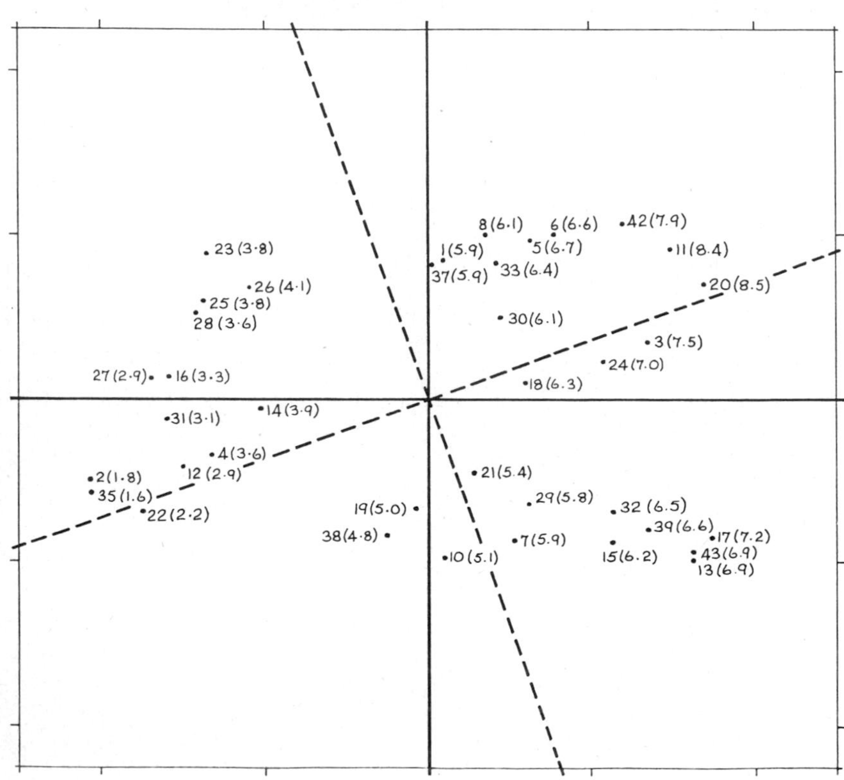

FIGURE 2 Multi-dimensional scaling of the goodness of example ratings of the general student group.

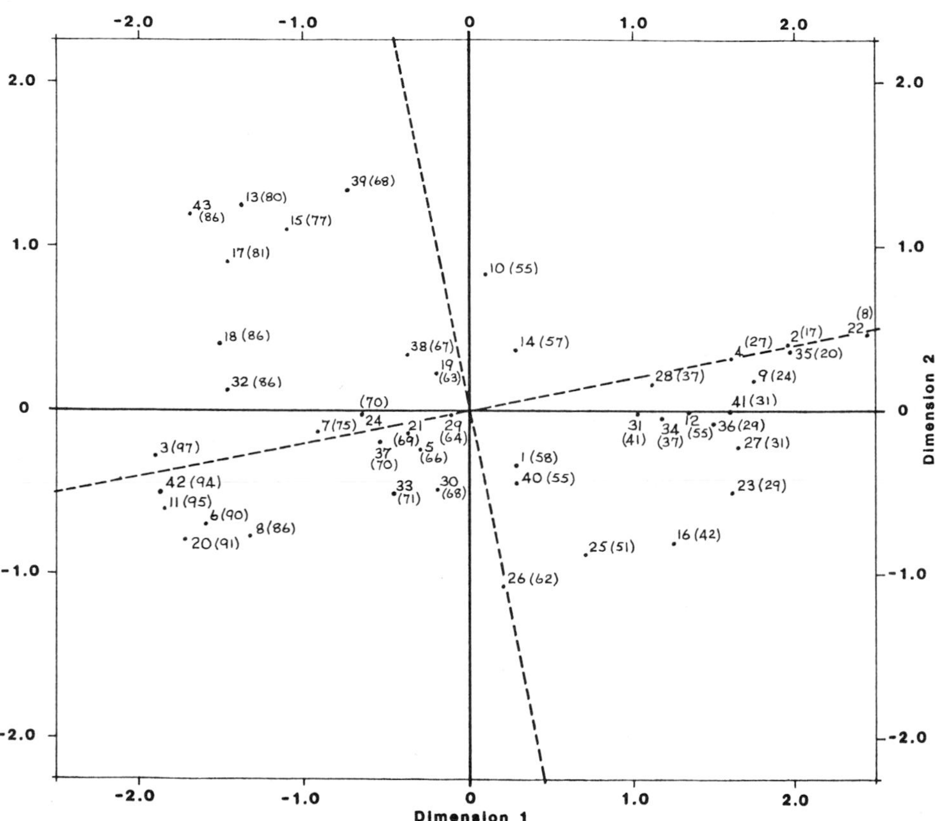

GOODNESS OF EXAMPLE

Again, two components accounted for 98% of the variance, however, in this case, factor I which accounted for 68% of the variance was most closely related to interest, attractiveness and preference, while goodness of example is most closely related to factor 2 which accounts for 30% of the variance. Architecture students therefore give greater emphasis to the interest dimension and their preference/attractiveness judgments are related to this dimension rather than the goodness of example dimension which was the case with the more widely selected student sample. However, the two sets of goodness of example judgments are quite closely related; they correlate 0.77. Clearly the basic organization of the material is the same in both cases; that is in terms of goodness of example and interest. The differences lie in the emphasis given to each and the relationship between these two dimensions and preference/attractiveness. This is even more apparent in the multi-dimensional scaling of the goodness-of-example data where the two configurations are very similar (See Figures 1 and 2).

Multidimensional Scaling Analysis

The second type of analysis discussed above was used to say something about which houses were good examples, attractive, preferred or interesting and what attributes of the houses led to these differing judgments. The approach used was multidimensional scaling. This takes the calculated similarity between all the pairs of houses for each judgment type and constructs a geometric model based on Euclidian distances in one or more dimensions. A measure of how well the model fits the similarities in each of the dimensions is calculated and this is used to decide how many dimensions are needed. In this case it was quite clear that two dimensions were sufficient for each type of judgment; and it is possible therefore to produce a map showing the positions of each of the houses in this space.

The goodness-of-example map or configuration for the general student sample is shown in Figure 2. The number in brackets next to the number identifying the stimulus is the mean rating for that slide. If the axes are rotated slightly as shown by the dotted lines in the figure (a permissible procedure as the position of the axes is not uniquely determined by the analysis) it is clear that Dimension 1 reproduces the goodness-of-example ratings with the highest at the left hand end and the lowest at the right. There is also clear evidence of a second dimension which, however, seems to be asymmetric with its top end closer to the best examples and its lower end closer to the worst examples.

Figure 3 presents the two-dimensional configuration for the interest judgments. Again the figures in brackets represent the average rating for each house. Here again the slightly rotated Dimension 1 reflects the order of interest ratings, in this case with the highest ratings at the right hand end and the lowest at the left. As well as rotations being permissible reflections also do not indicate any difference in the basic structure in this type of analysis. If the stimuli at each end of Dimension 1 are examined it becomes apparent that the stimuli at the high interest end (27, 26, 25, 16) are those at the lower end of Dimension 2 in the analysis of the goodness of example ratings. Similarly the least interesting examples (39, 17, 13, 43) are those at the top end of the second dimension in the goodness of example ratings. If either end of Dimension 2 in this analysis is examined it is found that they contain the same stimuli as the extremes of Dimension 1 on the goodness-of-example case. Note also that the Dimension 2 in the interest analysis is also oblique to Dimension 1.

FIGURE 3 Multi-dimensional scaling of the interest ratings of the general student group.

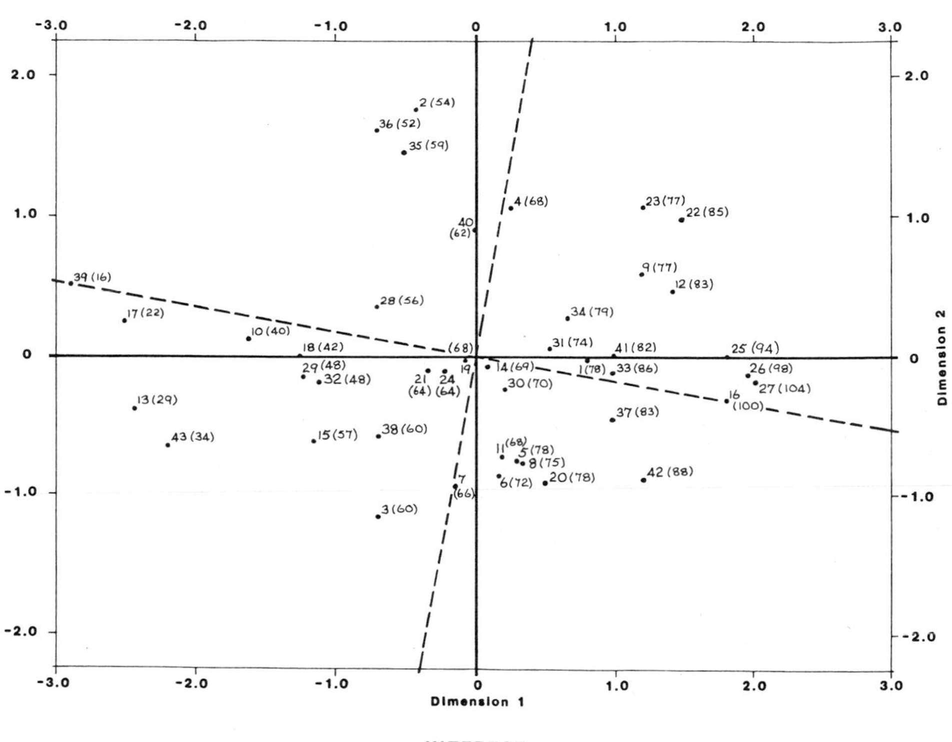

INTEREST

FIGURE 4 Multi-dimensional scaling of the attractiveness ratings of the general student group.

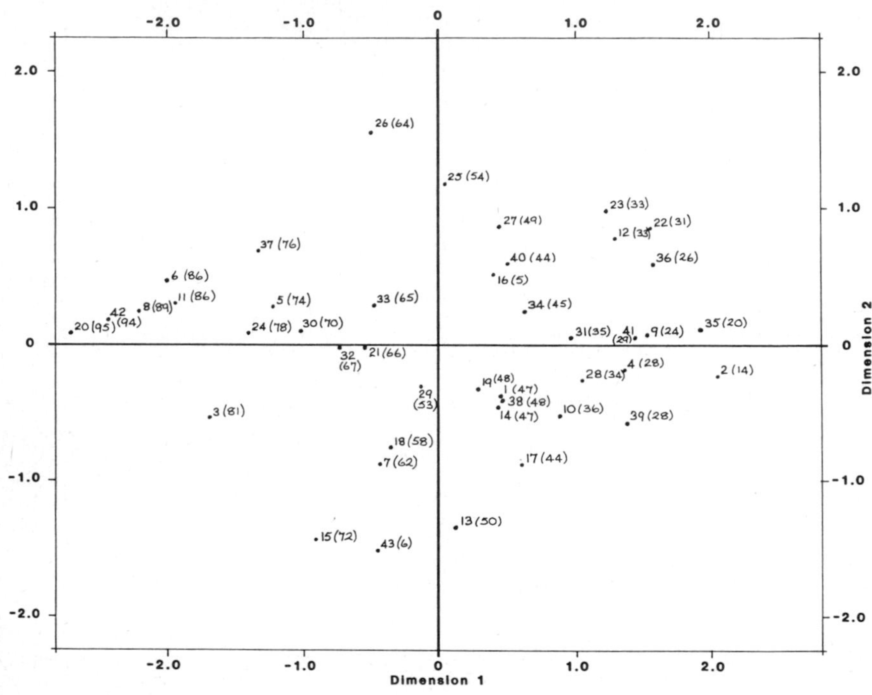

FIGURE 5 Multi-dimensional scaling of the preference ratings of the general student group.

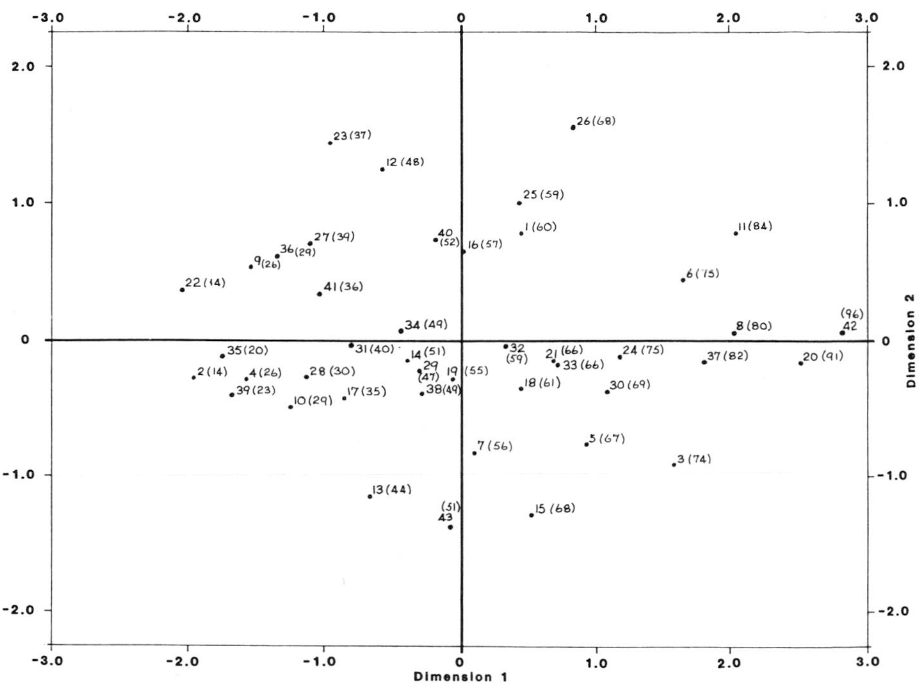

PREFERENCE

Here the best examples are closer to the interesting end while the worst examples are closer to the non-interesting end. It is as though in the two cases the same underlying psychological organization exists but that this is altered in opposite ways depending on the judgment being made. When a goodness-of-example judgment is made greater emphasis is put on this dimension which is reflected in the stretching of Dimension 1 and the shrinking of Dimension 2 in the first analysis. Conversely when interest judgments are being made what was Dimension 2 in the goodness-of-example receives less emphasis. It is clear, therefore, that the second dimension in the first analysis corresponds to an interest dimension and the lack of correlation between goodness of example and interest is misleading if interpreted as indicating no relationship. The two are closely related in a quite unique and meaningful way.

Figure 4 presents the analysis of the attractiveness ratings and again the figures in brackets represent the mean ratings for each house. At the left hand end of Dimension 1 are the most attractive houses (20, 42, 8, 6, 11) and these are the houses that are judged as the best examples (see Figure 2). Similarily the least attractive are also the worst examples. This reflects the high correlation between the two sets of judgments. The houses at the top and bottom of Dimension 2 in this case are also the houses at the top and bottom of Dimension 2 in the goodness-of-example analysis and at the top and bottom of Dimension 1 in the interest analysis. Thus the basic structure is the same in attractivenss as in the previous two analyses. It is interesting however that the asymmetry in the previous configurations has now disappeared and the overall configuration is less elliptical and more circular. This may indicate that on this judgment more equal emphasis is being given to the two dimensions although the stronger emphasis is on goodness of example as the correlations would suggest.

Figure 5 is the configuration for the preference judgments. An examination of this reveals exactly the same pattern as in the previous analyses. Here again the overall configuration is more circular but this time with a suggestion of a greater role for interest in the preference judgment.

In effect these results demonstrate a relationship which has been well documented in the aesthetic and environmental perception literature. In studies using the semantic differential technique two factors occur repeatedly although with varying degrees of clarity. The first is an attractive/pleasantness factor often linked with Osgood et al's (1957) evaluative factor and an interest factor often linked with Osgood's activity factor. These have been considered as independent aspects of psychological experience. However, as Ekblad (1980) has pointed out, the pattern of results of a large number of studies has a number of ambiguities. These results demonstrate that attractiveness and interest are important in such judgments but that they are not independent as previous models would require. Of perhaps far greater importance is the clear demonstration in this experiment of the absolutely basic importance of goodness of example in both attractiveness, preference and interest. It is this set of relationships which makes sense of the attractiveness/preference and interest results in previous studies.

It also provides significant evidence for the type of model discussed in the introduction which explicitly deals with the aesthetic response and its relationship to everyday experience. In brief the house category is prototypically arranged as illustrated in the ratings of goodness of example. However, these ratings are the result of two underlying processes - goodness of example and interest. Interest ratings exhibit exactly the same organization except that the axes show a differential stretching and rotation.

Attractiveness and preference also exhibit the same underlying configuration. However, here the axes are displaced slightly away from goodness of example towards interest for attractiveness and slightly more towards interest for preference. These relationships are exhibited in both the pattern of the correlation coefficients between judgment scales and in the multidimensional scaling of each set of judgments separately. Thus the relationships predicted from the model are clearly illustrated in this example. Attractive houses represent slight departures from the best examples: preferred houses are closely related to attractive houses but are relatively closer to interesting houses. Unattractive and least preferred houses are obviously the reverse of these relationships.

Housing Attributes and Aesthetic Response

While the discussion of the various analyses so far has supported the model of the aesthetic experience presented in the introduction it has not dealt in any way with the attributes or characteristics of houses which may make them more attractive, preferred, interesting or better examples or, given that the collection of houses used in the study included many examples where the architect's intent was specifically aesthetic, what the relationship is between the aesthetic response to these houses and the aim of the architects. Figure 6 contains black and white prints of each of the houses numbered in the order that they appear on the multidimensional scaling configurations. Given the similarity in the underlying organization of our experience of these houses the discussion of this aspect of the results is confined to Figure 5, the preference judgments.

The least preferred houses (22, 2, 35, 4 and 9, which are also the worst examples) are by some of modern architecture's most illustrious practitioners - Louis Kahn, Philip Johnson, Mies van der Rohe, Peter Eisenman. All of those houses lying along the central line and above it to Stimulus 26 are by modern architects with the exception of Stimulus 23 (a villa by Palladio) and Stimulus 1 (a house by Walter Burley Griffin). Houses with specific aesthetic intent as designed by architects therefore fail to communicate with this group of respondents in the sense of inducing positive aesthetic experience. Presumably it was not the architect's intent to induce negative experiences. Note however that House 39 which is also among the least preferred is a very low cost bungalow built by a public housing authority in Australia. Below the centre, with one or two exceptions, are typical plain suburban housing showing very traditional roof façade and material detailing. At the most preferred end of the configuration is a number of traditional Victorian/Georgian style house and traditional farmhouses.

A careful examination of the characteristics of the houses as a function of their position in the configuration reveals a number of clear trends. Starting with the least preferred houses, there are extremely simple house forms without a pitched roof, with unusual materials and with non-traditional windows and other details. As preference increases above the mid-line the houses become more complex in three-dimensional form and start to include typical house details such as a pitched roof or traditional material (stone) although these are used in unusual ways (note the most preferred examples of these architect designed houses, numbers 25 and 26 by

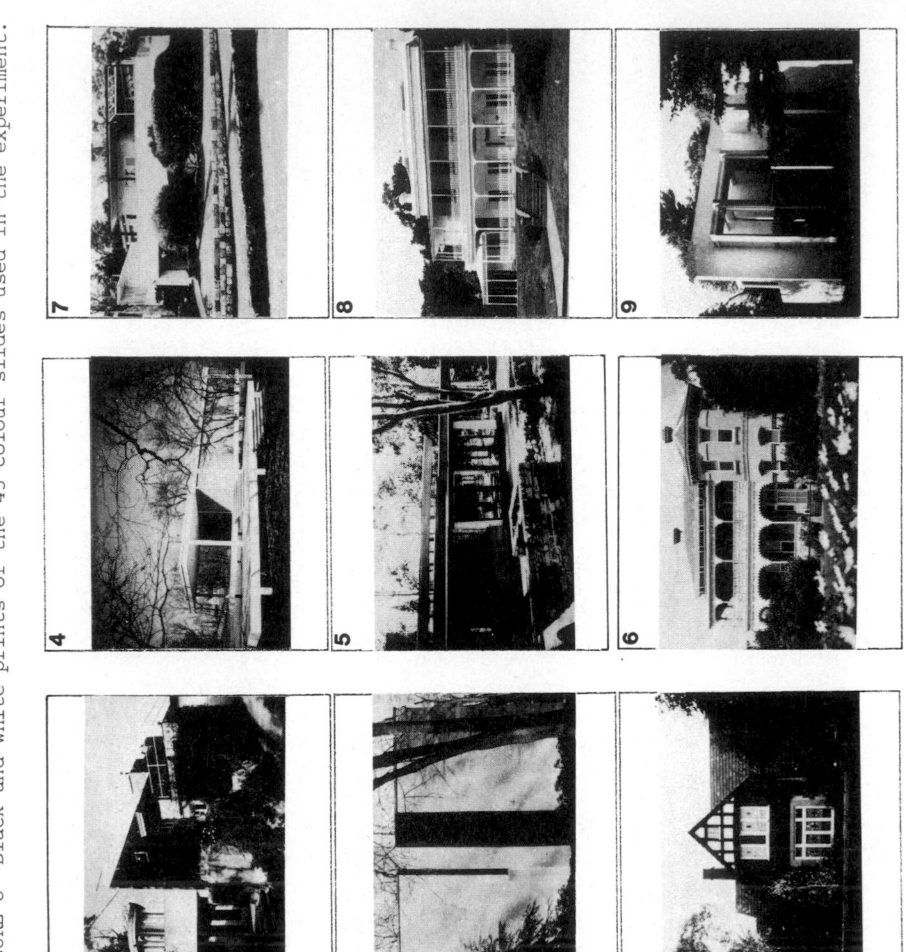

FIGURE 6 Black and white prints of the 43 colour slides used in the experiment.

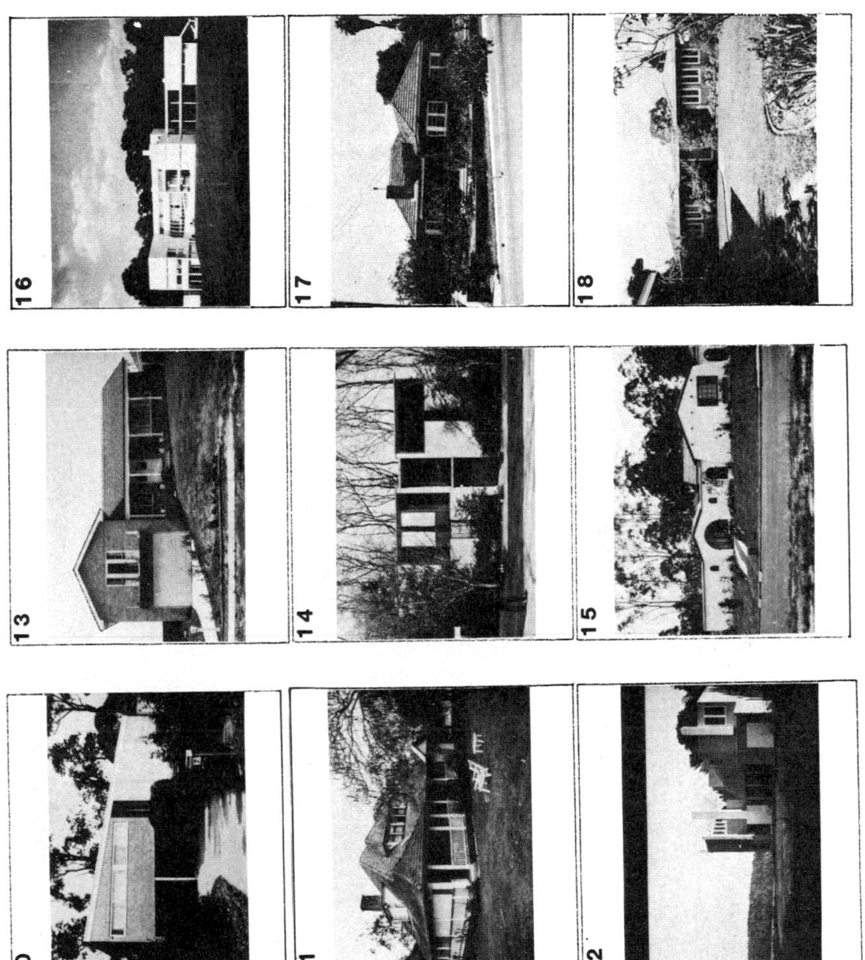
10
11
12
13
14
15
16
17
18

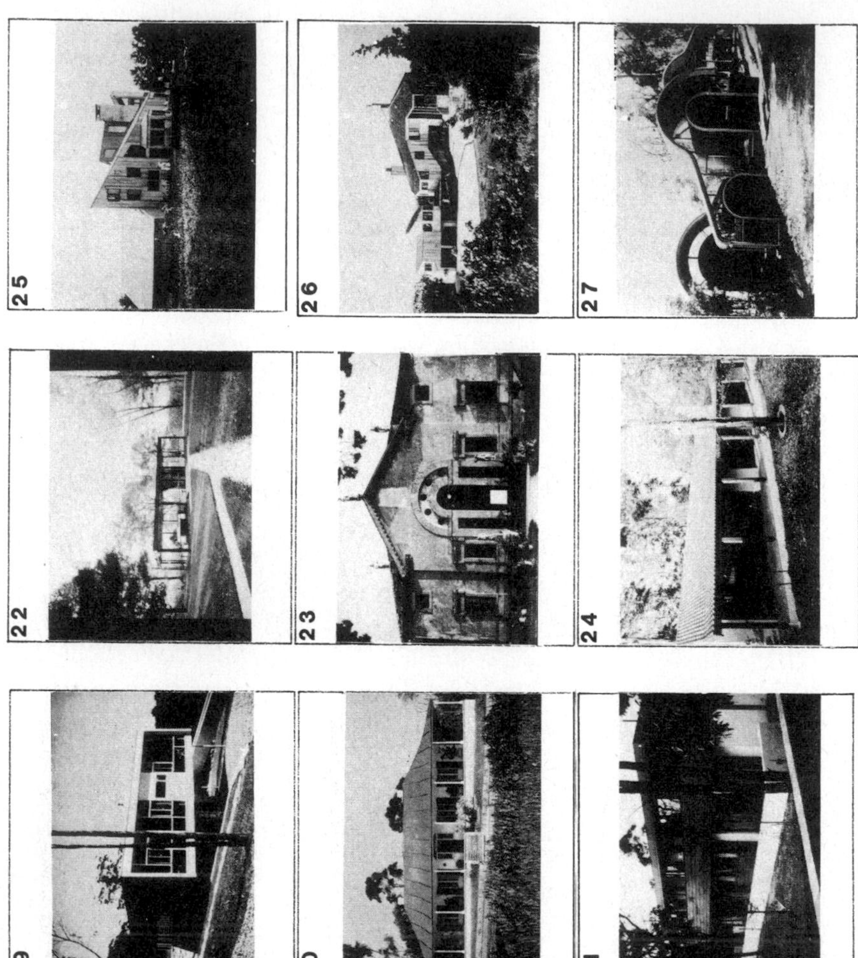
19
20
21
22
23
24
25
26
27

28
29
30
31
32
33
34
35
36

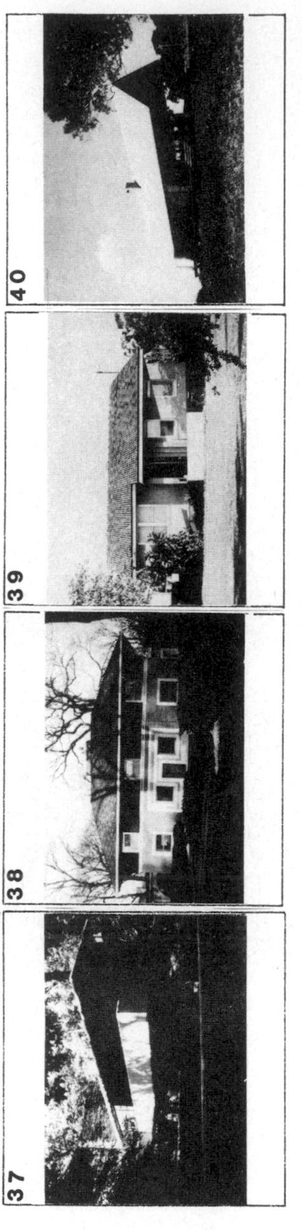
37
38
39
40

43

42

41

Charles Moore, are also among the most interesting houses).

Below the centre line are traditional house forms that lack complexity and are very simple. Towards the more preferred end in that part of the configuration are examples showing increasing façade complexity (3) or coherent perceptually well-organized houses which are also of increasing complexity even though they lack traditional attributes such as pitched roof (e.g., 30). Finally, the most preferred houses exhibit the use of traditional materials, conventional but strong three-dimensional building forms together with complex but perceptually well-organized detailing.

In conclusion, while the architects sought the essence of a house through the pursuit of aesthetic aims specifically by simplyfying and reducing the complexity of both form and detailing and the use of conventional materials, the essence of the experience of a house for the general student group lay in complexity of three-dimensional form and strong perceptual organization together with the use of traditional materials. The response to complexity of form and perceptual organization I would argue is a fundamental aspect of the way we organize our experience of the world. Stimuli which are both complex and perceptually well-organized are intrinsically interesting and attractive. The architect's search is entirely cognitive and intellectual. It will fail in relation to these groups in society who are not familiar with the aims of the designer and the moment in architectural history at which the works were produced; that is to say with groups who lack requisite schemas that would allow these houses to be seen as less extreme departures from the prototype - a prototype which on the evidence presented here may be shared between groups.

REFERENCES

Barron, F. (1958). The psychology of imagination. Scientific American, 199, 3, 150-169.

Berlyne, D.E., Robbins, M.C. and Thompson, R. (1974). A cross cultural study of exploratory and verbal responses to visual patterns varying in complexity. In: D.E. Berlyne (Ed.) Studies in the New Experimental Aesthetics. New York: Wiley.

Ekblad, G. (1980). The Curvex: Simple order structure revealed in ratings of complexity, interestingness and pleasantness. Scandanavian Journal of Psychology, 21, 1-16.

Eysenck, H.J. (1981). Aesthetic preferences and individual differences. In: D. O'Hare (Ed.) Psychology and The Arts. Brighton, Sussex: Harvester.

Fechner, G. (1876). Vorschule der Aesthetik. Leipzig: Breitkopf and Hortel.

Friedman, A. (1979). Framing pictures: the role of knowledge in automatized encoding and memory for gist. Journal of Experimental Psychology: General, 108, 316-355.

Guilford, J.P. and Holley, J.W. (1949). A factorial approach to the analysis of variances in aesthetic judgments. Journal of Experimental Psychology, 39, 208-218.

Humphreys, N.K. (1973). The illusion of beauty. Perception, 2, 429-439.

Mandler, G. (1975). Mind and Emotion. New York: Wiley.

Osgood, C.E., Suci, G. and Tannenbaum, P.H. (1957). The Measurement of Meaning. Urbana, Illinois: University of Illinois Press.

Rosch, E. (1977). Human categorisation. In: N. Warren (Ed.) Studies in Cross Cultural Psychology. Volume 1. London: Academic Press.

Rosch, E. and Mervis, B. (1975). Family resemblances: studies in the internal structure of categories. Cognitive Psychology, 7, 573-605.

Schachter, S. and Singer, J.E. (1962). Cognitive, social and physiological determinants of emotional state. Psychological Review, 69, 379-399.

Smith, E.E., Shoebem, E.J. and Rips, L.J. (1974). Structure and process in semantic memory: a featural model for semantic decisions. Psychological Review, 81, 214-241.

Wittgenstein, L. (1953). Philosophical Investigations. New York: Macmillan.

Cognitive Processes in the Perception of Art
W.R. Crozier and A.J. Chapman (editors)
© Elsevier Science Publishers B.V. (North-Holland), 1984

EVENT PERCEPTION, PERCEPTUAL ORGANIZATION AND EMOTION

Richard D. Walk

George Washington University

The key terms in this chapter title may seem somewhat disjointed. But, we are concerned here with a single topic, and it grew out of my interest in the new research on event perception and in trying to find new ways of looking at perceptual organization (Walk, in press). The core of the chapter is an experiment using body movement to depict dance and emotion in 'pure form' with points of light and the technique pioneered by Johansson (1973). Such an experiment has implications for the study of perceptual organization.

EVENT PERCEPTION

Johansson (1978) defines event perception as taking place over time. Motion perception takes place over time and is an example par excellence of event perception. Motion perception, as event perception, can be contrasted to the static perception of, as an example, the static visual illusions. Event perception utilizes a well-known word, 'event', with its synonyms of an 'occurrence' or a 'happening', and appropriates it for use in motion perception. But a 'static' perception, as of a still photograph, may take place over time since eye movements search the photograph, and a fine photograph or a fine painting may require more time for its information to be assimilated than does a motion sequence in which only time and different views can reveal the nature of the event. An example of photographs that are themselves an 'event' is Robert Capa's photograph of a Spanish soldier, caught by the camera at the moment he is killed by a bullet, Margaret Bourke-White's photograph of emaciated inmates when they were rescued from an internment camp in Germany, and the many photographs of Hollywood stars of the 1920s and 1930s, memorialized in such recent books as Kobal's 'The Art of the Great Hollywood Portrait Photographers' (1980), and the subject of a 1983 exhibition of over 100 such photographs at the National Portrait Gallery in Washington. Such stars as Marlene Dietrich, Jean Harlow, Rita Hayworth, Robert Taylor, Joan Crawford and Gary Cooper were as famous for their still photographs as they were for the movies in which they played. A comment by a former star, Gloria Swanson - 'We had faces then' - sums up the difference between the time when the studios invested tremendous sums in still photographs to advertize the stars and the present when the stars must be known by the projected moving image alone.

Event perception, in a larger sense, is on a continuum ranging from still pictures or photographs to motion perception of events that are meaningless without motion. The points of light that move in meaningful units as used in Johansson's research are examples of the latter (Johansson, 1973).

EMOTION

Emotion as studied in research is an example of the complexity of event perception. Emotion is often studied with the perception of facial expressions. The faces used are those of actors who depict the emotions in a static face frozen in time by a photograph. 'Real emotion' is not used because real emotion requires a context; it takes place over time, the face is more mobile, the body and its autonomic nervous system participate, and the participant subjectively interprets the emotion as do observers often. Participants in television shows that award prizes practice their unrestrained joy beforehand, before getting the correct answers and winning a prize such as a new television set. The practice is to ensure that their reactions fit the expectations of the television audience. The point is that the facial expression of emotion in a photograph for research is also an event that is captured at the correct moment to fulfil our cultural expectations of what the emotion should be. The photograph is not of a real emotion, but of what we think a real emotion should look like. The match between such photographs and real emotions as experienced by people in real-life situations is probably too complex a research question to be answered.

Since 'real emotion' is multisensory, involving the entire body over a period of time, we can also study the emotion as bodily expression, as essentially pure movement. To do this, we have used Johansson's method of outlining the body with points of light. This is emotion without facial cues, and the ease of identification of such emotion can be contrasted with Tomkins' position that 'affect is primarily facial behavior' (1980, p. 142).

The research with points of light that is described below has a number of implications for the study of perceptual organization; these implications are not specific to this type of 'event perception', but more general. They are discussed after the experiment on the bodily expression of emotion is described.

AN EXPERIMENT ON EVENT PERCEPTION

To investigate nonverbal dance and emotion we constructed a tape made with the sequences depicted in Johansson's points of light. We did this by having the performers wear twelve white cotton balls attached with tape at the shoulders, elbows, wrist, hips, knees and ankles. They wore dark clothing, including dark gloves, and a bag with eye holes over the head. The background was dark, matching the clothing. The only light was from a single bulb near the video camera in the back of the room. The video-tape had 13 trials in all, each separately numbered and photographed for 5 secs, then a blank of 5 secs, followed by an event sequence of dance or emotion that lasted 10-15 secs, then a blank of 5 secs that permitted a pause in the video-tape so subjects could write their reactions down. (EXAMPLE: 'Trial 4'-5 secs, pause - 5 secs, ballet sequence - 10 secs, pause - 5 secs.) For projection onto a 12 inch black and white television screen, the contrast on the television was turned almost to a maximum so only the white cotton balls were visible. The technique is similar to one described by Cutting and Proffitt (1978).

The events themselves were, in order: a still figure, jazz dancing, a waltz, ballet, rock and roll, walking, a drunken sequence, sadness, happiness, fear, surprise, anger and contempt. The first 6 sequences were performed to music where appropriate by Carolyn Homan, a co-investigator for the study, who

FIGURE 1 A person as represented by 12 points of light.

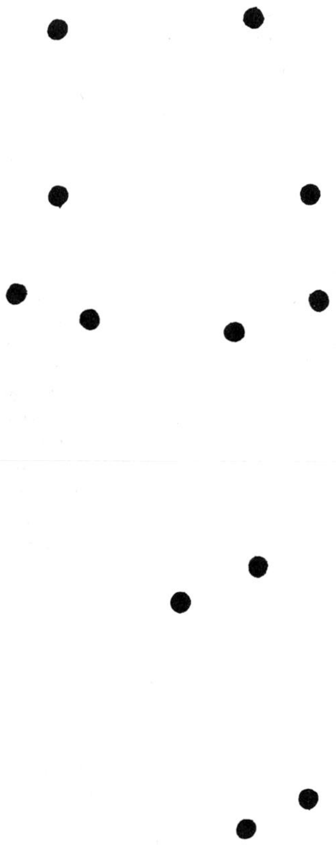

studied ballet for many years, and the next 7 by Jacqueline Samuel, who spent 2 years with a mime troupe in Holland before beginning the graduate study of psychology. The tape was projected silently to groups of 2-13 subjects at a time, undergraduate and graduate students at George Washington University. Each subject saw the tape twice. For the first tape showing subjects were instructed to describe what they saw; the second showing had the correct categories alphabetized in 2 groups (for trials 1-6 and 7-13) and subjects were told to pick their choices from them.

The spontaneous comments on first showing revealed a wide variety of interpretations. Some of these are described to give some flavour for the task. The results are presented in general terms and not trial by trial. We had 24 subjects in all (12 male, 12 female).

The first trial was of a still figure and 22 of the 24 subjects (92%) mentioned light patterns (2 vertical columns, 2 dice, a grid of dots, a cluster of stars, lights on a runway) while 2 mentioned a person; outline of a person, a person standing.

The 'jazz' trial was the first movement trial, and 92% of the subjects called it dancing with 17% calling it disco, jazz or modern dance. Waltz was correctly named by 42%, ballet 79% and rock and roll by 50%; most 'other'responses mentioned dance for all dance sequences except for rock and roll, where marching, machines moving up and down, swaying lights, and arms swinging got some responses. Both walking and drunkenness were correctly and specifically identified 92% of the time.

One has in this research an occasional subject who resists putting meaning in the light displays. This disappeared during the constrained identifications (the second showing), but it appeared during the first one. Responses like: lights move across screen, lights move up and down, lights back off, slow motion up and down, are examples. It is as if Titchenerian or structural psychology which tried to describe the stimulus without adding meaning, is a natural reaction for one or two of our subjects. (One cannot help but wonder if these roughly 10% of our sample might not warrant further study!)

The mimed emotional reactions gave much more variable reactions than did the dance patterns. Anger was easy to identify, though the names were slightly different (fighting, boxing), and fear was reasonably good (with cowering also counted), but many others were more difficult. Contempt and surprise, for example, were not identified spontaneously. Contempt was called fear more often than fear was (timid, afraid, retreating) and had other variable reactions: trying to hide, karate, female, fashion show, shy. Surprise seemed related to stage performance: blowing kisses, celebrating, singing, giving a speech, accepting applause, waving to the crowd, along with anger and pride. One subject called surprise, 'Luciano Pavorotti at the end of a performance.'

Happiness and sadness were intermediate, occasionally identified but with much inaccuracy. Happiness was also called aerobic dancing, jumping, hopping, running and the can-can, and sadness was identified as sneaking, staggering, limping, twisting, afraid, sick, posing like a body builder.

While it is obvious that the mimed emotions did elicit different reactions, the variability was marked. One cannot help but think of Gombrich's reprint of a New Yorker cartoon on nonverbal movement in the elementary classroom where the little girl with hands over her head thinks she is depicting a flower, but the balloons over the heads of the children in the class show that they interpret her pose as being a bee, a sailboat, an aeroplane, a bird, a plant, an octopus, a horse, a cow and a fish (Gombrich, 1972b).

The variability disappeared with the second showing of the tape. The only mistakes for the non-emotional sequences (Trials 1-6) were the confusion of jazz with rock and roll, each with the other, so each was correct 71% overall. This is not a surprising finding, since they are somewhat similar dances, with the rock and roll dance more static.

The emotional reactions settled down with labelling, though their identification was far from perfect. The first and second showings of the tape are shown in Table 1. One notes a marked jump in mimed happiness from 25% to 96% correct, and that anger stayed constant at 88% correct identifications while surprise and contempt, unidentified initially, were over 70% correct. Labels (and perhaps the context provided by the first showing) make for a remarkable improvement. Labels are also supplied with studies of facial expressions of emotion.

TABLE 1 Correct identification of emotions

EMOTION	FIRST SHOWING	SECOND SHOWING
Sad	8%	75%
Happiness	25%	96%
Fear	42%	71%
Surprise	-	79%
Anger	88%	88%
Contempt	-	71%

The women students were slightly better at identifying the correct depictions than were the men. We had 13 trials projected twice, or 26 possible correct responses. The female subjects averaged 17.6 correct responses as compared to 15.1 for the males. This is barely a statistically significant difference on a 2-tailed test ($p<.05$). One should, however, be cautious in leaping to conclusions from this result, based as it is on 12 males and 12 females, since the results could be due to other factors such as intelligence. Women may pay more attention to non-verbal cues than do men, and this task may reveal it, but one should not draw such a conclusion from the present study without more evidence.

The relation between this study and studies of identification of emotion in photographs of faces is shown in Table 2. The accuracy in identifying bodily expressions of emotion is remarkably accurate. The data in Table 2 were collected by Ekman and Friesen and are described in Ekman (1973). For the literate cultures the method was as follows: 'In every culture we studied the observers were given the words for these emotions in their own language and were required to choose on word for each picture (the only exception was that for disgust both the words 'contempt' and 'disgust' were used).' (Ekman 1973, p. 206). The Fore of New Guinea, a non-literate culture, were read a story describing an emotional situation (happiness, for example) and then were asked to pick the best picture from 3 pictures of which the target was one.

TABLE 2 This study, compared with studies of facial expression of emotion

	This Study	Ekman and Friesen's Data		
		U.S.	Literate Cultures	Fore of New Guinea
Happiness	96	97	92	92
Fear	71	88	74	80
Surprise	79	91	88	68
Anger	88	69	74	84
Disgust/ Contempt	71	82	84	81
Sadness	75	73	83	79
Number of Observers	24	99	356	189

NOTE Literate cultures were Japan, Brazil, Chile and Argentina. The percentages presented are a rough median of the per cent of the four cultures (e.g., 87, 97, 90, and 94 equals 92).

This study, one will recall, was that of identifying emotion from bodily cues where only points of light represented the body. Yet the results overlap with those of extensive research programmes of facial expression representing emotion. The results are particularly impressive when one considers that this is a first attempt, that the mimed emotions are the interpretation of only one performer, and that we have no extensive research programme that picked out the best mimed sequence.

DISCUSSION

The Sound of Silence

The figure with 12 points of light is 'seen' as a human being dancing, walking, retreating, jumping with joy - yet only 12 points of light are present in various combinations of relative and absolute motion. Almost all of the figure is seen as inferred, the bulk of the figure, as compared to real figures, is 'silent'. One might think of the body parts - say the head or the feet - as inferred from their effect on other parts, much as the existence of the planet Neptune was inferred from perturbations in the orbit of the planet Uranus. In other words, the motion of the points of light in relation to each other might only happen if a head and feet existed.

But silence is multi-sensory and the 'silence' in areas that are unseen yet inferred in points-of-light experiments leads one to think in more general terms about the organization of silence in perception in general. I first became interested in the organizing properties of silence in reading about research on speech perception (Liberman and Studdert-Kennedy, 1978). Simply by manipulating the interval between an s-sound and the syllable, 'lit', one hears, for a short interval, the word 'slit', as expected, but 'split' for a longer interval. The brain supplies a 'p' that is not there; the 'p' is added by the silence in this context.

An obvious and well-known example of the 'sound of silence' in visual perception comes from contour studies of subjective organization (see Figure 2). One sees a subjective contour that is not there in the square, a definite contour that is not present in the stimulus. Kanizsa (1976) states that the contour requires a meaningful figure, the outline must form a square, a triangle or other meaningful form; the same elements produce no subjective contour unless they outline a meaningful figure.

FIGURE 2 A square, the added contour is termed the 'subjective contour'

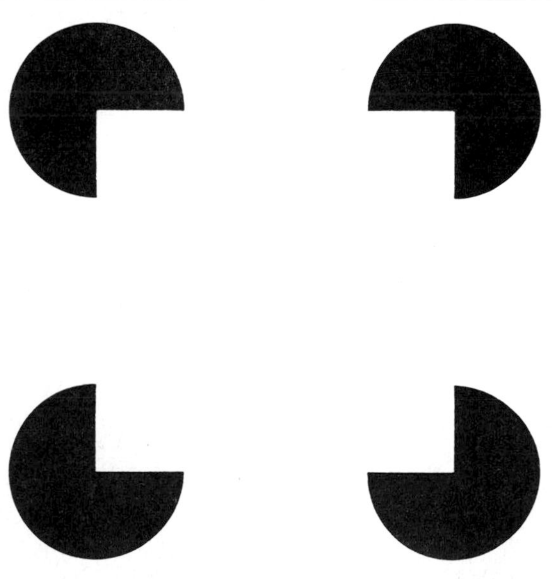

Multisensory influences of the sound of silence are present with beats. The heart beats rapidly when one is excited and slowly when one is calm. A dance tune is rapid and a funereal dirge is slow -- joy, excitement are fast beats and sad, calm states require slow beats. Visual or tactual beats would produce the same effects. The slow beats are not just slower; they also can produce tension, the interval is not blank but filled with tension.

Artists use the presence of a gap to produce tension, to make for a more dynamic work than would a joined element. Perhaps the best-known example is Michelangelo's painting 'The Creation of Adam' where God's hand reaches out to touch and create Adam, but the fingers do not quite touch, creating a dynamic union, a feeling that the energy from the Creator goes toward Adam, a force that is more powerful than it would have been had the Creator's finger touched Adam. Arnheim reproduced a drawing by Lipchitz, 'Prometheus Strangling the Vulture' and commented 'The contradiction between the solidity of the flesh suggested by the concavities and the lack of texture enhances the conflict that the drawing is meant to convey' (1954, p. 225). The sculptor Henry Moore leaves gaps and holes in sculptures of the human figure to enhance the dynamic effect, using outside space to create a more active figure. Moore (1981) commented on his own work: 'Eventually I found that form and space are one and the same thing' (p. 112); 'This space between each piece is terribly important and is as much a form as the actual solid ...' (p. 266). Gombrich (1972a) has written of the use of suggestion in Chinese drawing to create human figures with no eyes to see and those without ears that seem to listen.

In ballet, the gap between persons can be used to produce isolation or interdependence, depending on how it is used, just as figures close together may appear to belong together. A complete discussion of the perceptual organizing properties of 'silence' in all modalities is beyond the scope of this chapter, but this brief discussion suggests that it may be very fruitful.

The easy identification of all aspects of the human figure from 12 points of light creates an interesting theoretical discrepancy. A Helmholzian or constructivist view would say that the prior experience with figural movement of human beings leads the observer to infer the missing feet, hands, head, etc. in the figure. A Gibsonian (Gibson, 1979) or direct perception viewpoint, one favoured here, would predict that the moving action of the figure could only be produced in the way that it is by the addition of the missing parts, they are required by the present action just as Neptune was required by the action of the orbit of Uranus.

The Alarm Hypothesis

This hypothesis is based on prior research with odour and sound, and it states that non-verbal emotional behaviour has cross-species generality for the emotions related to fear and anger, emotional reactions that may threaten or warn other species. The pheromones for alarm among insects are broad. As broad pheromones they are interpreted by many social insects, while the sexual pheromones are more specific, attracting only the specific odours, disagreeable tastes or secretions that burn the skin that warn off many species, including human beings. Examples are the skunk, 'Bombadier beetles', stinkbugs, the Puss Moth and the Magpie Moth (Cott, 1940). Birdsongs are songs where the male sings both to attract a female and to warn off rival males, but birds also have a high pitched continuous whistle that is difficult for the predatory hawk, for example, to localize and warns many species of songbirds. Our research showed that the mimed emotions of anger and fear were the easiest to identify, without labels needed. The bodily action of threat or fear can be interpreted not only by human beings, but also by other species, just as we can interpret the behaviour of an angry bull, dog or lion. These are nonverbal bodily expressions, but happiness, while easily identified as a species-specific facial expression, does not generalize to other species.

Music is a species-specific trait of human beings. The extent to which music in one culture is identified for its emotional quality by other cultures is interesting but not crucial to the hypothesis. Sundberg (1982) does note that the amplitude-modulation characteristics of the voice are particularly efficient in communicating fear (80% identified correctly), sorrow (66% correct) and anger (60% correct), while neutral and joy seemed to be signalled along some other acoustic dimensions since they were only 24% and 8% correct respectively. Sundberg calls the amplitude-modulation characteristics 'mere translation into the acoustic domain of general patterns of bodily movements' (Sundberg, 1982, p. 94). This is some support for the alarm hypothesis, though it may be stretching it a little.

Best support for this alarm hypothesis with human beings comes from bodily postures. Facial expression is more species specific. Some sounds - the screams of alarm or the roar of anger - may also support the alarm hypothesis; the cooing of a lovesick human couple is species specific and one would expect little identification of it or interest in it by other species.

The Use of Labels

Most of the mimed sequences of emotion were ambiguous until a set of possible labels was supplied. Facial expressions of emotion also ask the subject to choose from a restricted set of labels the one that best applies to a facial expression, so our experiment is not different in principle from those. The early experiments on facial expressions of emotion in which the subject supplied the emotional labels had a wide range of names for each emotional expression (see Woodworth, 1938, Chapter XI). The range does not seem to be quite as broad, though, as that of the interpretations elicited by some of the mimed expressions.

Other experiments have noted the constraining effect of labels. Gombrich (1972b) referred to experiments by Krauss in Germany in 1930 and described them as follows:

> 'Subjects were asked to convey through drawn abstract configurations some emotion or idea for others to guess at. Not surprisingly, it was found that such guessing was quite random. When people were given a list of various possible meanings, their guesses became better, and they improved progressively with a reduction in the number of alternatives....' (Gombrich, 1972b, p. 96)

Roger Brown had a similar finding from studies of music. He asked musicians and non-musicians to pair musical selections in terms of similarity of emotional meaning. Neither group made spontaneous groupings that agreed with Brown, but when he supplied possible labels the instrumentalists agreed on pairings that matched his, while the nonmusicians, even with words supplied, never did. The words made a difference for the musically trained: 'With ... words, the instrumentalists, insofar as they agreed at all, made pairs that coincided with .. (my) .. intentions' (Brown, 1981, p. 252). Brown used a powerful illustration to show the usefulness of labels. If one crosses one's open hands and touches the thumbs, palms in, and spreads the fingers, and asks for guesses in the meaning for sign language, others do not guess correctly the label for the gesture. But if the label 'butterfly' is supplied, the appropriateness of the name to the sign is immediately perceived.

CONCLUSION

An experiment on event perception in which emotion is depicted by a mime and only visible through points of light is described along with similar depiction of dance and other movement sequences. The most important sequences, theoretically, were the emotional ones. Tomkins' (1980) statement that, 'affect is primarily facial behavior', should be changed to read 'affect is multisensory'. The affect expressed by the body, with no facial cues available and the body represented by 12 points of light is as accurately portrayed and understood as are facial expressions.

The study has implications for the study of perceptual organization. The body depicted only by moving points of light is necessarily mostly unseen, silent, not directly perceived. Thomas Carlyle wrote 'Silence is the element in which great things fashion themselves together', and the silence of visual gaps or of visual or auditory time intervals has been exploited for powerful effect by artists, dancers, musicians and perceptual psychologists. Rightly used, silence may enhance perceptual organization.

Emotion depicted in bodily motion helps support the 'alarm hypothesis', the hypothesis that the survival emotions of anger and fear are interpreted by other species, while species specific emotions (happiness, for example) do not have inter-species generality. In addition to body posture, the alarm hypothesis is supported by cross-species alarms in odour, audition and taste. As in facial studies of emotional expression, the use of labels constrains choices and helps accurate identification.

ACKNOWLEDGMENT

I thank Carolyn Homan for helping with the planning and execution of this study, Jacqueline Samuel for her fine mimed representations of emotion, and Jay Dowling for his helpful comments.

REFERENCES

Arnheim, R. (1954). Art and Visual Perception. Berkeley, California: University of California Press.

Brown, R. (1981). Music and language. In: Documentary Report of the Ann Arbor Symposium. Music Educators National Conference, Reston, Virginia.

Cott, H.B.(1940). Adaptive Colouration in Animals. London: Methuen.

Cutting, J.E. and Profitt, D.R. (1981). Gait perception as an example of how we may perceive events. In: R.D. Walk and H.L. Pick Jr. (Eds.) Intersensory Perception and Sensory Integration. New York: Plenum.

Ekman, P. (1973). Cross-cultural studies of facial expression. In: P. Ekman (Ed.) Darwin and Facial Expression. New York: Academic Press.

Gibson, J.J. (1979). The Ecological Approach to Visual Perception. Boston, Massachusetts: Houghton Mifflin.

Gombrich, E.H. (1972a). Art and Illusion: A Study in the Psychology of Pictorial Representation. Princeton, New Jersey: Princeton University Press.

Gombrich, E.H. (1972b). The visual image. Scientific American, 227, 82-96.

Johansson, G. (1973). Visual perception of biological motion and a model for its analysis. Perception and Psychophysics, 14, 201-211.

Johansson, G. (1978). Visual event perception. In: R. Held, H.W. Leibowitz and H.L. Teuber (Eds.) Handbook of Sensory Physiology, Volume VIII: Perception. Berlin: Springer-Verlag.

Kanizsa, G. (1976). Subjective contours. Scientific American, 234, 48-52.

Kobal, J. (1980). The Art of the Great Hollywood Portrait Photographers. New York: Knopf.

Liberman, A.M. and Studdert-Kennedy, M. (1978). Phonetic perception. In: R. Held, H.W. Leibowitz and H.L. Teuber (Eds.) Handbook of Sensory Physiology: Volume VIII: Perception. Berlin: Springer-Verlag.

Marler, P.R. (1972). The drive to survive. In: T.B. Allen (Ed.) The Marvels of Animal Behavior. Washington,DC: National Geographic Society.

Moore, H. (1981). Henry Moore Sculpture. New York: Rizzoli.

Sundberg, J. (1982). Perception of singing. In: D. Deutsch (Ed.) The Psychology of Music. New York: Academic Press.

Tomkins, S.S. (1980). Affect as amplification: some modifications in theory. In: R. Plutchik and H. Kellerman (Eds.) Emotion: Theory, Research and Experience: Volume 1: Theories of Emotion. New York: Academic Press.

Walk, R.D. (In press). Perceptual organization. In: R. Corsini (Ed.) Encyclopedia of Psychology. New York: Wiley.

Wilson, E.O. (1963). Pheromones. Scientific American, 208, 100-114.

Woodworth, R.S. (1938). Experimental Psychology. New York: Henry Holt.

Section 5

PERCEPTION OF MUSIC

Cognitive Processes in the Perception of Art
W.R. Crozier and A.J. Chapman (editors)
© Elsevier Science Publishers B.V. (North-Holland), 1984

COGNITION OF COMPLEX EVENTS: VISUAL SCENES AND MUSIC[1]

James C. Bartlett

University of Texas at Dallas

Rarely do students of memory have much to say about art. This is in contrast to students of perception, personality and social psychology, who currently are saying a great deal (see Crozier and Chapman, 1983). Although it might be argued that the silence of memory researchers on the topic of art is justified, in that the functioning of memory simply has nothing to do with art, this seems an unwarranted if not a downright preposterous claim. Art works are things that people remember, they are sometimes *about* memory, they are often intended to be highly memorable, and they depend upon memory for interpretation, appreciation and analysis. A more plausible claim is that currently available knowledge of memory has nothing to do with art -- that is that we know very little of the functioning of memory in naturalistic contexts that are relevant to art. This is a claim that makes much more sense. Indeed, it is simply a variant of the frequent pronouncement that -- despite approximately one hundred years of memory research -- we still know very little of the functioning of memory in any naturalistic context, whether relevant to art or not (Jenkins, 1977; Neisser, 1982a).

Although our knowledge of memory in naturalistic contexts is currently quite limited, a new tradition of memory research is emerging, and it promises to rectify matters. This can be termed a 'naturalistic' (Neisser, 1982a) or 'ecological' (Turvey and Shaw, 1979) tradition, which is linked historically to the ecological tradition in perception (Gibson, 1966; Neisser, 1976), and which stresses the importance of naturalistic stimuli and tasks. My goal in this chapter is to characterize the ecological approach as it has been applied to memory, and to describe two relevant lines of memory research. One line of research concerns memory for sequences of naturalistic photographs. It was motivated by a desire to develop some ideas that have been generated by the ecological approach. The second line of work concerns memory for melodies and effects of tonality upon such memory. Although it was not initiated with the ecological approach in mind, it obviously is relevant to problems in the psychology of art. Further, the melody-memory work turns out to be interpretable along ecological lines. Indeed, I make clear how both lines of work support the viability of an ecological approach and also its utility for generating ideas and questions for new research.

THE ECOLOGICAL APPROACH TO MEMORY

The ecological approach has become well-established in the domain traditionally known as 'perception' (Gibson, 1966, 1979; Michaels and Carello, 1981; Shaw and Pittenger, 1978). However, its applicability to memory has been much less thoroughly explored (Bransford et al, 1977; Jenkins et al, 1978; Johnston and Turvey, 1980; Turvey and Shaw, 1979). This hardly is surprising given that memory -- as a theoretical or explanatory construct --

is generally avoided by proponents of the ecological approach. In their writings on perception, Gibson and other ecologically-oriented thinkers have opposed the notion that information-'pick-up' is mediated by 'memories' of information previously 'picked-up'. Opposition to the memory construct is maintained in cases (indeed, especially in cases) where information pick-up is extended in time -- as when listening to a symphony, learning the layout of a city, or detecting the changes in a friend's ageing face (see Shaw and Pittenger, 1978; Turvey and Shaw, 1979). Gibson himself has expressed this opposition most clearly:

> Because we are led to separate the present from the past, we find ourselves involved in what I have called the 'muddle of memory' (Gibson, 1966). We think that the past ceases to exist unless it is 'preserved' in memory. We assume that memory is the bridge between the past and the present. We assume that memories accumulate and are stored somewhere; that they are images, or pictures, or representations of the past; or that memory is actually physiological, not mental, consisting of engrams or traces; or that it actually consists of neural connections, not engrams; that memory is the basis of all learning; that memory is the basis of habit; that memories live on in the unconscious; that heredity is a form of memory; that cultural heredity is another form of memory; that any effect of the past on the present is memory, including hysteresis. If we cannot do any better than this, we should stop using the word. (Gibson, 1979, p. 254)

Opposition to memory as a theoretical construct implies no judgment that the problems of memory are unimportant or impossible to address. People do show the phenomena of remembering and forgetting, and there is no denying the necessity of understanding just how and why such phenomena occur. The issues raised by ecologically-oriented writers concern the concepts we use to understand the phenomena of memory -- the challenge posed by the ecological approach is to conceptualize these phenomena without reliance on the notion of memory 'stores' containing countless numbers of 'engrams', 'images', 'traces', etc. This point is made clearly by Bransford et al:

> It seems reasonable to suggest that current uses of the term memory frequently involve tacit or explicit assumptions not too different from those noted by Ebbinghaus: for example, that memory can be broken down into a set of *memories*, that these consist of relatively independent *traces* that are stored in some *location*, and that these traces must be *searched for* and *retrieved* in order to produce remembering, and that appropriate traces must be 'contacted' in order for past experiences to have their effects on subsequent events. If memory is to be defined in this way, it becomes important to consider the possibility that the concept of memory (and memories) is simply one of many general hypotheses about the processes underlying remembering and the manner in which previous experiences have their effects on current events. (Bransford et al, 1977, p. 432)

So, what are some alternatives to a 'memory hypothesis?' Certainly one such alternative -- currently enjoying great popularity -- is that provided by schema theories (e.g., Bartlett, 1932; Mandler, 1979; Rumelhart, 1975; Schank and Abelson, 1977). According to such theories, memory is a product of incorporating or assimilating new information into previously developed structures or organizations of knowledge in long-term memory. Remembering, then, involves 'reconstructing' prior events based upon schemata, which themselves have been modified as a result of a person's experience of these prior events. Bartlett (1932) spoke of an organism's 'turning round' upon its own schemata in order to recall. Such an hypothesis is indeed rather different from that of searching for traces within a large memory 'store'. However, proponents of an ecological approach suggest or imply that to replace the memory concept with that of internal schemata is insufficient as a departure from traditional ways of thinking. Their proposals are more radical.

The ecological approach to memory phenomena might be made comparable with the concept of schemata (see Neisser, 1976). However, it appears to differ from the currently fashionable schema theories -- as well as most other theories -- in the emphasis it places on three 'core' ideas. These three ideas are: (1) that the units of perception and memory are temporally extended 'events'; (2) that the basis of perception and memory is the pick-up of invariants over time; and (3) that perception and memory are essentially veridical. All three ideas are derived from Gibson (1966, 1979). However, Idea-1 and Idea-2 have been elaborated by Bransford et al (1977), Jenkins et al (1978), Shaw and Pittenger (1978) and Turvey and Shaw (1979). Idea-3 has been developed more fully by Neisser (1976, 1982a, 1982b).

THE EVENT PERCEPTION HYPOTHESIS

From the perspective of memory researchers, Idea-1 is perhaps the most critical of those listed. The reason is that it speaks most directly to the status of memory as a theoretical construct, and departs most drastically from what many would argue is good common sense. It has been termed the 'event perception hypothesis', and is at once a claim that there is no clear dividing line between the traditional domains of perception and memory, and that the units of memory (perception?) can be greatly extended in time. Thus, 'events' are the appropriate units of analysis, whether they are 'fast' (pertaining to perception as traditionally conceived) or 'slow' (pertaining to memory as traditionally conceived). Some flexibility (and vagueness) to the event perception hypothesis is provided by the concept of 'embedding'. Fast events, for example a change in expression of face, can occur within slower events, for example the ageing of a face (see Jenkins et al, 1978; and discussion of the embedded nature of perceptual cycles in Neisser, 1976).

It might help considerably to understand the event perception hypothesis if the concept of 'event' were satisfactorally defined. It is not now (Jenkins et al, 1978), though this may soon change (see Shaw and Pittenger, 1978). We must work in the meantime with the intuitive notion that events 'are things that happen' (Pick, 1979, p. 145), involving 'changes in objects or collections of objects' (Michaels and Carello, 1981, p. 26). In the research that follows -- particularly that on apprehension of picture sequences -- the crux of the matter appears to be that sequences of stimuli extended in time might function as units in memory (perception?). Thus, a practical problem facing researchers is that of determining if a stimulus sequence has been unitized by the perceiver, and, simultaneously, that of determining the effects or manifestations of such unitization, if it occurs.

A strong form of the event-perception hypothesis does not stop with the notion that events are the primary unit of analysis. It continues to claim that all events -- both fast and slow -- are directly perceived (Michaels and Carello, 1981). Thus, Shaw and Pittenger argue that:

> The perception of change, even extremely slow change, is immediately experienced; there is no necessary intervention of mediating constructs such as specific memory for static objects or intellectual inferences, for it is certainly a philosophical conundrum to assume that the experience of change can somehow arise from the experience of static things. (1978, p. 188)

Conundrum or not, many psychologists might feel more comfortable with a weaker form of the event perception hypothesis, one which admits the possibility that memory and inference may in some cases contribute to event perception. In any event, the problem of determining the nature of events -- the conditions for their perception and the role they play in producing memory phenomena -- can be separated from questions of mechanism. This is the view of Jenkins et al (1978), who suggest that 'modeling of how people process information' and 'the specification of the units of analysis' are two different though interdependent tasks. This weaker form of the event perception hypothesis is that which is dealt with below.

INVARIANT PICK-UP

Idea-2 of the ecological approach to memory phenomena is that such phenomena reflect the invariants -- that is unchanging aspects -- of stimulus information. So fundamental is the concept of 'invariant' that perception itself is defined as the pick-up of invariant information over time (Gibson, 1966, 1979). Extending this idea to memory phenomena, Bransford et al (1977) argue that 'learning involves the detection of invariant information from a set of acquisition experiences, and that one's ability to accurately *remember* depends on what was learned' (p. 463). That is, remembering depends upon the prior detection of invariants from sets of stimuli or experiences, not upon prior storage of distinct representations of all of the aspects of these stimuli or experiences.

Although the concept of invariant appears much more concrete than that of event, it remains somewhat vague (Cutting, 1983), especially as applied to memory phenomena. The problem faced by memory researchers is our ignorance not simply of what can constitute an invariant of an event, but also of the effects to be expected if an invariant of an event is detected. Fortunately, clarification is added by Jenkins et al (1978), who suggested that the invariants extracted from a sequence of stimuli can in effect specify alternative stimuli besides those actually presented (Garner, 1974). Such alternative stimuli, if encountered subsequently, should be perceived as related to those originally experienced. Indeed, an entirely 'new' stimulus that matches invariants might be wrongly recognized as 'old'. In contrast, another new stimulus that mismatches invariants should be easily rejected as 'new'.

Aside from specifying sets of alternative stimuli, invariants have another important property -- they can pertain not only to static features of stimulus information -- such as an unchanging spatial lay-out -- but also to dynamic features -- such as the route of an observer across a spatial lay-out. The former invariants are termed 'structural', whereas the latter are termed 'transformational'. Whereas structural invariants pertain to unchanging (or slowly changing) features of stimulus information, transformational invariants pertain to 'styles of change' (Shaw and Pittenger, 1978), and underlie the perception of events. 'Thus, if an event is something happening to something, the "something happening" is presumed to be specified by transformational invariants while the "something" that it is happening to is presumed to be described by structural invariants' (Michaels and Carello, 1981, p. 26).

It is obvious from the foregoing that the concept of invariants and the concept of events are tightly intertwined. Indeed, it seems implicit in much current writing -- particularly in Jenkins et al (1978) -- that transformational and structural invariants act as a kind of 'glue' that can 'unitize' a sequence of stimulus information into a coherent 'event'. Indeed such a conception follows from Garner (1970, 1974), whose evidence shows that 'good patterns have few alternatives'. Stimulus patterns are perceived as belonging to sets (or subsets) of alternative stimuli, and a 'good' stimulus pattern is one for which the (sub)set of alternatives is small. Thus, to the degree that invariants of a sequence of stimuli specify a relatively small set of alternative stimuli, the sequence will function as memorability. In sum, it is plausible to suggest that a certain minimum amount of invariant structure within a sequence of stimuli may be a necessary prerequisite for an event to be perceived. Beyond this minimum, the amount or type of perceived invariant structure should determine the 'goodness' of the event.

VERIDICALITY OF MEMORY

Idea-3 of the ecological approach to memory phenomena is that memory -- if viewed in appropriate perspective -- is essentially veridical or accurate. Of course this is not to deny that errors of memory occur. Indeed, the framework suggested by Jenkins et al (1978) implies that certain types of memory errors are caused by the invariants extracted from perceived events. The point to be made is that subjects' performance in memory tasks -- even when this involves errors - is reflective of invariants they have (accurately) extracted from stimulus information. In discussing his analysis of John Dean's memory for events surrounding Watergate, Neisser (1982b) makes this point clearly:

> What he says about those 'episodes' is essentially correct, even though it is not literally faithful to any one occasion. He is not remembering the 'gist' of a single episode by itself, but the common characteristics of a whole series of events.
>
> This notion may help us to interpret the paradoxical sense in which Dean was accurate throughout his testimony. Given the numerous errors in his reports of conversations, which did he tell the truth about? I think that he extracted the common themes that remained invariant across many conversations and many experiences, and then incorporated these themes in his own testimony .. Except where the significance of his own role was at stake, Dean was right about what had really been going on in the White House. What he later told Senators was fairly cose to the mark: his mind was not a tape recorder, but it certainly received the message that was being given. (pp. 158-159)

The idea that memory is essentially veridical is important in distinguishing the ecological from alternative viewpoints, particularly that of schema theory. As mentioned earlier, it may be possible to incorporate the schema concept within the framework of an ecological approach to memory. However, at least one important process pertaining to schemata appears quite foreign to the ecological approach. This is the concept of 'assimilation', most closely identified with Piaget.

According to Flavell (1977), 'Assimilation essentially means interpreting or construing external data in terms of the individual's existing cognitive system. What is encountered is cognitively transformed to fit what the individual knows and how he thinks'. Assimilation can be contrasted with accommodation, which 'means taking account of the structure of the external data' (Flavell, 1977, p. 13). Although in Piaget's system both assimilation and accommodation are reflective of the functioning of schemata, it is possible to accept a role for schemata, and to agree that accommodation of these schemata to external information occurs, but to deny that assimilation is an important process in ordinary perception or memory. Thus, Neisser (1976), in a passage revealing of both the ecological orientation and his own acceptance of the schema concept, writes the following:

> Although accommodation certainly occurs, Piaget's companion concept of assimilation seems more dubious. Why should we suppose that the child alters the information he picks up? He finds out less about his environment than an adult would, but what he does discover need not be wrong. While he makes mistakes, as we all do, these may be incorrect extra polations from what he has seen rather than fundamental illusions. (Neisser, 1976, p. 66)

'Incorrect extrapolations' can presumably reflect perceived alternatives to presentation stimuli, that is veridical pick-up of invariants of these stimuli. This is consistent with an event perception hypothesis for memory phenomena.

The three core ideas of the ecological approach to memory -- that the units of memory are events, that memory phenomena reflect the pick-up of invariant information, and that memory is essentially veridical -- are supported by some of my own research efforts in two rather disparate domains. One of these domains is that of spatial memory, and the other is that of memory for melodies. Both lines of work have recently converged in suggesting that the perception of events and the pick-up of invariants have important effects upon 'memory' for sequences extended in time. These effects are qualitative in nature, and appear quite provocative for theory. They also appear to be generally consistent with the veridicality of memory for naturalistic materials.

RESEARCH ON MEMORY FOR PHOTOGRAPHIC SEQUENCES

Several landmark experiments on event perception were reported in the paper by Jenkins et al (1978). The approach taken in these experiments was to show subjects slide sequences depicting naturalistic events, such as a simple series of actions (e.g., a woman making tea, as viewed from one station point), or a 'walk' across terrain (e.g., successive pictures taken along a route across a college campus). The sequences were such that many intermediate stages of the events were not shown, though they presumably were implied by invariants extractable from what was shown. In subsequent tests of recognition memory, subjects saw three types of picture: ORIGINALS each of which was identical to a previously viewed slide; BELONGING items each representing an intermediate stage of an input sequence; and CONTROL items, each of which violated one or more invariants of the input sequence. The task was to recognize originals as 'old', and to reject belonging and control items as 'new'.

Coherence and Fusion Effects

The critical question that was asked in these experiments was whether subjects perceived the slide sequences as 'coherent' (unitary) events. The pattern of subjects' recognition responses appeared to suggest that the answer was 'yes'. Specifically, while subjects were accurate at recognizing the 'oldness' of original slides and rejecting the control slides as 'new', they frequently were fooled by belonging items. Such items frequently were judged to be 'old', though in fact they were 'new'. The results of a study by Pittenger and Jenkins (1979, cited in Jenkins et al 1978) were typical. Their input sequence comprised photographs taken from 13 points along a route across a college campus. In the subsequent recognition test, the hit rate to original pictures averaged .83, and the false alarm rate to control items averaged .08 (the control items included pictures taken on the campus but not along the route, and also pictures showing side views along the route). The false alarm rate to belonging items averaged .68, over 8 times that of control items. This type of pattern is described as 'coherence' by Jenkins et al. An even more striking pattern -- one termed 'fusion' -- also can occur. Fusion refers to cases in which original and belonging items are not reliably discriminated, that is cases in which the false alarm rate to belonging items is as high as the hit rate to originals (e.g., Allen et al, 1978).

An Event-Perception Hypothesis for Coherence and Fusion

The empirical phenomena of coherence and fusion led Jenkins et al (1978) to conclude that 'events can be primary units of analysis' (p. 142), and that these 'events are natural wholes that are, so-to-speak, perceived through the slides (of a picture sequence), rather than built up from the slides'. (p. 158). According to this view, subjects' false recognitions of new-but-belonging stimuli occur because some stimuli match the invariants of the apprehended event. Indeed, using terms reminiscent of Garner (1974), the authors suggested that new-but-belonging items are 'specified' by invariants as alternatives to the stimuli presented. And, 'Stimuli that are thoroughly specified are likely to be falsely recognized just because they fit all of the constraints or invariants of the system (the event) that has been apprehended' (p. 158).

The conclusions reached by Jenkins et al recently have been termed a 'fusion hypothesis' (Liebrich and White, 1983). This choice of label may be unfortunate as Jenkins et al use the term 'fusion' primarily to refer to an empirical outcome (zero discrimination between original and belonging items) rather than to a hypothetical process. Further, they were clear in suggesting that both the fusion pattern and the coherence pattern were evidence favouring event perception. According to Jenkins et al fusion is the limiting case in which 'specific knowledge' of what was seen in an experiment is totally dominated by 'extensive knowledge' of the event. In more typical cases, specific and extensive knowledge are thought to co-exist producing the coherence pattern.

Effects of Disordering Upon Coherence and Fusion

Although the empirical phenomena of coherence and fusion are provocative, they are not by themselves adequate to support an event perception hypothesis. The reason simply is that alternative interpretations of those two phenomena are possible. One such interpretation is based on the principle that similar stimuli are difficult to distinguish in recognition memory tasks.

Thus, the high false alarm rates to belonging items in the Jenkins et al (1978) experiments might reflect the fact that each of these belonging items was very highly similar to one or more of the originally presented items.

A second alternative interpretation for coherence and fusion pertains to possible problems with processes of retrieving information from memory. Assume, for example, that subjects store traces for individual pictures, but that they have difficulty retrieving just the right trace in response to just the right picture at test. In such a case, subjects might adopt a 'consistency' strategy (see Reder and Anderson, 1980). If a picture evokes retrieval of a trace, and appears to be consistent with information in this trace (e.g., if it looks like it could have been taken from along the same 'walk'), the subject might simply say 'old' on that basis. Hence, truly old items and new-but-belonging items would not be distinguished from each other, though both would be distinguished from control items, based simply on these 'consistency' tests (see also Moeser, 1982, for some related ideas applied to memory for complex verbal materials).

Jenkins et al (1978) were aware of alternatives to the event perception hypothesis, and developed a potentially powerful technique for testing the hypothesis further. The technique entailed a manipulation of ordering of the sequence of pictures presented at input. Instead of always presenting slides in correct temporal order, slides were sometimes presented in a disordered fashion. It is plausible that disordering in some cases can disrupt the process of extracting invariants, reducing the probability that a coherent event is perceived. If so, and if the perception of a sequence as a coherent event actually is responsible for coherence/fusion effects, such effects should be weakened in the disordered condition: that is, false recognitions of belonging items relative to control items, should be reduced in conditions of disordered presentation. Unfortunately, the predicted tendency for disordered presentation to reduce the coherence/fusion effect has sometimes been observed, but more often it has not (see Allen et al, 1978; Jenkins et al, 1978; Liebrich and White, 1983; Pittenger and Jenkins, 1979).

The inconsistent effects of the disordering variable were addressed by Jenkins et al (1978), who argued in essence that manipulations of ordering are not always effective in altering the way that events are perceived. However, ineffectiveness of the ordering variable is unlikely to be the only factor involved. In a recent experiment by Liebrich and White (1983, Experiment 4), the input sequence depicted a complex event involving people meeting people at a park bench. The event was contrived to be highly time-dependent, and yet not so intrinsically ordered that it could be extracted from a disordered sequence. Indeed, subjects' verbal descriptions of the input slide sequences showed reduced comprehension in a disordered presentation condition, as compared to a well-ordered condition. Despite this effect on verbal comprehension, the performance of subjects in a recognition test showed clearly the pattern of coherence, even with disordered presentation. Thus, the coherence phenomenon was shown to be separable from the perception of a slide sequence as an event.

Additional Evidence for Event Perception

The results of the experiment by Liebrich and White (1983) appear quite damaging to the event perception hypothesis as originally formulated by Jenkins et al (1978). Indeed, they raise the possibility that event perception simply does not occur, at least not with sequences of pictures of the type we have considered. However, a complete rejection of the event perception process appears to be unwarranted, as at least 3 existing studies have reported observations -- besides those of coherence of fusion -- which strongly support the event perception idea. The general finding of these 3 studies (Allen et al, 1978; Hock and Schmelzkopf, 1980; Kraft and Jenkins, 1977) is that viewing a set of pictures taken from a scene can give rise to rather detailed knowledge of invariant spatial relationships among the objects or features in the scene. This knowledge is accessible even in response to new-but-belonging pictures, not actually presented at input.

Perhaps the most impressive evidence for extraction of spatial relationships is provided by the Hock and Schmelzkopf (1980) study. Subjects were trained to classify photographs from a scene with respect to the station-point from which they were made (1 of 4 locations near a street intersection). In a subsequent test, subjects were able to judge whether 2 pictures -- with non-overlapping content -- were made from precisely the same station-point (with the camera pointed in different directions), versus 2 different station-points. The accuracy of these judgments was considerably greater than chance, even with pictures made from new station-points, that is station-points within the scene that were not used in training. It is difficult indeed to interpret such data without assuming some sort of unitization of information from the slides that were used during training. Such unitization is consistent with the hypothesis of event perception.

NEW RESEARCH ON EVENT PERCEPTION WITH PICTURE SEQUENCES

Some experiments performed by DeNeal and myself (Bartlett and DeNeal, in preparation; Wallace, 1982) were based on the hypothesis that sequences of pictures can indeed be perceived as coherent events, but that such perception does not generally produce the coherence and fusion phenomena. In order to test this simple hypothesis, we presented our subjects with sequences of slides depicting 'walks' across a terrain, and subsequently tested the ability of these subjects to distinguish in recognition (a) between original and belonging slides, and also (b) between correctly oriented and left-right-reversed slides. We also included both ordered and disordered presentation conditions. The procedure was in some ways similar to that of Kraft and Jenkins (1977), whose subjects showed excellent memory for the orientation of slides from a previously presented sequence.

A critical aspect of our experiment involved the ordering manipulation. As in prior research, half of our subjects saw input sequences in correct temporal order. The remainder of our subjects received a disordered presentation. However, we took steps to ensure that the manipulation of ordering would be an effective one. All of our 'walks' began from one location, proceeded in an approximately straight line to another location, and then returned to the starting location. And all 4 walks contained a salient feature (e.g., a chain link fence) that extended along one or the other side of the path of the route. The consequence was that all 4 walks included a salient feature that sometimes was on subjects' right-hand side, and sometimes was on their left-hand-side. Our assumption was that this aspect of our materials should maximize 'incoherence' in the disordered presentation condition.

The procedure of the experiment was straightforward. All subjects viewed 4 different walks at input -- with 10 slides per walk -- in either an ordered or a disordered sequence. The 16 subjects in the ordered condition saw all 10 slides from one walk, in correct order, followed by all 10 slides from the second walk, all 10 slides from the third and, finally all 10 slides from the fourth. The 16 subjects in the disordered condition saw the first slide from one walk followed by the first slide from a second walk, the first slide from a third, and the first slide from a fourth. Then, the tenth slide from each walk was presented, followed by the second slide from each walk, the ninth slide from each walk, and so on through presentation of the sixth slide from each walk. Slides were shown for 10 seconds each, and subjects were instructed to view each walk carefully in preparation for a subsequent test.

The recognition test was identical for the 2 experimental groups and included 20 original slides in correct orientation, 20 original slides in reversed orientation, 20 belonging slides in correct orientation, and 20 belonging slides in reversed orientation. Belonging slides were taken from along the same walks as originals, but at different station points. Reversals were created simply by placing slides 'backwards' in the slide projector tray. The task for subjects was to classify each slide with respect to 4 categories: (1) Old (original) and correct in orientation; (2) old (original) but reversed; (3) new (belonging) but correct in orientation; or (4) new (belonging) and reversed. Note that the old-new dimension and the correct-reversed dimension were logically independent and uncorrelated.

One prediction for the results of the study was that subjects experiencing ordered presentation would be more accurate in their judgments of orientation of slides than would subjects experiencing disordered presentation. However, we suspected that this effect might be weaker with old (original) slides (for which individual picture memory might be helpful) than with new (belonging) slides (for which individual picture memory should be relatively useless). We also made the negative prediction that subjects experiencing ordered presentation would not show more evidence for coherence or fusion.

Table 1 displays probabilities of 'same-orientation' judgments to each item type and in the ordered and disordered conditions. Same-orientation judgments are 'hits' when made to correct items, and 'false alarms' when made to reversed items. Thus, it is obvious that orientation hits exceeded orientation false alarms ($F = 77.9$; $df = 1.30$; $p<.0001$), demonstrating fairly accurate knowledge of the correct orientation of slides. What is perhaps more interesting is that hit rates exceeded false alarm rates even with new (belonging) pictures, that is those not presented on the input list. There was no statistical support for a main effect for oldness, or for an orientation x oldness interaction. This is consistent with findings of Kraft and Jenkins (1977), and suggests that orientation judgments are based at least partially on invariants of some type, not storage and retrieval of individual-picture representations.

Our prediction had been that the accuracy of orientation judgments -- that is the difference between hits and false alarms -- would be greater in the ordered than in the disordered condition, particularly with new items. In statistical terms, the prediction was that of a 2-way interaction between orientation and presentation-order, possibly qualified by a 3-way interaction involving oldness. The former interaction was only marginally significant ($F=3.49$; $df=1.30$; $p<.08$) and the latter did not approach significance. However, when the data from new items were analyzed separately, the orientation x presentation-order interaction was reliable ($F=5.86$; $df=1.30$; $p<.05$). Thus, the data presented in Table 1 provide suggestive evidence that ordered presentation improved extraction of orientation invariants.

Although the same-judgment data were encouraging, the old-judgment data provided more convincing evidence for a role of invariants in orientation memory. Table 2 displays the probabilities of such judgments to each item-type and in each order condition. Note that old judgments are hits when made in response to old items, and are false alarms when made in response to new items.

TABLE 1 Probabilities of Same-Orientation Judgments to Old (Original) and New (Belonging) Pictures, Presented in Correct and Reversed Orientation in the Ordered and Disordered Presentation Conditions.

	PRESENTATION ORDER AND OLDNESS			
ORIENTATION	ORDERED		DISORDERED	
	OLD	NEW	OLD	NEW
Correct	.82	.80	.80	.77
Reversed	.50	.48	.55	.59
Difference	.32	.32	.25	.18

The data in Table 2 show that the old-judgment hits were generally more probable than old-judgment false alarms, suggesting some ability to distinguish pictures shown at input from pictures not shown. However, this difference was virtually absent with reversed-orientation supported by a 3-way interaction in the analysis of variance ($F=10.8$; $df=1,30$; $p<.005$) (there also were main effects of orientation and oldness, and an orientation x oldness interaction, but all of these were qualified by the 3-way interaction). We note that the difference between old-judgment hits (to old items) and old-judgment false alarms (to new items) were statistically significant by t test ($p<.01$) in each combination of presentation-order and slide orientation, except that of ordered presentation and reversed pictures (where $p > .10$).

The old judgment data shown in Table 2 are not inconsistent with the results of prior literature. However, these data add to the observations made previously, and in fact place prior data in a new and interesting context. Research completed previously has examined probabilities of old judgments to original items presented in correct orientation, and to belonging items presented in correct orientation. The corresponding data from the present experiment are those displayed in the first and third columns of the Table. Looking only at these data, there clearly is no evidence for a qualitative difference between ordered and disordered presentation -- with either sort of presentation, old judgments to original items (hits) exceeded old judgments to belonging items (false alarms). Indeed an analysis of variance performed on just these data supported simply a highly reliable main effect for oldness ($F=64.3$; $df=1,30$; $p<.0001$) and a marginal main effect for presentation-order ($F=3.88$; $df=1,30$; $p<.06$); old judgments were slightly more frequent in the disordered condition . Thus, there was no suggestion in these data that ordered presentation -- and, by inference, event perception -- increased the false alarm rate to new-correct items. As in most prior research, and in accordance with predictions, ordered presentation failed to strengthen the coherence phenomenon.

TABLE 2 Probabilities of Old Judgments to Old (Original) and New (Belonging) Items Presented in Correct and Reversed Orientation in the Ordered and Disordered Presentation Conditions.

	PRESENTATION-ORDER AND ORIENTATION			
OLDNESS	ORDERED		DISORDERED	
	CORRECT	REVERSED	CORRECT	REVERSED
Old	.63	.53	.69	.63
New	.43	.50	.54	.47
Difference	.20	.03	.15	.16

What is new in our data is the pattern that is shown by the reversed-orientation pictures, displayed in the second and fourth columns of Table 2. Here, presentation-order had a qualitative effect. With disordered presentation, there was above-chance discrimination between old-reversed items and new-reversed items. With ordered presentation, there was not. Indeed, a separate analysis of variance of the reversed item data supported the main effect for oldness ($F=11.6$; $df=1,40$; $p<.002$) as well as an interaction between oldness and presentation-order ($F=6.66$; $df= 1,30$; $p<.02$), supporting the conclusion that the ordering of slide sequences affected discrimination between old-reversed and new-reversed items.

Despite the fact that we did not predict the pattern shown in the second and fourth columns of Table 2, it has, we would argue, considerable importance for at least two reasons. First, the simple fact that an ordering manipulation had a qualitative effect on recognition performance adds badly needed support to the general idea that sequences of pictures are perceived in some cases as wholistic events. Second, the pattern is important in suggesting a principle regarding the nature of the effects which event perception can have upon memory. Event perception is not generally the cause of subjects' confusions between original pictures and belonging pictures that match invariants of the event, that is old and new 'correct' items. Rather, event perception has a more subtle effect, impairing discrimination between original and belonging pictures that 'mismatch' invariants of the event. Apparently, when an input sequence is perceived by subjects as a unitary event, and when recognition-test stimuli violate invariants of this event, it can become difficult to detect similarities between these test stimuli and input items. Violations of invariants appear to disrupt the perception of similarities between stimuli.

Since completing our original experiment, DeNeal and I have performed additional studies which generally strengthen the conclusions reached above. One of these experiments was identical to our first study, except that elderly subjects were employed. Because of prior work on age differences in picture memory (Bartlett et al,1983), we suspected there might be age-related deficits in detecting invariants -- including orientation invariants -- from picture sequences. Indeed, accuracy of orientation judgments was relatively low in our elderly group, as compared to the young adult group. Of greater interest, the elderly subjects did not show the pattern of reduced discrimination between old-reversed items and new-reversed items, given ordered presentation at input (in fact, such discrimination was significantly greater than chance in the elderly group, though it was not in the young group). While strong claims regarding ageing effects are not warranted by these findings, they are important in demonstrating that the pattern of old-judgment data shown in Table 2 is reflective of processes of invariant pick-up, and not some artifact produced simply by turning pictures backwards. This same point has been made in another recent study, in which 12 young adult subjects viewed a presentation sequence in which the orientation of slides was not consistent: that is, half of the slides were shown reversed left-to-right at input (cf. Kraft and Jenkins, 1977). The subsequent test included old items shown in the same orientation as at input, as well as old items (in this design, it is impossible to designate a new item as either correct or reversed in orientation). The results were straightforward; old judgments to old items (hits) were at least as probable when these items were reversed (.75) as when they were presented in the same orientation as at input (.74). Old judgments to new items averaged .63. Apparently, when orientation invariants are impossible to detect -- because they do not exist -- reversing an old picture does not reduce its recognizability as old. Again, we conclude that the pattern of data shown in Table 2 is reflective of pick-up of orientation invariants.

A question begged by the preceding discussion concerns the nature of the invariants that are affected by ordering and involved in producing old judgments. Although the data in hand obviously are inadequate to answer this question fully, the distinction cited earlier between structural and transformational invariants suggests an hypothesis that warrants testing. Note that the type of invariants most plausibly susceptible to ordering effects are of the transformational type, that is the type specifying the routes of the walks. Indeed, there is evidence supporting the importance of route knowledge in the process of cognitive mapping (Allen et al, 1978; Thorndyke and Hayes-Roth, 1982). It is plausible to suggest that transformational invariants that specify routes are involved in the making of old-new judgments in recognition. Subjects who have knowledge of such invariants should have some ability to recall the routes that were followed at input, along with the 'stopping points' along these routes (e.g., perhaps they can 'mentally simulate' the original walk, see Thorndyke and Hayes-Roth, 1982). Recall of such knowledge might support discrimination between original-correct pictures and belonging-correct pictures, since only the former would match the perspectives of stopping points. However, recall of such knowledge might be useless for discriminating original-reversed pictures from belonging-reversed pictures, since neither of these would match the perspectives of stopping points. Thus, ordered presentation plausibly provides knowledge of transformational invariants that support discrimination between old and new pictures, so long as the old pictures match information derived from these invariants.

In summary, the results of our experiments have been highly informative concerning the nature of event perception and its effects upon spatial memory. We found no evidence in this research that the perceptions of a slide sequence as an event is associated with the phenomena of coherence and fusion. However, we did obtain evidence that event perception is associated with the extraction of invariants that specify left-right orientation. These orientation invariants, whatever their precise nature, produce, when violated, impaired detection of similarities that exist between stimuli.

MEMORY FOR MELODIES

The second line of research that I discuss in this chapter began quite independently of the first, and it has more immediate relevance to the psychology of art. It was carried out in collaboration with Dowling and derives from the literature on music cognition (see Deutsch, 1982). The research in this literature has now established the psychological reality of tonal structures, and the effects of such structures in a variety of musically-relevant tasks (see Dowling, 1978; Krumhansl, 1983; Shepard, 1982). It has been shown, for example, that tonal melodies -- relative to atonal melodies -- are relatively well remembered (Francès, 1972), that the perceived similarity between pairs of notes and pairs of chords is affected by the prevailing musical key (Krumhansl, 1979; Krumhansl et al, 1982), that subjects who have heard a short tonal sequence can generate notes of the appropriate musical scale (Cohen, 1978), that atonal (out-of-key) notes are used to reject lures in a transportation-detection task (Cuddy et al, 1979; Dowling, 1978) and that the distance between melodies around the circle of fifths has effects on judgments in this task (Bartlett and Dowling, 1980; Cuddy et al, 1979). It also has been shown that tonality of melodies -- and more specifically the conformity of melodies to musical scales -- systematically affects subjects' (even children's) aesthetic reactions to these stimuli (Cross et al, 1983; Krumhansl and Keil, 1982).

The focus of our own more recent studies has been on the effects of musical-scale information on memory for melodies, and specifically upon the question of why 'atonal melodies' -- by which we mean melodies that violate commonly used musical scales -- are difficult to remember. The specific hypothesis with which we started this research (see Dowling and Bartlett, 1981) was that internalized 'schemata' for musical scales can impair subjects' memory for atonal melodies through an assimilative process. We assumed this process could distort memory for atonal melodies in the direction of tonality. Our thinking was also that this process was time-dependent, one which might function through internal imagery or 'rehearsal' of melodies. It should be obvious from the preceding discussion that such an assimilation/distortion hypothesis is not highly compatible with the ecological approach to memory. Indeed, we soon were led to abandon this hypothesis in favour of one more consistent with ecological thinking.

An interesting prediction of the assimilation/distortion hypothesis is that of asymmetrical similarity relations (cf. Krumhansl, 1979; Krumhansl et al, 1982) between tonal and atonal melodies. Specifically, a time-dependent process of assimilation-distortion should cause an atonal melody to be more highly confusable with a subsequently presented tonal melody, than with a previously presented tonal melody, particularly if the melodies are in many respects similar. As an initial test of this line of thinking, we (Dowling and Bartlett, 1981) examined a situation in which subjects heard pairs of 5 note melodies, one tonal and the other relatively atonal, separated in time by a 5 second interval (the melodies themselves were presented at a 2.4 note-per-second rate). The tonal melodies within each pair were random permutations of the first 5 notes of the C major scale, always beginning on middle C (262 Hz). Their atonal mates were identical, save for a note that was changed by one semitone to fall outside the C major scale. For example, the tonal member of one melody pair was C, D, F, E, G. Its atonal mate was C, D♭, F, E, G. Given that time-dependent assimilative processes can distort subjects' memory for atonal melodies in the direction of tonality, melodies presented in the atonal-tonal order should be in effect more similar than those presented in tonal-atonal order.

Subjects in our first experiment performed one of two different rating tasks in response to the melody pairs. While one group of subjects responded to each pair with a similarity rating, another group of subjects responded to each pair with a same-different recognition rating (though all melodies were different, subjects were not informed of this). Both sorts of rating were made with a 6-point scale. The atonal-tonal pairs were rated as more similar than the tonal-atonal pairs, and also as the 'same' with greater confidence. These effects were stronger among moderately experienced subjects (2 or more years of formal training) than among virtually inexperienced subjects (less than 2 years training).

Originally, we felt that this asymmetrical similarity effect was due to assimilation, but we began to doubt that the assimilation concept was viable. In a second experiment reported by Dowling and Bartlett (1981), we varied the delay between the first melody of a pair and the second. This delay was either 5 or 0 seconds (beyond that imposed by the rhythm of presentation). Assuming that assimilation is a time-dependent process, enhanced by the process of internal rehearsal, we predicted that the magnitude of the asymmetry effect would be greater in the delay condition than in the no-delay condition. No such pattern was observed, however.

A NEW EXPERIMENT ON SIMILARITY OF MELODIES

Another experiment which questions the assimilation/disorder notion has been recently completed in our laboratory. Similarity and recognition judgments were examined under 4 different stimulus conditions, including the tonal-atonal and atonal-tonal conditions, as previously, but also a tonal-tonal and an atonal-atonal condition. It was the tonal-tonal condition, in comparison to the tonal-atonal and atonal-tonal conditions, that we considered most critical. The melodies within a tonal-tonal pair always differed by one note, but there was never a violation of key (the change was between F and E in the key of C). Thus, we saw no reason to assume that assimilation would alter the internal representation of the first melody presented in such pairs. In consequence, we reasoned that tonal-tonal pairs should strike the listener as obviously different. As a result, recognition (sameness) ratings -- and perhaps similarity ratings -- should be lower for tonal-tonal pairs than for atonal-atonal pairs, but these were included for exploratory purposes, and to create a statistically elegant tonality-of-first-melody x tonality-of-second-melody design.

All subjects heard recordings of pairs of 7 note melodies, presented at a rate of 3.6 notes per second, played on a piano. Each of the melodies within a pair began and ended on C, and were identical with respect to all other notes save one. Tonal melodies always included 6 of the 7 chromas of diatonic scale (excluding either E or F). Atonal melodies always included one non-diatonic note; an F# (in place of G), an A# (in place of A), or a C# (in place of D). The melodies within tonal-tonal and atonal-atonal pairs always were identical, except that a G, A, or D, in the tone melody was replaced by a F#, A#, or C#, respectively, in its atonal mate.

From each of 24 different tonal-tonal pairs, an atonal-atonal pair, a tonal-atonal pair, and an atonal-tonal pair was constructed (this was accomplished by replacing the G, A, or D in one or both melodies with the corresponding non-diatonic note (F#, A#, or C# , respectively). Thus, there was a total of 96 pairs, and every subject heard all 96 (for counterbalancing purposes, 4 different orderings of pairs were used).

The 28 subjects included 15 subjects of moderate musical experience (2 or more years of formal training on an instrument) and 13 of low experience. Approximately half of the subjects within each experience group rated the melodies in each pair for similarity, whereas the remainder of these subjects rated their confidence that the melodies were identical versus different. Both types of rating were on a six-point scale (6 = highest similarity, or highest confidence in 'sameness').

Results and Discussion

The average ratings for the 4 types of melody pairs and for moderately experienced and inexperienced subjects, are shown in Table 3. The data are collapsed over the type-of-rating variable (similarity versus recognition) which had no reliable effects. A comparison of the middle 2 columns shows that the asymmetrical similarity effect was replicated. However, contrary to predictions of the assimilation/distortion hypothesis, ratings in the tonal-tonal condition were virtually identical to those in the atonal-tonal condition. An analysis of variance performed on these rating data supported highly significant main effects for tonality of first melody and tonality of second melody, as well as the interaction: $Fs\ (1,24) = 40.2$, 39.1 and 14.6, respectively, all $p's < .001$. Further, there were reliable interactions between musical experience and tonality-of-first melody ($F = 4.96$; $df = 1,24$) and between musical experience and tonality-of-second-melody ($F = 5.98$; $df = 1,24$; $p < .05$). Indeed, a separate analysis of just the tonal-atonal and atonal-tonal conditions (those pertaining to the asymmetrical similarity effect), supported a highly reliable effect of condition ($F = 24.3$; $df = 1,24$; $p < .0001$) as well as a condition x experience interaction ($F = 7.7$; $df = 1,24$; $p < .01$). Thus, as in our previous experiments (Dowling and Bartlett, 1981), the effects of tonality were generally stronger with the more musically experienced listeners (cf. Dowling, 1978; Krumhansl and Shepard, 1979).

AN EVENT-PERCEPTION HYPOTHESIS FOR MELODY SIMILARITY

It was at this point that the ecological approach to memory, which had been supported in the picture memory experiments, began to shape our thinking about tonality effects. Indeed, while the perception of picture sequences as coherent events may still be open to debate, the perception of melodies as coherent events hardly seems questionable (Pick, 1979). As von Ehrenfels (1937) and the Gestalt psychologists (see Boring, 1942) argued long ago, melodies by virtue of their transposibility are prototypic examples of wholes that are different from the sum of their parts. It seems but a small step to refer to such wholes as 'events'.

TABLE 3 Average Ratings of Similarities/Sameness for the Four Types of Melody Pair Made by Moderate- and Low-Experience Subjects.

	Type of Pair			
	Tonal-Tonal	Tonal-Atonal	Atonal-Tonal	Atonal-Tonal
Moderately Experienced	4.65	3.56	4.76	4.32
Inexperienced	4.41	3.85	4.39	4.28

NOTE: On the 6-point 6 scales, 6 represented maximum similarity or 'sameness'.

Although the claim that melodies are perceived as events many not be controversial, it carries interesting implications nonetheless (Pick, 1979). One implication is that melodies allow for the extraction of invariants, and that these invariants contribute to their coherence as events, that is their perception as melodies versus unconnected sequences of notes. Further, according to the analysis of Jenkins et al (1978), the implication follows that melodies -- due to their invariants -- should serve to specify sets of alternative melodies that may or may not actually be presented in an experiment (Garner, 1974). And subsequent melodies that violate such sets should be perceived as 'different'. These implications appear quite relevant to interpreting the data in Table 3.

There is a good deal of evidence that the 'feature' of musical key can be 'picked-up' from simple melodies (Bartlett and Dowling, 1980; Cross et al 1983; Cuddy et al, 1979; Dowling, 1978, 1982). Thus, it is plausible, taking an ecological perspective, that key can function as an invariant of a melody, contributing to its perceptual coherence, and specifying alternative melodies that were not presented. This idea suggests a workable account of the asymmetrical similarity effect observed by Dowling and Bartlett (1981), and also in our more recent experiment (Table 3). Consider first the tonal-atonal condition (column 2 of the Table), in which the first melody is tonal and second is not. In this case it is plausible that subjects detect the notes of the key of C as an invariant of the first melody, so that they perceive it as a member of a set of melodies composed of those notes. The second melody of course falls outside this set, which plausibly leads to perceived dissimilarity or difference. The atonal-tonal condition is different in that the notes of C are violated by the first melody, and would not be detected as an invariant of this melody. The specified set of alternative melodies would in this case be quite large -- perhaps including all possible melodies with the same melodic contour -- and probably would include the second item of an atonal-tonal pair. Thus, an impression of great dissimilarity or difference would not be expected to occur. We should note that the concepts of inferred alternative sets (and subsets) of stimuli have previously been applied to asymmetrical similarities among non-musical stimuli (Garner, 1974; Handel and Garner, 1966).

The idea that key can function as an invariant of melodies, specifying relatively small sets of alternative melodies, is also useful in explaining the pattern of the tonality-of-first-melody x tonality-of-second-melody interaction, shown in Table 3. If the first of a pair of melodies is tonal, and is perceived as one of a relatively small set of tonal alternatives, it makes sense that a subsequent tonal melody -- which should be a member of this set -- should be perceived as more similar than a subsequent atonal melody -- which should not. If, on the other hand, the first of a pair of melodies is atonal, and is perceived as a member of a relatively large set of tonal and atonal alternatives, then obviously the tonality of the second melody should make little difference. Indeed, as shown in Table 3, the tonality of the second melody had a subsequently larger effect when the first melody was tonal than when it was atonal.

In summary, an event-perception hypothesis for melody memory -- buttressed by Garner's (1974) concept of inferred alternatives to presentation-stimuli -- provides a workable account of the asymmetrical similarity between tonal and atonal melodies, and of the interaction between tonality-of-first-melody and tonality-of-second-melody, obtained in the experiment just presented. It can also handle, at least in principle, the effects we found of musical experience. Proponents of the ecological approach frequently conceptualize effects of experience, or perceptual learning, in terms of the 'education of attention' to invariants (Gibson, 1966; Michaels and Carello, 1981). Thus it is arguable that more experienced listeners are somehow more attentive to invariants of key in melodies. Of course, the question by which attention contributes to extraction of key invariants is left unanswered by such statements. One is forced to wonder whether 'scale schemata' (Dowling, 1978) might be involved.

It is important to note that the event-perception hypothesis, as developed here, implies that the phenomenon of asymmetrical similarity between tonal and atonal stimuli, and that of an interaction between tonality of a first stimulus and tonality of a second, should generalize beyond melodies to events of different types and temporal extent. Indeed, these phenomena do generalize beyond melodies, as shown most convincingly in the pioneering research conducted by Krumhansl and her colleagues. In one experiment by Krumhansl (1979), musically sophisticated subjects judged the similarity of pairs of musical notes within the framework of a musical key (C major). Asymmetrical similarity effects were clearly in evidence, as the rated similarity between a diatonic note and a non-diatonic note was significantly higher when the non-diatonic note was presented first. Moreover, Krumhansl found in general that when the first note of a pair was a diatonic note (in C major), similarity was greater if the second note was diatonic than if the second note was non-diatonic. When, however, the first note of a pair was a non-diatonic note, it made little difference what the second was. This, of course, is consistent with our own findings of asymmetry, and with the tonality-of-first-stimulus x tonality-of-second-stimulus interaction shown in Table 3. It too can be interpreted in terms of sets of perceived alternatives to 'tonal' versus 'atonal' stimuli.

In a more recent study, Krumhansl et al (1982) had subjects listen to pairs of 7 chord sequences, and to judge whether or not a single chord had been changed (at least 6 of the 7 chords always were identical). The 'context key' (that of the 6 non-target chords of a sequence), was sometimes C, sometimes G, sometimes A, and sometimes B. However, of greatest relevance to our own research were the trials in which the context key was C, and a chord was in fact changed between the 2 sequences. Within this subset of trials, 4 different conditions were present: (1) Both 'target' chords could be in C; (2) the target chord of the first sequence could be in C while that of the second could be in F#; (3) the target chord of the first sequence could be in F# while that of the second could be in C; or (4) both target chords could be in F#. Note that these 4 conditions correspond fairly well to the tonal-tonal, tonal-atonal, atonal-tonal, and atonal-atonal conditions of our own experiment, though our study was conducted with 7 note melodies, not 7 note chords. I have estimated the probabilities of same judgments (false alarms) in each of the 4 conditions of Krumhansl et al (1982), using Figure 4 of that paper. The estimated probabilities were .41, .08, .39 and .22, respectively. The pattern is strikingly similar to that of ratings of similarity in Table 3. It clearly supports the asymmetry effect (which was tonality-of-first sequence x tonality-of-second-sequence interaction. (Krumhansl et al were concerned with other empirical issues, and did not assess the statistical reliability of this interaction.)

There appears to be converging evidence for the asymmetry pattern and the tonality-of-first-stimulus x tonality-of-second-stimulus interaction shown in Table 3. Both of these empirical phenomena are interpreted quite naturally with the general notion that tonal stimuli allow for the pick-up of key invariants and that these key invariants specify sets of alternative (tonal) stimuli. This notion itself derives from the view that musical stimuli -- including melodies, single notes, or sequences of chords -- can be perceived in some cases as coherent events. Thus, an event perception hypothesis appears to be viable in the music cognition domain. The hypothesis requires development, however, in order to deal adequately with several different aspects of music cognition. A few of these aspects are discussed below.

At a strictly empirical level, the event-perception hypothesis must be developed to handle a discovery of Krumhansl (1979), which is that pairs of (non-identical) stimuli that fall within a prevailing key are perceived as more similar than pairs of stimuli that do not. Although initially established with single-note stimuli, the phenomenon generalizes to chord sequences (Krumhansl et al, 1982), and apparently to melodies as well. Note in Table 3 that the average similarity of tonal-tonal melody pairs exceeds that of atonal-atonal melody pairs (and this difference was significant ($F = 8.2$; df=1,24; $p<.01$). Shepard (1982) has suggested that this sort of effect might reflect the general principle that pairs of more salient stimuli have more overlapping features than pairs of less salient stimuli (see Tversky, 1977). This notion might be taken to imply that the effect should hold more strongly with similarity ratings than with recognition or 'difference' ratings. However, although both recognition and similarity ratings were employed in our study (Table 3), they did not produce distinguishable patterns of data.

Another type of finding which is not yet handled by the event perception hypothesis is that of key distance effects (Bartlett and Dowling, 1980; Krumhansl et al, 1982). The sorts of phenomena discussed above apparently are not simple matters of atonal-atonal or diatonic-non-diatonic dichotomy, but of some sort of continuum extending from notes especially central to a key (C, E and G for the key of C), to less central notes within the key (D, F, A, B), to non-diatonic notes that are diatonic within relatively 'near' keys around the circle of fifths (B♭, for the key of F; F#, for the key of G) to non-diatonic notes that are diatonic only within more distant keys. Some explicit way of accommodating this continuum to the notion of invariants should be worked out.

A third area for development of an event perception hypothesis concerns the role played by sensory factors in memory for musical events. Deutsch (1982) has provided considerable evidence for a sensory memory system retaining absolute pitch information. Although memory for pitch within this system is apparently quite short-lived, the properties of the system are likely to constrain the pick-up of invariants from melodies, particularly invariants pertaining to key. Consider for example the well-established finding that short-term memory for the pitch of a tone is impaired if one tone in a subsequent sequence is a semitone removed in pitch. Such an effect might contribute to the results of our similarity-rating study, shown in Table 3. Each of the tonal sequences used in this experiment included one and only one semitone interval (that between C and the B below). In contrast, most of our atonal sequences included 2 semitone intervals each (the exceptions were 3 melodies including an F# but no F). Thus, it becomes arguable that what we have termed 'key invariants' might be based in part on 'pitch-set' invariants, and that -- due to sensory factors -- pitch-set invariants are easier to pick-up from tonal than from atonal melodies. Following the argument outlined above, a difference in the pick-up of pitch-set invariants from tonal versus atonal melodies might contribute to the asymmetrical similarity effect, and to the tonality-of-first-melody x tonality-of-second-melody interaction that we observed (Table 3).

Were sensory factors solely responsible for the effects of the tonality on similarity judgments, the effects we observed of musical experience would not be expected to occur. These effects of musical experience are strongly suggestive that key invariants of an abstract type are picked up from simple melodies. It is nonetheless plausible that sensory factors exert constraints upon the process of invariant pick-up, and this is a matter that should be addressed.[2]

A fourth area for development of the event perception hypothesis was suggested by the results of a new experiment, recently conducted by Dowling and myself, with which I close this chapter. The purpose of the experiment was to test an implication of the research on picture memory described earlier in this chapter. This implication was that invariants when violated, can impair the detection of similarities that exist between stimuli. If this implication generalizes to melodies, an interesting phenomenon might be expected. Detection of similarities between a tonal melody and an atonal melody might be superior if the first melody presented is the atonal item than if the first melody presented is the tonal item.

In order to test this prediction, we conducted an experiment similar in nature to that reported in Table 3. However, a major new feature was that one-half of the melody pairs in each of the 4 tonality conditions differed with respect to melodic contour. Melodic contour is known to be a highly salient attribute of melodies, and is usually defined, perhaps simplistically, as the sequence of ups and downs in a melody's pitch. Our manipulation of contour was straightforward -- all of our melodies had a G, but this was sometimes the G below middle C (197 Hz), and sometimes the G above it (393 Hz). When low, the G was the lowest note in a melody, and, when high, it was the highest. Hence, when a high G in one melody was changed to a low G in its mate, or vice versa, contour necessarily was changed.

The experiment included 17 subjects with moderate (2 years or greater) musical experience, and 35 subjects with low (less than 2 years) experience.

Their task was to listen to 48 melody pairs -- 24 same-contour items and 24 different-contour items -- and to make 2 judgments: (1) a judgment of same versus different contour; and (2) a global similarity rating, using a 1 to 6 scale for both.

The pattern shown by the similarity ratings was essentially the same as that shown in Table 3. Again, there was a main effect for tonality of first melody (F = 6.6; df=1,49; p<.01), a main effect for tonality of second melody (F = 41.4; df=1,49; p<.0001) and a tonality-of-first melody x tonality-of-second melody interaction (F = 4.54; df=1,49; p<.05). As expected, similarity ratings were higher for same-contour items than for different-contour items (F=211.0; df=1,49; p<.0001). Surprisingly, there were no reliable effects of musical experience.

The most interesting result of this experiment was the pattern of probabilities of same-contour judgments, shown in Table 4. These data were subjected to an analysis of variance, which showed a reliable effect for contour (F = 176.4; df=1,49; p<.0001) as well as a reliable effect of tonality-of-second melody (F = 38.6; df= 1,49; p<.001). Although the tonality-of-second melody effect appeared somewhat stronger with same contour items than with different-contour items, the interaction was only marginally reliable (F = 3.0; df=1,49; p<.10).

TABLE 4 Probabilities of Same-Contour Judgments to Pairs of Melodies with Same and Different Contour in Four Different Tonality Conditions.

Contour of Melodies	Type of Pair			
	Tonal-Tonal	Tonal-Atonal	Atonal-Tonal	Atonal-Atonal
Same	.68	.54	.70	.59
Different	.29	.21	.26	.20

Given the salience of the contour attribute in melody memory (Dowling, 1978), we find it impressive that judgments of this attribute are susceptible to tonality effects. Further, our predictions for the experiment were supported to the degree that same-contour judgments were more probable in the atonal-tonal condition than in the tonal-atonal condition, especially for same-contour items. However, the data are puzzling in that there were no effects involving tonality-of-first melody or involving the tonality-of-first melody x tonality-of-second melody interaction. Rather, the data suggested simply that same-contour judgments were generally more likely when the second melody was tonal.

Although further experimentation clearly is necessary, the effects of tonality upon contour judgments suggest interesting new directions for developing and testing an event perception hypothesis for music cognition. Specifically, these data suggest on the one hand that violating key invariants can disrupt the detection of similarities between stimuli, but, on the other hand, that atonal (non-diatonic) notes are not always perceived as violating such invariants. Apparently, the process of detecting key invariants, and of assessing violations to such invariants, are more complex then we once supposed.

As a starting point for refining an event perception hypothesis to cover tonality effects, I make a suggestion that is illustrated in Figure 1. The Figure shows a portion of Shepard's 'melodic map' (see Shepard, 1982, Figure 4), which provides a means of visualizing 2 important dimensions of pitch -- pitch height, and key distance. Using this map, I have illustrated the case in which the prevailing key is C, and an 'atonal' melody has been presented (see Dowling, 1978, for the metaphor of melodies being 'hung' upon scales). The melody shown is C, B, D#, G, E, A, C (its tonal 'mate' contained a D in place of D#). The suggestion I am making is that this 'atonal' melody -- depending upon context, listener experience and other variables -- can be perceived in either of two different ways. First, it can be perceived as containing a note that violates key, and/or signals a shift in key. Second, it can be perceived as including an 'accidental' or passing tone, within the key framework.

My suggestion for interpreting the data in Table 4 begins with the assumption that the 'atonal' note in tonal-atonal and atonal-atonal pairs is perceived as violating the invariant of key. Because a key invariant has been violated, the pitches of such melody pairs are perceived as spanning virtually the entire extent of the melodic map. Hence, no small set of within-key notes is useful as a framework for perceiving and remembering such melodies. Similarities between melodies, including similarities of contour might be difficult to detect in such cases. My suggestion continues with a second assumption, which is that the 'atonal' note in atonal-tonal pairs is perceived as an 'accidental' or passing tone, that is as a sharp or flat version of a within-key reference note that subsequently 'resolves' to this reference note. In consequence, the pitches of atonal-tonal pairs -- as well as of tonal-tonal pairs -- are perceived as residing within a relatively small region of the melodic map (that portion corresponding to the key of C). Hence, a relatively small set of within-key notes can be used as a framework for perception and memory, and similarities between melodies, including similarities of contour, might be easily detected. In effect, I am claiming that atonal melodies in atonal-tonal pairs are perceived as specifying relatively small sets of alternatives (Garner, 1974), despite the atonal note. Although clearly quite speculative, these suggestions for interpreting the data in Table 4 appear to be testable with current techniques. In any event, the sensitivity of contour judgments to aspects of tonal structure appears quite provocative for theory.

CONCLUDING REMARKS

The two lines of work in this chapter converge in suggesting that sequences of stimuli can be perceived as coherent events. The main substantive conclusion that was drawn from this research is that invariants extracted from stimulus sequences produce, when violated, global impressions of difference or dissimilarity. These global impressions appear to influence judgments that might be thought irrelevant to the invariants themselves. Thus, a violation of an orientation invariant can influence judgments that a picture is old versus new. Similarly, a violation of a key invariant can influence judgments that a melody has changed versus unchanged contour. The nature of invariants, the ways they can be violated, and the reasons they affect judgments of various stimulus properties are matters on which future research is possible. In general, the results encourage further exploration of memory for various types of complex sequences, including those used in art.

FIGURE 1 A portion of Shepard's (1982) melodic map, with dots representing diatonic notes within the key of C, and circles representing the pitches of an 'atonal' melody beginning on C, and continuing to B, D#, G, E, and A, before returning to C. The Figure illustrates two alternative ways of perceiving D#, as an out-of-key note, and as a 'sharp' version of D.

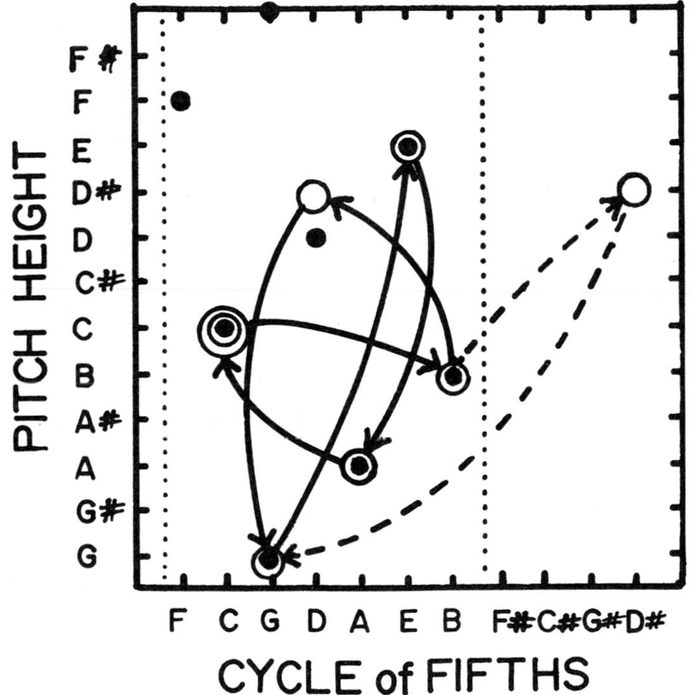

FOOTNOTES

1. I thank W.J. Dowling for many helpful discussions. This research was supported in part by Organized Research Funds from the State of Texas.

2. I thank Diana Deutsch for alerting me to the importance of sensory constraints on melody memory.

REFERENCES

Allen, G.L., Siegel, A.W. and Rosinski, R.R. (1978). The role of perceptual context in structuring spatial knowledge. Journal of Experimental Psychology: Human Learning and Memory, 6, 617-630.

Bartlett, F.C. (1932). Remembering: A study of experimental and social psychology. Cambridge: Cambridge University Press.

Bartlett, J.C. and Dowling, W.J. (1980). Recognition of transposed melodies: A key distance effect in developmental perspective. Journal of Experimental Psychology: Human Perception and Performance, 6, 501-515.

Bartlett, J.C., Till, R.E., Gernsbacher, M and Gorman, W. (1983). Age-related differences in memory for lateral orientation of pictures. Journal of Gerontology, 38, 439-446.

Boring, E. (1942). Sensation and perception in the history of experimental psychology. New York: Appleton-Century.

Bransford, J.D., McCarrell, N.S., Franks, J.J. and Nitsch, K.E. (1977). Toward unexplaining memory. In: R. Shaw and J. Bransford (Eds) Perceiving, Acting and Knowing: Toward an Ecological Psychology. Hillsdale, New Jersey: Erlbaum.

Cohen, A.J. (1978). Inferred sets of pitches in melodic perception. Paper presented at the Meeting of the Western Psychological Association, San Francisco.

Cross, I., Howell, P. and West, R. (1983). Preferences for scale structure in melodic sequences. Journal of Experimental Psychology: Human Perception and Performance, 9, 444-460.

Crozier, W.R. and Chapman, A.J. (1983). (Guest Editors). Leonardo, Volume 16, Issue 3, pp. 96. (Special Issue: Psychology and the Arts).

Cuddy, L.L., Cohen, A.J. and Miller, J. (1979). Melody recognition: the experimental application of musical rules. Canadian Journal of Psychology, 33, 148-157.

Cutting, J.E. (1983). Four assumptions about invariance in perception. Journal of Experimental Psychology: Human Perception and Performance, 9, 310-317.

Deutsch, D. (1982). The Psychology of Music. New York: Academic Press.

Dowling, W.J. (1978). Scale and contour: Two components of a theory of memory for melodies. Psychological Review, 85, 341-354.

Dowling, W.J. and Bartlett, J.C. (1981). Assimilation of brief atonal melodies to tonal prototypes: Asymmetrical effects on judgment. Paper presented at the meeting of the Psychonomic Society, Philadelphia, Pennsylvania.

von Ehrenfels, C. (1937). On Gestalt-qualities. (M. Focht, translation). American Journal of Psychology, 44, 521-524.

Flavell, J.H. (1977). Cognitive Development. Englewood Cliffs, New Jersey: Prentice-Hall.

Francès, R. (1972). La perception de la musique. Librarie Philosophique Journal, Vrin, Paris, second edition.

Garner, W.R. (1970). Good patterns have few alternatives. American Scientist, 58, 34-42.

Garner, W.R. (1974). The processing of information and structure. Hillsdale, New Jersey: Erlbaum.

Gibson, J.J. (1966). The senses considered as perceptual systems. Boston, Massachusetts: Houghton-Mifflin.

Gibson, J.J. (1979). The ecological approach to visual perception. Boston, Massachusetts: Houghton-Mifflin.

Handel, S. and Garner, W. (1966). The structure of visual pattern associates and pattern goodness. Perception and Psychophysics, 1, 33-38.

Hock, H.S. and Schmelzkopf, K.E. (1980). The abstraction of schematic representations from photographs of real-world scenes. Memory and Cognition, 6, 543-554.

Jenkins, J.J. (1977). Remember that old theory of memory? Well, forget it! In: R. Shaw and J. Bransford (Eds.) Perceiving, Acting and Knowing: Toward an Ecological Psychology. Hillsdale, New Jersey: Erlbaum.

Jenkins, J.J., Wald, J. and Pittenger, J.B. (1978). Apprehending pictorial events: An instance of psychological cohesion. In: C.W. Savage (Ed.) Minnesota Studies in the Philosophy of Science, Volume 9. Minneapolis, Minnesota: University of Minneapolis Press.

Johnston, T.D. and Turvey, M.T. (1980). A sketch of an ecological metatheory for theories of learning. In: G.H. Bower (Ed.), The Psychology of Learning and Motivation. Volume 14. New York: Academic Press.

Kraft, R.N. and Jenkins, J.J. (1977). Memory for lateral orientation of slides in picture stories. Memory and Cognition, 5, 397-403.

Krumhansl, C.L. (1979). The psychological representation of pitch in a tonal context. Cognitive Psychology, 11, 346-374.

Krumhansl, C.L. (1983). Perceptual structures for tonal music. Music Perception, 1, 28-62.

Krumhansl, C.L., Bharucha, J. and Castellano, M.A. (1982). Key distance effects on perceived harmonic structure in music. Perception and Psychophysics, 32, 96-108.

Krumhansl, C.L. and Keil, F.C. (1982). Acquisition of the hierarchy of tonal functions in music. Memory and Cognition, 10, 243-251.

Krumhansl, C.L. and Shepard, R.N. (1979). Quantification of the hierarchy of tonal functions within a diatonic context. Journal of Experimental Psychology: Human Perception and Performance, 5, 579-594.

Liebrich, J. and White, K.G. (1983). Recognition memory for pictorial events. Memory and Cognition, 11, 121-128.

Mandler, J.M. (1979). Categorical and schematic organization in memory. In: C.R. Puff (Ed.) Memory Organization and Structure. New York: Academic Press.

Michaels, C. and Carello, C. (1981). Direct Perception. Englewood Cliffs, New Jersey: Prentice-Hall.

Moeser, S.W. (1982). Memory integration and memory interference. Canadian Journal of Psychology, 36, 165-188.

Neisser, U. (1976). Cognition and Reality. San Francisco, California: Freeman.

Neisser, U. (1982a). Memory: What are the important questions? In: U. Neisser (Ed.) Memory Observed: Remembering in Naturalistic Contexts. San Francisco, California: Freeman.

Neisser, U. (1982b). John Dean's Memory: A case study. In: U. Neisser (Ed. Memory Observed: Remembering in Naturalistic Contexts. San Francisco, California: Freeman.

Pick, A.D. (1979). Listening to melodies: Perceiving events. In: A.D. Pick (Ed.) Perception and its Development: A Tribute to Eleanor J. Gibson. Hillsdale, New Jersey: Erlbaum.

Pittenger, J.B. and Jenkins, J.J. (1979). Apprehension of pictorial events: The case of a moving observer in a static environment. Bulletin of the Psychonomic Society, 13, 117-120.

Reder, L.M. and Anderson, J.R. (1980). A partial resolution of the paradox of interference: The role of integrating knowledge. Cognitive Psychology, 12, 447-473.

Rumelhart, D.E. (1975). Notes on schema for stories. In: D.G. Bobrow and A. Collins (Ed.) Representation of Understanding: Studies in Cognitive Sciences. New York: Academic Press.

Schank, R.C. and Abelson, R. (1977). Scripts, Plans, Goals, and Understanding Hillsdale, New Jersey: Erlbaum.

Shaw, R. and Pittenger, J. (1978). Perceiving change. In: H.L. Pick and E. Saltzman (Ed.) Modes of Perceiving and Processing Information. Hillsdale, New Jersey: Erlbaum.

Shepard, R.N. (1982). Geometrical approximation to the structure of musical pitch. Psychological Review, 89, 305-333.

Thorkdyke, P.W. and Hayes-Roth, B. (1982). Differences in spatial knowledge acquired from maps and navigation. Cognitive Psychology, 560-589.

Turvey, M.T. and Shaw, R. (1979). The primacy of perceiving: An ecological reformulation of perception for understanding memory. In: L. Nilsson (Ed.) Perspectives on Memory Research: Essays in Honor of Upsala University's 500th Anniversary. Hillsdale, New Jersey: Erlbaum.

Tversky, A. (1977). Features of similarity. Psychological Review, 84, 327-352.

Wallace, T.D. (1982). Age and context effects on memory for spatial orientation of real-world scenes. Unpublished Master's thesis. University of Texas at Dallas.

Cognitive Processes in the Perception of Art
W.R. Crozier and A.J. Chapman (editors)
© Elsevier Science Publishers B.V. (North-Holland), 1984

MUSICAL SPACE

Diana Deutsch

University of California, San Diego

THE HARMONY OF THE SPHERES

Those concerned with the study of music have always been fascinated by the connection between musical relationships and relationships in space. In ancient and medieval times, this was evidenced in the Pythagorean doctrine that music serves as a reflection of sounds produced by the heavenly bodies (Hawkins, 1853/1963; Hunt, 1978). The doctrine held that the sounds resulting from the motion of the planets must vary with their speeds and distances from the earth. It was further maintained that these speeds and distances were such that the combination of sounds produced must form a harmony. As Aristotle described this view in 'De Caelo':

> the motion of bodies that (astronomical) size must produce a noise, since on our earth the motion of bodies far inferior in size and speed of movement has that effect. Also, when the sun and the moon, they say, and all the stars, so great in number and in size, are moving with so rapid a motion, how should they not produce a sound immensely great? Starting from this argument, and from the observation that their speeds, as measured by their distances, are in the same ratio as musical concordances, they assert that the sound given forth by the circular movement of the stars is as harmony. (1930).

And as Alexander of Aphrodisias further wrote in his 'Commentary on Aristotle's Metaphysics':

> the sound which they (the planets) make during this motion being deep in the case of the slower, and high in the case of the quicker; these sounds then, depending on the ratio of the distances, are such that their combined effect is harmonious. (1972).

Figure 1 displays the Pythagorean view of the universe, showing the relative distances of the heavenly bodies to each other, in musical intervals. As can be seen, the distance from the Earth to the Moon comprised a whole tone; from the Moon to Mercury a semitone; from Mercury to Venus another semitone; from Venus to the Sun one and a half tones; from the Sun to Mars a tone; from Mars to Jupiter a semitone; from Jupiter to Saturn another semitone. It can further be seen that the entire distance between Earth and the Supreme Heaven comprised an Octave.

The theory of the Harmony of the Spheres immediately gave rise to the problem of why, if the heavenly bodies do indeed produce this harmony, we cannot hear it. One suggestion, fielded by Censorinus, was that the loudness of this sound is so great as to cause deafness. This view inspired the following lines by Samuel Butler in 'Hudibras':

Her voice, the music of the spheres,
So loud it deafens mortal ears,
As wise philosophers have thought,
And that's the cause we hear it not. (1973).

Another more sophisticated view, was that since this sound is present at all times, and since sound is perceived only in contrast to silence, we do not notice its presence. It is hardly surprising, however, that neither explanation met with general acceptance.

At all events, the link between music and astronomy in ancient and medieval times was so strong that the scientific half of the programme of higher education developed into the 'Quadrivium', of geometry, arithmetic, astronomy and music. The Copernican revolution, however, considerably undermined this relationship, since it became clear that the planets did not in fact form a harmony. Those seeking to understand musical phenomena therefore began to seek elsewhere to forge links between music and spatial relationships. This chapter examines several approaches to this issue, which have both strong theoretical and practical implications.

FIGURE 1 Pythagorean view of the universe, in musical intervals. (From Hawkins, 1963)

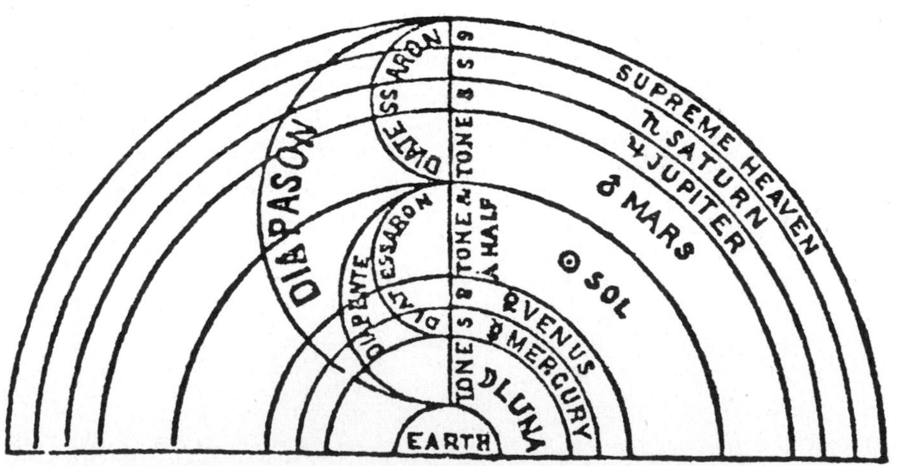

VISUO-SPATIAL ANALOGUES

The drawing of analogues between visual and musical percepts has been popular since the last century (Helmholtz, 1859; Koffka, 1935; Mach, 1894, 1906; von Ehrenfels, 1890). A detailed analysis of schemes for translation between visual and auditory configurations has been provided by Kubovy (1981).

This approach has proved particularly successful in the case of perceptual grouping phenomena: auditory analogues of visual grouping may readily be produced by mapping one dimension of visual space into pitch and another into time (Bregman, 1978; Deutsch, 1975, 1978; Divenyi and Hirsh, 1978; van Noorden, 1975). For example, when a single stream of tones is presented in rapid succession, and then those tones are drawn from 2 pitch ranges, the listener perceives, not a single stream, but rather 2 parallel streams. This is illustrated in the example shown on Figure 2, and it can be seen that the formation of perceptual groupings on the basis of proximity in pitch and time clearly emerges in the visual representation.

Now such rapid sequences of tones have several interesting properties. For example, they are poorly organized in the temporal domain. Temporal relationships are easily perceived between tones in the same pitch range, but are poorly perceived between tones in different pitch ranges. In one experiment by Bregman and Campbell (1971), subjects listened to repeating sequences of 6 tones which were drawn from 2 different pitch ranges. When these tones were presented at a rate of 10/sec, listeners found it very difficult to perceive their orders.

Even when order perception is readily accomplished, there is a gradual breakdown of temporal resolution as the pitch disparity between two alternating tones increases. For example, a rhythmic irregularity is quite apparent in a sequence of alternating tones that are close in pitch; but as the pitches of these tones diverge, this irregularity becomes gradually less perceptible (van Noorden, 1975).

At all events, the success of this visuo-spatial analogy for perceptual grouping phenomena leads us to enquire whether transformations may also be performed in such a musical space which are analogous to those in vision. We recognize visual shapes as equivalent when these are of different size or orientation or in a difficult position in the visual field. Do analogous transformations result in perceptual equivalences in music also?

Transposition provides one good example. A musical passage retains its perceptual identity when transposed to a different pitch range, provided that the relations between the individual tones are not altered. As pointed out by von Ehrenfels (1890), transposing a musical passage is like translating it to a different position in the visual field.

This example leads us to enquire whether further equivalences can be shown to exist in music that have counterparts in vision. Take size, for example. Early psychologists, such as Werner (1925), claimed that melodies will be recognized as equivalent when they are projected onto scales in which the octave is replaced by some other ratio, such as a fifth or two octaves; these micro- or macro-octaves being devided into 12 equal parts, so giving rise to micro- or macro-scales. Melodies which are projected onto such scales would then be analogous to shapes that have increased or decreased in size.

FIGURE 2 Grouping of melodic patterns by pitch proximity. The pitches that are heard correspond to fundamental frequencies whose relationships are here displayed. Two parallel lines are perceived, each in a different pitch range('From Beethoven's Six Variations on the Duet 'Nel cor piu non mi sento' from Paisiello's 'La Molinara'). (From Deutsch, 1982b)

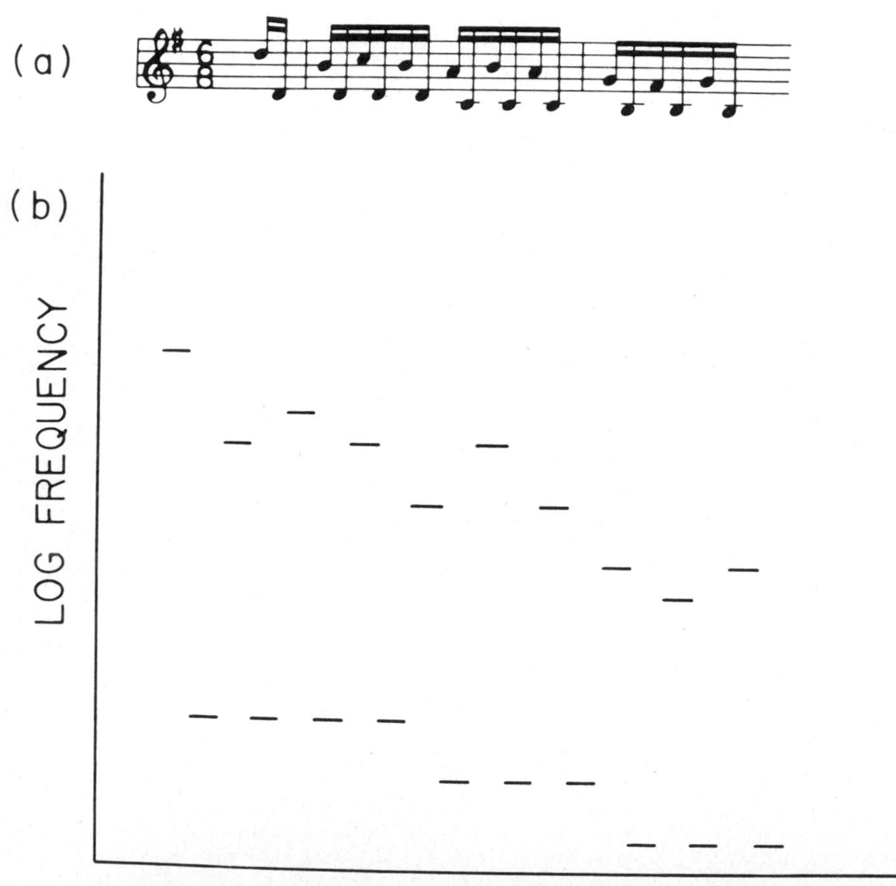

Recently, Vicario (1983) performed a study to determine how well listeners can recognize well-known melodies which have been transformed in this fashion. He varied the amount of compression of the octave down to 1 semitone, and the amount of expansion up to 2 octaves. The results of his experiment are shown on Figure 3. It can be seen that such transformations did indeed impair recognition, so that the intermodal analogy is not so successful here.

FIGURE 3 Percent correct recognition of melodies transformed by compressing and enlarging the melodic intervals to different extents. (Adapted from Vicario, 1983)

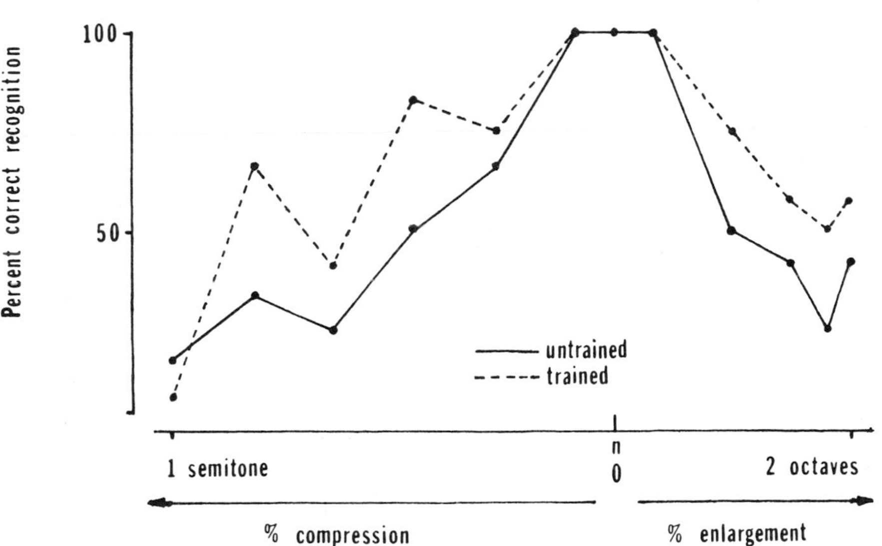

The composer Arnold Schoenberg approached the analogy in a different way. He placed strong emphasis on the perceptual equivalence of tones that are separated by octaves, and so envisaged the pitch dimension as collapsed across octaves. Further, he treated the horizontal dimension, not simply as time, but rather as succession. He went on to argue that,,within this musical space as he conceived it, transformations may occur that are analogous to rotation and reflection in vision. As he wrote:

> THE TWO-OR-MORE DIMENSIONAL SPACE IN WHICH MUSICAL IDEAS ARE PRESENTED IS A UNIT . . . The elements of a musical idea are partly incorporated in the horizontal plane as successive sounds, and partly in the vertical plane as simultaneous sounds . . . *The unity of musical space demands an absolute and unitary perception*. In this space . . . there is no absolute down, no right, or left, forward or backward . . . To the imaginative and creative faculty, relations in the material sphere are as independent from directions of planes as material objects are, in their sphere, to our perceptive faculties. Just as our mind always recognizes, for instance, a knife, a bottle or a watch, regardless of its position, and can reproduce it in the imagination in every possible position, even so a musical creator's mind can operate subconsciously with a row of tones, regardless of their direction, regardless of the way in which a mirror might show the mutual relations, which remain a given quantity. (Schoenberg, 1951)

On this basis, Schoenberg argued that a row of tones will be recognized as equivalent when it is transformed in such a way that all ascending intervals become descending intervals, and vice versa (this is termed 'inversion'), when it is presented in reverse order (this is termed 'retrogression'), or when it is transformed by both these operations (this is termed 'retrograde-inversion'). Figure 4 illustrates how Schoenberg made use of his theory in compositional practice (see also Babbitt, 1960).

It is interesting to note in this regard that prior to Schoenberg, much discussion had taken place concerning the perceptual relationships between inverted pitch sequences. Indeed Mach (1894) argued that it was self-evident that such sequences were not perceptually equivalent! He wrote:

> Now, in all the preceding examples, I have transposed upward into equal and similar steps downward: that is, as we may justly say, I have played for every moment which is symmetrical to it, yet the ear notices nothing of this symmetry . . The symmetry is there for the mind, but is wanting for sensation. No symmetry exists for the ear, because a reversal of musical sounds conditions no repetition of sensation. (Mach, 1894)

Returning to Schoenberg's scheme, we may note that this also assumes perceptual equivalence of tones that stand in octave relation. Contemporary music theorists refer to such tones as being in the same 'pitch class'. Analogously, psychologists refer to tones standing in octave relation as having the same 'chroma'. Drobisch (1846) suggested that the similarity of tones standing in octave relation be accommodated by deforming the rectilinear scale of pitch into a helix having one complete turn per octave. A version of this view, taken from Shepard (1982), is presented in Figure 5. In one degenerate case of the helix, it is compressed into a circle, so that there is total perceptual identity of tones that are separated by octaves.

Reasoning along these lines, Shepard (1964) synthesized a set of tones whose perceptual representation was in fact circular. Each tone consisted of many sinusoids which were separated by octaves. The amplitude spectra of the tones were such as to exaggerate the circular component and to minimize the dimension of height. When such tones are presented in ascending semitonal stops, they create the fascinating illusion of a set of tones that are endlessly climbing up an abstracted octave.

FIGURE 4 Illustration by Schoenberg of his theory of equivalence relations between pitch structures, taken from 'The Wind Quartet, Op. 26'. Schoenberg wrote: 'The employment of these mirror forms correspond to the principle of *the absolute and unitary perception of musical space*'. (From Schoenberg, 1951)

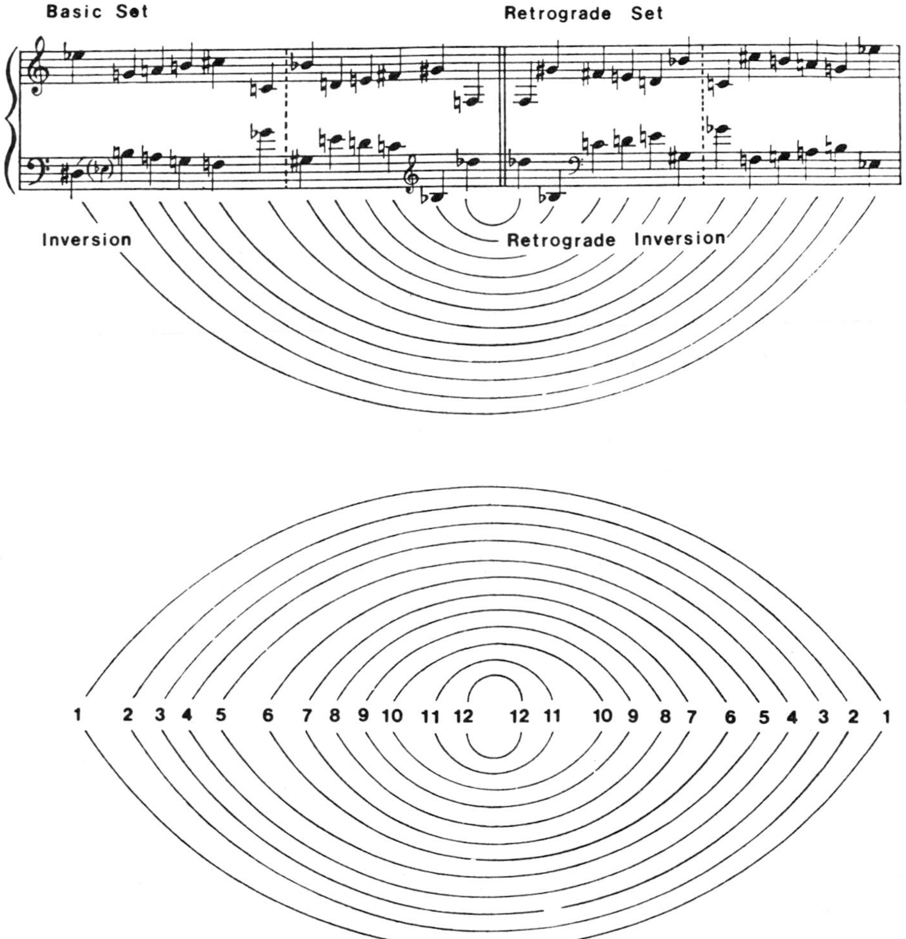

FIGURE 5 The helical model of pitch. (From Shepard, 1982)

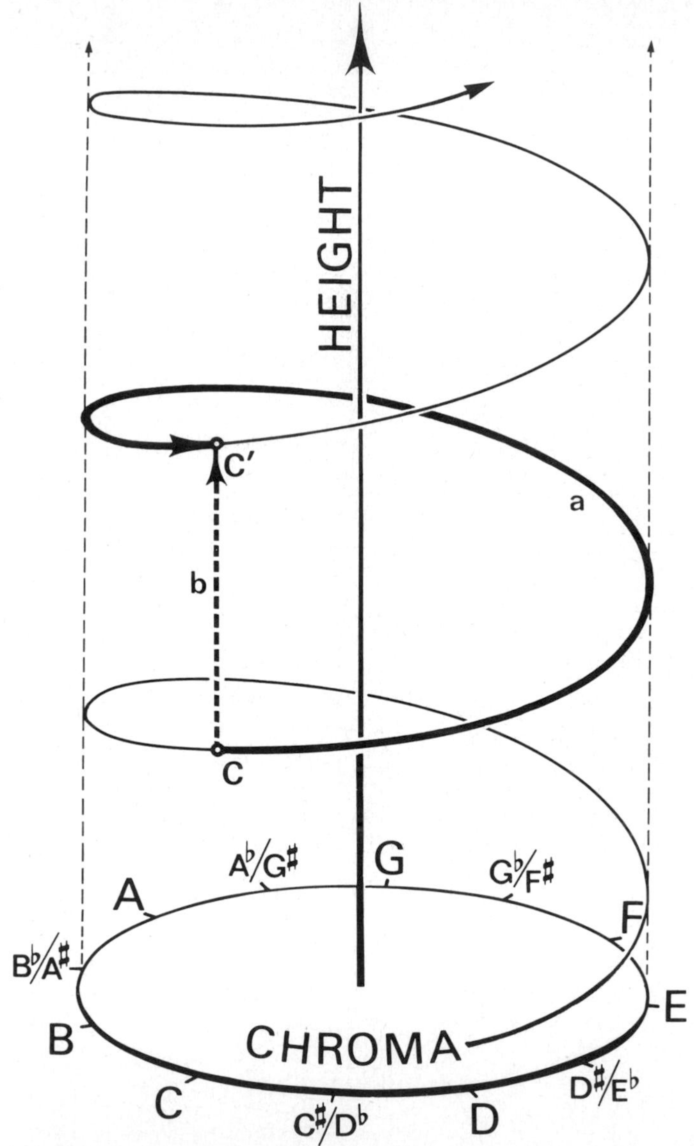

From these and other demonstrations, it is clear that powerful octave equivalence effects can be obtained in certain musical situations. But can we assume that pitch class identity holds true in general? Some time ago, I proposed a neurophysiological model for the abstraction of pitch relationships which assumes that this is not the case (Deutsch, 1969). According to this model such abstraction takes place along two separate and parallel channels, as shown in Figure 6. Along the first channel, there is convergence of information from neural units that underly tones which are separated by octaves; this produces octave equivalence effects. Along the second channel, no such convergence takes place; instead this channel mediates transposition of musical intervals and chords. The 2-channel model therefore makes a prediction which might seem rather implausible; namely that it should be very difficult to recognize well-known tunes in which pitch class is preserved, but the tones are placed randomly in different octaves. However, I tried this effect out using a variety of tunes, and found that indeed people had considerable difficulty in identifying them. So I carried out a formal test of the hypothesis (Deutsch, 1972).

The first half of the tune 'Yankee Doodle' was chosen as the test sequence. There were 2 reasons for this choice. First, it is extremely well-known; and, second,it contains very little rhythmic information. Other investigators had shown that people can guess the identities of tunes to a fair extent on the basis of rhythm alone; so it seemed necessary to minimize this factor.

The tune was generated under 3 different conditions: (1) it was produced without transformation in each of three adjacent octaves; (2) it was produced such that each tone was in its correct position within the octave (i.e., pitch class was preserved), but the octave placement of these tones varied randomly between these same three octaves; and (3) the tune was produced as a series of clicks, so that it contained no pitch information, but the rhythm was presented. This third condition therefore provided a measure of identification accuracy on the basis of rhythm alone. The different versions of the tune were presented to separate groups of subjects They were asked to listen to the sequence, and then to write down what they believed the tune to be.

Figure 7 shows the percent correct recognitions of the different versions of 'Yankee Doodle'. You can see that recognition was extremely poor for the randomized octaves version, with only around 12% of the subjects guessing it correctly. In fact, recognition here was even poorer than for the version where the pitch information was entirely removed, though this difference was not significant. However, when these same subjects were then played the untransformed version, recognition was immediate; and recognition was also easy once the subjects knew what to listen for.

The results of this experiment are in accordance with the 2-channel model of Deutsch (1969), and show that perception of pitch class, where melodic intervals are concerned, does not take place directly. Rather, in certain situations, pitch class perception can result from an active hypothesis testing process. The listener matches each incoming note with his mental image of the expected note, and so confirms or disconfirms a hypothesized pitch class.

For the reader who can play a musical instrument, this experiment is easy to repeat. Figure 8 presents a 'randomized-octaves' version of another well -known tune. When played as shown, subjects are generally unable to recognize it. But if all the notes are transposed onto a single octave, recognition is usually easy. (Be careful, if attempting this experiment, not to give away the name of the tune before your subjects hear it, or the effect will not work).

FIGURE 6 Two-channel model for the abstraction of pitch relationships One channel mediates transposition of intervals and chords, and the other channel mediates octave equivalence effects. (From Deutsch, 1969)

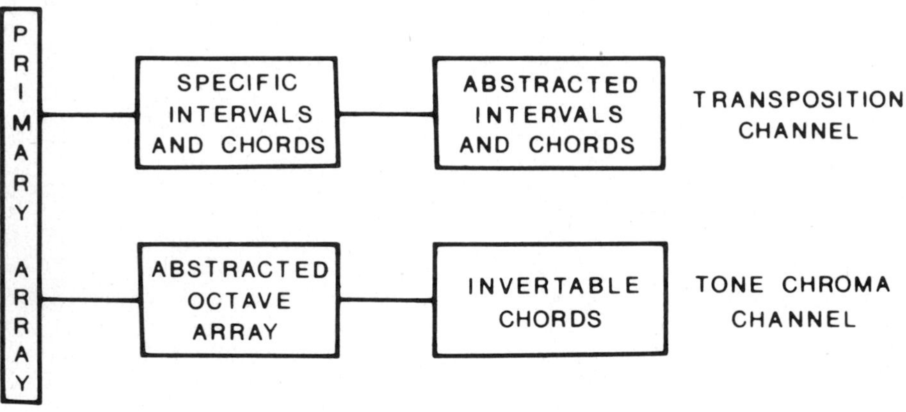

FIGURE 7 Percent correct recognition of different versions of 'Yankee Doodle'. (From Deutsch, 1972)

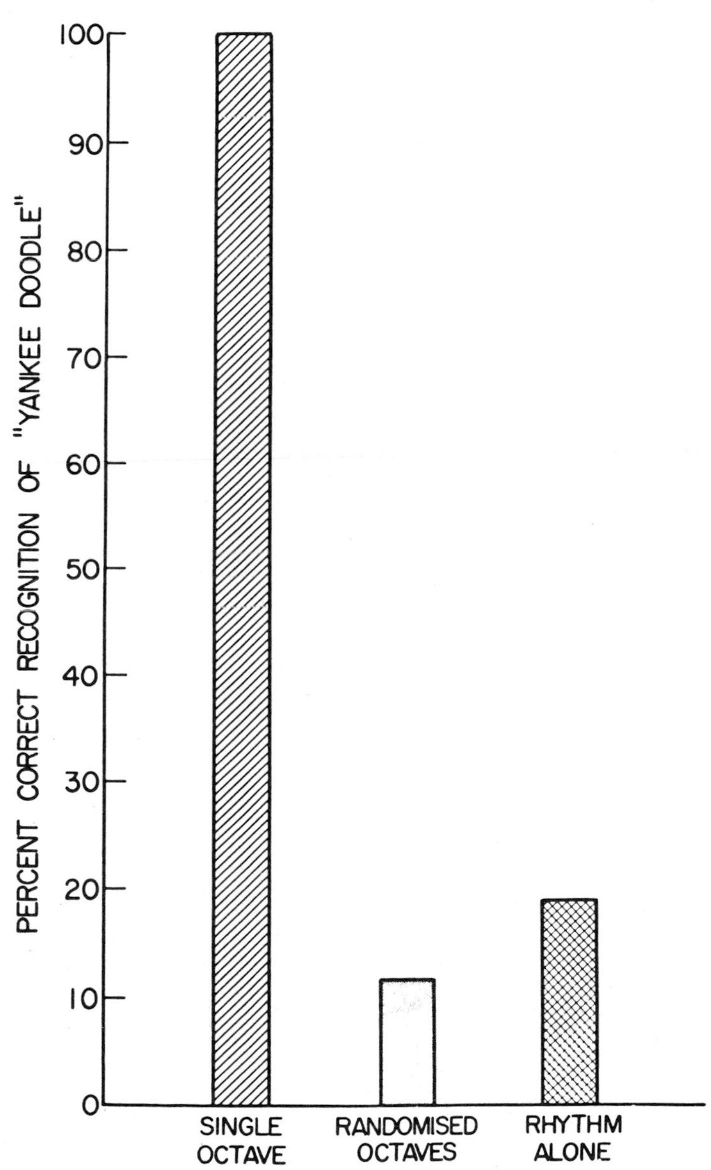

FIGURE 8 A 'randomized-octaves' version of a well-known tune. (See text for details)

Now it could be argued, and indeed it has been, that the failure to recognize or acquire melodies under octave displacement is due, not to an inability to perceive intervals directly where octave jumps are involved, but rather to a disruption of the recognition process by an alteration in melodic contour (Idson and Massaro, 1978; Kallman and Massaro, 1979; but see Deutsch, 1982a). So recently, I carried out an experiment to control for this. Instead of using a recognition paradigm, I presented musically literate subjects with novel sequences, and asked them to write down in musical notation what they heard.[1] Since a comparison judgment was not involved here, the involvement of contour as a cue could not arise.

There were three conditions in the experiment, and examples of sequences in these conditions are shown in Figure 9. In the first, all tones within a sequence were in a higher octave. In the second, all tones were in the adjacent lower octave. And in the third, tones within a sequence alternated between these 2 adjacent octaves. In the third condition, about two-thirds of the successive intervals involved octave jumps; the remainder spanned less than an octave. Also shown in Figure 9 are the percentages of tones that were correctly notated in their correct serial positions in these different conditions. It can be seen that performance levels were substantially lower in the condition involving octave jumps than in the other two. This result therefore shows again that we experience considerable difficulty in processing melodic intervals across octaves, so that octave equivalence cannot be taken to be a perceptual invariant (Deutsch, 1983a).

To conclude this section, visuo-spatial analogues have been found quite successful for certain aspects of musical processing, but not for others. It appears that the mechanisms underlying perception of pitch sequences have some points of similarity with those underlying perception of static visual arrays: but that important differences also exist.

FIGURE 9 Examples of sequences employed in experiment to examine the effect of octave jumps in the processing of melodic information. Also shown are the percentages of tones that were correctly notated in their correct serial positions in these different conditions. (From Deutsch, 1983a)

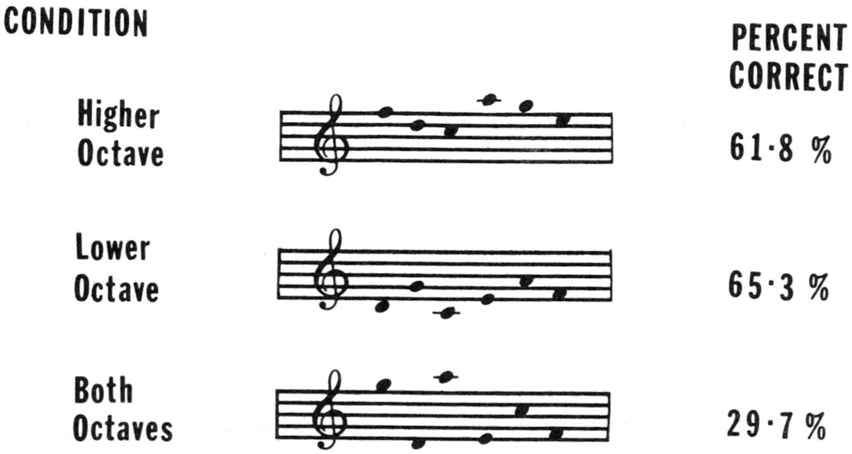

CONDITION	PERCENT CORRECT
Higher Octave	61·8 %
Lower Octave	65·3 %
Both Octaves	29·7 %

ABSTRACT GEOMETRIC REPRESENTATIONS OF PITCH STRUCTURES

Geometric representation of pitch structures have been popular among music theorists since Pythagorean times. The Renaissance theorist Gioseffo Zarlino (1517-1590) invoked a mathematical model to justify expanding the realm of the consonances beyond the currently accepted ratios of the octave (2:1) fifth (3:2) and fourth (4:3), so as to include also the major third (5:4), minor third (6:5) and major sixth (5:3). Figure 10 is taken from Zarlino's emblem, and depicts a cube which is inscribed by various lines that intersect so as to form the ratios of the consonances; namely, those ratios involving the first six numbers; the 'senario'. Above the cube is written **Οὐδέν χωρίς ἐμόν** meaning 'nothing outside me'. Zarlino argued that as long as the composer stayed within the senario he was safe. But outside was a wilderness of dissonances, which should be employed only under very restricted conditions (Palisca, 1961).

Later, theorists emphasized the advantages of considering pitch structures as existing in a 'tonal space' of 3 dimensions corresponding to the octave (2:1), fifth (3:2) and major third (5:4) (Bosanquet, 1876; Helmholtz, 1859; Rameau, 1721). Such spaces have frequently been invoked in debates over tuning systems (Barbour, 1951; Hall, 1973, 1974). They further provide the basis for current theorizing about the internal representation of tonal structures. Longuet-Higgins (1962a, 1962b, 1978) has argued for a model of key attribution involving such a space (Figure 11). He proposed that when a listener hears a musical passage, he selects a given region of this space; so attributing a key. However, if his choice results in his having to make large jumps within this region, he abandons it and selects instead a region in which the tones are more compactly represented; so attributing a new key.

FIGURE 10 Cube on Gioseffo Zarlino's (1517-1590) emblem. The lines on the cube intersect so as to form the ratios of the consonances. (Adapted from Palisca, 1961)

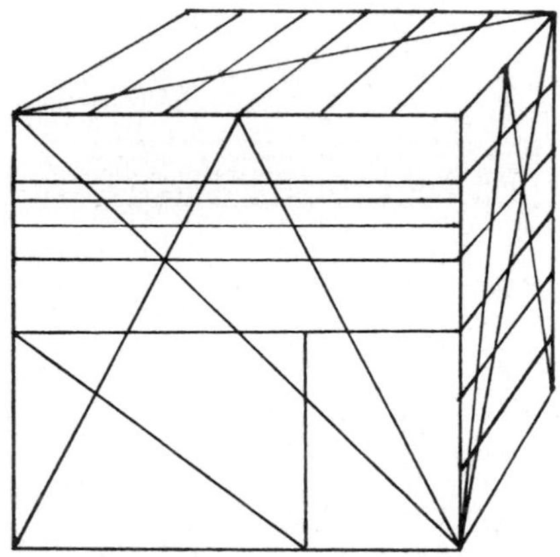

Shepard (1982) has also invoked the principle of proximity in arguing for a particular internal representation of pitch structures. His model of tonal space includes one dimension for pitch height, two for the octave relation and two for the circle of fifths. The resulting representation is of a double helix wrapped around a helical cylinder in 5 dimensions, as shown in Figure 12.

Krumhansl and Kessler (1982) performed a series of experiments to obtain a spatial representation of the relationships between keys. In the resulting representation, the points for the different keys are located on the surface of a torus in 4 dimensions. One circle of fifths was obtained on this surface for major keys, and another for minor keys; and these were aligned so as to reflect parallel and relative relationships between the major and minor keys. The authors argue that this spatial representation is similar in many respects to that proposed by Schoenberg (1969). For a review of this and related work, see Krumhansl (1983).

FIGURE 11 Representation of tonal space proposed to underly key attribution by Longuet-Higgins. (From Longuet-Higgins, 1978)

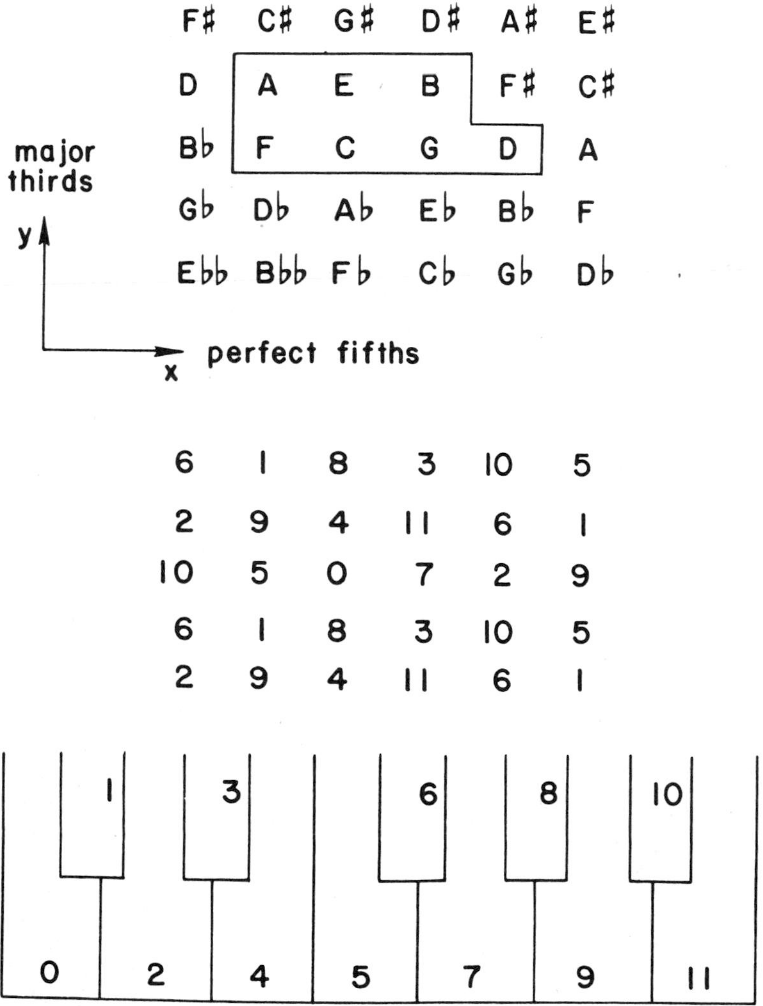

FIGURE 12 Representation of tonal space as a double helix wrapped around a helical cylinder in five dimensions, as proposed by Shepard. (From Shepard, 1982)

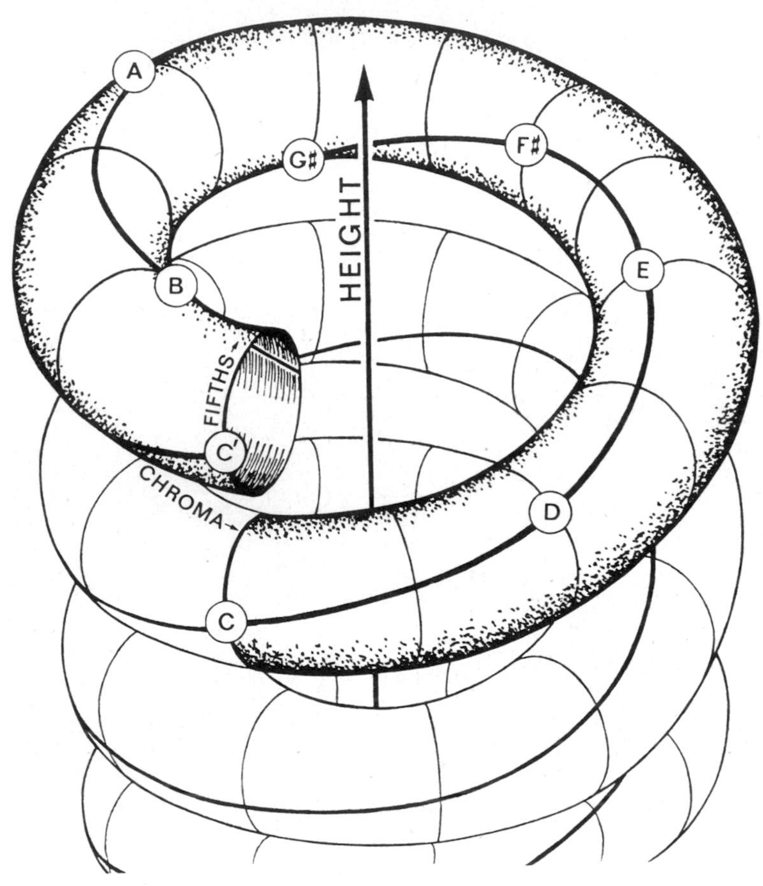

TIMBRAL SPACE

Spatial representations have been used successfully in the modelling of perceived instrument sounds. For example, Grey (1975) had subjects rate the similarities of pairs of such sounds, and from these ratings obtained the 3-dimensional representation shown in Figure 13. The first dimension related to the spectral energy distribution of the different tones. Tones with narrow bandwidths, and with a concentration of low-frequency energy appeared at one end; and tones with wide bandwiths and less concentration of low-frequency energy appeared at the other end. The second dimension was related to the distribution of energy in the attack segments of the tones. At one end, tones displayed high-frequency low-amplitude energy in the attack portion, and at the other end, no high-frequency precedent energy in the attack was found. Two alternative interpretations were proposed for the third dimension. Either this related to the form of onset-offset patterns; or the dimension was a cognitive one, in which the tones were arranged according to instrument family.

FIGURE 13 Three-dimensional representation of perceived similarities of instrument sounds. On the walls are shown the two-dimensional projections of the cubes in this space. O1, O2 = oboes; C1, C2 = clarinets; X1, X2, X3 = saxophones; EH = English horn; FH = French horn; S1, S2, S3 = strings; TP = trumpet; TM = trombone; FL = flute; BN = basoon. (From Grey, 1975)

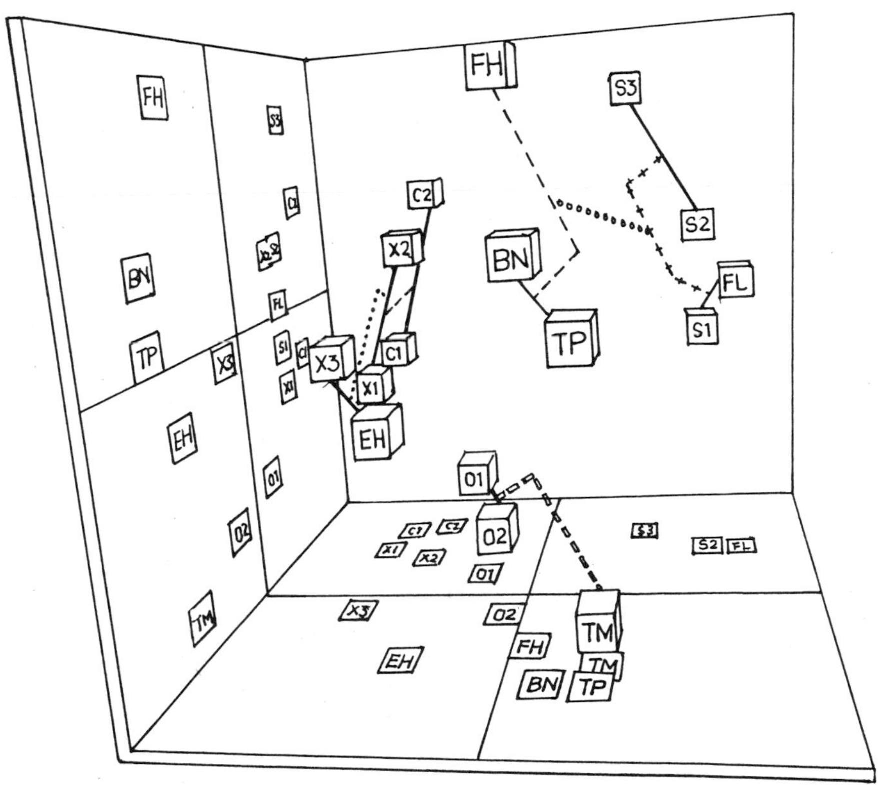

The multidimensional spatial representation of timbre was exploited by Ehresman and Wessel (cited in Wessel, 1979) in a study on the transportation of timbral relationships. As shown in Figure 14, the pattern of timbres A→B is ideally analogous to the pattern C→D in a timbral space. The authors examined whether such analogies are indeed produced by listeners, by presenting them with pairs of timbres, and having them rank-order 4 possible solutions of the form (A→B as C→D). A good correspondence was indeed obtained from the rank orders that were predicted and those derived empirically.

FIGURE 14 Parallelogram model of timbral analogies. A→B is a given change in timbre. C→D is the desired analogy when C is given. D is the point of ideal solution. The actual solutions offered to subjects were the points D_1, D_2, D_3 and D_4. (From Wessel, 1979)

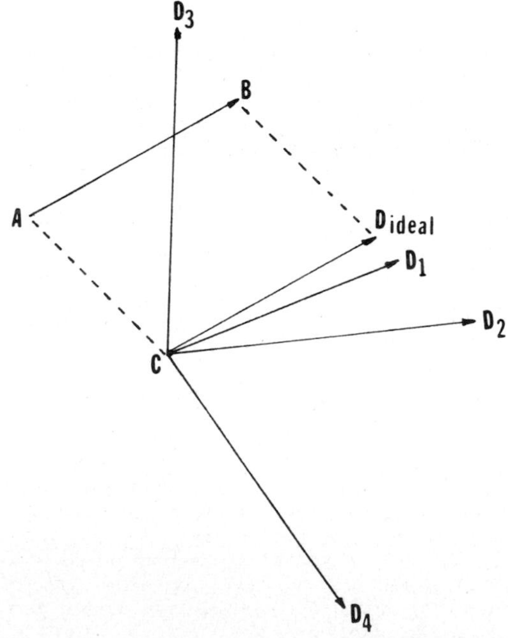

Such work is of direct interest to contemporary composers who are concerned with creating orderly patterns from sequences of timbres. Schoenberg in particular was interested in determining the rules governing systematic timbral transitions. As he wrote (Schoenberg, 1911):

> If it is possible to make compositional structures from sounds which differ according to pitch, structures which we call melodies, sequences producing an effect similar to thought, then it must also be possible to create such sequences from the timbres of that other dimension from what we normally and simply call timbre. Such sequences would work with an inherent logic, equivalent to the kind of logic which is effective in melodies based on pitch. All this seems a fantasy of the future, which it probably is. But I am firmly convinced that it can be realized.

Informal studies exploiting timbral spaces have proved very promising for such endeavours. For example, Grey (1975) created a series of tones that traversed his multidimensional space in small steps. This resulted in the listener first perceiving one instrument (such as a clarinet), and at some point in the series realizing that he was instead perceiving a different instrument (such as a cello). Yet the transition between the 2 types of percepts was quite smooth. Thus Schoenberg's concept of composing with timbres that are arranged along an orderly continuum appears realizable (see also Risset and Wessl, 1982, for an extended review).

MUSIC AND DISPOSITION IN PHYSICAL SPACE

The question of how the disposition of instruments in physical space affects the perception of music has been of particular interest to composers since the work of Berlioz in the last century. Following his lead, twentieth century composers such as Ives, Brandt and Stockhausen have paid particular attention to the positioning of instruments and instrument groups.

In laboratory situations, spatial relationships have been shown to interact with other musical attributes in striking ways. In one set of studies, I examined the perceptual effects of presenting 2 simultaneous sequences of tones, one to each ear. The following question was addressed. Does the listener, under such conditions of extreme spatial separation, perceive the sequence coming from one side of space or the other; or does the listener instead form the perceptual configurations on another basis? Instead of obtaining simple answers, a set of striking and paradoxical illusions was uncovered. A further surprise was that the type of illusion obtained correlates with handedness.

The pattern that I first employed (Deutsch, 1974, 1975a) is shown in Figure 15A. As can be seen, this consists of two tones, which are spaced an octave apart, and presented in alternation. The same sequence is presented to both ears simultaneously: however, when the right ear receives the high tone the left ear receives the low tone; and vice versa. So the listener is presented with a single continuous two-tone chord, but the ear of input for each component switches constantly.

It might be easily imagined how this sequence should sound if perceived correctly. But I have played it now to hundreds of listeners, and so far only 3 people have been able to guess what the stimulus was; and 2 of these had clear signs of neurological abnormality. With these 3 exceptions, an illusion was always obtained. The kind of illusion varied from listener to listener; but the most typical one is shown in Figure 15B. It can be seen that this consists of a single tone which alternates from ear to ear; and whose pitch simultaneously alternates between high and low. That is, a single high tone is heard in one ear, which alternates with a single low tone in the other ear.

FIGURE 15 (A) Sound pattern producing the octave illusion. This pattern is repeatedly presented without pause. (B) Representation of the illusion most commonly obtained. A single high tone in the right ear appears to alternate with a single low tone in the left ear. (From Deutsch, 1975a)

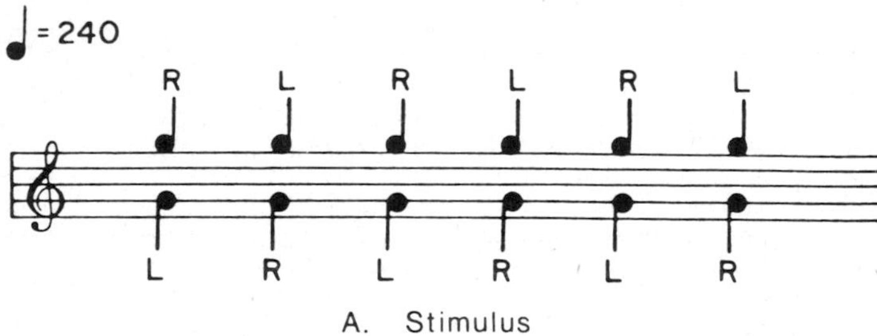

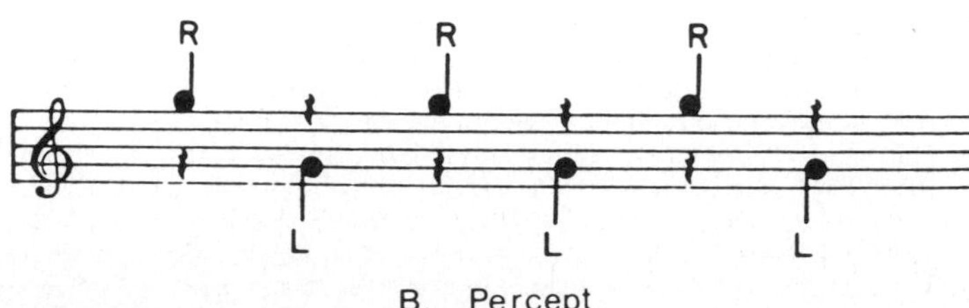

Clearly, there is no simple way to explain this illusion. The perception of alternating pitches can be accounted for by assuming that the listener attends to the input to one ear and ignores the other. But then both of the alternating pitches should be perceived as in the same ear. Or, the alternation of a single tone from ear to ear can be explained by supposing that the listener suppresses the input to each ear in turn. But then the pitch of this tone should not alter with a change in its apparent location. The illusion of a single tone that alternates simultaneously both in pitch and in location creates a paradox.

The illusion is even more unexpected when we consider what happens when the listener's earphones are reversed. Now exactly the same thing is heard by most people: the tone that appeared in the right ear continues to appear in the right ear and the tone that appeared in the left ear continues to appear in the left ear. So it is, though the earphone which had been emitting the high tone is now emitting the low tone, and the earphone which had been emitting the low tone is now emitting the high tone.

There is another surprising aspect to the illusion: right-handers and left-handers exhibit different patterns of localization for the 2 pitches at the 2 ears. Right-handers have a strong tendency to hear the high tone on the right and the low tone on the left; and to retain this percept when the earphones are reversed. But left-handers as a group do not show any such consistency. Now the left hemisphere is dominant in the overwhelming majority of right-handers; but this is true of only about two thirds of the left-handed population; the remainder being right hemisphere dominant (Goodglass and Quadfasel, 1954; Milner, Branch and Rasmussen, 1966; Zangwill, 1960). This pattern of results therefore shows that we tend to perceive the high tones as coming from the side of space that is contralateral to the dominant hemisphere, and that we tend to perceive the low tones as coming from the opposite side.

If we assume that separate brain mechanisms exist for attributing the pitch of a tone, and for attributing its location, we are in a position to provide an explanation for this illusion. The model is displayed on Figure 16. To determine the perceived pitches, the frequencies arriving at one ear are attended to, and those arriving at the other ear are supressed. But, to provide perceived locations, each tone is localized in the ear that receives the higher frequency, irrespective of whether the higher or the lower frequency is in fact perceived. Let us consider the listener who follows the frequencies presented to the right ear. When a high tone is presented to the right and a low tone to the left, this listener hears a high tone, because this is presented to the right ear. He or she also localizes the tone in the right ear, because this ear receives the higher frequency. But when a low tone is presented to the right and a high tone to the left, this listener now perceives a low tone, since this is presented to the right ear; but he or she localizes the tone in the left ear instead, because this ear receives the higher frequency. So the sequence as a whole is heard as a high tone to the right that alternates with a low tone to the left. It can be seen that reversing the position of the earphones would not change this basic percept. But for the case of the listener who follows the frequencies presented to the left ear instead, keeping the localization rule constant, this same sequence is now perceived as a high tone to the left that alternates with a low tone to the right. Further experiments have confirmed this model (Deutsch, 1981; Deutsch and Ross, 1976).

FIGURE 16 Model showing how the outputs of two brain mechanisms, one determining perceived pitch, and the other determining perceived location, combine to produce the octave illusion. Filled boxes represent high tones, and unfilled boxes represent low tones. (From Deutsch, 1981)

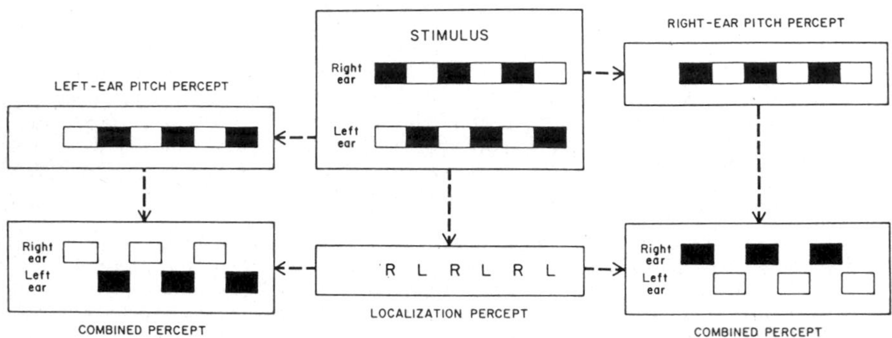

Informal work in my laboratory has demonstrated that this illusion also occurs when signals are presented through loudspeakers rather than through earphones (Deutsch, 1975a). Further, Wessel (1983) has shown that variants of the illusion may be generated with computer-synthesized musical instrument tones, in which pitch is held constant, and location and brightness are varied. For example, a very striking effect is produced by alternating tones which simulate French horn and muted trombone. It is highly probable therefore, that effects of this sort occur in listening to live music also.

What occurs if we present a pattern that consists of more than 2 tones? In one experiment I employed the sequence shown on Figure 17A; this constitutes a major scale, with successive tones alternating from ear to ear. The scale is presented simultaneously in both ascending and descending form, such that when a tone from the ascending scale occurs in one ear, a tone from the descending scale occurs in the other ear (Deutsch, 1975a, 1975b).

FIGURE 17 (A) Sound pattern producing the scale illusion. This pattern is repeatedly presented without pause. (B) Representation of the illusion most commonly obtained. The higher tones all appear as in the right ear, and the lower tones as in the left ear. (From Deutsch, 1975a)

This sequence also produces a number of illusions, which differ from listener to listener. The illusion most commonly perceived is represented in Figure 17B. The correct sequence of pitches is heard, but as 2 separate melodies, that move in contrary motion. Furthermore, all the higher tones appear to be emanating from the right earphone, and the lower tones from the left. This percept is still maintained when the earphone positions are reversed. It thus appears to the listener that the earphone which had been emitting the higher tones is now emitting the lower tones, and that the earphone which had been emitting the lower tones is now emitting the higher tones.

Effects of this kind can be obtained in listening to live music. A passage from the final movement of Tschaikowsky's Sixth Symphony is shown in Figure 18. It can be seen that the theme and accompaniment are each distributed between the two violin parts. But the theme is heard as emanating from one set of instruments and the accompaniment as from the other. I have experienced this illusion very powerfully when listening to this passage seated in front of an orchestra arranged in nineteenth century fashion, that is with the first violins on one side of the orchestra and the second violins on the other.

How can such illusions be accounted for? We live in an auditory environment that is very complex. Because of the presence of echoes and reverberation, it is difficult to assign sounds correctly to their sources. So when both ears are stimulated simultaneously, first-order localization cues alone are generally not sufficient to determine which portions of the total spectrum should be assigned to which source. Similarity of spectrum provides an important additional cue: similar sounds are likely to be coming from the same source, and different sounds from different sources. So with such musical passages it is reasonable for the listener to assume that tones in one range of the spectrum are coming from a different source. The tones are therefore perceptually reorganized in space in accordance with this assumption.

What happens when the sounds arriving at the 2 ears or from the 2 locations are not simultaneous? To investigate this question, subjects were presented with 2 simple melodic patterns, and on each trial they identified which one they had heard (Deutsch, 1979). The patterns were generated in 4 different ways, as shown in Figure 19. In the first condition, the melody was presented simultaneously to both ears. It can be seen that identification performance was here very good. In the second condition, the component tones of the melody were distributed between the ears in quasi-random fashion. It can be seen that identification performance was now, in contrast, very poor. At the subjective level, it is easy to listen to the pattern coming either from one earphone or from the other, but it is very difficult to integrate these 2 patterns into a single percept. The third condition was just as the second, except that now the melody was accompanied by a drone. Whenever a tone from the melody was in the right ear the drone was in the left ear; and vice versa. So both ears now received input simultaneously, even though the melody was greatly improved here, and at the subjective level the melody emerges perceptually without effort. In the fourth condition, the melody was again accompanied by a drone. However, the drone was now presented to the same ear as the tone from the melody, so that input was again to only one ear at a time. As can be seen, identification performance was here again very poor.

FIGURE 18 Passage from last movement of Tschaikowsky's Sixth Symphony. The Violin I and Violin II parts in combination produce the percept shown on the upper right. The Viola and Violoncello parts in combination produce the percept shown in the lower right. (From Butler, 1979)

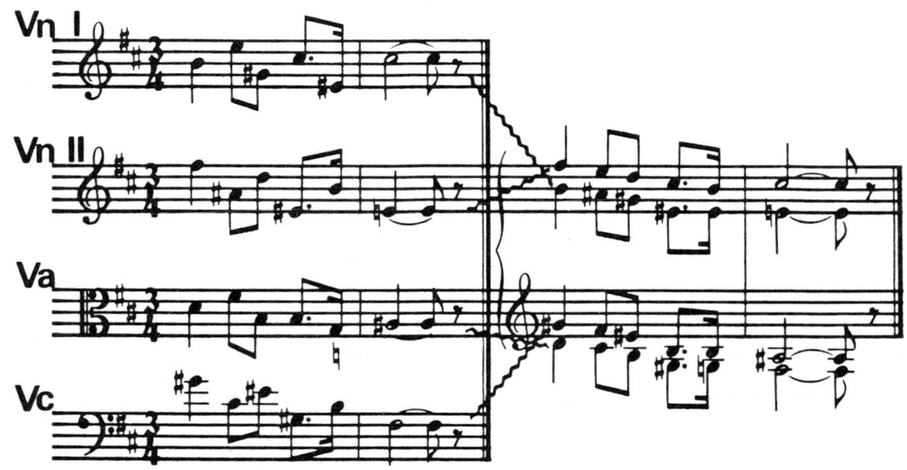

FIGURE 19 Examples of distributions between ears of melodic pattern and drone. Also shown are error rates in melody identification obtained in the different conditions. Where input was to both ears simultaneously (Conditions 1 and 3), performance levels were very high. But where input was to one ear at a time (Conditions 2 and 4), performance levels were very low. (From Deutsch, 1979)

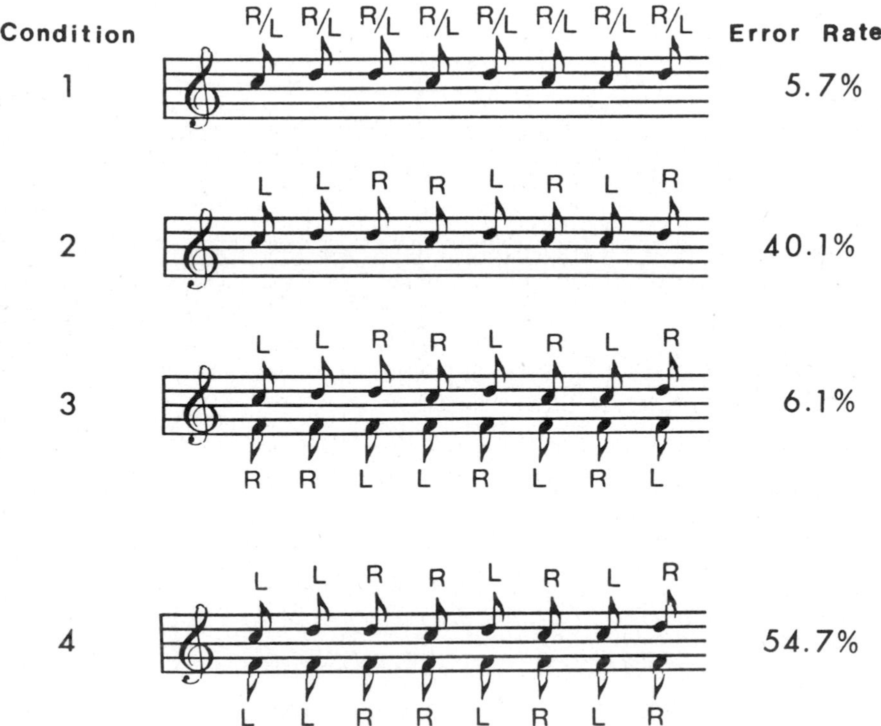

This experiment demonstrates that, with signals coming from different spatial locations, temporal relationships between them are important determinants of grouping. Where the 2 ears received input simultaneously, grouping by frequency range was easy, with the result that melody identification readily occurred. However, when these signals were clearly separated in time, grouping by spatial location virtually obliterated the subjects' ability to integrate the signals into a single perceptual stream.

What happens when the signals arriving at the 2 ears are not strictly simultaneous? In a second experiment I presented various conditions of onset-offset asynchrony between the notes of the melody and the contralateral drone. Performance levels here were found to be intermediate between those in conditions which the 2 ears received input strictly simultaneously and where the ears received input one at a time: performance was poorer than in the former case, but better than in the latter.

How can these findings be explained? The relationships between wave-form envelopes of sound signals are important cues as to whether these signals are coming from the same source or from different sources (Tobias, 1972). We should therefore expect that the clearer the temporal separation between the signals arriving at the 2 ears, the greater should be the listener's tendency to treat the signals as coming from separate sources, and so the greater should be the tendency to group them by spatial location. If such grouping is sufficiently powerful, it should prevent the listener from forming perceptual linkages between signals coming from different sources. In performing auditory shape analyses, it is necessary that we do not link together the components of different signals; otherwise nonsensical percepts result. In relating these findings to listening to live music, it is interesting to consider the following passage from Berlioz's 'Treatise on Instrumentation' (1948):

> I want to mention the importance of the different points of origin of the tonal masses. Certain groups of an orchestra are selected by the composer to question and answer each other; but this design becomes clear and effective only if the groups which are to carry on the dialogue are placed at a sufficient distance from each other. The composer must therefore indicate in his score their exact disposition. For instance, the drums, bass drums, cymbals and kettledrums may remain together if they are employed, as usual, to strike certain rhythms simultaneously. But if they execute an interlocutory rhythm, one fragment of which is given to the bass drums and cymbals, the other to kettledrums and drums, the effect would be greatly improved and intensified by placing the two groups of percussion instruments at the opposite ends of the orchestra; i.e., at a considerable distance from each other.

The experiments described above essentially confirm Berlioz's picture: the spatial disposition of instruments should indeed have profound effects on how music is perceived. When there is a clear spatial separation between two groups of instruments, and in addition a clear temporal separation between the sounds produced by these instruments, the perceptual dissociation that results may be so strong as to prevent the listener from integrating the different sounds into a single stream. Perceptual integration will, however, be facilitated by some temporal overlap between the different instruments. Yet there is a trade-off: As the temporal overlap increases, spatial distinctiveness will be gradually lost; and as simultaneity is approached, spatial illusion will begin to occur.

We finally return to the question of how, in a sequential setting, perception of 2 simultaneous tones may be affected by whether the higher is to the right and the lower is to the left, or whether this configuration is reversed. As already mentioned, in the scale illusion, right-handers tend strongly to perceive high tones as on the right and low tones as on the left, irrespective of their true locations. In other words, combinations of the 'high-right/low-left' type tend to be accurately localized, and combinations of the 'high-left/low-right' type tend to be mislocalized. A further experiment has confirmed this finding in a more general setting (Deutsch, 1983b). We can then ask: given the impairment in localization accuracy for 'high-left/low-right' combinations, compared with 'high-right/low-left' combinations, is there also perhaps an impairment in perceptual accuracy for tones in these combinations regardless of how they appear localized? To examine this issue, Deutsch (1983b) presented musically trained subjects with 2 sequences of sine wave tones, one to each ear, and they wrote down in musical notation what they heard, without regard for ear of input. An example of a pattern employed is given in Figure 20. It can be seen that this can be described as a sequence of dyads, each of which is either of the 'high-right/low-left' type, or the 'high-left/low-right' type.

FIGURE 20 Example of pattern used in experiment to determine perceptual accuracy for tones forming 'high-right/low-left' dyads compared with tones forming 'high-left/low-right' dyads. (From Deutsch, 1983b)

Figure 21 displays the percentages of tones that were correctly notated in their correct serial positions, classified by whether they came from 'high-right/low-left' dyads, or from 'high-left/low-right' dyads. Performance was significantly better for the former type of dyad than for the latter (Deutsch, 1983b). We can see, therefore, that there is an advantage to a spatial disposition in which higher tones are to the right and lower tones to the left, compared with the reverse. This is true both of how well the tones are perceived, and also how well they are localized.

This leads us to the following line of reasoning, with which this chapter concludes. In general, seating arrangements for contemporary orchestras are such that, taken from the viewpoint of the performer, instruments with higher registers tend to be to the right, and instrument with lower registers to the left. As an example, a seating plan of the Chicago Symphony, viewed from the orchestra, is shown in Figure 22. In the strings section, the first violins are to the right of the second violins; and these are to the right of the violas; and these are to the right of the cellos; and these are to the right of the basses. In the case of the basses, the trumpets are to the right of the trombones; and these are to the right of the tuba. It is also the case in general that, within specific instrument groups (such as trumpets), those playing in higher registers tend to be to the right, and those playing in lower registers to the left. The same principle tends to hold for choirs and other singing groups also. Since it is important that performers should be able to hear each other as well as possible, it is probable that such arrangements have evolved by trial and error because they are conducive to optimal performance.

FIGURE 21 Percentages of tones that were correctly notated in their correct serial positions, classified by whether they were from 'high-left/low-right' dyads, or from 'high-right/low-left' dyads. (From Deutsch, 1983b)

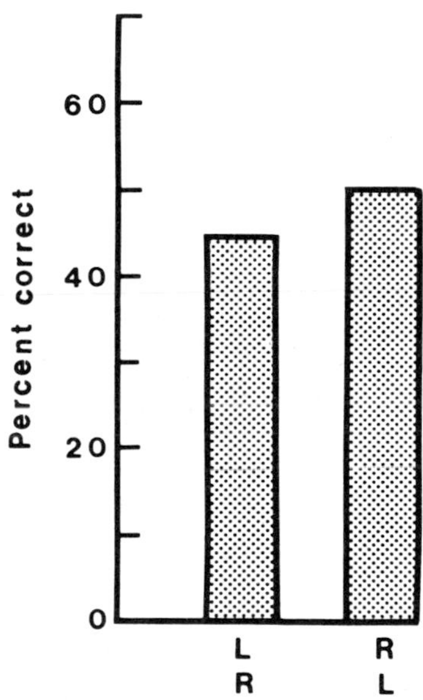

However, this gives rise to an interesting paradox. Since the audience sits facing the orchestra, this left-right disposition is from their point of view mirror-image reversed: instruments with higher registers now tend to be to the left, and instruments with lower registers to the right. So from the point of view of the audience, this spatial arrangement is such as to cause perceptual difficulties. The greatest problem should occur from instruments with low registers which are to the audience's right: these should tend to be poorly perceived and localized (Deutsch, 1983c). Indeed, phenomena such as the 'mystery of the disappearing "cellos"' which unaccountably plague some concert halls, may be based in part on this effect.

FIGURE 22 Chicago Symphony seating plan; viewed from the orchestra. (Adapted from Machlis, 1977)

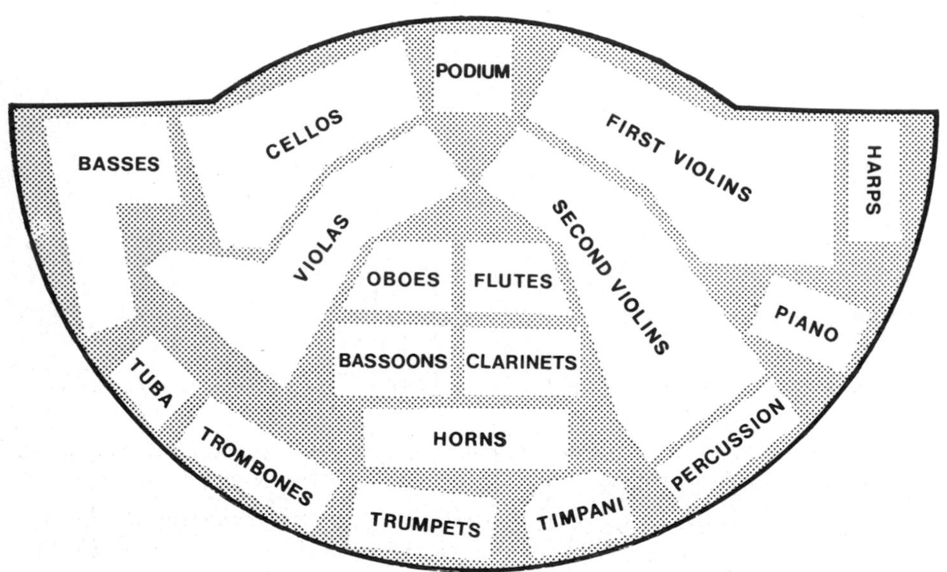

It is not at all clear what can be done about this. We cannot simply mirror-image reverse the orchestra, because the performers would then not be able to hear each other so well. Suppose instead that we placed the orchestra with their backs to the audience. This would provide no solution either, since the brasses and percussion would then be closest to the audience, and so would drown out the strings. Suppose, then, that we 'retrograde-inverted' the orchestra, so that they had their backs to the audience, but the strings would be closest to them and the brasses and percussion farthest away. This would again provide no solution, because the conducter would not be able to hear the strings, and so would not be able to conduct efficiently. One solution that has been suggested is to keep the orchestra as it is, and have the audience hanging upside-down from the ceiling, as shown in Figure 23[2]. Unfortunately, such a solution is unlikely to be popular with concert-goers!

FIGURE 23 Proposed seating arrangement for concert halls, designed to accommodate the perceptual advantage for 'high-right/low-left' dispositions over 'high-left/low-right' dispositions; considering the percepts of both performers and audience.[3]

Although there is no ready solution to this problem where listening in concert halls is concerned, the perceptual advantage to 'high-right/low-left' dispositions has obvious practical implications for the broadcasting and reproduction of stereophonic sound. If the channels were so arranged that from the listener's point of view, higher frequencies tend to be to the right and lower frequencies to the left, this should lead to enhanced perceptual clarity and so, presumably, to greater listener enjoyment.

CONCLUSION

This chapter has considered a number of different approaches to music and spatial relationships. All have been shown to provide useful insights into the nature of music and its processing. This connection will doubtless continue to be a fruitful source of theoretical speculation and empirical investigation.[4]

ACKNOWLEDGMENTS

1. Richard Boulanger provided able assistance in running the subjects in this experiment.

2. This solution was suggested to me by Professor Robert M. Boynton.

3. Cartoon by Janet Loken.

4. This work was supported by USPHS Grant MH-21001.

REFERENCES

Alexander of Aphrodisias. (1932). Commentary on Aristotle's Metaphysics; translated in Sir Thomas L. Heath, Greek Astronomy. London: J.M.Dent & Sons.

Aristotle. (1930).(De caelo.) (J.L. Stocks, translation). In: The Works of Aristotle, Volume 2. Oxford: Oxford Univeristy Press.

Babbitt, M. (1960). Twelve-tone invariants as compositional determinants. Musical Quarterly, 46, 246-259.

Barbour, J.M. (1951). Tuning and Temperament. East Lansing, Michigan: Michigan State University.

Berlioz, H. (1951). Treatise on Instrumentation, (Ed.) R. Strauss: translation by T. Front. New York: E.F. Kalmus.

Bosanquet, P.H.M. (1876). Elementary Treatise on Musical Intervals and Temperament.

Bregman, A.S. (1978). The formation of auditory streams. In: J. Requin (Ed.) Attention and Performance. Volume VII. Hillsdale, New Jersey: Erlbaum.

Bregman, A.S. and Campbell, J. (1971). Primary auditory stream segregation and perception of order in rapid sequences of tones. Journal of Experimental Psychology, 89, 244-249.

Butler, D. (1979). Melodic channeling in a musical environment. Research Symposium on the Psychology and Acoustics of Music, Kansas.

Butler, S. (1973). Hudibras, Parts I and II, and Selected Other Writings. Editors: J. Wilders and H. de Quehen. Oxford: Clarnedon Press.

Deutsch, D. (1969). Music recognition. Psychological Review, 76, 300-307.

Deutsch, D. (1972). Octave generation and tune recognition. Perception and Psychophysics, 11, 411-412.

Deutsch, D. (1974). An auditory illusion. Nature, 251, 307-309.

Deutsch, D. (1975a). Musical illusions. Scientific American, 233, 92-104.

Deutsch, D. (1975b). Two-channel listening to musical scales. Journal of the Acoustical Society of America, 57, 1156-1160.

Deutsch, D. (1978). Delayed pitch comparisons and the principle of proximity. Perception and Psychophysics, 23, 227-230.

Deutsch, D. (1979). Binaural integration of melodic patterns. Perception and Psychophysics, 25, 399-405.

Deutsch, D. (1981). The octave illusion and auditory perceptual integration. In: J.V. Tobias and F.D. Schubert (Eds.) Hearing Research and Theory. Volume 1. Academic Press: New York.

Deutsch, D. (1982a). The processing of pitch combinations. In: D. Deutsch (Ed.) The Psychology of Music. New York: Academic Press.

Deutsch, D. (1982b). Grouping mechanisms in music. In: D. Deutsch (Ed.) The Psychology of Music. New York: Academic Press.

Deutsch, D. (1983a). Dichotic listening to musical sequences: Relationship to hemispheric specialization of function. Journal of the Acoustical Society of America, in press.

Deutsch, D. (1983b). Octave equivalence in the processing of tonal sequences. Journal of the Acoustical Society of America, in press.

Deutsch, D. (1983c). Auditory illusions, handedness, and the spatial environment. Journal of the Audio Engineering Society, 31, 607-617.

Deutsch, D. and Roll, P.L. (1976). Separate 'what' and 'where' decision mechanisms in processing a dichotic tonal sequence. Journal of Experimental Psychology: Human Perception and Performance, 2, 23-29.

Divenyi, P.I. and Hirsh, I.J. (1978). Some figural properties of auditory patterns. Journal of the Acoustical Society of America, 64, 1369-1386.

Drobisch, M.W. (1846). Uber die mathematische Bestimmung der musikalischen. Intervalle.

Goodglass, H. and Quadfasal, F.A. (1954). Language laterality in left handed aphasics. Brain, 77, 521-543.

Grey, J.M. (1975). An exploration of musical timbre. Unpublished doctoral dissertation, Stanford University, California.

Hall, D.E. (1973). The objective measurement of goodness-of-fit. Journal of Music Theory, 17, 273-290.

Hall, D.E. (1974). Quantitative evaluation of musical scale tunings. American Journal of Physics, 42, 543-552.

Hawkins, Sir J.A. (1963). General History of the Science and Practice of Music. Volume 1. London: Dover. (Originally published in 1853.)

Helmholtz, H. von (1954). On the Sensations of Tone as a Physiological Basis for the Theory of Music. Second English Edition. New York: Dover. (Originally published in 1859).

Hunt, F.V. (1978). Origins in Acoustics. New Haven, Connecticut: Yale University Press.

Idson, W.L. and Massaro, D.W. (1978). A bidimensional model of pitch in the recognition of melodies. Perception and Psychophysics, 24, 551-565.

Kallman, H.J. and Massaro, D.W. (1979). Tone chroma is functional in melody recognition. Perception and Psychophysics, 26, 32-36.

Koffka, K. (1935). Principles of Gestalt psychology. New York: Harcourt.

Krumhansl, C.L. (1983). Perceptual structures for tonal music. Music Perception, 1, 24-58.

Krumhansl, C.L. and Kessler, E.J. (1982). Tracing the dynamic changes in perceived tonal organization in a spatial representation of musical keys. Psychological Review, 89, 334-368.

Kubovy, M. (1981). Concurrent pitch-segregation and the theory of indispensible attributes. In: M. Kubovy and J.R. Pomerantz (Eds.) Perceptual Organization. Hillsdale, New Jersey: Erlbaum.

Longuet-Higgins, H.C. (1962a). Letter to a musical friend. Music Review, 23, 244-248.

Longuet-Higgins, H.C. (1962b). Second letter to a musical friend. Music Review, 23, 271-280.

Longuet-Higgins, H.C. (1978). The perception of music. Interdisciplinary Science Reviews, 3, 148-156.

Mach, E. (1943). On symmetry. In: Popular Scientific Lectures. (T.J. McCormack, translator). Fifth edition, La Salle, Illinois: The Open Court Publishing Company. (Originally published in Germany, 1894.)

Mach, E. (1959). The Analysis of Sensations and the Relation of the Physical to the Psychical. (C.M. Williams, translator; W. Waterlow, review and supplement). New York: Dover. (Originally published in Germany, 1906.)

Machlis, J. (1977). The Enjoyment of Music. Fourth Edition. New York: Norton.

Milner, B., Branch, C. and Rasmussen, T. (1966). Evidence for bilateral speech representation in some nonrighthanders. Transactions of the American Neurological Association, 91, 306-308.

Palisca, C.V. (1961). Scientific empiricism in musical thought. In: H.H. Rhys (Ed.) Seventeenth Century Science in the Arts. Princeton, New Jersey: Princeton University Press.

Rameau, M. (1721). Traite de l'harmonie reduite a des principles naturels.

Risset, J-C. and Wessel, D.L. (1982). Exploration of timbre by analysis and synthesis. In: D. Deutsch (Ed.) The Psychology of Music. New York: Academic Press.

Schoenberg, A. (1911). Harmonielehre. Leipzig and Vienna: Universal Edition, Number 3370.

Schoenberg, A. (1951). Style and Idea. London: Williams and Norgate.

Schoenberg, A. (1967). In: G. Strong (Ed.) Fundamentals of Musical Composition. New York: St. Martin's Press.

Schoenberg, A. (1969). Structural Functions of Harmony. Revised edition. New York: Norton.

Shepard, R.N. (1964). Circularity in judgments of relative pitch. Journal of the Acoustical Society of America, 36, 2345-2353.

Shepard, R.N. (1982). Structural representations of musical pitch. In: D. Deutsch (Ed.) The Psychology of Music. New York: Academic Press.

Tobias, J.V. (1972). Curious binaural phenomena. In: J.V. Tobias (Ed.) Foundations of Modern Auditory Theory. Volume II. New York: Academic Press.

van Noorden, I.P.A.S. (1975). Temporal coherence in the perception of tone sequences. Unpublished doctoral dissertation. Technische Hogeschoel Eindhoven, The Netherlands.

Vicario, G.B. (1983). Micro- and macromelodies. Paper presented at the Fourth Workshop on the Physical and Neuropsychological Foundations of Music, Ossiach.

von Ehrenfels, C. (1890). Uber Gestaltqualitaten Vierteljahrschrift fur Wissenschaftliche Philosophie, 14, 249-292.

Werner, H. (1925). Uber Mikromelodik und Mikroharmonik. Zeitschrift fur Psychologie, 98, 74-89.

Wessel, D.L. (1979). Timbre space as a musical control structure. Computer Music Journal, 3, 45-52.

Wessel, D.L. (1983). Timbre control in research on melodic patterns. Paper presented at the Fourth Workshop of Physical and Neuropsychological Foundations of Music, Ossiach.

Zangwill, O.L. (1960). Cerebral Dominance and its Relation to Psychological function. Edinburgh: Oliver and Boyd.

Cognitive Processes in the Perception of Art
W.R. Crozier and A.J. Chapman (editors)
© Elsevier Science Publishers B.V. (North-Holland), 1984

THE AUDITORY IMAGE: A METAPHOR FOR MUSICAL AND PSYCHOLOGICAL RESEARCH ON AUDITORY ORGANIZATION

Stephen McAdams

Institut de Recherche et Coordination Acoustique/Musique

INTRODUCTION

Imagine that you are walking blindfolded through the streets of a city. What do you hear? A combination of chugging and whirring metal and the popping of rubber on cobble stones is heard as a passing car. A rhythmic clicking of toe nails and jangling of small metal medallions is heard as a dog trotting by. A small herd of children goes giggling and screaming by on bicycles. You walk past a jack-hammer pounding the street with metal and your ears with painful pressure waves. Do we merely hear these sources as a collection of 'sound events' (p. 50)? Or do we hear each of these complex sound constellations as an 'object'? I would opt for the latter claim. I do not just hear a jangling and clicking. I also hear a trotting dog with a well adorned collar. There is a certain coherence in the collective behaviour of these events that I have learned and which allows (even induces) me to group them into the auditory image of the dog or the jack-hammer or the herd of children.

As organisms functioning in a not always so hospitable environment, it is important that our auditory systems -- as well as our visual systems -- be able to objectify the elements of that environment. That is, we must be able to parse, or separate, the complex acoustic array into its many sources of sound if we are to be able, on the one hand, to separate dangerous from innocuous or friendly objects and, on the other hand, to pay attention to a source in order to extract meaningful information from its emanations. In fact, the auditory system is so biased towards this parsing behaviour that we have difficulty hearing the sound environment as other than filled with objects. This is like trying to look at a landscape and seeing only patterns of coloured light instead of trees, flowers, mountains, clouds, etc.

But now let us move to the world of sound artifice and enter (still blindfolded) a concert hall, where a full symphony orchestra is playing. What do you hear? At one level you probably hear the sound objects making up the orchestra; trumpet, violin, flute, tympani, contrabassoon, etc. Under many conditions you can 'hear out' these various instruments whether they are playing melodically or in chords (though less so in the latter case depending on the voicing of the chord). One set of cues that is useful in separating the instruments is associated with their occupying different positions in space. This certainly facilitates the auditory system's task. But imagine the same orchestra being recorded with a microphone and then replayed over a single speaker. Now there is a single physical source emitting a very complex waveform. What do you hear? It is still relatively easy to hear out trumpets, violins, etc., though there is certainly a loss of acuity in denser orchestrations. Somehow we are able to parse the single physical source into multiple 'virtual source images' and to selectively focus on their separate behaviours.

This is only one level of 'grouping' or 'parsing' of a musical sound environment. If three or more instruments play different pitches simultaneously, these events may be heard as a group. The composite would be experienced as a chord having a certain functional quality in a sequence of other chords. The single chord may, in some sense, be conceived as an object, as might the sequence of chords defining a certain harmonic progression. The harmonic function of any of these chords depends on the component pitches being taken perceptually as a group. A chord can also be perceptually 'collected' from a sequence of pitches across time as with arpeggios. One might hear several groups of instruments that are blocked into differently textured organizations, for example, rapid staccoto winds against rapid legato arpeggios in the strings and a unison choral melody line. Here the 'objects' would be accumulated by attending to a certain playing characteristic or movement as well as to various timbral characteristics.

The point is that many different levels of organization are possible and even desirable in a musical composition. One is less interested in hearing the physical objects (the instruments) than the musical objects (melodies, chords, fused composite timbres, group textures, etc.). Nevertheless any listener brings into the musical situation all of the 'perceptual baggage' acquired from ordinary in-the-world perceiving. And this will certainly influence the way the music is listened to and organized by the listener.

Assuming an interest on the part of the composer in volitional act of perceptual organization that may take place within each listener, one might ask the following questions: (1) What might possibly be paid attention to as a musical image? (By implication, what are the limits of musical attention?); (2) What processes can we conceive as being involved in the act of auditory organization?; and (3) What cues would a composer or performer need to be aware of to effect the grouping of many physical objects into a single musical image, or, in the case of music synthesis by computer, to effect the parsing of a single musical image into many?

Several concepts have been introduced in these opening paragraphs which need to be explicated further, such as the formation and distinction of auditory source images (objects), simultaneous and sequential auditory organization, and attentional processes. I discuss these concepts further in an attempt to clarify what we have to work with in approaching answers to or rephrasings of the questions posed.

THE METAPHOR: AUDITORY IMAGE

It is important where music and psychology meet to develop metaphors for communication and cross-fertilization. In the search for a metaphor that embodies the combined aspects of auditory 'impressions' from perception, memory and imagination, the notion of the 'auditory source image' has proven fruitful to me in describing the results of auditory organizational processes to composers, musicians and psychologists. In particular, and directed toward my main interests, this metaphor has allowed the development of a common language for talking about the role of perception in musical processes that are to be embodied in compositions. While my own work to date has been limited to the study of images deriving from sound stimulation, many composers with whom I have worked find the metaphor and the delineation of its properties and implications useful for the imagining of musical possibilities at both conceptual and perceptual levels.

To summarize briefly, the auditory image is a psychological representation of a sound entity exhibiting a coherence in its acoustic behaviour. The notion of coherence is necessary, if rather general at this point. Since any natural and interesting sound event has a complex spectrum evolving through time, often involving noisy as well as periodic and quasi-periodic portions, it is important to consider the conditions under which these acoustically disparate portions cohere as a single entity. For example, all of the physical sources listed in the first paragraph were quite complex acoustically and some even involved multiple sources of sound. But each of these could be perceived as a whole, as a single image. Certainly we could listen only to the jangling medallions or the clicking nails of the right forefoot. But the temporal nature of the pattern as a whole is what gives us the coherent auditory image of a domesticated trotting dog.

Here, at the outset, I have introduced what I consider to be the most powerful asset of the metaphor. It allows for a hierarchical or multi-levelled approach to auditory organization. We can consider a single trumpet tone as an image and speak of its properties as a tone, for example, pitch, brightness, loudness. We can consider a whole sequence of trumpet tones as an image and speak of its properties as a melody and of the functional properties of the articulation of individual tones as parts of the melody. We can consider a collection of brass tones, many occurring simultaneously, others in succession, as an image and speak of the properties of a brass choir as an ensemble or of the properties of a particular piece written for brass choir with harmony, polyphony, rhythm, force, *panache*, etc. All of this is to say that the metaphor allows the development and application of a broad set of criteria for musical coherence to be applied to music as a grouping and parsing of sound events into multi-tiered musical images.

Next let us consider the application of this metaphor to psychological research on auditory organization. I select several pertinent examples to circumscribe the nature of sequential and simultaneous organizing processes and to illustrate the essential differences between them. Then I return to the notions of the auditory image and the coherence of behaviour of a sound entity to see how far we can push the metaphor at this stage.

SEQUENTIAL ORGANIZATION

Research on sequential organization of sound is concerned with how the structure of a sequence of events affects the perceived continuity of the sequence. That is, under what conditions is a sequence of sounds heard as one or more 'streams'? Bregman and Campbell (1971) employed the metaphor 'stream' to denote a psychological representation of a sequence of sounds than can be interpreted as a 'whole', since it displays an internal consistency, or continuity. Van Noorden (1975) termed this continuity 'temporal coherence', that is the events in the sequence cohere as a perceptual structure through time. In general, we may consider that a stream represents the behaviour of a real and vital source of sound. This is consistent with the notion of image - a stream is an image of a source whose emanations are extended across several events in time, that is a melody is a stream is an image. Implied here is the possibility that a single sequence of tones can be organized (grouped) as more than one stream. This case is particularly common in music for solo instruments of the Baroque period (cf. the violin partitas of J.S. Bach). In these compositions, the soloist sometimes alternates rapidly between registers or strings on successive notes and what one hears is two melodies that appear to overlap in time.

It is also possible to have a situation where a listener can switch between hearing a sequence as one or two streams by changing attentional focus. Many of the more interesting instances of this in music have such multiple perceptual possibilities. It is an important point psychologically to note that, in such cases, a listener may hear one organization or the other but not both at once. In other words, I can hear the sequence as one stream or as two streams (and switch my attention between each of the two streams at will), but I cannot hear the sequence as both one *and* two streams simultaneously. These are mutually exclusive organizations.

There are several important properties exhibited by a stream. These are discussed more fully elsewhere (McAdams and Bregman, 1979), so I merely summarize them.

1. It is possible to focus one's attention on a give stream and follow it through time; this means that a stream, by definition, exhibits temporal coherence.

2. The parsing of a sequence into smaller streams takes a certain amount of time to occur; it generally takes several notes into a compound melody line until the separate registers are relegated to different streams. It appears that the perceptual organizing processes assume things are coming from one source until they accumulate enough information to suggest a different interpretation of how the world is behaving.

3. It is easily possible to order the events of a stream in time, but it is more difficult to determine the relative order of events across streams. Two streams resulting from the same sequence of notes appear to overlap in time, but it is hard to say exactly how they are related temporally. Since temporal ordering of notes is an essential determinant of a melody, this means that a melody is, by definition, a stream, that is a melody has a perceptual unity (temporal coherence). This also implies that not just any arbitrary sequence of tones constitutes a melody; if the sequence is not temporally coherent, it is not heard as a melody (but maybe as two or more melodies).

4. A given event can be a member of one or of another concurrent stream but not both simultaneously. As mentioned above, one might switch between hearing an event, belonging to one organization and then to another. The important point here is that several parsing schemes cannot be used at the same time.

The main acoustic factors which have been found to be used by the perceptual systems to build descriptions of streams include frequency, rate of occurrence of events (tempo), amplitude, and spectral content and form, that is the frequencies present in a complex tone and their respective amplitudes. It is not possible to go into great detail about all of these factors. Simple illustrations are given here and the reader is referred to review articles (Bregman, 1978, 1982; McAdams and Bregman, 1979).

Frequency Separation

It has been shown repeatedly with sine tone sequences that the relative frequency separation between tones influences the formation of stream organization (Bregman, 1981; Bregman and Campbell, 1971; Bozzi and Vicario, 1960; Dannenbring and Bregman, 1976; Deutsch, 1975; Van Noorden, 1975, 1977; Vicario, 1965, 1982). At a given tempo, tones that are farther apart in frequency are more likely to be heard in separate streams than those that are closer together. Also, at a given frequency separation the role of tempo is such that faster sequences have more of a tendency to split into multiple streams than slower sequences. There is a kind of trade-off between tempo and frequency separation.

FIGURE 1 The tones of parts of two common nursery rhyme melodies are interleaved. In (a) the frequency ranges of the two melodies are similar and the sequence is heard as one, unfamiliar melody. In (b) the frequency ranges of the melodies are non-overlapping and each melody is heard independently. The dotted lines indicate temporal coherence (perceived sequential organization). (derived from Dowling, 1973)

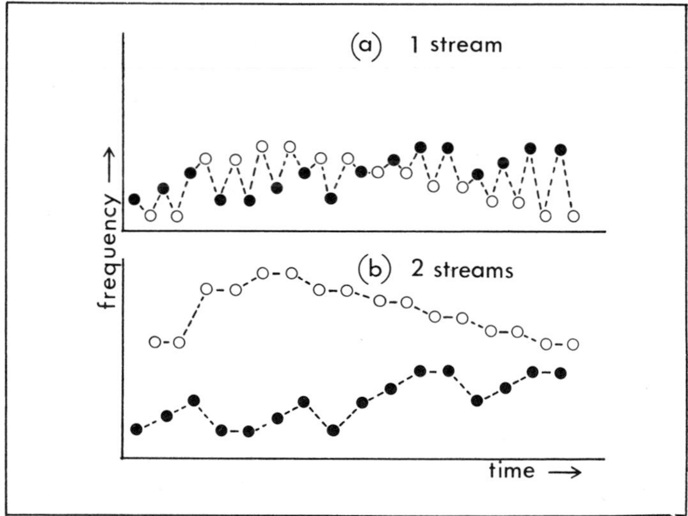

A compelling example of the frequency separation effect is illustrated in Figure 1. This example is based on an experiment by Dowling (1973) where he interleaved (alternated) the notes of two familiar nursery rhyme melodies. When the ranges of the pitches of the two melodies are the same (see Figure 1a) it is difficult to hear out the separate melodies and one melody is heard which is a combination of the two. However, when the frequency ranges are sufficiently separated, one easily discerns the two melodies as is indicated in Figure 1b. In this and similar succeeding figures the dashed lines between tones indicate temporal coherence. For example, in Figure 1b the third tone is perceived as following the first tone rather than the second tone. In Taped Example 1[1], the two melodies are played at four

FIGURE 2 Illustration of the different percepts resulting from the alternation of two sinusoidal tones of identical frequency and duration, when the amplitude of tone A is varied relative to that of tone B. The shapes in the figure represent the amplitude envelopes of the tones. (from Van Noorden, 1975)

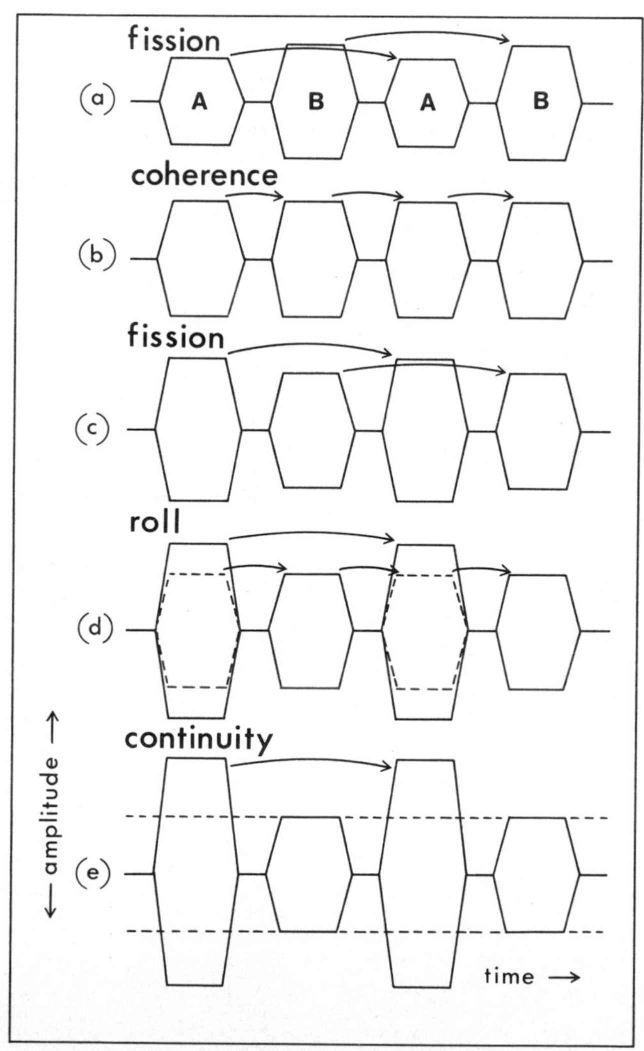

different separation values; the first and last are as shown in Figure 1. Here the identification of the melody as a whole entity is dependent on being able to separate its elements from the other melody and hearing them as a group. The streams that are formed on the basis of frequency separation are the melodies.

Amplitude Differences

Another factor that can contribute to a stream formation is the relative amplitude of the tones. Though this is a much weaker effect than the rest. Van Noorden (1975), for example, has demonstrated many perceptual effects resulting from the alternation of two identically pitched pure tones which differ in amplitude, and they range from hearing: (1) a fission of the sequence into two pulsing streams (one soft and one loud; Figure 2a, c); (2) to a coherent stream at twice the tempo (Figure 2b); (3) to a single loud stream at one tempo plus a soft stream at twice that tempo ('roll'; Figure 2d); (4) to a loud pulsing stream plus a continuous soft tone ('continuity' Figure 2e). These amplitude-based effects are also dependent on tempo and frequency separation.

FIGURE 3 Effect of differences in spectral composition on sequential organization. In (a) all tones are sinusoidal and the frequency separation between them is adjusted so that a single stream percept may be heard, as indicated by the dotted lines. In (b) the third harmonic is added to one pair and the spectral difference causes two streams to form, each with a different timbre. Each of these 4-tone patterns was recycled continually. (McAdams and Bregman, 1979)

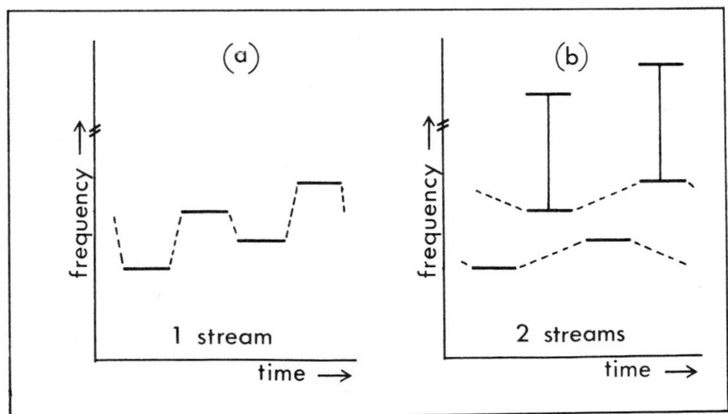

Spectral Form and Content

The last factor to be discussed that contributes to stream formation is spectral form and content. A stimulus sequence can be constructed where the spectral composition is very similar (all tones are sinusoidal, as in Figure 3a) and the frequency variation from tone to tone is small enough so that the sequence can be heard as one stream. By adding a harmonic (the third, in this case) to certain tones in this sequence, those tones are made to form a separate stream (Figure 3b). The solid vertical bar denotes the fusion of the spectral components into one percept. In Taped Example 2, you may hear first the stimulus cycle in Figure 3a and then the cycle in Figure 3b. Note also that the tempo of the new streams is half that of the original stream. This illustrates that perceived rhythm is also dependent on the stream organization, that is rhythm may be considered as a quality of a given stream.

FIGURE 4 When all of these tones are played by the same instrument ascending pitch triplets are heard (solid lines). But when two instruments with different spectral forms each play the X's and O's respectively, descending triplets are heard (dotted lines). (from Wessel, 1979)

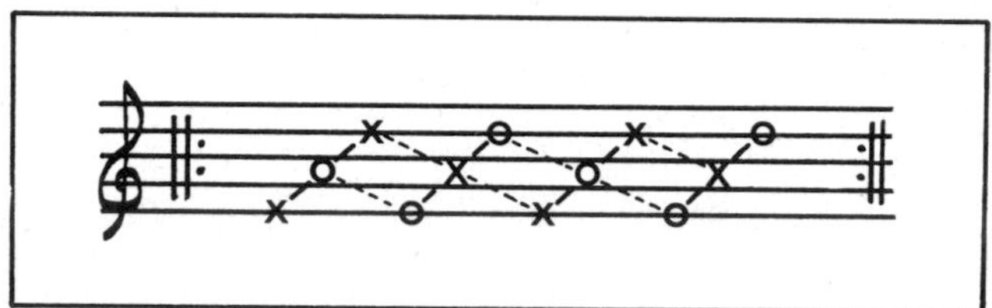

Another example of stream formation based on spectral form is illustrated in Figure 4 which is taken from Wessel (1979). In the first part of Taped Example 3 you may hear the ascending three-note sequence played by one instrument. Then, in the second part, the tones marked X are played by one instrument and those marked O by another. After a couple of cycles of the three-note figure (and as the sequence is sped up) the percept splits into two overlapping sets of descending triplets being played by the two separate instruments with very different spectral characteristics. Note here that not only the rhythm, but also the direction of the triplet changes when the sequence is parsed into multiple images.

Spectral Continuity and Sequential Organization

At first consideration, there would appear to be three basic factors used to organize monodic (single-voiced) sequences of sound. One might try to explain the parsing as being based on the differences in perceptual qualities of the separate organizations. For example, a series of sine tones that form two separate auditory streams may be said to be parsed on the basis of pitch differences. A series of complex tones that form separate streams when they have different spectral forms but do not stream when they are sinusoidal may be said to be parsed on the basis of timbre differences. A sequence of tones of equal pitch and timbre which differ in amplitude and form separate streams may be said to be parsed on the basis of loudness differences. However, Bregman has proposed (cf. Bregman and Pinker, 1978) that the perceptual qualities themselves are derived from the stream organizations, or source image groupings. That is, the auditory system first groups the complex acoustic array into source sub-groups, and then the qualities of these sub-groups are derived from their respective properties. We then hear a continuity or proximity of those qualities within a given stream.

I have proposed (McAdams, 1981, 1983; McAdams and Wessel, 1981) that sequential organization is based on a context dependent criterion of spectral continuity. All of the three acoustic factor criteria proposed earlier in this section may be reduced to this one criterion. Particularly for experiments done with sine tones or complex tones with constant amplitude relations among the partials, spectral continuity and pitch-height continuity are perfectly correlated (Wessel, 1983). But van Noorden (1975) and Bregman (1982) have shown that when one constructs stimuli with a sequence of alternating tones where the pitch sensations are identical but the spectral compositions are very different, they form separate perceptual streams due to the discontinuity of the spectral change, or of the place of stimulation in the auditory periphery. For experiments with complex tones whose spectral structure changes from tone to tone, the spectral discontinuity and timbral discontinuity are well-correlated. In Taped Example 4, composed by Wessel (1979), you may hear the effects of continuity of spectral form on the organization of a sequence of tones. This sequence has a different instrument playing each note. In the first case, the instruments are chosen to maximize the spectral discontinuity and, not surprisingly, it sounds discontinuous, like a series of melodic fragments strung haphazardly together. In the second part, the instruments are chosen to maximize spectral continuity while still changing instruments from note to note. (The pitches and apparent spatial location of the notes were also varied to make the example more musically interesting.)

Any musical passage that is changing in pitch, timbre and loudness on a note to note basis is creating spectral discontinuities all the time. And yet we rarely have trouble following melodies or other kinds of musical figures. We cannot rule out the influence of higher level musical constructs such as rhythmic and harmonic function on our organization of sequential material. Certain rhythmic figures can be especially strong 'groupers' of events with diverse spectral compositions as anyone who has heard the marvellous complexity, and yet perceptual unity, of a brazilian *batucada* will testify. To my knowledge, there have been no systematic investigations of the effect of strength of metric field or rhythmic pattern on sequential organization.

Of musical interest is the suggestion that the principal factor for sequential organization can result in several different perceptual qualities which can then set up interesting paradoxes in musical streams. The ear follows spectral continuity and not necessarily a given sound source that is being composed with (though most musical sources tend to be relatively continuous spectrally as used in common practice). One might compose for example in a polyphonic setting certain patterns that jump around in pitch for individual instruments. But these may be reorganizable by the ear into several meaningful melodic patterns, each being a different *klangfarbenmelodie* (hear Taped Example 5). The important fact is that while the principle of spectral continuity is simple, spectral organization in music implies a vast complexity of musical possibilities.

SIMULTANEOUS ORGANIZATION

Spectral continuity of event sequences is not the only source image organizing principle. We must also investigate how it is that complex tones such as those produced by musical instruments are heard as single sound images and not as compounds of many sinusoids. Also, how are we able to separate complexes from one another that are sounding at the same time?

My recent work has been concerned with determining the processes that contribute to the formation and distinction of concurrent source images. And of particular musical interest, the relation between these processes and the derivation of the perceptual qualities of sources. At least four classes of acoustic cues may be shown to contribute to auditory image formation: (1) coherence of amplitude modulation across a sub-group of spectral components belonging to the same source; (2) coherence of frequency modulation across a spectral sub-group; (3) stable resonance structure forming the amplitudes of a spectral sub-group; and (4) localization in space of a spectral sub-group. The first three have been shown to contribute to 'spectral fusion', that is the perceptual fusion of spectral components into a unified percept or source image.

Amplitude Modulation Coherence

By amplitude modulation, I mean the low-frequency modulations we consider as the amplitude envelope (attack and decay functions, and fluctuations in the intensity) of natural sounds. In a musical situation, this would also include tremolo. Two aspects of the coherence of amplitude behaviour of spectral components are important for grouping decisions: onset synchrony of spectral components and amplitude fluctuations across these components during a sustained tone.

Onset Synchrony. It has been demonstrated several times that when the onsets of the partials of a tone complex are asynchronous by as little as 20-30 msec, the perceived fusion decreases and the ability to hear out individual partials increases (Bregman and Pinker, 1978; Dannenbring and Bregman, 1976; Rasch, 1978, 1979). The minor asynchronies observed in the partials of musical instrument tones are generally less than 20 msec (Grey and Moorer, 1977). Helmholtz (1885, 1954) reminded us in the last century that with natural tones all of the partial tones tend to start together, swell uniformly and cease simultaneously. 'Hence no opportunity is generally given for hearing them separately and independently' (p. 60).

With computer synthesis techniques, one has easy control over the relative onsets of individual partials. In Taped Example 6 you may hear a series of tones which are identical except for the synchrony of onset of the partials. The extremes of the series are represented schematically in Figure 5. Beginning with perfect synchrony the exponential envelope of the inharmonic partials of this bell-like tone are progressively desynchronized until you can hear each partial separately. Note that the change is one from a fused rich sound to a more chord-like quality, even though the frequency relations are identical. Here, the coherence of the amplitude behaviour is progressively destroyed which results in the destruction of the image's unity (or, alternatively, in the creation of a multiple image).

Kubovy and Jordan (1979) produced a similar kind of effect by suddenly changing the phase relation of one harmonic of a 12-harmonic tone relative to the phases of the rest of the harmonies. In this case the single harmonic is separately audible as a pure tone if the phase difference is at least 30 degrees. It seems likely that a sudden phase shift like this might be interpreted as an onset asynchrony by the auditory system, thus causing the single harmonic to be heard as a separate source.

Amplitude Fluctuations. Increased fusion can also be obtained even in inharmonic tone complexes by imposing a common amplitude modulation on the components. Von Békésy (1960) reported getting fused images lateralized to one side of the head when he presented sinusoids of differing frequencies (one to each ear over headphones) and imposed an identical low-frequency (5-50 Hz) sinusoidal amplitude modulation (100% modulation depth) on each tone component.

FIGURE 5 The role of onset synchrony in spectral fusion. When the amplitude envelopes of all spectral components of this inharmonic sound start synchronously (a), a single, fused, bell-like image occurs. When the onsets of these partials are spread out in time (b), each partial is heard as a separate source image. (from McAdams and Wessel, 1981)

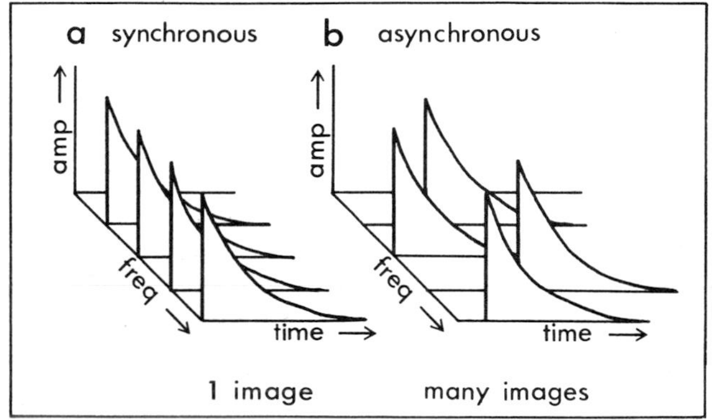

FIGURE 6 The role of amplitude modulation coherence in spectral fusion. When the amplitudes of all partials fluctuate together (a) a fused image is heard, but when the onsets are asynchronous and the amplitude fluctuations are incoherent, several images are heard. (from McAdams and Wessel, 1981)

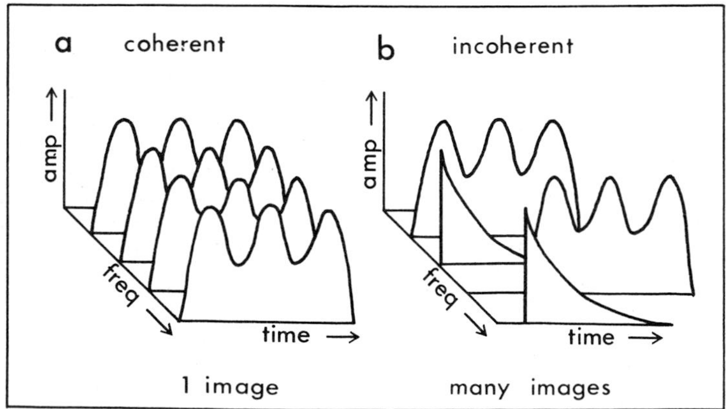

As far as I am aware no systematic study has been done on the necessary modulation depth or the limitations of the modulation frequencies which can cause tone complexes to fuse. Bregman, Abramson and Darwin (1983) performed an experiment in which a pure tone alternated with a two-tone complex (a stimulus configuration similar to that shown in Figure 6). The pure tone and the upper of the two tones in the complex were amplitude modulated at 100 Hz. The modulation rate of the lower of the two tones varied between 95 and 105 Hz. The best fusion of the tone complex occurred when the modulation rates were the same and the modulation waveforms were in phase. The frequency relation between the tones of the complex did not affect the fusion. Only the coherence of the amplitude modulation had an effect on the fusion. This same result was reported by von Békésy and implies that it is the coherent fluctuation that is the unifying criterion rather than the harmonicity of the side bands created by the modulation.

To illustrate the effect of AM coherence, McAdams and Wessel (1981) synthesized a series of tones where the amplitude envelopes of the partials fluctuated at approximately 3 Hz. When all of the partials (the same inharmonic partials as in Taped Example 6) fluctuate coherently (see Figure 6a), that is in exactly the same manner, one hears a fused tone. However, when these fluctuations are not in phase or are completely different (see Figure 6b) one hears the individual partials. In Taped Example 7 you may hear again the fused exponential envelope tone from the previous example, then a coherent 3 Hz fluctuation (50% modulation depth) and then different mixtures of dephasing of the periodic fluctuations and addition of the exponential envelopes on some of the partials. Again, when the amplitude behaviours of the components are coherent, the spectral components are fused into a single source image, but when they are incoherent, or unrelated, they tend to be heard as separate sinusoidal sources.

Frequency Modulation Coherence

The types of frequency modulation I am referring to here include musical vibrato (periodic modulation), jitter (aperiodic modulation)[2], and slow pitch glides such as in voice inflections or musical portamento. In all natural, sustaining vibration sources, any perturbation, periodic or otherwise, of the fundamental frequency is imparted proportionally to all of the harmonies. There are, of course, minor departures due to various non-linearities in such acoustic systems, but in general as the fundamental frequency changes, all of the harmonics change with it maintaining their harmonic relations. Thus, what I call 'coherent frequency modulation' is modulation maintaining the frequency ratios of the partials. With the computer synthesis, this can be applied to sustained inharmonic tones as well as to harmonic tones.

It is difficult to do an experiment to show that frequency modulation actually fuses a tone complex. But it is certain that for music synthesis it adds a liveliness and naturalness to otherwise dead and electronic sounding images. In fact, I was first put on this course of research by hearing the examples of McNabb (1981) and Chowning (1980) who were trying different methods of synthesizing sung vowels. They had synthesized all of the spectral form (speech format) parameters correctly, but without modulation the tones were still unsatisfactory for musical purposes. When jitter and vibrato were added, the vocal sounds became life-like and imbued with the musical richness the composers were seeking. This effect can be heard in Taped Example 8 where a vowel-like sound is unmodulated, then modulated, then unmodulated and then modulated again with a spectral change to a different vowel. Note that the natural voice quality goes away, and one can actually hear out individual harmonics, when the modulation is not shown.

It can be seen that if a frequency modulation (vibrato or jitter) is imposed on the partials of a harmonic tone complex such that the ratios are not maintained, the complex 'defuses'. In one experiment (McAdams, 1983), I asked the question whether coherence could be had simply by moving all the harmonics in the same direction at the same time or whether it was really necessary to maintain the frequency ratios. Subjects were asked to compare among harmonic complex tones with different modulation schemes. One tone had a modulation that maintained constant frequency ratios among the 16 harmonics. The other tone had a modulation that maintained constant frequency differences among the harmonics. These stimuli are illustrated schematically in Figure 7. The logarithm of the frequency variation is plotted as a function of time. Note that on a logarithmic scale, constant ratios maintain a constant distance, whereas constant differences do not. We know that the basilar membrane resolves frequency components in the inner ear roughly on a log frequency continuum. Thus a constant ratio modulation would maintain the relative distances between the places of maximum stimulation on the membrance due to the various harmonics.

When the rms modulation width[3] was at least 12 cents[4], listeners more often chose the constant difference tone as having more sources, or images, or distinguishable entities in it. In these tones, one experiences a modulating fundamental with the rest of the tone being relatively stationary particularly at larger modulation widths. It should be noted also that the frequencies of the components making up these tones move in and out of a harmonic relation. For the constant ratio tones, the percept is very unified even at rather large modulation widths. In Taped Example 9 you may hear one series of each type of modulation (constant ratios, constant differences). The series starts with no modulation and then progressively increases the modulation width up to 56 cents (3.3%,a frequency excursion of about a quarter tone on either side of the centre frequency). This experiment demonstrates that the maintenance of constant ratio is an important part of the definition of coherence for frequency modulation.

In another experiment (McAdams, 1983c) I modulated 15 of the harmonics of a 16-component tone coherently and modulated one harmonic incoherently. In these tones, I used a jitter modulation. The statistical characteristics of the modulation on the 15 coherent harmonics and that on the incoherent harmonic were very similar, but the random waveforms were independent. Several perceptual effects resulted depending on which harmonic was modulated and on what the overall modulation width was. Either certain partials stand out as separately audible (lower partials), or a kind of 'choral effect' results where an illusion of multiple sources is heard (higher partials). You may hear a similar effect in Taped Example 10. The vibrato modulation is added to a single harmonic and then removed. This is done for each harmonic in turn from the lowest up to the sixteenth. Note that even the pitch of the sixteenth harmonic can be heard when it is modulated independently of the rest of the tone complex.

The choral effect in the higher partials is not surprising if we stop to imagine the behaviour of several instruments playing sustained tones simultaneously: five violins for example. Each acoustic source has its own independent jitter modulating all of its harmonics. When we add all of the sources together we get these random movements of the frequencies beating against one another creating quite a complex situation acoustically. In addition, as one moves into the higher harmonics, the patterns of stimulation on the basilar membrane move closer and closer together until they are heavily overlapping.

FIGURE 7 The role of constant ratio frequency modulation in spectral fusion. A spectrographic diagram of constant frequency ratio and constant frequency difference modulations is plotted on a log frequency scale. In (a) a fused, modulating image is heard. In (b) the lowest frequency separates perceptually from the rest, which are perceived as barely modulating.

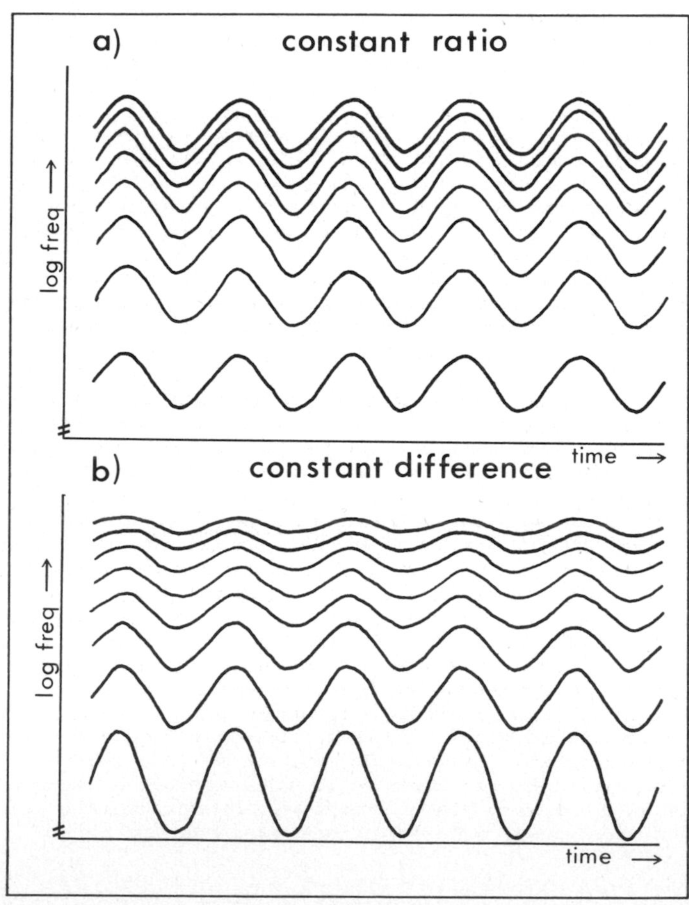

In these regions, the incoherent movement of adjacent harmonics is creating a complex stimulation for any given auditory nerve. You can imagine that if enough of these violins are playing the same pitch, there is a limit to how many sources you can pick out. The difference between 15 and 16 violins is very small indeed and after about 8 to 10, we generally just hear 'many'.

I have reported previously (McAdams, 1980, 1981, 1982a, 1982b, 1983a, 1983c) that FM serves not only to group simultaneous components into a source image, but serves as a cue to distinguish concurrent sources as well. The presence of independent modulation patterns on separate sub-groups gives two types of cues for the presence of multiple sources: (1) adjacent partials belonging to separate sources are incoherently modulating with respect to one another; and (2) the modulation across the partials belonging to a single source is coherent. It seems likely to me that the auditory system makes use both of the local incoherence between partials to detect the presence of multiple sources and global coherence among partials to accumulate the appropriate spectral components into a source image. This may be one reason soloists, particularly opera singers, use vibrato to the extent they do, that is to separate themselves from the rest of the ensemble. Of course, as mentioned before, if things are too crowded temporally and spectrally the system may have trouble distinguishing individual source images and tracking their behaviour. This would be due to the limitations of spectral and temporal resolution in the auditory system.

Another cue related to frequency that interacts to a certain extent with modulation coherence is the harmonicity of the frequency components. This is particularly evident with sustained sounds. A harmonic series, in most contexts, gives an unambiguous pitch sensation. Sustained inharmonic sounds tend to elicit a perception of multiple pitches. In many cases, the perception of multiple pitches can be interpreted as the presence of multiple sources (Cutting, 1976; Scheffers, 1983).

In a laboratory situation, unmodulated, sustained harmonic sounds can be perceptually analysed into their harmonics for harmonic numbers up to the fifth, sixth or seventh depending on the fundamental frequency. This means listeners can reliably hear out individual harmonics and identify their pitches. But a pilot study I have recently performed suggests that when these tones are modulated, listeners are no longer able to hear out the harmonics, indicating that the image is fused and unanalysable perceptually. In this case the only pitch heard is the pitch of the fundamental. This may be interpreted as support for the notion that the grouping processes (including *spectra fusion*) influence our perception of the qualities of source images (including pitch). There remains, however, the possibility that pitch detection also influences source image formation under certain conditions. It is still unclear at this point whether it is the presence of a number of pitches that indicates the number of sources, or whether the presence of *multiple harmonic series* indicate multiple sources and give rise to multiple pitches. I am more inclined toward the latter interpretation given the preliminary result of reduction of perceptual analysability of harmonic complexes in the presence of frequency modulation.

Spectral Form

Most sustaining musical sound sources have resonance structures that are relatively stable, or very slowly changing, compared to the frequency fluctuations mentioned in the previous section. These structures are due to resonant cavities that filter the sound before it radiates into the air, for example, vocal cavities, body resonance for string instruments and tube resonance for winds. Each resonance has a particular frequency to which it responds the greatest. The frequency is related to the volume of the cavity, and the size of the opening. Other frequencies are attenuated (made less intense), or are not passed as easily, relative to this resonant frequency. Also, different shapes and the nature of the walls of the resonant cavities influence which frequencies near the resonant frequency are allowed to pass. When it allows a larger number of frequencies around the resonant frequency to pass we say it has a larger bandwith.

These resonance regions are called formants in voice sciences. And the placement of the formant (centre) frequencies, their relative amplitudes and their bandwiths are thought to determine which vowel is perceived. This is particularly true for the arrangement of the first three formants.

Now let us imagine what happens when a singer sings with vibrato. All of the frequencies are moving back and forth in a coherent manner. And what happens to their relative amplitudes? Well, since the resonances come after the point in the system where the vibrato is introduced, the amplitudes must follow the contour of the formant structure. This is illustrated schematically in Figure 8. The horizontal axis represents linear frequency and the vertical axis, amplitude. There are three formants(bumps in the curve) represented here. Notice that for a given frequency excursion of the fundamental frequency, there are progressively greater excursions for the higher harmonics. This is due to the linear frequency scale used in the diagram. Each harmonic is moving a constant percentage lower and higher, so while the excursions at higher harmonics is greater when measured on a linear scale, it still maintains a constant ratio distance from all of the other harmonics.

The overall form of the resonance structure is indicated by dotted lines. The amplitude by frequency trajectories of each partial are indicated by solid lines. In a sense, we can consider that as the frequencies modulate, their amplitudes change such that each partial *traces* a small portion of the *spectral envelope* , that is, the frequency-amplitude curve describing the overall spectral form. This complex coupling of frequency and amplitude modulation serves to define the spectral contour and in certain cases may actually reduce the ambiguity of the resonant identify of the sound source.

In Figure 9 is another spectral form. This corresponds to the vowel /a/. The fundamental frequency is quite high here so that not very many harmonics fall into each formant region. In this case the formant structure is not well defined and accordingly, the perception of the vowel sound would be weak if at all existent. However, when the spectral components are made to modulate in frequency, their amplitudes trace the spectral envelope and the auditory system then has access to the *slopes* of the formants around each partial. This adds important (even essential) information which the system can use to identify the nature of the source. So one important function of frequency modulation is to reduce the ambiguity of the nature of the resonance structure defining the source. This has been verified experimentally, particularly for higher fundamentals where definition of spectral form is lacking (McAdams, 1982a, 1983c).

Another experiment has shown that if the spectral envelope with the frequency modulation, that is, the amplitudes of the components remain constant, a kind of timbral modulation occurs. With vowel envelopes one hears a whistling sound which seems associated with the perceptual decomposition of the higher formants. This occurs for modulation widths in excess of 1/8 to 1/4 tone

(25 cents to 50 cents). This result has some interesting musical possibilities for sound synthesis methods based on formant structures. This is discussed later.

But now let us imagine the following perception problem. The ear receives a complex spectrum as shown in Figure 10. There is no modulation on any of the components. Listeners sometimes report hearing certain vowels embedded in this complex and report as many as 6 - 8 different pitches. You may hear six such configurations in Taped Example 11. Without some cue to help us group the elements of this complex, it sounds like a tone mass. If, however, we add some frequency modulation coupled to the resonance structures the elements are grouped perceptually. We hear the images more clearly as being a certain vowel at a certain pitch. What the auditory system may then have access to spectrally is represented in Figure 11. It now knows that there are three sources each with different vowel quality and pitch. The stimuli actually presented are notated in Figure 12. You may hear these same configurations of three vowels at three pitches, but with vibrato this time, in Taped Example 12.

FIGURE 8 The dotted line represents the spectral form created by a 3-formant resonance structure. As the harmonics are modulated in frequency, their respective amplitudes fluctuate as a function of the spectral envelope. This is indicated by the solid portions on the dotted line. Note that these trace out the formant shapes and in the case of f_1 and f_2 these shapes 'point' toward the formant peak.

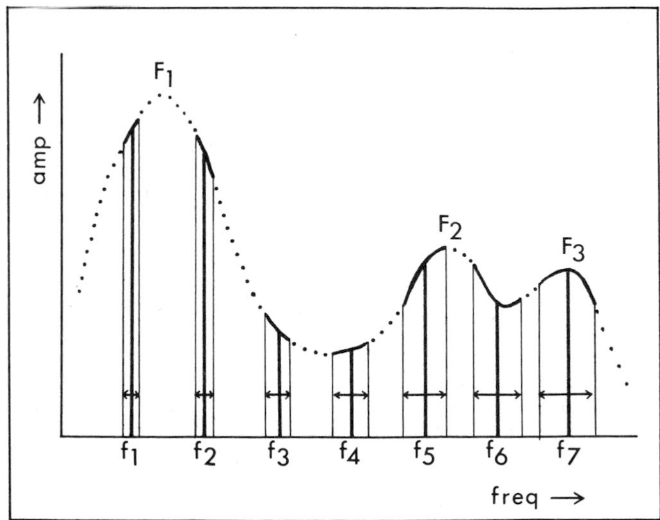

FIGURE 9 The vowel /a/ is plotted with a high fundamental frequency where there are few harmonics present. Without modulation (a), the inferred spectral form (dashed line) would be very different from the actual spectral form (dotted line). With modulation (b), the spectral slopes give a much clearer indication of the spectral form.

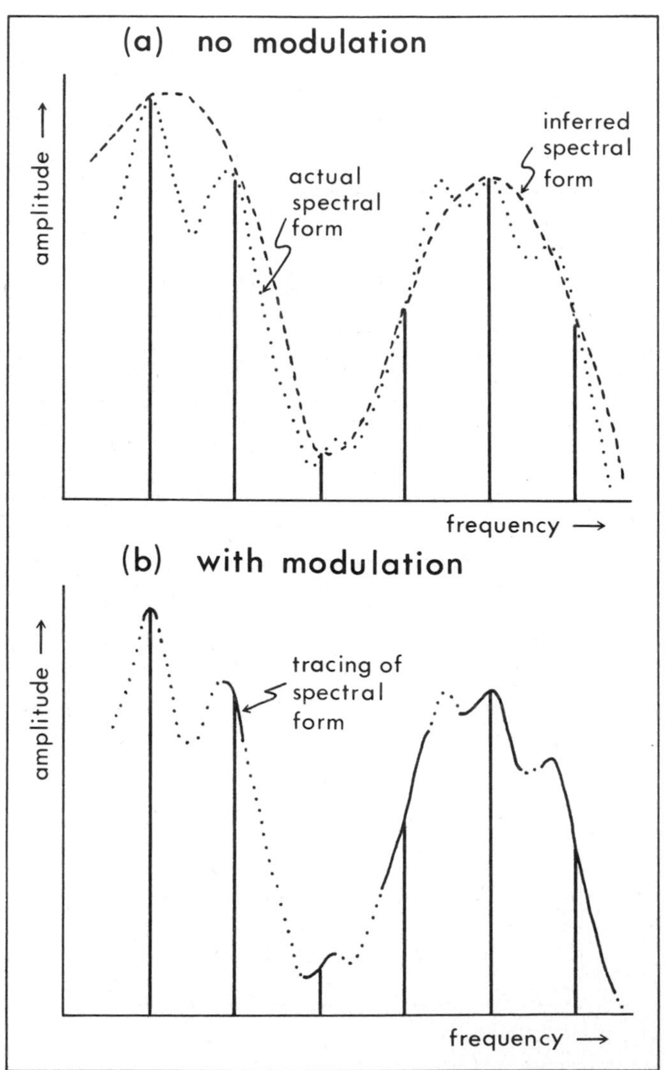

FIGURE 10 Complex spectrum resulting from several unmodulated sustaining harmonic sources.

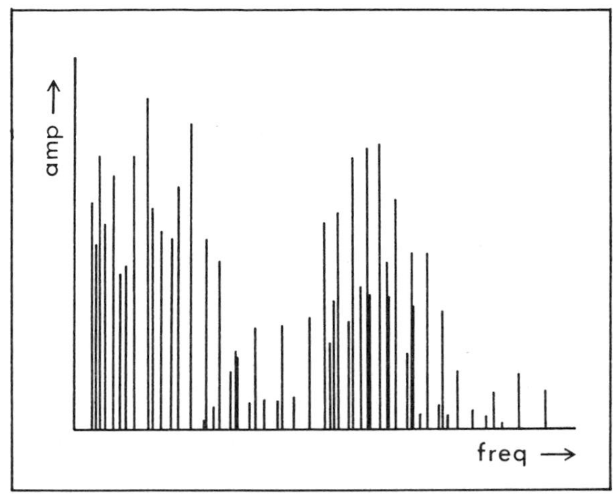

FIGURE 11 Spectral forms extracted by the auditory system when the individual sources are modulated, thereby increasing the information pertaining to the number and nature of the sources.

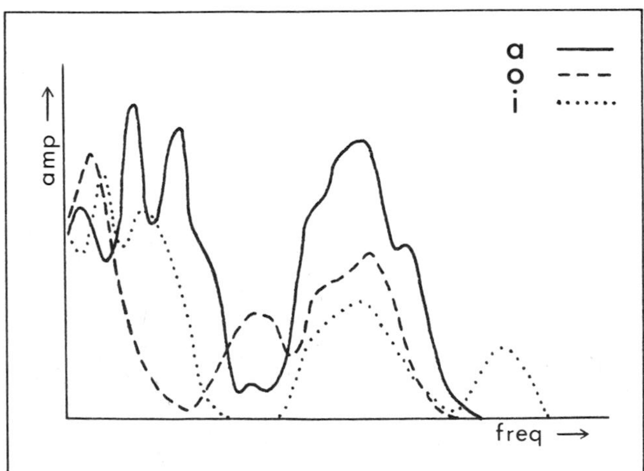

FIGURE 12 Permutations of three vowels at three different pitches. These chords may be heard in Taped Examples 11 and 12.

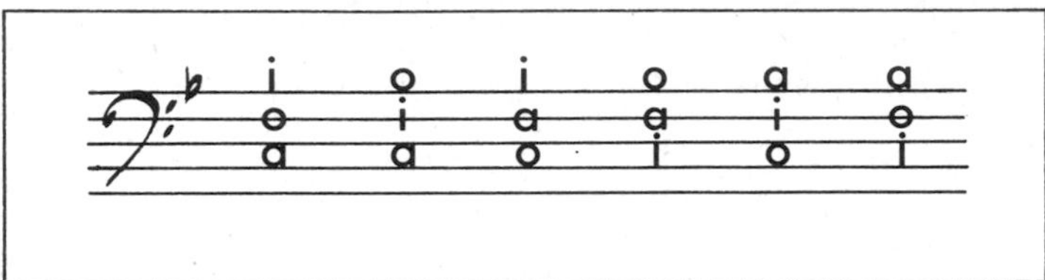

It is important to remark here that without the grouping information to select a certain subset of spectral components, one does not have access to the particular spectral form which gives the vowel quality. The overall spectral form is heard, which does not really correspond to any vowel[6]. But when the modulation is added and the partials trace the individual spectral envelopes, both the coherent harmonic behaviour and the reduced ambiguity of spectral form can be used to hear out the vowels.

In an experiment using stimuli similar to these, listeners judged the vowels to be more prominent and the pitches less ambiguous when the 'sources' were modulating. But there was also a surprising result. In some conditions all three vowels at their respective pitches were modulated coherently, maintaining the exact routes between all harmonics of all vowels. Given the putative criterion of frequency modulation coherence for grouping, I expected it to be more difficult to hear out the vowels in this situation. However, there was no difference between modulating the vowels coherently or incoherently between them. But remember that even when their frequencies are moving coherently, the amplitudes of the partials of each vowel are tracing the spectral envelope of the vowel alone. Thus each vowel is still being unambiguously defined by the amplitude movement. Listeners' results indicated that there was no effect of the coherence of modulation of the three vowels. As long as they were being modulated at all, they were more prominent perceptually.

This suggests the possibility that perception of vowel identity is independent of a source forming process, that vowel identification (or speech sound identification in general) is performed in parallel with source image processing. This suggestion is supported by the work of Cutting (1976). The stimulus he used is shown in Figure 13. A schematic, two-formant speech sound (consonant-vowel syllable) was split up and presented dichotically over headphones. The first formant and steady state portion of the second formant were presented to one ear. The second formant transition responsible for the perception of the /d/ phenome was presented to the other ear. When the temporal alignment of the transition sound was appropriate, subjects reported hearing a /da/ syllable in the ear with the steady state portion. When the transition was not presented at all, subjects reported hearing a /ba/ most of the time. So the transition in the opposite ear was contributing to the percept of the /da/ syllable, the whole of which was located in one ear. However, many subjects also reported hearing a chirp sound (the percept elicited by the second formant transition alone) in the opposite ear as well. A two source percept resulted where one element of acoustic information was contributing to the qualities of both sources simultaneously.

FIGURE 13 Schematic representation of the formant trajectories in the stimulus used by Cutting (1976). The second formant transition for the /da/ syllable was presented to one ear and the rest of the signal was presented to the other ear. The resulting percepts and their perceived located are indicated at the bottom.

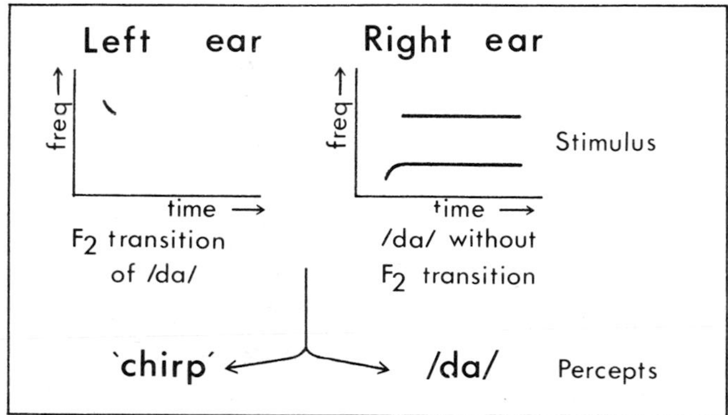

I now present a musical example where the same kind of effect takes place. Namely, the behaviour of the overall spectral form is extracted as meaningful speech information, while the actual spectral contents are perceived as being several sources. Taped Example 13, is a fragment composed by Alain Louvier for the dance theatre piece, '*Casta Diva*', by Maurice Béjart and is taken from a recent record of extracts from compositions and research done at IRCAM (1983). The example was realized by Moorer using linear predictive coding techniques for analysis and resynthesis of voice. In the analysis phase, the voice is modelled as a source of acoustic excitation (a periodic sound produced by the vocal chords and the noise produced by breath, etc.) and a series of filters (the vocal cavities) which change in time. These can be resynthesized exactly as analysed in which case one recovers a sound very much like the original. Or one can perform a resynthesis (called 'cross-synthesis') where the normal vocal chord excitation stimulating the vocal tract is replaced by a more complex, computer-synthesized waveform. Both kinds of resynthesis can be heard in the Taped Example.

What is fascinating musically and psychologically in this kind of example is the demonstration of the multipotentiality of the imaging process. One can synthesize the behaviour of the overall spectral form and hear intelligible speech. At the same time one can analyse the spectral contents into multiple source images.

Spatial Location

Sounds in the environment stimulate two sense organs, our two ears. Except for sound sources lying in the median place, equidistant from the two ears, the signals received at the two eardrums are slightly different. When a source lies to the right side of the head, the sound reaches the right ear first. It is also more intense in the right ear at higher frequencies since the head casts a sound shadow which attenuates the sound before it arrives at the left ear. Also, the two pinnae (the outer ears) modify the sound significantly depending on the azimuth and elevation of the sound source relative to them. These modifications, that is, the introduction of certain reflections due to the structure of the outer ear, would again be slightly different for each ear when the sound was not in the median plane. The pinna modifications are considered to be particularly important for detecting the elevation of a sound and for making back/front distinctions.

At any rate, what I am pointing out here is that in most cases, the sounds arriving at the two eardrums are not exactly the same. But the two sources of stimulation are heard as one source, and the disparities between the ears influence certain qualities of the source image, for example its location in azimuth and elevation, the characteristics of the acoustic environment (large reverberant cathedral *versus* open air space, for example; and I am sitting next to a wall rather than being in the middle of the auditorium,) etc.

When sounds are presented over headphones or speakers, where two or more physical sources are present, the placement of a virtual source image between the physical sources can be simulated by adjusting the relative intensities and onset times at each speaker or headphone. For example, over headphones (where the sound is usually heard inside the head but can be moved from side to side) a time onset difference of only 0.6 msec is sufficient to make the sound appear to come entirely from the leading earphone (cf. Mills, 1972). If the onset difference is increased to a few msec one begins to hear two separate events (cf. Schubert, 1979; editors's comments pp 255-257). With speakers in a moderately reverberant room, the difference must be in the order of 30 msec for separate events to be perceived. Thus, in the temporal domain, there are some rather narrow limits to the fusion of separate events into a single image. Also, if the spectral and temporal characteristics of the events are quite different, the disparities necessary to hear the events as separate are smaller.

Often, in room listening, echoes (which are repeated versions of the same sound, but coming from different directions and transformed by the room acoustics) do not affect the apparent location of the sound source. They are ignored in this respect by the auditory system, but contribute instead to the perception of the acoustic properties of the environment. This is called the 'precedence' effect to indicate that the event which precedes its replications (echoes) is used to determine the nature and location of the source, and the replications that follow are perceptually fused with the direct sound.

Now let us consider the extent to which spatial location helps us to distinguish among sound sources. Cherry (1953) studied the ability of listeners to attend to and extract meaningful information from a speech stream embedded in a noisy background (a cocktail party) of many other speakers (people speaking loudly, not loudspeakers). When at the party itself, we can use the location of the source, speech characteristics of the voice being listened to, semantic constraints and additional visual information, such as lip reading, hand gestures and the like, to reconstruct information masked or covered up by the noisy environment. When we listen to the same person speaking in the same environment but recorded on a stereo tape recorder (in order to preserve the directionality of the various sources) intelligibility decreases somewhat but a significant amount can still be distinguished. However, when only one channel of sound is presented, intelligibility of the target speech stream is reduced drastically.

This suggests that the sounds that mask the target signal in the monoaural case are not as effective as maskers when the auditory system can relegate them to separate spatial locations. Thus, spatial location is a cue that can be used to attend to and follow the emanations of a given sound source. There is a well-developed area of study in 'classical' psychoacoustics addressing the improvement in detection that occurs when two ears are used instead of one. This improvement is called a masking level difference (MLD cf. Durlach, 1972; Jeffress, 1972), since it is a difference between monaural and binaural listening conditions in the level that is necessary to hear a target signal in the presence of a masking signal.

There arise certain situations in music where a composer desires a great complexity of material and, at the same time, a great clarity or distinguishability of the elements in that complexity. The spatial separation of key elements can help a listener to differentiate between them. A good example of this is the recent piece '*Repons* ' by Pierre Boulez (1981/1982). He has six soloists playing percussive instruments (for example piano, xylophone, harp) which are arranged around the perimeter of a rectangular hall. Each soloist's sound is modified electronically and sent to six speakers also in the perimeter of the hall. A small orchestra is placed in the centre of the hall. The audience is distributed around the orchestra and thus positioned between the acoustic orchestra and the electronically modified soloists. At one point near the beginning of the piece the transformed sounds from each soloist are echoed many times and sent bouncing around to the speakers. What results is a marvellously rich, crystalline texture of timbral arpeggios that nonetheless has a kind of clarity due to the timbral elements being distributed in space. After hearing the first performance of this work, I then heard a stereophonic recording of the same concert. The carefully woven, multi-mirrored reflections and the intricacy of the electronic modifications of the soloists' notes were reduced to a dull, ambient mush. The spatialization had been an essential compositional element in the hearing of the piece. This was something akin to seeing a photograph of a Monet painting of the water-lilies at Giverny in low-contrast black and white. In the case of '*Repons*', two electronic 'ears' were not enough to preserve the clarity because in a concert hall the human ears are attached to a movable globe and the act of moving itself helps to distinguish different sources by creating a continually changing disparity between the ears which is unique for each source of sound. This changing disparity is a very strong cue for the invariance in location of the source.

Coherent Behaviour of Sound Objects and Simultaneous Organization

All of the factors discussed above contribute to a general coherence of the elements belonging to a physical sound source. And this coherence may be considered in turn as a by-product of the behaviour of the physical system producing the sound. I propose that much of the organization our perceptual systems perform is based on (but by no means limited to) a learning of the normal behaviour of physical objects in the world around us. I would not want to limit the possibilities of perceiving to such object-based learning, but I would suggest that this whole realm of normal perceiving heavily influences our perception of music. Further, I have found, in my own perceptual analyses of several pieces of music, that extensions of these various criteria of 'behavioural coherence' have proven useful in predicting when different kinds of reorganization of the physical objects are possible, for example, the recombination of several instruments into a fused composite timbre, and so on.

To summarize briefly the elements treated in this section, there are (at least) four factors contributing to the fusion and separation of simultaneous source images. These are: (1) a common (or closely correlated) global amplitude modulation (low frequency amplitude fluctuations and amplitude envelope); (2) a common (or closely correlated) frequency modulation which maintains the frequency ratios among the components (periodic: vibrato, aperiodic: jitter, or slow pitch glides: inflection); (3) a complex coupling of amplitude and frequency modulation which defines a spectral envelope, implying a stable resonance structure (such as vowel formants); and (4) a common spatial location (the dynamic maintenance of similar time, intensity and spectral disparities at the two ears for all elements of a source whether the source is moving or the head is moving).

With computer music synthesis one can independently control the degree of coherence for any of these factors and even play them against one another. In Taped Example 14 a slowly evolving, but stable vocal spectral form is pitted against incoherent random amplitude modulation on each of the harmonics of the complex tone. This modulation occurs around the main spectral form as illustrated in Figure 14. Three different versions are played, each with a progressively greater modulation depth. Note that the effect moves from one of a kind of chorus effect to a crow-like image. Since the average spectral form is the same for each condition, the vowel sounds are maintained. But the incoherence of amplitude behaviour gives the impression of many sources and so an image of a crowd trying to say the same vowels results.

For Taped Example 15, the sound of an oboe was analysed by phase vocoder. You would first hear the original oboe sound on the tape. The output of this analysis describes the amplitude and frequency behaviour of each harmonic. From these data the sound can be resynthesized either exactly as analysed or with certain modifications. In this case, the even and odd harmonics are sent to separate channels in order to be played over different loudspeakers. Initially the same vibrato and jitter patterns are imposed on the two groups of sounds. Then, slowly, the frequency modulation pattern on the even harmonics is decorrelated from the pattern on the odd harmonics. This is illustrated in Figure 15.

As you may hear, the initial image of an oboe between the speakers gradually pulls apart into two images and in the two speakers: one of a soprano-like sound an octave higher (the even harmonics) and one of a hollow, almost clarinet-like sound at the original pitch (the odd harmonics). Following this, each channel is played separately and then the two channel version is played again. It is extremely important that the levels of the two channels be properly adjusted for the effect to work. This example was used in a composition by Roger Reynolds '*Archipelago*' (1983) and was realized at IRCAM by Lancino. Here we have a case where the coherence of frequency modulation at the beginning of the sound overrides the spatial separation of the two subsets of harmonics and one hears a single image of the oboe, more or less localized between the speakers. But as the modulations become incoherent, the images move to their rightful places and the sounds now appear to come from where they were originally coming from.

As discussed in the section on spectral form, the auditory system is very sensitive to the behaviour of the overall spectral structure. With Rodet's (1980a,b) time-domain, formant-wave synthesis called CHANT (from the French word for 'sing') one has flexible and independent control over the behaviour of each formant. Barriere (1983) used this capability in a series of studies for his piece '*Chréode*' realized at IRCAM. He manipulated the way the individual formants changed in time to make the spectral forms either coalesce into vowels or disintegrate into the several formants as individual images. In Taped Example 16 you may hear some voices modelled after Tibetan chant that are slowly disintegrated by decorrelating the formant movements until, at the end of the fragment, individual formants can be heard whistling around across the harmonics.

All of these examples are intended to show that the constellation of factors contributing to the organization of simultaneous elements into auditory source images is quite complex. They also demonstrate that the factors can interact and that some factors can override the effects of others, as was demonstrated in the split oboe example.

FIGURE 14. The amplitudes of each harmonic are modulated randomly above and below their central value, defined by the vowel spectral envelope. The modulation pattern on each harmonic is independent of that on any other harmonic. In Taped Example 14 the modulation depth is varied. As the modulation depth is increased, the central spectral form is deformed to a greater degree. Note also that in the Taped Example, the central spectral form is actually evolving as well and that this evolution is not depicted here.

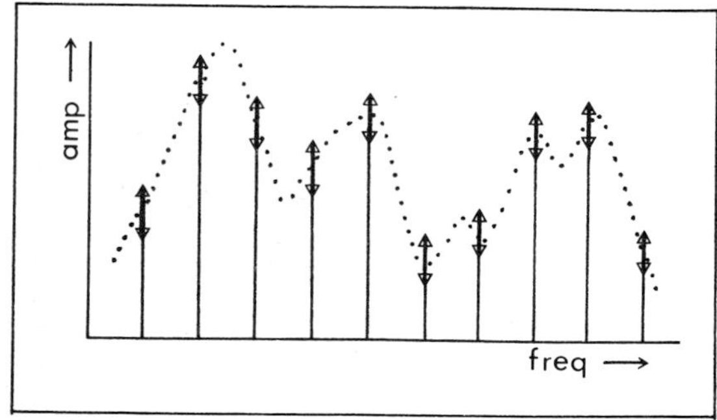

FIGURE 15 The parsing of even and odd harmonies of an oboe sound. Initially, all harmonics are modulated coherently. Then the even harmonics are slowly decorrelated from the odd harmonics until they have an independent modulation pattern. The triangle and square waves are only used for easy visualization. Vibratos of different rates and independent jitter functions were used in Taped Example 15.

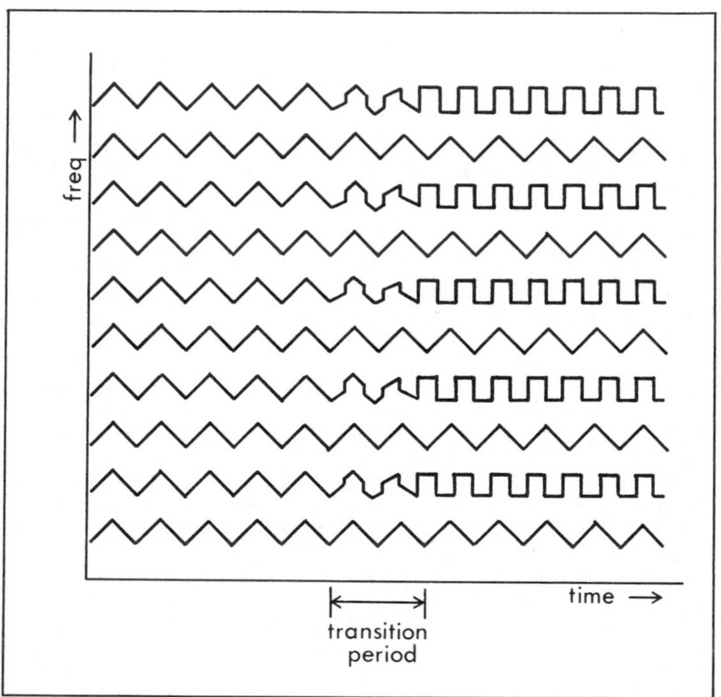

The important similarities among these factors are that they are dynamic, that is they change with time, and the coherence of change indicates a common source origin while incoherence of change indicates diverse source origins. I consider the spatial location factor to be dynamic because in normal listening both the head and the sound source are moving to some extent and the dynamic coherence of the result, with respect to the two ears, becomes a relatively unambiguous cue for place of origin of the sound source. Indeed, 'place' becomes an invariant quality of the sound image when this coherence is maintained.

What I think we need as a general and subdividable principle is the notion of the coherence of behaviour of the elements belonging to a source. Again, as an explanatory metaphor, this notion can be applied at several levels of description and defined with respect to the factor being considered, as I have demonstrated in the previous sections. It is also important to consider that the 'meaning' of coherence can be dependent on the previous experience of a listener. We can learn the behaviour of various sound sources. And we can incorporate the instances and relations between instances of its sound emanations into a model of coherence for that object and for physically similar objects.

I find myself returning often to consider the behaviour of physical objects for reasons of both 'ecological validity' (perceptual systems are 'meant' to operate in the physical world) and personal experience with electracoustic music. In listening to several hundred hours of electronic and computer music I have often been struck by a particular, natural (almost default) mode of listening which remarks that electronic sounds most often *sound like something*. Which is to say that my perception, being always influenced by memory and learned patterns of categorizing and identifying, tries to hear with respect to the *already heard*. I return to this point shortly, but now I consider the interactions of sequential and simultaneous organization.

INTERACTIONS BETWEEN SEQUENTIAL AND SIMULTANEOUS ORGANIZATION

It is no news to musicians that there is some essential distinction to be made between these two types of organization, which are traditionally denoted as 'horizontal' and 'vertical' in reference to the page of the musical score. In music we see different kinds of compositional principles in operation for writing that tends more toward homophony and that which tends more toward polyphony. But, of course, the most interesting music arises where these come into counterplay - either converging on similar propositions of perceptual organization, or proposing separate, conflicting organizations. It is the creation of tension and functional ambiguity that, among many other things, brings an exhilaration to me as a listener.

In a sense, there are two separate propositions before our ears in this kind of counterplay. It appears that sequential and simultaneous organization are determined by separate criteria: sequential elements are organized according to spectral continuity, simultaneous elements are organized according to coherence of dynamic cues. That they are organized by separate criteria suggests the possibility that they may conflict, even compete, with one another. This was tested experimentally by Bregman and Pinker (1978). The stimulus they used is depicted in Figure 16.

A pure tone A alternated with a two-tone complex B and C. The frequency of tone A was varied to make it more or less likely to form a sequential stream with B. The onset time of tone C was varied to make it more or less likely to fuse, that is form a simultaneous organization with tone B. Thus, both tones A and C were competing for the membership of tone B. Two judgements were collected from subjects: (1) whether A and B formed one stream or two; and (2) whether C was perceived as being more pure or more rich. When A and B were in close frequency proximity (tending to be perceived as one stream) and B and C were asynchronous (tending to be perceived separately), judgements indicated that A and B more often formed one stream and C was perceived as being more pure. When A and B were distant in frequency (tending to be perceived as two streams) and B and C were synchronous (tending to be perceived as a group), judgements indicated that A was heard in a stream by itself and C was perceived as being richer (being fused with

B). These two cases may be heard in Taped Example 17 in the order described above.

This was an important experiment in two respects. It demonstrated the separate kinds of organization and their interaction in the final perceptual result. And it also demonstrated that a perceived quality of source, for example the timbre of C, was dependent on how the elements were organized. When tone B was not grouped (fused) with C, the latter was more pure. But when they were fused, C was perceived as being rich. Thus timbre, and, as I demonstrated with the oboe in Taped Example 16, pitch are properties of source images that are derived after the concurrent elements have been organized into those images.

FIGURE 16 The stimulus used by Bregman and Pinker (1978) to demonstrate the competition of sequential and simultaneous organizations. Tone B is potentially a member of a sequential organization with A or a simultaneous organization with C. See text for more detailed information.

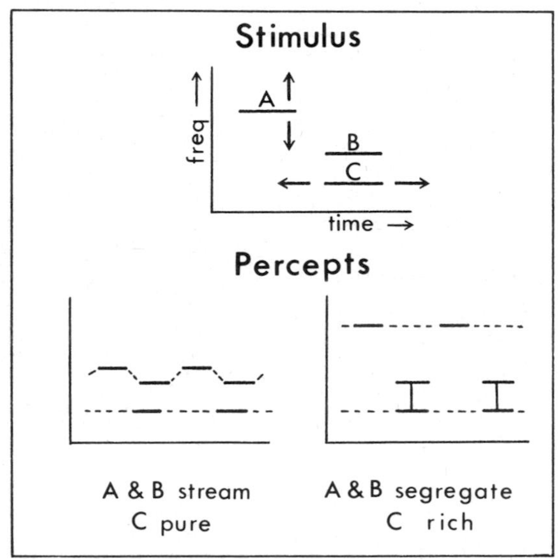

Another example to demonstrate the organizational dependency of timbre is schematized in Figure 17. This sound configuration is played in two separate contexts which greatly affect the perceived timbre of tone A. In the first part of Taped Example 18, tone A (4 components) is initially played alone. And then tones B and C (two components each) gradually fade in. At first the percept is that shown in Figure 17 as (a). Tones B and C form one stream and tone A forms another. Note the timbre of tone A. But as the intensities of B and C approach that of A, the components of A are captured and pulled into separate organizations by B and C. At this point the original timbre of A is more difficult to hear. It is replaced by a double timbre and the rhythmic pattern is as shown in percept (b).

FIGURE 17 Depending on the intensity of tones B and C and on the context, A may be heard as a fused tone with its own timbre, or it may be split into two simultaneous tones, A_b and A_c as indicated by the dotted lines in the stimulus diagram. In the former case, the resulting rhythm is (a); in the latter case, the rhythm is (b).

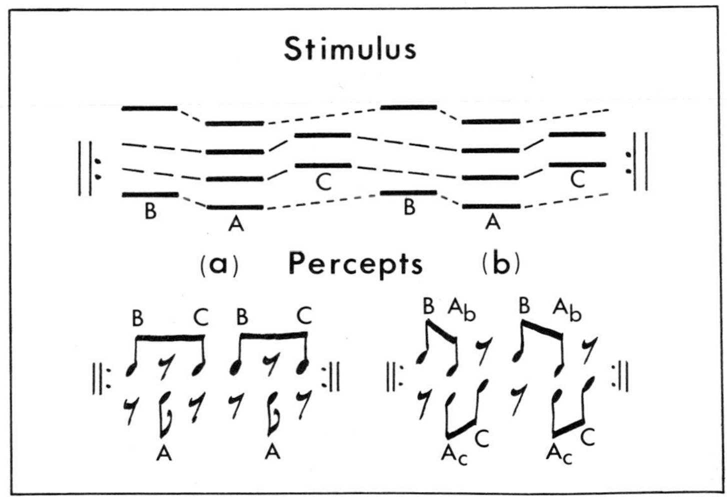

But now let us reverse the procedure. The second part of Taped Example 18 starts with tones B and C and the tone A is gradually faded in. This time it never reaches (for my ears anyway) a point where it is pulled apart by tones B and C. Somehow the crescendo movement of A seems to keep it stable as a separate stream and stays at percept (a). So with as simple a sound configuration as this we already have some rather complex effects of context on the way the elements are organized and the timbres are perceived. Demonstrations such as this support the proposition of Bregman (1977, 1980) that perception is an active process of composing the sensory data into some kind of interpretation of the way the world is behaving. The composition process draws from a large number of elements in the perceptual field that interact in complex ways to produce a final percept (Bregman and Tougas, 1979).

Where this becomes interesting musically is in its implication that, with computer synthesis techniques, processes of horizontal and vertical musical organization can be carried into the sound microstructure. The composer can play with the processes of perceptual organization that underly the heard musical surface. This sets up the possibility of composing situations where sequential and simultaneous organizations compete for individual spectral components to be part of the structure of a musical image. With a careful consideration (or better yet, embodiment and subsequent intuitive use) of these principles of perceptual organization, the composer has access to a whole realm of mutability of the heard 'image'. Convergences and divergences of the musical functionalities of individual elements allow the development of microstructural (and pre-perceptual) ambiguity. These possibilities are evidenced in the last Taped Example (no. 19), created by Rodet with the CHANT computer-synthesis program.

SUMMARY

I have proposed that there are separate groups of criteria that determine the way one organizes acoustic information sequentially and simultaneously. This distinction perhaps reflects the involvement of different types of perceptual mechanisms. Sequential information is organized according to criteria of spectral continuity. A sequence of events that maintains spectral continuity is more easily followed as a source image than a sequence that is discontinuous. In the latter case one is more likely to reorganize the sequence into two or more streams. Simultaneous information is organized according to criteria of coherence of dynamic cues such as amplitude and frequency modulation that indicate common source origin, the tracing of spectral form that indicates a common spatial origin. Spectral components that behave coherently in these ways are more likely to be heard as originating from a common source and will thus form a unified, fused auditory image. As this coherence of behaviour is maintained across time, the image can follow in time as well. However, since the criteria for sequential and simultaneous organization are different, it is possible to construct situations where they come into conflict. In situations of conflict, either one criterion overrides another and the organization follows accordingly, or situations of organizational ambiguity result.

Given the extensibility of the auditory image metaphor and the principles of continuity and coherence, it should be possible to develop a psychologically relevant theory of musical attention and organization that covers the range from the formation of the image of a single event to the accumulation of the 'image' of a musical form, passing through many intermediate levels of organizational polyvalence (each element is potentially a member of several concurrent organizations) and the construction of composite musical objects that have a complex evolution through time. I feel that structural and functional ambiguities are a very important part of musical organization and if well understood can be used with great effectiveness and power in musical composition.

So where do we stand with respect to the initial questions? As concerns what might possibly be attended to as a musical image, a good start has been made with an understanding of certain basic principles of sequential and simultaneous organization, at least at the level of source organization.

There remains much work to be done on the effects of higher level organizing principles, such as underlying metric and rhythmic structure and underlying harmonic structure, on what can be followed throught time as a coherent entity and on what can be grouped as musically meaningful conglomerates or composite images. With respect to the second and third questions, the principles outlined here are certainly an important group of processes that are involved in the act of auditory organization. Again, what needs to be further researched (as much in musical as in psychological paradigms) is the extent to which the active, creative involvement of the listener can play a role in the organizing of complex constellations of sound events into musical images.

As I am prone to reiterate ad nauseum, each listener still carries into the musical situation 'normal' tendencies of hearing that are going to act as defaults in the organization of musical sound. However, what is most compelling as a result of all of the research on auditory organization is the fact that the will and focus of the listener play an extraordinarily important role in determining the final perceptual results. Musical listening (as well as viewing visual arts or reading a poem) is and must be considered seriously by any artist as a creative act on the part of the participant. As mentioned previously, perceiving is an act of composition, and perceiving a work of art can involve conscious and willful acts of composition. What this proposes to the artist is the creation of forms that contain many possibilities of 'realization' by a perceiver, to actually compose a multipotential structure that allows the perceiver to compose a new work within that form at each encounter. This proposes a relation to art that demands of perception that it be creative in essence.

ACKNOWLEDGMENTS

Some of the research reported in this chapter was conducted while the author was supported, in part, by a research grant from the Minister of Foreign Affairs of the French Government. I would like to express appreciation to Al Bregman for kindly communicating unpublished research to me and for a continually stimulating, dialogue on principles of auditory organization. I continue to draw heavily from his example and his work. Finally, I would like to thank Wendy Lindbergh, Tod Machover and David Wessel who provided helpful critques of this manuscript.

FOOTNOTES

1. A cassette tape of the sound examples described in this text is available by writing to the author.

2. Vibrato is approximately sinusoidal modulation with modulation rates between about 3-10 Hz. Jitter is an aperiodic modulation generally found in all natural sustained-vibration sources like voices, bowed strings and winds: the frequency spectrum of the modulation itself usually has a low-pass characteristic, that is has a greater predominance of lower frequencies, particularly those below 30-50Hz (McAdams, 1983).

3. Rms stands for root-mean-square which is a measure of the overall deviation from the centre frequency of a given partial. Several

different experiments have shown that this is a good measure since vastly different modulation waveforms, like vibrato and jitter, can be equated for amount of deviation with this measure (Hartmann and Klein, 1983 ; McAdams, 1983c).

4. 1 cent = 1/100 of a semitone; 12 cents is approximately 0.7% of the frequency.

5. This, however, has been shown by Cohen (1980) to be dependent to some extent on the form of the amplitude envelope. Inharmonic (and by implication multi-pitched) sounds are most often heard as fused, single sources when they have exponentially decaying amplitude envelopes as one finds with many kinds of struck sound sources, for example, strings, bars, tubes, plates, etc.

6. For many listeners, the vowel /a/ is always more prominent than the vowels /o/ and /i/, even when there is no modulation. This is most likely due to the fact that the individual vowels were equalized for loudness before mixing into the complexes. The formants for the vowel /a/ are grouped into two spectral regions and thus their energy is more concentrated and the harmonics in these regions stand above those of the other two vowels whose spectra are more spread out. Listeners thus have access to several formant features for the vowel /a/ even when it is not being modulated.

REFERENCES

Barriere, J.B. (1983).'Chréode' for computer generated tape. Paris: IRCAM.

Békésy, G. von. (1960). Experiments in Hearing. New York: McGraw-Hill.

Boulez, P. (1981/1982). 'Repons' for orchestra, soloists, live electronics and computer generated tapes. London: Universal Editions.

Bregman, A.S. (1977). Perception and behavior as compositions of ideals Cognitive Psychology, 9, 250-292.

Bregman, A.S. (1978). The formation of auditory streams. In J. Requin (Ed.) Attention and Performance. Volume 7. Hillsdale, New Jersey: Lawrence Erlbaum.

Bregman, A.S. (1980). The conceptual basis of perception and action. In Perception and Cognition II: Presentations on Art Education Research. Volume 4. University of Montreal: Concordia.

Bregman, A.S. (1981). Asking the 'what for' question in auditory perception. In: M. Kubovy and J. Pomerantz (Ed.), Perceptual Organization. Hillsdale, New Jersey: Lawrence Erlbaum.

Bregman, A.S. (1982). Two-factor theory of auditory organization. Journal of the Acoustical Society of America, 72, S10 (A).

Bregman, A.S., Abramson, J. and Darwin, C. (1983). Spectral integration based on common amplitude modulation. Unpublished manuscript, McGill University, Montreal.

Bregman, A.S. and Campbell, J. (1971). Primary auditory stream segregation and the perception of order in rapid sequences of tones. Journal of Experimental Psychology, 89, 244-249.

Bregman, A.S. and Pinker, S. (1978). Auditory streaming and the building of timbre. Canadian Journal of Psychology, 32, 19-31.

Bregman, A.S. and Tougas, Y. (1979). Propagation of constraints in auditory organization. Unpublished manuscript, McGill University, Montreal.

Bozzi, P. and Vicario, G. (1960). Due fattori di unificazione fra note musicali: La vincinanza temporale e la vincinanze tonale. Rivista de Psychologia, 54, 235-258.

Cherry, E.C. (1953). Some experiments on the recognition of speech with one and with two ears. Journal of the Acoustical Society of America, 25, 975-979.

Chowning, J.M. (1980). Computer synthesis of the singing voice. In: Sound Generation in Winds, Strings, Computers. Royal Swedish Academy of Music, Publication number 29, Stockholm.

Cohen, E.A. (1980). The influence of non-harmonic partials on tone perception. Unpublished doctoral Dissertation, Stanford University.

Cutting, J.E. (1976). Auditory and linguistic processes in speech perception: Inferences from six fusions in dichotic listening. Psychological Review, 83, 114-140.

Dannenbring, G.L. and Bregman, A.S. (1976). Stream segregation and the illusion of overlap. Journal of Experimental Psychology/Human Perception and Performance, 2, 544-555.

Deutsch, D. (1975). Two-channel listening to musical scales. Journal of the Acoustical Society of America, 57, 1156-1160.

Dowling. W.J. (1973). The perception of interleaved melodies. Cognitive Psychology, 5, 322-337.

Durlach, N.I. (1972). Binaural signal detection: Equalization and cancellation theory. In: J.V. Tobias (Ed.), Foundations of Modern Auditory Theory. Volume 2. New York: Academic Press.

Grey, J.M. and Moorer, J.A. (1977). Perceptual evaluations of synthesized musical instrument tones. Journal of the Acoustical Society of America, 62, 1493-1500.

Hartmann, W.M. and Klein, M.A. (1980). Theory of frequency modulation detection for low modulation frequencies. Journal of the Acoustical Society of America, 67, 935-946.

Helmholtz, H.L.F von (1954). On the Sensations of Tone as a Physiological Basis for the Theory of Music (Dover, New York, from 1885 edition of English translation by A.J. Ellis).

IRCAM: Un Portrait. (1983). Recorded disc with accompanying text. Paris: IRCAM.

Jeffress, L.A. (1972). Binaural signal detection: Vector theory. In J.V. Tobias (Ed.) Foundations of Modern Auditory Theory. Volume 2. New York: Academic Press.

Julesz, B. (1971). Foundations of Cyclopean Perception. Chicago, Illinois: University of Chicago press.

Kubovy, M. and Jordan, R. (1979). Tone-segregation by phase: On the phase sensitivity of the single ear. Journal of the Acoustical Society of America, 66, 100-106.

McAdams, S. (1980). The effects of spectral fusion on the perception of pitch for complex tones. Journal of the Acoustical Society of America, 68, S109 (A).

McAdams, S. (1981). Auditory perception and the creation of auditory images. Paper presented at Informatica e Composizione Musicale, Festival Internazionale di Musica Contemporanea, La Biennale di Venezia, Venice.

McAdams, S. (1982a). Contributions of sub-audio frequency modulation and spectral envelope constancy to spectral fusion in complex harmonic tones. Journal of the Acoustical Society of America, 72, S11(A).

McAdams, S. (1982b). Spectral fusion and the creation of auditory images. In: M. Clynes (Ed.) Music, Mind and Brain: The Neuropsychology of Music. New York: Plenum.

McAdams, S. (1983a). Acoustic cues contributing to spectral fusion. Proceedings of the International Congress of Acoustics, Paris, France, 3, 127-130.

McAdams, S. (1983b). L'image auditive: Un métaphore pour la recherche musicale et psychoacoustique. In: 'Un Portrait': IRCAM. Paris: IRCAM.

McAdams, S. (1983c). Spectral fusion, spectral parsing and the formation of auditory images. Unpublished doctoral dissertation, Stanford University, California.

McAdams, S. and Bregman, A. (1981). Hearing musical streams. Computer Music Journal, 3, 26-43.

McAdams, S. and Wessel, D. (1981). A general synthesis package based on principles of auditory perception. International Computer Music Conference, Denton, Texas.

McNabb, M. (1981). Dreamsong: The composition. Computer Music Journal, 5, 36-53.

Mills, A.W. (1972). Auditory localization. In: J.V. Tobias (Ed.), Foundations of Modern Auditory Theory. Volume 2. New York: Academic Press.

Noorden, L.P.A.S. van (1975). Temporal coherence in the perception of tone sequences. Unpublished doctoral dissertation. Tech, Hogeschool, Eindhoven, The Netherlands.

Noorden, L.P.A.S. van (1977). Minimum differences of level and frequency for perceptual fission of tone sequences ABAB. Journal of the Acoustical Society of America, 61, 1041-1045.

Rasch, R. (1978). The perception of simultaneous notes such as in polyphonic music. Acustica, 40, 21-33.

Rasch, R. (1979). Synchronization in performed ensemble music. Acustica, 43, 121-131.

Reynolds, R. (1983). 'Archipelago' for orchestra and computer-generated tape C.F. Peters, New York.

Rodet, X. (1980a). CHANT Manual. Paris: IRCAM.

Rodet, X. (1980b). Time-domain formant-wave-function synthesis. In: J.C. Sinon, (Ed.) Spoken Language Generation and Understanding. Reidel, Dordrecht, Holland.

Scheffers, M. (1983). Sifting vowels: Auditory segregation and pitch perception. Unpublished doctoral dissertation, University of Groningen, The Netherlands.

Schubert, E.D. (1979). Psychological Acoustics. Stroudsberg, Pennsylvania: Dowden, Hutchinson and Ross.

Vicario, G.B. (1965). Vicinanza spaziale e vincinanza temporale nella segregazione di eventi. Rivista di Psicologia, 59, 843-863.

Vicario, G.B. (1982). Some observations in the auditory field. In: J. Beck (Ed.), Organization and Representation in Perception. Hillsdale, New Jersey: Lawrence Erlbaum.

Wessel, D. (1979). Timbre space as a musical control structure. Computer Music Journal, 3, 45-52.

Wessel, D. (1983). Timbral control in research on melodic patterns. Paper presented at the Fourth International Workshop on the Physical and Neuropsychological Foundations of Music, Ossiach, Austria.

Cognitive Processes in the Perception of Art
W.R. Crozier and A.J. Chapman (editors)
© Elsevier Science Publishers B.V. (North-Holland), 1984

CREATIVITY AND TRADITION IN ORAL FOLKLORE OR THE BALANCE OF INNOVATION AND REPETITION IN THE ORAL POETS ART[1]

Vaira Vīķis-Freibergs

University of Montreal

The study of creativity by psychologists has tended to focus on creativity as a stable and enduring characteristic of individuals, a sort of psychological commodity which some possess more of, and others less. The interest in binary classification of individuals into the creative and the non-creative and in the measurement of individual differences in this trait has tended to emphasize *who* is or is not creative, sometimes to the neglect of the *how* of the creative process, the statics of creativity thus tending to overshadow its dynamics.

A different way of approaching the problem of creativity would be to work backward from the creative product to make inferences about the psychological processes that must have been at work in producing it. This descriptive approach has a respectable tradition in structural anthropology, especially that of the French school (notably the work of Levi-Strauss). It also has affinities to the concept of the 'natural experiment' as understood in the French tradition of clinical psychology. This assumes that any unobserved phenomenon or body of data is an equally legitimate object of scientific study, independently of how it was obtained. While data produced at the instigation of experimenters and recorded under their very eyes have all the advantages that the experimental tradition has rightfully ascribed to them, this should not preclude our interest in data produced by series of 'natural' events outside our direct control. Thus, in the clinical setting, the study of individuals with brain lesions can be equally instructive independently of whether the lesions were surgically produced in the laboratory or produced by assorted traumas outside it. The experimental approach offers greater control and precision; the descriptive approach offers greater breadth and scope.

The field of literature offers wide opportunities for psychological study, which have been happily exploited by scholars in many disciplines but totally neglected by psychologists (Vīķis-Freibergs, 1982). Thus, the fundamental question of what distinguishes the 'high' language of literature as art (*die Kuntsprache*) from the 'low' language of ordinary usage has been the object of heated scholarly debate over several centuries. Psychology, which has little enough to say about the complex structure of ordinary language, has been all but mute on the subject of language as a medium for artistic expression. Another topic widely debated by scholars has been the question of the particularities (if any) of oral, as distinguished from written, literature. On this point, too, psychology has been silent.

The historical reasons for this difference are clear enough: a new discipline that was striving to establish itself as a 'hard' science would naturally shy away from topics that had traditionally been identified with scholarship in the humanities. So scholars have had the field to themselves and, contrary to trained psychologists, have not feared to deal with many challenging and fascinating problems of a decidedly psychological nature. Their disadvantage has been in having little knowledge of what psychology as a discipline was more and more able to offer, as well as an unfamiliarity with (and, hence, severe mistrust of) all forms of quantitative methods. No wonder that other scholars might find such ventures more than faintly suspect, objecting to psychological speculation as 'something which is never proved and which anyway comes very close to being a tautology' (Finnegan, 1976, p. 142).

With the solid grounding in objective methods which psychology has to offer, combined with the enormous strides of cognitive science in recent decades, the time seems propitious for a new interdisciplinarity in which worthwhile contributions from both science and scholarship could be fruitfully united. Such an attempt, of course, is not without its dangers, not the least of which is that of falling between two stools. To some it would be nothing less than a betrayal of the scientific method. As Hebb (1973) has had occasion to put it bluntly, 'Mixing humanism and science ruins both'. Needless to say, the research programme described here rests on the contrary conviction that at least certain branches of psychology as a science can be enriched by the contributions of scholarly disciplines, and that psychology has something to contribute in return. Something not unlike such a programme had already been envisaged by Wundt (1900-1920), better known as the founder of academic experimental psychology. He had called it *Völkerpsychologie*, meaning by it not 'folk' psychology in the sense of common wisdom, but rather a psychology dealing with the cultural products of nations or social groups namely, language, myths and customs.

ORAL LITERATURE: CREATIVE OR IMAGINATIVE?

Within the very broad field that is literature, there is a subfield of study variously referred to as folk literature (by extension from W.G. Herder's 'folksong' and the brothers' Grimm 'Folk tales'), oral folklore or, more recently (reference to 'folk' having become old fashioned) - as 'oral literature'.[2] This refers to artistic creations in either verse or prose encountered in traditional (i.e., pre-industrial and frequently pre-literate) societies, which are preserved and transmitted through the medium of the sung or spoken word, without recourse to written records. Following the original impetus given by the interest of the German Romantics in the artistic creations of 'the common people', such traditions have been recorded in most countries of Europe and, more recently, on other continents.

Folk literature is of potential interest to psychology from a number of points of view. First, it presumably reflects a record of live performances and thus has a more circumscribed and more 'behavioural character' than the more diffuse and elaborate constructions of written literary creations. More importantly, traditions that are carried entirely in human memory without any external mnemonic aids are of obvious relevance to a science that would have something to say about long-term retention and retrieval. Indeed, from a descriptive point of view, one may consider any corpus of folkloric texts as a 'natural experiment' in memorization conducted on the grandest of scales: with a cast of thousands performing across periods of centuries.

When a singer sings a song from a live oral tradition, the performance reflects underlying processes which present a challenge to theoretical explanation. What is it precisely that the singer is doing? Is it the rote recitation of material handed down from others and merely learned by heart? Or, at the other extreme, is it an act of spontaneous creation, each line being improvised anew in the heat of performance, with nothing but the general story and the metric mould of the verse for guidelines?

European scholarship (since the German Romantics) has tended to focus on the imitative and repetitive aspect of folklore, which implies the existence of a canonical text version - the text as it was at its moment of creation by some individual X. The Finnish school of folklore, with its interest in the geographical distribution of motifs and the history of their 'borrowings' between different peoples, is one prominent example. Somewhat as a reaction against this tradition is work of the so-called Harvard school (Lord, 1951, 1964; Parry, 1930, 1932) which has emphasized that the idea of a fixed text is the product of the literate mentality, but unknown in oral traditions, where a song is a fluid thing and each separate rendition an equally legitimate expression of it (Lord, 1976). (The idea that no version of an oral text is more legitimate than any other is also very strong among American folklorists.)

By a curious paradox, the concept of the oral poet as endlessly creative rather than passively repetitive arose out of Parry's work on the repetition of stereotyped expressions (formulae) in the *Iliad* and the *Odyssey* of Homer. This stereotypy is particularly striking in the case of the constant epithets, which seem as if glued to the name of the God or hero they are linked with: Dawn is 'rose-fingered Dawn', Hera is white-armed or ox-eyed, Achilles is fleet-footed, Athena owl-eyed, etc. These had always been an embarrassment to some classical scholars, who found it hard to reconcile Homer's undisputed poetic genius with such hackneyed stereotypy of diction. Parry proposed the explanation that such formulaicity is a sign that these epic poems originated in an oral tradition: It is precisely because the true creative singer (aioidos) is re-creating the epic song at each new singing that the singer needs repeated recourse to fixed formulae as a quick and convenient means of expressing the same idea within the confines of the same metric slot in the hexameter verse. If this performer were reciting a memorized text, as a 'mere rhapsode' would do, there would have been leisure enough to weed out such repetitions, much as is done by an author in written literature, where repetitions have come to be considered as inelegant.

To test this idea, Parry went to do field-work in Yugoslavia, recording epic songs from the still-live Serbo-Croatian tradition. After Parry's untimely death, Lord took over the work, refining and amplifying the original position and emphasizing, among other things, that the formulae can embrace much larger units of text than the well-known noun-epithet combinations. Lord's book, the *Singer of Tales* (1964) had an enormous impact in the English-speaking world, where the idea of formulaicity as proof of the oral origins of a text was seized upon eagerly by scholars in many different disciplines.

An interesting extension of Lord's ideas has been presented by Nagler (1974) in his analysis of the Homeric epics. According to Nagler, the oral poet works from a sort of Gestalt or mental template, which is used to generate similar passages of text in similar situations. Just like in Chomskian grammar the text of a sentence is generated by a set of syntactical rewrite rules, so in the oral poet's performance the text is being generated by a poetic grammar, embracing a higher-order set of rules of composition. The generative aspect is what gives spontaneity to the oral performance but the generative rules themselves are traditional. It is this combination of spontaneity and tradition which makes oral singers appear as simultaneously creative and imitative in their art. What is not entirely clear from such an account is how to explain the numerous verbatim repetitions which can be observed in any composite folkloric corpus, that is, an accumulation of songs from many different singers. The whole idea of the generative approach is that a limited number of rules should be able to produce a large number of different surface structures, that is a variety of different strings of particular words. But when fifty singers are found to produce verbatim the identical string of words fifty time over, one may be forgiven for wondering whether some rather Skinnerian learning by imitation and repetition may not be involved as well (Skinner, 1957).

Along the same lines of argument, closely similar (even if not identical) variants of the same text could hardly have arisen by a process of spontaneous generation in a number of different singers in isolation from each other. An oral tradition is, after all, a social phenomenon. Like language, it is an important means of communication in traditional societies. It is a stylized, ritualized, poeticized transformation of ordinary language, yet it is a language nonetheless. As such, it must be learned at some point by those who would use it, and in mastering any given tradition, the learner must necessarily have models to follow. If we would capture something of the interaction between the individual singer and his or her models, we must necessarily go beyond the repertoire of any single singer and examine a body of tradition as a whole. By analogy with de Saussure's (1916) conception of language, we may consider a corpus as a whole as one approximation to that abstract entity, *la langue* , which is like a composite dictionary existing collectively in the minds of all its speakers or, in our case, an abstract representation of the basic structural characteristics of the poetics of the tradition in question. Any specific song or text then becomes the analogue of a concrete speech act (*la parole*), the behavioural expression of the singer having mastered the abstract symbolic system that is the tradition.

The research reported here, using Latvian folksong texts as material, rests on this basic postulate of the poetic tradition as a heightened form of language, the study of which may hopefully provide some insights into the processes of literary creativity as well as those involved in the mastery of language at any level.

THE TRADITION

According to the testimony of foreign observers, as well as that of the songs themselves, singing was an integral part of everyday life in traditional Latvian society. Most of the singing was done by women, but groups of men or mixed groups were not excluded. Good singers, just like eloquent speakers, were much admired and held high social status. Typically, singing was done in a social setting, with the texts sung or chanted by a lead singer (*teicēja*) and accompanied by a chorus providing a *basso continuo* or *bourdon* with 'ah' or 'ooh' and joining in on the refrain and repetition. A *vikēja* (or several) singing in harmony or dissonance and adding grace-notes and melodic ornamentation was an optional feature. Group singing in unison was mostly a late nineteenth century development, under the influence of choir masters trained in Western musical traditions.

THE CORPUS

The main printed sources of Latvian folksongs texts (unaccompanied by melodies) span the period of 1807 to the nineteen-thirties, with the bulk of the material collected in the second half of the nineteenth century. The classical reference is the monumental work by Krišjānis Barons (whose sesquicentennial will be marked in 1985), which appeared as six volumes in eight tomes between 1894 and 1915. Barons developed a highly lucid and logical thematic classification, arranging the song texts in a hierarchically ordered system of major themes and subthemes. Songs closely resembling each other were grouped in clusters under the same reference number. One modal text was chosen as the 'type-song' and printed in ordinary type, and variants of it, consecutively numbered (e.g., Var. 1, Var. 2. ...) were printed in smaller type. For each printed text, a number of subvariants were listed giving only those words in which they differ from the text printed in full. This method allows for the presentation of extraordinarily large quantities of information in a compact and economical manner.

The Barons collection contains 35,789 consecutively numbered 'type-songs' and approximately 182,000 variants and subvariants. A four-volume supplement edited by P. Šmits was published between 1936 and 1939, bringing the number of type-songs to 60,080 but adding only 7,758 variants. Both these standard reference works were combined in a twelve volume edition published in Copenhagen between 1952 and 1956 (Švābe, Straubergs and Hauzenberga-Šturma, were the editors). This latter collection has been transcribed in computer-accessible form and constitutes a corpus of over 60,000 numbered song texts with selected variants, for a total of approximately 100,000 texts (V. Bērziņš et al, 1982). This is a composite corpus, recorded from many different singers in different parts of Latvia and represents the collective expression of a particular folk tradition.

The computerized corpus as a whole consists of 11.2 million characters, which includes song texts, identifying numbers and the geographical codes for the area in which they were recorded. The songs are stored on tape in the same order in which they appear in the twelve published volumes from which they were transcribed. The texts are stored line-by-line in character format, ASCII, a standard format for character representation which can be read by all computing machines. Search times for the complete corpus vary with the facilities available. A search takes two hours on a PDP 11-45 with a UNIX operating system, which has many programming tools which can be tailored to work most efficiently on a specific application (e.g., the LEX program which carries out selection based on various lexical criteria, such as all songs containing a given root-form). On an ICL 2988, using the Oxford Concordance Program, it takes five to six hours. This is largely because the OCP is a general program which is less effective for specific needs and also less effective on a very large corpus such as this one.

THE METRICAL STRUCTURE OF THE DAINA

In his system of classification, Barons chose the quatrain strophe as the basic, identifiable daina unit. The quatrain is a semantically complete, self-contained entity, built around an almost mathematically rigorous quadratic symmetry. Versification follows a number of very strict rules, which have been extensively studied by scholars, notably Bērziņs (1959). Over 90% of all dainas follow a trochaic meter, the remainder being loosely classified as dactylic. The dactylic songs stem from the Western part of Latvia (Kurzeme) and are strongly linked to ceremonial rituals and dances. The quatrain structure of these two types of meters may be represented by the following simplified schemas, where / marks the stresses syllables or arses and ◡ marks the unstressed syllables or theses.

TROCHAIC QUATRAIN

	Colon 1	Colon 2	
Line 1	/ ᴗ / ᴗ	/ ᴗ / ᴗ	Couplet 1
Line 2	/ ᴗ / ᴗ	/ ᴗ /	
Line 3	/ ᴗ / ᴗ	/ ᴗ / ᴗ	Couplet 2
Line 4	/ ᴗ / ᴗ	/ ᴗ /	

DACTYLIC QUATRAIN

	Colon 1	Colon 2	
Line 1	/ ᴗ ᴗ	/ ᴗ ᴗ	Couplet 1
Line 2	/ ᴗ ᴗ	/ ᴗ	
Line 3	/ ᴗ ᴗ	/ ᴗ ᴗ	Couplet 2
Line 4	/ ᴗ ᴗ	/ ᴗ	

The quatrain can be seen to consist of two metrically identical couplets. In the trochaic metre, each line contains two dipodia or cola separated by a caesura. There is enjambement across lines and line-end rhymes are exceptional. The caesura cannot fall in the middle of a word, which means that words longer than four syllables cannot be used. The caesura of the shorter dactylic line is not so strong, so that five-syllable words may be encountered (see Vīķis-Freibergs, 1981, for further background information on the dainas).

In some sense, the couplet, rather than the quatrain, constitutes the most basic metric building block of the daina. It is also the unit of text carried by one repetition of the melody. However, it is the quatrain which constitutes a semantic whole, presenting one unified statement or idea. The metric parallelism of the two couplets is reiterated at the morphological syntactic and semantic levels. Representative types of this multiplicity of complex correspondences have been recently analysed by Vīķis-Freibergs (1983). Most typically, the first half of a quatrain presents an image from nature, followed by a metaphorical parallel from culture, but the two couplets may also represent a question and an answer, a general statement followed by a particular example, etc. (cf. Bičolis, 1934, for an inventory of the various possible relationships).

POETICS AND STYLE

The dainas are characterized by a highly stylized, concentrated form of expression, which follows certain discernible principles (cf. Vīķis-Freibergs, (1983), but is exceedingly difficult to render in translation. Texts which are strikingly beautiful and moving in Latvian may sound flat, even silly, when rendered into another language. Because Latvian is a highly inflected language, word order is very free and many words may be understood as implicit without having to be spelled out, as in English. Readers of English translations of the dainas should therefore bear in mind that they are getting a reflection of the content, but not of the form of the originals.

GENERAL METHOD

Since texts from an oral tradition are characterized by the frequent repetition of stereotyped elements, we have used repetition as an empirically defined phenomenon to determine the nature and size of functionally meaningful units in our corpus. Thus, searching for strings of identically repeated words of increasing string sizes reveals the size of the functional units which form the repertoire of traditional stereotypes. An exhaustive analysis of a smaller thematic sub-corpus (Vīķis-Freibergs and Freibergs, 1978) had shown these functional units in the dainas to be the colon, line, couplet and quatrain, thus reflecting the division of the metrical structure. Longer, thematic or narrative modules are also found in the longer songs. Since the smaller units are not embedded in the larger ones and are relatively independent of them, the corpus of texts as a whole may be considered as a hierarchically ordered system, built up of modular interchangeable units at each level of analysis..

For retrieving text units of any given size (e.g., lines, couplets, etc.) we have developed a collection of reference materials which are simply listings of all exemplars of the unit, listed in alphabetical order and accompanied by their frequency of occurrence. This allows one to see at a glance clusters of lines, for instance, that are identical or even closely similar, as well as indicating the prevalence of a given formulaic element in the corpus. The reference number of the song in which the unit appears may be programmed to appear next to it in the print-out, or obtained by referring to a separate concordance. The full text of any required song can be either obtained in a print-out or projected on a video-screen terminal. Naturally it can also be readily looked up in the printed sources, thus gaining access (where needed) to all the minor subvariants which have not been transcribed into the computerized corpus.

DEFINITIONS OF FORMULAE

The original and much-quoted definition of a formula (Parry, 1930) is 'A group of words which is regularly employed under the same metrical conditions to express a given essential idea'. This brief definition is sufficiently ambiguous to have occasioned a wide variety of different, sometimes conflicting interpretations (cf. the review by Rogers, 1966). In an attempt to make the concept of formula more operational, Vīķis-Freibergs and Freibergs (1978) have proposed to distinguish three quite different types of formulae. The simplest to define are syntagmatic formulae, which refer to any syntagmatic string of words occurring at least twice in any given corpus. To comply with Parry's idea of a formula, the repeated strings must fit into the same metric slots within a line of verse. The repetitions should be, strictly speaking, exactly identical. Where minor variations are accepted, these should be explicitly specified (for instance, one may decide to accept all inflected forms of a word as being equivalent). More complex is the notion of a paradigmatic formula, which is defined as a set of syntactically identical phrases in which one or several members of the string can be substituted for in a paradigmatic manner. Typically, in a paradigmatic formula, some members of the string will remain constant, which others suffer substitution. The paradigmatic substitution is based on similarity within a semantic class or along some definable dimension (e.g., substituting the name of one tree for another, the word 'big' instead of 'small' etc.). Finally there is a type of formula in which two expressions may not have even one word in common, but seem to have been generated according to some discernible syntactical pattern and in which paradigmatically equivalent members of the string tend to belong to some identifiable semantic category.

ILLUSTRATIVE EXAMPLES OF FORMULAIC SYSTEMS

In order to show how formulaic elements function in Latvian folk poetry, some illustrative examples are here analysed in detail. This is on the assumption that the structural principles thus derived will be representative of the whole daina tradition.

The 'Rosy cheeks, blue eyes' Formulaic System

Let us take, as a convenient point of departure, a syntagmatic formula occurring four times in our corpus, the line *Sārti vaigi, zilas acis*, 'Rosy cheeks, blue eyes'. The first thing one notices in the alphabetic line print-out is that the same formula crops up yet another three times, but with the two elements in reverse order: 'Blue eyes, rosy cheeks'. Since metrically each of these word pairs forms a colon, it would appear that this formulaic line is actually constructed out of the agglutination of two one-colon formulae, the order of these being freely reversible.

In addition to these seven lines composed of four identical words in two different word orders, the corpus contains a series of related lines in which one or another of the words has suffered a paradigmatic replacement. Thus, in place of the word 'rosy' (*sārti* , adjective, masculine, plural), we find in two instances the phonetically and semantically similar 'red' (*sarkan'* abbreviated form of *sarkani* , adjective, masculine, plural), once in each of the two colon orders (C1, C2 and C2, C1). Similarily, there are nine lines in which some other colour than blue is substituted for it (*brūnas* 'brown', *melnas* 'black', *rudas* 'reddish brown', *raibas* 'mottled'). This line cluster thus forms a paradigmatic formula which may be summarized as follows:

(ROSY/RED) Cheeks, (X_{colour}) EYES

or

(X_{colour}) EYES, (ROSY/RED) CHEEKS

The frequency distribution of the different realizations of this formula in the corpus are presented in Table 1.

In one single instance we find the line 'Wide eyes, rosy cheeks' (*platas acis*). In this case it is apparent that the singer has broadened the range of substitutable elements in the formulaic colon (X_{colour}) EYES by changing it to a new formula: $(X_{\text{qualifier}})$ EYES.

One question that might be raised at this point is whether the order of formulaic colons making up a line is entirely random and arbitrary or whether it is regulated and lawful. One binary dimension in the content of these songs which might conceivably be linked to colon order is the sex of the individual to whom these qualities are attributed.

Fitting the cluster of eighteen lines into the appropriate contingency table we find that, indeed, the formula 'Cheeks, eyes' is twice as frequent when applied to a girl than when applied to a young man. The reverse form of the formula, 'Eyes, cheeks', which occurs only half as often, is distributed equally across the sexes. The actual frequency distribution may be shown in a contingency table as follows:

	BOY	GIRL	TOTAL
Eyes, cheeks	3	3	6
Cheeks, eyes	4	8	12

There is thus a tendency for one of the forms to be the preferred one when talking about a girl, but this is not systematic enough to be considered a general rule.

TABLE 1

The 'Rosy cheeks, blue eyes' Formulaic System

COLON 1	COLON 2	FREQUENCY
S̄ARTI VAIGI (Rosy cheeks)	ZILAS ACIS (Blue eyes)	4
SARKAN' VAIGI (Red cheeks)	ZILAS ACIS (Blue eyes)	1
SARKAN' VAIGI (Red cheeks)	BRŪNAS ACIS (Brown eyes)	1
S̄ARTI VAIGI (Rosy cheeks)	BRŪNAS ACIS (Brown eyes)	1
S̄ARTI VAIGI (Rosy cheeks)	MELNAS ACIS (Black eyes)	2
S̄ARTI VAIGI (Rosy cheeks)	RUDAS ACIS (Ruddy eyes)	1
SORKONS VAIGS (Red cheek))	RAIBAS AC'S' (Mottled eyes)	1
ZILAS ACIS (Blue eyes)	SARKAN' VAIGI (Red cheeks)	1
ZILAS ACIS (Blue eyes)	S̄ARTI VAIGI (Rosy cheeks)	3
MELNAS ACIS (Black eyes)	S̄ARTI VAIGI (Rosy cheeks)	1
PLATAS ACIS (Wide eyes)	S̄ARTI VAIGI (Rosy cheeks)	1

An interesting thing about the most frequently occurring version of this formula is that it exhibits a strong degree of phonetic patterning, which is weakened in those versions occurring only once or twice each. Thus, the vowel pattern of the 'Rosy cheeks, blue eyes' line runs as follows:

$$\bar{A} - I\ AI - I,\ I - A\ A - I$$

(where A is pronouned as in the English *far* , I as in *deep*, and AI as in *fire*). As it is, the vowels in ZILAS, 'blue' are an inversion of the A-I pattern found in the other three words. The vowel sounds in the words for other colours of eyes, AI-A, U-A and E-A, represent much further departures and weaken considerably the sense of phonetic unity in the line as a whole.

The frequency of the strongly patterned line suggest that such devices may increase the likelihood that a line will be encoded in memory at the phonetic level, thus increasing the probability of its being repeated in identical form by some other singer who had heard it. The paradigmatic substitutions within the semantic category of eye colours, on the other hand, suggest that a line (or some of its components) may be encoded at a more abstract level of the semantic category. At the moment of decoding this information, so as to re-create the surface structure of the trochaic line, the singer may then choose other members of the category than the one originally heard (so long as they fit the number of available syllables in the metric template).

Given the repetition of a line in several song texts, how will such a stereotyped line be used in context of the quatrain? Let us compare two such texts, the one recorded as an isolated quatrain, the other as the first lines of a very long song.

48623

No tālienes es pazinu	*I can tell at a distance*
Nākot savu īsto māsu:	*That it's my sister who's coming*
Sārti vaigi, zilas acis,	*Rosy cheeks, blue eyes*
Dzelteniem matiņiem.	*/A head of/yellow hair*

33632

Man bij daiļis arājiņis	*My husband (lit. 'ploughman') is handsome*
Par visiem arājiem:	*Above all men:*
Zilas acis, sārti vaigi,	*Blue eyes, rosy cheeks,*
Iedzeltāni matu gali.	*Yellowish tips to his hair.*

We can see from just these two examples that our original syntagmatic formula may be inserted into a larger, tripartite structure, which could be expressed as follows:

ROSY CHEEKS, BLUE EYES, YELLOW HAIR

where the sequence of three colours could serve as a mnemonic aid, but in which the third element, although conceptually identical, is expressed through different surface structures. Note also that the string of stereotyped characteristics is applied to a close family member in both instances ('true sister', i.e., sibling and husband) and that the emotional tone is one of undisguised self-satisfaction that someone emotionally and socially close to the 'lyrical I' is possessed of such physical attributes as apparently are desirable in that society.

Another text, more different on the surface, still shows a recognizable family resemblance at a more abstract level:

43387

Šai ciemā man patika,	*I like this village,*
Šitās ciema zeltenītes:	*The girls of this village:*
Sārti vaigi, zilas acris,	*Rosy cheeks, blue eyes.*
Skaidra zīles valodiņa	*Clear, bird-like* language.*

*Literally: 'tit-like language', which might be misconstrued in English.

The first couplet again introduces the individuals (this time in the plural) to whom the stereotyped attributes are to be ascribed. They are still part of an in-group, albeit a larger one than the family. The reference formula fills the same logical slot in the quatrain, occuping the third line, and again constitutes the first two elements of a tripartite description. The attribute to form the third element in this series, however, is radically different from that used in the preceding examples.

As can be seen from these examples (and numerous similar ones which could be adduced), the degree of similarity between two different texts may be expressed as a function of the levels of processing of the information that they have in common. If the information to be carried in memory is to be encoded at the phonetic and morphological level, verbatim repetitions of identical strings of words will be produced. If the encoding is by semantic categories, then different members of the category can be expected to appear in different variants of the song. And, finally, if the level of encoding is more general still, groups of songs will be created which can be shown to have similarities of structure, yet which are quite distinct from each other in their specifics. Our descriptive approach thus yields results which can be readily compared to those obtained from laboratory studies. The levels of processing implied by the degrees of similarity in our texts have close parallels in those that have been manipulated experimentally, either with isolated words and sentences (notably the two levels of phonemic processing and sentence processing in the 1972 Craik and Lockhart study) or on continuous text (as in Kintsch's work on comprehension and recall of studies e.g., Kintsch, 1975).

The descriptive approach, however, can be extended to encompass considerations which are not so readily revealed in the laboratory setting. Consider again the group of texts containing the formulaic element (X_{colour}) EYES. Sorting these according to their contents reveals a binary division which may be expressed as follows: BLUE EYES versus DARK EYES. Desirable husbands are described as being blue-eyed, rosy cheeked and as having yellow hair, these stereotyped attributes being a metonymic way of expressing both healthy good looks and the preferred phenotype for physical colouring in a person. Dark eyes, on the contrary, are a sure sign of poor husband material, being indicative of a drunkard, a 'drinker of tears' or even a wife-beater. One text also mentions wide eyes as a sign of an evil temper. Including this text in our system would extend the formulaic distinction from BLUE vs DARK to BLUE EYES vs NON-BLUE EYES. A similar binary division between socially desirable and undesirable traits is drawn in the texts referring to women. Blue-eyed girls are seen as physically attractive, with yellow hair, a fine figure, a tiny nose ... and also as socially accomplished: witty and sparkling in their speech or being good singer. A brown-eyed or black-eyed girl, on the contrary is described as *sīva* or *bārga*, which means something like harsh, abrasive, unkind, cruel. Only one text out of the 18 in this group, a longer song (Nr. 26367), mentions brown eyes in a woman as part of a relatively neutral description of her appearance. Blue eyes thus become a symbol for a 'good' person and dark eyes come to symbolize 'badness'.

To sum up, what may be said about the way in which such a formulaic system was used by carriers of the daina tradition? The weight of the tradition is certainly evident and this at every level of structure of the text: phonetic, metric, lexical, syntactic, semantic, symbolical. To understand the symbolic level, the texts must be seen in their broader social setting in which they become the vehicle for expressing the belief systems of the ambient culture. At family feasts and calender festivities (such as the midsummer solstice celebration), a good singer was expected to act as a mouthpiece for religious beliefs, ancient myths, ritual procedures and a wide assortment of generally accepted items of folk wisdom. In spite of all these constraints, however, the tradition is certainly not a body of immutable texts which each singer memorizes and reproduces verbatim. Being the carrier of a folk tradition means being in possession of all the skills and tricks of the trade needed to generate strings of text which fit the myriad internal rules and preferences of the genre and tradition. But the singer still has many degrees of freedom of choice at each structural level

TABLE 2

The XX (Colon 1), ROSY CHEEKS (Colon 2) System

COLON 1	TRANSLATION	FREQUENCY
BALTA MUTE	White mouth (=face)	1
BALTA SEJA	White face	1
DRĪZ BIJ MANI	Soon will be my	2
KUR NU MANI	Where now my	4
NEBŪT MANI	Would not be my	2
NEKĀ MANI	Rather than my	2
NOBĀL MANI	Grow pale my	3
TĀ BĀL MANI	Thus grow pale my	1
TĀ DZELT MANI	Thus grow sallow my	1
PAZŪD MANI	Disappear my	1
SEN BŪT MANI	(They) would have long since	1
ŠOGAD MANI	This year my	1
VAI JŪS MANI	Oh you, my	1
DIŽENS PUISIS	A striking young man	1
JAUNAM PUIŠAM	To a young man	1
SMUKS PUISĪTIS	A handsome young man	2
TEV, PUISĪTI	To you, young man	1
TOV, PUISĪTI	To you, young man	1
KUR PALIKA	Where have gone	2
TUR PALIKA	There have gone	1
MAN PAŠAI	I myself have	1
TĀDI POŠI	Just the same	1
TO MAN DARA	This I get from	1
NI SAULĒ	Nor in the sun	1

of text generation. This, combined with the multiplicity of such levels, helps to explain the wide range of differences which obtain between different texts, even as they exhibit various degrees of similarity at one or the other of the levels. Just like a limited number of syntactic rules do not prevent the generation of an infinite number of different sentences, so the structural exigencies of a folklore tradition do not prevent the generation of a potentially limitless number of acceptable texts, of which the texts actually recorded are but a sample.

The example we have just analysed shows but one miniscule slice of the formulaic complexity in the dainas. Formulaic systems such as the one we have examined may be regrouped into yet larger systems. Consider, as an example, the formulaic colon 'Rosy cheeks'. It may occur as the second half of a line in combination with a wide variety of other expressions than the 'Blue eyes' we have seen. The full range of these expressions is listed in Table 2. The expression itself occurs 25 times in the standard form, nominative case in apposition, once in the instrumental plural ('with rosy cheeks') and three times in the accusative plural. Of the expressions it combines with, six contain some form of the word for 'young man', whereas 19 use the extended formula 'XX my rosy cheeks'.

In addition, we find a whole range of closely related formulaic expressions such as 'red little cheeks', 'with red little cheeks', 'little cheeks of red roses', 'with the rosy cheeks', 'ruddy of face', 'You, young girl (young man), red-cheeked one'... It is clear from these examples that the daina tradition does not place strong constraints on its singers as far as the actual form of an expression is concerned. Quite the contrary, there is a veritable riot of expressions for the same basic idea. The true stereotype here seems to be a conceptual one: the use of 'rosy cheeks' as a metonymic figure of speech for expressing a young person's vitality, youth, good health and good looks. This is an accepted part of the tradition, dear to both singers and audience alike. It is at the level of expressing this idea that the skill of the singer can manifest in the different ways of saying the same thing. The basic concept may also be used in combination with other elements to express something new and creative. How this may be done we turn to briefly in the next section.

THE VERBAL FORMULA AND THE POETIC IMAGE

Let us examine two different texts linked by a common syntagmatic formula in the second line of the stanza:

Saule brida pa mākoni,	*The sun wades through the clouds.*
Es pa ļaužu valodām;	*(And) I, through people's gossip;*
Izbrien saule no mākoņa,	*The sun breaks through the clouds,*
Es no ļaužu valodām	*(And) I - through people's gossip.*

(Nr. 8870)

Gulbis peld pa ūdeni,	*The swan swims through the water*
Es pa ļaužu valodām;	*(And) I - through people's gossip;*
Ni ūdens gulbim lipa,	*The water does not stick to the swan,*
Ni man ļaužu valodiņas.	*Nor to me - people's gossip.*

Although only one line is identical in both these quatrains, their overall structure can be seen to fit into the same formulaic mould. This mould is syntactico-semantic for the first couplet and may be tentatively expressed as follows:

LINE 1: REALM OF NATURE

SUBJECT 1	VERB 1	OBJECT 1
X From Nature	Motion through viscous or obscuring medium	Medium of motion

LINE 2: REALM OF CULTURE

SUBJECT 2	VERB 2	OBJECT 2
'Lyrical I'	(Ellipsis: Same as Verb 1, implicit)	Medium of motion: Metaphorical human analogue of Object 1.

In the second couplet, the correpondences between the two texts are not so evident, and only appear at the more abstract level of poetic imagery. The human element in both cases presents the image of a young girls's reputation emerging unscathed from an onslaught of malicious gossip. This is placed in parallel with a vivid, concrete image from the world of nature: either the brightness of the sun, emerging undimmed from behind a cloud, or the image of a water-bird, emerging dry out of the water.

In the genesis of this type of related songs, the concerns and preoccupations of the 'Lyrical I', conditioned by local customs, living conditions, etc., could be seen as the motivating moment in the creation of the quatrain. (Here the vulnerability of a young girl's reputation and the potential harm malicious comments from neighbours might cause to her marriage prospects.) With this as a starting point, the folk singers could generate a series of conceptually related parallel images from nature, which would serve as a sort of poetical exorcism to the emotional concerns in question. (Here images emphasizing the maintaining of integrity under conditions which appear to threaten it).

Frameworks such as these would appear to leave much more scope to the singers for introducing novel images and comparisons into the traditional repertoire. It would be quite possible, for example, for a singer to hear a poetically doubtful or mediocre image and use the underlying framework to produce a far better one. Similarily, a mediocre singer might debase a poetically powerful image by adopting it in an unskilled way.

Other groups of songs suggest the reverse pathway for text generation, in which a constant general image from the realm of nature can serve as the starting point for generating a series of parallel images from the realm of culture. One of the more productive of such generative systems in the dainas is the broad metaphorical parallel between the sun's course in the sky (whether diurnal or annual) and the course of a human life. Reflecting a sense of intimate correspondence between the macrocosm and the microcosm, it it an integral part of the ancient Latvian philosophy of life, and all singers would have been acquainted with it from earliest childhood. But this does not mean that a singer had no choice but to repeat those poetic images already in the tradition. On the contrary, knowledge of the framework could be used to generate new, original images which would fit into the archetypal pattern. This would be done by reducing the overall general parallel to an intermediary conceptual level, which, in turn, would be expressed through more specific concrete imagery, as in the following examples:

23077

Spožа saule uzlekdama,	*Bright was the sun on rising,*
Ne tik spožа tecēdama;	*Not so bright throughout its course;*
Mīļš tautietis precēdams,	*Loving was my husband on marrying,*
Ne tik mīļš dzīvodams.	*Not so loving throughout our life.*

6556

Kam, saulīte, spodra leci,	*Why, oh sun, did you rise so brightly*
Kad tik spodra netecēji?	*If as brightly you would not shine on?*
Kam, meitiņa, skaista augi,	*Why, my sister, did you grow up so lovely,*
Kad ar godu nedzīvoji?	*If with honour you could not live on?*

The common propositional content of the two examples quoted is the idea of early promise not fulfilled, of something originally bright and attractive which subsequently becomes blighted. At the next step of concretization, this intermediary level image can then be applied to a whole series of analogous human problems: an initially loving husband becoming indifferent or hostile over the years, a brilliant young girl losing her honour, etc., etc.

Our last set of examples was chosen to show traditional stereotypy reduced to a mimimum, with one single concrete image as the common element in songs otherwise showing great latitude for different topics and treatments. The common image used is that of sweat and tears placed in parallel through the common sensory property of being drops of liquid. This image is then focused on in the text, making it a metonymic expression of hardship and sorrow. In the first quatrain, the 'I' is a woman (as indicated in the original by grammatical suffixes) and it is sung to a tune masterful in its sadness and simplicity:

Ai tu, manu grūtu mūžu,	*Life of mine, life of hardship,*
Kā es tevis nodzīvoš?	*How am I to live you through?*
Sviedrus slauku tecēdema,	*I wipe sweat from my brow when moving,*
Asariņas stāvēdam'.	*I wipe tears from my eyes when I'm still.*

The first couplet has an unusually free construction, with a continuous sentence running through both lines. The second couplet follows the more traditional parallel construction, with ellipsis of the verb in the last line. Within the condensed and laconic scope of the fourteen words of the original, this text manages to convey a remarkable sense of physical hardship, exploitation and despair.

The next example keeps the image of sweat and tears placed in parallel, but the attribution and context is totally different:

Augsti kalni, karsta saule	*High the hills, hot the sun*
Smagi kunga vezumiņi;	*Heavy the loads of the master;*
Kumeļam sviedri lija,	*Sweat pours from my horse,*
Man birst gaužas asariņ's	*Bitter tears run down my cheeks.*

This daina refers to a specific historical period when peasants were required to use their own horse and wagon to convey a fixed number of loads per year to Riga for their landlord. The landlords would typically overload the wagons, often ruining the peasant's only horse for subsequent labour in his own fields and thus endangering the survival of his family.

While in the first example the sweat and tears were attributed to the same person, thus emphasizing the extent of her misery, the second example broadens the story-telling scope of the quatrain by splitting the redundancy in the parallel. It is the horse that is sweating while the man cries tears of shame, despair and frustration at seeing it pine away under his very eyes. The folk poet does not explicitly have to state what everyone knows in his culture, which is that the horse, since most ancient times, has been considered a noble animal, that mistreating a horse is a most heinous offence and that a well-fed, prancing horse is the ultimate expression of a man's pride and manhood. The simple images chosen by the folk poet thus act as stimuli evoking a whole series of associations of ideas, relying for this on the common background of singer and audience, in what I have called the centrifugal technique of evocation in the dainas (Vīķis-Freibergs, 1983). This is why the text can suggest, in a mere fourteen words, a sense of psychological humiliation, of emasculation, in addition to the more explicit material hardship and social despair, and gives this brief lyrical quatrain an impact that is almost epic in its scope. Interestingly enough, the first line of this daina is strongly reminiscent of the first line in several *laisses* of the mediaeval French epic *Chanson de Roland:*

Halt sunt li pui e li val tenebrus	*High are the mountains and dark the valleys*

The creative possibilities of the same conventional image are extended even further in our very last example, in which only the tears remain as a common element, now placed in parallel with something entirely different. This is a very popular orphan song, also possessed of several hauntingly beautiful melodies. It is quoted here in full so as to give a better idea of the insertion of a specific image in the broader composition of a song:

I was so young, I did not see
Where my mother was buried.
Now I found her resting place
Out yonder in the pasture.
Oh rise, dear mother from your grave,
And I will lift the green-sward.
I'll tell you through my bitter tears
Of my step-mother's cruel treatment:
She sends me to the apple tree
For branches as rods for beating:
I lean against the apple tree
As if it were my mother;
White blossoms fall from the apple tree,
Bitter tears fall from my eyes.

The parallel between tear drops and falling apple blossoms is linked to the parallel between the dead mother and the apple tree, established in the preceding couplet. As background information, it would have been common knowledge to those hearing this song that fine birch branches are what is normally used for spanking children - they hurt, but do not damage. Apple-tree branches are hard and knobbley and would be likely to produce bruises.

Furthermore, needlessly cutting the branches of a fruit tree would be considered as something akin to vandalism in this culture. The earlier context of the song thus establishes the step-mother as acting against 'natural law' not just in her family relationships, but in the widest sense of that term. Against this background, the orphan's seeking solace from a mute, immobile tree is again a metonymic way of condensing the whole misery of her life into one vivid, concrete image. She sees a sympathetic response in the tree's shredding of its blossoms - what is known in poetry as the pathetic fallacy - and the image takes on true pathos by showing graphically that this child has nowhere else to turn for comfort. This song, compared to the two preceding examples shows the broad scope for individual creativity available to the folk poet, even while using certain fixed elements which are drawn from the tradition.

CONCLUSIONS

In evaluating the creativity of traditional singers, one must be careful to do so in the social context within which it flourished, and avoid judging it by the standards of modern written literature. The folk poet differs from the modern poet in several ways. First, she or he had a functional role to play in everyday occurrences and did not cater to a selected elite of the population. In this role, they were expected to exhibit a high degree of skill in performance, but there were no demands from society that they be original or necessarily different from other singers. Second, the skills the poet was expected to acquire were highly technical ones, allowing them to function within a rigorously defined metrical and stylistic framework. This, of course, is something that modern poetry has turned its back on. The folk poet was thus expected to acquire something like a poetic metalanguage, a process probably not unlike that of learning a second language. Indeed, certain insights derived from a study of folk traditions might be usefully applied to a better understanding of the processes of foreign language acquisition. The concept of formulaicity, especially, is closely analoguous to that of idiomatic expressions and turns of phrase which which must be mastered if one is going to sound like a native speaker of a tongue. Finally, the traditional poet of the Latvian dainas, although using the poetic convention of the 'lyrical I', is much more intent on expressing folk wisdom and beliefs about various aspects of the human condition than on giving vent to any personalized, individually subjective feelings. The folk poet thus functions within a very regulated and partially redundant system which directs poetic expression in predetermined, well-worn channels. This does not mean, however, that the folk singer has no other choice than to memorize and repeat songs heard from others. This certainly happens, and forms part of the training of a singer, but it need not stop there. The structure of the tradition is open-ended enough so that the mature singer who has mastered the tradition may, if they have enough talent, introduce entirely new elements into the common repertoire of ideas, images and expressions.

FOOTNOTES

1. The work reported in this chapter is part of a broader research programme which is the object of a book on the Structure of the Latvian Dainas. The support of grants from the Social Science and Humanities Research Council of Canada (Grant No. 410-81-0319 as well as earlier ones) is hereby most gratefully acknowledged.

2. The expression of 'oral literature' has received the sanction of usage

in spite of what purists would consider an inner contradiction of terms In expressions like 'the scientific literature', the term has kept the etymological meaning of something conveyed through letters - the written word. But if 'literature' is used in the sense of *belles lettres*, there is no reason not to distinguish written artistic productions from those that are transmitted by word of mouth.

REFERENCES

Bērziņš, L. (1959) Ievads latviešu tautas dzejā. (Introduction to Latvian folk poetry) Chicago, Illinois: Baltu Filologu Kopa.

Bērziņš, V., Freibergs, I.F., Konrāde, K., Strazds, G. and Vīķe-Freiberga, V. (1982). The computer-accessible corpus of Latvian folk songs (M.I.T., Boston and Université de Montreal). A transcription of A. Švābe, K. Straubergs and E. Hauzenberga-Šturma (Eds.), Latviešu tautas dziesmas (Imanta, Copenhagem, 1952-1956). 12 Volumes.

Bičolis, J. (1933). Par latviešu tautas dziesmu struktūru (On the structure of the Latvian folk-songs). Filologu biedrības raksti, 13, 152-156.

Craik, F.I.M. and Lockhart, R.S. (1972). Levels of processing: A framework for memory research. Journal of Verbal Learning and Verbal Behavior, 11, 671-684.

Finnegan, R. (1976). What is oral literature anyway? Comments in the light of some African and other comparative material. In: B.A. Stolz and R.S. Shannon (Eds.), Oral Literature and the Formula. Ann Arbor, Michigan: University of Michigan.

Hebb, D.O. (1973). Invited address at the 81st Annual Convention of the American Psychological Association.

Kintsch, W. (1975). Memory representations of text. In: R.L. Solso (Ed.), Information Processing and Cognition. Hillsdale, New Jersey: Lawrence Erlbaum.

Lord, A.B. 91964). The Singer of Tales. Cambridge, Massachusetts: Harvard University Press.

Lord, A.B. (1965). Yugoslav epic folk poetry. In: A. Dundes (Ed.), The Study of Folklore. Englewood Cliffs: Prentice-Hall.

Lord, A.B. (1976). Response to R. Finnegan's paper. In: B.A. Stolz amd R.S. Shannon (Eds.), Oral Literature and the Formula. Ann Arbor, Michigan: University of Michigan.

Nagler, M.N. (1974). Spontaneity and Tradition: A Study in the Oral Art of Homer. Berkeley, California: University of California Press.

Parry, M. (1930). Studies in the epic technique of oral versemaking: I. Homer and the Homeric style. Harvard Studies in Classical Philology, 41, 73-147.

Parry, M. (1932). Studies in the epic technique of oral versemaking: II. The Homeric language as the language of poetry. Harvard Studies in Classical Philology, 43, 1-50.

Rogers, H.L. (1966). The crypto-psychological character of the oral formula. English Studies, 47, 89-102.

Saussure, F. de (1916). Cours de linguistique générale. (Payot, Paris, 1967).

Skinner, B.F. (1959). Verbal Behavior. New York: Appleton-Century-Crofts.

Wundt, W. (1900-1920). Völkerpsychologie: Eine Untersuchung der Entwicklungsgesetze von Sprache, Mythus und Sitte. 10 Volumes. Leipzig: Wilhelm Englemann.

Vīķis-Freibergs, V. (1983). The poetic imagination of the Latvian dainas. Mosaic: A Journal for the Comparative Study of Literature, 6, 209-221.

Vīķis-Freibergs, V. (1981). Daina, Latvian. In: H.B. Weber (Ed.), The Modern Encyclopedia of Russian and Soviet Literatures. Academic International Press. Volume 5. Pp. 41-49.

Vīķis-Freibergs, V. (1982). Expressing the inexpressible and measuring the incommensurable: On language, literature and psychology. Canadian Psychology, 23, 1-10.

Vīķis-Freibergs, V. (1983). The logical structure of the Latvian dainas. Paper presented to the Language and Folklore Sector of the Academy of Sciences of Soviet Latvia, Riga.

Vīķis-Freibergs, V. and Freibergs, I. (1978). Formulaic analysis of the computer-accessible corpus of Latvian Sun-Songs. Computers and the Humanities, 12, 329-339.

Cognitive Processes in the Perception of Art
W.R. Crozier and A.J. Chapman (editors)
© Elsevier Science Publishers B.V. (North-Holland), 1984

COGNITIVE PROCESSES IN IMPROVISATION

Jeff Pressing

La Trobe University

To the extent that we are unpredictable, we improvise. Everything else is repeating ourselves or following orders. Improvisation is thus central to the formation of new ideas in all areas of human endeavour. Its importance experientially rests with its magical and self-liberating qualities. Its importance scientifically is that it presents us with the clearest, least-edited version of how we think, encoded in behaviour. From this one might well imagine that improvisation would be a phenomenon much-studied by psychologists. Yet this is emphatically not the case. A search through 'Psychological Abstracts' reveals a nearly complete absence of research, even in areas, such as creativity research and artificial intelligence, of presumably direct relevance.

There seem to be methodological problems right from the start. For example, since no action can be completely free of the effects of previous training, how does one reliably distinguish learned from improvised behaviour? How can one construct a useful model (one that makes testable predictions) to describe that which is by definition unpredictable? Experienced improvisers most commonly operate within highly specialized artistic domains - how will the non-specialist psychologist assess the results of such improvisations when the specialists may disagree among themselves? Furthermore, the fact that improvisation involves substantial body movement makes psychological measurements (e.g., EEG, GSR, evoked potentials) a highly dubious approach due to the production of muscular artifacts.

THE ARTISTIC PERSPECTIVE

On what can we then base a study of improvised behaviour? The single largest source of information is unquestionably the activities of improvising artists. The primary materials - the improvised artistic products - have been and are being recorded at this very moment on vast numbers of audio and video recording tapes. There is no shortage of data. Furthermore, improvising performers in general have access, by introspection, proprioception and self-observation, to additional information about such issues as learning, training, the usefulness of imagery, muscular coordination, and cognitive processing. The result of this is that there exists a large literature on improvisation in the arts, consisting mainly of: (a) descriptions by artists of their own improvisation processes; (b) analyses (e.g., by musicologists) of the recorded improvisations of artists; and (c) prescriptive teaching manuals written by artists. The first part of this chapter therefore consists of an analysis of this extensive body of writings which in Western culture dates back at least to the ninth century A.D.

This literature is very unevenly distributed over the various artistic disciplines, and with good reason. For an additional sense of the word improvisation is that it concerns actions whose effects are indelible. If erasing, painting over, or non-real-time editing exist, improvisation does not. Hence the visual arts are normally excluded, though there are always exceptions, such as the Japanese painting form that requires that the brush never leaves the paper until the painting is finished.

It is among the time-based arts, namely music, dance, theatre and mime that we find the greatest literature. From a survey of this material, certain facts emerge quite consistently, and allow the formulation of plausible cognitive models for improvisation. What is particularly striking is the similarity of general cognitive processes employed in many different areas of endeavour, when one penetrates beyond the specific language and traditions of each artistic discipline.

While no such cognitive overview has been made by any previous author, the extraction of field-specific improvisational principles has been clearly formulated in several areas, most notably in the pioneering works of Ferand (1938, 1961), which concern pre-1900 European music. Also noteworthy for their cognitive implications are the recent works by Bailey (1980) which contain perceptive interviews and commentary on a number of musical traditions, the thesis by Sperber (1975) which examines improvisation in contemporary music, dance and theatre, Duke's (1973) comparison of eighteenth and twentieth century musical improvisation teaching methods, Mettler's (1960) extensive prescriptive text on modern dance, and articles by Nettl (1974) and Hood (1975) on non-Western musics. A study of these and other references leads to the following conclusions about time-embedded art forms: (1) There is a continuum of possibilities between the extreme hypothetical limits of 'pure' improvisation and 'pure' composition. These limits are never obtained in live performance because no improviser (even in 'free' improvisation) can avoid the use of previously learned material, and no re-creative performer can avoid small variations specific to each occasion.

The very approximate placement of a number of traditions along the composition-improvisation axis is indicated in the diagram below.

(2) Central to improvisation is the notion of the 'referent'. The referent is an underlying formal scheme or guiding image specific to a given piece, used by the improviser to facilitate the generation and editing of improvised behaviour on an intermediate time scale. The generation of behaviour on a fast time scale is primarily determined by previous training and is not very piece-specific. If no referent is present, or if it is devised in real-time, we speak of 'free' or 'absolute' improvisation. This is much rarer than referent-guided, or 'relative' improvisation.

Much of the variety of improvisation comes from the many different types of referent which may be used, and the many kinds of relationships the improviser may choose to set up between the referent and the sounds, movement, words, etc., that constitute the improvised behaviour. For example, the referent may be a musical theme, a motive, a mood, a picture, an emotion, a structure in space or time, a guiding visual image, a physical process, a story, an attribute, a movement quality, a poem, a social situation, an animal - virtually any coherent image which allows the improviser a sense of engagement and continuity. In contemporary improvisation practice just about anything is possible. But, historically, referents most commonly take the following forms for the indicated fields:

TYPICAL REFERENTS

Music : musical structures or motives, mood.
Dance: music, kinetic or structural images, movement qualities, stories, emotions.
Drama: social situations, stories, emotions.

The referent typically functions either as a source for material, which is then repeated, transformed, varied or developed, or as a focus for the production and organization of material from other sources.

FIGURE 1

Heuristic classification of selected artistic traditions on the basis of improvisation content.

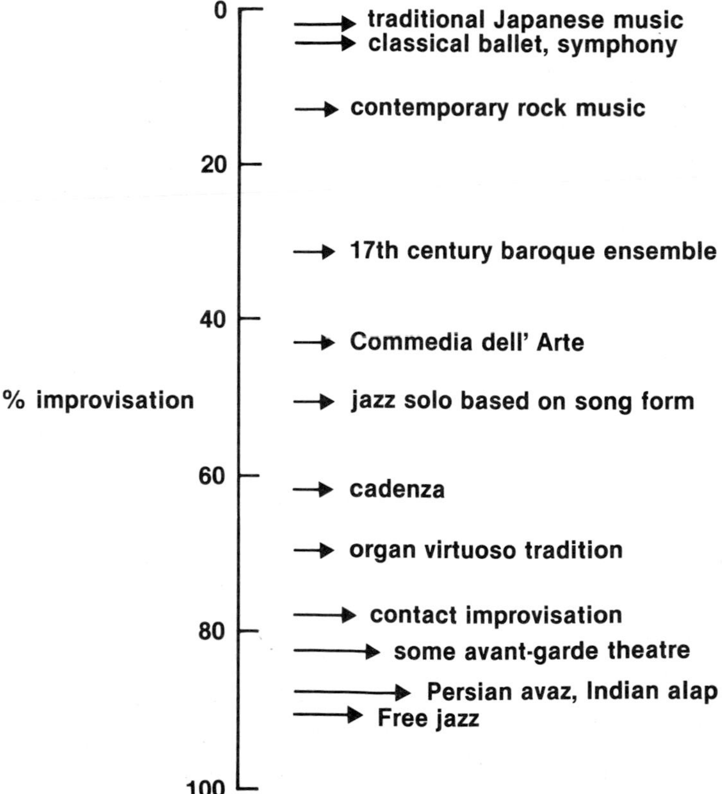

Those referents which have an associated time dimension (e.g., a story or a chord progression) also serve a place-keeping function, which is particularly useful in co-ordinating ensemble improvisation. These may be called 'in-time' referents, as distinguished from 'out-of-time' referents. A further distinction in the class of in-time referents is between those that contain precise durational information (e.g., musical rhythm or clock-measured cueing)and those that merely consist of a specified sequence of events or a process that does not have a well-defined time scale (e.g., a story or a sequence of crawling movements). The first group of such in-time referents requires the construction of an internal cognitive clock, which is not necessary in the second situation. These may be termed 'clocked' and 'sequenced' in-time referents respectively.

The relationship between improvised behaviour and referent is variable. It may be imitative, metaphoric, allegorical, antagonistic, canonic, contrapuntal, variational or independent, just to mention a few possibilities; and the time scale for behavioural response may vary from very short to long. In strict improvisation contexts compatability between referent and behaviour is continuous, in freer contexts the expressive continuity of the improvised material may cause temporary abandonment of the referent.

To see these distinctions more clearly, we look at a variety of historical examples of improvisational practice. Most examples are musical, as this is the field with the greatest literature and most extensive history.

(a) The Ornamented Melody

Here a given melody is used as referent, and some aspects of it are changed while others essential to the preservation of its identity are maintained. Stereotyped ornamentation formulae typically develop, alongside free embellishment. This is found in virtually all cultures and all histroical epochs.

(b) The 'Melody Type'

This very ancient improvisation style lies at the heart of many Oriental and Middle Eastern music traditions, such as the Indian 'raga', the Arabic 'magam' and the Persian 'dastgah'. Its influence extends also to early Western 'chant', ancient Greek 'tonoi', many traditional Jewish melodies, and the Byzantine 'echoi'. These musics are basically monophonic (consisting of one melodic line) and the loosely in-time referent is in the first instance a repertoire of melodic motives arranged in different registers. Yet beside these large-scale motives, standard ornamentation formulae are employed, which may be transposed at will. Furthermore, each different tone contained in the melody type of a given piece has a specific function - one is a final tone, one is a reciting tone, another is a characteristic highest note, and so forth. The result is a powerful system of melodic improvisation.

(c) The Thoroughbass

This technique originated about 1600 in baroque chamber ensembles and the in-time referent consists of a composed bass line above which one or more players improvise chords and counterlines. The improvisation was often further restricted by the addition of figures above the bass notes, indicating the permissible chord types, producing a figured bass.

(d) Theme and Variations Form

Very common in many styles, from sixteenth century England to tonal jazz. The referent is in-time and may consist of the chord progression, song melody, and distinctive rhythmic features. In short, all the developmental possibilities of the theme may be exploited.

(e) 'Free' Jazz

A twentieth century phenomenon beginning in the 1940's. Normally no referent, although sometimes a very loosely structured out-of-time one is used, not based on traditional tonal musical structures. The task of such improvisers often involves finding a shared context. To this end each experienced free jazz performer creates (by practice) a personal repertoire of usable musical gestures and procedures which may be adapted to fit into almost any situation.

(f) Silent Film Accompanists

Before audio-visual technology was able to cope with the synchronization of music and film, theatre organists (either solo, or as leaders of groups of musicians) had to improvise accompaniment to all silent films. They used every conceivable Western musical style and the in-time referent was generally considered to be the 'mood' and story line of the film (Hanlon, 1975).

(g) Commedia Dell' Arte

This Italian improvised theatre form flourished from the sixteenth to eighteenth centuries throughout Europe. It is a comedy based upon a standard cast of characters and the barest outline of a plot, which serves as the referent for the improvised dialogue. For example, Pantalone is a doddering elderly parent or guardian of the heroine; Columbina is the maid of the heroine who connives with her to arrange meetings for the two central lovers; the Harlequin is a jester who speaks the truth in parables; and so forth.

(h) Contemporary Theatre

Twentieth century theatre has seen the wide scale use of improvisation in training and teaching, and somewhat less frequently, in performance. A few important names are those of Constantin Stanislavski, Charles Dullin, Peter Brook and Jerzy Grotowski. For example, Grotowski's Actor's Training includes bird and kangaroo improvisations, foot and mime exercises, imitation of natural sounds with the voice, expression of conflicting emotions in different parts of the body, and the cultivation of an ability to exploit errors - a widely mentioned feature of improvisation. His techniques are designed not to promote the accumulation of skills but the eradication of expressive blocks (Grotowski, 1968).

(i) Ballet and Much Modern Dance

Here music is the common in-time referent, and the amount of improvisation varies from very little in ballet to considerable in some modern dance. Often the music-dance relation is fairly imitative, with direct movement responses on the basis of musical rhythm, pitch contour, timbre, harmony, dynamics, activity level and mood. For example, fast tempi usually give rise to quick movements. The dance-referent relation may also be much more indirect or abstract.

(j) Some Contemporary Dance (e.g., Martha Graham; Mary Wigman; Alwin Nikolais; Anna Halprin; Barbara Mettler - See Mettler, 1960.)

Music is no longer automatically the referent. The referent may be, for example, a physical object - with focus either in its structure or associations: for example, box, arch, church, crossbow, water, earth, cloud, frog, insect, lathe, sunrise, fire. It may also be based on properties or qualities, such as permanent, buoyant, lazy, cautious, peaceful, flippant, rough: or on abstractions like gravity, force, energy, beauty, flow, continuity. Very common are referents based upon specific movement qualities such as the following verbs: wriggle, sway, curl, slouch, sprint, burrow, jog, burst, congeal, effervesce, boil, pluck, fling, grope, trample, caress, linger, repulse, wither, hesitate. And, finally, emotions are used: anger, love, hate, indifference, etc. This list is far from exhaustive and except for the case of specific movement qualities these are out-of-time referents.

(k) Contact Improvisation

This is an improvised ensemble dance form that became popular in the United States in the 1970's. It is a fairly free form, as the single agreed-upon constraint (a token referent) is that each dancer must at all times remain in physical contact with (at least one of) the other dancers. The journal 'Contact Quarterly' is devoted to this form.

Most commonly the referent is stated in some form by performers alongside the improvised material. However, the situation is variable and in other cases (e.g., h,j, above) the referent may be imperceptible.

(3) On a faster time scale than changes in the typical in-time referent, intact behaviour-encoded ideas, motives or 'seeds' are produced and manipulated by the performer. These 'seeds' come from the referent, the performer's memory, or are freshly created. Those originating from the performer's memory may be subdivided into those he or she has personally created, and those that are copies of the work of others - that is, innovative or imitative seeds, respectively. The aesthetic evaluation in many traditions favours innovative seeds, but this is by no means always so.

(4) All referent-guided improvisation systems, and even some free ones, stand in clear relation to a parallel repertory of compositions. That is, each such improvisation tradition has an associated group of devices used for development of ideas or seeds and those devices are in general very similar to those of the allied compositional practices. (In fact, early Christian music and that of many traditional non-Western cultures fail to make any distinction between composition and improvisation). These developmental devices may be consciously learned by training but more typically are inferred by playing repertoire and the imitation of teachers. One common teaching system is always to present several versions of each new concept or movement sequence, so that the student intrinsically thinks of variation and a certain controlled fuzziness.

The development of seeds normally is based on repetition, juxtaposition and variation, wherein some aspects of the seed are held fixed while others change. This has been most clearly documented in the case of music since many (ethno) musicologists (e.g., Jones, 1959; Locke, 1979; Nettl and Reddle, 1974; Owens, 1974) have made detailed transcriptions of improvised music from around the world. Subsequent analysis is useful in inferring cognitive processes, but this is only reliable in conjunction with corroborating information, such as discussion with the performers. The problem otherwise may be likened to trying to infer the details of the machinery in a factory by looking at the finished products alone.

(5) The generation of seeds is an associative process. That is, each new seed generated will almost always be the result of combining previously learned gestures, movement patterns or concepts in a novel relationship or context. The conservatism of this process derives largely from the limited resources of cognitive processing available for real-time composition. But all or nearly all improvisation traditions also proclaim the notion that completely new and unprecedented seed ideas sometimes spontaneously occur. The origin of such material is often ascribed to God, mysterious higher forces, or undefined transpersonal powers.

Another factor limiting the kinds of seeds or improvised behaviour the performer will present is the goal of the occasion. A professional performer in a concert situation will edit or filter his or her behaviour much more stringently than someone doodling at the piano at home. Hence we may distinguish the product orientation of an improviser whose primary goal may be pleasure, therapy, education, artistic discovery or spiritual development. The most common aesthetic stance of the professional improviser is a balance between adherence to structure and self-expression, whereas the most common goal is to make appropriate music/movement/words that support the sense of occasion.

(6) As a general rule, the larger the performing ensemble, the more restricted the scope for successful improvisation, and the more necessary a detailed referent to achieve overall coherence. That is, the referent is more likely to include information about relationships between improvisers. A soloist. either alone, or surrounded by fixed elements, is accorded the greatest latitude of action. An ensemble without agreed-upon common referent (e.g., free music ensemble) frequently results in a presentation of co-existing rather than inter-relating streams.

This then is the information provided by artists and analysis in the arts, on improvisation.

THE PSYCHOLOGICAL PERSPECTIVE

The next step is to interpret the above conclusions on the basis of existing research in psychology. The most relevant areas appear to be skilled performance, attention and memory, which are discussed below. Before that I give an abbreviated general description of improvisational cognitive process, couched in psychological language. It is convenient to use the language of a specific field, in this case music. With some appropriate modifications the following descriptions may also be applied to dance, theatre, etc.

Let us consider the case of the instrumental improviser. Motivation to improvise is an obvious pre-requisite. Given this, the improviser awaits some impulse to begin, which may come from the surroundings, or may be internally generated. This results in the production of some seed or idea appropriate to the performance context, along with some idea of how the idea might be developed. The idea is the result of the player's interaction with the instrument and the performing context, and has meaning on at least three

FIGURE 2 Major factors influencing the production of improvised musical behaviour.

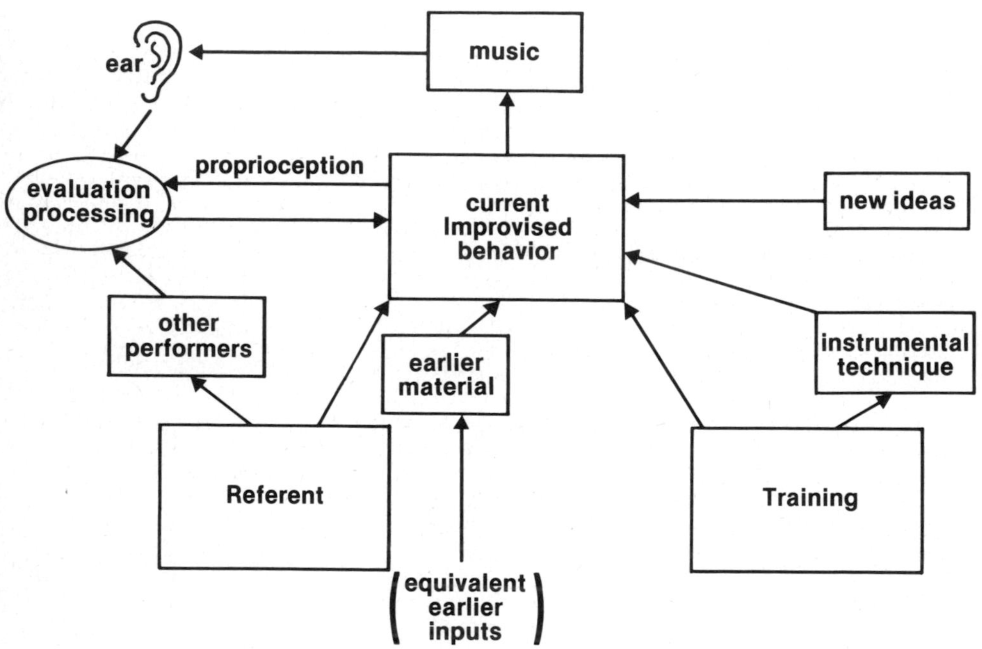

levels of structure - as a musical structure, as an acoustic stimulus and as a pattern of muscular movement. The player may attend to any of these levels of meaning (and there may well be others, such as an associated emotion or movement metaphor) with the aim of development or continuity. Attention is also periodically directed to the referent and sounds produced by other musicians. The development of this seed and the introduction of new ideas is continually modified by the associated cognitive strategies employed, the sounds being produced and the direct proprioceptive feedback. The primary feedback link is, however, the evaluation of musical stability by some sort of evaluation processor. This judgment of suitability is coloured by goals, previous training, what has gone before, and the sounds produced by other musicians. The major factors influencing the production of improvised behaviour are indicated in Figure 2. The origins of all actions are considered to be long-term memory (referent, training, some earlier material), short-term memory (some earlier material) and the ever-mysterious 'new ideas'.

It is possible to view the course of the improvisation as a succession of creative impulses mapped onto music and adapted to the acoustical surroundings. At this point in research such a perspective cannot be proved -- it merely sounds plausible. Given this, the factors that affect the transformation of impulses into sound are legion and include the extent of knowledge of composition and theory, instrumental technique, the ability to link theory and practice quickly (achieved through practice), the speed and scope of the player's imagination, memory, attention, depth and span, attention strategies used, the nature of the instrument used, beliefs about what is possible, set, setting, state of consciousness and goals. A diagram incorporating all such factors would contain numerous levels of feedback and look messy. A simple description of the process might run as follows: ideas are generated and realized into sound via technique. This produces continuous aural and proprioceptive feedback, which allows continuous evaluation, on the basis of which the current ideas are either repeated, developed or discarded. In this way a long-term improvisation can be built up.

IMPROVISATION AS SKILLED PERFORMANCE

The body of psychological research most relevant to an understanding of improvisation is probably work on skilled performance. That is, improvisation may be viewed as a special kind of aesthetically constrained motor performance that maintains a commitment to high levels of real-time decision making. Sophisticated perceptual, intellectual and motor skills are required for success. In common with other kinds of skilled performance, improvisation then involves a chain of mechanisms leading from sensory input to motor output: first, perceptual coding of incoming sensory data; second, evaluation of possible responses and choice of response; and, third, execution and timing of chosen actions (Welford, 1976). The dedicated unpredictability of improvisation and the consequent high levels of continuous decision-making mean that the improviser will seek to operate all three stages as efficiently and as concurrently as possible.

The automaticity of certain motor sequences (discussed further below) shows that stage 3 can occur simultaneously with other processing. That is, the results of one decision can be performed while a new set of sensory data are being processed. However, whether or not Stages 1 and 2 can run concurrently is uncertain. The view that they can run concurrently is supported by the fact that fluent musical improvisers can produce unbroken complex and coherent melodic strings of notes of nearly arbitrary length at speeds of up to ca. 10 notes/sec. This is close to the limiting reported values of kinesthetic reaction times of 119-136 msec (Chernikoff and Taylor, 1952; Glencross, 1977; Higgins and Angel, 1970). On the other hand it is possible that incoming sensory data of their perceptual representations (stage 1) could be stored in short-term buffers to avoid intrinsic interference with evaluation processing (stage 2). It is also possible that such concurrent processing is feasible for simpler improvisation tasks but unviable for more complex ones.

In any case feedback is crucial to the control of skilled improvisation. In the case of instrumental music, while aural feedback is clearly most important, proprioception, touch and vision are also significant. In vocal music improvisation, only hearing and proprioception are relevant. In a fixed task, such feedback is oriented towards the detection (and subsequent correction) of errors. In improvisation, only certain kinds of small errors can really be 'corrected' - as, for example, in music when a violinist grasps for a high note, misses the correct spot slightly and quickly adjusts the intonation according to a cognitive representation of the correct pitch. This sort of process goes on continually (and in fixed tasks as well), wherever there is a continuous variable which can be fine-tuned for error correction, such as pitch, distance along a fingerboard, or embouchure. Commonly, however, larger improvisational errors occur, such as striking an unintended key on the piano, plucking the wrong string on a guitar, or executing an inappropriately chosen (incorrectly pre-heard) motor sequence on an instrument; errors that are so noticeable and discrete that correction is impossible. Rather, such actions must be accepted as part of the irrevocable chain of acoustical events, and contextually justified after the fact by reinforcement or development. The ability to handle such errors is a crucial component in the array of cognitive skills the improviser brings to the performance. Without such a skill no long-scale musical development would be possible, and the sense of relaxation required for efficient and effective improvisational performance would be difficult to achieve.

An interesting and long-standing controversy connected with feedback in skilled performance is the so-called peripheralist-centralist debate: are the fine muscular movements of skill controlled by central motor programs (disregarding sensory input) or by continuous sensory monitoring? The issue has been clearly stated by Glencross (1977, p. 25):

> 'On the one hand, very precise patterns of movement can be made by the human operator at a speed too fast for sensory feedback to be processed and thus cannot be controlled by continuous sensory monitoring. But as soon as the feedback is blocked or even distorted, finely graded and temporally precise skill is lost in other movements. What these findings suggest is that for a central control process (e.g., a motor program) to be fully effective, it must be integrated with peripheral sensory information at some stage. But how does this integration occur and in what precise way is the feedback used to facilitate the ongoing organization?'

To give a plausible answer to this question, it is necessary to first look at the effects of training and practice on the development of improvisatory skill. The first point here is a distinction between what may be called 'object memory' and 'process memory': that is, the musical improviser typically practises in two rather distinct ways. One method is to practise the execution of specific forms, motives, scales, arpeggios or less traditional musical gestures, so that such musical objects and generalized representations of them are entered into long-term 'object memory' in conceptual, muscular and musical coding. A second method is to practise the 'process' of compositional problem-solving: transitions, development and variation techniques, and methods of combining and juxtaposition are practised in many musical contexts and with many different referents. This experience (along with actual performance) forms the basis for long-term 'process memory'.

One result of the first practice method is the creation of a number of small motor programmes or units of action. Continued practice refines these programmes, producing even greater economy of action. These programmes can be temporally integrated to form a continuous response (Bryan and Harter, 1899), and they may be combined by further practice to form composite units of action. The continuation of this process builds eventually an elaborate sequence and hierarchy of composite motor units that can encompass at its limit the whole of a task. This is the basic technique of skill acquisition for a fixed task. In an improvisation task, on the other hand, where there is no fixed ordering of action units, the construction of habit hierarchies is still crucial, but not sufficient. For a task entailing a relatively limited amount of improvisation, such as ordinary motoring, it may be sufficient to appreciate the various possible linear sequences of required action. For a more ambitious project, like jazz improvisation, it will be necessary for the performer to actually find, by practise, appropriate procedures for linking up novel combinations of action units in real-time and changing chosen aspects of them. In other words, the ability to construct new, meaningful pathways in an abstract cognitive space must be cultivated. Each such improvised pathway between action units will sometimes follow existing hierarchical connections, and at other times break off in search of new connections. It is the second practice method which builds this venturesome second possibility.

It should be emphasized that such motor action units are stored in higher cognitive as well as muscular coding. This means that practising them will also increase the size of units used in perceptual coding, that is, in stage 1 of the three-stage skill model mentioned earlier. Comparable effects will also be obtained (to use the language of music again) by listening to recorded improvisations, particularly one's own improvisations. This improved coding will tend to reduce central processing load, since many aural data are now partially 'pre-processed'. In effect training increases the appreciation of redundancy in the incoming sensory information.

To return to the question of how feedback is used, the best existing model applicable to improvisation is probably the model of Glencross (1977). He proposes that the first two stages of Welford's (1976) three-stage model constitute an executive control system that is feedback dependent, while the final motor output stage, once initiated, normally runs its full course without further sensory or central intervention. This seems eminently satisfactory if one adds the proviso that for improvisation, central interruption of motor programmes may be much more frequent due to the unpredictability of the task demands. The time scales given by Glencross for the operation of this executive control system are 300-500 msec for complex sequences of signals and decisions, and 150-200 msec for discrete responses which are in line with the practising improviser's experience of the real-time processing limits.

Here one must also note the notions of feedforward, so-called 'corollary discharge' and other concepts that postulate a pre-setting of the sensory systems for the anticipated consequences of chosen motor actions (Teuber, 1974). With improvisation, the ability to 'pre-hear' internally a chosen motor action without relying on either memory or subsequent auditory feedback is widely recognized as a critical component of musicianship. In improvised jazz melody, for example, a skillful pre-hearer is complimented by saying that his or her instrumental lines are 'singing'.

What are the limits to such real-time processing? Despite the effects of training, feedback and feedforward, there can be no doubt that there are practical limits to the possible complexity of improvised behaviour. Two critical variables are usually considered to be attention and memory. Yet attention is a notoriously difficult concept to pinpoint, and the principal historical theories of early selection or filtering (Broadbent, 1959), late selection (e.g., Deutsch and Deutsch, 1963; Norman, 1968), and attenuation (Treisman, 1964) are clearly inadequate as models here, because they do not allow for the attentional flexibility characteristic of successful improvisation. Less well-defined than those theories but heuristically more useful here is the notion of attention as the allocation, from a limited pool, of cognitive processing capacity. Kahneman (1973) and Norman and Bobrow (1975) are the developers of this so-called resource allocation model. We propose here, following this idea, that conscious attention is the allocation of central cognitive processing (stage 2 decision-making) and that unconscious or automatic attention is the allocation of peripheral cognitive subroutines: perceptual analysis (stage 1) and pre-coded motor sequences (stage 3). The experience of virtually all improvisers, that automatic (not consciously monitored) activity can spontaneously occur, makes this division of attention into conscious and unconscious types unavoidable. This distinction has been proposed previously by Broadbent (1977).

Evidence of the usefulness of considering attention to be resource allocation may be seen by considering the long-standing problem of multiple attention, a critical one for improvisation. Is it possible to attend to two things at once? Many researchers have answered 'no' (Broadbent, 1959; James, 1890; Welford, 1976), preferring to believe that (a) one task is 'automated' while attention tracks the other task; or (b) attention alternates rapidly between the tasks (time-sharing); or (c) the two tasks are time-integrated (often by training) and reconceptualized as one task. These explanations have behind them the idea of attention as a 'single channel' processing capacity. While it is undeniable that all the above possibilities do occur, Shaffer (1975) has criticized such explanations as either begging the question of what attention is (point a) or being untestable (point b). Point (b) is also open to criticism when one considers that an experienced jazz drummer can perform a double-stroke drum roll of at least 20 strokes/second and simultaneously improvise complex patterns with both feet, This would require continuous attentional shifting of the order of 20-50 msec, which although possible seems most unlikely in view of introspective 'evidence' and other measured times associated with cognitive processing. Point (c), the time integration mechanism, undoubtedly has considerable validity in learning processes in general (e.g., Welford, 1976, and see below) but is most unlikely to be a general explanation inasmuch as experienced inprovisers can perform two improvised tasks in novel time relation without rehearsal. Psychologists seem to have ignored such facts because of the dearth of non-specialist publications on improvisation. For example, Welford (1976, p. 94) has stated:

> 'The child's trick of patting the head with one hand while making circular motions with the other is an example; the actions are different, but nobody seems able to perform them simultaneously without making the one a unitary multiple of the other.'

On the contrary, the present writer and other practising improvising musicians whom I have contacted, have little difficulty in rubbing the stomach with one hand in a circular motion at one tempo and patting the head with the other at an apparently continuous graduation of tempi.

Other cognitive research, notably by Hirst et al (1980), also appears to mitigate the likelihood of point (c) as an ultimate explanation. These researchers trained two adults to read and take dictation simultaneously. Attention to the reading material (short stories) was monitored by frequent tests of comprehension. The dictation entailed writing down simple sentences like 'a fire alarm went off' that were simultaneously dictated at a rate of 25-30 words per minute, admittedly rather slow. Initially the tasks interfered, but after extensive training, both subjects were able to read at the same levels of speed and comprehension whether they were taking dictation simultaneously or not. These results are in accord with earlier reports, such as those of Paulhan (1887), who could write one poem while reciting another; Allport et al (1972) who demonstrated that music students can sight play piano music while shadowing prose; and Moray and Fitter (1973) who showed that two different auditory targets could be simultaneously detected in different spatial locations as accurately as either could alone. Finally, the impressive performances of simultaneous translators further bolster the idea that attention is not exclusively single-channel.

Hirst et al. (1980) went on to propose that there are no obvious capacity limits in performing two tasks at once. However, the experience of keyboard improvisers from before the time of Bach to the present day suggests this is false. No one in this long period has been able to improvise complex polyphonic music at the level of rigour and symmetry attained by the finest composers. Apparently in the limited space of a lifetime, training in real-time decision making cannot equal the privilege of editing available to the composer for certain styles. (Let this not be taken as proof of the superiority of composed music over improvised. Certain other styles cannot really be written down in notation and can only be properly realized by improvisation.)

Most of the above fits very well with a resource allocation model of attention. This predicts that one can perform two tasks concurrently without interference if the cognitive load of the two tasks does not exceed available resources. Likewise two tasks can interfere if their total processing demands exceed existing capacity. The result of task rehearsal is thus to convert processing routines requiring conscious attention into automatic routines requiring only unconscious attention. As James said in 1890, 'habit diminishes the conscious attention with which our acts are performed' (p. 114). This process is indicated schematically in Figure 3.

FIGURE 3

Results of improvisational training: a progressive decrease in central processing load and required conscious attention.

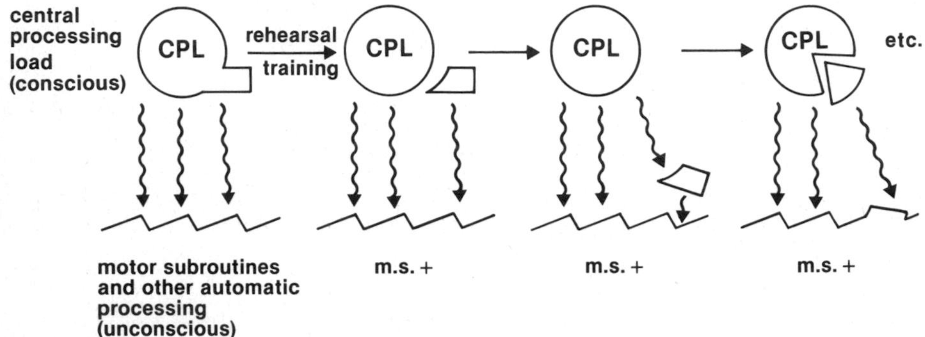

Fitts (1965) labelled this the 'autonomic phase', while Schmidt (1968) referred to it as 'automatization'. The result for the performer is a sensation of automaticity, an uncanny feeling of being a spectator to one's own actions, since increasing amounts of cognitive processing and muscular subroutines are no longer consciously monitored (Welford, 1976). Attention allocation becomes increasingly more task-driven, increasingly less volition-driven. This accords well with introspective reports of improvising musicians (see, for example, Bailey, 1980), which may be summarized as follows. The experience of some improvisers is that attention shifts fairly quickly between different levels of meaning and structure - from referent to timbre to rhythm to remembered motives to melodic development to the sounds of other musicians to body movements to completely extraneous topics like sex or politics. All such resources are useful, but there are too many of them to be efficiently allocated to conscious attention. The danger with this attention strategy is that one factor will be tracked at the expense of others. This is a well-known phenomenon in the training of airplane pilots, called 'chasing the needle', where the student pilot follows one dial of the instrument panel too closely and allows others to drift to extreme ranges.

As the other extreme from this policy of rapid alternation is a strategy of conscious attention that focuses exclusively on overall musical stability - a global and diffuse attention strategy that attempts to leave all detail under the control of unconscious processing (presumably located at lower levels of the central nervous system). At its limit this approaches a meditation-like state, where the player's consciousness mainly 'stays out of the way' of the developing music. This attention strategy is normally considered to produce better music than the first.

Two points remain which are not clearly covered by resource allocation. The first is the question of modality: it has been shown that it is usually easier to divide attention between sensory modalities than within one. Treisman and Davies (1973) concluded that attention capacity is limited in (at least) two different stages: one stage modality specific and a second shared between modalities. Such a distinction is supported by the experience of musical improvisers. For example, a pianist playing a repeating left-hand figure and improvising with the right hand will commonly use visual feedback to assist the execution of one or the other of the hands or the relation between them. Or, the performer may rely on the tactile and proprioceptive 'feel' of the left-hand pattern and divert conscious (aural) attention predominantly or exclusively to the right. If non-aural feedback is reduced, accuracy may drop.

The second point is time behaviour, and there are two relevant issues. First, the model of improvisational attention given above is centred around the near future and the near past. We have spoken about the loading of motor action units, and their discharge while conscious control reverts to the central decision-making stage and fresh data are considered and fresh actions planned, using both feedback and feedforward. This process means that little if any decision-making is concerned with long-scale structure. Indeed this is a criticism sometimes levelled against improvised art and it is sometimes justified. This explains the use of long-term memory in the form of the referent as a guide over longer time scales. The central short-term decision-making processor has only a few options in one sense: repeat the last motor action unit, vary it, introduce contextually new material, or rest.

The second part of this issue is timing. It is known that, as mentioned earlier, simultaneous fixed tasks are often voluntarily integrated into a single time-line to facilitate performance. Musical tasks often require the performance of two sets of timed motor actions, each simple in itself, but difficult to do together. For example, tapping two rhythms in 5:4 relation is far more difficult than tapping either one alone. Simple resource allocation does not explain this. One most postulate the necessity of building an integrative cognitive routine that puts both actions on a common time-scale, either by forming a composite rhythm or using one tapping rate as an automated conceptual ground into which one inserts the other taps at appropriate points. In general it appears that required relationships between subtasks must be considered in determining the overall difficulty of a composite task.

The other variable requiring further comment here is memory. The traditional distinction into short- and long-term stores is adequate for many purposes. Long-term memory critically shapes the kind of sound ideas the performer will produce, and the way in which they will be developed. This memory ranges over musical theory and composition concepts, 'auditory images', specific pieces and motives, and memorized muscular sequences (action units), corresponding roughly to the traditional music labels of theory, musicianship, repertoire, and technique. Each of these areas allows the cognitive organization of many events under smaller umbrella concepts like scale, modulation, interval of a major sixth, mordent, 'swing' time, etc. The reader will recall the earlier distinction between object and process long-term memory. It is long-term memory that is also critical to interaction with the referent, and in establishing long-term musical relations in an extended improvisation.

Short-term memory shapes improvisation primarily by the limitation of the magic number 7 plus or minus 2 - the number of 'chunks' that may be retained in short-term memory (Miller, 1956; Woodworth, 1938). This well-known limit implies that few, if any, performers can take all of a sequence of, say, 15 newly-presented notes not arranged in any standard sequence and improvise successfully with them. There are just too many independent variables. Of course, if these notes can be conceptionally 'chunked' into larger groupings, this statement is no longer true. For example, if each adjacent group of 3 notes belongs to a different major chord, played in a consistent order, then only 5 objects must be memorized and the experienced improviser would have no difficulty in manipulating the material. Without knowledge about theory, musicianship, repertoire and technique the limits of short-term memory would make sophisticated musical development and impressive technical displays impossible.

Yet at the same time that the development and training of memory is liberating it is restricting. For the improviser yields the detailed control of fast events to previous (non-spontaneous) decisions, and introduces an element of composition. Thus, as stated earlier, fast time-scale decisions cannot be very piece-specific; they are training-specific.

CONCLUDING COMMENTS

This chapter has contained two main sections. First, it has reviewed the extensive literature on improvisation in the arts for its implications for cognitive process. Focusing then largely on music, it has blended these results with existing psychological research data, primarily with regard to skilled performance and attention, to create a general sketch of a theory of improvised musical action. Many issues have been left unresolved, for this is really a new field. In this spirit, let me end by proposing some questions deserving further reflection: (1) Is it possible to define a logic or grammar of the generation and transformation of improvised action in the arts? Perhaps even a mathematical formalism of association?; (2) Could improvisation be approached as a problem-solving activity (for which there is an extensive literature) that does not permit editing?; (3) Can methods used to teach improvisation in the arts be adapted to facilitate creative action in other fields, like science, industrial skills or sport?; (4) By detailed analysis of the transcriptions of improvisations can we refine our knowledge of the limits of attention and short-term memory?; and (5) Pupil size appears to be a sensitive index of momentary fluctuations in the expenditure of mental effort (Kahneman, 1973). Mental effort is clearly related to conscious attention allocation. Could pupil monitoring be used to track the attentional processes occurring in improvisation?

REFERENCES

Allport, D.A., Antonis, B. and Reynolds, P. (1972). On the division of attention: A disproof of the single channel hypothesis. Quarterly Journal of Experimental Psychology, 24, 225-235.

Bailey, D. (1980). Improvisation: its nature and practice in music. London: Moorland.

Broadbent, D.E. (1959). Perception and Communication. Oxford: Pergamon Press.

Broadbent, D.E. (1977). The hidden pre-attentive process. American Psychologist, 32, 109-118.

Bryan, W.L. and Harter, N. (1899). Studies on the telegraphic language. The acquisition of a hierarchy of habits. Psychological Review, 6, 345-375.

Chernikoff, R. and Taylor, F.V. (1952). Reaction time to kinesthetic stimulation resulting from sudden arm displacement. Journal of Experimental Psychology, 43, 1-8.

Deutsch, J.A. and Deutsch, D. (1963). Attention: some theoretical considerations. Psychological Review, 70, 80-90.

Duke, J.R. (1972). Teaching musical improvisation: a study of 18th and 20th century methods. Unpublished doctoral thesis, George Peabody College for Teachers.

Ferand, E. (1938). Die Improvisation in der Musik. Zurich: Rhein-Verlag.

Ferand, E. (1961). Improvisation in nine centuries of Western music. Arno Volk Verlag, Hans Gerig KG, Cologne.

Fitts, P.M. (1965). Factors in complex skill training. In: R. Glasser (Ed.) Training Research and Education. New York: Wiley.

Glencross, D.J. (1977). Control of skilled movements. Psychological Bulletin, 84, 14-29.

Grotowski, J. (1968). Towards a Poor Theatre. London: Methuen.

Hanlon, E.S. (1975). Improvisation: theory and application for theatrical music and silent films. Unpublished doctoral thesis, University of Cincinnati.

Higgins, J.R. and Angel, R.W. (1970). Correction of tracking errors without sensory feedback. Journal of Experimental Psychology, 84, 412-416.

Hirst, W. Spelke, E.S., Reaves, C.C., Caharack, G., Neisser, U. (1980). Divided attention without alternation or automaticity. Journal of Experimental Psychology: General, 109, 98-117.

Hood, M. (1975). Improvisation in the stratified ensembles of south-east Asia. Selected Reports in Ethnomusicology (UCLA), 2, 25-33.

James, W. (1890). The Principles of Psychology. Volume 1. New York: Henry Holt.

Jones, A.M. (1959). Studies in African Music. London: Oxford University Press.

Kahneman, D. (1973). Attention and Effort. Englewood Cliffs, New Jersey: Prentice-Hall.

Locke, D. (1979). The music of Atsiabeko. Unpublished doctoral thesis, Wesleyan University.

Mettler, B. (1960). Materials of Dance. Tucson, Arizona: Mettler Studios.

Miller, G.A. (1956). The magical number seven plus or minus two: some limits on our capacity for processing information. Psychological Review, 63, 81-97.

Moray, N. and Fitter, M. (1973). A theory and the measurement of attention: tutorial review. In: S. Kornlum (Ed.) Attention and Performance. Volume IV. New York: Academic Press.

Nettl, B. (1974). Thoughts on improvisation. Musical Quarterly, 60, 1-19.

Nettle, B. and Riddle, R. (1974). Taqsim Nahawand: a study of 16 performances by Jihad Racy. Yearbook of the International Folk Music Council, 5, 11-50.

Norman, D.A. (1968). Towards a theory of memory and attention. Psychological Review, 75, 522-536.

Norman, D.A. and Bobrow, D.G. (1975). On data-limited and resource-limited processes. Cognitive Psychology, 7, 44-64.

Owens, T. (1974). Charlie Parker: techniques of improvisation. Unpublished doctoral thesis, UCLA.

Paulhan, F. (1887). La simultanéité des actes psychiques. Revue Scientifique, 39, 684-689.

Schmidt, R.A. (1968). Anticipation and timing in human motor performance. Psychological Bulletin, 70, 631-646.

Shaffer, L.H. (1975). Multiple attention in continuous verbal tasks. In P.M.A. Rabbitt and S. Dornic (Ed.) Attention and Performance. London: Academic Press.

Sperber, M. (1975). Improvisation in the performing arts: music, dance and theater. Ed.D. Thesis, Columbia University.

Treisman, A.M. (1964). Selective attention in man. British Medical Bulletin, 20, 12-16.

Treisman, A.M. and Davies, A. (1973). Divided attention to ear and eye. In: S.Kornblum (Ed.) Attention and Performance. Volume IV. New York: Academic Press.

Teuber, H.L. (1974). Key problems in the programming of movements: Concluding session. Brain Research, 71, 535-538.

Welford, A.T. (1976). Skilled Performance. Glenview, Illinois: Scott, Foreman and Co.

Woodworth, R.S. (1938). Experimental Psychology. New York: Holt, Rinehart and Winston.

Section 6

ISSUES IN EXPERIMENTAL AESTHETICS

Cognitive Processes in the Perception of Art
W.R. Crozier and A.J. Chapman (editors)
© Elsevier Science Publishers B.V. (North-Holland), 1984

A GENERAL NOTION OF BEAUTY USED TO QUANTIFY THE AESTHETIC ATTRACTIVITY OF GEOMETRIC FORMS

Frans Boselie and Emanuel Leeuwenberg

University of Nijmegen

The question to which this chapter addresses itself is: What makes things beautiful? Through the centuries many writers have set about the task of characterizing beauty (For an overview of many such theories, see Berlyne, 1971, or Lindauer, 1981). The theories vary widely in the character and number of terms employed to deal with the determinants of the aesthetic experience. Nevertheless, certain themes come back again and again. Many theories for instance have in common that they conceive of beauty as a function of two opposing factors. One factor might be represented by concepts like order, lawfulness or unity, the other one by concepts like complexity, multiplicity or diversity. Also, another point they have in common is that none of them is stated in a formal way, so they cannot be falsified unequivocally. The work of Birkhoff (1933) forms a notable exception in this respect. He was the first to express the idea that beauty is a function of two factors in an exact form. He maintained that our pleasure in any work of art depends on the amount of order (O) and of complexity (C) in the object. He argued that the amount of pleasure (M) is best represented by the ratio $M = O/C$. Birkhoff himself has worked out this formula in detail for polygonal forms, case outlines, lines of poetry and melodies. The definiteness of his propositions is rather uncommon in the field of aesthetics, and makes it possible to challenge his proposals. His formula has been tested in many experiments and it is clear that it gives a rather poor prediction of the actual aesthetic judgments of subjects (Eysenck, 1941; McWinnie, 1968).

Other quantitative models have been proposed. Rashevsky (1938) based a model on avowedly speculative neurophysiological postulates. Some information-theoretic aestheticians (Bense, 1969; Gunzenhauser, 1965) have provided for information-theoretic equivalents of Birkhoff's O and C. However, they introduced subjective quantities, which should vary with learning and motivation and which have to be assessed empirically. Eysenck's (1942, 1968; Eysenck and Castle, 1970) extensive research in this area has till now been one of fact finding and of empirically determining regression equations, rather than an endeavour to develop a formal theory. He suggested that the equation $M = O/C$ should be replaced by $M = O \times C$. His rules for computing O and C are entirely empirically determined and in fact differ between experiments as do the weights of O and C in his regression equations. Summarizing the foregoing: at the moment there is no theory based on generally accepted assumptions from which a quantitative measure of the beauty of simple geometric forms can be derived.

In this chapter we develop a new quantitative index for the beauty of geometric forms that fits better with known facts than Birkhoff's equation. We start from a simple idea concerning the nature of the aesthetic experience.

The broad applicability of this notion is demonstrated by means of several examples. Then a quantitative specification of the beauty of geometric forms is given based on the general notion from which we started. Evidence is presented that the theoretical measure we propose corresponds to a considerable degree with the actual judgments of people.

BEAUTY AS A FUNCTION OF MEANS AND EFFECT

In many situations people draw a distinction between means applied and effect attained; or between materials and finished product; or they differentiate between investment and profit. Sometimes an effect displays a property which is thought improbable given the means to attain the effect. On observing such a phenomenon one will be surprised. Here are some examples. A conjurer shows us the material that is going to be used: an empty hat. *Et voila* ! He manages to draw a rabbit out of the same hat. It is magic. Michelangelo's 'Slaves' (1519-1532) are in the Academia at Florence. We see human bodies larger than life-size. They are perfectly proportioned and sculptured in a very precise manner in unyielding stone. The precise forms contrast strongly with the hardness of the material from which they are cut. The bodies emerge from huge pieces of marble which show the rough cuts caused by hammer-blows. Thereby the hardness of the material is made perceptually very salient. Another example of attaining an effect by unlikely means is formed by theories based on a few simple assumptions which describe a wide range and diversity of phenomena. Looking at such simple assumptions they do not seem suited at all for the purpose they serve.

We believe that the feelings of surprise and amazement stirred by events and objects like the ones mentioned in these examples are at the very heart of all aesthetic experiences. This hypothesis can be formulated more precisely as follows: an object will give rise to an impression of beauty when it is cognitively represented as having two qualities which, according to the knowledge embodied in the representational system, are incompatible. Such a feeling of surprise will only come into being when the qualities which are taken as incompatible are represented in a clear and unambiguous way (Boselie, 1983). It is because of this prerequisite that a magician makes it perceptually very convincing that the hat used in fact is empty. The rabbit too has to be shown clearly, not just for a moment, neither blurred by a screen of smoke. Besides that, it must be beyond doubt that the whole trick is performed with only one hat, that the rabbit pops up from the empty hat. Looking at a sculpture we only can be amazed by the combination of the stone and the precision of its form when both qualities are cognitively represented in a prominent way. The presence of the raw material from which Michelangelo's 'Slaves' emerges enhances the visibility of the hardness of the material from which the bodies are cut and in that way the beauty of these forms is increased by the unfinished character of these works.

When the condition of unambiguousness of means applied and effect attained is met, we will be the more surprised as the improbability of the effect given the means applied increases. To return for a moment to the example of an elegant theory: a theory based on just a few assumptions and explaining many phenomena will stir stronger feelings of surprise than a theory having a less favourable ratio between the number of assumptions and the number of phenomena explained.

The foregoing can be summarized as follows: when an object is cognitively represented as having two incompatible qualities it will be thought more beautiful as these qualities are represented in a more unambiguous way and as they more strongly contrast with each other. This can be formulated briefly as :

$$M = Um \times Ue \times Cm, e \quad (1)$$

M = amount of beauty
Um = amount of unambiguousness of the means
Ue = amount of unambiguousness of the effect
Cm, e = the amount of contrast between means and effect

In addition to the examples already given we now analyse the aesthetic appeal of several other types of stimuli in the terms of this formula.

When we watch ballet dancers in motion, it sometimes appears as if they succeed in overcoming gravity. When a dancer leaps, for example, there is no motion at the height of the leap although this moment forms part of an ongoing motion. So at the height of a leap the dancer manages to attain the perceptual effect of stillness by the improbable means of motion. This remarkable combination of perceptual qualities is expressively worded as 'frozen motion' by Lasher et al (1983). Another moment of frozen motion can be observed when the body of a dancer, performing an arabesque, attains its most extreme extension. These moments of frozen motion contribute to the exciting quality of ballet. This only holds on the condition that the means applied to attain the stillness of the body are perceptually unambiguous. When the spectator suspects that the stillness is achieved by means of special appliances and not by the unaided human body, the effect is spoiled. In the eighteenth century 'invisible' wires and pulleys were introduced to enhance the duration of the stillness by attaching dancers to the wires. These tricks, however, were quickly abandoned (Kreitler and Kreitler, 1972).

A fine line-drawing has aesthetic appeal. For example, in Figure 1 we see a face. This effect is attained by means of a number of thin lines. They do not form a closed contour. There is no trace of shading to indicate the fullness of the face, the presence of flesh. Nevertheless we see a figure that stands out from the background. The surface structure of the figure looks different from that of the background. This effect is attained with an unlikely means, that is the same empty paper surface is used for both figure and background. One wonders how a few marks of ink can have such strong illusory effects. That the awareness of the surface pattern of a drawing or painting is clearly of great importance from an aesthetic point of view has been stressed by many authors (Arnheim, 1954; Gombrich, 1956; Pirenne, 1970; Tolnay, 1972).

Another demonstration of the broad applicability of the notion that aesthetic merits are related to the way effects are attained is given by Figures 2A and 2B. The square of Figure 2A is divided by heavy lines into a number of smaller squares. Each of these squares in turn is subdivided by thin lines in exactly the same way as the square we started with. Figure 2B is constructed in the same way as Figure 2A with the exception that all divisions are made with thin lines.

FIGURE 1

A face.

FIGURE 2

Two squares divided into a number of smaller squares. In 2A heavy lines indicate the main division.

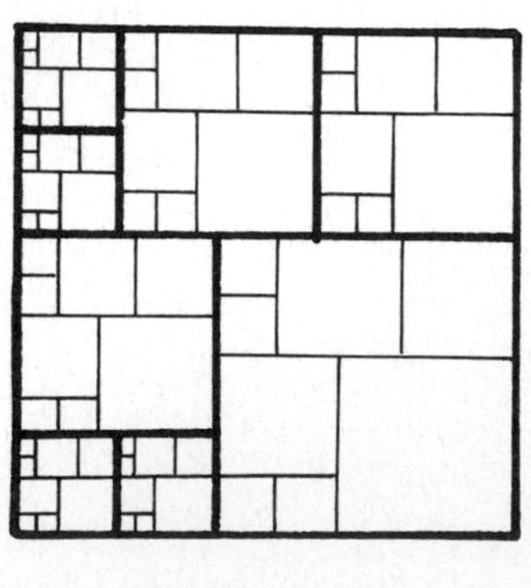

A

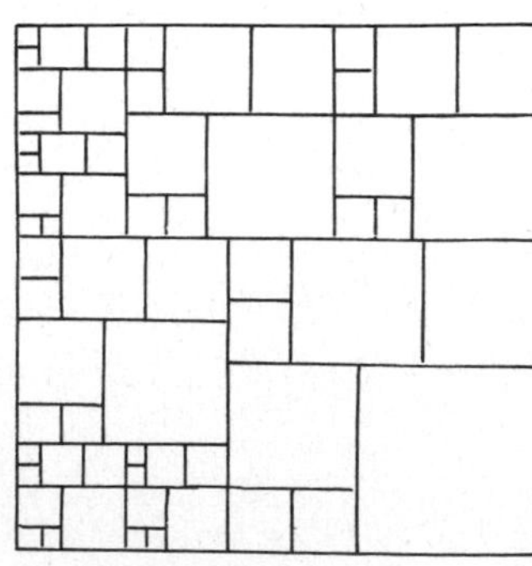

B

Both drawings exemplify the very efficient use of means in forming structures, namely recursion. Both are aesthetically attractive but according to expert opinion (see Naredi-Rainer, 1982; Slebos, 1939) pattern 2A is the better one: main divisions and subdivisions have to be kept apart. This prescription of beauty is easily understood on the basis of the means-effect metaphor as specified by our formula. Both patterns display the peculiar charm that, in spite of the fact that the whole pattern is made up from only one shape, the square, the overall impression is one of variety in unity. But besides that, Figure 2A stands out from Figure 2B by displaying more unity and more variety than that pattern. The combination of heavy and thin lines makes Figure 2A more complex than Figure 2B but at the same time this difference in thickness forms the means by which the order imposed upon the pattern by the two-fold recursion is made perceptually salient. The squares of the main division of Figure 2B are not sufficiently prominent to make it clear that the whole pattern is made up of a two-fold recursion. Recursion plays an important role in design, architecture and music and can be frequently found in nature. Recently it has been proposed that the perception of self-repeating patterns in coastlines, rivers, trees, clouds and so on lies at the root of our appreciation of nature's beauty (Gardner, 1978; Mandelbrot, 1977, 1981).

An example of a rather different kind of situation in which the same criterion of aesthetic value operates is given in a study by Margulies (1977). He asked expert chess-players to examine pairs of check positions. In both members of a pair a move was shown leading to checkmate, but the members differed in the means applied to attain this end. The experts were asked to select the more beautiful checkmate of a pair. As a result of his study Margulies formulated seven principles of beauty. They all can be reduced to the one notion of beauty formulated above. Here, we confine ourselves to two of his principles. The first one says: use the weakest possible piece to checkmate your opponent. Why is checkmate by a pawn judged more beautiful than checkmate by a queen? It is because in chess-theory the pawn clearly is appraised as the weakest and for that reason least important of all pieces. But in the on-going chess match this unimportant piece does the only thing that matters: it checkmates the king. Another principle formulated by Margulies says: use all of the piece's power. This rule is demonstrated by Figure 3.

In Figure 3A more of the queen's power is used to checkmate the king than in Figure 3B. Checkmate 3A is judged the more beautiful one. This result fits in with our notion of beauty as a function of the amount of contrast between qualities of a situation. The two relevant qualities here are: the actual position of the queen and the position where her influence becomes apparent. The distance between these positions is the most plausible index of the degree in which the positions contrast when brought together in the representation of one chess-piece.

To conclude we apply a similar analysis to the kind of emotion which accompanies the sudden discovery of the solution to a problem. The emotion at the moment of discovery is one of surprise, and the 'aha-experience' forms an instance of aesthetic experiencing. It is important to note that the discovery of a solution only gives rise to an impression of beauty when it is preceded by a period of hard but unsuccessful work. Why is this? Our interpretation of this phenomenon is as follows. The information processing during the unsuccessful attempts to solve the problem results in a representation in which one feature of the problem situation is outstanding, namely that it does not meet the requirements of the much sought solution. Take this problem for instance (see Figure 4; Dreistadt, 1969).

FIGURE 3

More of the queen's power is used in 3A than in 3B

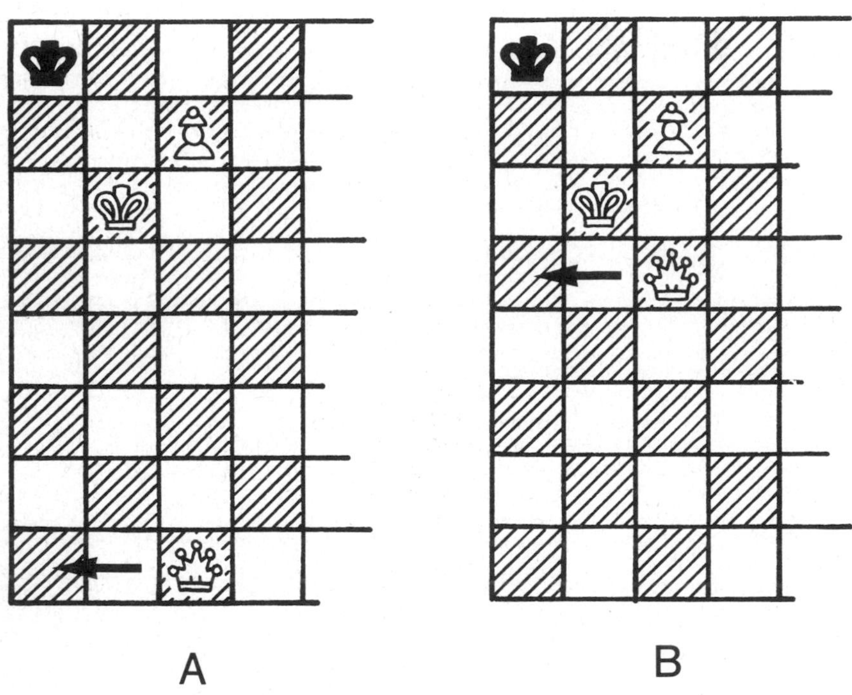

FIGURE 4

Divide this area into four parts which have the same size and shape:

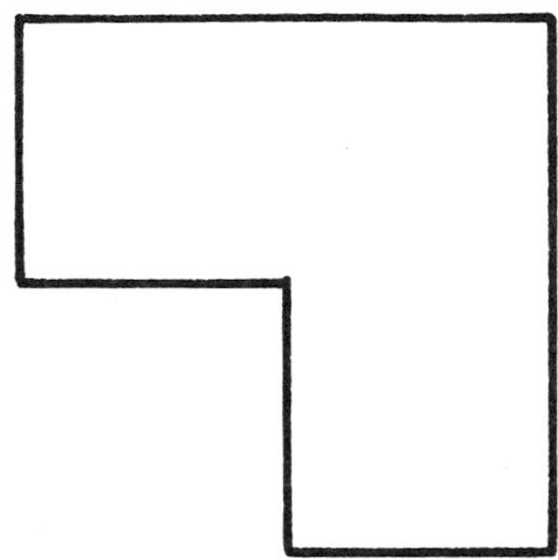

This is not an easy problem to solve. Try it. When you give up, you are aware that your representation of the problem situation does not form the appropriate means to *restructure perceptually the pattern into four parts of the same size and shape.* The moment you see the solution without anybody's assistance your representation in fact is appropriate. This surprises you. As regards this particular problem: at the moment you see the solution the representation of the shape of Figure 4 has two contrasting qualities. It is the shape you did perceive all the time and it is the shape you sought for all the time. This extra contrast makes the solution an aesthetic one. (The solution is shown in Figure 11.)

In our opinion, these examples, to which other ones from the field of literature, music, etc. could be easily added, strongly suggest that the aesthetic appeal of objects originates from contrasting qualities which form part of the cognitive representation we make of them.

JUDGMENTS OF BEAUTY

The foregoing analyses give credit to our hypothesis. Nevertheless, we are not yet in a position to predict successfully the judgments of beauty subjects actually make. Prediction will fail because of a number of very divergent reasons. First, we do not yet have a measure of the amount of unambiguousness and incompatibility of contrasting qualities. Second, cognitive representations sometimes will display several pairs of contrasting qualities. How are we to combine the effect of these different sources of surprise? A picture, for example, may have aesthetic merits at at least two levels. First, there can be a contrast between the means used (canvas, formless strokes of paint, etc.) and the illusionistic effect attained (a woman). This contrast belongs to the art of depicting. Second, the woman herself may be very beautiful. The contrasts that make her beautiful belong to nature.

This leads us to another factor that makes judgments of beauty difficult to predict. In our conception aesthetic feelings are stirred by a 'formal' quality of cognitive representation, by the relation between means and effect. According to that view beauty does not depend in a direct way on the effect or 'content' of an object. It is obvious however that people attribute different values to objects just because they differ in content. When the content of a painting evokes strong feelings of approval or disapproval these feelings may push the aesthetic feeling of surprise caused by contrasting qualities to the background. When subjects are asked to rate such paintings on a scale of beauty their ratings may first of all reflect this emotional reaction to their content. So in an experiment Rembrandt's well-known painting of a slaughtered animal hanging out from a scaffolding at a butcher's shop may not score high on a scale of beauty, because the scene depicted evokes repulsion, whereas a mediocre landscape may score high because it represents a peaceful scene. Höge (1983) reports an experiment in which this effect is demonstrated very clearly. He found that pictures rated as expressing happiness score higher on a scale of beauty than pictures expressing sadness. It is evident that such ratings are too complex to be predicted on the basis of our hypothesis. Still another biasing factor is that subjects will differ in the way in which they represent qualities of an object. A combination of qualities that is represented as being incompatible by one subject may be taken as ordinary by another subject. Such differences in cognitive appraisal are likely to occur on the basis of differences in familiarity. So a painting in the photo-realistic style may have aesthetic appeal for a layperson because seemingly the effect attained is very improbable, whereas a connoisseur may not be surprised by this kind of realism at all.

This enumeration of factors makes it clear that most of the time the formal quality of contrast between means applied and effect attained will not be sufficient to account for actual judgments of beauty. Besides there are still more factors that play a part;for example, the prestige attributed to a work of art (its financial value or expert opinion) or the conformity to group norms (for an overview of these effects, see Crozier and Chapman, 1981). From this it can be concluded that for the moment our hypothesis can only be tested by using stimulus material that, as regards content, is as neutral as possible. Simple geometric forms come up to this requirement. In fact we could use the set of polygons published by Birkhoff (1933). They have the adventitious advantage that they have been judged already in many experiments. In the next section therefore we specify a measure of beauty M for geometric forms and test it against preference-judgments of Birkhoff's polygons.

THE BEAUTY OF GEOMETRIC FORMS

Almost every visual pattern can be interpreted in various ways. Some interpretations will be simple, others will be complex. According to the law of Prägnanz (Koffka, 1935) we will always perceptually organize a pattern in the simplest possible way. It is important to note that an interpretation nearly always forms an incomplete description of a pattern. It represents a pattern as an element of a class of patterns. For example: when we interpret Figure 5A as two identical rectangles, placed orthogonally and symmetrically around axis S, one rectangle occluding the other, we actually describe this pattern as an element of a class of patterns of which Figure 5B and 5C also are elements. Thus, an interpretation nearly always leaves some parameters of a pattern free to vary.

FIGURE 5

A class of patterns.

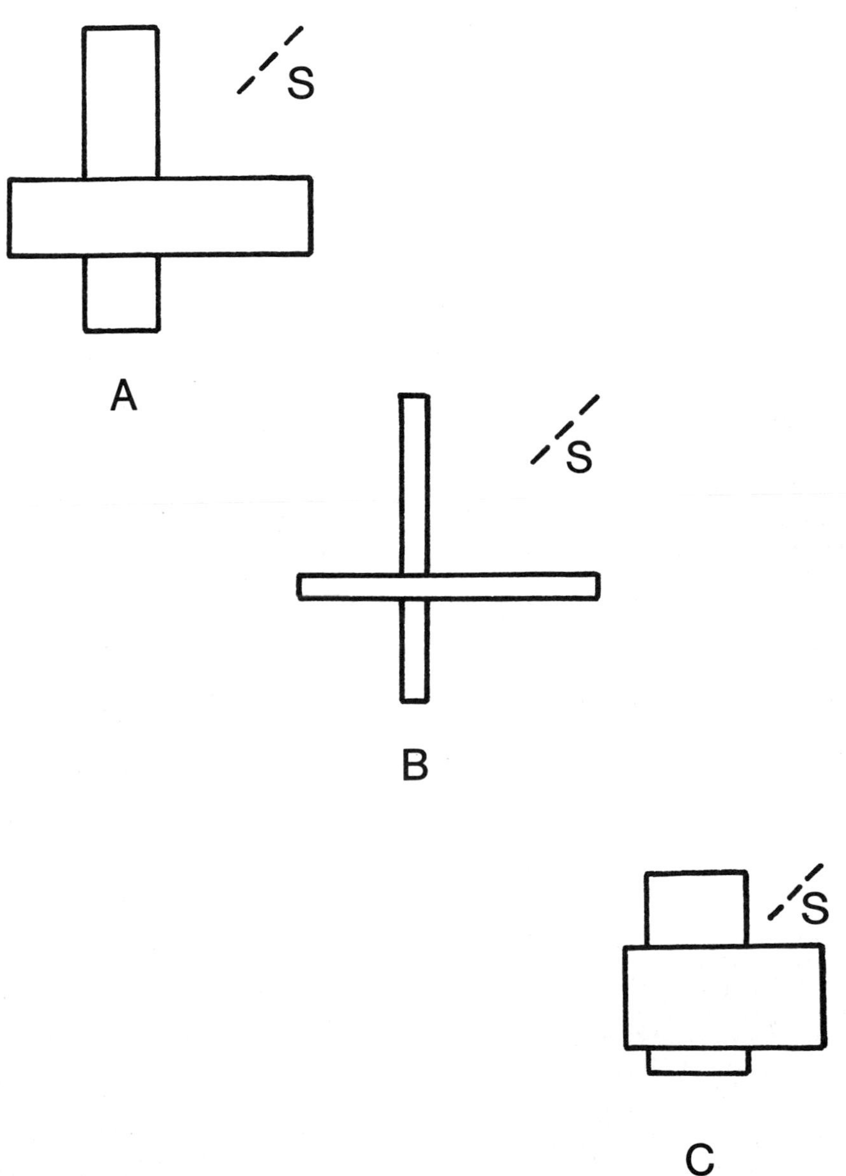

Simple interpretations will take into account the regularities of a pattern in an efficient way. That does not mean however that the simplest interpretation always includes all of a pattern's regularities. For example: the simple interpretation of Figure 5A we just gave does not reflect a regularity that can be observed in this pattern, namely that rectangle R1 = R2 (See Figure 6).

FIGURE 6

In A a regularity can be observed which is illustrated in B. R1 = R2.

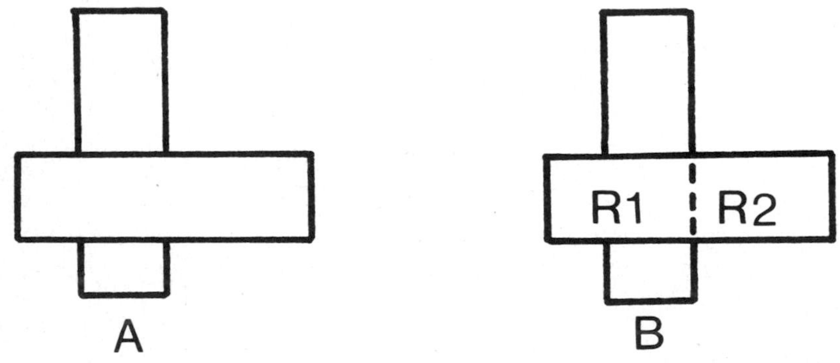

There is reason to believe that regularities that do not show up in the simplest interpretation of a pattern often will be perceived and will affect the impression a pattern makes (Arnheim, 1954; Bouleau, 1963; Pirenne, 1970). On perceiving such an additional regularity one will be mildly surprised, because it is in no way implied by the simplest interpretation. Indeed one might say that adding an extra regularity to the simplest interpretation gives rise to a contrast within the representation of a pattern because an additional regularity specifies a parameter which the simplest interpretation leaves free to vary. Thus the presence of a free parameter which in fact is restricted by an additional regularity will enhance the perceived beauty of a pattern.

Let the number of free parameters of the simplest interpretation be represented by the symbol P, the number of additional regularities that is perceived by the symbol R. Then we can specify the amount of incompatibility Cm,e (see formula 1) between the indeterminacy of the simplest interpretation and the definiteness of the additional regularities by the ratio (1 + R)/P. Figure 7 gives an illustration of the steps involved.

FIGURE 7

An arrow-like pattern and an illustration of its perceptual representation. The simplest interpretation describes a class of patterns, four of which are drawn. Detection of an additional regularity reduces the size of the class.

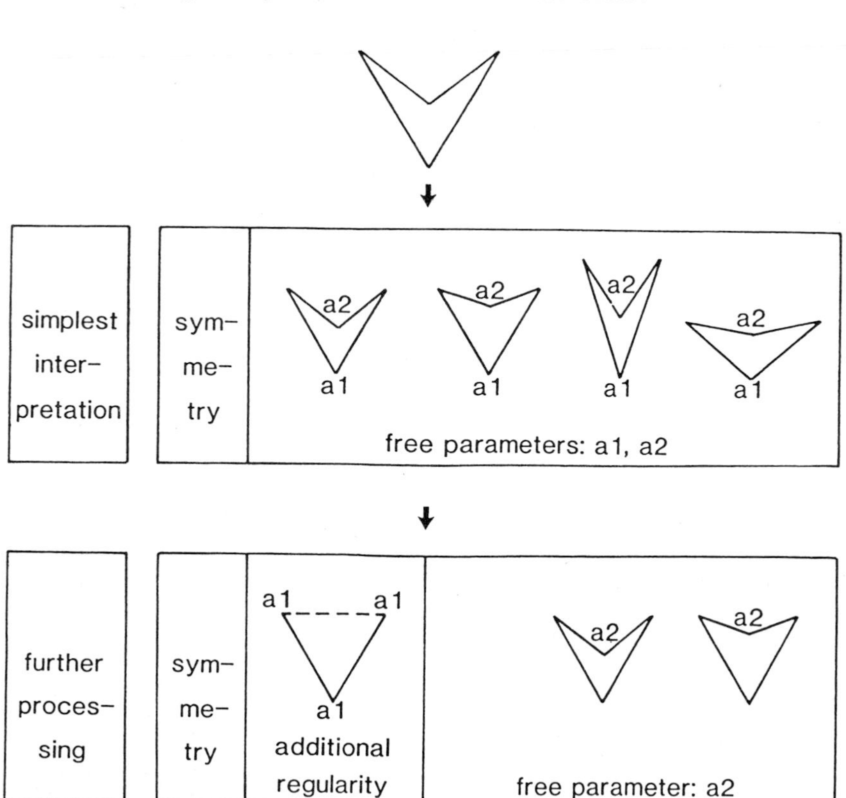

The simplest interpretation of the pattern shown in Figure 7 is: an arrow-like pattern which is symmetrical around a vertical axis of symmetry. This interpretation does fix the pattern in some respect (its symmetry) but not in others (the actual size of its angles). In fact it does not specify the size of the angles a1 and a2. So the number of free parameters of this interpretation equals two, P = 2. The simplest interpretation, however, does not represent the fact that the envelope of the pattern is a very regular one, it is an equilateral triangle. Thus there is an additional regularity by which the parameter a1 is specified: the angle of the point of the arrow equals the other angles of the envelope. No other regularities can be found in the pattern and thus R = 1. The amount of contrast between indeterminacy and lawfulness thus is represented by Cm,e = (1 + 1)/2. Note that as the number of additional regularities of a pattern increases, the number of free parameters of its representation decreases.

The descriptions of figures we gave thus far represent our subjective way of interpreting patterns. To proceed in a more objective way one needs a formal method to identify the simplest interpretation of a pattern. Given the simplest interpretation the number of free parameters P is fixed. Then, in order to specify R, one needs an objective procedure to identify any possible additional regularity. Further one has to specify the degree to which a free parameter or additional regularity is perceived in an unambiguous way. All these questions are dealt with in the following section.

TOWARDS A FORMAL MEASURE OF BEAUTY

The Maximally Constraining Code of a Pattern

A tool to represent pattern interpretations by pattern codes is provided by Leeuwenberg's coding language (Leeuwenberg, 1969, 1971; Restle, 1982). It has been shown (Buffart et al, 1981; Van Tuyl, 1980) that the perceptually preferred interpretations of patterns can be adequately reflected by means of Leeuwenberg's coding language. Here we introduce the construction of pattern codes informally and only as far as it is necessary to understand its application to Birkhoff's polygonal forms. For a more definitive treatment we refer to the studies mentioned above and to Boselie and Leeuwenberg (1983).

In Leeuwenberg's coding language it is assumed that perceiving a pattern means classifying it. A code, thus, represents a class of patterns and the code elements referring to line-lengths and angle-sizes do not denote specified values. A code describes a surface enclosed by a contour. A surface can be thought of as composed of a number of smaller adjacent surfaces, each enclosed by a contour of its own, which together make up the contour of the whole pattern. The first step in making a code of a pattern is to trace the contours of the surfaces and to represent the successive lengths of the line elements and the angles between them by means of symbols. This series of symbols is called a primitive code. If a primitive code shows redundancy, it can be rewritten in a simpler form by means of a set of coding rules, also called operators. If possible, the simplified code may be reduced further in this way. Two kinds of symbols thus can be distinguished in such a code: (1) operators and (2) symbols referring to the lengths and angles of a pattern. As those last-mentioned symbols do not denote specified metric values, they are called the 'free parameters of a code'.

The number of symbols of a code needed to specify the shape of a pattern is called the 'information load I'. When a code is reduced, its information load becomes less. For a given pattern a code with the lowest possible information load is called a 'minimum code'. The minimum code with the lowest number of free parameters is the code that maximally constrains a pattern. This is the code we need to compute M. For the maximally constraining code is the one which has to be complemented with a minimum of additional regularities. Should we compute M starting from another code, the number of additional regularities possibly would be inflated.

Recurrent elements in a code are the basic source of redundancy, which can be extracted by coding rules, five of which are presented in Table 1. As a case in point we show the coding of one of Birkhoff's polygons. The elements which contribute to I are indicated by dots.

TABLE 1

Examples of Coding Rules

CODING RULE	PRIMITIVE CODE	REDUCED CODE	I
iteration	a a	2*a	2
symmetry	a b b a	SYM (a b)	3
symmetry	a b c b a	SYMM (a b (c))	4
distribution	a b a c	<a>\< b c >	3
continuation	a a ...	@*(a)	1

The primitive code of Figure 8A overleaf is
l a l b k c l a l b k c l a l b k c l a l b k c (I=24) (1)
which, by continuation, equals
@*(l a l b k c) (I= 6) (2)
and, by distribution, equals
@*(<l>\<a b> k c) (I= 5) (3)
which is a minimumcode.

The regularities specified by this code are the rotational symmetry of the pattern (specified by the continuation rule) and the repetition of the lengths and angles denoted by l, a, b, k and c. The code thus has five free parameters.

Additional Regularities

There is a whole class of patterns answering to the description given by the minimum code (3), Figure 8B is one of them. It is evident that Figure 8A displays more regularities than Figure 8B and thus it does have regularities not accounted for by code (3), that is additional regularities. Several types of additional regularities may arise. We now illustrate those which occur most frequently. They can be made conspicuous by drawing auxiliary lines in a pattern. Examples of this kind of regularity are shown by Figure 9.

FIGURE 8

A: Birkhoff polygon and some of its coding elements
B: This pattern answers to the same minimum code as pattern A.

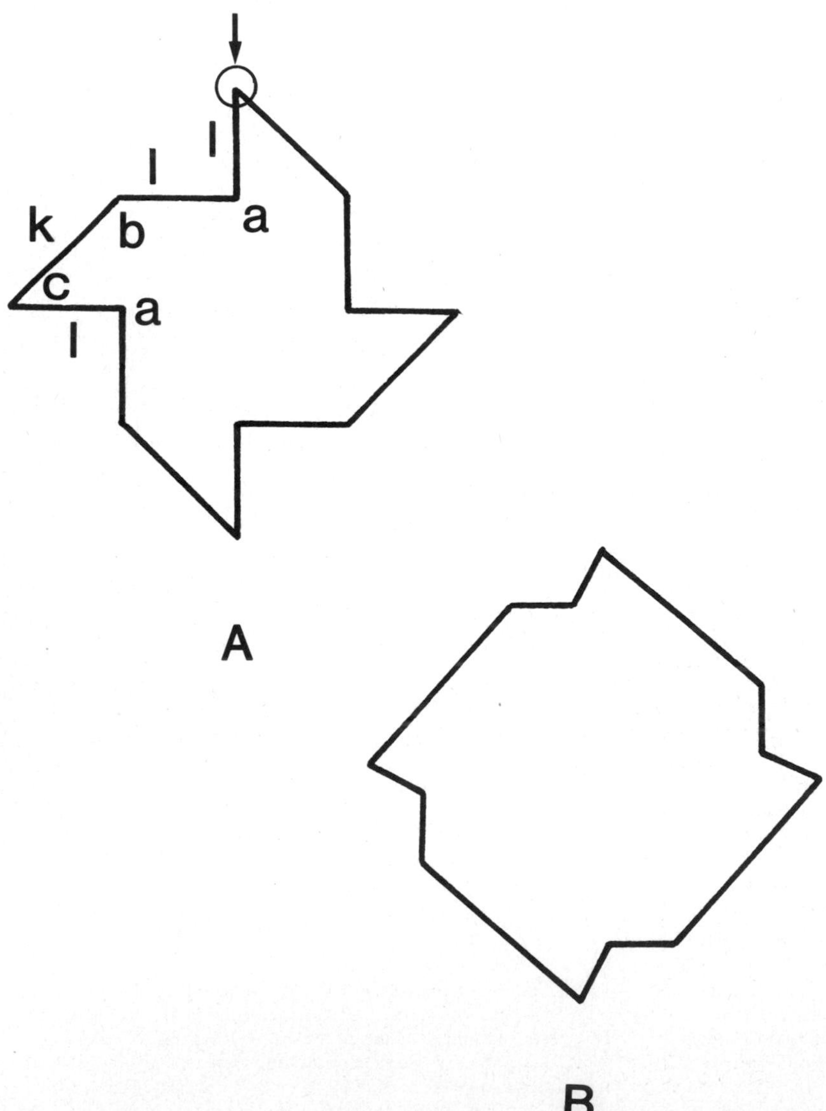

FIGURE 9

Examples of two kinds of additional regularities. A and C display an additional regularity whereas B and D do not.

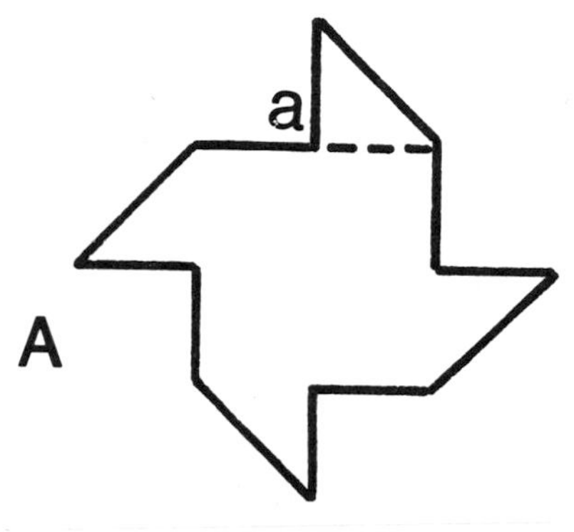

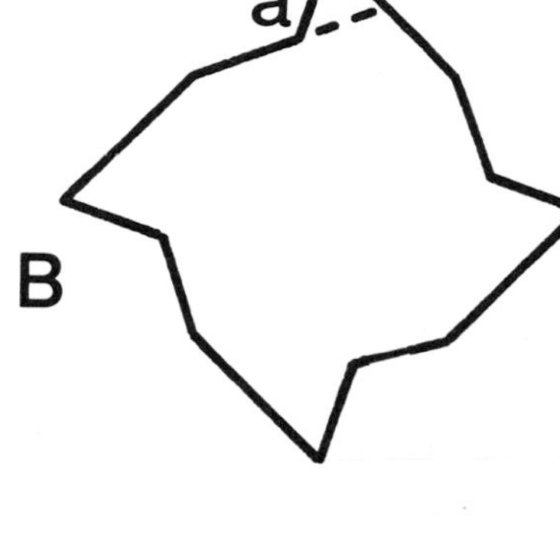

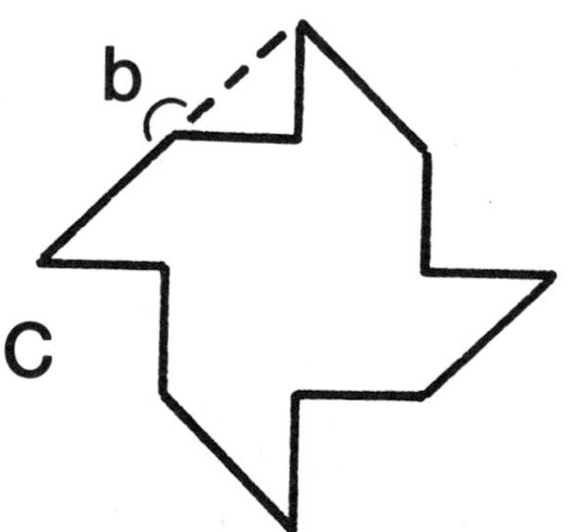

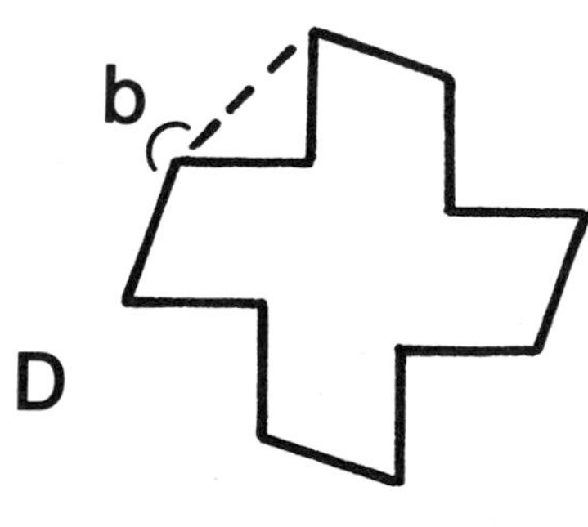

b = 360 - b

They pose a problem here, because little is currently known about the spontaneous perception of this kind of order. Indeed it is generally agreed that the perceptual structure by which an observer represents a drawing might contain orientations, angles and lengths that are not actually drawn (Buffart et al, 1981; Piaget, 1963) and that, when this happens, regularities might be perceived that are more or less hidden (Arnheim,1954; Bouleau,1963; Ogden,1937). But it is not possible to infer from the published evidence which regularities will and which will not be perceived in an unambiguous way. We therefore have to rely on intuition as regards the type of concealed regularities people might sense. We supposed that the sides and angles of the contour of a pattern form the starting point from which human observers look for additional regularities. They may proceed in two ways: (1) by continuing orientations of sides; and(2) by connecting corners which are not next to each other on the contour. In that way only regularities that one comes across starting from the orientations of sides and corners described by the maximally constraining code are taken into account.

Figure 9A illustrates an extra regularity that can be found in the pattern of Figure 8 by continuing one of its sides inwardly. This regularity is not present in Figure 9B. By connecting corners of Figure 8 another additional regularity comes to the fore (see Figure 9C). Given these rules, the additional regularities of a pattern can be identified. Sometimes regularities will be mathematically dependent. To compute R only mathematically independent regularities will be counted. We do not yet have a measure of the degree of unambiguousness by which additional regularities are cognitively represented. For the time being we assume that regularities that can be found by the two rules specified above will be perceptually prominent enough to contrast with the free parameters of the simplest code. The same restriction applies to the way the unambiguousness of the free parameters is dealt with here. A first requisite in order to make a code of a pattern and to identify free parameters is that a pattern should be unambiguous with respect to the length of its sides and the size of its angles. These have to be either the same as or clearly different from other lengths and sizes. Only then the unambiguousness of the free parameters is ascertained. To dispose of ambiguities we proceed as follows. All sides and angles differing less than 7.5% in length or size will be interpreted as equal to each other. Patterns with sides or angles differing more than 7.5% and less than 15% will be taken as being ambiguous. These cutting points roughly coincide with three bits of selective information, which is, as is generally assumed, approximately the maximum amount of information transmission per dimension (Garner, 1962). Having no measures of unambiguousness to specify Um and Ue, we had to make it probable in this provisional way that the free parameters and additional regularities of the patterns we are going to use to test our hypothesis will be perceived. Thus for the present we have to reduce formula (1) to

$$M = (1 + R) / P$$

Computation of M

We are now in a position to compute M for simple geometric forms. Figure 10 gives an example. The four patterns shown all answer to the minimumcode (3) of Figure 8. The number of parameters left free to vary by this maximally constraining code, five, is the same for all patterns, thus P = 5. Figure 10A through 10D form a series of patterns in which every pattern exhibits one additional regularity more than the one preceding it. The value of R for the patterns of this series amounts to 0, 1, 2 and 3 respectively. The M values therefore are 1/5, 2/5, 3/5 and 4/5 respectively.

APPLICATION TO BIRKHOFF'S POLYGONS

We computed M for 37 polygons of Birkhoff's set (details of this study are given in Boselie and Leeuwenberg, 1983). The set of polygons was made up as follows. We started from the research of Eysenck and Castle (1970). Theirs is the most extensive study on preference judgments for Birkhoff's polygons. More than eleven hundred subjects (art students and controls) rated each polygon for aesthetic pleasingness on a seven point scale. The correlations between Birkhoff's M and the judgments were very low, 0.28 for the art students and 0.04 for the controls. Eysenck and Castle divided Birkhoff's set of polygons in two groups. One group contains thirty-two polygons that show marked differences between the two kinds of subjects they used, art students and controls, the other group (fifty-eight patterns) contains the polygons on which their subjects show marked agreement. We restricted ourselves to this last set of polygons. Several of Birkhoff's polygons do not meet the requirement that a pattern has to be unambiguous with respect to the length of its sides and the size of its angles. We disposed of these ambiguous patterns by applying the procedure we described above. Doing so, we retained 37 out of the 58 patterns. For this set we computed Spearman's correlation coefficient between our theoretical measure (1 + R)/P and the judgments of aesthetic pleasingness given by the art students and controls. Correlations are 0.76 for the art students and 0.71 for the controls ($p < .001$). The correlations between Birkhoff's M and the judgments for this set of patterns are 0.15 and 0.02 for art students and controls respectively. The fact that our tentative measure M accounts for about half the variance of these judgments suggests the adequacy of formulating the beauty of geometric patterns as a function of the contrast between free parameters and additional regularities.

CONCLUSION

In our opinion the notion that an impression of beauty arises when an effect is attained with means that do not seem appropriate to that end has great heuristic value. The analysis we gave of the perception of geometric patterns is a case in point. The distinction between the simplest interpretation and additional regularities not only nicely fits in with the means-effect metaphor, the simplest interpretation being the necessary but insufficient condition for additional regularities to appear. What is more, the distinction is a decisive one when it comes to predicting the actual judgment of subjects by means of the concepts of order and complexity. Both Birkhoff and Eysenck tried to formulate beauty in terms of the contrast between order and complexity. But they failed to notice that the effect of order has to be attained with respect to pattern-parts that already are represented in a more complex way in the simplest interpretation. This 'hidden' order thus implies both order and complexity and differs both from the conspicuous order of the simplest interpretation and from the complexity of unconstrained irregularities. We thus might discern different kinds of order and complexity: (1) the order of the simplest interpretation, 'simple order'; (2) additional regularities, 'complex order'; (3) free parameters constrained by additional regularities, 'lawful complexity'; and (4) unconstrained free parameters, 'random complexity'. These distinctions originate from the means-effect metaphor. They are missing in Birkhoff's and Eysenck's formulations.

FIGURE 10

A series of patterns in which every pattern exhibits one regularity more than the one preceding it.

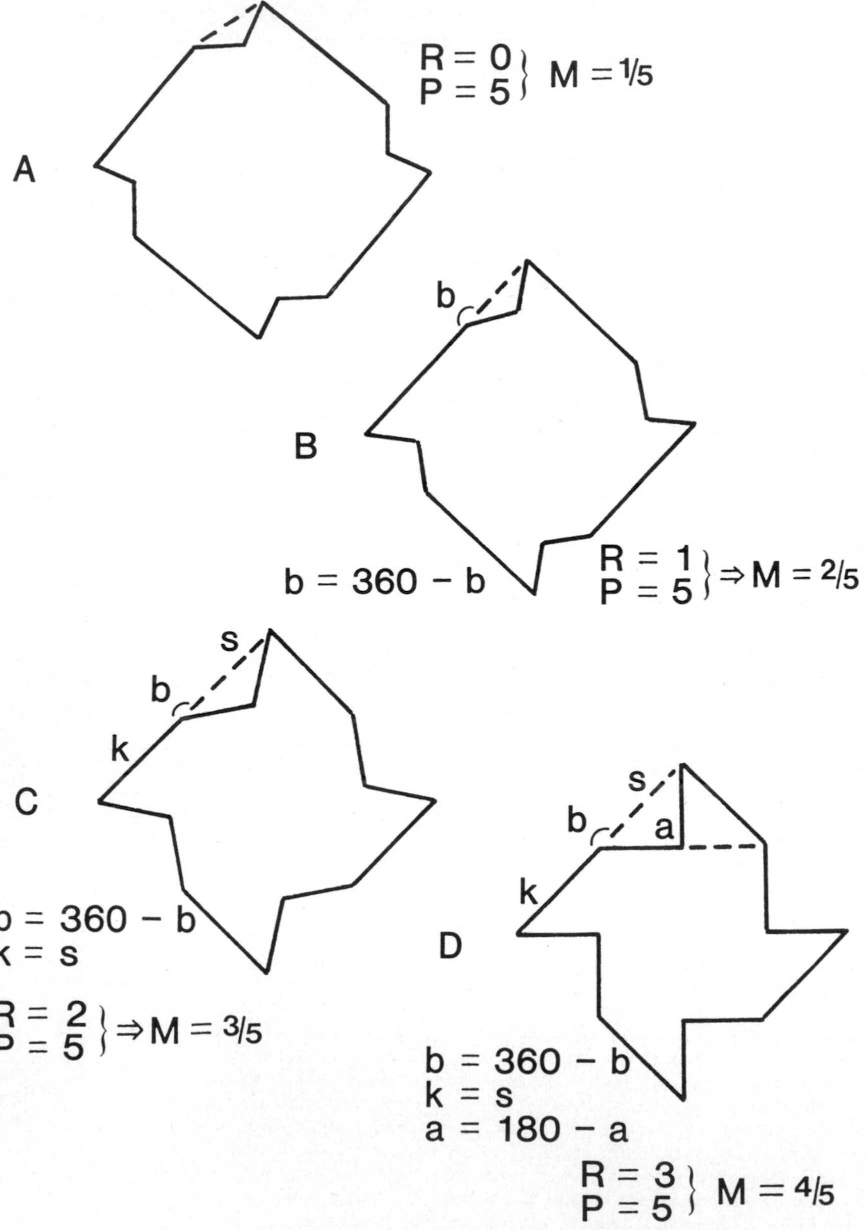

FIGURE 11

The solution to the problcm givcn in Figurc 4.

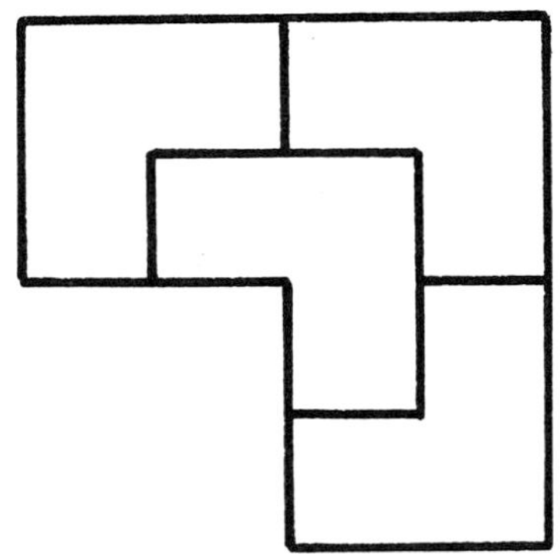

REFERENCES

Arnheim, R. (1954). Art and Visual Perception. Berkeley, California: University of California Press.

Bense, M. (1969). Einfuhrüng in die informationstheoretische Asthetik. Hamburg; Rowolt.

Berlyne, D.E. (1971). Aesthetics and Psychobiology. New York: Appleton-Century-Crofts.

Birkhoff, G.D. (1933). Aesthetic Measure. Cambridge, Massachusetts: Harvard University Press.

Boselie, F. (1983). Ambiguity, beauty and interestingness of line drawings. Canadian Journal of Psychology, 37, 287-292.

Boselie, F. and Leeuwenberg, L.(1983). Birkhoff revisited: beauty as a function of effect and means. Internal Report, 83-10. Nijmegen: University of Nijmegen. Department of Psychology.

Bouleau, C. (1963). The Painters Secret Geometry: A Study of Composition in Art. New York: Brace and World.

Buffart, H., Leeuwenberg, E. and Restle, F. (1981). Coding theory of visual pattern completion. Journal of Experimental Psychology: Human Perception and Performance, 7, 241-274.

Crozier, W.R. and Chapman, A.J. (1981). Aesthetic preferences: prestige and social class. In: D. O'Hare (Ed.) Psychology and the Arts. Brighton, Sussex: Harvester.

Dreistadt, R. (1969). The use of analogies and incubation in obtaining insights in creative problem solving. Journal of Psychology, 71, 159-175.

Eysenck, H.J. (1941). The empirical determination of an aesthetic formula. Psychological Review, 48, 83-92.

Eysenck, H.J. (1942). The experimental study of the 'Good Gestalt' - a new approach. Psychological Review, 49, 344-364.

Eysenck, H.J. (1968). An experimental study of aesthetic preferences for polygonal figures. Journal of General Psychology, 79, 3-17.

Eysenck, H.J. and Castle, M. (1970). Training in art as a factor in the determination of preference judgments for polygons. British Journal of Psychology, 61, 65-81.

Gardner, M. (1978). White and brown music, fractal curves and one-over-fluctuation. Scientific American, 238, 16-32.

Garner, W. (1962). Uncertainty and Structure as Psychological Concepts. New York: Wiley.

Gombrich, E.H. (1956). Art and Illusion. Princeton, New Jersey: Princeton University Press.

Gunzenhaüser, R. (1965). Das äesthetische Mass Birkhoff's in informations-ästhetischer Sicht. In: H. Ronge (Ed.) Kunst und Kybernetik. Köln: Dumont.

Höge, H. (1983). The emotional impact on aesthetic judgments: an experimental investigation of a time-honoured hypothesis. Paper presented to the British Psychological Society, Welsh Branch, International Conference on Psychology and the Arts, Cardiff.

Koffka, K. (1935). Principles of Gestalt Psychology. New York: Harcourt.

Kreitler, H. and Kreitler, S. (1972) Psychology and the Arts. Durham: Duke University Press.

Lasher, M., Carroll, J.M. and Bever, T.G. (1983). The cognitive basis of aesthetic experience. Leonardo, 16, 196-200.

Leeuwenberg, E.L.J. (1969). Quantitatve specification of information in sequential patterns. Psychological Review, 76, 216-220.

Leeuwenberg, E.J.L. (1971). A perceptual coding language for visual and auditory patterns. American Journal of Psychology, 83, 307-349.

Lindauer, M.S. (1981). Aesthetic experience: a neglected topic in the psychology of the arts. In: D. O'Hare (Ed.) Psychology and the Arts. Brighton, Sussex: Harvester

Lindauer, M.S. (1981). Aesthetic experience: a neglected topic in the psychology of the arts. In: D. O'Hare (Ed.) Psychology and the Arts. Brighton, Sussex: Harvester.

Mandlebrot, B. (1977). Fractals: Form, Chance and Dimension. New York: Freeman.

Mandlebrot, B. (1981). Scalebound or scaling shapes. Leonardo, 14, 45-47.

Margulies, S. (1977). Principles of Beauty. Psychological Reports, 41, 3-11.

McWhinnie, H.J. (1968). A review of research on aesthetic measure. Acta Psychologica, 28, 363-375.

Naredi-Rainer, P. von (1982). Architektur und Harmonie. Zahl, Mass und Proportion in der äbenlandischen Baukunst. Köln: Dumont.

Ogden, R.M. (1937). Naive geometry in the psychology of art. American Journal of Psychology, 49, 198-216.

Piaget, J. (1961). Les Mecanismes Perceptifs. Paris: PUF.

Pirenne, M.H. (1970). Optics, Painting and Photography. Cambridge:University Press.

Rashevsky, N. (1938). Contribution to the mathematical biophysics of visual perception with special reference to the theory of aesthetic values of geometrical patterns. Psychometrika, 3, 253-271.

Restle, F. (1982). Coding theory as an integration of Gestalt psychology and information processing theory. In: J. Beck (Ed.) Organization and Representation in Perception. Hillsdale, New Jersey: Erlbaum.

Slebos, J.C. (1939). Fundamentals of Aesthetics and Style. Amsterdam: Ahrend.

Tolnay, C. de (1972). History and Technique of Old Master Drawings. New York: Hacker.

Van Tuyl, H. (1980). Perceptual interpretation of complex line patterns. Journal of Experimental Psychology: Human Perception and Performance, 6, 197-221.

Cognitive Processes in the Perception of Art
W.R. Crozier and A.J. Chapman (editors)
© Elsevier Science Publishers B.V. (North-Holland), 1984

EFFECTS OF MERE EXPOSURE, COGNITIVE SET AND TASK EXPECTATIONS ON AESTHETIC APPRECIATION

J.E. Temme

University of Utrecht

More than a century ago Fechner (1876) postulated that familiarity would have a positive effect on aesthetic appreciation. Although, according to Fechner, 'Uebersättigung' (supersaturation) would lead to a temporary aversion, comparable with over-eating, the more familiar aesthetic object would be liked more than the less familiar. Some corroboration for this hypothesis is reported in a number of older studies; for example, Meyer (1903) found avant-garde music was liked better when heard more often. Pepper (1919) reported increased appreciation for unusual colour combinations after familiarization had taken place. Preference for the more familiar of two paintings by the same artist was found by Maslow (1937). Research on the effect of familiarity on affect was revitalized by Zajonc's (1968) monograph in which the hypothesis was examined that: 'mere repeated exposure of the individual to a stimulus is a sufficient condition for the enhancement of his attitude toward it. By 'mere exposure' is meant a condition which just makes the given stimulus accessible to the individual's perception' (Zajonc, 1968, p. 1).

Experimental evidence supporting the hypothesis that the attractiveness of a stimulus is enhanced by mere repeated exposure is reported by Harrison (1968), Harrison et al (1971), Harrison and Zajonc (1970), Janisse (1970), Matlin (1970), Zajonc (1968), Zajonc and Rajecki (1969), Zajonc et al (1971). These findings suggest that familiarity, the result of mere exposure, does not breed contempt but comfort (Zajonc, 1970). Other researchers however have reported negative effects of familiarity on appreciation (e.g., Cantor, 1968; Cantor and Kubise, 1969; Faw and Pien, 1971; Lemond and Nunnally, 1974; Siebold, 1972). Enhancement followed by a decrease of attractiveness, an inverted-U relationship, has also been reported. Harrison and Crandall (1972) found this relationship between familiarity and affect when they repeatedly presented the same stimuli and had them rated immediately after the last presentation. Inverted-U relationships between familiarity and attractiveness are also reported by Saegert and Jellison (1970) for simple stimuli, and by Zajonc et al (1972) for abstract paintings.

To explain the contradictions between empirical findings, Berlyne (1970) has postulated a two-factor theory. The first factor 'positive habituation' leads to an increase of attractiveness, while the second factor 'tedium' decreases attractiveness. Positive habituation as well as tedium are a result of familiarization, but because the positive effect of habituation starts immediately and the negative effect of tedium somewhat later, their joint effects on attractiveness lead to an inverted-U function between familiarity and affect. This function relates the 'hedonic value' of stimuli with their arousal potential, the latter being dependent on the novelty and complexity of the stimuli.

According to Berlyne (1967, 1971, 1973) the arousal potential of stimuli is a result of their degree of complexity, which is a function of collative variables such as ambiguity, incongruity, and novelty. The more complex a stimulus, the more arousal potential it will have. The relationship between arousal potential and hedonic value, for example the degree of aesthetic preference, has the shape of an inverted-U. Very high as well as very low arousal potential is supposed to have aversive effects and therefore stimuli of an intermediate level of complexity will be preferred. The unbroken lined curve in Figure 1 is a graphic representation of this relationship. The dotted line in Figure 1 represents the linearly increasing function of the logarithm of exposure frequency of the stimulus, first reported by Zajonc (1968).

FIGURE 1

Hypothetical relationships between frequencies of exposure and preference.

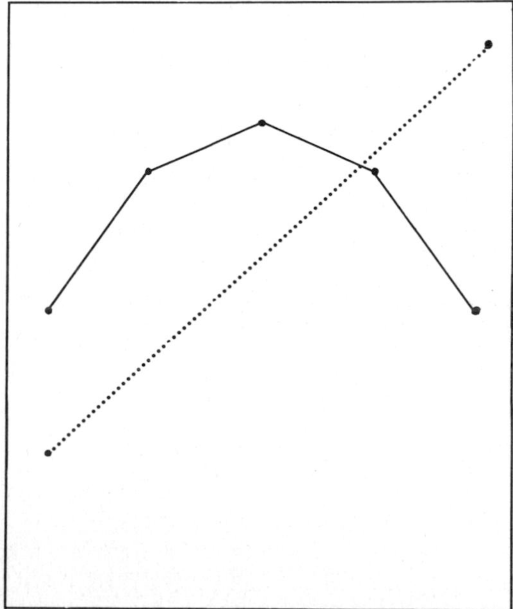

According to Zajonc, Crandall, Kail and Swap (1974), Berlyne's (1970) two-factor theory only explains the affective influence of familiarization on exploratory approach reactions. They interpret the inverted-U function as a combined result of a permanent positive effect and a transitory boredom effect. The latter only influences 'exploratory approach reactions', the 'affinitive approach reactions' resulting from repeated exposure to the same stimulus are not subject to the affect lowering influences of boredom. To give support to this interpretation Zajonc, Crandall and Kail (1974) report an experiment in which stimuli were presented 0, 1, 9, 27 or as many as 243 times and then rated on a number of scales, with good-bad representing affinitive approach reactions and interesting-boring, like-dislike and harmful-beneficial representing exploratory approach reactions. The good-bad scale, supposed to be most free of exploratory components, indeed showed the most positive ratings for the stimuli that were exposed 243 times. The 3 other scales showed a drop at the highest frequency of presentation. According to Zajonc et al (1974) this drop had disappeared after a one-week delay. The curve resumed monotonicity when subjects were again asked to rate on a liking scale, the stimuli they had seen with different frequencies a week before. These results support the interpretation that tedium has only a transitory effect and then only on the exploratory components of attractiveness.

The effect of tedium might explain the results of Harrison and Crandall (1972) and Saegert and Jellison (1970). They showed an inverted-U relation between exposure and attractiveness, probably because both experiments used paradigms in which tedium is likely to appear. In the Harrison and Crandall experiment the same stimuli were repeated in homogeneous presentation sequences and there was overlap between exposure and rating phases because each stimulus was rated immediately after its maximum exposure was attained. In the Saegert and Jellison experiment the stimuli were simple - one to three brush strokes of the type of which Chinese characters are composed. According to Harrison (1977, p. 45) a positive effect of mere exposure on rated attractiveness 'is less likely when (1) the stimuli are simple; (2) the stimuli are presented in homogeneous sequences; and (3) the exposure and rating phases overlap.' This overall pattern was used by Harrison (1977, p. 47, 50) to explain as follows:

> 'Many of the studies bearing on the mere exposure hypothesis have dealt with people's reactions to musical selections, art works, and other aesthetic stimuli. Compared with the investigations thus far reviewed, these studies have often suggested that low frequency or intermediate frequency stimuli are best liked ... Thus, a sizable proportion of the studies which have assessed people's reactions to aesthetic stimuli have yielded results which appear to conflict with the mere exposure hypothesis. However, when complexity, presentation sequence, and time of rating are taken into account, they do not conflict with a previously noted overall pattern.'

It may be true that simple stimuli, homogeneous presentation sequences and overlapping exposure and rating phases appear in many studies dealing with aesthetic appreciation (e.g., all three in Berlyne, 1970).

None of these three factors, however, is present in the experiment by Zajonc et al (1972) in which abstract paintings were used as stimuli. These paintings were not what is usually considered as simple stimuli: they were not presented homogeneously and rating took place after the exposure phase, so there was no overlap. Nevertheless an inverted-U function was found between amount of exposure and liking of the paintings. Zajonc et al (1972) tried to explain this unexpected result by the high degree of stimulus discriminability of the abstract paintings. In their paper they reported three other experiments, one with highly similar 'paintings' (in fact one reproduction cut in 12 pieces) and two with highly discriminable stimuli photographs of men's faces and nonsense words. Results showed that appreciation for the highly similar paintings dropped when they were seen in the highest frequency (25), but such a drop was not found for the highly discriminable other types of stimuli. Discriminability does not explain the inverted-U relationship between exposure and liking of paintings. Perhaps, according to Zajonc et al this relationship is a result of the interestingness of the paintings. Subjects are eager to become acquainted with all the paintings and feel frustrated by the frequently exposed stimuli. In terms of Zajonc, Crandall, Kail and Swap (1974) this would mean that paintings, more than other types of stimuli, instigate exploratory approach reactions. It has already been mentioned that, according to Zajonc et al (1974), these type of reactions are more subject to tedium than are affinitive approach reactions. If presenting abstract paintings in a mere exposure experiment indeed leads to a higher than usual inclination to explore the stimuli, this would explain the inverted-U relationship between exposure and the appreciation of paintings in such an experiment.

EXPERIMENT 1

In the present experiment the hypothesis was tested that presenting abstract paintings in a mere exposure experiment induces an explorative, aesthetic set. To test this hypothesis, abstract paintings and Chinese ideographs were rated after being presented in different frequencies, both types of stimuli in two different ways. Half the subjects were asked to indicate their aesthetic appreciation, the other half to guess the meaning of the stimuli. It was expected that presenting aesthetic stimuli in the form of abstract paintings, would induce an aesthetic set in which exploratory approach reactions are presumed to be preponderant. Presenting another type of stimuli, Chinese ideographs, would induce another set in which affinitive approach reactions supposedly dominate. An attempt was made to change these original sets by asking half the subjects who had seen the paintings to guess their meaning instead of judging them aesthetically and asking half the subjects who had seen ideographs to judge them aesthetically instead of guessing their meaning. If the sets, induced by the type of stimuli presented, could be altered by these instructions in such a way as either to maximize or to minimize the influence of affinitive or exploratory reactions this would lead to the same results for abstract paintings and Chinese characters: a negative or inverted-U relationship between amount of exposure and affect when the stimuli are judged aesthetically and a monotonic positive relationship when the meaning of the stimuli is guessed.

Procedure

The material used to test these predictions consisted of 12 colour slides of abstract paintings by Appel, Corneill, de Kooning and Pollock and of 12 colour slides of Chinese ideographs painted with a brush on off-white, textured paper. The slides were projected (at a size of approximately 60 x 90 cm) by way of a carrousel-type projector on which a time switch, set at 5 secs, was installed.

All 72 subjects were first told they would be shown a number of slides and asked to pay close attention. They were shown 10 out of 12 slides of either paintings or characters, counterbalanced over the frequencies 0, 1, 2, 4, 8 and 16 (two slides, the zero-frequency, were seen for the first time when they were being rated). Half the number of subjects saw slides of paintings, rated them, were given a filler task, and then saw slides of characters. The other half of the subjects started with characters and ended with paintings.

Manipulation of Set

Because presenting paintings was supposed to induce an aesthetic set, half the number of subjects who had seen paintings were simply asked to rate them on a scale 'beautiful-ugly'. The other half of the subjects were told they had just seen some examples of abstract expressionism, which could be considered a mode of non-verbal communication. They were asked to guess which meaning was expressed by each of the paintings and instructed to do so on a 'favourable-unfavourable' scale.

After seeing Chinese ideographs half the subjects were given the instruction used by Zajonc (1968): they were told that the characters stood for adjectives, and that the meaning of each adjective could be indicated on a scale 'favourable-unfavourable'. The other half of the subjects were told they had seen some examples of Chinese calligraphy and were instructed to rate them aesthetically on a scale 'beautiful-ugly'.

All 12 slides were now presented in a random order and were rated on the appropriate scale. The subjects were then given a filler task (the Baron-Welsh figure preference test) while the experimenter changed the slides. After the filler task the subjects were shown the second type of stimuli and asked to rate them aesthetically if they had done so with the first type of stimuli or guess the meaning of the stimuli if this had been their first assignment.

Results with Paintings

For both types of stimuli a separate analysis of variance for complex Latin squares was performed (Winer, 1971). The results of this analysis for abstract paintings showed that the manipulations of both set ($F=4.04$; $df=1,60$; $p<.05$) and frequencies ($F=3.07$; $df=5,660$; $p<.01$) were effective. The significance of the effect of set resulted from the difference in ratings between aesthetic and meaning judgments. The latter were, averaged over frequencies, lower than the aesthetic judgments. Also statistically significant ($F=2.88$; $df=5,660$; $p<.05$) was the interaction between these two factors: inducing either an aesthetic or a meaning set leads to different exposure effects.

The exposure effects on abstract paintings when judged aesthetically or when the meaning of the stimuli were guessed are shown graphically in Figure 2. The hypotheses about the shape of the relationships between exposure and ratings were tested with trend analyses. For the aesthetic judgment only the linear trend component proved significant ($F=15.32$; $df=1,660$; $p<.001$). As can be seen in Figure 2 this concerns a negative relationship as was hypothesized. Guessing the meaning of the pictures, however, did not have the hypothesized effect on the influence of mere exposure on the ratings of the stimuli. In this case, only the quadratic component was significant ($F=6.48$; $df=1,66$; $p<.05$). As can be seen in Figure 2, this curve is U-shaped and not monotonic as predicted in the hypothesis.

FIGURE 2

Effects of frequencies of exposure and set induction on affective rating of abstract paintings.

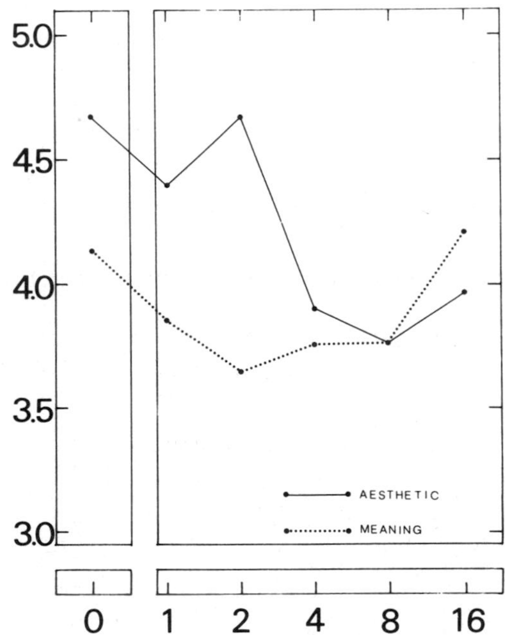

Results with Characters

As with paintings, manipulations of set (F=10.45; df=1,60; p<.005) and frequencies were effective. Again, averaged aesthetic judgments were significantly (F=10.45; df=1,60; p<.005) higher than meaning judgments. However, the interaction between these two factors was not significant when ideographs were used as stimuli.

Exposure effects on Chinese characters are shown in Figure 3. Trend analysis of the curve shown in Figure 3 gave support to the hypothesis that guessing the meaning of characters would lead to a positive effect of exposure. Only the linear component was highly significant ($F=15.79$; $df=1,660$; $p<.001$). No confirmation was found for the hypothesis about the aesthetic judgment of the characters. In this case there was only a tendency towards significance of the linear component ($F=3.08$; $df=1,660$; $p<.10$). The predicted negative or inverted-U relationship was not found.

FIGURE 3

Effects of frequencies of exposure and set induction on affective rating of characters.

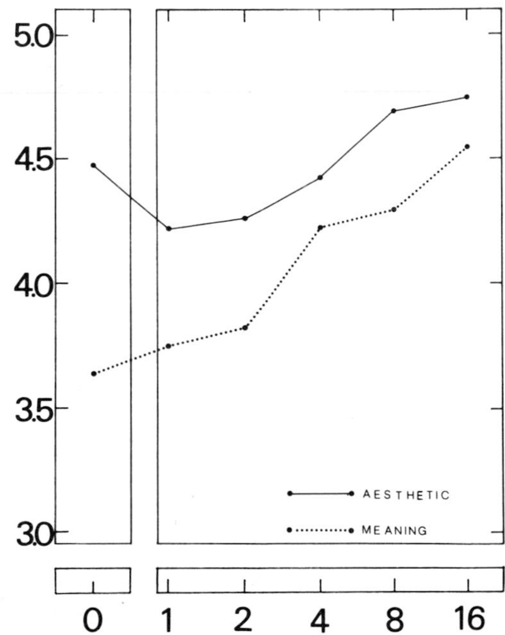

EXPERIMENT 2

In the first experiment the effects of mere exposure on the aesthetic judgments of abstract paintings and the judgments of the meaning of Chinese characters supported the hypotheses about the effects of an aesthetic set (exploratory approach) or a meaning set (affinitive approach). On the other hand, the results of the conditions in which stimuli were judged in a non-standard way did not support the hypotheses. For both hybrid conditions a (non-inverted) U-shaped relationship between exposure and preference was found, be it that with characters as stimuli this relationship was not significant at the 5% level.

A possible explanation for the unpredicted effect of mere exposure in the two hybrid conditions could be that the original set, induced by the stimuli, is too strong to be sufficiently overcome by the instruction to guess the meaning of abstract paintings or the instruction to judge Chinese characters aesthetically. Therefore a second experiment was performed in which the instructions to judge the stimuli aesthetically or to guess their meaning were given before the stimuli were presented in different frequencies. This was done in the first place to strengthen set induction. It also had the advantage that an experimental method results which is a mixture of the methods normally used by Zajonc (e.g., 1968) and by Berlyne (e.g., 1970). Berlyne used to instruct his subjects, before any stimuli were presented, that the stimuli would be rated on a scale after a number of presentations. In a typical Zajonc mere exposure experiment the normal procedure is to give the instructions concerning the rating of the stimuli after presenting them in a number of different frequencies.

As mentioned before Zajonc and his co-workers (with the notable exception of Zajonc et al, 1972, who used abstract paintings and found an inverted-U relationship between exposure and liking) usually find positive relationships between exposure and affect. Berlyne (1967, 1970, 1971) on the other hand reported negative or inverted-U relationships between familiarity and 'hedonic value'. By comparing the results of our first and second experiment the possible effects of instructing the subjects either before or after presenting the stimuli can be taken into account.

Like in the first experiment, a negative or inverted-U relationship between exposure and liking of abstract paintings was hypothesized. When subjects were instructed to guess the meaning of abstract paintings it was expected that this instruction would overcome or at least reduce the implicit aesthetic set evoked by these type of stimuli. Therefore a positive relationship, based on affinitive reactions, between exposure and preference, was hypothesized for this condition.

A third hypothesis, based on the results of the first experiment, was tested: aesthetic judgments, averaged over frequencies, would be higher than meaning judgments.

Procedure

To test these hypotheses the same procedure as in Experiment 1 was used, with the following exceptions. Instead of 12 slides, counterbalanced over 6 frequencies, 10 slides were counterbalanced over 5 frequencies: 0, 1, 3, 8 and 27. Instructions about how to judge the stimuli were given before (instead of after) presenting them in different frequencies. Like in the first experiment there were two instructions, one to judge the paintings aesthetically and the other to guess their meaning. Eighty subjects were randomly divided over these two conditions. After presenting the slides, a booklet was handed out with an instruction as to how to rate the paintings on the first page, followed by 10 pages with a 7-point scale: pleasing-displeasing. The same scale was used in both conditions. All 10 slides were presented once more and rated on the scales in the booklet. After completion subjects addressed two further questions in the booklet, about the task: (Did you find the task easy-difficult/boring-interesting?) and these also had to be answered on 7-point scales.

Results

These are graphically presented in Figure 4. Again manipulations of set ($F=8.73$; $df=1,70$; $p<.05$) and frequencies ($F=6.15$; $df=4,630$; $p<.001$) were effective, but the interaction between these 2 factors was not statistically significant ($F=2.32$; $df=4,630$; $p=0.06$). The first two hypotheses concerned the shapes of the two curves in Figure 3. The curve representing the effect of mere exposure after an aesthetic set had been induced was supposed to be inverted-U shaped or negative, while the curve representing the effect of a meaning set was supposed to be monotonically positive. The latter was not found.

Trend analysis showed that the curve representing aesthetic judgment had a significant linear component ($F=4.10$; $df=1,390$; $p<.05$) as well as a significant quadratic component ($F=16.51$; $df=1,390$; $p<.05$). This curve can best be described as an inverted-U relationship with a downward tendency, which is in support of the hypothesis. Of the curve representing the judgment of meaning only the linear component was significant ($F=16.17$; $df=1,390$; $p<.001$). Quite contrary to the hypothesis this is a monotonic negative relationship.

The third hypothesis, that aesthetic judgments would be higher than meaning judgments, was supported by the results. Averaged over frequencies the mean aesthetic rating of the stimuli is 4.38 and the mean rating of their meaning is 3.99 and this difference is significant beyond the .005 level.

Two additional questions concerning difficulty and interestingness of the rating task were examined. Rating the paintings aesthetically was easier for the subjects ($t=2.61$; $df=78$; $p<.01$). Although guessing the meaning of the paintings was rated as slightly more interesting the results were not statistically significant ($t=1.37$; $df=78$; $p<.20$).

Discussion

The most striking result of this experiment is the unexpected finding that exposure has a negative effect on ratings of the ascribed meaning of paintings when the subjects are told beforehand they can expect such ratings. Asking for this kind of rating after stimuli have been exposed in different frequencies usually results in a positive effect of exposure. This was found not only in the first experiment reported here but also in many studies by Zajonc and his co-workers. Goodness of ascribed meaning is supposed to be representative of affinitive approach reactions and the most free of the effects of tedium (Zajonc et al, 1974). To account for this unexpected result, two more experiments were performed and they are described below.

FIGURE 4

Effects of set induction and frequencies of exposure on pleasingness of abstract paintings.

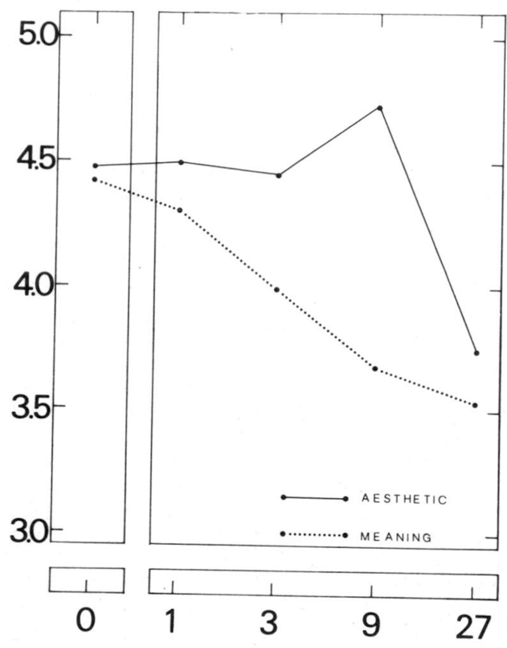

EXPERIMENT 3

In the instruction, given before the stimuli were presented in the second experiment, it was suggested that a correct answer was possible to the question how pleasing or displeasing the meaning of each of the paintings was. In this respect, the condition in which the meaning of the paintings had to be guessed was different from the aesthetic judgment condition. In the latter condition no correctness of judgment was implied. Subjects in a psychological experiment generally try to perform their task as well as possible; they want to look good in the eyes of the experimenter. In this context, Rosenberg (1965) has referred to 'evaluation apprehension'. When subjects are told they will have to rate the meaning of abstract paintings, every repeated presentation of the stimuli is a confrontation with the difficulty of this task. This is not the case when aesthetic judgments are asked. Aesthetic judgments are probably perceived as subjective and contrary to ratings of meaning, no objective, correct judgment is assumed. As the saying implies, tastes do not have to be accounted for. Giving the instruction to judge paintings aesthetically before or after presenting the stimuli in different frequencies does not make much difference, and this was shown in the results of our first and second experiment. In both experiments exposure eventually had a negative effect on aesthetic appreciation, regardless of whether subjects were instructed before or after the exposure phase.

When subjects were told after the exposure phase that they had to guess the meaning of abstract paintings, there resulted a U-shaped relationship between exposure and assumed-favourableness-of-meaning. When instructions were given before exposure, a monotonic negative effect of exposure was found. Evaluation apprehension could explain the negative effect of exposure when subjects are instructed beforehand that they are to indicate the meaning of abstract paintings. If this explanation is correct, giving instructions before starting exposure to Chinese ideographs of which the meaning has to be guessed must also lead to a decrease in rated pleasingness of the meaning of the characters shown in the higher frequencies. Like abstract paintings, ideographs do not contain objective information about their meaning, at least not to European subjects. If subjects are asked to guess the meaning of this type of stimuli they are faced with a task as impossible as guessing the meaning of abstract paintings. Therefore, if evaluation apprehension explains the negative effect of exposure to paintings combined with knowledge of the task, a negative effect of exposure to ideographs should also be found when instructions are given before exposure. Because Chinese characters are less easily discriminated than abstract paintings an initial increase in pleasingness of rated meanings should be expected. This initial increase could be caused by the positive influence of learning to discriminate the stimuli which are perceived as contributing to task performance. It should be followed by a decrease in appreciation of the frequently presented stimuli, caused by frustration to fulfill the task of correctly guessing their meaning.

This hypothesis was tested in Experiment 3, which is similar to the second experiment except for the stimuli used: viz. Chinese characters instead of abstract paintings. Again, half the subjects were asked to judge the stimuli aesthetically and the other half to rate their meaning. The hypothesis concerning the latter is described above. Between exposure and aesthetic appreciation again an inverted-U or negative relationship was expected. Further hypotheses to be tested were: (1) aesthetic rating would be higher than rated meaning; and (2) rating the meaning of the stimuli would be more difficult and also more interesting than aesthetic rating.

Procedure

The procedure was the same as in Experiment 2. Only the instructions to rate stimuli aesthetically or to guess their meaning were adapted to be used with Chinese characters instead of abstract paintings.

Results

Significant main effects for set ($F=7.16$; $df=1,70$; $p<.01$) as well as frequencies ($F=3.93$; $df=4,630$; $p<.005$) were found. These effects are graphed in Figure 5. In both conditions an inverted-U relationship between frequencies of exposure and ratings was hypothesized. Trend analysis of the ratings of meaning showed the quadratic component to be significant ($F=10.65$; $df=1,390$; $p<.005$). In support of the hypothesis, this curve can best be described as an inverted-U.

FIGURE 5

Effects of set induction and frequencies of exposure on pleasingness of Chinese characters.

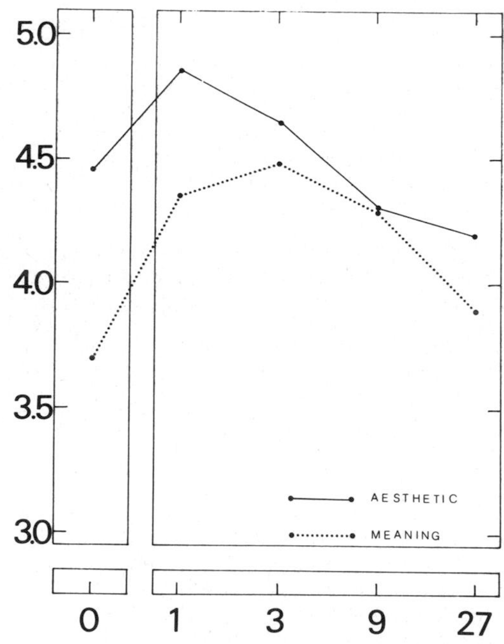

No significant component of trend was found for the condition in which aesthetic ratings were performed, although both the linear component ($F=3.56$; $df=1,390$; $p<.10$) and the quadratic component ($F=2.91$; $df=1,390$; $p<.10$) tended towards significance, thus supporting the hypothesis of the inverted-U relationship.

In support of the further hypotheses, aesthetic ratings were significantly higher than the ratings of meaning; rating the meaning of the stimuli was considered more difficult ($t=2.58$; $df=78$; $p<.01$) and more interesting ($t=2.01$; $df=78$; $p<.05$).

Discussion

As in the foregoing experiment, the more interesting result of the present experiment is the finding that exposure does not have the usual positive effect on ratings of the ascribed meaning of stimuli when such ratings are expected because instructions are given before presenting the stimuli. In the condition in which the meaning of Chinese characters had to be guessed the instruction was, with the exception of the part in which repeated presentations were announced, an exact translation of the instruction used in the original Zajonc (1968) experiment. This original experiment has been replicated several times with modifications intended to find limiting conditions of the mere exposure effect (Brickham et al, 1972; Harrison and Crandall, 1972; Zajonc, Crandall, Kail and Swap, 1974; and Zajonc et al, 1971). Despite the search for limiting conditions, three of the four studies report positive exposure effects when Chinese ideographs were used as stimuli. The one exception is the Harrison and Crandall (1972) study in which an inverted-U relationship between affective ratings of ideographs is reported under conditions of maximum homogenity of exposure sequence and immediate ratings; that is the same stimulus is presented until the maximal intended exposure of that particular stimulus is reached and then rated.

Harrison and Crandall (1972) explained their results by suggesting the influence of tedium is enhanced by homogeneous presentation followed by immediate ratings. The results of the second and third experiment reported here suggest another possible explanation: inverted-U or negative relationships between exposure and appreciation of stimuli arise when subjects know, or at least expect, that their task will be to rate the stimuli. Whether this expectation results from an explicit instruction given before stimuli are presented or from the implicit information when the first rating has been done and subjects are exposed to the following stimuli, seems to be of minor importance. Even if no explicit instruction about rating the stimuli is given before exposure, presenting abstract paintings results in inverted-U or negative relationships between frequency of presentation and appreciation of this type of stimuli (Zajonc et al, 1972; first experiment reported here). Therefore, a fourth experiment was performed to find out whether presenting painting is, like ratings interspersed in the exposure sequence, a way of implicitly instructing the subjects that rating the stimuli will be their experimental task.

EXPERIMENT 4

In the first experiment reported here, no support was found for the hypothesis that inducing an aesthetic set before rating more or less frequently presented stimuli would lead to explorative reactions while inducing a meaning set would evoke affinitive reactions. In the second experiment it was tried to strengthen set induction by giving the appropriate instructions before presenting the stimuli. The effect of exposure on aesthetic appreciation was not influenced as was expected, but the effect of frequency of presentation on the rated meaning of abstract paintings was quite contrary to expectations. Rather than the hypothesized positive relationship between exposure and appreciation of stimuli, a negative relationship was found. The more often a painting was presented, the more negative was the rating of the meaning ascribed to that painting. Results of the third experiment confirmed that instructing the subjects before starting the exposure sequence also has a negative effect on the appreciation of frequently presented Chinese ideographs. It seems that the inverted-U or negative relationship between frequency of exposure and appreciation, typically found when aesthetic stimuli are used in a mere exposure experiment (e.g., Brickman et al, 1972; Zajonc et al, 1972; experiments reported here) is a result of the information about the experimental task implicitly given by presenting this type of stimuli. This notion led to the hypothesis to be tested in the present experiment: when abstract paintings are used as stimuli in a mere exposure experiment, more of the experimental subjects will expect that their task is to rate the stimuli than when Chinese characters are used in the same type of experiment. Additional hypotheses to be tested were: (a) between frequency of exposure and appreciation of abstract paintings there is an inverted-U relationship; and (b) between frequency of exposure and appreciation of Chinese characters there is a monotonic positive relationship. Because expressing one's appreciation of Chinese characters is a less common task than the appreciation of paintings, it was expected that the appreciation of Chinese characters would be perceived as a more difficult task than the appreciation of abstract paintings.

The task to rate paintings was perceived as more interesting in Experiment 2 than the rating of ideographs was in Experiment 3. One the other hand, ratings of meaning, which are more plausible for ideographs than for paintings, tend to be perceived as more interesting than aesthetic ratings. Because in the present experiment no instruction to guess the meaning of either type of stimuli was to be given, it was expected that the appreciation of abstract paintings would be perceived as a more interesting task than the appreciation of Chinese characters.

Procedure

After the subjects were seated they were told they would be shown a number of slides, and they were instructed to pay close attention. Slides were projected in the same frequencies as in Experiments 2 and 3. Twenty subjects saw slides of paintings, the other 20 were shown slides of ideographs. After the exposure sequence, subjects were asked to write down their expectations about what would happen next. When this question was answered, ten 7-point scales were presented to rate the degree of pleasingness of each of the stimuli, which were shown once more in a random order. The only instruction given was how to mark the scale point considered to be most appropriate for the stimulus just seen. Three more 7-point scales were presented to rate the degree in which the rating task accorded to expectations about the experimental task, and the degree to which the rating task was perceived as difficult and as interesting.

Results

The main hypothesis of the present experiment concerned task expectations of the subjects. Corresponding to this hypothesis, more subjects who had seen paintings instead of ideographs expected that rating the stimuli would be their task. After being exposed to the stimuli in different frequencies, twenty-five percent of the subjects shown paintings as compared to 5% of the subjects shown ideographs used the term 'rating' (of the stimuli) or an equivalent of this word in answering the question about their expectations as to what would come next. However impressive a ratio of 5:1 may be, we are still left with 75% of incorrect answers in the exposure of paintings condition (to be compared with 95% of incorrect answers in the exposure of ideographs condition).

After being analysed, the 75% of incorrect answers in the exposure of paintings condition could be divided into two categories. Forty percent of the subjects in this condition expected that their task would be to recognize the stimuli. The remaining 35% gave somewhat ambiguous answers, which did not completely meet the criterion of using the word 'rating' in their answers.

Two out of the 20 subjects exposed to ideographs answered the question about task expectations by stating they did not have the slightest idea. The remaining 85% expected they would be asked to recognize the stimuli.

After performing the rating task, subjects were asked to indicate the degree to which this task accorded to expectations. Subjects who had seen paintings averaged 3.65 on a 1 (not at all) to 7 (completely) scale, subjects shown characters only averaged 1.45 ($t=3.16$; $df=38$; $p<.005$). Like the results on the first question about task expectations this result supports the hypothesis that a rating task will be expected more often after exposure to paintings than after exposure to ideographs.

Differences in attitude towards the task also sustained the relevant hypotheses. Rating Chinese characters was perceived as more difficult, a mean score of 3.10 on a seven-point scale, than rating abstract paintings, which averaged 2.15 ($t=1.89$; $df=38$; $p<.05$). This supports the notion that the rating of paintings is a more usual task than the rating of characters.

Rating paintings was considered more interesting ($\bar{X}=4.60$) than the rating of characters ($\bar{X}=3.75$) ($t=2.13$; $df=38$; $p<.025$). In Experiments 2 and 3 the rating of meaning was perceived as more interesting than aesthetic rating. Therefore this result supports the idea that the possible meaning of the characters was not considered when rating them.

Frequency of exposure had different effects on the appreciation of paintings and characters ($F=2.72$; $df=4,390$; $p<.05$), and these effects are presented in Figure 5. The shape of the curves support the hypotheses: a highly significant linear trend component for the relationship between frequency of exposure and appreciation of Chinese characters ($F=12.17$; $df=1,390$; $p<.001$). Between frequency of exposure and the appreciation of paintings, the relationship satisfied the hypothesized inverted-U shape, but there was only a tendency towards significance of the quadratic component ($F=3.26$; $df=1,390$; $p<.10$).

The positive effect of mere exposure on the appreciation of characters appears, even when degree of pleasingness of the stimuli is rated instead of degree of goodness of assumed meaning. Pleasingness suggests rather an aesthetic rating than a rating of meaning, so it seems superfluous to induce a meaning set to find a positive effect of mere exposure on the appreciation of characters. An inverted-U relationship between frequency of exposure and appreciation of abstract paintings is also found without any instruction inducing an aesthetic set.

FIGURE 6

Effects of frequencies of exposure on rated pleasingness of abstract paintings and Chinese characters.

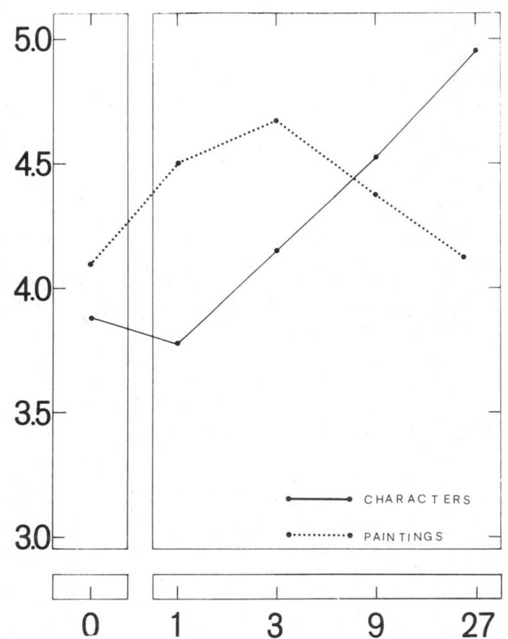

Discussion

The four experiments reported here were performed in an attempt to explain an unexpected result, reported in a study by Zajonc et al (1972). Using the same experimental method which had yielded monotonic positive effects of exposure on attitudes towards Turkish words, Chinese ideographs and photographs of men's faces (Zajonc, 1968) they found an inverted-U relationship between exposure and appreciation of abstract paintings. An explanation for this result might be that aesthetic stimuli somehow trigger more exploratory reactions than other types of stimuli. According to Zajonc, Crandall, Kail and Swap (1974) exploratory approach reactions are more sensitive to the negative effect of tedium on the appreciation of repeatedly presented stimuli than are affinitive approach reactions. The study by Zajonc et al (1974) was a reply to a study by Berlyne (1970).

Berlyne (1967, 1970, 1971) has formulated a theory about the relationship between pleasingness of stimuli, their 'hedonic value' and arousal potential. Stimulus familiarity, the result of exposure to the stimulus, decreases the amount of arousal potential. Because the relationship between arousal potential and pleasingness is supposed to an inverted-U function, familiarity will eventually have a negative effect on pleasingness. According to Berlyne (1967) the arousal potential of either too novel or too familiar stimuli is either too high or too low to bring an organism to its optimal level of arousal. Berlyne (1970) maintained that familiarity has lasting negative effects on pleasingness, while Zajonc et al (1974) asserted that any negative effects of familiarity on affect are only temporary.

Both Berlyne (1970) and Zajonc et al (1974) have reported evidence sustaining their points of view. However, according to the results of the presently reported experiments, neither lasting effects of tedium (Berlyne, 1970) nor temporary effects of frustrated exploratory approach reactions (Zajonc et al, 1972, 1974) are to be considered as causal factors explaining negative effects of high exposure frequencies on the appreciation of stimuli in an experiment. It seems that these negative effects are obtained when experimental subjects feel that further presentations of the same stimulus do not contribute to their performance of the expected task. In other words, negative effects of exposure rather than positive effects (Stang, 1974) are an experimental artefact. Stang's (1974) criticism of Zajonc (1968) that the positive effect of mere exposure is an artefact of the experimental situation was refuted by the results of an experiment by Moreland and Zajonc (1976). In that experiment, demand characteristics, which according to Stang (1974) caused the mere exposure effect, were eliminated by a between-subjects design. Different groups of subjects viewed novel stimuli at different frequencies, so the subjects were not aware of differences in exposure frequencies. Nevertheless increasing exposure had a positive effect on the ratings of the stimuli.

According to Burgess and Sales (1971) and Grush (1976) the effect of mere exposure can be considered as a process of attitude formation. Depending on the associations, linked to every repeated exposure, a positive as well as a negative effect can be explained. The results of experiments by Saegert et al (1973), and by Zajonc, Markus and Wilson (1974), however, showed that negative associations do not always lead to negative exposure effects. In the Saegert et al (1973) experiment exposure was manipulated by varying the number of encounters among subjects. Positive or negative associations were manipulated by having the subjects taste either pleasant or noxious solutions. Both conditions resulted in a positive relationship between number of encounters and interpersonal attraction. Negative associations did not result in negative exposure effects. Similar results were obtained by Zajonc, Markus and Wilson (1974). They showed their subjects photographs of faces of Chinese men in different frequencies. In the positive association condition these men were announced as famous scholars and scientists: in the negative association condition they were announced as criminals. With every stimulus presentation the scientific contribution or the committed crime was mentioned. Liking for 'scientists' as well as for 'criminals' increased with frequency of exposure.

Although these results suggest negative associations do not influence the positive effect of mere exposure, there still is reason to believe the attitudinal effects of frequency of exposure are partly a result of associations during the presentation of stimuli. However, these are not the kind of associations generated by presenting stimuli in a positive or negative context. Rather than the objective contextual associations, it seems the subjective associations resulting from task expectations contribute to the results of an exposure experiment. Not the associations generated by the experimenter, but the associations generated by the subject decide whether frequency of exposure will have a positive or a negative effect.

The subjects in Zajonc et al's (1974)experiment who were shown photographs of Chinese men probably expected they would be asked to recognize the faces, like the majority of subjects in the fourth experiment reported here who expected they would be asked to recognize the Chinese characters shown them. Whether presented as scientists or as criminals, Chinese faces are easier to recognize when seen more often by Western folk. Like the Chinese ideographs used in the experiments reported here, Chinese faces are, certainly for European subjects, stimuli that are hard to discriminate from one another. When subjects expect their task will be to recognize the stimuli, frequent presentation of stimuli that are low on discriminability will be a positive experience. Thus positive associations with every repeated stimulus presentation will be generated when hard to discriminate stimuli are presented and a recognition task is expected.

Even when no recognition task is expected, exposure does have positive effects on attitudes. Examples are the study by Saegert et al (1973) in which the subjects thought their task was the tasting of pleasant or noxious solutions, and the field experiment by Zajonc and Rajecki (1969). In this latter experiment students rated the goodness-of-meaning of nonsense words. These words had appeared in different frequencies in a number of university newspapers. A positive effect of frequency of exposure was found, although during exposure, subjects had not been aware of their participation in an experiment.

Task expectations are not to be considered as the causal factor which explains the effects of mere exposure. At the most, they contribute to positive effects when frequent exposure is perceived as a positive contribution to performance of the expected task. On the other hand, it seems that task expectations interfere with the mere exposure effect when frequent exposure is perceived as not contributing to or even hindering task performance. The mere exposure effect is probably not hampered when Chinese ideographs are presented before any instructions about rating them are given. The typical result of such an experiment is a monotonic positive relationship between frequency of exposure and appreciation. Presenting abstract paintings in the same way, however, results in an inverted-U or even negative relationship between frequency of exposure and appreciation.

The difference in the results obtained when either characters or paintings are used as stimuli seems to be partly caused by different task expectations evoked by the two types of stimuli. After viewing Chinese characters, a vast majority of the subjects expect they will be asked to recognize these stimuli. After viewing abstract paintings, task expectations are less unanimous. Twenty-five percent of the subjects shown paintings expected an aesthetic judgment task, 40% a recognition task, the remaining 35% could not unambiguously be categorized. However, basically the same relationship, an inverted-U, between exposure and appreciation was found for all three groups of subjects (because of the small number of subjects in each group and the stimuli no longer being counterbalanced over frequencies, no statistical comparison between the three groups was performed).

The results of the group expecting an aesthetic judgment task might be explained as follows. Certainty about an aesthetic judgment seems to be achieved after a relatively small amount of exposure. Kunst-Wilson and Zajonc (1980) reported an experiment in which polygons were presented five times during one millisecond. Together with an as yet not presented polygon, the stimuli then were presented again and subjects were asked to indicate which one of each pair they preferred (an aesthetic judgment) and which one of each pair they had seen before (a recognition judgment). Subjects also indicated their degree of certainty about both judgments. Certainty about the aesthetic judgment was greater than certainty about the recognition judgment. This result indicates that subjects need very little time to reach certainty about an aesthetic judgment. Consequently, high exposure frequencies are unnecessary for the performance of an aesthetic judgment task and thus will be perceived as not contributing to an adequate performance of such a task. Low or intermediate exposure frequencies will be considered the most appropriate by subjects expecting their task will be to judge the paintings they are viewing. According to the subjective association hypothesis this will yield a negative or inverted-U relationship between exposure and appreciation. For the group of subjects expecting this task an inverted-U relationship was indeed found.

An inverted-U relationship was also found for the group of subjects who, after viewing paintings, expected a recognition task. On the other hand, for subjects who expected recognition of Chinese characters a positive relationship was found. As compared to characters, paintings are far more discriminable stimuli and hence lower levels of exposure are probably sufficient to achieve certainty about the ability to recognize them. Again, the subjective association hypothesis would predict an inverted-U relationship.

Additional to the results already outlined, the following seem worth mentioning. In the first three experiments either an aesthetic or a meaning judgment was asked. In all three experiments the stimuli, paintings as well as characters, were rated significantly higher when they were judged aesthetically. However, between the ratings of paintings and characters in the fourth experiment no such difference was found. Asking to guess the meaning of stimuli involves some expectations of correctness which is not involved in aesthetic judgments. This might explain why aesthetic ratings are higher than ratings of meaning. The latter task was also perceived as more difficult and interesting than aesthetic judgments in Experiments 2 and 3. In the fourth experiment on the other hand, rating paintings was found more interesting than rating characters. Although in this experiment rating characters was seen as more difficult than rating paintings, the mean difficulty equalled the mean difficulty of rating characters aesthetically and was significantly lower than the difficulty of rating the meaning of characters.

CONCLUSION

According to Zajonc (1980) the positive effect of mere exposure may well be explained without assumptions about prior cognitions. However, when stimuli are presented well above recognition threshold, interactions between affect and cold cognitions will occur (Zajonc, 1968). Such interactions could explain the controversy between Berlyne's and Zajonc's results. As was shown in the experiments reported here, Berlyne's method of instructing subjects before exposure to the stimuli leads to inverted-U shaped or downward relationships between frequency of exposure and preference: not only when the experiment concerns liking for paintings but also when the instruction to guess the meaning of Chinese characters is given that was used in Zajonc's experiments.

The difference in results obtained when either characters or paintings are used as stimuli in a mere exposure experiment does not seem to be caused by a higher degree of exploratory reactions when aesthetic stimuli are presented. Results of the four experiments reported here indicate there is no basic difference between the effects of mere exposure on the appreciation of aesthetic stimuli as compared to other types of stimuli.

The negative or inverted-U function found when abstract paintings are used as stimuli in a mere exposure experiment can be explained by two specific qualities of this type of stimuli. The first is that presenting paintings more often then presenting other stimuli evokes the expectation of a rating task. If the same task is evoked by explicit instruction, when other types of stimuli: Chinese characters, are to be rated, an inverted-U relationship results. The second quality is the high degree of discriminability of paintings. Even when recognition is expected, fewer exposures than with other types of stimuli are needed to achieve certainty about task performance.

REFERENCES

Berlyne, D.E. (1967). Arousal and reinforcement. In: D. Levine (Ed.) Nebraska Symposium on Motivation. Lincoln, Nebraska: University of Nebraska Press.

Berlyne, D.E. (1970). Novelty,complexity and hedonic value. Perception and Psychophysics, 8, 279-286.

Berlyne, D.E. (1971). Aesthetics and Psychobiology. New York: Appleton-Century-Crofts.

Berlyne, D.E. (1973). The vicissitudes of aplopathematic and thelematoscopic pneumatology. In: D.E. Berlyne and K.B. Madsen (Ed.) Pleasure, Reward, Preference. New York: Academic Press.

Brickman, Ph., Redfield, J., Harrison, A.A. and Crandall, R. (1972). Drive and predisposition as factors in the attitudinal effects of mere exposure. Journal of Experimental Social Psychology, 8, 31-44.

Burgess II, T.D.G. and Sales, S.M. (1971). Attitudinal effects of 'mere exposure'; a reevaluation. Journal of Experimental Social Psychology, 7, 461-472.

Cantor, G.N. (1968). Children's "like-dislike" ratings of familiarized and nonfamiliarized visual stimuli. Journal of Experimental Child Psychology, 6, 651-657.

Cantor, G.N. (1972). Effects of familiarization on children's ratings of pictures of whites and blacks. Child Development, 43, 1219-1229.

Cantor, G.N. and Kubose, S.K. (1969). Preschool children's ratings of familiarized and nonfamiliarized visual stimuli. Journal of Experimental Child Psychology, 8, 74-81.

Faw, T.T. and Pien, D. (1971). The influence of stimulus exposure on rated preference: effects of age, pattern of exposure, and stimulus meaningfulness. Journal of Experimental Child Psychology, 11, 339-346.

Fechner, G.T. (1976). Vorschule der Aesthetik. 2 Teile. Leipzig: Breitkopf and Hartel.

Grush, J.E. (1976). Attitude formation and mere exposure phenomena: a nonartifactual explanation of empirical findings. Journal of Personality and Social Psychology, 33, 281-290.

Harrison, A.A. (1968). Response competition, frequency, exploratory behavior and liking. Journal of Personality and Social Psychology, 9, 363-368.

Harrison, A.A. and Crandall, R. (1972). Heterogeneity-homogeneity of exposure sequence and the attitudinal effects of exposure. Journal of Personality and Social Psychology, 21, 234-238.

Harrison, A.A, Tutone, R.M. and McFadgen, D.G. (1971). Effects of frequency of exposure on response competition and affective ratings. Journal of Psychology, 75, 163-169.

Janisse, M.P. (1970). Attitudinal effects of mere exposure: a replication and extension. Psychonomic Science, 19, 77-78.

Kunst-Wilson, W.R. and Zajonc, R.B. (1980). Affective discrimination of stimuli that can not be recognized. Science, 207, 557-558.

Lemond, L.C. and Nunnally, J.C. (1974). The influence of incongruity and preexposure on the familiarity effect in visual selection of children. Journal of Experimental Child Psychology, 18, 373-381.

Maslow, A.H. (1937). The influence of familiarization on preference. Journal of Experimental Psychology, 21, 162-180.

Matlin, M.W. (1970). Response competition as a mediating factor in the frequency-affect relationship. Journal of Personality and Social Psychology 16, 536-552.

Meyer, M. (1903). Experimental studies in the psychology of music. American Journal of Psychology, 14, 456-476.

Moreland, R.L. and Zajonc, R.B. (1976). A strong test of exposure effects. Journal of Experimental Social Psychology, 12, 170-179.

Pepper, S.C. (1919). Changes of appreciation for color combinations. Psychological Review, 26, 389-396.

Rosenberg, M.J. (1965). When dissonance fails: on eliminating evaluation apprehension from attitude measurement. Journal of Personality and Social Psychology, 1, 28-42.

Saegert, S.C. and Jellison, J.M. (1970). Effects of initial level of response competition and frequency of exposure on liking and explorating behavior. Journal of Personality and Social Psychology, 16, 553-558.

Saegert, S., Swap, W. and Zajonc, R.B. (1973). Exposure, context and interpersonal attraction. Journal of Personality and Social Psychology, 25, 234-242.

Siebold, J.R. (1972). Children's rating responses as related to amount and recency of stimulus familiarization and stimulus complexity. Journal of Experimental Child Psychology, 14, 257-264.

Stang, D.J. (1974). Intuition as artifact in mere exposure studies. Journal of Personality and Social Psychology, 30, 647-653.

Winer, B.J. (1971). Statistical Principles in Experimental Design. New York: McGraw-Hill.

Zajonc, R.B.(1968). Attitudinal effects of mere exposure. Journal of Personality and Social Psychology Monograph, Supplement 9 (2, Pt. 2), 1-27.

Zajonc, R.B. (1970). Brainwash: familiarity breeds comfort. Psychology Today, 3, 32-62.

Zajonc, R.B. (1980). Feeling and thinking: preferences need no inferences. American Psychologist, 35, 151-175.

Zajonc, R.B., Crandall, R., Kail Jr., R.V. and Swap, W. (1974). Effect of extreme exposure frequencies on different affective ratings of stimuli. Perceptual and Motor Skills, 38, 667-678.

Zajonc, R.B., Markus, H. and Wilson, W.R. (1974). Exposure effects and associative learning. Journal of Experimental Social Psychology, 10, 248-263.

Zajonc, R.B. and Rajecki, D.W. (1969). Exposure and affect: a field experiment. Psychonomic Science, 17, 216-217.

Zajonc, R.B., Shaver, P., Tavris, C., and Van Kreveld, D. (1972). Exposure satiation, and stimulus discriminability. Journal of Personality and Social Psychology, 21, 270-280.

Zajonc, R.B., Swap, W.C., Harrison, A.A., and Roberts, P. (1971). Limiting conditions of the exposure effect: satiation and relativity. Journal of Personality and Social Psychology, 18, 384-391.

Cognitive Processes in the Perception of Art
W.R. Crozier and A.J. Chapman (editors)
© Elsevier Science Publishers B.V. (North-Holland), 1984

REVERSAL THEORY, COGNITIVE SYNERGY AND THE ARTS

Michael J. Apter

University College, Cardiff

Reversal theory is a general psychological theory of motivation, the emotions and personality; and it can be used to throw light on a wide variety of everyday activites. Among other things, it can provide a broad perspective on all those kinds of experience, behaviour and objects which are associated with the arts, and this is the theme of the present chapter.

This is not the place to describe reversal theory in detail, or to attempt to justify it, but some of the principal ideas are introduced before turning to questions of aesthetics. The reader interested in learning more is advised to consult *The Experience of Motivation* (Apter, 1982a) which provides a complete and detailed account of the theory as it stands at present. While reversal theory integrates previous data from a number of fields in psychology it has also engendered its own programme of new research. In this respect, supportive evidence will be found in such papers as Apter (1976), Murgatroyd et al (1978), Fontana (1981), Svebak et al (1982), Walters et al (1982) and Wicker et al (1982).

One of the key concepts of the theory is that of 'metamotivational mode'. A given metamotivational mode is a particular 'state of mind' which structures and interprets in its own distinctive way that part of conscious experience which is to do with motivation. These modes are called 'metamotivational' because they are not themselves motivational but, rather, they are about motivation. It is postulated that they go in pairs and that one or other member of each pair is always operative, with switching between them occurring from time to time under certain conditions. Since the members of each pair of modes are regarded in the theory as opposites, such switching can be seen as involving a reversal from one to the other: hence the name of the theory.

For example, there are two different ways in which the relationship between goals and means can be structured within experience. In one case the goal has overriding importance and the means are chosen in relation to it; if a particular means is not effective another means may be chosen, but the goal remains the same. In the other, the centre of interest is the activity in itself; the goal here is no more than an excuse to perform the activity, or a way of organizing it, and if it turns out not to be appropriate for some reason then some other goal may be chosen instead. In other words, in one case the situation is 'serious' and in the other it is 'playful'; in the former the goal is significant beyond itself and therefore cannot be changed; in the latter the whole situation is 'encapsulated' and treated as a kind of game. Another way of putting this is to say that the goal is the figure of the 'phenomenal field' in one case, with the activity part of the ground; that is, the goal 'stands out' and dominates experience, the activity being organized around it. In the other case, the activity is the figure in the 'phenomenal field' and the goal the ground: in this case the activity 'stands out' and goals are organized around it. The first of these two 'states of mind' or 'modes' (the one in which the goal is primary) is called the 'telic mode', and the second (the one in which the activity is primary) is called the 'paratelic mode'.

Another pair of metamotivational modes concern different interpretations of the feeling of arousal. In one of these, high arousal is preferred, and is felt as excitement; the lack of high arousal in this state is felt as boredom. In the other, low arousal is preferred and is experienced as relaxation; in this state the lack of low arousal is unpleasant and is felt as anxiety. In other words, the whole range of arousal is experienced in opposite ways in these two modes, and as a reversal takes place so a switch occurs in the way in which the prevailing level of arousal is experienced at that moment. If arousal is high it is experienced, depending on which mode is operative, as some degree of anxiety or excitement; and if the arousal is low it is experienced as some degree of boredom or relaxation. These relationships are summarized in the accompanying figure. It will be realized that this formulation differs considerably from that of 'optimal arousal theory' (stemming from Hebb, 1955) in which there is a single mode, the preferred level of arousal in this mode being supposed to be somewhere in the middle of the arousal dimension.

Of course all emotions may be said to involve arousal in proportion to the intensity with which the emotion is experienced. This means that, in the mode which seeks high arousal, any emotion can be enjoyed, even such emotions as anger, horror, fear or revulsion. These emotions are supposed in common sense terms to be unpleasant, and indeed they usually are because it is difficult to maintain the mode in which high arousal is enjoyed in the face of events of the type which include such emotions. However, it is nevertheless possible in certain circumstances to maintain this mode and enjoy these emotions, as witness the way in which we enjoy them empathically when we go to the theatre or watch a film. When such supposedly unpleasant emotions are experienced as pleasant they are referred to in reversal theory as 'parapathic emotions'.

The two arousal modes just described can be regarded as a pair of metamotivational modes in their own rights: the 'arousal-avoidance' and 'arousal-seeking' modes. However, there does seem to be a close connection between these two modes and the telic and paratelic modes respectively. If the primary characteristic of the mode is goal-orientation, as it is in the telic case, then anxiety appears to be felt if arousal is high; and the more important the goal is perceived to be, and the more the difficulties which arise in its attainment, the greater the anxiety which is likely to be experienced; but when the goal is achieved arousal subsides and pleasant relaxation is experienced instead. If, on the other hand, the primary characteristic is activity-orientation, as it is in the paratelic mode, then excitement of one kind or another appears generally to be felt in relation to the activity if arousal is high, and boredom if high arousal cannot be derived from the activity. From this point of view, then, the arousal-avoidance and arousal-seeking modes can be conveniently regarded as aspects of the telic and paratelic modes respectively, and they will be regarded in this way here. So the telic and paratelic modes can come to be seen as complexes with a number of features. In fact, a number of further features of these metamotivational modes also become apparent when they are conceived in this broad fashion. In particular, the telic mode is seen as one in which the individual is generally oriented towards the future and prefers to plan

FIGURE 1 'States of mind', reversal and arousal.

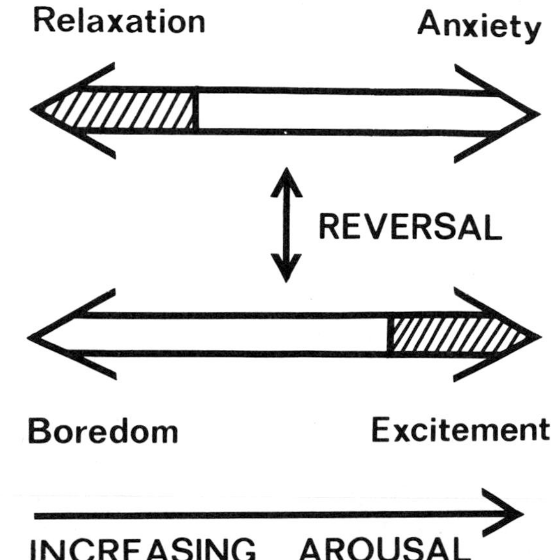

ahead as far as possible, whereas the paratelic mode is one in which the individual is more concerned with the present moment and prefers to act in a relatively spontaneous way. Also the paratelic mode is concerned with increasing, and the telic mode with decreasing, not only felt arousal but also the intensity of sensations of any kind.

Another pair of metamotivational modes is the pair which have been labelled 'negativistic' and 'conformist'. The negativistic mode is defined as a mode in which one wants, or feels a need to act against, some external source of pressure or requirements. It is described in everyday language by such phrases as 'feeling awkward' or 'cussed' or 'being bloody-minded'. The conformist mode can most simply be characterized as the absence of this feeling. Both the negativistic and conformist mode can occur in combination with either the telic or paratelic modes: thus there are both provocatively playful and grimly serious forms of negativism. An example of the former might be having an argument with someone for the fun of the argument itself, while an example of the latter might be arguing with someone on some important topic, like religious belief, with the sole aim of changing the other's point of view. In principle, many actions can be interpreted as being simultaneously both for something and against something. Thus if one votes for someone in an election, one is ipso facto voting against others who are standing. Or if a teenager conforms to a peer group he may, in doing so, be defying adult authority in some way at the same time. But the question is which way the individual involved sees what he or she is doing at the moment in question. If the focus of attention is on the conformist aspect of the action, then the conformist mode is the one which is operative and if the negativistic aspect is at the focus of attention, then the negativistic mode is the one which is prevailing at that time.

Although everyone is expected to experience both members of each pair of metamotivational modes at different times, individuals will not necessarily spend the same amount of time in each mode. And the amount of time which is spent in each mode will, at least in part, be a reflection of an underlying personality predisposition: other things being equal, a given individual will tend to spend longer periods in one mode than the other. The degree of innate bias towards one mode rather than its opposite is referred to in reversal theory as the 'dominance' of that mode, so that someone who is, for example, highly 'telic dominant' will be expected to spend much more time in the telic than the paratelic state over a given sample period. How much time is actually spent in a given mode will be determined by an interaction between the innate forces which determine the degree of dominance of that mode and such environmental forces as tend to induce either it or its opposite.

To complete this brief introduction to some of the central ideas of reversal theory, one other concept needs to be added: that of 'cognitive synergy'. Cognitive synergy is that which occurs in experience when something is seen to be possessed of opposite or mutually-exclusive properties, either simultaneously or in quick succession. For example, the experience of a man dressed as a woman would be synergic in this sense, as would be a cane which turned into a scarf during a conjuring trick. Synergies are generally enjoyed in the paratelic mode because they tend to increase arousal and the intensity of experience. Of course, to the degree to which they are enjoyed in the paratelic mode, they are disliked in the telic mode in which they are often referred to by such perjorative terms as 'dissonant' and 'incongruous'. The part which cognitive synergy plays in art is a central theme in this chapter, and a fuller account is given below.

ART AS A PARATELIC PHENOMENON

Many of the phenomena of human culture would appear to be essentially paratelic. That is to say, much of civilized life, and the institutions which support it, can be seen as being in the service of the paratelic mode in that they help to induce it, maintain it for periods once it has been induced, and provide the means by which pleasurably intense experience, including the experience of high arousal, may be achieved while it endures. Consider sport, for example, which undeniably plays a central part in the lives of large numbers of people. The institutionalization of sport into different 'games' with their own rule structures, techniques, venues and history provides a framework which, once entered, provides a context which tends to induce the paratelic state in participants and spectators. The uncertainty of the outcome of a particular game, or of the moves which will take place within it, and the challenge of the struggle and the risks which may be taken, may then be enjoyed even if, as is the case with spectators, the experience is based only on empathy.

What seems to happen in such a case is that the activity is 'cut off' from real life with its genuine threats, dangers and worries, and exists in a special psychological space of its own which is clearly demarcated. In this space the 'lead of anxiety' is transmuted into the 'gold of excitement' and this is possible because (and only if) crossing the threshold from 'real life' to the 'game' triggers the paratelic state. If it does not do so, if the game is experienced as 'real life' and the individual remains aware that failure can lead to serious consequences, as may be the case for professional sportspersons, then the experience of the game will be quite different: it will be telic, it will be 'work' rather than 'play', and real untransmuted anxiety and fear will be felt as arousal increases.

The situation is essentially the same for entertainment of all kinds. While it is possible to have fun in a variety of self-made and spontaneous ways, culture provides many ready-made contexts which systematically help to induce the paratelic state and within which paratelic satisfactions and pleasures may then be experienced. Such contexts include the fairground, the cinema, the circus, the night club, the casino, the betting shop, the slot machine arcade, the bull ring, the discotheque, or simply the space in front of a television set.

The same would appear to be true of art, using this term in its widest sense to include painting, music, poetry, theatre, fiction and all 'the arts'. Various devices are used in connection with the different arts, each in its own way, to help to induce the paratelic rather than the telic mode. The main effect of these is to encapsulate the situation, removing it from the domain of serious action for the spectator so that the experience of the artwork can be enjoyed in itself. This typically involves 'framing' the situation in some way, especially through the use of special locations which are dedicated to the form of art in question, such as galleries, theatres, and concert-halls. And, within each of these locations, many distinctive cues are used to make the situation different from the world outside. Consider all the cues which one encounters on a visit to the theatre. First of all there is the foyer with its attendants in evening dress, programmes for sale, and posters; then there is the main area of the theatre in which one sits in a plush seat and observes the curtains and the often garish, and in any case distinctive, decor; finally when the curtain goes up the action takes place within the literal form of the proscenium arch, and follows conventions of its own with respect to lighting, costumes, manner of speech, and so on. All of these ever serve to mark off what happens in the theatre from everyday life.

Of course a work of art may in itself contain enough cues to induce the paratelic state. But these are often not sufficient to guarantee this state, so that if the artwork is encountered in some other, 'real-life' surroundings, the spectators' mood may remain telic and the work instead be experienced as threatening, or irritating or embarrassing. Hence the annoyance of hearing serious music as background in a supermarket, the embarrassment caused by 'street theatre', or the irritation of seeing reproductions of famous works of art hanging on the wall in a dentist's waiting room.

THE ENJOYMENT OF ART

Within the protective framework just described, it is possible for the work of art to produce enjoyably intense experiences in the spectator. This can be achieved in a variety of ways, of which the following would appear to be some of the main ones:

Use of Stimulus Properties

These have already been discussed by other writers and are now a central part of the field of the psychology of art, and figure prominently in the present book. For example, Berlyne (1971) lists three general ways in which arousal may be increased: (1) Through psychophysical properties, including their intensity (brightness, loudness, etc.) and in some cases their physical size (e.g., in important buildings); (2) Through ecological properties, which are properties which elicit responses, including increased arousal, because of their psychological meaning -- for example, spiders may produce revulsion, and the female form may elicit sexual arousal in males; and (3) Through what Berlyne calls 'collative properties' such as complexity, incongruity and novelty.

It should be reiterated that the reversal theory view is that these are used in the attempt to raise arousal to a high level, whereas in optimal arousal theory (which is the theory which Berlyne was developing) it is supposed that they are used to raise it only to some intermediate level on the arousal dimension.

Use of Negativism

By negativism is meant behaviour which defies convention, expectations, rules, etc. It is of course this type of behaviour which is enjoyed in the negativistic mode as defined earlier. If the work of art itself is clearly a result of negativism, and the negativistic mode can be induced in the spectator, then the negativism can be enjoyed empathically. But more than that, it is also likely to increase arousal because it can produce novel and even unexpected effects (a point which is returned to below), and if the conventions or rules are rigid enough the very fact of breaking them can in itself create a pleasurable frisson. The conventions may be those of art itself, and it is these which the avant-garde in any movement set out to destroy: in this respect the work of art is effectively defined as any object which poses the question 'What is a work of art?'. Or the conventions may be those of society, in which case the work of art may be seen by others to be breaking some taboo and may become labelled as, for example, debased, pornographic, corrupting, or subversive. Either way, the artist can be seen as a kind of intellectual psychopath.

There is always the danger in using this technique to increase arousal, that the spectator will be offended or threatened and revert to the telic mode (and perhaps the conformist mode too), when unpleasant feelings of anxiety or guilt or anger may be experienced instead of excitement. But if the paratelic frame can be maintained so that the negativism is understood for what it is - playful provocativeness, defiance and denial - the technique may be extremely effective.

Use of Techniques to Induce Parapathic Emotions

Provided that the paratelic 'frame' is sufficiently strong to maintain the paratelic mode in the spectator, the most threatening features of the real world may be harnessed to the production of intensely pleasurable experiences - so that crime, torture, war, accidents, natural disaster, death and dying of all kinds, loss of freedom, physical danger, and so on, may all be the subject-matter of works of art and used for the positive purposes of aesthetic experience, and particularly for the increased arousal which they can generate.

It is at this point that the notion of parapathic emotions, as defined earlier, becomes relevant. For the increased arousal produced by subject-matter of these types is likely to be experienced as a variety of parapathic emotions each of which has its own flavour and which may be described by such words as 'anxiety', 'anger', 'grief', 'horror', and 'guilt'. Indeed, the whole gamut of emotions which are normally unpleasant may be experienced within the paratelic frame. But within the frame, as already explained, they take on a special quality (and this is the reason they are placed in inverted commas above) which allows them to be experienced as pleasant. And the stronger the emotion (within limits), the more enjoyable it will be expected to be.

This is at least part of the reason why plays and novels seem so often to be characterized by violence and tragedy, and why a large part of the Western tradition of painting has dealt with such topics as natural calamity, battle, rape, abduction and execution - including, of course, crucifixion.

Use of Cognitive Synergy

The use of cognitive synergy could appear to be particularly widespread in art, and the whole of the next two sections of this chapter are therefore devoted to an examination of different types of 'aesthetic synergy' and the use to which synergies are put in different artforms.

THE NATURE OF COGNITIVE SYNERGY

Before looking in more detail at the part which synergy plays in aesthetic experience it is necessary first to define it. 'Synergy', or more precisely 'cognitive synergy', is defined in reversal theory as that which occurs in experience when a given identity (e.g., object, person, situation) is seen to have opposite or mutually-exclusive characteristics, either simultaneously or in quick succession (Apter, 1982a). It is argued that it constitutes a kind of conceptual contrast effect in which the contradictory components which go to make up the synergy enhance each other phenomenologically, in much the same kind of way as placing complementary colours like red and green next to each other makes both of them seem more vivid. In the case of cognitive synergy, cognitively dissonant components are brought into the same conceptual space so that they, and the identity with which they are associated, are experienced more intensely. The term 'synergy' is used to describe this process because the components work together to produce an effect which they could not have produced independently (the word being derived from the ancient Greek 'syn' meaning 'together' and 'ergon' meaning 'work'). Not only do the incompatible properties, when brought together, interact and mutually enhance each other in this way, but they also appear to provide a special phenomenological quality over and above this which tends to be described (when the quality is desired) by such words as 'fascinating', 'intriguing', or 'amazing'. The process is therefore synergic in this sense too.

In order to make the concept more concrete, here are a few examples of cognitive synergies:

(1) In a conjuring trick, as Zajonc (1960) has pointed out, something which is thought to be impossible turns out, at least in appearance to be perfectly possible; so there is a paradoxical conjunction of impossibility and actuality.

(2) In playing with a toy like a model car or aeroplane the child is pretending that it is something other than what it really is, and must in some sense be aware of both of these aspects - real and the pretence - at the same time.

(3) When one puts on fancy dress one imagines oneself to be different from what one really is, and enjoys the resulting clash of incompatible self-concepts.

(4) In looking at some ancient object in an archeological museum one is aware of both its 'here-and-now-ness' and its 'there-and then-ness'. (In relation to this, see the article on the enjoyment of antique collecting by Smith and Apter, 1977).

(5) A religious person visiting a sacred place will experience it at one and the same time as both natural and supernatural, geographical and spiritual. (See Apter, 1982a, Chapter 12 for a discussion of such 'sacredness synergies').

(6) A joke involves a special kind of switch between seeing some identity in one way and seeing it in another. The whole process is complex (see the detailed analysis in Apter, 1982a, Chapter 8), but a simple example would be the way in which puns involve a single word being used with two different meanings.

(7) A wedding is the meeting point of the states of being unmarried and being married and, like all other 'transitional states' (to use the anthropologists' term), it is experienced as something 'special'.

It will have been noticed that in these examples there is no necessary logical contradiction between the different meanings involved in a given synergy: either the different meanings are assigned in quick succession, or they are experienced simultaneously but are no more than different possible interpretations of the same situation. But it must be emphasized that the present analysis is phenomenological, not logical, and the point is that opposite meanings for the same identity are *experienced* together, and related to each other in the person's 'phenomenal field'.

Cognitive synergies are encountered so widely throughout the arts that one is forced to suppose that they may be a necessary component of aesthetic experience itself. Indeed, there are some general types of synergy which appear time and again in all the arts, and it is these ubiquitous types of synergy which are at the focus of attention here. It should be noted that it is not being claimed that these general synergy types will be present in all art forms, or all styles within a form of art, but rather that any type of art or style will be likely to take advantage in its own way of some subset of them. They can be labelled as 'signifier/signified synergy', 'empathy/alienation synergy', 'ambiguity synergy', 'metaphoric synergy' and 'structural synergy'. Let us now look at each of them in turn.

TYPES OF SYNERGY IN ART

Signifier/Signified Synergy

The two terms used here to describe this type of synergy come from linguistics, in which signs are seen to consist of a signifier (e.g., a word like 'rose') and a signified (i.e., that which is depicted by a word like 'rose'). Although these concepts were initially developed to deal with spoken and written language, they are now used more widely to refer to any kind of sign (e.g., a road sign, or a gesture which someone might make).

In receiving communications one is usually aware more of that which is signified in the communication than the signified, or medium of the communication, the latter tending to be 'transparent'. Signifier/signified synergies involve bringing both aspects of the sign to awareness simultaneously (or in quick succession), which is usually accomplished by drawing attention in some way to the otherwise unnoticed signifier. What this comes to in terms of art, is that the work of art plays with, and makes maximum use of, the possibilities for confusion and confrontation between the artwork itself (the signifier) and that which is represented by it (the signified). This type of synergy therefore is particularly likely to be made use of in figurative art and is more or less intrinsic to representational art of any type, be it painting, sculpture, theatre or fiction.

To give an illustration, consider landscape painting as a genre. A particular landscape is, in an experiential sense, both a flat surface covered by a layer of paint, and an open air scene. It is at once a relatively small, movable object and a large immovable terrain. It is both two-dimensional and three-dimensional, enclosed by a frame and open to the sky; and if the scene depicts something moving -- a flowing river, a galloping horse, a bird on the wing -- there is both stillness and motion.

None of this constitutes a logical paradox, since one set of features only represents or indicates the other; but phenomenologically the various oppositions indicated are brought together and made to interact synergically. At least part of the fascination of a painting such as landscape, then, is this incongruity which one perceives between these two aspects, as one moves backwards and forwards (sometimes literally, in front of the canvas) seeing it now one way, now another. And it is this which landscape artists play on, each after their own fashion, one emphasizing the smallness of the means as aginst the grandeur of the subject, another the drama of movement against the static nature of the paintwork, yet another making much of the way in which the eye can be tricked into seeing depth and distance where there is nothing but flat surface. And all landscape painting involves making the intangible tangible: the sky, spring, even the characters of mythology, take concrete form and can be possessed.

The same kind of argument can be carried over into other genres of painting - the portrait, the battle scene, and so on. Any by extension it relates to any form of artistic representation. The dual nature of representation is therefore something which art can work on, and it is one of the features of art that it tends to keep the observer aware of the medium. Thus language itself is 'foregrounded' in poetry (to use the term suggested by Murkarovsky 1964), as is the 'theatricality' of the stage in drama. Operas and ballets likewise tell their stories in highly stylized ways which cannot help but draw attention to themselves.

Finally, artists have ingenious ways of playing double-tricks' on us, increasing both the complexity of the synergy and with it the shock-value or the richness of their work. Thus it is possible to have a painting of a painting (as in interiors with paintings on the walls), plays within plays (as in Hamlet), novels about the writing of a novel (as in Proust's great work), people acting as sculptures (Gilbert and George), materials which represent the material themselves (collage), and objects which represent themselves (objets trouvés)

Empathy/Alientation Synergy

If signifier/signified synergy is about the relationship between the artwork and that to which it refers, empathy/alientation synergy is about the relationship of the artwork to the person who observes it. Now although it would appear to be a characteristic of works of art that they evoke strong feelings of empathy, even tenderness, many works of art also, at moments, seem to involve some element of strangeness which rebuffs the observer. Since we must assume that the artist does wish to communicate, the function of such alientation where it occurs must presumably be to provide another element of synergy for the spectator to enjoy. Among other things this explains why those artists such as Bertolt Brecht or Jean-Luc Godard, who deliberately go out of their way to alienate, nevertheless can produce such fascinating plays and films.

There are a number of devices which can be used to alienate the observer (at least temporarily), and they include the following:

(1) The creation of 'puzzles' which the spectator must work out, or bafflement which must be overcome in order to 'understand' the 'message'. It will be noticed that any original style will initially have this effect and therefore cannot avoid at first making use of this type of synergy.

(2) The placing of emphasis on the medium, and the techniques being used, at the expense of any content which the spectator might find it easy to identify with. In this respect the resulting synergy is the same as the signified/signifier synergy, in which the medium is foregrounded as much as possible.

(3) The breaking up of the narrative or pattern, for example, by

the intrusion of the creator, as in those books in which the author intersperses his own comments about the book he or she is writing, such as *The French Lieutenant's Woman* by John Fowles. Similarly, using different styles within the same artwork draws attention to stylistic convention and prevents the easy flow of experience in relation to the work, for example, a painting like Picasso's *Les Demoiselles d'Avignon* in which some faces are painted in the style of African masks and others in the manner of early Spanish painting.

(4) Making the content inherently uninteresting or even repellent, so that the observer 'holds himself or herself back'. (There is also the chance here for a further synergy between an ugly content and beautiful means of representation). Needless to say, this technique is only likely to work for short periods otherwise artists lose their audience.

(5) By making the subject-matter itself strange or bizarre or uncanny, as in so much surrealism and the 'theatre of the absurd'.

Ambiguity Synergy

If an ambiguity is a situation in which something can be interpreted (identified, evaluated, etc.) in distinctly different ways, then all ambiguities are synergies (although not all synergies, it should by now be apparent, are ambiguities). This is because different and even mutually exclusive meanings are being assigned to a single aspect of the situation, and one is aware of these in such quick succession that the meanings in some sense interact with each other. For example, if one sees a distant figure on a misty day and cannot make out which of two people it might be, then one is aware of both these people in relation to the figure. Or if a child has broken a vase and one is not sure whether it was done deliberately or by accident, one will be aware of both interpretations in relation to the action.

The importance of ambiguity in art has been argued by a number of writers, including William Empson who wrote the classic 'Seven Types of Ambiguity' (1930). One only has to think of such masterpieces as Hamlet, the Venus de Milo and the Mona Lisa, or to consider such diverse modern art movements as Cubism or Op Art, to realize what a central part ambiguity plays in aesthetic experience. This whole topic has been discussed at more length elsewhere in the context of reversal theory (Apter, 1982a, Chapter 6).

Metaphoric Synergy

Ambiguity and metaphor can be seen as constituting a pair of symmetrical opposites. If the essence of ambiguity synergy is that one identity has two contradictory properties, the essence of metaphoric synergy is that two different identities are shown to have the same property. This is synergic because the two identities will also have many properties which are different, and these differences will clash when the two identities are brought together into the same conceptual space. In ambiguity synergy, then, X is shown to have mutually-exclusive properties A and B. In metaphoric synergy, identities A and B are shown to have a common property X. But in the latter case, A and B will also have opposing properties, say P and Q respectively, and these properties will also be brought together when A and B are equated.

When an aeroplane is spoken of as if it were a bird, or a woman as if a flower, or a General as if a chess player, the phenomenological effect is more intense and interesting than saying that the aeroplane flies or the woman is beautiful or the General is clever; and the reason for this is that a synergic nexus of differences has been created by means of the similarity between the pairs in each case. An aeroplane is like a bird in that it has wings and flies but is also opposite in many obvious ways. To put this metaphorically, a metaphor builds a bridge over which a battle can then be fought. (This has been discussed in more detail in Apter, 1982b).

Metaphor need not be restricted to verbal discourse, but can also be visual. For example, if one looks at the portrait of Elsbeth Tulcher by Durer, one sees that everything which the sitter is wearing is stylistically mirrored by features in the background: her necklace is painted in the same way as the trees, her brocade in the same way as a meandering path, and there is a pattern of two 'W's beneath her brooch which relate to mountains in the background which form two inverted 'W's. Here different identities are linked by means of the painter's stylistic representational devices.

Structural Synergy

For the final type of synergy to be discussed here, we turn to the way in which synergies may be formed from the formal patterns which exist within the work of art. This type overlaps with the two previous types, since such pattern synergies may either involve a given pattern having, as it were, different interpretations (which is a form of ambiguity synergy) or two different patterns being related to each other (which is a form of metaphoric synergy). In music, for example, the first type is exemplified by variations on a theme, since each such variation is both the theme and something other than the theme. The second is exemplified when two different themes have something in common (for example, a common chord sequence, which is the basis of all jazz).

Both types of structural synergy are also prevalent in paintings. Thus given identity within the painting may partake simultaneously of two different patterns in the painting. In seascapes, for example, the sails of sailing ships often link in with two types of pattern within the painting: a swirling or rococo structure of clouds and waves on the one hand, and on the other the horizontal/vertical structure of the horizon and masts. And two different identities in a painting may be linked visually in some way which brings them together even though they are very different in other respects. For example, a building in the background of a landscape may be painted in the same colours as the trousers of a figure standing in the foreground, so that these contrasting structures are chromatically linked.

There is a sense in which nearly all art involves at a fundamental level two contrasting types of structure which may be labelled 'main-structure' and 'counter-structure'. The main-structure is the framework within which the artwork has its being. This is usually relatively simply and symmetrical, such as the literal frame of a painting, or the rhythm and key of a piece of music. These may be further enhanced within the body of the artwork itself -- for example by means of vertical and horizontal lines in the painting, and by means of a rhythmic accompaniment in music. The counter-structure is the most obvious overriding structure of the work, and it tends to overpower the structure, especially in 'romantic' rather than 'classical art. It is generally more complex than the main-structure, and typically asymmetrical. It cannot, however, exist without the main-structure, otherwise it would be merely 'noise' or randomness: that is, it only has meaning within the context provided by the main-structure. The work of art as a whole, however, can be seen to involve a synergy between these two general types of structure and to derive its life and interest at least in part from the interplay between them. Thus a good tune escapes from the rhythm which underlies it, while at the same time remaining tied to it. The dominant lines in a painting may be diagonal, but the diagonals are only fully perceived as diagonal within the structure of a verbal/horizontal frame.

The points which have been made here could of course be developed, elaborated and exemplified at length. But enough has probably been said to give a flavour of the way in which the concept of 'cognitive synergy' can be used in the analysis of particular works of art, or in the general attempt to understand the structure and function of artworks in general.

It is possible that particular artworks may make use of types of synergy other than those which have been listed here. But these five types would appear to be those of which most widespread use is made throughout the arts.

CREATIVITY IN ART

Reversal theory is relevant not only to an understanding of the appreciation of art, but also to an understanding of its creation (and indeed to creativity in general).

For one thing, it can be suggested that it is easier to be original in the paratelic than the telic mode. There are several reasons why this may be supposed to be the case. For one, if the artist is thinking about some problem in that paratelic mode then his thinking is likely to be playful, being engaged in it for its own sake, and if he 'plays around' with ideas, inferences and presuppositions for their own sake and follows them wherever they lead without worrying about their serious implications or practicalities he may be more likely to follow new paths than he would do if he was thinking about a problem in the goal-oriented telic mode. In other words, his thinking is more likely to be sensitive to a variety of possibilities which might be excluded at an early stage in telic thinking, and so he is in a better position to overcome the effects of 'set'. To put this in terms of contemporary jargon, 'lateral thinking' (Do Bono, 1968) would seem to be easier in the paratelic than the telic mode. An analogy would be going for a walk: if one takes the most direct route to a destination because the most important thing is to get there, one is less likely to make discoveries about the terrain than if one wanders around because one is enjoying the walk, and perhaps even loses one's way: indeed, it is even possible that one might discover a better and more direct route to the destination in this way.

A second, and related, reason, is that thinking which increases arousal will be enjoyed in the paratelic mode, and therefore those trains of thought which produce jolts of arousal will be less likely to be avoided than they would be in the telic mode. These might include topics which are normally anxiety-provoking (and therefore not well thought through in the telic mode) and also ways of thinking which produce surprise and some degree of unpredictability to the thinker. So one is more likely in the paratelic mode to ask oneself 'What if?' questions, even if they are silly, or entertain 'Suppose that' thoughts and pursue them without inhibition, and in both these ways the result may be the emergence of unusual and even shocking ideas which can be recognized and faced rather than immediately suppressed. Of course, there is more to the creation of a work of art than originality or novelty and much hard work, planning and 'testing' may be needed. Much of this may occur, and perhaps occur more appropriately, in the telic mode, so that one would expect an alternation between the two modes during the production of a work of art. The point is that the originality is most likely to occur in the paratelic phase.

If it is easier to be original in the paratelic mode, it can also be suggested that one is more likely to come up with novel ideas, and ways of doing things, in the negativistic than the conformist mode. As Picasso is reported to have said, 'Every act of creation is first of all an act of destruction' (May, 1976). If an artist therefore is in the negativistic mode he may be more likely to be iconoclastic, defy convention, break through normal barriers and taboos, re-examine hallowed beliefs and assumptions, deny what is generally believed to be desirable or possible, disregard the rule book, set new challenges to struggle against, and so on. In all these ways he opens himself more to the possibility of coming up with new and interesting definitions of his art, and with novel techniques and original effects than would have been the case if he had remained in the conformist mode and 'mould'. (In this respect, see Dreistadt, 1970.) And if he is negativistic dominant, in other words a generally 'awkward', 'difficult' and 'combative' kind of person, it would follow that he stands the chance of producing novel work more frequently than someone who is not - unless his negativism is continually 'displaced' onto non-artistic issues.

Both the negativistic and paratelic modes, then, might be expected to be associated with originality and creativity more than the two other modes. Presumably the most productive state in this respect will be that in which both these modes occur together, as is the case when negativism is used to help achieve excitement or when playful activity is undertaken to allow for the expression of negativism in the negativistic mode. It is also possible incidentally, that the playful denial of some aspect of a situation (which could occur in the negativistic/paratelic combined state), and its substitution in imagination by some opposite quality, may be one of the principal ways in which cognitive synergies are created.

ART AND ENTERTAINMENT

A criticism of the reversal theory account of art, as given here, might be that it treats art as if it were mere entertainment: that is, as if it were to speak disparagingly, no more than another way of passing the time, deriving immediate gratification or obtaining a temporary thrill.

The first thing to say in response to such a criticism would be that there is nothing wrong with entertainment and that the ability to enjoy it is an essential part of a healthy mental life. To say that art is entertainment, is not to condemn it. However, if art is entertainment, it is clearly a special form of entertainment and one that requires an openness to a new experience, a willingness to learn and an ability to concentrate, which are not always necessary for the full appreciation and enjoyment of other more passive forms of entertainment. None of this contradicts any part of the analysis which has been given here. In particular, art differs from other forms of entertainment, according to reversal theory, in the degree to which it makes use of certain identifiable types of cognitive synergy. Indeed, it is precisely the deliberate use of one or more of the types of synergy discussed here which distinguishes work which aspires to be treated as serious art from that which is intended to be no more than entertainment. In such entertainment as, for example, the general run of 'soap opera' series on television, signifier/signified synergies are avoided, the medium being an unobtrusive as possible; the viewer is encouraged to identify more or less completely with the principal characters and hence alientation, for this and other reasons, is minimized and empathy/alienation synergy is unlikely to be experienced; ambiguities are generally avoided and as a result the characters become 'cardboard' and their actions raise few real moral problems; and while there are often interesting patterns of similarity and difference between characters that might allow for metaphoric synergy, and complexities of plot line which give rise to the possibility of structural synergy, these possibilities are rarely taken advantage of fully; one is not invited to see similarities between highly dissimilar characters, for example, and plot complexity is usually used to allow cuts between subplots which keep attention from flagging rather than to bring interesting comparisons between subplots. This is to make no value judgment as between art and entertainment, nor to imply that there is a sharp cut-off point from one to the other, but rather to identify some dimensions of difference which help one to understand what it might mean to say something is, or is not, a 'work of art'.

The fact that art is at least in part produced in the paratelic mode, and in normal circumstances wholly consumed in that mode, does not mean that it cannot be used for serious telic purposes. There is no doubt that a work of art can have enduring effects on the spectator's attitudes and opinions, and indeed, in a more subtle but all-pervasive way, change the manner in which he views the world. This means that it can be used for religious, political, commercial, educational, or other ends by those who commission the artist or purvey his work, by the artist himself at certain times during the planning and production of the work, and also by the consumer who, in deciding to expose himself to the influence of the work, may well do so in the serious-minded expectation that it will have long-term beneficial effects, and in some way or another be 'improving'. And of course it may have serious effects even when not deliberately or consciously designed to do so by the artist. But none of this changes the fact that for the work of art to function as a work of art it must do so through the medium of the paratelic mode. Without the sheer joy and exhilaration which art can provide it can accomplish nothing. One of the paradoxes of art is that unless it is enjoyed for its own sake, it cannot be used for the sake of anything else.

ACKNOWLEDGMENT

The author is indebted to Dr. K.C.P. Smith for discussions on reversal theory and art out of which arose a number of the concepts described in this chapter.

REFERENCES

Apter, M.J. (1976). Some data inconsistent with the optimal arousal theory of motivation. Perceptual and Motor Skills, 43, 1209-1210.

Apter, M.J. (1982a). The Experience of Motivation: The Theory of Psychological Reversals. London: Academic Press.

Apter, M.J. (1982b). Metaphor as synergy. In: D.S. Miall (Ed.) Metaphor: Problems and Perspectives. Brighton, Sussex: Harvester Press.

Berlyne, D.E. (1971). Aesthetics and Psychobiology. New York: Appleton-Century-Crofts.

De Bono, E. (1968). The Five-Day Course in Thinking. Harmondsworth, Middlesex: Allen Lane the Penguin Press.

Dreistadt, R. (1970). Reversing, using opposites, negativism and aggressiveness in creative behavior in science and philosophy. Psychology, 7, 38-63.

Empson, W. (1930). Seven Types of Ambiguity. London: Chatto and Windus.

Fontana, D. (1981). Obsessionality and reversal theory. British Journal of Clinical Psychology, 20, 299-300.

Hebb, D.O. (1955). Drives and C.N.S. (Conceptual Nervous System). Psychological Review, 62, 243-254.

May, R. (1976). The Courage to Create. London: Collins.

Mukarovský, J. (1964). Standard Language and Poetic Language. In: P.L. Garvin (Ed.) A Prague School Reader on Aesthetics, Literary Structure and Style. Washington, DC: Georgetown University Press.

Murgatroyd, S., Rushton, C., Apter, M. and Ray, C. (1978). The development of the Telic Dominance Scale. Journal of Personality Assessment, 42, 519-528.

Smith, K.C.P. and Apter, M.J. (1977). Collecting antiques: a psychological interpretation. Antique Collector, 48, 64-66.

Svebak, S., Storfjell, O. and Dalen, K. (1982). The effect of a threatening context upon motivation and task-induced physiological changes. British Journal of Psychology, 73, 505-512.

Walters, J., Apter, M.J. and Svebak, S. (1982). Color preference, arousal, and the theory of psychological reversals. Motivation and Emotion, 6, 193-215.

Wicker, F.W., Thorelli, I.M., Barren, W.L. III. and Willis, A.C. (1981). Studies of mood and humor appreciation. Motivation and Emotion, 5, 47-59.

Zajonc, R.B. (1960). Balance, congruity and dissonance. Public Opinion Quarterly, 24, 280-296.

Cognitive Processes in the Perception of Art
W.R. Crozier and A.J. Chapman (editors)
© Elsevier Science Publishers B.V. (North-Holland), 1984

SYNESTHESIA AND THE ARTS

Lawrence E. Marks

Yale University

ON SYNESTHESIA

In his account of the exhibition of painting in Paris known as the *Salon de 1846*, the poet Charles Baudelaire wrote of colour as follows:

> But immediately great blue shadows rhythmically pursue in front of them the throng of orange and fragile rose tones, which are like the distant, enfeebled echo of light. The great symphony of yesterday, that succession of melodies, where infinity generates variety, that complex hymn goes by the name of colour.
> In colour there is harmony, melody, counterpoint (Baudelaire, 1889, p. 89)

By means of synesthesia involving colour and sound, Baudelaire employs words to translate into music the colours of the paintings he viewed in the exhibition.

Synesthesia serves as a means to unify the arts through a psychological unity of the senses. Synesthesia refers to the transfer of qualities from one sensory domain to another, to the translation of texture to tone or of tone to colour, smell or taste. Because the various modes of art -- poetry,painting, music, sculpture, dance -- rest on and appeal to different senses, synesthesia correspondences among the senses thereby can point to similarities and analogies -- as well as to differences -- among the artistic forms.

In this chapter I review the role of synesthesia in response to works of art, especially to poetry -- though I also touch upon painting and music. First, it is important to clarify and delineate synesthesia itself. To start, we should note that synesthesia comes in a variety of forms. One form consists of a widespread, perhaps even universal, appreciation about the ways that perceptions in different modalities can 'match up'. If you ask people the question, 'Which is brighter, a cough or a sneeze?', virtually everyone readily responds 'a sneeze' -- even though most are not sure how or why they know this. The answer to the question how they know this probably is that this knowledge comes through an understanding of synesthetic relationships between auditory and visual experiences. Sneezes are typically higher in pitch than coughs, and high pitched sounds correspond to brighter colours.

But synesthesia also comes in a strong perceptual form, as a phenomenon in which people claim to experience the qualities of one sensory modality in terms of qualities of another -- as when synesthetic individuals say that the sounds of speech or music actually take on shapes or colours or flavours (Marks, 1975). Sneezes truly 'look' brighter than coughs. A synesthetic person may ascribe colours to spoken names or words -- it typically being the vowel sounds that determine the hues associated with a given name or word. Shapes may wax and ebb with the flow of sound, now larger and rounder when tones are softer and lower in pitch, smaller and sharper when the tones are louder and higher in pitch (Karwaski and Odbert 1938; Marks, 1975). In its most potent manifestations, synesthetic perception is part and parcel of the person's phenomenological experiences, so ineluctable and integral a part of those experiences that synesthesia has sometimes (mistakenly) been considered virtually pathological. Reports of such synesthesias began to appear frequently in the medical literature of the last century (for reviews, see Clavière, 1898, and Marks, 1975).

SYNESTHESIA AND THE ARTIST

What might be the consequences of strong synesthesia for art? One is the possibility that synesthetic artists will inject their cross-modal associations into their works. Baudelaire (1923), for example, appears to have experienced synesthesia on at least some occasions, for he described these experiences as having occurred upon partaking of hashish. Baudelaire attended some of the meetings of the 'hashish club', meetings that took place on Ile St. Louis in Paris at the Hôtel Pimodan, the same building in which Baudelaire lived. His fellow poet and critic Théophile Gautier also attended these meetings, and Gautier too described, in vibrant and florid prose, the synesthetic consequences of eating hashish, which was served in a green paste:

> The notes quivered with such power, that they entered my breast like luminous arrows; then the air being played seemed to come out of my very being; my fingers rambled over a nonexistent keyboard; the sounds gushed out blue and red, in electric sparks; Weber's soul had been reincarnated in me (Gautier, 1846, p. 530).

For Baudelaire the existence of synesthetic connections between different senses was a doctrinal tenet. His sonnet *Correspondences* describes 'scents, colours, sounds speaking to each other,' through 'smells as fresh as children's skin, sweet as oboes, green as prairies'. As I have indicated elsewhere (Marks, 1978), Baudelaire believed that these equivalences in sensory perception had a deep meaning, that they represented an essential underlying unity in the universe. It is significant that Baudelaire did not mistakenly attribute synesthetic perception to the drugged state itself. 'Sounds cloak themselves in colours, and colours contain music', he wrote, 'yet every poet's brain, in its normal and healthy state, easily conceptualizes these analogies' (1923, p. 218). In this, Baudelaire showed considerable psychological acumen. Some synesthetic correspondence, some connections between what is seen and what is heard, are indeed universal.

It is presumably because some synesthetic experiences are so powerful that synesthetic individuals, including synesthetic artists, may be convinced of their significance. Among composers, Scriabin and Rimsky-Korsakov were synesthetic and Scriabin's synesthesia is evident in his musical work.

Alexander Scriabin (1911) composed his *Prometheus* for orchestra and piano, with choir and colour-keyboard; the work was intended to express through a coloured music his vision of the synesthetic relationships between tone and hue: In *Prometheus*, each note of the scale has a colour to which it is 'naturally' connected. The notion that notes and colours match up one to the other goes back at least two-and-a-half centuries, to Louis-Bertrand Castel (1735), who proposed and built a colour organ, this invention being guided by Newton's (1704) analogy between the seven notes of the diatonic scale and the seven putative primary colours of the spectrum. Castel was convinced, as was Scriabin much later, that by an appropriate correspondence of visual colours and auditory notes, it is possible to produce a colour music that is perceptually the 'same' to the two sense modalities. For Scriabin, as for Baudelaire, the artistic works seem to reflect in part their creator's synesthetic mode of perception.

Among painters, Wassily Kandinsky gives evidence of having been synesthetic. To be sure, many of his paintings were constructed on musical themes, their bright colours and dynamic shapes indicating the flow of notes. More significant to the inference that he was synesthetic are Kandinsky's written accounts. Kandinsky's descriptions of the relationships between colour and form on the one hand and sound on the other typify synesthetic perception. In his works *Concerning the Spiritual in Art* (1977) and *Point and Line to Plane* (1979) Kandinsky argued that music and painting, in part through their elements, serve much the same role of expressing feeling. Music and painting can do this because colour, form and tone alike are linked to one another and to emotions. (A similar doctrine was expressed by several of the Futurists, for instance, by Bruno Corra (1973), who described his explorations of coloured music, and by Carlo Carra (1973), who gave a written account of his translation of sounds, noises and smells into painting. It should be noted, however, that there is little either in the art or in the documents of the Futurists to suggest strong perceptual synesthesia as a basis to their multimodal art).

For Baudelaire, for Scriabin, and for Kandinsky, the synesthetic correspondence between or among the senses was doctrinal: multimodal sensory experiences not only served as a source for a particular set of artistic devices, but synesthesia also became part of the subject matter that these artists attempted to communicate to the spectators of their works.

GENERALITY OF SYNESTHETIC ASSOCIATIONS

Synesthesia comprises both the general and the specific, the universal and the idiosyncratic. Although it is of interest to consider the role that strong synesthetic perception may play in the work of a given artist, it is perhaps even more important to the arts to consider the role that weaker but more pervasive kinds of synesthetic associations may play in the response of the spectator. Early in this century, Martin (1909) conducted an experiment in which she presented reproductions of works of art to her subjects, asking them for verbal reports of sensory images. Many of the responses were synesthetic, consisting of descriptions of kinesthetic, thermal, tactile, gustatory, olfactory, and auditory images accompanying the visual perceptions of the art reproductions.

Even among the vast majority of individuals who never or rarely experience strong synesthetic perception, there is a widespread comprehension of certain similarities among different sensory qualities, these similarities forming a fabric of interrelatedness that can play a subtle but pervasive role in the apprehension of art. To a large measure, it seems that both the strong synesthetic perceptions experienced by at most only a few percent of the population and the weaker associations recognized by virtually everyone stem largely from the same source: an intrinsic unity of the senses.

CHARACTERISTICS OF SYNESTHETIC ASSOCIATION

Two primary principles govern perceptual synesthesia. The first is that while much in the way of synesthetic perception is idiosyncratic and individual, marking the 'personal equation' of the synesthetic person, much else in synesthetic perception is universal, with synesthetic perceivers agreeing on many of the intersensory relationships (Marks, 1975). The second principle is that synesthesia largely involves systematic relationships between different sense modalities, where sensations of one modality translate by a regular rule into sensory images or qualities of another. Often, synesthesia consists in the alignment of dimensions on different modalities (Karwoski et al, 1942; Marks, 1975; Riggs and Karwoski, 1934). Significant too is the fact that the alignments of sensory dimensions characterize the perceptions and associations both of strong synesthetic perceivers and of others who acknowledge only weaker bonds between the senses (Karwoski and Odbert, 1938; Marks, 1975, 1978).

The subject, S, who was studied by Luria (1968) largely for his prodigious memory, was also synesthetic. Luria provides the following description:

> Presented with a tone pitched at 50 cycles per second and an amplitude of 100 decibels, S. saw a brown strip against a dark background that had red, tongue-like edges. The sense of taste he experienced was like that of sweet and sour borscht, a sensation that gripped his entire tongue ...(p. 45).

Clearly the association of sound with the taste of borscht is idiosyncratic; moreover, this association presumably was made possible only through S's upbringing in Russian culture. Many synesthetic associations are idiosyncratic to individuals; many are specific to given cultures.

But others are not. Despite the diversity, there is a significant core of synesthetic experience that is pervasive and widespread, acknowledged and appreciated by virtually everyone. To synesthetic individuals who attribute colours to musical notes, there may be little or no agreement as to specific correlations: C may be green to one person, red to another; G may be blue or yellow: Yet, typically, synesthetics will agree that as a note increases by octaves, say from middle C to high C, the colour, whatever it is, becomes brighter (Marks, 1978). By analogy, nonsynesthetic individuals judge sounds with higher pitches to correspond to lighter and brighter colours (Marks, 1974; 1978). To the extent that this is so, to the extent that there are generally appreciated rules of cross-modal association, there exists the potential for a reliable 'translation' from one modality to another. In this sense, Baudelaire, Scriabin and Kandinsky were quite on the mark in their interpretation of synesthetic responses to colour or shape or sound. In synesthesia artists can find both form and substance to communicate to their audience.

UNIVERSALS IN SYNESTHESIA

The sources for universal synesthesia can be diverse. Simply because associations are universal, for example, does not require them to be inherent or innate. Universal connections could be made through common experiences. A review of some of the major types of universal synesthesia correspondences is in order.

Warm and Cool Colours

One of the most widely recognized relations across modalities is that between temperature and colour, with reds, oranges, yellows and browns designated as 'warm colours' and blues and greens as 'cool colours'. In paintings the greater warmth of reds, oranges and yellows compared to blues and greens is readily apparent even in works that are similar in composition; compare, for instance the several versions of Monet's *Haystacks*, or contrast Claude Lorrain's *The Herdsmen* with Corot's *View near Epernon*. And in many of Renoir's paintings, not only the subject matter but the pink tones of skin impart an irresistible glow.

Poets often capitalize on the 'cold light' of the moon in contrast to the 'warm light' of the (yellower) sun. Shelley, in *To the Queen of my Heart* describes how the 'pale moonbeam .../ Sheds a floor of silver sheen .../ As the cold ray strays/ O'er thy face.' With such metaphors, the explanation may be rather simple: The light of the moon often is experienced in conjunction with the relatively colder temperatures of night. More generally, we perceive bodies of water -- lakes and oceans, as both blue-green to the eye and as cool to the touch. Conversely, many objects when heated give off a yellow-red glow, this colour being seen in conjunction with the felt, thermal perception of warmth. Such common alliances in the natural world, and our experience of them, can serve as the basis for colour-temperature associations learned on a transcultural basis. Consistent with this view is the finding that the normative colour-temperature associations are not appreciated until late in childhood or even adolescence (Morgan et al, 1975).

Intensity

By way of contrast, other synesthetic associations are appreciated quite easily by both children and adults. Just as widely acknowledged by adults as the warm and cool colours, these associations are, moreover, comprehended by children at an early age, and therefore may be based on intrinsic similarities between qualities of experience in different modalities. Intensity, for instance, is commonly considered a universal attribute of perceptual experience, applicable to visual, auditory, tactile, gustatory, and olfactory sensations alike. Swinburne wrote in *Erechtheus:* 'Like fire are the notes of the trumpets/ That flash through the darkness of sound'. Synesthetic perceivers may find colour images brighter or taste images stronger when sounds are louder: The synesthetically perceived qualities tend to follow the intensity as an attribute for cross-modal translation, but so do nonsynesthetic individuals. When people are asked to select visual and auditory stimuli that 'match', they align soft sounds with dim lights, loud sounds with bright lights (Marks, 1978), this rule of cross-modal equivalence being in direct parallel to the ways that synesthetic people perceive.

Brightness

Even more universal than intensity is the attribution of brightness to sensations of different modalities. In *Astrophel*, Swinburne rhapsodized synesthetically on music:

> Music bright as the soul of light, for wings an eagle,
> for notes a dove
> Leaps and shines from lustrous lines where through
> thy soul from afar above
> Shone and sang till darkness rang with light whose fire
> is the fount of love.

Indeed, in the visual-auditory form of strong perceptual synthesia (which is by far the most frequently encountered form of that rather infrequently encountered phenomenon), it is the translation of the dimension of brightness from one sensory modality to another that appears most regularly and reliably, both in individuals and over individuals. To a synesthetic in whom sounds engender visual images, there is a systematic relationship based on brightness: Bright sounds produce bright visual images. Brightness in sound is largely determined by pitch; hence low pitched sounds are dim, dark, or dull, high pitched sounds bright. The very same relationship is readily acknowledged by nonsynesthetic individuals asked to 'match' visual and auditory stimuli (Marks, 1974, 1978; see also Wicker, 1968).

Size

Size too forms a bond connecting different senses, both in synesthetic perception and more generally in the ways that nonsynesthetic people perceive and judge perceptual experience. To synesthetics and nonsynesthetics alike, sounds that are louder and sounds that are lower in pitch are also associated with greater size or volume. Soft, high pitched sounds are associated with smallness. Hence Wallace Stevens' *Parochial Theme* could note '... sounds blown by a blower into shapes,/ The blower squeezed to the thinnest *'mi'* of falsetto.'

Thus, in addition to colour and its association with temperature, there are three other kinds of general, intersensory, synesthetic correspondence, these being based on intensity, brightness, and size. (Three is not the limit: Important synesthetic connections also make use of similarities in the temporal aspects of perception. Synesthetic individuals frequently report that changes in their visual images are synchronized with changes in sounds; although this is especially pertinent to music, nothing more will be said about this here). Not surprisingly, these correspondences also readily reveal themselves in works of art, and notably in spectators' responses to works of art.

SYNESTHESIA IN POETRY

Though a truism, it is nevertheless true that the apprehension and comprehension of poetry intertwines perceptual, affective, and cognitive responses. Two significant features that help to characterize poetry are the intimation of meaning by sound and the potency of figurative language, especially metaphor. Both the intimation of meaning by sound and the implication of meaning by metaphor can reflect the operation of universal synesthetic tendencies, a potent current of similarity across the senses.

I will consider first the central role played by words themselves, in particular the close relation between the sound of a word and its meaning in the context of the poem. Sound symbolism or phonetic symbolism -- the evocation of meaning by sound per se-- has been thought to play an important role in the reader's or listener's response to poetry.

SOUND SYMBOLISM

Doubtless there are several sources to sound symbolism besides intrinsic synesthetic correspondences. Some relationships may be learned. It is perfectly possible that the meanings of words impart to their bearers -- to the sounds of those words -- those very meanings, rather than the sounds *sui generis* imparting meaning. Does the broad a of 'grand' impart great size, compared to the compact e and i of 'petit'? Or does the speaker of French infer, implicitly, some connection between a and large, between e and i and small? Whatever the nature of the relationship of sound to meaning, it is a dynamic one, for the sound symbolism, to whatever extent it may operate in natural language, does not act wholly on its own, but perforce interacts with the denotative and connotative meanings given by the words themselves.

Still, the question of origins bears some consideration. There is a long dispute over this matter. For instance, to Alexander Pope's precept (from *An Essay on Criticism*) that 'The sound must seem an echo to the sense,' Samuel Johnson (1778) responded, 'The fancied resemblances I fear, arise sometimes merely from the ambiguity of words; there is supposed to be some relation between a soft line and a soft couch, or between hard syllables and hard fortune' (p. 182).

Even when the relations between sound and meaning are not learned or inferred they may still be indirect. It may not be speech sounds per se that transmit meaning, but the kinesthetic or proprioceptive sensations aroused through the motor action in producing speech that is crucial. As Grammont (1930) noted, the consonantal combination 'sp' at the beginning of many words that signify emission or expulsion (e.g., sputter, spit) is produced by a plosive motion. Vladimir Nabokov commented on his own synesthesia that 'I present a fine case of "colored hearing"'.. Perhaps hearing is not quite accurate, since the colour sensation seems to be produced by the physiological act of my orally forming a given letter while I imagine its outline' (1949, p. 33).

Despite the range of sources of sound symbolism, nevertheless the role of synesthetic, cross-modal associations between sound itself and other sensory qualities is clear. The evidence is substantial that a general sound symbolism utilizes cross-sensory connections between pitch on the one hand and brightness and size on the other. Low pitched vowels such as (u) and (o) suggest darkness and largeness, while high pitched vowels such as (e) and (i) suggest brightness and smallness. Several empirical studies using nonsense words in which vowels were systematically substituted within the constant contexts of consonants (Bentley and Varon, 1933; Newman, 1933; Sapir, 1929; For reviews see Dogana, 1983; Marks, 1975, 1978) found low pitched vowels to imply largeness and darkness/dimness, high pitched vowels smallness and brightness. It is particularly important to note that these rules of sound symbolism apply broadly to associations made by native speakers of a variety of languages.

To the dichotomy between low pitched, dark, and large versus high pitched, light, and small, there is attached a constellation of affective associations. In an experimental application, Hevner (1937) constructed sets of pseudoverse (nonsense words put into metrical form) in which she systematically varied the consonant and vowel structure; subjects were asked to describe the 'meanings' of the pseudoverse. The vowels were especially significant in determining meaning, with the high pitched vowels and diphthongs -- (i), (ai), and (ei), characterized as the 'light' vowels -- suggesting to the subjects greater playfulness, delicacy, and happiness, as compared to the low pitched or 'dark' vowels -- (u), (o), and (a). It may be that the affective or emotional associations help bind the cross-sensory connections, as Osgood, Suci and Tannenbaum's (1957) work suggests; alternatively, it may be that synesthetic connections among the senses help maintain the network of affective and emotional meanings.

Although several examples from poetry suggest themselves, I will cite just one. Consider the contrast between the following two couplets from E.E. Cummings' *What if a much of a which of a wind:*

> what if a dawn of a doom of a dream
> bites this universe in two

and

> what if a keen of a lean wind flays
> screaming hills with sleet and snow

where the low pitched vowels in the first couplet face the high pitched ones in the second, reinforcing the darkness and profundity of the one, the sharp piercing brilliance of the other.

The cross-modal component to sound symbolism shows itself clearly in Macdermott's (1940) investigation. Macdermott assessed the meanings, on a line by line basis, in nearly 200 poems, and then related these meanings to the use of low and high pitched vowels. Sensory qualities are prominent. Low pitched vowels, she found, are associated with heaviness, roundness, warmth, roughness, slow movement, greatness, and the affective qualities of solemnity and deep, mature love, whereas high pitched vowels are associated with lightness, angularity, and the affective qualities of gaiety and light-hearted youthful love. It may well be that sensory qualities become bound to affective ones -- for instance deep, mature love becomes associated with largeness and heaviness, youthful love with lightness. And once this happens then the already present synesthetic connections - based on fundamental sensory similarities -- make possible an expansion of the realm of sound symbolism, so that sounds can not only engender other sensory meanings, but can evoke a whole gamut of nonsensory meanings that themselves are connected with the synesthetically aroused qualities.

SYNESTHETIC METAPHOR

The cross-modal connections just described also show themselves, at another level, namely in certain metaphors. In everyday speech, expressions like 'loud colours', 'sharp tastes', and 'bitter cold' are synesthetically metaphoric, taking a word whose primary meaning applies to one sense modality and transferring the meaning to another. Metaphors in poetry as well as in everyday speech often use cross-modal elements, and the interpretation of cross-modal metaphors may rely at least in part on the implicit comprehension of synesthetic perceptual associations. For certain poets, like Swinburne, the use of cross-modal or synesthetic metaphors is a common device. In others, notably the Symbolists, such metaphors held a special place. As I already noted, Baudelaire employed synesthesia as a central motif in the sonnet *Correspondences* -- the poet not only using cross modal metaphor as trope but treating cross-modal equivalences as a subject suggesting that our implicit knowledge of intersensory connections can lead in some mystical fashion to an understanding of the nomena underlying mere phenomena.

Be this as it may, it nevertheless seems clear that our understanding, whether implicit or explicit, of cross-modal similarity makes it possible to comprehend certain synesthetic metaphors. Shelley's lines in *Prometheus Unbound* describing 'undernotes/ Clear, silver, icy, keen, awakening tones' conveys through the visual and tactual modalities that the tones are loud, are brief, and undoubtedly are high pitched. A similar example: When we interpret Poe's 'sound of coming darkness' (from *Al Aaraaf*) as relatively soft, it is because darkness is weak in intensity. Another simple example: Swinburne's line describing 'Bright sound of battle ... / Loud light of thunder' (*Birthday Ode*) gives directly -- literally -- the visual and auditory qualities, both of which represent high intensity.

Do people actually comprehend cross-modal metaphors in a systematic manner that is consistent with universal synesthetic association? To answer this question empirically, I conducted an experiment where subjects read several synesthetic metaphors selected from a variety of poetic sources (Marks, 1982 b). The poetic lines are listed in Table 1.

TABLE 1 Synesthetic (sound-light) metaphors from poetry examined by Marks (1982b)

A. the murmur of the gray twilight (Poe)
B. the sound of coming darkness (Poe)
C. the quiet-coloured end of evening (Robert Browning)
D. sunset hovers like the sound of golden horns (Edwin Arlington Robinson)
E. the world lay luminous; every petal and cobweb trembled music (Conrad Aiken)
F. a soft yet glowing light, like lulled music (Shelley)
G. music, sister of sunrise, smiled as dawn (Swinburne)
H. music suddenly opened like a luminous book (Conrad Aiken)
I. the notes entered my breast like luminous arrows (Théophile Gautier)
J. music bright as the soul of light (Swinburne)
K. the silver needle-note of a fife (Joseph Auslander)
L. thy voice is loud as, when night is bare, /the moon rains out her beams (Shelley)
M. bright sound of battle, loud light of thunder (Swinburne)
N. sunlight above roars like a vast sea (Conrad Aiken)
O. the dawn comes up like thunder (Kipling)

The experimental task for the subjects was to set the brightness of a light and the loudness of a tone to the levels implied or indicated by each poetic excerpt. As expected, there was a strong association between the brightness settings and the loudness settings, implying in part a perceptual equivalence in terms of intensity (see Figure 1). For instance, 'the sound of coming darkness' was rated low in loudness, the implied softness no doubt engendered by the darkness. Indeed, 'the sound of coming darkness' behaved, at least with regard to loudness and brightness, virtually identically to Poe's direct statement in the same poem, of 'the murmur of the gray twilight'.

FIGURE 1: Average settings of luminance (brightness) and sound pressure (loudness) to each of a 15 sound-light metaphors from poetry, as listed in Table 1. The linear relationship expresses a synesthetic correspondence between brightness and loudness. Data of Marks (1982b).

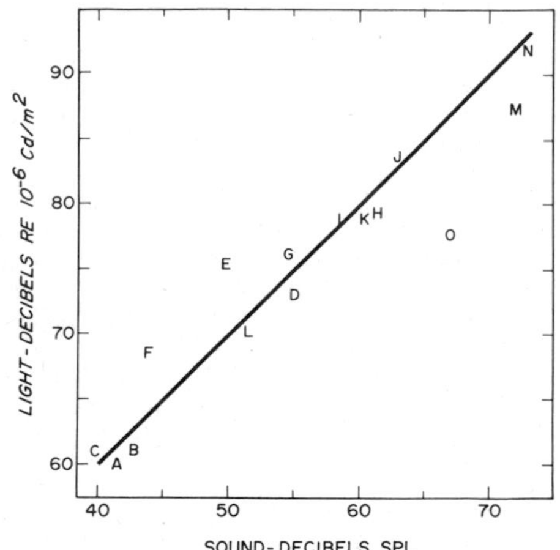

The straight line in Figure 1 expresses the typical relationship obtained in sensory psychophysical experiments where subjects are simply told to match loudness and brightness to each other (Stevens and Marks, 1965). The sound and light settings obtained when poetic metaphors were stimuli adhere well to this psychophysical relationship. It appears, then, that a prototypical perceptual relationship based on intensity in the two modalities underlies the comprehension of these poetic metaphors. When the reader or listener encounters a synesthetic metaphor, a metaphor of light and sound, the loudness tends to imply a perceptually equivalent level of brightness, or the brightness a perceptually equivalent level of loudness, in accordance with an implicit or explicit sensory correspondence between these two instantiations of intensity.

MULTIPLE MEANING IN SYNESTHETIC METAPHOR

Even within the relatively narrow domain of synesthetic metaphors, it is important to keep in mind the multifariousness of perceptual experiences. Intensity is, for example, only a single aspect of sense perception. Even in the limited and carefully selected metaphors studied by Marks (1982b), other perceptual attributes are important. When 'the dawn comes up like thunder,' dawn not only suggests a particular brightness, but Oriental dawns that 'come up like thunder' conjure up a variety of other connotations -- notably the coloured glow and the rapid, almost explosive, way the sun rises over the horizon. And, of course, as in the case of sound symbolism, synesthetic metaphors can spread far beyond the sensory, to include affective and other dimensions. While the dawn that comes up like thunder expresses energy and activity, the quiet colours of evening invoke the calm of a spreading, almost anesthetic, restfulness. It seems the very nature of metaphor to extend itself and thereby to extend meanings by ever expanding networks, as, in Wallace Stevens' terms, 'the poliferation of resemblances extends an object' (1951, p. 78).

WHERE DO SYNESTHETIC CORRESPONDENCES COME FROM?

In sum, evidence from a variety of sources -- ranging from cross-modal perception to poetic texts -- suggests the pervasive presence of a synesthetic component to meaning on at least two levels, namely in sound symbolism and in metaphor. An important question concerns the source(s) of these connections among the senses. I have argued (1978) that several of them represent intrinsic properties of perceptual experience; if this is so, then accordingly loudness-brightness, pitch-brightness and pitch-size relationships alike (as well as perhaps others) should be evident in perceptual matching and (maybe) in verbal behaviour of children as well as adults. An alternative view is that some or all of these cross-modal connections derive from or depend crucially upon experience; in particular, others (e.g., Brown, 1958) have argued that the inverse relation between pitch and size is learned through our experience with sizes of resonating bodies (larger objects in general emit lower sound frequencies; grown-ups typically have deeper voices than children). If some or all synesthetic connections are learned -- and especially if they are learned relatively slowly -- then this would bear on such matters as children's sensitivity to sound symbolism and cross-modal metaphor.

CROSS-MODAL SIMILARITY: LANGUAGE AND PERCEPTION

So far, I have characterized synesthesia as representing a pervasive mode of perception, in which dimensions of sensory experience in different modalities align themselves one to another. I have also characterized sound symbolism and synesthetic metaphor in poetry as resting on implicit perceptual knowledge about synesthetic correspondences, this implicit knowledge presumably shared by artist and audience. Missing at this point -- save for the study of Marks (1982b) -- is direct evidence concerning people's verbal understanding of perceptual synesthetic relationships. Do people translate descriptions of sensory experiences by the rules of synesthetic association? And do children understand the rules as adults do?

Over the past several years, my colleagues and I have collaboarated on an ongoing series of experiments, where we have tested a total of more than 400 children between the ages of 4 and 13 years and more than 100 college-aged adults on their recognition of cross-modal associations between loudness and brightness, pitch and brightness, and pitch and size (Marks, 1982a; Marks et al, in preparation). Two kinds of understanding were evaluated. Perceptual understanding was assessed by asking the children and adults to make pairwise cross-modal matches; given, for example, two sounds differing in pitch and two lights differing in brightness, the task was to decide which sound and which light 'match'. Verbal understanding was assessed by asking the children and adults to judge each of a variety of cross-modal metaphors on a scale of perceptual meaning: given, for example, the expressions 'sunlight whispers', 'sunlight roars', 'moonlight whispers', and 'moonlight roars', the task was to rate the expressions on a graphic scale of either brightness or loudness. If there is a synesthetic association between brightness and loudness, then 'sunlight' should not only literally be brighter but also metaphorically louder than 'moonlight', and 'roars' should be not only literally louder but also metaphorically brighter than 'whispers'.

In the rating procedure, the subject is given a 200-mm long rating line, anchored by appropriate descriptive adjectives (e.g., 'very very soft'; 'very very loud'). The subject marks the line to indicate the location of the meaning of each phrase.

Consider the following paradigm as applied to adults. Subjects judge a set of words on a rating scale of loudness. Because adults have conceptual prototypes of perceptual events, they know that a 'trumpet note' is louder than a 'piano note', and the ratings reveal this. When these same nouns are modified by the adjectives 'loud' and 'soft', the ratings of loudness increase or decrease in turn. When the modifications are cross-modal -- that is, metaphorical -- those modifiers that imply greater loudness also imply greater brightness, and those modifiers that imply greater brightness also imply greater loudness; the modifiers exert cross-modal effects that are about as large as the literal effects. For instance, the adjective 'soft' means 'dim' and the adjective 'dim' means 'soft'; 'loud' means 'bright' and 'bright' means 'loud'. This is evident in Figure 2, which shows examples of the literal and metaphorical effects that the adjectives exert on the meanings of nouns. Note that the nouns too exert metaphorical effects: Sunlight is louder than moonlight, as well as being brighter. Various syntactic combinations show these synesthetic shifts in meaning, not only combination of adjectives with nouns but also combinations of nouns with verbs (Figure 3).

FIGURE 2 Average judgments by adults of loudness and of brightness given to synesthetic metaphors in which auditory adjectives combine with visual nouns. Data of Marks (1982a).

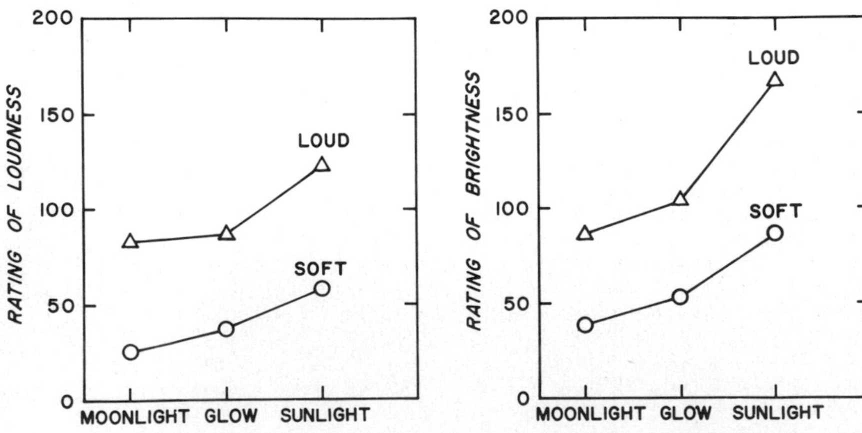

FIGURE 3. Average judgments by adults of loudness and of brightness given to synesthetic metaphors in which visual nouns combine with auditory verbs. Data of Marks (1982a).

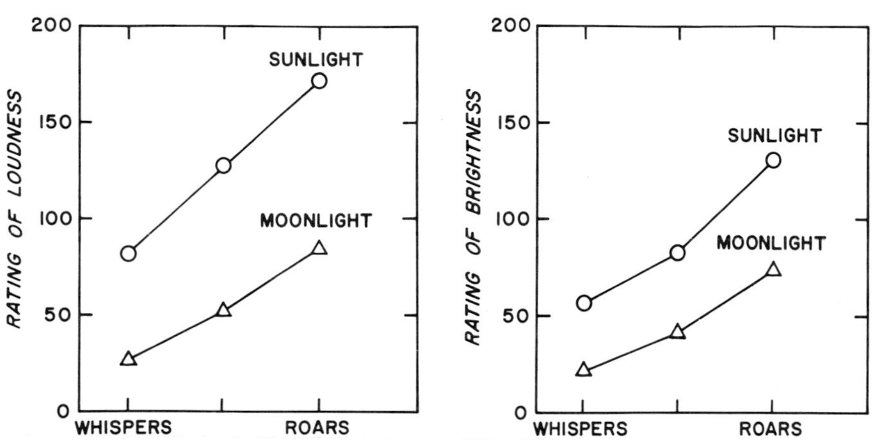

Loudness and brightness show an equivalence in verbal meaning -- these studies show -- just as earlier work revealed an equivalence in perceptual meaning. The translations between modalities are complete and symmetrical.

So too do pitch and brightness. It does not matter whether the visual dimension represents luminous objects (brightness) or reflecting surfaces (lightness), adults interpret greater pitch to imply -- synesthetically and metaphorically -- both greater lightness and brightness, and greater lightness and brightness to imply -- synesthetically and metaphorically -- greater pitch. This is true for a wide range of adjective-noun combinations, as well as for metaphorical (cross-modal) judgments of single words. For example, colours have pitches as well as brightness. At least our conceptual prototypes of colours have pitches as well as brightnesses and lightnesses; for, as Figure 4 shows, it is these visual qualities that directly, immediately and virtually completely determine their metaphorical pitch: 'Black' and 'brown' are dark, therefore low pitched;'white' and 'yellow' are light, therefore high. Similarly, our prototypes of acoustic events sort themselves out by pitch, and the pitch determines, metaphorically the lightness or brightness of the sound (Figure 5). 'Coughs' are dimmer and darker than 'sneezes', and 'thunders' dimmer and darker than 'whispers'.

FIGURE 4. Average judgments of pitch versus corresponding judgments of brightness (filled circles) or lightness (open circles) of colour names. Data of Marks (1982a).

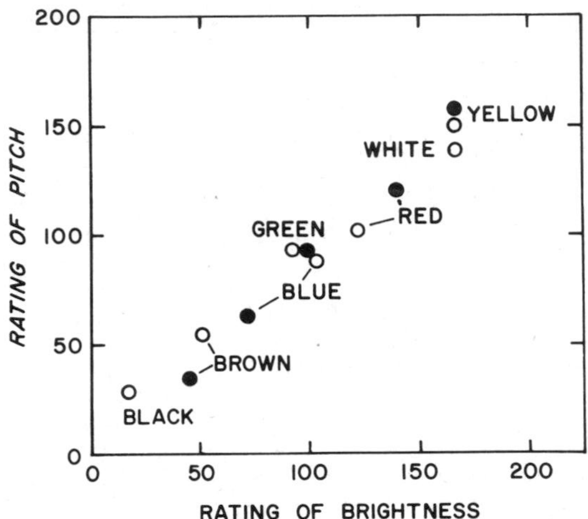

FIGURE 5. Average judgments of pitch versus corresponding judgments of brightness (filled circles) or lightness (open circles) of auditory names. Data of Marks (1982a).

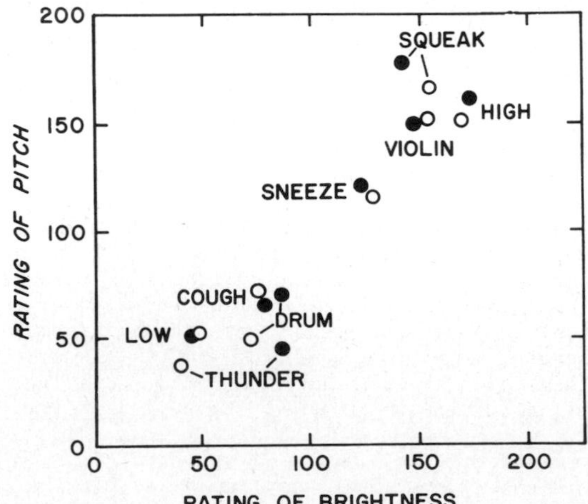

FIGURE 6 Average judgments by adults of pitch given to synesthetic metaphors in which size adjectives combine with auditory nouns.

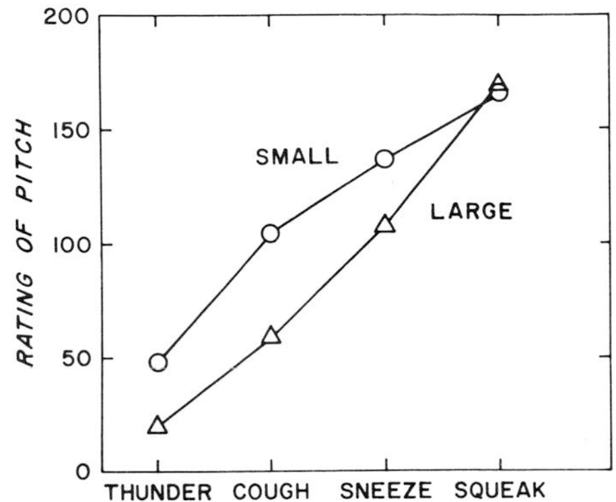

Pitch and size too form a metaphorical pair, with lower pitch synesthetically implying greater size and greater size synesthetically implying lower pitch (see Figure 6). 'Small' is high pitched, 'large' is low. In behaving this way, the metaphors function much like sound symbolism.

CHILDHOOD ORIGINS OF CROSS-MODAL SIMILARITY

Where might these similarities some from? One hypothesis (Hornbostel, 1931; Marks , 1978) says that these relationships are intrinsic to sensory-perceptual experience itself. The similarities may derive from elemental properties of experience as experience, perhaps residing in common properties of the underlying neural code. Another possibility is that these similarities derive from certain universal environmental correlates, which make it possible for most of us to learn that, say, *ceteris paribus* larger objects resonate at lower sound frequencies than do smaller objects, and thus have lower pitches (Brown, 1958). Maybe, as already was mentioned, we form kinesthetic or proprioceptive associations through the movements and positions of our lips and tongue when we speak. Or perhaps the cross-sensory connections come from learned affective mediators (Osgood et al, 1957).

One way to get a handle on the sources of cross-modal similarity is to look at origins in childhood. It was for this reason that we have extended the metaphor tasks to 4/13-year-old children. The verbal experiments used the same graphic-rating scale we used with adults (though with a smaller corpus of expressions, and often with simpler words). In addition, we have conducted perceptual matching studies. Given two visual stimuli and two auditory stimuli, we asked each child simply to indicate which sound and which light or shape 'match up' best.

The findings can be summarized fairly succinctly. First of all, and most importantly, children even as young as 4 or 5 years can readily translate the perception or the language of one sense modality into that of another, much in the way that adults do. Nevertheless, some differences between children and adults do appear. Children, especially young children, do not always make so fine distinctions as do adults. Still, children 'know' so to speak, that louder and higher pitched sounds are brighter than are softer and lower pitched sounds, and that brighter objects are louder and higher pitched than dimmer ones. (Figures 7-10 give examples.) Children know this perceptually. And they know it verbally.

FIGURE 7 Average judgments by children of brightness given to synesthetic metaphors in which auditory adjectives combine with visual nouns. Diamonds: age 5; circles: 6; squares: 8; triangles: 10.

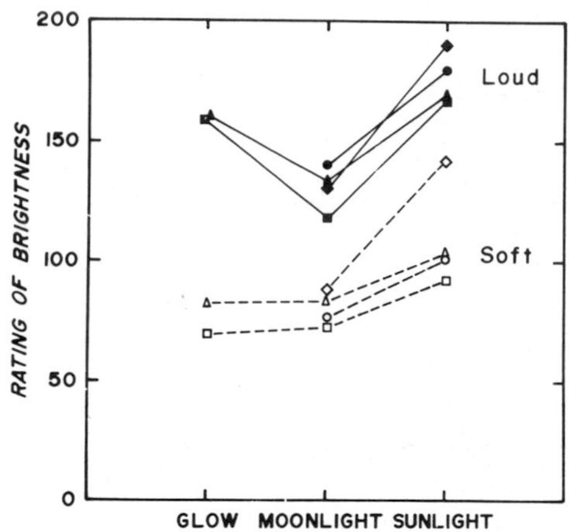

FIGURE 8 Average judgments by children of loudness given to synesthetic metaphors in which visual adjectives combine with auditory nouns. Symbols as in Figure 7.

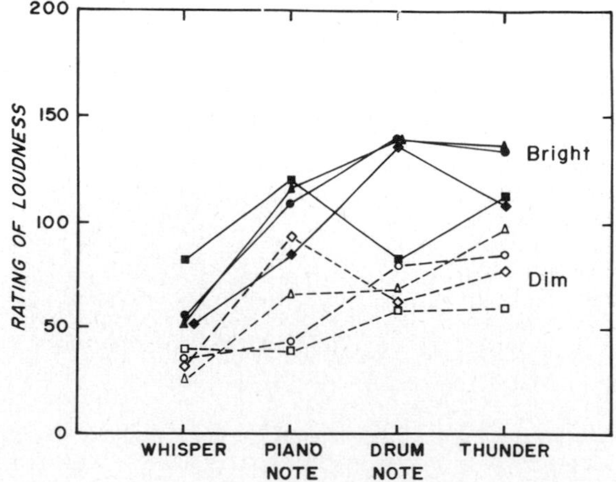

FIGURE 9 Average judgments by children of brightness given to synesthetic metaphors in which auditory adjectives combine with visual nouns. Symbols as in Figure 7.

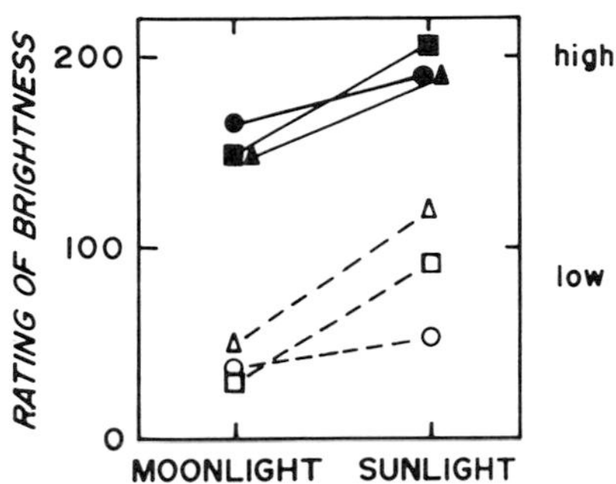

FIGURE 10 Average judgments by children of pitch given to synesthetic metaphors in which visual adjectives combine with auditory nouns. Symbols as in Figure 7.

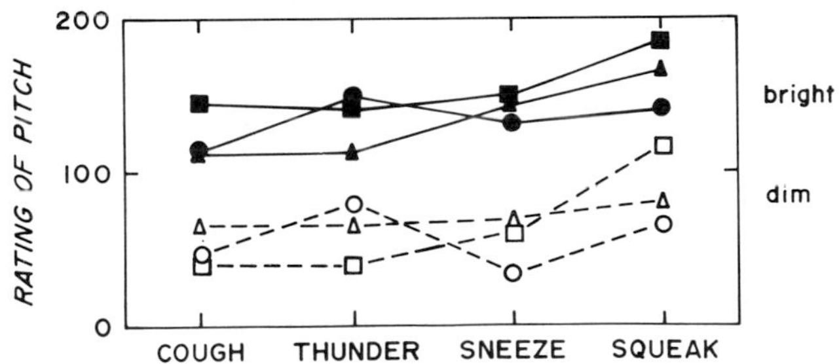

Just when -- at what age -- children know these similarities, however, does depend on the particular cross-modal relationship in question. Table 2 displays the development of cross-modal understanding. The percentages in this table represent the proportions of children who performed in accord with 'normative rules', that is, in accord with the majority of adults. By far the strongest, clearest, most regular and reliable relationship is that between pitch and brightness. By 4-5 years, the earliest age we have yet examined, virtually all youngsters know that high pitched sounds are bright, low pitched sounds dim. Four-year-old children reveal this knowledge most clearly in their perceptual matches, the children being a little less reliable in their performance on the verbal task.

TABLE 2 Percentages of children and adults who yielded similarities in accordance with 'normative rules' (majority of adults) in perceptual (P) matching and verbal (V) comprehension tasks.

	PITCH-BRIGHTNESS low = dim high = bright			LOUDNESS-BRIGHTNESS soft = dim loud = bright			PITCH-SIZE low = large high = small		
AGE	N	P(%)	V(%)	N	P(%)	V(%)	N	P(%)	V(%)
4-5	16	94	74	23	74	43			
6	32	94	94	35	71	63			
7-8	34	95	92	25	76	80	27	56	52
9-10	34	100	100	30	90	93			
11-12	35	97	94	34	94	86	26	85	69
13							34	91	74
Adult	16	100			16	100		16	75
	17		100	16		100	16	88	

Not even the relation between loudness and brightness is as clear at so young an age as is that between pitch and brightness. While it is true that the majority of 4/5-year-olds understand loud to resemble bright, soft to resemble dim, at the verbal level performance runs 50-50, that is, at a random level. By age 7, though, the similarity between loudness and brightness appears also in language. I will note that, as a general principle, perceptual performance tends to lead, verbal performance tends to lag, as if it can take some time for perceptual knowledge to become available to or accessible through language. (This interpretation assumes that the two tasks are comparable in difficulty.)

That very young children quite readily recognize both loudness-brightness, and, especially, pitch-brightness similarity suggests to me, though of course it does not yet prove, that these cross-modal correspondences are built-in, are intrinsic to perceptual experience. Research on infants may tell us with greater certainty whether this is so. It is encouraging in this respect that Lewkowicz and Turkewitz (1980) found evidence, as measured by habituation in a heart-rate response, for an equivalence between brightness and loudness in three-week-old infants. Even though much of the evidence is at this point somewhat scanty and circumstantial, it seems reasonable to hypothesize that some cross-modal -- which is to say synesthetic -- relationships are innate, intrinsically given in the functioning of the sensory apparatus.

Surprising to me were the findings on the relationship between pitch and size. Not until age 11 does a majority of children appreciate this similarity. It is hard to square this finding with my original view -- that pitch-size similarity is built into the hardware of our senses. Instead, it seems more reasonable to conclude that the pitch-size relationship is acquired, and acquired rather slowly at that. The implications of the difference between these similarities that appear early -- pitch and brightness, loudness and brightness -- and those that appear later -- such as pitch and size -- for young children's sensitivity to sound symbolism and synesthetic metaphor are, I think, apparent.

Whatever the origin of cross-modal similarities -- and it seems perfectly reasonable to me that the multifarious similarities can have different sources, some learned and others unlearned -- whatever their origin, it is clear that these similarities form part of our store of implicit knowledge. It is through such shared knowledge, whether learned or whether based on intrinsic similarities, that many cross-modal metaphors become effective, that the artist, strongly synesthetic or not, can succeed in conveying meaning through implication and through metaphor. By means of a 'unity of the senses', we can acknowledge the propriety of Joseph Auslander's description (in *Steel*) of the 'silver needle note of a fife,' we can appreciate with Conrad Aiken the contrasts between 'the violins ...weaving a weft of silver' and 'the horns ... weaving a lustrous brede of gold' (*The House of Dust*), and we can know -- indeed, we can almost hear -- Shelley's 'undernotes', these being, as he called them, 'clear, silver, icy, keen, awakening tones'.

SUMMARY

Synesthesia -- the transfer of qualities or meanings from one sensory modality to another -- is salient in visual art, music and poetry. Pervasive in much poetic expression are sound symbolism and synesthetic cross-modal) metaphor. In part, both sound symbolism and synesthetic metaphor rest on widely appreciated similarities between qualities of phenomenal experience in different sense modalities. Although some of these similarity relationships are likely learned, others probably reflect intrinsic resemblances that are part and parcel of the nature of sensory perception. By means of characteristics common to different senses, such as intensity and brightness, sounds can intimate nonacoustic meanings, and metaphors can translate freely among the visual, auditory and tactual. That metaphors of loudness and brightness and metaphors of pitch and brightness are readily understood even by young children (4/6-year-olds) carries two main implications. First, it points to the early origin of these cross-modal similarities. And, second, it suggests that young children share with adults the potential sensitivity to respond to sound symbolism and synesthetic metaphor in poetry.

REFERENCES

Baudelaire, C. (1889). Salon de 1846. In: Curiosités Esthetiques, (Calmann Lévy, Paris).

Baudelaire, C. (1923). Les Paradis Artificiels. In: J. Crépet (Ed.) Oeuvres Complètes de Charles Baudelaire 3. Paris: Gallimard.

Bentley, M. and Varon, E.J. (1933). An accessory study of 'phonetic symbolism'. American Journal of Psychology, 45, 76-86.

Brown, R. (1958). Words and Things. New York: Free Press.

Corrà, B. (1973). The painting of sounds, noises and smells. In: U. Apollonio (Ed.) Futurist Manifestos. New York: Viking.

Castel, L-B., Nouvelles experiences d'Optique & d'Acoustique, Mémoires pour l'Histoire des Sciences et des Beaux Arts n.v. (1735) 1444-1482; 1619-1666; 1907-1939; 2018-2053; 2335-2372; 2642-2768.

Corra, B. (1973). Abstract cinema - chromatic music. In: U. Apollonio Futurist Manifestos. New York: Viking

Clavière, J. (1898). L'audition colorée. Année Psychologique, 5, 161-178.

Dogana, F. (1983). Suono e Senso. Milan: Angeli.

Gautier, T. (1846). Le club des hachichins. Revue des Deux Mondes, 13, 520-535.

Grammont, J. (1930). La psychologie et la phonétique. Journal de Psychologie Normale et Pathologique, 278, 544-613.

Hevner, K. (1937). An experimental study of the affective value of sounds in poetry. American Journal of Psychology, 49, 419-434.

Hornbostel, E. von. (1931). Ueber Geruchshelligkeit, Pflüg. Archives Gesellschaft Psychologie, 227, 517-538.

Johnson, S. (1778). The Lives of the Most Eminent English Poets with Critical Observations on their Works. Volume 4. London: Bathurst et al.

Kandinsky, W. (1977). Concerning the Spiritual in Art. New York: Dover.

Kandinsky, W. (1979). Point and Line to Plane. New York: Dover.

Karwoski, T.F., Odbert, H.S. and Osgood, C.E. (1942). Studies in synesthetic thinking. II. The role of form in visual responses to music. Journal of General Psychology, 26, 199-222.

Lewkowicz, D.J. and Turkewitz, G. (1980). Cross-modal equivalence in early infancy: auditory-visual intensity matching. Developmental Psychology, 16, 597-607.

Luria, A.R. (1968). The Mind of a Mnemonist. New York: Basic Books.

Macdermott, M.M. (1940). Vowel Sounds in Poetry: Their Music and Tone-colour. London: Kegan Paul.

Marks, L.E. (1974). On associations of light and sound: the mediation of brightness, pitch and loudness. American Journal of Psychology, 87, 173-188.

Marks, L.E. (1975). On colored-hearing synesthesia: cross-modal translations of sensory dimensions. Psychological Bulletin, 82, 303-331.

Marks, L.E. (1978). The Unity of the Senses: Interrelations among the Modalities. New York: Academic Press.

Marks, L.E. (1982a). Bright sneezes and dark coughs, loud sunlight and soft moonlight. Journal of Experimental Psychology: Human Perception and Performance, 8, 177-193.

Marks, L.E. (1982b). Synesthetic perception and poetic metaphor. Journal of Experimental Psychology: Human Perception and Performance, 8, 15-23.

Marks, L.E., Hammeal, R.J., and Bornstein, M.H. (In preparation). Synesthetic metaphor: Developmental processes in comprehension of cross-modal similarity.

Martin, L.J. (1909). Ueber ästhetische Synästhesie. Zeitschrift, Psycholische, 53, 1-60.

Morgan, G.A., Goodson, F.E. and Jones, T. (1975). Age differences in the associations between felt temperatures and color choices . American Journal of Psychology, 88, 125-130.

Nabokov, V. (1949). Portrait of my mother. New Yorker, 25, 33-37.

Newman, S.S. (1933). Further experiments in phonetic symbolism. American Journal of Psychology, 45, 53-75.

Newton, I. (1704). Opticks: or, A Treatise of the Reflexions, Refraxions. Inflexions and Colours of Light. London: Smith and Walford.

Osgood, C.E., Suci, G.J. and Tannenbaum, P.H. (1957). The Measurement of Meaning. Urbana, Illinois: University of Illinois Press.

Riggs, L.A. and Karwoski, T. (1934). Synaesthesia. British Journal of Psychology, 25, 29-41.

Sapir, E. (1929). A study of phonetic symbolism. Journal of Experimental Psychology, 12, 225-239.

Scriabin, A. (1911). Prométhee, le Poème du Feu, Pour Grand Orchestre et Piano avec Orgue, Choeurs et Clavier à Lumières. Berlin: Breitkopf und Härtel.

Stevens, J.C. and Marks, L.E. (1965). Cross-modality matching of brightness and loudness. Proceedings of the National Academy of Science, 54, 407-411.

Stevens, W. (1951). The Necessary Angel. New York: Knopf.

Wicker, F.W. (1968). Mapping the intersensory regions of perceptual space American Journal of Psychology, 81, 178-188.